# 10,000 Dreams

## EXPLAINED

### HOW TO USE YOUR DREAMS TO ENHANCE YOUR LIFE AND RELATIONSHIPS

PAMELA J. BALL

ARCTURUS

I would like to thank all those who have made this book possible. Firstly, Fiona who has balanced the dual roles of daughter and editor with admirable aplomb and who has realized that the frustration is not directed at her; secondly, Jacob who epitomizes the generations to come and hopefully will find the book useful in future years; thirdly, my publishers, who gave me the confidence to set out on this labyrinthine road in the first place and, finally of course, you the readers, who continue to be the source of much of the material in the book itself.

ARCTURUS

This edition published in 2009 by Arcturus Publishing Limited
26/27 Bickels Yard, 151–153 Bermondsey Street,
London SE1 3HA

ISBN: 978-1-84837-087-6
AD000015EN

Printed in the UK

# CONTENTS

## KEY TO ENTRIES

    spiritual meaning

    psychological, emotional perspective

    everyday material aspects

    gender-specific meanings

# INTRODUCTION

*'The man who will not listen to the sublime whisper of his Overself during his waking hours will respond more easily during his dreaming ones, when the veil is thinner, partly because his egoistic will is more relaxed and partly because he is actually nearer the source of consciousness.'*

PAUL BRUNTON

Paul Brunton was one of the finest mystics of the 20th century, bridging the gap between the spiritual and physical realms in his own inimitable way. For him, dreams began within the spiritual and manifested in the physical. We are more able to listen to, and understand, the inner self in sleep in ways we are not able to do in waking life.

He went on to say, 'It is dreams of this superior and spiritual character which bear good fruit after the man awakes.' He, then, was aware that interpretation of dreams was an integral part of understanding the spiritual dimensions and the spiritual self.

Dreams are perhaps one aspect of the human mind which are an integral part of all aspects of knowledge, but which still hold their mystery no matter which way we look at them. Regarded from a spiritual perspective they help us to understand the Divine; from the psychological point of view they enhance our understanding of ourselves and from a mundane viewpoint they make sense of the world in which we live.

Following Brunton's lead, we lay out each interpretation as follows:

First, there is the spiritual meaning indicated by the symbol ✵, then the psychological/emotional perspective with the image ♥, followed by the more everyday material aspects with the ▣ emblem. Some entries also have a fourth interpretation which gives gender-specific meanings ⬒. There can never be a 'one-fits-all' theory – we must all be honest enough to admit that we do not know and then be prepared to take from each theory what seems right for us.

We can use this book then as a dictionary, first listing those components that we need to understand and then, if necessary, reconstructing the dream so we understand the whole story. To enhance your understanding and your dream vocabulary there is extensive cross-referencing throughout the A to Z section: sometimes to similar images, sometimes to other entries which have similar meanings. Often, the entries refer back to this introduction to the

Archetypes (a proven source of images) and to Symbology and Spiritual Imagery. Gradually you will build up your own categories of meaning and hopefully will find as you do so that the content of your dreams becomes more meaningful and part of your everyday life.

## MODERN DREAM INTERPRETATION AND ANALYSIS

The word 'interpret' is, we discover, of unknown origin but probably comes from a Sanskrit word meaning 'to spread among'. Therefore dream interpretation would mean 'to spread our dreams among others'. The common factor that is shared by all dream interpreters is that the original material from which dreams are fashioned is hidden.

The renowned and extremely influential psychoanalyst Sigmund Freud's work was based on the belief that dreams were disguised expressions of what went on below the surface of the mind. Carl Jung, who was originally a pupil of Freud's, had a more spiritual perspective and said, 'Dreams may give expression to ineluctable truths, to philosophical pronouncements, illusions, wild fantasies... anticipations, irrational experiences, even telepathic visions and heaven knows what besides.' Herbert Silberer, a contemporary of the two, took a much more mystical approach and studied the state between waking and sleeping. He formed the theory of Intraversion, which necessitates the descent of the individual into the soul/psyche from which a great deal of information and knowledge can be drawn.

Calvin Hall in the mid-20th century developed a cognitive (relating to intellectual activity) theory of dreams which states that dreams express 'conceptions' of self, family members, friends and social environment. With Robert van de Castle he developed the quantitative analysis of dream content, perhaps the first time that truly scientific methods had been applied to dream analysis. He also saw dream content as metaphor – one thing conceived as representing another: a symbol.

Then, in the late 1960s, Fritz Perls developed his own philosophy of Gestalt which means 'wholeness'; he believed that it was possible to reclaim those parts of our personalities which had become lost or hidden. He called dreams 'the royal road to integration'. If each image in the dream is an alienated part of ourselves, then it is wise to look at the necessity of giving each part of the dream its own voice and the opportunity to express itself, and therefore to become whole. Those wholenesses can then be integrated to become a greater whole. This approach ties in with Jung's theory of Archetypes about which we shall learn more later.

Calvin Hall's method of dream analysis gave rise to much research, and arguments still rage today as to whose theories of dreaming are right. For the layman, it would seem that the arguments can be divided into two camps, broadly how we dream and why. Much still remains hidden because those who believe that dreaming is purely neurological in origin cannot give a reasonable answer as to how the images are put together to form a dream. They appear to believe that the process is essentially chaotic and possibly meaningless. Those who believe that dreaming is a function of the cognitive brain – that which knows – have difficulty in explaining the randomness of the images.

G William Domhoff of the University of California, who has used Hall's methods to good effect, has come to probably the most easily understood conclusion that:

'Dreaming is best understood as a developmental cognitive achievement that depends upon the maturation and maintenance of a specific network of forebrain structures. The output of this neural network for dreaming is guided by a "continuity principle" linked to current personal concerns on the one hand and a "repetition principle" rooted in past emotional preoccupations on the other.' [Domhoff, G. W. (2001). A new neuro-cognitive theory of dreams. *Dreaming, 11,* 13–33.]

It has been discovered that, in the front part of the brain (forebrain), the necessary nerve connections for what might be called coherent dreaming are not really sufficiently mature until around the age of nine years old. This suggests that the night terrors that very young children have are a function of the immature brain.

The personal concerns of the dreamer – that which is happening to him in the here and now – is linked by the dreaming mind with what has happened in the past and had an effect on him emotionally. Setting aside for the moment the argument that the brain itself must mature before it can process information, one supposes that a child would not have enough waking life experience to be able to make such links.

When the dreaming mind makes connections and brings together images from similar experiences (Freud called it condensation), this is metaphor. Metaphor in dreams is basically a noting and expressing of similarities. Dreams then, according to Ernest Hartmann, one of the chief proponents of this idea, are explanatory metaphor. Through the highlighting of the similarity we gain understanding. Mostly, dreams will work with what is occurring at the time in our lives, but they will also pick up past images, ideas and concepts in an effort to have us understand and deal with what disturbs us. This then allows us to uncover the hidden meaning more objectively.

Dream metaphor takes a somewhat abstract idea such as fear and turns it into a recognizable picture (a monster). The best interpreter of these pictures obviously is the dreamer himself, but it can be of help to know the common meanings of such pictures. The language of dreams is universal.

## SPIRITUAL DREAMING

Dreams can be a useful tool, giving us a much wider perspective and fuller appreciation of what is happening both in our world and the wider world in general. The knowledge and information that we acquire in dreams opens up a whole library of creativity which is ours to use if only we have the courage. Unfortunately, it is all too easy to forget the content of a dream on waking. We need to learn to record our dreams and an easy-to-follow method is shown below.

Dreams also give us access to another dimension of being – spirituality and the intrinsic use of power. Many Eastern cultures see sleep as a preparation for death and therefore a learning experience. One definition of spirituality is 'the awareness of other dimensions of existence beyond that of the purely physical, tangible realms'.

Dreams are an expression of the spiritual realm and also a bridge between that and the tangible. Interestingly, many authors, artists, poets, scientists and engineers are able to use their dreams creatively. Such people tend to be more lateral in their thought processes and are more likely to remember their dreams, which allows them to make something of a quantum leap in understanding. Scientists and engineers do tend to be more logical and linear in their thought processes and will not necessarily accept their dreams without being able to prove the reality in waking life.

However, it has happened. An excellent example of this process is scientist Friedrich Kekule's dream of the structure of the benzene molecule. Trying to solve the mystery of this structure, Kekule dreamt that the most important aspect was that the molecules formed a complete ring which he saw as a snake eating its own tail. Remembering that this dream occurred in the latter part of the 19th century when less was known about chemistry, this dream certainly constituted a breakthrough in knowledge.

This benzene ring provided the basis for the whole science of molecular chemistry. This particular dream symbol echoes the ouroborus (the symbol of the cycle of existence), which is often used in magical workings as a protective device.

## INSPIRED DREAMING

Today, many people will admit to having creative flashes of inspiration following dreams. It is as though a missing piece of jigsaw suddenly fits into place, allowing them to see the whole picture and therefore to make sense of a creative problem. Often a fragment of music, poetry or apparent doggerel will linger in the mind, which on consideration is not as beautiful or pertinent as it once seemed in the dream, but it may contain the key for moving an idea or a project forward.

The mind can open up to possibilities and potentials far beyond the waking consciousness. Meditation can often aid in this process of creative dreaming, whether we use it before sleep to open up to the creative self or use it after dreaming to gain a greater understanding.

Part of the process of using inspiration as a dream tool is to be able to remove the restrictions placed on us by the society in which we live. We need to know and understand ourselves what makes us the unique individuals that we are, as well as what we need to do to bring out our best qualities. The way a child grows in understanding as it matures is a good matrix for spiritual and creative growth.

As adults, with the realization that we are very much part of a greater whole, we can begin to take responsibility for the creation of a better, fuller existence for ourselves and finally accept that, by doing so, we can build a better and more stable future. Whatever stage of understanding we may have reached, dreams can help and encourage us or indicate that we are going down a particular route which may not be worthwhile.

Dreams can be taken as events in their own right and be interpreted as such. Whether they make sense, or whether we choose to act on the information given, is decided by us and us alone. We can also accept dreams as an expression of the unconscious creative self, which can contain a message given either in an easy-to-understand form or in the language of symbolism, where initially the meanings are not easily discernible.

It is when we begin to recognize the creativity behind the process of dreaming that we open ourselves up to different ways of approaching our own talents and abilities in a novel way.

## THE HYPNAGOGIC AND HYPNOPOMPIC STATES

With practice, the states between waking and sleeping (or indeed sleeping and waking) can also be a time when wishes and desires can be given substance and brought into reality in a particularly magical way.

Briefly, the hypnagogic state is one which occurs between waking and sleeping, whilst the hypnopompic occurs between sleeping and waking. The best explanation of these two states comes from the realms of Spiritualism. The Astral Planes are those levels of awareness where the various thought-forms which have occurred are stored, and in the hypnagogic and hypnopompic states the mind has some access to those realms, without actually seeing spirit form.

Herbert Silberer sought to fuse contemporary ideas with mystical thought processes using the 'in-between states'. This is part of the process of the spiritual 'transmutation of the soul' found in most of the mystical traditions of the world. His book, *Problems Of Mysticism And Its Symbolism*, becomes a work of mysticism in its own right and is no longer a purely scientific work or psychological study.

While dream interpretation itself does not necessarily require an understanding of the 'hypno' states or vice versa, we can often use dream images and the hypno states to enhance our spiritual workings. The half-and-half awareness of consciousness and the semi-dream state that we have within the hypnagogic state gives us an opportunity to follow a line of thought which can clear away problems in an almost magical way. Learning to use incantations, blessings or prayers as well as colour and symbolism in this state can be highly productive. One such mantra might be:

*May the good I have done remain,*
*May the wrongs I have done be washed away.*

During the hypnogogic state, the mind is in idling mode when a review of the day can lead to insights about our behaviour or beliefs in surprising ways. By using this pre-sleep state to 'download' each day's material, the mind can then bring forward deeper and more meaningful images in dreams, the understanding of which eventually allow us to take more control of our lives. We learn to dream spiritually and creatively rather than simply using dreaming as a dumping ground. We then start the next day with a clean slate and can use the hypnopompic state to bring order to the coming day.

This can be an exciting time, and can open up all sorts of possibilities, such as the exploration of telepathy, ESP (Extra Sensory Perception), healing and so on. It is our choice which route of exploration we wish to undertake.

By their very nature, flashes of ESP are symbolic and indistinct and take on a hallucinatory quality. When they occur spontaneously in the 'hypno' states, they are more readily accepted as valid and open to interpretation in the same way as dream images. By becoming more practised at working in that state, we become more able to use the magically spiritual and psychic senses if we so wish. We are able to make use of a far more creative input than our 'normal' awareness.

## Hallucinations

When dreaming, there is an hallucinatory quality about everything that we see anyway. We usually accept what we experience as real and, in the actual dream state, do not question it. It is only when we consider the dream afterwards that we realise how odd this may be. During dreams, things can take on qualities of other objects and of other feelings.

Dreams can create a reality of their own, they do the unexpected – which in normal waking life would be totally illogical and surreal; it seems simply that we observe what is going on. Even our own actions can take on an oddness about them and we can be liberated enough to create a totally different concept of our own abilities, our thought patterns and even our own past. We can often dream that we have done things in the past which we have never done, or more importantly we can prepare ourselves to do things in the future which again we would never expect to do.

The hallucination that we experience in dreams can also be the result of direct messages from the unconscious – psychologically freeing the mind so it can 'roam' at its own speed, allowing hidden memories, images and thoughts to surface in such a way that we can handle the input when perhaps in real life we might not have been able to do so. We create a reality which suits an action, rather than creating an action which suits the reality.

## SLEEP DISORDERS

There are a number of sleep disorders that are worthy of note, particularly since any such disorder affects the quality and quantity of our dreaming.

## Insomnia

This is probably the best-known sleep disorder and one from which many people suffer. The causes range from depression through stress to physical problems. To understand our own insomnia it would be necessary to recognize the underlying causes and to do what we can about them. In the case of physical problems, ensuring habits such as regular bedtimes can be helpful, as can all the well-known ways of handling the problem which include hot baths and massage.

It is worth noting that Chinese medicine holds the theory that some energy lines within the body are soothed or stimulated at certain times of the day and night, and that certain imbalances when identified and treated, will aid the management of insomnia. The organs of the body each govern certain psychological and physiological processes and understanding this, working with the principle and using alternative methods of management such as acupuncture, creative visualization or meditation can help. It has been said that ten minutes of meditation is worth four hours' sleep at night, so being able to make adjustments to our lifestyle could be of great help. Insomnia is a very difficult thing to deal with, not least because it can affect not only the individual's life, but also the lives of others round about.

### Sleep Apnoea

Another sleep disorder is sleep apnoea. This occurs when the sleeper stops breathing for anything up to a minute. This then brings arousal from sleep, and the individual seldom has restful sleep. This condition does need qualified medical attention.

### Narcolepsy

The study of narcolepsy, which is a condition where people can fall asleep in the middle of conscious activity, has yielded information on muscular movement in sleep. Under normal circumstances there is an area in the brain which suppresses muscular movement. This is called the *pons*. If this part is damaged or suppressed, then full muscular movements in connection with the dream occur. Such movements do not seem to be survival techniques or socially motivated, but are a form of release mechanism to enable the dreamer to deal with emotions and trauma. As part of that process, spontaneous movement and speech can occur. This is akin to automatism which can occur in changes of consciousness connected with many religious practices.

### Nightmares

Nightmares and anxiety dreams have an intensity of emotion about them which we seldom feel at any other time. The commonest characteristic is the need for flight, i.e. to run away from the situation. The physiological reaction to fear of fright, fight, flight (then in the waking state, submission) seems to be involved here, except that we usually wake up before submission. It is almost as though it would be too painful to get into that submission state. Almost inevitably, on waking there is huge relief that one has escaped. Nightmares do appear to arise from six main causes. These are:

a Childhood memories of intense emotions. These are often centred around loss, and it has been suggested that such dreams are to do with the birth process and the severance from mother.

b Childhood fears, perhaps also centred around the same situation, though the fears at this stage also include the fear of being attacked, and also anxiety about our internal drives. This may be to do with the child's need for survival and to satisfy the basic needs for food, warmth and shelter. (It has been noted that, if those needs are not satisfied, the child withdraws into a world of its own. If, therefore, the rage it experiences is suppressed, this could surface later in nightmares.)

c In Post-Traumatic Stress Syndrome, where again the basic need for survival is threatened, it has been found that the anxiety experienced can still surface a long time afterwards. Some people are still experiencing such nightmares many years after the event. It would appear that the brain has not been able to discharge the trauma sufficiently for the sufferer to be at peace.

d The ordinary everyday drive to survive can surface in adults as fear of the future, or fear of change and growth. Essentially, it is fear of the unknown.

e Some nightmares are centred around an apparent sense of foreboding. Whether these come under the title of precognitive dreams is not decided. What does seem true is that the human being is capable of picking up information on a subliminal level, without being able to understand that information.

f Serious illness with all its fear surrounding death can obviously cause nightmares. Some help could be gained from therapy and counselling.

*Recurring Dreams*

Recurring dreams can have an element of anxiety about them. Indeed, it may be that they are triggered off by anxiety. The setting of the dream may always be the same. The characters in the dream may not vary, or the theme may always be the same. It is often not until we begin to explore our dreams that the anxieties and attitudes begin to change, and there is no longer a habitual response.

*Sleep Talking and Walking*

Sleep talking and sleep walking both seem to occur as part of a response to stimuli. Sleep talking seems to play a part in clearing the mind of worries and concerns.

Sleep walking also apparently has a purpose, in that if left alone the sleepwalker will attempt to complete whatever action was started.

## TYPES OF DREAM

It is generally recognized that dreams tend to be of two types, those that Jung called 'big' and 'little' dreams. With practice we can record these in different ways; for example if we choose to write down our dreams by using two different books. Important dreams are usually easily remembered and we recognize the relevance fairly quickly, whereas the significance of lesser dreams may not become apparent until all the themes and dimensions have been explored. Frequently, it is worthwhile comparing important and less important dreams. The themes which are first presented in 'big' dreams are often enhanced and better understood by subsequent 'little' dreams. The more proficient we become at recording our dreams, the more easily they are remembered.

A further way of categorizing dreams is by dividing them into 'good' or 'bad' dreams. With a greater degree of knowledge, the dreamer can often change the outcome of a bad dream into a good one. This is called RISC technique and was developed in America as a therapeutic tool. The four steps are:

1) Recognize a bad dream while it is occurring.
2) Identify the bad feeling.
3) Stop the dream.
4) Change negative into positive. Initially, it may be necessary to wake up in order to undertake any of these steps. Gradually, with a greater proficiency, we are able to do this while remaining asleep.

Because change takes approximately six weeks to occur on a psychological level, we need to be patient with ourselves while learning these new techniques. Often, we notice changes in attitude fairly quickly, but they do not become habit until about six weeks later, since it takes time for them to become fixed in our minds. Given that we are prepared to change, it is often we ourselves who are most surprised by the shift in awareness. We may become better able to deal with issues which have previously proved difficult, or find that inner conflict is more easily and efficiently handled. By beginning to work with opposites – however they may present themselves – those opposites become more easily appreciated and handled in waking life.

Sometimes in dreams there is an intensity of emotion which can be extremely frightening. We may be incapable of feeling such an emotion in everyday life, but for some reason we can allow ourselves, for instance, to be terrified in nightmares. It is almost as though we know we can escape from the situation simply by waking up.

*Anxiety Dreams*

One of the most frequent dream themes is that of some form of anxiety. Anxiety dreams – while less intense than nightmares – often allow us to replay, and thus capture, those aspects of our lives which cause us difficulty. Disturbing elements in our dreams arise from our memories, stray thoughts or impressions and our own emotions which we deliberately suppress during waking hours.

Subliminal worries and problems can be allowed to surface with safety in anxiety dreams. While the images may appear to be the important part of such a dream, it is actually the emotion experienced which needs to be faced and recognized. By doing this, we are able to handle ordinary, everyday anxieties. Dreams associated with grief, particularly surrounding the death of a partner, are a particularly poignant form of anxiety dream and are a necessary part of recovery.

Dreaming can allow us deliberately to access and explore our anxieties. If we cannot meet our feelings of fear or emotional pain we allow ourselves to be controlled by them. Often by deliberately facing our hidden anxieties, dreams will give us information on what action needs to be taken to enable us to avoid making mistakes. Expectations of the future may be revealed through hidden anxieties.

*Precognitive Dreams*

Precognitive dreams are an interesting phenomenon. Opinions vary as to whether there really are such things. Suffice to say that when anxieties are dealt with and further insights gained, the dream function will often access the best course of action available and give the information through images. That course of action is then usually chosen by the dreamer, though it may be that the conscious mind does not readily accept the situation.

*Magical and Spiritual Dreams*

Magical dreams and spiritual dreams are also part of the framework of awareness, though there are those who will deny their existence. Dreams have often been proved to give information in more esoteric ways. Number and colour, and all of the symbolism contained therein, are a valid part of dream interpretation and, with a little knowledge, can create a structure which allows access to what would otherwise be hidden information.

Tradition which is based on wisdom, and rituals and ceremonies built around a knowledge of symbolism, are thus accessed. Personal management of the creative side of oneself becomes possible both through dreams and the directed use of power in the waking state, and dreams can act as a monitor for correct behaviour.

## KEEPING A DREAM JOURNAL

Keeping a dream journal – that is, recording each and every one of the dreams we can recall – can be a fascinating but somewhat difficult task. Over a period of time, while it can give us information from all sorts of angles, it is an extremely efficient tool in dream interpretation.

We may find that we go through a period when most or all of our dreams seem to be around a particular theme, for instance that of the gods and goddesses. When we feel that we have understood that series of dreams, we can explore the same theme in waking life and enhance our knowledge.

It can be interesting to discover months or perhaps years later that the same pattern and theme recurs, with additional information and clarity. By keeping a dream journal at the same time as recording the methods and results of our contemplations, we are able to follow and chart our own progress in becoming a spiritual adept.

The dreaming self is highly efficient in that it will keep presenting information in different ways until we have finally got the message. Equally, that same dreaming self can be very inefficient in that the information can be shrouded in extraneous material and symbolism which will need teasing out of the rubbish. It is up to you to decide which explanation is more relevant, so if you are using your dreams as a spiritual or psychic tool you will interpret them in that light.

There are now a number of software programmes to help in the quantifying of dream content. Some people are prolific dreamers, others less so, and many more have 'big' dreams very rarely. In fact, we all dream at some point every night, often without remembering, though it does appear that the more we learn to remember our dreams, the more proficient we become at dreaming. It is as though the more we use the 'muscle', the better it responds.

A dream journal allows us to assess not just the content of our dreams, but also the pattern of our dreaming. Below are several steps necessary for you to keep a dream journal efficiently:

Any paper and writing implements can be used – whatever you prefer, although it will probably make things easier for you if you just use one journal at a time. You might also like to keep your writing implements separate from any others.

Always keep your recording implements at hand. You can also if you wish use a tape recorder to record your dream. 'Speaking' the dream fixes it in your mind in a particular way, enabling you to be in touch with the feelings and emotions of the dream. It is sometimes easier to explain the dream in the present tense. For instance, 'I am standing on a hill' rather than 'I was standing on a hill'.

Write the account of the dream as soon as possible after waking. Keeping an account – particularly of the more inexplicable or 'way-out' kind – is helpful.

Use as much detail as you can remember. A hastily scribbled dream is much less easy to decipher than one which goes into more detail.

Be consistent in the way that you record your dreams. One simple scheme is given below.

## RECORDING YOUR DREAM

This is an easy way for you to record your dreams, which echoes that used by Calvin Hall. Obviously, the first three parts only need to be recorded if you intend to share your dream with others who do not know you.

If you intend to keep your dream journal private, this method gives you the opportunity to look carefully at each of your dreams and return to them at a later date if necessary, perhaps to compare content, scenarios or other aspects. It can also allow you to assess your progress in the art of self-development.

*Name*

*Age*

*Gender*

*Date of dream*

*Where were you when you recalled the dream?*


*What was the content of your dream?*

*Write down anything that strikes you as odd about the dream (e.g. size, bizarre situations etc.).*

*What were your feelings in/about the dream?*

## DREAM MANAGEMENT

If you are just beginning to record your dreams, the important thing is not to try too hard. Being relaxed about the whole thing will give you far more potential for success than getting worked up because you cannot remember your dream or because you do not appear to have dreamed at all. The more you practise, the easier it becomes.

If you do decide to keep a journal, it is worthwhile incorporating it in the preparation for your night's sleep. Making these preparations into something of a ritual can help to concentrate your mind on the activity of dreaming, and thinking over a situation before you go to sleep, or meditating on it, can help to open the doors of the unconscious to some of the answers you are seeking. So, carefully laying out your tools, re-reading some of your old dreams, using deep relaxation methods, assisted by relaxing oils or herb teas, and even asking the superconscious for useable material can all assist in the creative dreaming process.

Try to wake up naturally, without the shrill call of an alarm clock or booming music. There are various devices on the market such as daylight simulators which come on gradually, dimmer switches, and clocks which have a soft alarm, graduating in intensity, which can help with this. Even a radio, tape recorder or mobile phone programmed to play soft relaxing music can be used. Using such waking aids can help us eventually to hold on to the hypnopompic state and use it creatively. Some dreamers report that the spoken word seems to chase away a dream, so gentle music is probably best.

On waking, lie as still as possible for a moment, and try to recall what you have dreamt. Often it is the most startling thing or feeling which you will remember first, followed by lesser elements. Transcribe what you remember into your journal, and write the 'story' of the dream. This may well give you an initial perception which is sufficient for your needs, both in the everyday and from a spiritual perspective.

Later, list alphabetically the elements of the dream, and decide first on the individual meanings of each aspect of the dream. Then look for the theme of the dream, and which part of your life it applies to. Often the theme is presented in more than one form, so that you 'get the message'. Next, reconstruct the dream and interpret it on a deeper level so you understand what kind of dream it is – that is, whether it is giving information as to the state of things as they are at the moment, whether it is suggesting a particular course of action or whether it is offering an explanation of what is happening within your Superconscious.

## GAINING INSIGHT AND CLARIFICATION

There are several ways to gain insights through dreams, and this process is not necessarily the same as interpreting the dream. We can start off by defining the conventional meaning of something which comes up in a dream which will help us to understand our situation. Let us suppose that we are standing on a clifftop looking out to sea. The conventional explanation is that we are on the edge of something, perhaps a new experience (the clifftop). This experience may be to do with the emotions, since often water symbolizes emotions in dreams.

Insight comes when we apply conscious rationality to the dream scenario. Thinking about it allows the order and clarity to be seen, rather than the fact that everything is a complete jumble. On this occasion we are aware of the vastness and depth of the sea, and therefore understand that the emotions are far deeper and more meaningful than previously realized. This is an insight into our personality. The dream has been of use when we are able to apply that insight in everyday life.

We are aware in our dream state that we cannot decide whether to jump off the cliff (take a risk) or move away from the clifftop (refuse to face the situation or move away from danger). We then discover ourselves at the foot of the cliff. The interpretation is that we have achieved what we felt was right, and have taken the appropriate risk. The insight is that it did not matter how we did it; we simply trusted our intuition. By keeping the interpretation simple, the insight may be more telling.

Given the basic meaning of the dream action or symbol, it is possible to find out the necessary information to understand the dream. Having such information offers an interpretation of the dream; working with the interpretation gives insight. The dream vocabulary is both diverse and specific to each individual dreamer, and each person is so multi-faceted that several simultaneous explanations are possible, all of which may be equally valid. It will depend on the person who has the dream which one has the greatest validity.

Working at dream interpretation with other people, whether known to us or not, can be a highly illuminating experience. Taking the time to explore all facets of the dream – and bring into conscious memory all aspects of it – can deepen the insights that we obtain as we work with our dreams. Someone who knows us well may be able to see the relevance of some image in a dream to a situation we face in everyday life, whereas we are too close to the situation to be able to understand. Someone who does not know us well may have the degree of objectivity needed to round off an interpretation so that we can move forward.

The support offered through the insights that friends gain in interpreting our dreams can make a tremendous difference to our lives and theirs. Sometimes acting out a dream with friends and perhaps including the dream in a consideration of what may happen next can be helpful and can clarify a course of action for us. This does not simply mean using the imagination. We have the opportunity to work interpretations through more fully using our own techniques. We may choose to use meditation, guided imagery or other methods since these share much of the symbolism of dream imagery.

## SYMBOLOGY

Dream image as metaphor is possibly the most potent form of symbology there is – it is what people will believe in. Frequently, there seems to be no context in which to place the figures which appear. The shapes manifest apparently at random yet, as we become more and more involved in the interpretation of our dreams, we discover they contain a message in themselves. They are an aspect of sacred geometry (the measurement of perfect proportion in the physical world) and, put simply, are the way in which the physical world reflects the spiritual. There are many images which demonstrate such a concept; below are the ones that are most likely to appear in dreams:

**Circle** – the circle symbolizes the Universe; a circle with a dot in the centre can signify the soul in its entirety and is sometimes taken to represent Woman or the essential feminine. A circular object – such as a ring – has the same meaning as the circle.

**Crescent** – information on the origins of this symbol are difficult to ascertain, but most sources agree that ancient celestial symbols were in use by the peoples of Central Asia and Siberia in their worship of sun, moon, and sky gods many thousands of years ago.

**Crooked Line** – deviance from the norm in a spiritual sense can be a falling away of the standards we have set ourselves. If we are aware of this on a spiritual level, a crooked line will often appear in a dream. The line may be any sort of line, such as a queue of people, a line of cars or whatever.

**Cross** – the cross shape gives rise to many images. Moving through the symbol of the sword with the crossbar at the bottom through the equal-armed cross, from there to the cross of suffering and crucifixion and finally to the Tau of perfection, the cross symbolizes the lessons the soul must learn. Through experience it overcomes the obstacles to spiritual progression. The arms of a cross signify conflict, anguish and distress, finally reaching perfection. The intersection signifies the reconciliation of opposites. The three upper arms are said to stand for God the Father, Son and Holy Ghost, but more properly they indicate any Divine Trinity. The hung cross with the figure of Christ represents the sacrifice of self for others.

**Spiral** – when the spiral moves towards its centre, it shows we are approaching our own spiritual centre via an indirect route. A clockwise spiral, moving outwards to the right, is a movement towards consciousness and enlightenment. If the spiral is moving anti-clockwise, it shows a degree of introspection towards the unconscious, and possibly regressive behaviour. The spiral convolutions on a shell have often been associated with perfection and therefore plenty. The conch shell was, and still is, used as a trumpet in certain societies, hence it may be seen as a warning. The spiral representing a flow of energy has a connection with the navel or solar plexus as the centre of power.

**Square** – a figure within a square is the Self or Perfect Man, perhaps the most recognizable image is Leonardo da Vinci's representation. A simple square signifies energy given expression within the physical world. A square within a circle suggests the actual act of 'becoming' or taking on form. Any square object signifies the enclosing and feminine principle.

**Star** – the five-pointed star or pentagram evokes personal magic, and all matter in harmony. Ideally, the star should point upwards. In dreams it signifies our acceptance of our own magical qualities and aspirations. If it is pointing downwards, it symbolizes evil and misuse of power. The six-pointed star, or Star of David, is made up of one triangle pointing upwards and another pointing downwards: the physical and the spiritual are thus joined together in harmony to create wisdom. Human nature moves towards the Divine and Spirit seeks expression through the physical. Twelve stars signify both the Twelve Tribes of Israel and the Apostles.

**Swastika** – this is a form of cross which, revolving clockwise, symbolizes positivity and the Wheel of Life. Revolving anti-clockwise it has a more negative connotation often connected with the misuse of power.

**Tau Cross** – spiritually, the Tau Cross signifies the key to Supreme Power and living a truly successful life. In the psychological sense, it signifies the meeting of the physical and the spiritual and all that that entails. Worn as a talisman, it protects from evil, and will often be perceived in this way in a dream.

**Triangle** – the triangle can represent family relationships, that is, father, mother and child. If the triangle points upwards, it is reaching towards the Divine, and symbolises Duality reaching Unity. If it is pointing down, it is any two polarities finding expression through the act of creation.

## SPIRITUAL IMAGERY

Below we explain archetypes. For the purpose of this section we have defined these spiritual images and imagery as those which have arisen from the various systems of belief around the world. These frequently surface in dreams and are part of what Jung called the Collective Unconscious. These images are often recognizable, half-remembered and, once we have identified them, easily understandable. Obviously, in a book of this size we regrettably have not been able to include all such images, but hope that this short cross-section will whet your appetite for further research of your own.

So that it gives you, the reader, a proper flavour of how the entries in the book are laid out, we should point out that first part is a spiritual explanation, the second a slightly more emotionally slanted one – in these cases the popular meaning – which has developed over a number of years. Finally, the third section gives more down-to-earth information as to why we need these images in our lives and our dreams. Below that is a section on spiritual imagery, an important part of any dreamer's vocabulary. Some of the images also have individual entries in the body of the book which will further enhance your understanding.

✿ If spirituality is taken to be an inner truth, and religion as that which links us back to Source, then it must be the case that religious, or perhaps more accurately, spiritual imagery partly assists us in recognizing truths which we have long accepted as genuine. They are archetypal images which belong to everyone but resonate – or have a particular effect on each of us – in slightly different ways. Dreams have a way of introducing – or rather reintroducing – us to these images and when they begin to surface it is time to widen our appreciation of them perhaps by reading, perhaps by study, but probably most importantly by simple contemplation which helps decide what relevance they have to us. Using images that seem primarily to have a spiritual application allows us to integrate spirituality fully into our lives and does away with the idea that it is something separate from our daily lives but is, and always will be, an intrinsic part of who we are. Because the images are so specific they may be startling, but having the patience to work with them enhances first our understanding of ourselves and then our dream lives.

◈If we are prepared to accept that each truth will have its own personal slant, and that we must get back to the basic Truth, all dreams can be interpreted from a spiritual point of view. This is especially true of spiritual imagery. Most interpretations here are stated only in general terms and are given only as guidelines. When you feel like throwing away the book and saying that the interpretations are not valid, then you will be able to take on personal responsibility and will only need the book for verification.

**Angel** – in spiritual terms the angel symbolizes pure being and freedom from earthly matters. Angels tend to be androgynous, and are not recognized either as male or female. There is a hierarchy of angels: Angels (the realm closest to the physical), Cherubim, Seraphim and finally the Archangels, Michael, Gabriel, Raphael and Uriel. As more and more people seek spirituality, there are those who have become more aware of the angel form, particularly in dreams. It is vital that we are able to differentiate between the personalized aspect of the Higher Self and the angelic form, since they are similar but different. To put it as simply as possible, the aspect known as the Higher Self has a stronger affiliation with the physical domain, while the Angels have a greater affiliation with the spiritual. The Dark Angels are reputed to be those angelic beings who have not yet totally rejected the Ego or earthly passions. When this image appears in a dream, we are being alerted to a spiritual transgression, which often has already happened. Angels who issue warnings usually symbolize what should not be done in the future.

**Buddha** – the figure of Buddha appearing in dreams highlights the necessity to be aware of the Qualities of Being which Buddha taught. These are the four Noble Truths. It links us to the power of renunciation and of suffering, but in the sense that experience of suffering is valid.

**Breastplate** – the breastplate of Aaron was a jewelled protection where the jewels had certain esoteric meanings and were also said to represent the Twelve Tribes of Israel. When we experience ourselves as wearing some form of protection around the heart, we are usually protecting our right to love unconditionally and protect ourselves spiritually. If we are particularly aware of the gems or jewels, they can also have a great deal of relevance

**Ceremonies/Rituals** – ceremony and ritual are all part of the heightening of awareness which occurs on the path to spirituality. In dream ceremony the images are even more vivid.

**Consecration** – any act of consecration, blessing or prayer is dedicating an aspect of ourselves to the service of our God. In dreams, consecrating an object is ensuring that it is used solely for spiritual purposes.

**Christ** – the ideal Christ is that part of ourselves which is prepared to take on our portion of the sufferings in the world by working within the world. We do not need to be crucified physically to suffer. Appearing on the cross, Christ signifies redemption through suffering. The anarchic Christ is the part of us whose love and lust for life permit us to break through all known barriers. The cosmic Christ is the part that is prepared to take on Cosmic Responsibility – that is, to be connected with the Universal Truth. While these aspects have been spoken of particularly in Christian terms, they are also present in all religious leaders.

**Church or Religious Music** – these sounds, dedicated to the perception of God that we have, are sacred sounds, creating a vibration which expands consciousness. This creates a different state of awareness and is a way of expanding the spirit.

**Corridor or any passage** – this signifies a state of spiritual limbo, of transition, possibly moving from one state of mind to another, or perhaps between two states of being.

**Crucible** – manifestation of spiritual or psychic energy can be perceived as a crucible, a transforming receptacle linking with receptivity, intuition and our creative side. As a container which is capable of withstanding great heat, it is the aspect which can contain change and make it happen.

**Crucifixion images** – in a dream, these links typify the human being's need to sacrifice himself through passion and through pain. The image of Man hung upon a tree is a very ancient one and is seen in stories of Odin, the Norse God who hung upon the World Tree for nine days in order to obtain Knowledge.

**Devil** – in dreams, the Devil represents temptation. This often arises from repressed sexual drives, animal drives and the lust for life which all demand attention. It may also signify the Shadow.

**Ghosts** – these arise from independent forces within, which are separate from the will. It will depend on personal beliefs whether we accept the appearance of ghosts as psychological or spiritual apparitions.

**Gods/Goddesses** – we are each given the opportunity to make real our fullest potential. In doing so, we must undertake an exploration of, and possibly a confrontation with, our perception of gods and goddesses, whichever pantheon we may believe in.

**Hell** – a state of being where nothing is ever as it seems and, alternatively, this could be thought of as continually existing in a state of negative illusion. Reputedly, it is a state of spiritual agony where our worst dreams are fulfilled. It is thought that the same actions are often repeated over and over again ad infinitum.

**Heaven** – a state of being where the energy is of such a high frequency that there is no suffering. In dreams, it appears when we are transmuting our awareness into the spiritual dimensions. It is reputedly a place where bliss exists and is also known as Nirvana and Samadhi.

**Holy Communion** – the belief that Christ's body was transmuted into heavenly food – symbolized by the Last Supper – appears in dreams as the intake of spiritual sustenance. Holy Communion represents a sacred sharing. Most systems of belief have evidences of feasts and celebrations where the whole community participates in a meal which has certain rituals attached to it. This is one example of transubstantiation.

**Icon** - an icon is a representation of a religious figure or concept. It can, through usage, become revered as a holy object in its own right. In dreams, it can signify the belief itself.

**Incense** – an offering to the gods and a physical form of prayer through perfume and smoke.

**Initiation** – this occurs when we are ready to enhance our knowledge and understanding so that we can 'be' – that is, use the power we have – in a different, more effective, way. Spontaneous initiation can occur in dreams. We transcend something within ourselves.

**Mary, the Mother of God/Virgin Mother** – the symbolism of Mary, both as the maiden and as the mother, is a potent one. She epitomizes all that is Woman, and all that is holy.

**Moses** – appears in dreams as the holy figure who will lead us out of difficulty. He often symbolizes a flaw in our personality for which there must be some kind of 'sacrifice'.

**Ouroborus** – the symbol of the cycle of existence. As the snake that eats its own tail, it is circular in shape and therefore has the same symbolism as the circle. It signifies eternal existence.

**Religious books and Sacred Texts** – there is a repository of knowledge available to us all. In dream imagery, this will often appear in the form of books such as the Bible, the Koran or the Torah. Other sacred texts will also appear in dreams at certain stages of development to help us towards understanding.

**Priest/Prophet** – a priest as a man of God belongs to the present, whereas a prophet will foretell events to come. Both are interpreters of Divine Will, so in dreams, if they appear together, they represent a conflict between the present and the future.

**Religious Buildings** – this includes churches, chapels, mosques, synagogues and temples. We all are aware of our need for sanctuary from the batterings of the everyday world. Within the religious building, we are free to form a relationship with our own personal God. Dreams are often one of the places where we first discover this sense of sanctuary. In dreams, we may also come to the realization that our body is our temple.

**Religious Festivals** – each system of belief has its own celebration, whether that be the Wheel of the Year, Christian festivals, Hindu celebrations or Shinto. Associated with these festivals are certain traditions such as Diwali sweets or the sharing of food. One such tradition is the Christmas tree which initially symbolizes the tree of rebirth and immortality (the World Tree), the return of the light and the beginning of a new phase of life.

**Religious leaders** – appearing in dreams, they epitomize the recognition of the ability to reconcile the physical and the spiritual, God and Man. They personify Perfect Man, a state to which we all aspire. Each religious leader has their own quality or particular perspective on spirituality which will resonate with us and which will manifest unexpectedly in dreams. Most often we will first meet the religious figure who belongs to our own early system of belief later widening out to include others as our awareness increases. So someone brought up as Christian may first perceive the Christ figure, someone of the Hindu faith might perceive Lord Krishna.

**Religious Service** – the act of worship which is used to bring people together. It is recognized in dreams, perhaps as an act of integration of the whole self, and as an illustration that the whole is greater than the parts.

**Rose/Rosette** – the rose in dreams carries with it a great deal of symbolism. It suggests Perfection and Passion, Life and Death, Time and Eternity. It also represents the heart, the centre of life and as a psychological symbol symbolizes perfection. It contains within it the mystery of life and its grace and happiness.

**Sackcloth** – the act of mourning in olden times often indicated some public show, and so sackcloth was taken as the substance to show the spiritual poverty of the people concerned – that they had lost something very valuable. Sackcloth in dreams indicates repentance and an outward show of such repentance. We may feel that we have humiliated ourselves, and wish to show the world that we have repented of an action or deed.

**Seance** – we need the qualities of patience and determination to contact our own spiritual self. Dreaming of being at a seance, or sitting, can suggest a need to explore the psychic side of our nature. Remembering that psychic means 'being in touch with self', this can suggest being aware of our intuition.

**Sheaf** – as the symbol of the goddess Demeter, the sheaf represents Mother Nature in her guise of the nurturing mother. It can also suggest a dying world, in that Demeter refused to nurture 'her' humans when her daughter Persephone was taken into the Underworld by Pluto. Previously, a sheaf, particularly of corn, would signify a harvest or good husbandry. Now it is more likely to suggest old-fashioned ways and methods of operating.

**Shaman** – when this figure appears in a dream he epitomizes the ability to travel with guidance through otherworldly realms. His totem animal will transport, guard and protect him as he seeks knowledge often on behalf of others. He will, in waking life, interpret dreams and will dream on behalf of the whole community or tribe.

**Spirits** – during spiritual development, our perceptions widen from the ordinary everyday to other aspects and dimensions of knowledge. The spiritual self has access to the Collective Unconscious in its entirety. When spirits appear in dreams, their function may be to help us through various states of transition. A kindly or helpful spirit signifies that we can move on. Seeing the spirits of dead people generally means we need reassurance.

**Tabernacle** – this is a place where a sacred object is kept for safety, represents a temple and therefore becomes a World Centre. To dream of a tabernacle is therefore to be trying to understand our own need for sanctuary and safekeeping.

**Talisman** – mankind has a deep connection with objects he believes to be sacred. In most Pagan religions, objects such as stones and drawings were, and indeed still are, given magical powers by special techniques which empower them. They retain the ability to protect the wearer throughout time. When such an image appears in a dream we are linking spontaneously with ancient magic.

**Third Eye** – this represents developed clairvoyant perceptiveness, or the clarity of vision that comes with spiritual development. It is the Third Eye of Buddha and symbolizes unity and balance. It is often represented in symbolism by the Eye of Horus. In no case does it represent a physical quality, though it is thought to link with the pineal gland.

**Transfiguration** – this is a phenomenon which can occur during altered states of consciousness. It is as though a light enters the personality and changes it; for this to happen suggests that there is some special purpose or Divine intent. In the waking state, it is taken to suggest being used as a spiritual channel. Spiritually, we need to be aware that we are all part of a greater whole, and this dream can occur as we are working through stages of transition in our lives.

**Transformation** – this takes place in spiritual terms when freedom of thought or action is indicated, or when higher impulses are substituted for lower reactions. As the growth to spiritual maturity takes place, there are many transformations which occur. These are often depicted in dreams as immediate changes, rather like a time-stop film sequence of a flower opening. Transubstantiation is a form of transformation which takes place through Divine Intervention when a substance 'becomes' something else.

**Totem/Totem Animal** – a totem is an object or objects revered as sacred; they will have particular significance for the owner. When they are given enough spiritual power by a joint belief, the objects are perceived as taking on a power of their own. A totem animal, similar to a guardian angel, appears when we are ready to accept that there are dimensions other than our own, which can be visited with the animal's guidance.

▦ When we, through deliberate or spontaneous neglect, deny ourselves access to the store of spiritual imagery in waking life, dreams will often react to this lack and try to compensate by jolting us back into an awareness of our inner spirit. In today's society it is very easy to fasten on to the hypocritical aspects of religion and to accept that hypocrisy. It is also easy to make the assumption that the outward forms of religion often deny the existence of a true inner reality. If spirituality – the inner truth that we all hold – is neglected, it will not go away: it will simply reappear in its negative and terrifying form. In waking life, the closest image we have to that is the Devil, or the more vengeful Indian gods. Our own personalized demons can be more frightening than those. It is not until we accept responsibility for our own existence that true spirituality emerges.

## ARCHETYPES

Archetypes are basic pictures that each of us hold deep within our unconscious and belong to what Jung called the Collective Unconscious. They are, in a sense, 'psychic' blueprints. These blueprints – while potentially perfect – can become distorted by childhood experiences, socialization and even parental experience. Throughout the book you will see various cross-references to certain archetypes and characters. They are the stuff of which dreams are made and closely approximate to the 'lost' parts of the personality that Fritz Perls decreed could be rescued. Because they are universal, archetypes can present in many guises, yet ultimately with thought are totally recognizable.

Three facets of our personality show themselves separately in dreams. Sometimes they appear as people we know, sometimes as fictitious or mythical characters or beings, and sometimes as other images.

The most difficult side we all have has been called the Shadow and is the personification of our worst faults and weaknesses. It is the part of us that is the same sex as us, but has been suppressed because it is frightening and unmanageable. Then there is the Anima, or in a woman, the Animus – this represents the opposite sex within the dreamer. In a man it is all that is instinctive, feminine and sensitive. In a woman, it is her masculine attributes of logic and objectivity. Finally, there is the ideal or True Self, which holds our highest possible creative potential and is most likely initially to communicate through dreams. Although the Self first appears as potential belonging to the future, as the other aspects become properly integrated the individual may then become the whole, real and many-sided Self.

If we are prepared to work with the archetypal images and to understand them, the dream figures can help to create a sustainable reality that exists beyond any of them. They will then have fulfilled their function, and so will be unlikely to reappear in dreams except in times of stress. Because the most important quality of our inner being is energy, which can then become power, each of these dream images represents a different aspect of those vital forces we have at our disposal, and each in its own way can stimulate this energy into action.

For an understanding of the archetypal figures and their functions, it is important to keep the aim of personal growth in focus. Personal growth takes place as we learn to understand and integrate each of these facets of our character. Each aspect of the personality must grow in its own sphere without disturbing the function of the others. As each aspect matures, we are able to understand more and more about ourselves. When conflict does arise between them, while the process may be painful it should not be destructive. The interaction between them should both enhance and hone the character; those parts, having first been seen as separate entities and then understood, should become familiar and properly integrated into the whole personality. Then it really is a case of the 'whole being greater than the sum of the parts'.

### The Ego

When are dreaming and are observing what is going on, the part that observes is the Ego. Because it is our most conscious aspect, we tend to be more aware in dreams of the conflicts it has with our other aspects. When it has become split off or separate from other parts of the personality, we do not experience the world correctly. When this process goes too far, other aspects 'kick back' as it were, and try to redress the balance through dreams.

The Ego assesses our external reality but, if we are not careful, the need for an 'inner rightness' – an exaggerated need for fantasy – can overtake this reality. Developing objective self-criticism, observation of our fantasies and patience can create a balance.

The proper balance necessary between the inner and the outer, between logic and intuition or reason and imagination means that the Ego must be brought under control, although it can never be given up altogether.

### The Shadow (a figure of the same sex as the dreamer)

This appears in a dream as the person whom we fail to recognize, a vague instinctual figure, sometimes standing behind the dreamer. Often this figure initially appears to be the opposite sex to the dreamer and can therefore be confused with the Animus and Anima. It is only later that it is recognized as the same sex. It is the part of our potential that we have never developed; it is our neglected side. It contains those aspects of our character that have already been thwarted and frustrated, but above all parts which have never been recognized.

Everyone has his or her individual Shadow, and it is nearly always the worst side of us that we have failed to recognize. Meeting the Shadow is painful: it is the shock of seeing ourselves as we really are at our worst. When we are able to face this dreadful entity with humility, we can accept ourselves, and from that acceptance learn to see the rest of reality honestly. We can then often resurrect those normal instincts, appropriate reactions and creative abilities that we have consciously suppressed and buried along with the malicious and destructive sides of the personality. When harnessed and understood, this vital energy becomes a force for forward movement rather than a dangerous enemy.

The Shadow will often appear in dreams as someone we heartily dislike, are afraid of or envy, but whom we cannot ignore. We begin to grow when we realize that some change in circumstance has given us an opportunity to bring it to the surface rather than ignore it in the hope that it will go away. When we work with these frightening dream images, we can often stop projecting the negative aspects outwards and use the energy formerly spent protecting or suppressing them for growth and creativity. We can begin to mature and be real.

When we are not prepared to explore both sides of our personality, we lose a great deal because the way in which we have experienced life most comfortably becomes more difficult. The extrovert discovers that he is unable to cope with the outside world, and the introvert loses his sense of inner peace.

Dreaming can enable us to integrate the Shadow into the personality in such a way that we are able to live more fully both on an inner level and on an outer level. Dreams can both alert us to the need for integration and also assist in the process.

### *Anima/Animus (a figure of the opposite sex to the dreamer)*

No one can quite approximate to the ideal feminine within the man or the ideal masculine within the woman. This confusion of the inner ideal with the outer reality can cause a problem throughout life in any male/female relationship. These inner figures have been called the Anima and the Animus. If we can come to terms with them and accept them for what they are, they become the origin of our understanding of the opposite sex as well as helping us to open up to the inner realms. If this potential for androgyny (inner union) is neglected or abused, in later life the individual is likely to be cut off from contact with the important aspects of the opposite sex. It is possible that the suppressed inner function may come to the fore, making a man behave in an unstable fashion, whereas a woman may, for instance, become quarrelsome.

#### *Anima*

This is the emotional and intuitive side of the male's nature. Principally his mother, but additionally all the women the individual has known, will help to form his image of the feminine and give focus to all the feminine forces within him. In dreams this female figure may show herself as a completely unknown woman, aspects of women the dreamer has known, or as feminine deities.

Dreams make an attempt to offset unbalanced conscious attitudes. The Anima will often appear when a man is neglecting the feminine side of himself, for instance by forcing everything he is into the masculine which puts the qualities of tenderness, obedience and sensitivity beyond his grasp. If he fails to integrate these feminine attributes of warmth and genuine feeling properly, he will be perceived as rigid, world-weary or irresponsible. The suppressed feminine may also erupt into moodiness and temper tantrums rather than the more positive attributes.

When she is thwarted, the Anima turns into the completely negative feminine illusion who destroys all around her. The Anima becomes the guide to inner wisdom only when man confronts his destructive side and learns how to handle the energy he has available.

*Animus*

This part of the personality is the masculine part within a woman's character. When a woman learns how to integrate this properly, she is able to develop her logical, deliberating side, along with the ability to enhance self-awareness. This inner masculine is affected by a woman's early contact with the masculine around her. Interestingly, if the men around her have not been particularly adept in their own understanding of themselves, a woman's Animus can reflect that lack of understanding.

The Animus usually manifests itself in dreams to highlight the woman's need to develop the masculine traits in her personality. Only when she is able to develop her own judgement can she then use the masculine within to good effect without over-developing the need to compete with men, or equally to be destructive to other women.

If the negative side of the Animus dominates a woman's ability to think and plan, she may become obstinate and self-seeking, feeling that life, and particularly men, owes her success. When in dreams the Animus surfaces over and over again in one form or another, she must develop that side of herself that can judge without being judgmental, create strategy without being rigid, and can deliberately rather than instinctively maintain a hold on her inner reality.

Dreams allow us access to the peculiar characteristics which make each of us unique. When we have accessed the Animus or Anima we can allow ourselves to manage them in waking life and to take advantage of the energy released. There may be conflict between the masculine attributes and the feminine ones, but once some kind of a balance is established the integration of the whole character can take place. This leads to a much greater awareness, and ease of life.

*The Self*

The Self is the archetype of potential. It has in fact always been present, but gets hidden behind the necessary development of the personality, and can occasionally become confused with the Shadow. While the Shadow and Animus/Anima have almost deliberately been neglected, the Self holds the true secret of the properly integrated personality, which can only be revealed by working with it. Because the true potential beckons from the future, the first experience in dream form of the Self may be a figure encouraging us to move forward. Later, it becomes a symbol of wholeness, an ideal that we can work with in the here and now to create a sustainable future for ourselves.

As man begins to reach out further and further to understand the world he inhabits, a whole area of material becomes available to him which, if he dares, he is able to access and make use of. This is the unknown, unknowable higher spiritual quality held within us all. Each experience of it is unique, but its knowledge is truly universal. It is the inner guidance which we need to understand and trust. By learning to access this information, we learn once again that we are part of a greater whole with all its attendant glories.

We are often initially aware of it as a holy figure or some aspect of the particular god we have worshipped – Christ, Buddha, Krishna and so on. We exist through time and space as an entity, but are also involved in all things. It is often perceived as a knowledge we have already had without being fully conscious of it. We interact not just with other people but also with everything – we are ultimately all part of one greater whole. It is, as it were, a two-way traffic between the uniqueness and the glory of our being.

When images of this archetype – such as a guru, a god, a saintly animal, a cross, a mandala or other geometric shape – begin to appear in dreams, we are ready to face the process of becoming whole. This non-egocentric greater reality becomes so much part of our personal experience that we stand in danger of confusion. We belong to the human race and must live within our created world. We also belong to the spiritual world and have a personal responsibility within that realm. Only by achieving a balance between the two, and a full interaction, can we hope to be whole.

When negative or destructive images occur connected with this part, we are aware that we are neglecting the power of the Self. It is often at this point that we make a decision to advance and to change for the better. If we do not, often change will be forced upon us.

### The Great Mother/Mother Earth

This archetype is the embodiment of all the aspects of femininity, both positive and negative. It suggests total wholeness in a woman, and is the ability to make use of all areas of her personality. In reaching for this perfection, woman must use and clarify all the separate functions of her being. She must learn to use sensation, feeling, thinking and intuition as her tools rather than as weapons. This archetype is not the exclusively mothering side of woman, but is a much more spiritual inner sense of Self. All life, and the instinctual awareness of its processes, is her domain, and can be cultivated in many different ways.

### A Woman's Self

Every woman is the embodiment of feminine energy, ultimately seeking full expression in the Great Mother. Her focus is on the intangible side of life, on instinct and on feeling. Her abilities express themselves through the functions of sensation, feeling, intellect and intuition. She knows and understands the processes of life and death and of rebirth. Her images tend to be of fullness and nurturing, but also of the erotic and earthly.

She seeks to procreate, but at the same time knows she holds within the ability to destroy. She can be ruthless when it comes to destruction, seeing no point in maintaining that which she considers imperfect. In each individual woman there is a striving to express each function as fully and completely as possible, and she will tend to compensate for what she feels to be her own inadequacies by seeking balance through her man. Thus, the mothering type of woman seeking union with a man who needs mothering is often perceived, as is the virago with the hen-pecked husband. The interesting thing is that these relationships work until such times as either partner recognizes that they can develop other sides of their personality.

### The Wise Old Man

This is the prime archetype for the man's whole Self, in all its aspects. Like the Great Mother for the feminine, he is the composite figure of all the masculine attributes, properly understood and integrated. When a person recognizes that the only appropriate guidance is that which comes from within, the Wise Old Man often appears in dreams. It is as though his appearance is triggered by desperation on the part of the dreamer. By pulling on the deep reserves of the unconscious, a guardian and friend appears to be a source of inspiration and understanding, to give advice and to support necessary decisions. Within the Wise Old Man are combined the functions of sensation, feeling, thinking and intuition.

### A Man's Self

A man's Self will express itself much more through intellect, logic and conscious spirit. The civilized world and a technological society can mean that men are forced into the position of having to make decisions and judgements, which completely deny the intuitive function.

Primitive tribes had a much greater affinity with the earth and therefore less need to use intellect, but there is a tendency now to have the pendulum swing totally the other way. Each individual again grows into maturity by developing the functions of thinking or intellect, sensation, emotion and intuition. In this day and age as man understands more of the process of separation from the mother as a process of individuation and growth, so also he appreciates his need to be separate from, and yet connected with, his unconscious self. Provided he does not try to overcompensate by developing the macho side of himself at the expense of everything else, he will eventually reach a state of balance which allows him to relate to the rest of the world on his own terms. He will achieve an integration which allows him to function properly as a human being. If he loses himself too much on an intellectual level, his dreams will begin to depict the danger he is in.

The unconscious mind appears to sort information by comparing and contrasting. When we are aware of conflict within ourselves – whether this is between the inner and the outer selves, the masculine and feminine or whatever – we may dream in pairs of opposites (e.g. masculine/feminine, old/young, clever/stupid, rich/poor). It is as though there is some kind of internal pendulum which eventually sorts out the opposites into a totally unified whole.

The juggling that goes on in this way can take place over a period of time. A dream clarifying the masculine side of ourselves may be followed by a dream clarifying the feminine. Often in dream interpretation, looking at the opposite meaning to the obvious can give us greater insight into our mental processes.

### Functions of the Archetypes

Jung began studying archetypes and dividing function into thinking, feeling, sensation and intuition. Initially, he did not consider the feminine aspect of this work. Following various advances made by his pupils, it became possible to build up a type of 'map' of the interaction between all of these functions and to discover where distortions occur.

Each function has a 'positive' and 'negative' quality which is perhaps better described as 'greater' and 'lesser'. Each of the masculine and feminine sides of the personality has these four functions, thus there are 64 (8 x 8) interactions possible. Where a distortion has occurred, we tend to project on to those around us the archetype with which we have most difficulty (often the Shadow). Consequently, there will be a tendency to repeat situations over and over (e.g. the woman who continually finds herself in close relationships with a father figure type, or the man who continually finds himself at odds with women executives) until we learn how to cope with – and understand – our distortion. The obverse of this is that, with awareness, one is able to accept other's projections on to oneself without being affected by them. Perfect balance would be achieved by using all aspects of the personality as shown below.

❦ *The feminine archetypes are:*

**Kindly Mother** – this is the conventional picture of the caring mother figure, forgiving transgression and always understanding. Because much has been made of this side of femininity, until recently it was very easy to overdevelop this aspect at the expense of other sides of the personality.

**Destructive Mother** – this woman may be the 'smother-mother' type or the frankly destructive, prohibitive mother. Often, it is this aspect who either actively prevents or – because of her effect on the dreamer – causes difficulty in other relationships.

**Princess** – this is the fun-loving, innocent, childlike aspect of femininity. She is totally spontaneous, but at the same time has a subjective approach to other people.

**Siren** – this type is the seductress, the sexually and sensually aware woman who still has a sense of her own importance. In dreams, she often appears in historic, flowing garments as though to highlight her erotic power.

**Amazon** – the self-sufficient woman who feels she does not need the male; she often becomes the totally career-focused woman. She enjoys the cut and thrust of intellectual sparring.

**Competitor** – she is the woman who competes with all and sundry – both men and women – in an effort to prove she is able to control her own life.

**Priestess** – this is the highly intuitive woman who has learnt to control the flow of spiritual information and use it for the common good. She is totally at home within the inner world.

**Witch** – the intuitive woman using her energy to attain her own perceived ends. She is subjective in her judgement and therefore loses her discernment.

*The masculine archetypes are:*

**Kindly Father** – this side of the masculine is the conventional kindly father figure who is capable of looking after the child in us, but equally of being firm and fair.

**Ogre** – the angry, overbearing, aggressive and scary masculine figure, often arising from the dreamer's relationship with their father or father figure.

**Youth** – the fun-loving, curious aspect of the masculine is both sensitive and creative. This is the 'Peter Pan' figure who has never grown up.

**Tramp** – this is the real freedom lover, the wanderer, the gypsy. He owes no allegiance to anyone and is interested only in what lies around the next corner.

**Hero** – the hero is the man who has elected to undertake his own journey of exploration. He is able to consider options and decide his next move. Often he appears as the Messianic figure in dreams. He will rescue the damsel in distress, but only as part of his growth process.

**Villain** – the villain is completely selfishly involved, not caring who he tramples on in his own search. He is often the aspect of masculinity that women first meet in everyday relationships, so can remain in dream images as a threatening figure if she has not come to terms with his selfishness.

**Priest** – the intuitive man is the one who recognizes and understands the power of his own intuition, but who usually uses it in the service of his god or gods. He may appear in dreams as the Shaman or Pagan priest.

**Sorcerer** – this is the man who uses discernment in a totally dispassionate way for neither good nor evil, but simply because he enjoys the use of power. In his more negative aspect he is the Trickster or Master of Unexpected Change.

Spiritually, when we have access to all the archetypes, we are ready to become integrated and whole, and our dreams will reflect this.

The next section of the book – the main part – is a 'dictionary' listed in A to Z order. At times some of the entries may seem somewhat idiosyncratic and indeed what you are expecting to find may be missing. By and large, as stated previously, it should be possible to find entries similar to the ones you are looking for. You will then be able to develop your own individual slant and will begin to recognize your own very personal set of themes and motifs which occur again and again. We would suggest that, as part of your record keeping, you devote some pages of your journal to a listing of your own personal meanings. It is fascinating in later years to see how you have worked through your issues in different ways.

May I wish you Happy Searching.

## ABACUS

Over thousands of years numbers have taken on a mystical and magical quality, which has helped man to understand his world and eventually led to scientific discovery. Numbers and mathematics have a great deal of significance within spiritual development and thus anything which represents counting or classification bears careful interpretation. An abacus, which allows you to learn about numbers and such concepts as addition, subtraction, multiplication and division, is today more of a child's toy than a scientific instrument. Though basic, it often suggests keeping some kind of a tally.

Counting is an extension of language and the psychological significance of a measuring tool such as an abacus is often linked with the idea of learning new skills. A broken abacus may signify the ending of childhood or of innocence.

An abacus may simply be a reminder of times past which were perhaps less stressful than they are now.

An abacus is an introduction to logic, a masculine quality, rather than intuition, a more feminine one. When a man dreams of an abacus, it may be that he is being reminded of the more logical side of his personality, or the need to calculate risk, whereas a woman may need to become conscious of her more objective qualities rather than rely on her emotions.

*Additional information can be gleaned by reading the entries for Calculator, Numbers and Toy.*

## ABANDONMENT

There are actually several meanings of abandonment that can give rise to dream images. The first links with the idea of being able to let go completely – to be without restraint – and links with the Dionysian concept of abandoning the serious for fun, entering into a state of ecstasy and achieving an altered state of consciousness. The second meaning has a more negative connotation and deals with a sense of loss and deprivation. From a spiritual perspective this can arise from the initial separation anxiety that a baby may suffer when it is first born and realizes that it is no longer in the safe environment of the womb. There can also be a strong sense, as we progress spiritually, of having been abandoned or of having lost something important, perhaps our relationship with the Divine. Dreams can often help us to reconnect as we become more conscious of needing to find a safe haven.

⊗ To be abandoned, i.e. without restraint, within a dream may mean that we are seeking freedom or have issues with the idea of being constrained in some way. We are looking for the freedom to be ourselves.

▦ Similar to the sense of being rejected, the sense of having been abandoned represents how we experienced not being wanted or not fitting in with others when we were young. Such a feeling can occur as a result of trauma. For instance, a child having had to go into hospital may have recurring dreams in adulthood of being abandoned and may have problems in forming plans for future success. In such dreams there is seldom a sense of closure, often a sense of unfinished business. When we ourselves abandon something, we are becoming aware that we no longer need a particular way of thinking or being.

⊡ A child's first and most important relationship is with its mother, so being abandoned in a dream will have slightly different connotations in a man's dream to those of a woman. For both, however, there will be security issues. Grief at the loss of a partner or family member can trigger dreams of abandonment, perhaps bringing to the fore many unresolved issues.

*You may find it helpful to read the entries for Lost, Hospital and Mother.*

**ABBEY** – *see* **RELIGIOUS BUILDINGS IN BUILDINGS**

**ABCESS** – *see* **BODY**

**ABDUCT**

⊛ Abduction in a spiritual sense suggests being taken over by a force that cannot be contained and there is a stage in development where your dreams reflect the awareness of a spiritual force far greater than anything you have ever known. Many people believe that they have been abducted by aliens, and are radically changed by their perception of the experience.

⊗ Abduction signifies being taken away against our will, forced to do something that goes against the grain. The two aspects of victimization and vulnerability come together in an act of abduction, reflecting an element of powerlessness in everyday life.

▦ If we appear to be the victim of abduction in dreams, we usually have an issue with authority, whether that is in a work situation or in our personal lives. It may be helpful to explore such difficulties to be free of the vulnerability this brings. If we ourselves are doing the abducting we should explore our need for control.

For Joyce:

Thank you Francis!
and the list goes on...

Tue March 10th
Wed March 11th      For
Friday March 13th   Jean
Tue March 17th
Wed March 18th

7am to 4pm

Thur. March 5th - 7am to 4pm

⚡ Often in an intense relationship there is a sense of being overcome. For a woman this may result in dreams of abduction whereas a man is more likely to actually play the part of the 'knight in shining armour'.

*You may find it helpful to read the entries for Alien, Hostage, Jailer, Kidnap and Prison.*

## ABNORMAL

🌑 The abnormal or strange traditionally has possessed magical powers, possibilities or opportunities. In dreams we tend to lose the logical scientific side of ourselves and to tap into the more aware open side. Such things used to be beyond understanding and, therefore, appear abnormal and, even today, can make us aware of potential beyond the obvious. In dreams abnormality often represents something that we instinctively feel is wrong, not balanced properly or out of kilter. With an understanding of spirituality we are more able to put the balance right.

♥ An awareness of abnormality alerts us to the fact that we should be paying particular attention to areas in life that are not in line with the way we feel they should be. To dream of a giant, for instance, can indicate that our attention is being drawn to particular issues to do with size or deformity. There is something in our life that may be too big or too distorted to handle.

▣ If the abnormality is extraordinary, such as an abnormal feeling or sound, it is the strangeness that needs to be explored. Inappropriate behaviour or distortion of what we consider to be normal can give us information helpful in managing a situation in everyday life.

⚡ In the balance within us of masculine and feminine, both men and women can find that, as they reach for a better understanding of themselves, dreams bring to the surface traits of character which we consider to be abnormal or deviant.

*Considering the meaning of Magic/Magician and Size may widen your understanding of your particular dream.*

## ABORTION

🌑 Pregnancy is a time of waiting and an abortion is an enforced ending of that time. The modern phrase 'termination of pregnancy' is much closer to the spiritual implications of a dream about an abortion. Generally we must give up a cherished project or idea that has not yet come to full maturity in favour of something else, which ultimately is more important.

♥ The need to look clearly at what we have undertaken to do or to be in our lives becomes apparent. We are in a position to make decisions that will get rid of what is no longer needed, or free us from responsibilities that we cannot handle. We have internalized a new way of thinking or of being, which, on further consideration, may need to be rejected.

▨ There may be a need to reject a feeling, emotion, belief or concept that could be troublesome in some way. A risk has been taken which has not worked – often in relationships – and we must now make a conscious decision to restore the status quo.

▤ When a woman is pregnant and dreams of abortion, particularly during a first pregnancy, she is often trying to come to terms with her new status and any fears and doubts she may have. Such a dream is not usually precognitive. When a man has such a dream he may be beginning to come to terms with some kind of emotional trauma, feelings that he needs to understand and perhaps mourn.

*Additional information might be gleaned by consulting the entries for Baby, Family and Pregnancy.*

**ABOVE –** *see* **POSITION**

**ABROAD**

🌣 Going or being abroad is all about new spiritual experiences. We are moving away from mundane earthly experiences, breaking new ground and transcending boundaries. If we are aware of the country we are in or travelling to, then there is a particular quality or character trait that may be developed in us.

♡ There is a psychological need to get away from, or leave, a situation. We are perhaps travelling towards something new. Our minds are more than capable of accepting new input and experience and will often do so on a subliminal level. We then become aware through dreams of what we have learnt, or what we have to do.

▨ To dream about being or going abroad gives us an understanding of our feelings towards the widening of our horizons, or making changes in our lives. Such dreams may also be connected with beliefs about the country in the dream (See Places). We are dreaming about personal freedom or the ability to move freely around our universe.

▤ Where the dreamer often travels in his or her workaday life, going abroad for a man may simply signify how he gets from A to B – a logical progression. For a woman her issues may be about security and emotional commitment.

*Since the method of travel may be of significance, you may like to consult the entries for Aeroplane, Boat, Car, Journey and Transport.*

**ABSENCE**

🌣 To experience an absence, or sense of nothingness, suggests the Void. This is more easily accessed in the dream state, since our waking brain receives too much input via our senses to be able totally to shut out any stimulation.

♥ We are in a situation where we may suffer loss or where we may reject something we need. The type of dream where we are in a familiar environment, but a much-loved article or person is missing, suggests we may have a feeling of impermanence.

▦ A dream about someone being absent, or of the absence of something one would expect to find, indicates that the unexpected may happen. We may be looking for something that we have already lost. Our feelings about the absence (e.g. fear or anger) may also be important. A child experiences a strong sense of loss when mother is first absent from his perceived environment and this can cause extreme distress.

*You might like to consult the entries for Abyss and Lose/Loss/Lost.*

## ABUSE

✺ Spiritual abuse suggests that our sense of rightness has been violated. Perhaps our beliefs or faith have been held up to ridicule. We do not have the resources to be able to withstand such an onslaught.

♥ Emotional abuse in ordinary life can be experienced in dreams as violence and brutality.

▦ Physical abuse can give rise to nightmares and other terror dreams, further depleting our resources due to both broken sleep patterns and the over stimulation of the Fright, Fight, Flight response.

*Also consult Anxiety Dreams in the Introduction.*

## ABYSS

✺ The Underworld, which contains ghosts, ghouls, demons and inferior matters, has been pictured so often as frightening that it often appears in dreams as the abyss. On a very profound level, the Void or abyss is the Unknowable, that part of the Cosmos that is beyond our understanding. Considering the meaning of the Void or abyss and exploring doubts and fears may help with interpretation of your dream.

♥ There is a fear of losing control, of a loss of identity, or of some type of failure. More positively, it is possible to go beyond our own boundaries or present experience. Also the abyss indicates our coming to terms with opposites such as right and wrong, good and bad. To be on the edge of the abyss suggests having to come to terms with our own fears.

▦ To dream of an abyss indicates that you recognize within yourself the so-called bottomless pit or void. This is an aspect of the unknown which all of us must face at some time or another in our lives. It signifies risky action which must be taken without knowledge of what the outcome is going to be.

*Consult the entry for Empty for further information.*

**ACCENT – *see* VOICE**

**ACCIDENT**

From a spiritual perspective there is no such thing as an accident, so in dreams such an occurrence signifies Divine intervention, or interference from an authoritative source.

Such dreams may highlight anxieties to do with safety or carelessness, or fear of taking responsibility. When the accident happens to us our vulnerability is highlighted, when it happens to others we are made aware of the thoughtlessness of others.

Dreams of being injured, murdered or killed occur relatively frequently and seem to be a response to threat. Attention, therefore, needs to be paid to the specific circumstances of the dream. We are usually receiving a warning to be careful or to be aware of hidden aggression, either our own or others'.

*Also consult the entries for Fall/Falling.*

**ACHE – *see* BODY**

**ACID**

It is the symbolism of acid that is important in a spiritual interpretation. As a corrosive substance which may or may not have a positive effect, there is an ambivalence in any interpretation. An act of corruption and potential destructiveness eats away at our integrity, yet may leave us feeling cleansed.

Psychologically there is an awareness that self-confidence and our usual sense of well-being is being eroded by outside influences.

A corrosive influence in our lives may be bad but the eventual outcome can be cleansing or healing. There could be the feeling that we are being 'eaten away' by some action or concept. We should become aware of something – perhaps words or actions – that must be used with caution, depending how and on whom they are being used.

**ACORN**

Life, fertility and immortality are symbolized by the acorn, as is the androgynous. In the seed cup is the feminine and in the nut the potential for all life. The two together suggest individual life.

The germ of an idea is present. There is also a need for patience in dealings, either with ourselves or others (the acorn requires a long gestation period to grow into the mighty oak).

When we dream of acorns there is a huge growth process beginning to emerge from small beginnings. There is a new potential for strength and spirituality. Since acorns appear in autumn, there may be the need to harvest or gather up the ideas before they can be stored, in order to give them time to work.

⚐ Androgeny is inherent in the acorn along with the close relationship between the masculine and feminine principles with its potential for growth. This often means that this symbol should be interpreted by the male as fertility (normally a feminine realm) and by the female as tenacity and strength (usually perceived as masculine traits).

## ACQUIT

✹ Any dream about a judicial process is usually to do with your own internal sense of right or wrong, so to dream that you have been acquitted of a crime suggests that spiritually you feel you can justify your own actions.

♥ Whether we have chosen to develop it or not, there is an inner mentoring process which goes on in the background of our lives. Self-justification is not always possible on a conscious level, but dreams give us the opportunity to sort out our fears and doubts about our own moral conduct.

▦ On a more mundane level, to dream that you are acquitted of a crime denotes the possibility of legal action. To see others acquitted in your dream signifies that you are able to find compassion and forgiveness over others' misdemeanours.

*You may find clarification by reading the entries for Authority Figures in People, Guilt and Juror/Jury.*

## ACTOR

✹ There is an idea that we write our own scripts in life, so to perceive an actor on stage suggests that we each need to take responsibility for our actions and the act of living. Such an image may also suggest that we are somewhat dissociated from reality.

♥ We each are actors in our own play, so to see ourselves as actors suggests we may be projecting a particular persona or specific aspect of ourselves. We may not yet feel that we are in control of our own destiny, but are being ruled by the circumstances around us. We are being given the opportunity to make changes and become a different person.

▦ To dream of an actor, particularly a famous one, is to become aware of the ego in oneself. Very often we become conscious of the roles we are acting out every day and recognize that we are perhaps not playing the part we really want to in life.

⚐ In a man's dream an actor can represent the public figure while an actress will suggest one of the feminine archetypes and his Anima. In a woman's dream an actor may represent her Animus and an actress a hidden, perhaps unrecognized part of herself.

*You might also like to consult the entries for Celebrity, Famous People and Theatre.*

**ADDER – *see* SNAKE AND SERPENT IN ANIMALS**

**ADDICT/ADDICTION**

� Spiritually, this is connected with the pleasure seeking, hedonistic aspect of the Self, which seeks a change of consciousness for the better. The story of Dionysus, who taught men how to grow and tend the vine and to make wine because he felt that man deserved the ecstatic experience, epitomizes man's search for a better world, and the need to understand his own passionate nature.

♦ Awareness of addiction in dreams is an identification of the hold our own passions may have over us. We fear loss of control (that is, control over ourselves), but also our control of other people. To be with a group of addicts suggests we do not understand our own behaviour in social situations. We may be conscious of the fact that we tend to become the victim in everyday life.

▦ Such a dream allows us to recognize and acknowledge obsessive behaviour in ourselves or others. We may be subconsciously aware or have an anxiety that someone or something is taking us over. To be addicted to someone is to have abdicated responsibility for ourselves. To be addicted to a substance such as tobacco, alcohol or drugs in a dream suggests an inability to relate properly to the world we live in and that we cannot function without some sort of a prop or psychological crutch.

*Also consult the entries for Alcohol/Alcoholic and Drugs.*

**ADDRESS – *see* EMAIL, LETTER AND PARCEL**

**ADOLESCENT – *see* PEOPLE**

**ADOPT**

� To adopt a person or a way of life is to draw it towards you – to make it your own. From a spiritual perspective this suggests a process of learning to be comfortable within a given set of circumstances – to accept a way of being.

♦ It may be that an aspect of your life needs adjustment and the circumstances surrounding a dream of adoption need exploring. To dream of being adopted may reveal a basic insecurity over your sense of self.

▦ Dreaming of adopting a child suggests you may have doubts about taking on new responsibilities. Conversely such a dream may signify that you are now in a position to take on a new project or concept.

▐ In a man's dream, being adopted may suggest fear of emotional closeness, whereas in a woman's dream, she may actually be seeking such closeness. Your own personal circumstances will often give further clarification.

## ADVERTISEMENT

☀ The dreaming mind will often use a well-known object or device to drive home its message and an advertisement is one of those devices. Information received psychically needs acknowledgement so we can move forwards.

♥ There is a need to put ourselves on the line and to be acknowledged for who we are. If we ourselves are the subject of the advertisement, we should expect to be more upfront and open about our activities. If someone we know is advertising themselves in our dream, we may have become aware that they have the ability to help us in our activities. Conversely, our subconscious may be alerting us to their need for help.

▦ Depending on the other content of the dream, this indicates those areas in our lives that need to be acknowledged or recognized. For instance, an advertisement on a hoarding might mean a way of working in the world, whereas a television advert would represent a way of thinking. To dream of reading an advertisement in a newspaper might have a more personal impact than any other type of message.

## ADVICE

☀ We all have an inner awareness. The Higher Self or spiritual part of ourselves will often manifest itself as a figure that is giving advice, sometimes a figure of authority or a parental figure.

♥ In dreams, accepting advice helps us to acknowledge the need for change – perhaps to be doing something you don't necessarily want to do. Giving advice is recognizing that you are aware that you have information that can be helpful to others.

▦ Receiving advice in a dream means we should consider guidance from within, possibly from a part of ourselves that is unrecognized. A little thought will usually reveal which circumstances in our daily lives are under consideration.

⊞ In a man's dream, if he is receiving advice from a woman he may find it helpful to identify with which aspect of his Anima he is working. In a woman's dream, she may wish to consider her Animus as an ally rather than as an opponent.

*Additional information can be gleaned by reading Archetypes in the Introduction and the entry for Family.*

## AEROPLANE

☀ By association with the winged chariot, the aeroplane represents a spiritual journey. However as more and more people use this form of transport, the aeroplane can simply suggest the need for quick action or change of circumstance. Like the bus, it can represent a group purpose.

An aeroplane denotes a search for psychological freedom, a move towards independent being. It also suggests transcendence of the mundane, a need to 'lift off' into new ways of thinking.

Dreams of aeroplanes can represent sudden or dramatic life changes. An aeroplane taking off represents a leap into the unknown and taking risks. An aeroplane landing indicates the success of a new venture or the outcome of a calculated risk. An aeroplane crashing suggests the failure of a venture or life dream.

In some cases the aeroplane can suggest a phallic symbol or the assertive masculine. A man may choose this interpretation at the beginning of a new relationship, whereas a woman is more likely to use this interpretation as she progresses further into the relationship and understands her partner's ambition and drive.

*You may also like to consult the entries for Abroad, Airport, Bus, Journey and Transport.*

## AFFAIR

Dreaming of an affair shows we are seeking to integrate opposite polarities within ourselves: male/female, drive/receptivity, good/bad. Such integration and an understanding of the dynamics leads to wholeness and an ability to access hidden aspects of our personality.

We could be actively seeking emotional satisfaction in a way that is unacceptable in our waking lives. In dreams, to be having an affair with someone we don't know suggests that we should perhaps reassess our own needs and desires. If the affair is with someone we know but would not normally consider in that light we are perhaps looking for different sorts of satisfaction.

We need to come to terms with our own sexual needs and desires for excitement and stimulation. Dreaming of an affair allows us to release such feelings. We may feel the need to do something naughty or something that means we have to take emotional risks.

When a woman dreams of an affair, it is likely that she has registered that connection before becoming consciously aware of it. A man will tend to be more physically attracted before dreaming of an affair. Men tend to be better at analyzing systems while women tend to be better at reading the emotions of other people. They have an increased ability to bond and be connected to others.

*For further clarification you might like to read the entries for Family and People.*

**AFRAID** – *see* ANXIETY DREAMS IN THE INTRODUCTION

**AGATE** – *see* GEMS/JEWELS

**AGGRESSION –** *see* **ANGER**

**AIR**

    Spiritually, air signifies the Breath of Life and is the second element in the four creative elements of Fire, Air, Water and Earth, which together are part of the manifestation.

    Air represents the intellect and psychologically allows us to bridge the gap between the spiritual realm and the physical. As breath, it is a necessary part of life which tends not to be thought about until there is a problem. In dreams we will become conscious of air as a breeze or a wind of some sort.

    From a pragmatic point of view, air is a force which supports and surrounds all that we do, so in dreams to be conscious of bellows or a pump suggests that we need to use strategy and power to achieve our ends.

*Consult the entry for Wind for further clarification.*

**AIR FORCE –** *see* **ARMED FORCES**

**AIRPORT**

    An airport, because of its transitory nature, is a place for new experiences. We are ready to consider our spiritual progression, to move into a new way of perceiving life and all it has to offer. It signifies the desire for freedom, high ideals, ambition and hopes.

    Being delayed at an airport suggests that conditions are not yet right for what it is you wish to begin. We are being put in a position where our values may need to be reassessed in the light of our own – or someone else's – authority.

    In dreaming of an airport we are entering a stage of transition, making decisions to move into new areas of life. It may also indicate we are, or should be, making a fresh assessment of our own identity. Watching planes take off from an airport lounge suggests that we are – or fear – being left behind.

**ALBATROSS –** *see* **BIRDS**

**ALBINO –** *see* **COLOUR**

**ALCHEMY**

    Alchemy is the science of transformation and refinement, when crude material is turned into pure. While it is understood by most to be the turning of lead into gold, the spiritual significance is, in fact, the refinement of the spirit through understanding into a state of awareness approaching Divinity and the knowledge of Eternal Life.

    Alchemy from a psychological perspective is a philosophy of the cosmos and of mankind's place in the scheme of things. It is the refinement of thought, having the key through the Archetypes to unlocking an understanding of the innermost and unconscious part of the psyche. As an agent for change it has a relevance in dreams through both its symbolism and processes.

▦ Alchemy began as a rudimentary form of chemical technology, exploring the nature of substances, and in so doing developed a series of semi-scientific procedures in order to find the essence of those substances. It has that significance in dreams of a mundane nature when we are trying to get to the bottom of problems and situations.

## ALCOHOL/ALCOHOLIC

✿ Alcohol as 'spirit' or essence is the conjunction of opposites, a combination of the principles of fire and water. It is a means of changing consciousness. In dreams where alcohol is a feature there is an element of attempting to transcend the ordinary and approach the Divine (the Essence).

♡ When the normal constraints we put on ourselves in waking life are removed, we can often reach our own truth. Alcohol as a symbol of the removal of restraint enables us to accept dream ideas we might otherwise reject. There is the recognition of the potential for emotional confusion out of which can come clarity. To dream of an alcoholic suggests that we need to look at the way we handle excess and obsession in our daily lives.

▦ When alcohol appears in a dream it suggests that in a mundane sense we may need or require a largely pleasurable experience or influence. We have available means of changing perception. We can afford to let go and 'go with the flow' of what is happening to us.

⬒ As the use of alcohol becomes more prevalent in the everyday, it can have the effect of changing the quality of dreams, bringing more frightening or incomprehensible images to the fore. Often these images need to be interpreted in the way that they were in previous times, as gremlins and hidden fears and anxieties. Men tend to be less inclined to interpret such images and to dismiss them as being irrelevant, women may choose to take note of them.

*You may like to consult the entries for Abandonment, Drunk and Wine.*

## ALIEN/ALIENATED

✿ From a spiritual perspective an alien thought suggests one that goes against the grain. An alien being may be a manifestation of evil or, as something different and not yet understood, the Occult.

♡ To recognize that you feel alienated within a dream suggests that there is the potential in everyday life for experiencing oneself – or a part of oneself – as not belonging. To feel alienated from the dream scenario is the realization of being different from others in the way we live our lives.

🔲 To dream of an alien being suggests that there is something unknown and frightening which needs to be faced. We have never encountered the strangeness of the being that appears in our dream and we must handle whatever happens.

**ALLERGY – *see* ILLNESS**

**ALMOND – *see* FOOD AND NUT**

**ALONE**

🔅 Spiritually, dreaming of being totally alone suggests that we have reached a state of completeness, of wholeness. We have dissociated ourselves from the ordinary and the mundane.

♦ We have developed the ability to recognize the need to deal with our own emotional make-up without the help of others. By and large such a dream occurs within the framework of learning to meditate and highlights our individuality.

🔲 Dreaming of being alone can highlight being single, isolated or lonely. More positively, it represents the need for independence. Loneliness can be experienced as a negative state, whereas being alone can be very positive. Often in dreams a feeling is highlighted in order for us to recognize whether it is positive or negative.

⊟ In both men's and women's dreams, feeling alone can highlight the state of our relationships. When someone dies or a relationship comes to an end, such a dream can signify grief.

**ALTAR**

🔅 In most religions the altar signifies a sacred space where we commune with the Divine In the presence of the Divine, we can give thanks and be at one. Spiritually an altar signifies both the barrier and the link between the physical realms and the spiritual.

♦ The act of sacrifice, or rather of making our lives sacred, needs to be acknowledged and can be done through ceremony. An altar is an appropriate place to carry out such ceremonies, so in dreams it signifies a special place of great meaning. What is placed on the altar is significant and can be interpreted in the light of your religious belief or lack of such belief. Psychologically, it is worthwhile considering what is being sacrificed or given up, either willingly or unwillingly, in everyday life.

🔲 An altar in a dream represents the means or need to give ourselves up to something that is more important than the immediate situation. It can also represent the centre of your world, the starting point for a new life, or the giving up of an old one.

⊞ Within the framework of the differences between men's and women's dreams, working at an altar can highlight the difference between the archetype of the sorcerer, who tends to use power dispassionately, and the priestess, whose caring is more intuitive and in tune with what is needed.

*Also consult the entry for Table as well as the information on Spiritual Imagery in the Introduction.*

**AMBER –** *see* **GEMS/JEWELS**

**AMBULANCE –** *see* **TRANSPORT**

**AMBUSH**

✷ Any dream that contains an image representing a force greater than ourselves suggests an inability to handle circumstances around us. The most outstanding element of an ambush is its surprise, highlighting the unexpectedness of such a situation. Spiritually this may be, for instance, emotions and feelings about past events or traumas, with which we may consider we have come to terms but which re-emerge to trap us.

♡ Dreams of being ambushed suggest that we are subconsciously aware of being in danger. Our way forward is blocked until we deal with the problem. Waiting to ambush someone else suggests an element of cruelty in our make-up and that we are waiting for someone to make a mistake.

▦ Circumstances around us are not what they seem and we can expect the unexpected. Whether we can deal with what happens depends on our strength of character and ability to handle crises.

*You may also like to consult the entry for Kidnap and Prison.*

**AMERICA –** *see* **PLACES**

**AMETHYST –** *see* **GEMS/JEWELS**

**AMPUTATION**

✷ Spiritually any amputation signifies a loss of some sort – we may be attempting to disfigure the perfect. Often dreams show by their symbolism what is not right or good and a dream of amputation suggests that we need to take action to rectify the situation.

♡ We are suffering from a loss of power or ability and may, in the process, find that we have cut short an experience. Since pain is often a consequence of an amputation, we are trying to come to terms with pain or unpleasantness which has occurred in waking life.

▦ When we dream of the amputation of one of our own limbs, we risk or fear losing or cutting off, by repressing, a part of ourselves. There is loss of a facility or something we value. To dream of amputating someone else's limb indicates our ability to deny others their right to self-expression.

⚡ Arising from the patterning laid down in the womb, dreams of amputation of a limb can often have a sexual or gender specific meaning. In a man's dream there is an aspect of emasculation occurring, whereas in a woman's dream, she may be experiencing problems with aspects of her Animus.

*You might also like to read the entries for Guillotine and Operation as well as the information on Archetypes in the Introduction.*

## AMULET – *see* BADGE AND GEMS/JEWELS

## ANALYST

☀ When we dream of visiting an analyst or therapist we are in contact with the transformative power within, the monitor that alerts us to the need to analyse our actions and reactions. Spiritually that part of us that can heal us is making itself felt.

♥ The presence of an analyst in dreams alerts us to the fact that we are not acting appropriately in a situation in waking life. Also, if we are undergoing therapy in real life, the professional person can become a figure of authority in dreams.

▦ By analysing our actions and ideas – and breaking them down into manageable parts – we can improve our everyday lives.

⚡ Often in dreams an analyst will appear as a member of the opposite sex, so it is worthwhile taking careful note of what the interaction is between you and other people in the dream scenario.

## ANCESTORS – *see* FAMILY

## ANCHOR

☀ From a spiritual perspective the symbol of the anchor is particularly significant as it represents a boat and mast and hence the union of masculine and feminine. Its appearance in a dream shows we are working towards a time of a future tranquility. The anchor can also be the symbol of security and in Early Christian art was used as a representation of the Cross.

♥ Psychologically we need encouragement to develop the ability to 'hold fast' during a period of instability. If we can ride out the storm we shall survive. When an anchor is being dragged during a dream, the external forces are too great for us.

▦ When an anchor appears in a dream it usually means the necessity to remain stable in emotional situations. We need to catch hold of a concept or idea which will give us a point of reference in difficult situations.

⚡ In a man's dream the anchor can sometimes suggest his sexuality or perhaps his more creative urges. In a woman's dream it suggests either her nurturing side, intuitive abilities or perhaps the security of relationship, either personal or Cosmic.

*You might also like to consult the entry for Boat/Ship.*

## ANDROGEN/ANDROGENY

✸ From the very earliest times the idea of two polarities being able to unite in perfect harmony has been inherent in all spiritual belief. The union of the masculine and feminine principle into one perfect being is a principle presented in various forms in art and literature. The androgen in dreams, at a certain stage of development, can indicate a perfect spiritual balance, a state of autonomy and primordial perfection.

♥ We need an understanding of how our emotional selves can balance our personalities. The presence of an androgen in dreams suggests that we need to reconcile opposing thoughts and feelings within ourselves to achieve a balanced progression.

▦ If we dream of someone and cannot decide if they are male or female we are making an attempt to reconcile the opposite sides of ourselves. We are searching for completion and wholeness.

⸬ In both a woman's dream and a man's dream androgeny represents a coming to terms with the dynamic that can be created when we have an understanding of all aspects of our personality. We have, on some level, succeeded in what psychologists term 'integration'.

## ANGEL

✸ Nowadays, with a greater acknowledgement of the appearance of angelic figures, they are once again accepted as messengers of the Gods – heavenly powers and enlightenment. Traditionally perceived as beings of light, their appearance in dreams indicates that we are seeking a spirituality and purity of being that goes beyond the mundane. In almost all religious belief angels stand as intermediaries between us and the Divine. Archangels are a higher order of angels, each with their own responsibilities, and are more likely to appear if you are undertaking esoteric studies.

♥ From a psychological perspective the angel is the personification of the relationship with mother or mother figure and needs to be looked at as a separate entity to both her and the dreamer, i.e. as though it were a living, breathing being.

▦ Dreaming of angels indicates we are searching for a parental figure who gives unconditional love and support, or that we need to develop these qualities ourselves. We may be trying to introduce religious concepts into our lives.

⊡ Angels' appearance in dreams – for both men and women – suggest that we need to look at concepts that are particularly spiritual in origin. Both angels and archangels are traditionally identifiable by their attributes.

*You might also like to consult the information on Spiritual Imagery in the Introduction for further clarification.*

## ANGER

❀ Throughout history societies have believed that if their gods are displeased they will show their anger. If a dream figure is angry, therefore, we may feel that we are offending our own code of conduct or are suffering Divine displeasure. Often anger is symbolized in dreams by, for instance, a flaming torch or a raging animal.

♥ We can give ourselves permission to feel passion or aggression, which could be sexual or otherwise. Often the way we express emotion in dreams can give us information as to appropriate behaviour in everyday life. If someone is angry at you in dreams in an uncharacteristic way you may have offended them without consciously being aware that this has happened.

▦ Anger in a dream can often represent other passionate emotions. Aggression (an unprovoked attack) can be perceived as an extreme form of anger. We are struggling with the right to express that which is distressing us. We probably are unable to express emotion appropriately in waking life, but can do so in dreams. Annoyance is a mild form of anger which is a reaction to a perceived threat. It reflects our feeling that we are being denied what is ours by necessity or by right.

*Consult the entry for Argue/Arguments.*

## ANIMA/ANIMUS – *see* ARCHETYPES IN THE INTRODUCTION

## ANIMALS

❀ By understanding animals and their symbolism we approach life in a more simplistic and natural way. In Shamanism, one of the most ancient belief systems, animals are an intrinsic part of the shaman's (wise man or priest) journey into other realms. They are protective as well as being teachers.

♥ When we need some sort of understanding of our own psychological urges, animals will appear in dreams – and sometimes in everyday life – which symbolize those qualities. These are:

**Antelope** – the antelope represents speed, grace and beauty.

**Badger** – the badger is both well loved and much maligned. It signifies a hierarchical family structure and, because of its nocturnal habits, the basic wisdom belonging to the underworld.

**Bear** – the mother appears in dreams in many forms, the bear being one of them. The image may be of the possessive, devouring mother or of the all-caring mother. If it is recognized in the dream that the bear is masculine, the image may then be of an overbearing person, or possibly the father. *Also consult the entry for Family.*

**Beaver** – as a builder/gatherer the beaver suggests industriousness, preservation and best use of resources.

**Bull** – usually the bull in a dream denotes the negative side of behaviour, such as destructiveness, fear or anger (for example, a bull in a china shop). However, more positively, the bull is recognized as sexual passion or creative power. Slaying the bull indicates initiation into the world of the mature adult who succeeds in mastering his instincts, and can also represent the sign of Taurus in the Zodiac.

**Cat** – to dream of cats is to link with the feline, sensuous side in human beings, usually in women. Goddesses such as Bast the Egyptian cat goddess are usually represented as having two sides to their natures, one devious and one helpful, so the cat often denotes the capricious side of the feminine. The elegant but also the powerful yet overly self-sufficient aspect of woman, may also be perceived as the cat.

**Chameleon** – we are recognizing either in ourselves or others the ability to adapt and to change according to surrounding circumstances.

**Cow** – the eternal feminine, especially the mother or mother figure, is often depicted by the cow. This is partly because it provides milk and nourishment. *Also consult the entry for Family.*

**Deer/Reindeer** – the deer and the reindeer herd have a strict hierarchical structure. The deer symbolizes pride and nobility. We recognize our place in the world.

**Dinosaurs** – *see individual entry and also the entry for Monster.*

**Dog** – we may recognize a faithful and constant companion, a protector or, more negatively, somebody we can't shake off and who might make trouble. Dreaming of a dog we once owned or knew at a previous time in our lives shows that there may be memories associated with that period of our life, which hold clues to present behaviour. A huntress with dogs indicates we are making a connection with one of the feminine archetypes, that of the Amazon. A dog guarding gates or being near a cemetery signifies the guardian of the threshold and creatures that must be put to sleep, tamed or brought under control before there can be an initiation into the secrets of the underworld.

*You may also wish to consult the individual entry for Dog.*

**Elephant** – to see an elephant in a dream is to recognize the qualities of patience, long memory, strength and fidelity. In the more esoteric sense it signifies radiant and glowing wisdom.

**Fox** – a fox in a dream tells of hypocrisy, cunning and slyness. We should be aware of someone around us whom we do not particularly trust.

**Frog** – because a frog transforms (from a tadpole and moves on to the land), one appearing in a dream indicates a period or act of transformation. There is something unpleasant which eventually transmutes into a desirable asset (e.g. a frog into a prince). *Consult the entry for Reptiles in this section for further clarification.*

**Goat** – to dream of a goat is to recognize creative energy and masculine vitality. It may also represent the dark side of human nature, promiscuousness and sexuality. To be riding a goat is to be trying to come to terms with our relationship with the dark side of our nature. The goat may also represent the Devil or Satan, as seen in old woodcut images. It is also the symbol for the astrological sign of Capricorn.

**Gorilla** – in being so similar to the human being, gorillas have represented the more frightening aspects of mankind. As time passes, we recognize familiar aspects of a somewhat undeveloped personality coupled with a strong sense of family.

**Hare** – the hare highlights intuition, spiritual insight and intuitive 'leaps'. Intuition may be debased into 'madness' or capriciousness by fear or ignorance. Because of its association with the moon, the hare can, in its negative aspect, signify the Priestess/Witch aspect of femininity or the Priest/Sorcerer of the masculine. In its positive imagery, however, it is the radiant hare (often holding its baby in a cave) and thus the Mother of God. *Also consult the information on Archetypes in the Introduction.*

**Hedgehog** – the hedgehog can represent nastiness and bad manners, or quite literally our inability to handle a prickly situation.

**Horse** – the horse in a dream represents the energy at our disposal. A white horse depicts our spiritual awareness, a brown one the more pragmatic and down-to-earth side, while a black horse is the passionate side of our nature. A pale horse has the same symbolism as the figure of Death with this scythe. A winged horse depicts the soul's ability to transcend the earthly plane and, therefore, pass through the astral planes. If the horse is under strain or dying there is a severe weakening of the dynamic power that carries us forward. Too much pressure may be being experienced in our lives. If the horse is being harnessed to a cart we may be concentrating too hard on thoroughly utilitarian objectives. In a man's dream a mare will denote the Anima, a woman, or the realm of the feminine. In a woman's dream, being kicked by a horse may indicate the Animus or her relationship with a man. A horse that can get through any door and batter down all obstacles is the collective Shadow – those aspects of the personality that most people attempt to suppress. The horse as a beast of burden is often the Great Mother or mother archetype. Even though the horse has been superceded in waking life by the car, it still has huge significance in dreams. *Also consult the entry for Car as well as the information on Archetypes in the Introduction.*

**Hyena** – the hyena is generally taken in dreams to signify impurity, instability and deviousness.

**Jackal** – esoterically the jackal assists in allowing us to access past lives and the astral planes. The jackal-headed Egyptian god Anubis weighed the souls of the departed in the Judgement Hall. It is this that gives the jackal its quality of scavenger.

**Jaguar** – the jaguar's main qualities are its speed and balance. It stands for the balance of power between the dark and light forces.

**Kangaroo** – this animal often symbolizes nurturing, caring and motherhood. It also represents innate strength.

**Lamb** – the lamb is the innocent side of man's nature. It is said that evil cannot withstand such innocence.

**Leopard** – the leopard represents cruelty and aggression and traditionally the deviousness of wrongly used power.

**Lion** – the lion stands for majesty, strength and courage. It can also represent the ego and the passions associated with it. If we are struggling with the lion there should be a successful development as long as we are not overpowered, or the lion killed. A man-eating lion shows that an aspect of our personality has slipped out of alignment, putting both us and our surroundings at risk. A lion lying with a lamb shows there is a union, or compatibility of opposites; instinct and spirit going hand in hand.

**Lizard** – the lizard appearing in a dream represents instinctive action or 'one-track' thinking. *Also consult the entry for Reptiles in this section.*

**Lynx** – the main quality associated with the lynx is its keen eyesight, thus in a dream it can often portray objectivity.

**Monkey** – the monkey characterizes the infantile, childish and arrested side of our character. The qualities of mischief, impudence and inquisitiveness all belong to the monkey. While these are often seen as regressive tendencies, this quality of lively curiosity maintains a necessary lightness of spirit.

**Mare** – *consult the entry for Horse in this section.*

**Mole** – the mole is often taken to represent the powers of darkness, but can often signify the blind persistence and determination that enables us to succeed.

**Mouse** – the mouse's quality of timidity can often be addressed in the dreamer, if it is recognized that this can arise from turbulence and lack of understanding. *Also consult the entry for Vermin in this section.*

**Otter** – the otter is uniquely equipped to exist within its chosen element of water and to be able to gain subsistence from its surroundings, all things we may need to develop.

**Ox** – the ox depicts the ability to be patient and to make sacrifices for others.

Panther – the panther is a strong symbol for feminine energy, particularly in its freedom-loving aspect. It also signifies regenerative power: death and rebirth.

**Pig** – the pig is taken in Western belief to indicate ignorance, stupidity, selfishness and gluttony. We may be beginning to recognize these unattractive qualities in ourselves; without such recognition there can be no transformation or mastery of them. Ultimately, however, it is the qualities of intelligence and cunning that prevail. If we dream of pigs and jewels together it shows there is a conflict between the lower, basic urges and higher spiritual values. Perhaps there is a failure to appreciate spiritual values. Big litters of piglets can represent fruitfulness, although sometimes without result, since the sow can depict the Destructive Mother. *Consult the information on Archetypes in the Introduction for further clarification.*

**Rabbit** – rabbits appearing in a dream can mean one of two things: the obvious connection with fertility could be important, or it could be that the Trickster aspect is coming to the fore. A white rabbit may show us the way to the inner spiritual world and, as such, act as a guide. *Also consult the entry for Hare in this section.*

**Ram** – the ram is a symbol of masculine virility and power and, by association, has those qualities of the sign of Aries in the Zodiac.

**Rat** – the rat signifies a tainted or devious part of our personality or a situation we are in. It can also represent something that is repulsive in some way. We may also be experiencing disloyalty from a friend or colleague. *Also consult the entry for Vermin in this section.*

**Reptiles** – to dream of reptiles indicates that we are looking at the more frightening lower aspects of the personality. The unfeeling, inhuman aspect of the instincts, usually recognized as being destructive and alien, is often portrayed by reptiles and other cold-blooded animals. We may have no control over these instincts, and could, therefore, be easily 'devoured' by them. We learn to understand deceitful behaviour. Though we are afraid of Death or the death process, we recognize that we must go through a process of change in order to be reborn.

**Seal** – the seal is most beautiful in its own element of water, thus to dream of one shows that we are at one with our own domain. We are capable of progressing through our emotions.

**Serpent** – the serpent is a universal symbol which can be male or female, or it can be self-created. It can signify death or destruction or conversely life and also rejuvenation. It is the instinctive nature and equally is also potential energy. When the power of the instinctive nature is understood and harnessed we come to terms with our own sexuality and sensuality and are able to make use of the higher and more spiritual energies that become available. In a man's dream a serpent or snake may appear if he has not understood the feminine or intuitive part of himself, or when he doubts his own masculinity. In a woman's dream the serpent may manifest if she is afraid of sex, or sometimes of her own ability to seduce others. Because of its connection with the Garden of Eden, the serpent is the symbol of duplicity and trickery and also of temptation. *Also consult the entry for Snake in this section.*

**Sheep** – the sheep is renowned for its flock instinct and it is this interpretation that is most usually accepted in dreams. The helplessness of the sheep when off balance is also another aspect that is recognizable, as is the apparent lack of intelligence. The god-fearing, 'good sheep' and also the passive and 'sheepish' may have relevance within the context of the dream. To dream of sheep and wolves or of sheep and goats is to register the conflict between good and evil.

**Sinister Animals** – to find any animal threatening in a dream indicates the fears and doubts we have over our ability to cope with the stirrings of the unconscious. Such dreams are relatively common when starting out on personal spiritual development.

**Snake** – in common with serpent dreams, snake dreams occur when we are attempting to come to terms with our more instinctive self. Inevitably this has to do with the recognition and harnessing of energies that have been suppressed and thwarted. Since the most primeval urge is sexuality, the image of the snake is the most primitive one available. Because snakes are such a low form of life, while also being in some cases poisonous, they have become associated with death and all that man fears.

A snake twined around the body or limb indicates some form of bondage, possibly being enslaved to the passions. A snake, or worm, leaving a corpse by its mouth sometimes represents the sexual act (the little death), but can also signify our control of our libido. A snake in the grass image denotes disloyalty, trickery and evil. The image of a snake with its tail in its mouth is one of the oldest available to man and signifies completion and the union of the spiritual and physical. Being swallowed by a snake shows the need and ability to return to the ultimate and lose our sense of space and time. Dreaming of a snake twined around a staff or similar suggests that the unconscious forces that drive us are being released to create healing, rebirth and renewal. The colours of the snake may give additional insight into the meaning of the dream. *Also consult the individual entries for Caduceus, Colour, Eating and Shapes/Patterns, as well as Serpent in this section*

**Squirrel** – the squirrel represents the hoarding, acquisitive aspect of our personalities.

**Tiger** – the tiger signifies royalty, dignity and power and is both a creator and a destroyer.

**Toad** – dreaming of toads connects us with whatever we may consider ugly in life, or in our behaviour. However, implicit in that ugliness is the power of transformation and growth into something beautiful. For a toad and an eagle to appear is to note the difference between earthly and spiritual values. *Consult the entry for Reptiles in this section for further clarification.*

**Unicorn** – as a symbol of purity the unicorn traditionally could only be owned and perceived by virgins. It is a return to, and a resurgence of, an innocence necessary in self-understanding and it often suggests the control of the ego and selfishness.

**Vermin** – in dreams, vermin represent the enforced contemplation of something that is unpleasant and unnecessary or that has invaded our personal space.

**Whale** – as a mammal that lives within water, the whale symbolizes the power of resurrection and rebirth – man's ability to surpass personal trauma.

**Weasel** – the weasel traditionally highlights the devious, less than honest side of ourselves.

**Werewolf** – *See Sinister Animals and Transformation of Animals in this section.*

**Wild animals** – usually wild animals stand for danger, dangerous passions or dangerous people. There is a destructive force arising from the unconscious, threatening our safety. Such a dream may be a way of helping us understand and highlight particular anxieties. Dreaming of domesticating wild animals shows that we may have come to terms with our wilder, more unrestrained side.

**Wild Boar** – the wild boar depicts the archetypal masculine principal, and often the negative masculine in a woman's dream. We may be evading an issue that should be challenged and dealt with more daringly. *You may wish to consult the individual entry for Boar and also for Pig in this section.*

**Wolf** – dreaming of wolves may indicate that we are feeling or being threatened. This may be by a single predatory individual or by a pack of like-minded people. The she-wolf can be taken to represent the hussy, the unrestrained feminine, but also the carer for orphans and rejected young.

**Zebra** – this animal has much the same significance as the horse, but with the additional meaning of balancing the negative and the positive in a very dynamic way.

When animals appear in a dream they tend to represent an aspect of the personality that cannot be properly understood except on an instinctive level. Below are some common images that occur in dreams.

**Animal with a cub** – this represents motherly qualities and, therefore, the mothering instinct.

**Baby animals** – the childlike side of our personality, or possibly children known to us, can give us information about innocence and naivety.

**Composite animals** – to dream of composite animals could indicate some confusion in sorting out what qualities we need to use in waking life. The qualities of the various animals need to be assimilated and integrated in order to progress; there are two potentials of further development. If a half-animal, half-human is seen it shows that the dreamer's basic instincts are beginning to be recognized and humanized.

**Deformed animals** – the dreamer realizes that some of his impulses are out of kilter.

**Domesticated (tame) animals** – when we dream of domesticated animals we are aware of those parts of ourselves with which we have already come to terms. There are passions which are being used in a controlled way, although there is the suggestion that those passions were never very formidable.

**Eating the animal** – such an image is often about the 'demons' we create which can only be overcome by assimilating them in a constructive way. Shamanic societies believe that one takes on certain aspects of the animal that are superior – in certain respects – to ordinary human attitudes.

**Godlike, talking, awe-inspiring or wise animals, or those with human characteristics** – animal wisdom is simple and uncomplicated and, therefore, is innocent. In dreams and myths we personalize this quality. It is always important to pay attention to this aspect of animal life in fairy tales and dreams, since we need to be in touch with that part of ourselves.

**Helpful animals** – the figures of animals are an easy way for us to accept the help the subconscious and spiritual realms can offer. Your totem animal is traditionally your 'guide' through the unconscious realms.

**Hurt young animals** – we are perceiving a difficulty in behaving maturely or confronting issues in waking life.

**Killing the animal** – this is symbolic of destroying the energy derived from the instincts. It is trying to eradicate the very raw power of basic behaviour. Taming or harnessing the animal shows the efforts made to control our instincts and, if possible, make them productive and useful.

**Parts of animals (the limbs, eyes, mouth, etc)** – these all have the same significance as parts of the human body. If the four legs are particularly emphasized – possibly in contrast with a three-legged animal – the whole rounded personality with all four functions of the mind fully developed is being highlighted. *You may also like to consult the entry for Body for further clarification.*

**Transformation of animals** – in dreams, the metamorphosis of the dreamer or other people into animals and vice versa shows the potential for change within any situation. Coincidentally, magical techniques allow 'shape-shifting', permitting magicians and shamans to adopt animal form, and dreams give us an understanding of that process.

**Trapped by animals** – to dream of trying to find some refuge from animals, whether by building defences or perhaps by running away, is indicative of our struggle with our animal instincts and whether the action being taken is adequate. Such instincts may be threatening or damaging to aspects of our life.

**Vertebrates** – just as the human skeleton gives us an understanding of the 'structure' of our lives, animals with backbones often give an understanding of the organizational qualities associated with that animal. The smaller and lower orders of animal (such as rodents) signify the unconscious, the higher orders the emotions.

**Wounded and/or trapped animals** – this suggests that we have been wounded, either emotionally or spiritually, or perhaps that our natural instincts are not being allowed free expression and are, therefore, not functioning properly.

## ANKH

❂ The ankh is a key to the way to knowledge of hidden wisdom. Traditionally it is also a symbol for life and for the universe. As you progress in spiritual knowledge, dreams bring hidden information to the surface and the ankh in dreams often signifies a new level of awareness.

The symbolism of the ankh is that of all-encircling power and protection throughout the trials and tribulations of physical life. It is the link between the human and Divine and for many is a magical symbol signifying initiation into such mysteries.

On a mundane level the symbolism is similar to that of a cross. It represents the dreamer's concept of the universe, or his religious beliefs.

Formed as it is from the symbols of Egyptian deities Isis and Osiris – and, therefore, representing the generative principle – in a man's dream the ankh can suggest the power of resurrection, whereas in a woman's dream it is more likely to suggest the power of life.

*You might also like to consult the entry for Cross in Shapes/Patterns and Spiritual Imagery in the Introduction.*

**ANNOY** – *see* **ANGER**

**ANOINT** – *see* **SPIRITUAL IMAGERY IN THE INTRODUCTION**

**ANT** – *see* **INSECTS**

**ANTELOPE** – *see* **ANIMALS**

**ANTHEM** – *see* **MUSIC AND SING**

**ANTIQUE** – *see* **OLD**

**ANTLERS**

Supernatural powers, fertility and nobleness of spirit are represented by antlers. An attribute of the primeval Horned God and his lust for life, they suggest power over nature.

Psychologically these represent awareness of the potential for conflict between our nobler self and the baser instincts. The antler with ten points is the mark of the shaman or holy man.

The deer is a noble animal, so the interpretation differs if the antlers are mounted, as in a trophy, or are seen on the animal. If the latter, then the interpretation is that of something that is supernormal and they may represent intellectual powers. If the former, then they may be interpreted as attempting to achieve high status.

Antlers in dreams may always be considered to represent virility and sexual prowess, whether in a man's or woman's dream.

*Consult the entry for Horns to enhance your understanding of your dream.*

**ANVIL**

The anvil is an attribute of the forge Gods such as Thor, Vulcan and Hephaestos. The symbolism is that of forging new life, creating new beginnings and so on, so signifies creativity in its rawest sense.

As an image associated with the spark of life and of initiation, the anvil was once a very potent symbol. As time progresses, other objects, more pertinent to the times in which we live, appear in dreams, but the anvil will still appear as we return to basics.

🔲 Depending on the dream circumstances, the anvil can represent the basic force of nature, brute force or a way of creating an initial spark. By creating a situation in our lives where we are going to be tried and tested, we are pitting ourselves against natural forces.

🔲 In both male and female dreams the anvil can be seen as a form of resistance which allows us to use our individual creativity to fashion our lives.

## APE

🔅 As science discovers just how closely associated we are to the ape, it is hardly surprising that over the centuries this creature has had projected upon it aspects of our own character that we find difficult to handle. The ape in dreams, therefore, can suggest the Trickster, the mischievous side of wrongdoing, and irresponsibility. However, in Hindu belief the character of Hanuman the Monkey God teaches us of the unlimited power that lies unused within each one of us.

💟 One of the qualities of the ape is its ability to mimic, to copy and to learn by experience. To dream of apes may alert us to this ability, or for the need for us to learn by example.

🔲 Traditionally, to dream of apes or monkeys links with the mischievous side of ourselves. However, as perception changes, the symbolism is more of natural intelligence.

*Also consult the entry for Monkey in Animals for further information.*

## APOCALYPSE

🔅 The end of the world as we know it is such a potent image that it is part and parcel of almost every religion's belief system. In dreams the apocalypse (literally 'the lifting of the veil') is often the revelation of hidden meaning. It has much to do with our fears, with the survival of the fittest and a reshuffling of those aspects of life that are important to us. In such dreams it will be your beliefs and your faith that is the saving grace. Usually there is a particular symbol associated with your own basic belief which separates you from others in the dream.

💟 Apocalyptic dreams tend to be more prevalent at times of great change, either personal or otherwise. You may need to protect yourself from others and hold fast to an inner conviction in order to overcome opposition. The sense of knowing something or having information that no-one else does is a feature of dreams of the apocalypse.

🔲 Dreaming of an apocalypse is quite simply marking a transition period, moving away from a former course of action or way of being. Instinctively you may feel that the risks you must take are too great, or that you can only effect change by a massive shift in circumstances.

*You may wish to read the entries for Atom Bomb, Disaster and Nuclear Explosion.*

### APOLOGY

✦ Spiritually an apology is an act of self-justification – an understanding of rightness – and it is this meaning that comes across first of all in dreams of such an act. To dream that we apologize to someone means we acknowledge a lack of integrity in ourselves. To receive an apology suggests a recognition of that same integrity.

✦ It is important that we feel good about ourselves and, as dreams are a way of righting an imbalance, we have a mechanism through apology to put right an act or deed, either our own or others', which has upset us.

▦ If we dream about giving or receiving an apology we are aware of having offended our own personal code in everyday life and can work out what we need to do to restore the status quo.

### APOSTLE – *see* SPIRITUAL IMAGERY IN THE INTRODUCTION

### APPLE

✦ Spiritually the apple is the fruit of temptation, yet it is also a magical fruit containing the seeds of knowledge and awareness. An apple suggests a new beginning and a freshness of approach. In many traditions it is the fruit of immortality. Apple blossom is a Chinese symbol of peace and beauty.

✦ Eating an apple symbolizes the wish to take in information or knowledge. This has an obvious connection with Eve's temptation of Adam. As with many natural symbols, the phrases we use in the everyday can give rise to dream images. Thus to be giving someone an apple can suggest showing appreciation, whereas to pick up a rotten apple can signify meeting someone who is not good for us.

▦ Apples on a purely mundane level can signify fruitfulness, fertility, love and temptation. Sometimes in dreams they can suggest a particular time of year.

⊞ It is mainly by association that the apple has come to represent the feminine principle and sometimes the maternal breast. It is more likely to have this meaning in a man's dream than in a woman's. As a symbol of carnal knowledge it represents fertility.

*The entries for Food and Fruit may give further clarification.*

### APPOINTMENT

✦ Time is a man-made concept so, from a spiritual perspective, when we dream of having to keep an appointment we need to make use of time in the most spiritually effective way. There may be an issue to do with our self-discipline.

♥ We can perhaps give ourselves a gift or a reward for good work. There is something that has to be accomplished within a certain time limit. Often the person we have the appointment with may be important.

▦ Dreaming of going to an appointment indicates we need to have an aim or a goal. The dream is bringing to our notice something our inner self feels we need to deal with. Missing an appointment suggests we are not paying enough attention to detail.

*You might like to consult the entries for People and Time.*

## APPRENTICE

✿ An apprentice is technically assigned to a worker in order to learn a trade or profession. In spiritual terms, we all learn by example and, should an apprentice appear in dreams, we need only discover what it is that we should be learning.

♥ Life is a learning process and an apprentice suggests that a commitment has been given to enable us to learn more – to put our knowledge to good use and ultimately to pass on our own knowledge.

▦ To be learning as an apprentice suggests that we need more information in our working life. To be teaching an apprentice can suggest that we feel a promotion is appropriate.

⦂ Previously apprenticeships were more valid for men than for women, so to an extent the interpretation for a man or a woman will differ according to their age group. An older man might dream of his own apprenticeship whereas an older woman may feel that someone around her is lacking skill. Today's apprentices will not necessarily perceive a division in labour.

## APRON

✿ An apron can represent a badge of office and, as in Freemasonry, this suggests craftsmanship; in ancient China it was part of sacrificial regalia. It also has the symbolism of dividing the body into the upper, nobler part and the lower, baser instincts.

♥ If you are wearing the apron this may indicate the need for skill. If worn by someone else the part of you that is represented by the dream person may need protecting.

▦ The apron can represent family ties, constraints or outmoded ideas.

⦂ It depends on the gender of the dreamer and the content of the dream whether this image is negative or positive. In a woman's dream it might signify her nurturing side. In a man's dream it is more likely to represent his relationship with his mother.

*You may like to consult the entries for Body, Family and People for clarification.*

**AQUARIUM –** *see* **FISH**

**ARCH**

⚙ Since the arch can suggest the yoni, the feminine receptive principle, this image usually suggests that we are experiencing a form of spiritual initiation. We are being born again, given a fresh start.

♥ The arch marks a turning point; if we pass through we have passed a test. If we do not then our circumstances must remain the same. We may be being protected by authority.

▦ When we dream of arches or doorways we are often moving into a different environment or way of life. We have to go through some form of initiation or acceptance ritual in order to succeed.

⊡ In a man's dream, passing through an arch suggests that he is learning to use his intuitive side more successfully, whereas in a woman's dream it is more likely to signify that she is becoming aware of her own heritage and mystery.

**ARCHANGEL –** *see* **ANGEL AND SPIRITUAL IMAGERY IN THE INTRODUCTION**

**ARENA**

⚙ Today sport is often used as an energy release, so we are more likely to dream of a sports arena or football pitch rather than an ancient arena. Spiritually an arena suggests a ritualized form of combat and sometimes sacrifice, but can also suggest the need for space in which to expand or enjoy group activities.

♥ We are developing a new focus of attention or an area of conflict. This conflict may need to be brought out into the open for due consideration.

▦ Dreaming of being in an arena, either as a player or as a spectator, highlights the fact that we may need to make the decision to move into a specifically created environment, one which gives more room for self-expression and creativity or theatricality.

*You might like to look at the entries for Competition, Games and Rite/Ritual.*

**ARGUE/ARGUMENTS**

⚙ Two aspects of an argument are worth noting from a spiritual perspective. You are trying to resolve some internal conflict or unsettled issue which may not yet have come to conscious knowledge. If you are arguing with only one person the conflict is likely to be between two polarities of thought in you; with more than one person the issue is probably one connected with a wider, more global belief or concept.

❤ When challenged it is often difficult to state our case properly. Dreaming of an argument can help us to vocalize coherently in ordinary life.

▦ Dream scenarios often mimic everyday problems, so the atmosphere during a dream argument can give us clues about our passion or real feelings over an issue. To be having an argument with someone with whom you normally have a good relationship suggests you are unsure of your motivation in actions you are taking.

⊟ Arguments with members of the opposite sex suggest that some adjustment needs to be made in the way you approach relationships. Men may need to understand their own aggression whereas women may need to be less emotional. Certainly something is out of balance.

*Consult the entry for Conflict.*

## ARMED FORCES

✸ Any armed force is a disciplined group made up of many elements. It is this bringing together of the correct balance of factors which gives us a spiritual interpretation – a strong force, usually for good, a coherent whole with a joint purpose.

❤ To be in the armed forces in dreams signifies belonging to a trained team; to be facing an army highlights our doubts about or refusal to accept a carefully thought out plan of action. While this may be for the greater good, in itself it may be dangerous. By its association with the sea, the navy in dreams signifies a more disciplined response to emotional matters, whereas the air force suggests the need for a targeted response to intellectual and philosophical matters.

▦ The idea of fighting for a common cause suggests developing qualities which we would not necessarily foster in isolation. As organizations that accept all types of people and develops their potential, the armed forces are not just fighting units but are, in theory, agents for change.

⊟ In today's climate where everything is less regimented, a man dreaming of an army (or being a member of the armed forces) is likely to be about self-discipline, whereas a woman's dream is more about the aspect of belonging to a group of like minded people.

*Consult the entries for Conflict, Sailor, Tank, Uniform and War for further clarity.*

## ARMOUR

✸ Armour, particularly the old style suit of armour, signifies chivalry, protection and the need to protect or be protected.

❤ We may be protecting ourselves from something we feel is threatening us. Our way of protecting ourselves may, however, be outdated and inappropriate in the present circumstances. In today's climate of terror, to be wearing body armour suggests trying to protect ourselves against the wrongdoing and aggressive actions of others or against our own fears.

▦ We need to be aware of emotional and intellectual rigidity in either ourselves or others around us. If we are wearing armour we may be overprotecting ourselves, whereas if others are in armour we may be overly aware of their defence mechanisms.

## ARMS

❀ Arms are significant as a symbol of surrender, wisdom or action. One arm upraised denotes commitment but sometimes also suggests vengeance. Two arms raised sideways signify supplication; raised forwards suggest welcome.

✾ Arms – in the sense of weapons – are used to protect and defend. In olden times there were quite a series of rituals and stages of initiation with the Page becoming the Knight and making the transition from the arms bearer to the user of weapons. Dreams can mirror these initiatory rituals.

▦ It is worth noting the significance of the placing of the arms. If they are placed across the chest we are defending ourselves. If we are held in or by someone else's arms it suggests a need for security. A coat of arms or other such insignia suggests a form of recognition.

*Also consult the entries for Body, Sword and Weapons.*

## ARMY – *see* ARMED FORCES

## ARRESTED

❀ There are times when spiritually we are aware we are not acting according to our own beliefs. There is a need for a higher authority and we need to be stopped from coming to harm or creating problems. That higher authority is often the moral or spiritual aspect of ourselves.

✾ When in everyday life we are unsure of our motives in an action we are contemplating, dreaming of being arrested suggests we should stop and carefully consider our behaviour before we act.

▦ When we dream of being arrested, there may be a lack of integrity or good judgement. To dream of arresting someone else would indicate our instinctive disapproval of certain actions.

## ARROW

❀ Arrows as weapons suggest power, energy and expertise. As a means of pointing the way we should go, they will often hint at the next steps we need to take in personal development.

◆ Communications that we make could be damaging to other people. We could either hurt or be hurt by directness. Arrows indicating direction can suggest the quickest and easiest route.

▣ If we dream of shooting arrows we are aware of the consequences of actions, either our own or other people's, that cannot be recalled or revoked. Interestingly enough, arrows can also symbolize words in dreams.

▣ The arrow often suggests masculine power in a woman's dream while it is more suggestive of drive and ambition in a man's dream.

*You might like to consult the entries for Barb, Bolt, Direction, Shot/shooting and Weapons for further clarity.*

## ARTIST

✹ We tend to personalize our ideas of the Creator, or the Guiding Principle, and this often manifests as the artist in dreams. In the sense that an artist or creative person interprets a divine picture or idea as best he/she can, in dreams an artist represents the interpretive side of ourselves.

◆ We need to make use of our desire or ability to be creative in our own right – often not necessarily by painting pictures. We may also be linking with that part of ourselves that records events for posterity, literally leaving our mark on life.

▣ The artist in a dream makes us recognize the artist or creative ability in us. We are aware of the aspect of ourselves that is in contact with, and can interpret, the irrational, creative side of the unconscious.

*Consult the entries for Broom/Brush, Paint/Painting and Picture or other creative tools as appropriate.*

## ASCENDING/ASCENSION

✹ We are searching for spiritual awareness. Ascension is an altered state of consciousness which can occur as a result of meditation and spiritual practices. Ascension frequently follows the experience of a descent into the Underworld. In dreams it is seen as acceptable and real and is often accompanied by symbols of Paradise.

◆ We are becoming conscious of being able to exercise control over passion or sexual pleasure. The transition from expressing our energy through sex to expressing it in self-awareness is often shown as ascending. The act of Ascension is a breakthrough to a new spiritual plane which transcends the state of being human. It is an awareness of different levels of concentration, which give a fresh perspective to being human.

▣ If we are climbing stairs, or going up in an elevator or lift, we are making a movement towards waking or becoming more aware; we are making an escape from anxiety or being down to earth and are freeing ourselves from physical constraints.

**ASCETIC**

☀ There is an attempt to find the spiritual in our lives and also a development of the will to be 'pure'. In a dream, to meet an ascetic or holy man is to meet our higher self and to recognize the part of ourselves that is continually seeking unity with the Divine.

♡ Psychologically we are searching for purity in ourselves or in others. Equally we may be afraid of that purity within ourselves and need to come to terms with it. As an archetype Jung frequently mentions his Wise Old Man who was present when he needed guidance.

▦ There is some conflict with natural drives. There may be an avoidance of sex or contact through fear or the need for restraint. We may be looking for simplicity.

*Consult the entries for Hermit, Monk and Mystic for further information.*

**ASHES**

☀ Ashes represent purification and death and symbolically the perishable human body and mortality.

♡ A memory or a learnt wisdom needs to be retained in order for us to use information. After an event or person has gone or disappeared from our lives we may dream of a fire that has burned out, leaving ashes.

▦ Ashes in a dream often indicate penitence and sorrow. We are aware that we have been overanxious and stupid within a situation and that there is little left to be done. That situation has outlived its usefulness. The ashes are what remains of our experience, which will enable us to make the best of a situation.

**ASK – *see* QUESTION**

**ASP – *see* SNAKE IN ANIMALS**

**ASSAULT – *see* ATTACK**

**ASTRONAUT**

☀ Any figure that is not 'of this world' alerts us to the possibilities of other dimensions of being, spiritually lifting us away from the mundane into other areas of consciousness.

♡ In that an astronaut moves among the stars but cannot do so without some sort of protective covering, we are alerted to the discipline and skill needed when working within spiritual and psychic realms.

▦ From a mundane perspective we perhaps need to recognize that before moving into the unknown we need skill and protection.

**ASYLUM/ASYLUM SEEKER**

⚜ To be seeking asylum suggests the recognition that we need a sacred space. In the old-fashioned sense an asylum was an institution, so it may be that we are seeking safety in structure and proscribed boundaries.

♦ An enclosed space where we have to abide by rules imposed by others can give a sense of safety and security. Seeking asylum where one is not living in danger from our peers and compatriots suggests we are conscious that our thoughts and beliefs are not in tune with others. This may reflect a working situation.

▦ When an asylum seeker appears in dreams it is probable that we are neglecting part of our persona and putting it at risk.

**ATLAS** – *see* **MAP**

**ATOM BOMB**

⚜ We have become aware of the uncontrollable forces of life and the unconscious.

♦ There is a fear of irrationality and of power that could be used wrongly. An atom bomb is a deliberately engineered explosion designed to be destructive. We may feel that someone else may destroy and nullify our carefully constructed life.

▦ Where anxiety regarding the external world is experienced, we need to be aware that the end of a particular way of life is imminent in an especially dramatic fashion. Often there is a sense of an explosion of destructive energy before everything must be rebuilt.

*Consult the entries for Apocalypse, Bomb and Nuclear Explosion for further clarification.*

**ATTACK**

⚜ There is a spiritual or psychic threat. We often become aware on very subtle levels of threats or challenges to our beliefs and ideals and these can manifest as warnings of, or actual, attacks.

♦ If we are the attacker we need to defend ourselves by positive self-expression – we are making attempts to destroy some urge or feeling in ourselves or others.

▦ Being attacked in a dream indicates a fear of being under threat from external events or internal emotions. Unknown impulses or ideas force us into taking a defensive attitude. If we are being attacked by animals we are turning our own aggression and/or sexuality inwards; we have fear of our own natural urges.

⊞ In a woman's dream, being attacked will often be to do with her feelings of vulnerability. In a man's dream, being attacked perhaps highlights his poor self-image. In both men's and women's dreams, playing the part of the attacker suggests frustration and lack of control.

*You might also like to consult the entry for Wound.*

**ATTRACTION** – *see* **SEX/SEXUAL IMAGES**

**AUDIENCE**

✵ Spiritually, an audience tends to be either the multiple parts of our personality, all of which are answerable to the Higher Self, or represents the external world to whom we are accountable in a spiritual sense.

♡ We need to be considering an aspect of our lives carefully, particularly one that takes place in public and needs expression. We are the creators of our own play and an audience may also represent the various parts of our own personality that we have created.

▣ If we are standing in front of, or broadcasting to, an audience, we are probably having to deal with important issues in our lives. We need to reach a wider audience. If we are in the audience, we are witnessing an emotion or process of change in ourselves. To dream of listening to a broadcast means we should be listening to the message that other people are trying to get across.

*Also consult the entry for Theatre.*

**AUDITION** – *see* **EXAM/BEING EXAMINED AND TEST**

**AUNT** – *see* **FAMILY**

**AURA**

✵ The aura is an energy field, perceived clairvoyantly as bands of colour, which surrounds the physical body. It is an expression of the Self. When we become conscious of an aura in dreams, we are becoming more aware of others spirituality.

♡ The aura is a representation of the power we hold within, the force field of our essential energy with which we attract and ward people off. Because in dreams we are more sensitive, we become more conscious of such subtle emanations.

▣ To perceive an aura in a dream indicates how powerful we consider ourselves, or others, to be.

*Also consult Spiritual Imagery in the Introduction for further information.*

**AUSTRALIA** – *see* **PLACES**

**AUTHORITY FIGURES (SUCH AS TEACHERS, DOCTORS ETC.)** – *see* **INDIVIDUAL ENTRIES AND ALSO AUTHORITY FIGURES IN PEOPLE.**

**AUTOGRAPH** – *see* **SIGNATURE**

**AUTOPSY** – *see* **OPERATION**

**AUTUMN**

Symbolically autumn signifies a time of introspection when we can gain benefit from previous actions. We have the advantage of experience and maturity.

Psychologically by recognizing the cycles of growth and decay that occur in our own lives, we learn that some of these can be brought to fruition without harm.

We are being made conscious of the sense of something coming to an end. We recognize that the good in a situation can be 'brought in' and made use of, but the rest must be given up.

*Consult the entries for Harvest, Spring, Summer, Seasons and Winter for additional clarification.*

**AVALANCHE**

The power of our own nature and emotions that have frozen could overwhelm us and stop our spiritual progress.

Psychologically we need to regain control of forces outside ourselves. We are in a position that puts us in some kind of danger, most likely from old ideas and attitudes which have become 'frozen' by continuous use.

If we witness an avalanche in our dreams we are experiencing a destructive force. If we are in the middle of an avalanche we are being overwhelmed by circumstances.

**AXE**

The axe represents power, thunder, conquest of error and sacrifice. As a symbol it is seen in most religions usually representing divine, supernatural power.

From a psychological perspective, an axe, particularly a double-headed one, represents feminine supremacy and intuitive power, often in the role of the huntress.

When we dream of an axe we need to differentiate between whether it is being used against us or if we are using it. If it is used against us we feel we are being threatened by someone's greater power. To dream of using an axe indicates that we need to become aware of the destructive forces within us.

**AZTEC –** *see* **INDIGENOUS PEOPLES**

## BABBLE

When we are conscious of a babble of noise within a dream it suggests that there is too much information for us to be able to sort out what is relevant. The significance comes from the story of the Tower of Babel when communication is said to have become impossible. Spiritually, babble has the added significance of perhaps 'speaking in tongues' – receiving information from a hidden source.

Confusion in dreams usually alerts us to the need to categorize or sort out those things we do not understand. When we ourselves are babbling, we are not communicating properly; when others babble, we are not taking in information properly in everyday life.

As babies are learning to speak, they tend to babble as first experiments, as though trying out language. Babbling in dreams has this same connotation. We perhaps need to speak out more clearly. Talking in your sleep seems to be the mind's way of expressing suppressed material, or concerns that you have not been able to deal with properly.

## BABY – *see* PEOPLE

## BABYSITTING

Babysitting is an activity which crosses the divide between the spiritual and the physical. Spiritually it suggests the nurturing, caring side of the personality or that part which is ready to take responsibility for others.

Viewed from a psychological perspective, babysitting in dreams suggests that there may be a part of our personality which has not yet matured fully and needs looking after.

For many teenagers, babysitting is an ordinary, mundane activity and thus provides a dream scenario in which they can work out their attitude to other responsibilities in their lives. For others it may highlight their attitude to family responsibilities or to parenthood.

In a man's dream, to be babysitting suggests an increase in responsibility which may not necessarily be family related, whereas in a woman's dream it is more likely to be.

## BACHELOR

A bachelor or someone we know to be 'footloose and fancy free' appearing in a dream highlights the side of our personalities which prefers to have no particular ties. We are not tied down by mundane responsibility.

❤ We need to open up to the masculine side of ourselves in order to accomplish our destiny. Similar to the knight in tales of old, we sometimes have to challenge the status quo in order to achieve a breakthrough of some sort.

▦ To dream of meeting a bachelor indicates that we are searching for freedom either within our emotions or in our love life.

◧ In a man's dream it shows he may be wishing for the freedom to achieve something he might find difficult in partnership. In a woman's dream it indicates she may be feeling constrained by a relationship.

*You may find further clarification in the section on Archetypes in the Introduction.*

## BACK

❀ Spiritually, sometimes we have to turn our back on the past and reject the known. It will be up to you to decide which elements of the past need rejecting. In certain dreams the backbone – because it is the most stable part of our structure – signifies the Self. Backache in dreams, if not due to a physical cause, suggests that we are under some pressure, vis-à-vis a moral or spiritual issue.

❤ If we dream of turning our backs we are rejecting the particular feeling being experienced in the dream. There is a possibility that we are repressing our own urges or do not want to look at our inner feelings. We are in touch with the past and with memories. Intellectually we need to consider our firmness of character and recognize what has brought us to our present condition.

▦ Dreaming of seeing someone's back suggests we should identify the more private elements in our character or those around us. We may also find that we are vulnerable to the unexpected. If the backbone is particularly noticeable in the dream we need to consider our main support structure.

*You might like to consider the entries for Body and Stab.*

## BACKWARDS

❀ To look back into the past can sometimes be detrimental, and at other times helpful. In dreams, to be looking or moving backwards may suggest that answers to our present dilemma lie in the past. Past behaviour patterns may not be appropriate.

❤ When she looked backwards, despite being warned, Lot's wife was turned into a pillar of salt. To be looking back in dreams suggests that mentally we are not using our best faculties or are not looking to the future.

▦ To dream of going or walking backwards indicates that we may be withdrawing from a situation, or slow to learn from it. We may need to recognize that to continue in a particular situation will, at worst, stop our progress and, at best, impede it.

**BAD**

&#9733; Spiritually, anything that is bad or decaying has finished a positive cycle and is entering a negative one. Whilst a perfectly natural process, we do well to acknowledge this and dreaming of a 'bad thing' enables us to move on.

&#9826; If we dream of food being bad, we are not taking sufficient care of our inner needs. A bad smell in dreams could mean that our environment is not supporting us. Bad as in bad behaviour suggests we are rebelling in some way.

&#9632; When we dream of something being bad we are being made aware that the dream object is now worthless or defective. Feeling bad can have two meanings: one in the sense of being naughty and the other not feeling right. We are off balance in some way.

**BADGE/BROOCH**

&#9733; A badge signifies an emblem or insignia of office, an acknowledgement or reward for effort. Dreaming of such an object shows our need to be accepted, not just as ourselves, but also as part of a greater whole. A brooch also signifies an acknowledgement of value.

&#9826; We have been singled out for particular recognition, possibly because we have certain qualities. A badge can also have the same meaning as an amulet, a protective device against evil.

&#9632; To have our attention drawn to a badge makes us aware of our right to belong to a group. If a badge is recognizable in a dream we perhaps should try to assess what our feelings are about the organization or group involved. Brooches are often formed of precious or semi-precious gems and can impart a particular message.

*You might like to consult the entries for Gems/Jewels, Keepsake and Jewellery.*

**BADGER –** *see* **ANIMALS**

**BAG**

&#9733; A bag spiritually signifies the secret, the hidden and the occult. Long known as a symbol of femininity because of its association with the womb, it can also suggest intuitive wisdom. Occasionally it will suggest the elements of wind and air.

&#9826; Depending on the actual bag (e.g. a handbag, a shopping bag) and what is in it, we are probably hiding certain aspects of ourselves from public consideration. To be emptying a bag suggests that we are attempting to get rid of old concepts or ideas or other aspects which may be holding us back. To have lost a bag signifies that we have temporarily suppressed certain character traits.

&#9632; You may be having problems with the more feminine elements in your identity such as compassion or nurturing. There is an ability to use the social graces to achieve, and to cope with whatever occurs. A torn or broken bag may alert you to a health problem or to there being too much to deal with.

⚑ Whereas previously men carrying bags were seen as effeminate, this is no longer the case, so in dreams a man carrying a bag can symbolize his attitude to his responsibilities. In a woman's dream a bag is more likely to represent her inner feelings.

## BAGGAGE

⚙ Feelings of sorrow or of being overburdened can manifest in dreams as baggage. The type of baggage will be important, bulky suitcases being less easily dealt with than a simple bag. The spiritual implication is that you are perhaps holding on to inherited or learned ideas, beliefs and concepts which are for you no longer valid.

♥ You are under some psychological stress and may have to decide that some projects or feelings can be left behind in waking life. When you have been carrying luggage or baggage in a dream and find it has disappeared, you have successfully dealt with the problem.

▦ To be carrying extra baggage in a dream suggests that you may be carrying an extra load, either emotional or practical. You are expecting too much of yourself or of others and are carrying past hurt or trauma, possibly from as far back as childhood.

*For further clarity consult the entry for Luggage.*

## BAGPIPES – *see* MUSIC AND MUSICAL INSTRUMENTS

## BAILIFF

⚙ The bailiff in dreams signifies retribution, Karma or a backlash of some kind. Our integrity is being called into question.

♥ We have put ourselves at risk and have not fulfilled our obligations, or have not acted in an ethical manner. Unless we take responsibility for what we have done, we could be 'punished' by material loss and loss of status.

▦ When a bailiff appears in our dream, we doubt our own ability to manage our resources, both emotional and material. We are aware that we have overstepped the mark in a particular way and must be accountable to a higher authority.

*You may also like to consult Authority Figures in People for further clarification.*

## BAIT

⚙ Spiritually, when we are strong enough, we must 'tempt' negativity in some way in order to trap and ultimately control it.

♥ There is an aspect of our lives which needs bringing out into the open. We have to coerce that part of ourselves that is failing to co-operate into making progress. There is some kind of enticement which has to take place.

Baiting an animal in dreams suggests a degree of cruelty which needs addressing. If we are laying bait then the implication is that we are, at least in part, aware of the problem. If the bait is already in position then it is a warning to be careful.

In a woman's dream, putting down bait can be an indication of her doubts about her own ability to attract a partner. She may feel that she has to entrap or ensnare a partner. In a man's dream the more practical side recognizes the need to capture an elusive idea or concept.

## BAKE/BAKER/BAKERY

Since baking is a creative act, combining ingredients to make something new, it suggests the Creative Urge. As a baker knows his craft, in dreams he may be seen as an aspect of the Higher Self. The bakery in dreams represents a dedicated area or sacred space.

Our creative ability may need to be enhanced or lightened in order for us to achieve success. If the ingredients we use seem strange or bizarre, we may need to transform our mindset vis-à-vis what we are doing in ordinary life.

We all have within us the ability to alter our approach or attitude to situations in our lives. Dreaming of a baker alerts us to this ability, of a bakery, to changes to our environment, and of baking, the methods we must use.

If a woman dreams of baking she will recognize this as her need to nurture. By and large in the case of a man he may be dealing with his own professionalism.

*You might like to consult the entries for Cooking, Food and Oven.*

## BALANCE

Spiritually, balance represents fairness and impartiality. To be thrown off balance suggests that we have received a sufficiently bad blow or emotional shock for us to lose that impartiality. Balanced scales are a representation of the zodiac sign of Libra. This suggests an equilibrium between two polarities – often man's higher and baser nature. Justice – and, therefore, a balanced viewpoint – is symbolized by the scales.

To have the feeling that we are looking for the balance of a quantity of goods indicates we have more mental assets than we had first realized and need to start using them.

When we dream of trying to maintain our balance or of being balanced in a difficult position, we are searching for stability. To dream of searching for the balance in a financial account means we are looking for something which, at present, remains unrecognized and unknown.

⊡ In terms of spiritual progression in both men's and women's dreams, a representation of balance suggests an equilibrium between masculine and feminine qualities.

*You may also like to consult the entries for Scales and Zodiac.*

## BALCONY

⦿ When we dream of being raised above the ground in some way, we are beginning to recognize our spiritual competence or progression. There is perhaps an element of danger or arrogance in such a position.

♡ Psychologically we are searching for power within a situation in which we feel powerless.

▦ To dream of being on a balcony suggests that we are searching for a higher status than we have at present. To dream of being underneath a balcony indicates that we are aware of other people's need for status. At the same time we may be hiding from our own responsibilities.

⊡ In a man's dream, being on a balcony suggests an awareness of his need for status. In a woman's dream this suggests a degree of protection. In both it can represent the need for far-sightedness.

## BALD

⦿ Priests used to shave their heads to show they had nothing to hide. Before it became simply fashionable in today's world to be bald, baldness in a dream signified the attainment of spirituality with its attendant humility, and signified honesty.

♡ To dream of being bald when we normally have hair can be somewhat ambiguous. It suggests a loss, usually of intellectual prowess, but can also symbolize intelligence.

▦ To dream of someone who is bald when they normally have hair suggests we are being made aware of a degree of dullness in life.

⊡ Many men nowadays choose to shave their heads when they are losing their hair and are taking a practical step to deal with a problem. In a man's dream, therefore, when he is bald it will have less of an emotional impact than it will when a woman finds herself in that position.

*Consult the entries for Hair and Head in Body and Hat/Cap in Clothes.*

## BALL – *see* GAMES AND SPORT

## BALLERINA/BALLET DANCER

⦿ The figure of a ballerina is dreamlike in waking life, so in dreams a ballerina symbolizes music, fluidity and the inner aspect of spiritual feeling.

♡ We are aware of the creative side of ourselves and the need for controlled movement, yet in some ways it is separate from us. We are in touch with the expressiveness of our own inner being.

▦ The fairylike appearance of the classical ballerina within a dream shows we are making a connection with the creative energy within. Also we are searching for balance and poise.

▣ Modern ballet is a powerful medium with which to signify emotion, so in a man's dream a male ballet dancer will represent his more powerful emotions, whereas a ballerina is more likely to suggest his Anima. In a woman's dream, however, the male dancer might suggest the Animus, while the ballerina suggests the more elusive side of her personality.

*You might like to consult the entries for Dance and Theatre.*

**BALLET – see DANCE**

**BALLOON**

🌑 A balloon has a similar connotation as the sphere and the ball from a spiritual perspective but with the added symbolism of 'light spirited' joy, or indeed the spirit rising. Thus an ascending balloon – whether it is child's or hot-air – suggests that you may be making some kind of transition in your life.

♡ Balloons were once made of pig's bladders and were used by the court jester to lighten up the atmosphere around the king and to remind him that he was human. In dreams they may introduce a note of fun amid seriousness. A descending balloon suggests that there is a situation in life in which you need to be grounded and practical.

▦ Very often it is the colour of balloons in our dreams which are important. The number of balloons may also be significant, indicating a party mood or a celebration. A deflating or deflated balloon suggests that the energy has run out of a particular project.

*Consult the entries for Colour and Numbers for further clarification.*

**BALLOT – see VOTE**

**BAMBOO**

🌑 Man is symbolized by the bamboo, inherently perfect yet able to be pliant – to bow before the storm. The bamboo also signifies gracefulness and friendship. In China, the seven-knotted bamboo denotes the seven stages of initiation undergone before becoming an adept.

♡ Intellectually, bamboo represents good breeding, long life and a fulfilling old age. On top of that, it highlights the ability to yield when under pressure.

▦ The pliability of bamboo indicates yielding but enduring strength. It is used as a cure in Feng Shui (the art of placement) because it is fast-growing, sturdy and will thrive in a variety of conditions. It will now have gained much of that significance in dreams.

⊡ In both male and female dreams the bamboo plant can suggest androgeny. *Also consult the entry for Androgen/Androgeny.*

**BANANA**

☀ The banana generally symbolizes fertility and fecundity, but can also suggest sensuality. At one time it would have suggested the exotic.

♡ In conjunction with other fruit, it can be taken to mean fertility or sustenance – a bunch of bananas signifies a good harvest. Green bananas means a plan has not yet come to fruition.

▦ Most dreams about fruit are to do with sexuality or the harvesting of past actions. Conventionally, the banana, because of its shape, signifies the penis. However, it is also considered, because of its yielding nature, to represent the correct management of masculine sexuality.

⊡ Other circumstances of the dream will enable you to make a full interpretation. A single banana is more likely to be interpreted by a man in terms of the penis whereas a woman may interpret the same symbol as a caring (nurturing) action.

*Consult the entries for Food and Fruit.*

**BAND**

☀ Dreaming of a band as a group of musicians suggests harmony within the Self. All parts of the personality are integrated. If the image of a band is that of a stripe, there is some limitation within your circumstances which needs to be recognized, and you may need to work within well-defined guidelines.

♡ There is harmony on a psychological level which you can access. However, this requires practice and imagination.

▦ A band of material or stripe may be highlighting a division between two parts. If, however, the image is that of a group of musicians, this would indicate the need for teamwork.

*Also consult the entries for Orchestra/Orchestrate and Music/Rhythm.*

**BANDAGE**

☀ Bandages in dreams can signify preservation – as with the bandages of a mummy – as well as healing. It is likely that an aspect of your life needs caring attention.

♡ We may have been made sick or uncomfortable by a difficulty within our lives and need to pay attention to our ability to be healed. If the bandage is coming or being taken off we may have overcome the difficulty, or we may have been careless.

▦ If a bandage is being applied in a dream this shows the beginning of a healing process. There may be hurt feelings or emotional injuries which need attention. The area that is being bandaged may give information as to what the problem is.

*For further clarification, read the section on Body and also the entries on Doctor, Hospital and Operation.*

**BANG** – *see* **EXPLODE/EXPLOSION AND SHOT**

**BANK/BANKER**

◎ A bank suggests a secure space, where our spiritual resources are stored and increased with effort. It may also signify a place where an exchange of energy or power takes place. The banker represents the controlling, knowledgeable part of ourselves and thus our right to have personal management of our spiritual assets.

◈ Our internal resources need to be available to us in such a way that we have energy in reserve. Our emotional resources, such as self-confidence, social ability and wisdom, are secure, although there may be some insecurity over the actual management of those resources.

▦ Money and personal resources tend to be the things with which most people have difficulty. In our everyday life our financial, mental or spiritual resources may need careful management from a professional perspective. Our sense of security, without which it is difficult to venture into the world, needs to be properly managed and monitored. Our need for an authority figure to help us deal with problems that arise are usually symbolized by the banker or bank manager in dreams.

▢ In a woman's dream a banker may represent a type of father figure and the bank, depending on her own inherent personal abilities, a secure space. A man's dream is more likely to depict his own relationship with the material world.

**BANKRUPT/BANKRUPTCY**

◎ To dream of going or being bankrupt suggests that we have lost or cut ourselves off from a source of spiritual energy.

◈ Formerly, going bankrupt carried a great deal of stigma. Such a dream, therefore, highlighted our fears and doubts about our own abilities. In today's climate where there is less disgrace, dreaming of bankruptcy simply indicates a problem that needs to be dealt with – not necessarily a financial one.

▦ Since bankruptcy signifies a lack of the necessary resources, we will need to look at circumstances around us that reflect this state of mind.

**BANNER**

◎ A common standard of spiritual behaviour might be expected by those who gathered under a king's or knight's banner. A banner in dreams has this connotation and can also suggest a message to be put across to others.

❦ Psychologically we may adopt – or need to adopt – some kind of crusade or special cause. We need to know we have a common cause to fight for which is organized and specific.

▦ If the banner in the dream is a commercial one, such as a street, advertising or protest type, it represents the need to have something, which we may previously have ignored or rejected, brought to our attention. If the banner is an old fashioned one – as used in medieval battles – it indicates a need to consolidate thoughts and actions.

*You might like to consult the entry for Flag for further clarification.*

**BANQUET –** *see* **FEAST, FOOD AND MEAL**

**BAPTISM**

❈ Baptism is symbolic of many things: initiation, death and rebirth, regeneration and renewal. A rite of passage, baptism can signify acceptance by a group of people with specific knowledge. The method of baptism in the dream is also significant: water suggests cleansing, fire purification and air or wind renewal of the spirit.

❦ When a ceremony or ritual signifies new beginnings, our way of thought needs to change in line with what we now know to be true. We can ascribe to a common belief.

▦ To dream of being baptised indicates a new influence entering our lives, cleansing away old attitudes and opening up to many inner possibilities. To dream of baptising someone means you are ready to pass on knowledge to other people.

*Also consult the entry for Rite/Ritual and Spiritual Imagery in the Introduction.*

**BAR**

❈ Since strength is a feature of any bar, such an image becomes the symbol of our spiritual power, and power in everyday life. Interpretations can vary; a blockade, for instance, prevents us from wrong action, whereas a public house suggests a relaxed atmosphere and attitude.

❦ An iron bar suggests that we should look at how rigid or aggressive we are being in our behaviour. To be standing at a bar may represent a barrier to our sexual enjoyment or an awareness that we should preserve the status quo in our lives.

▦ We need to handle ourselves with strength of purpose and are seeking acceptance from our peer group in some aspect of everyday life.

⬔ In a man's dream an iron bar might suggest an assertive nature, whereas in a woman's dream it is more likely to signify aggression or to have sexual connotations.

*Also consult the entry for Barrier.*

## BARB/BARBED WIRE

The barb is traditionally the fork that the Devil carried with him, with which to goad us into action. Sometimes seen as the trident, it can represent the trinity of body, mind and spirit. Barbed wire might be seen as an entanglement which is not appropriate.

Intellectually, there are two potential meanings. Firstly, we are trying to be too smart. Equally we may be trying to force other people to do something they do not want to do. A barbed comment is one which is specifically designed to hurt the recipient and can take on this physical representation of a barb or barbed wire in dreams.

To be surrounded by barbed wire in a dream indicates that we are being prevented from moving forward by either our own, or others', hurtful remarks.

In both men's and women's dreams a barb can suggest aggressive male sexuality, whereas barbed wire is more likely to represent the legendary '*vagina indentata*' or all-devouring female.

## BARBER

The old idea that one's spiritual power was held in the head gives rise to the idea that a barber signifies control of spiritual strength.

An influence is becoming more apparent in our lives which indicates a need for change. That change needs to be dictated by the way we perceive ourselves, rather than dictated by an outsider.

When we dream of visiting a barber we are considering a change of attitude, thought or opinion about ourselves.

*Also consult the entry for Hairdresser.*

**BARE** – *see* NUDE

**BARGE** – *see* PUSH AND TRANSPORT

**BARK** – *see* DOG, FOREST, TREE AND WOOD

**BAR MITZVAH** – *see* CEREMONY AND RITE/RITUAL

**BARREL** – *see* CASK

## BARRIER

In spiritual terms, any barrier suggests a division between two states, e.g. the spiritual and the mundane, or the physical and emotional. The implication is that it has been placed there for a purpose, to alert us to a duality.

As a barrier signifies an obstacle to be overcome, or a difficulty to be recognized, the nature of the barrier and our reactions will clarify any action that needs to be taken. In our most vulnerable emotional states we may need some sort of buffer between us and the rest of the world.

🔲 If the barrier is a safety barrier we perhaps need to stop and consider our actions. To run into a buffer may indicate the need for caution. It suggests a parameter beyond which there is danger.

**BASE**

🔆 Spiritually, base material suggests crudeness and the unformed – something which has not yet taken shape. Our 'basic instincts' may be brought into play, requiring that we go back to original material.

♦ To dream of base material or metal indicates that we are dealing with something that is not of the best quality and needs refining in some way.

🔲 If our attention is drawn to the base of an object we may need to go back to the starting point of a project in which we are involved in waking life. We should consider how stable we are in any situation.

*You might like to read the entry for Foundations.*

**BASEMENT – *see* BUILDINGS AND HOUSE**

**BASKET**

🔆 Baskets traditionally represent the seasons. A full one, for instance, is full fruition and abundance, a time of harvesting. As a container, a basket can also represent the feminine closing or receptive principle.

♦ To be attempting to fill a basket can mean that we are trying to increase our talents and abilities. Somehow we feel we do not have 'enough'.

🔲 If the basket is full of bread it can represent sharing – as in a sacramental meal. If the contents are spilt, it signifies the possible failure of a venture or sometimes the premature ending of a project.

🔳 Because of its connection with the feminine, in a man's dream a basket can suggest domesticity or his caring nature. In a woman's dream, if she finds the basket heavy, she may be finding her responsibilities a burden.

**BAT**

🔆 A flying bat can represent discernment or obscurity of a spiritual kind. The meaning is often ambiguous, but being a nocturnal animal usually veers towards the negative interpretation. The vague unpleasantness may also suggest some idiosyncrasy within ourselves. A bat used in sports has the same interpretation as a weapon or tool.

♦ To dream of bats attacking us shows the need to confront our fears of madness. Because of their mouselike bodies and birdlike wings, bats are seen as having a dual nature. When the image is of a sports bat, such as cricket or baseball bat, the suggestion is that we are not able to use implements without some kind of training. To dream of using such a bat indicates a learnt degree of competence.

🔲 Because popular belief has it that bats are frightening, to dream of bats indicates that there are thoughts and ideas within the unconscious that may reveal themselves with frightening potential. Dreaming of a cricket bat or other such implement will give an indication of our attitude to controlled aggression, or to how we deal with external forces.

*You might like to consult the entries for Mouse in Animals, Birds, Games, Tools, Vampire and Weapons.*

## BATH/BATHING

From a spiritual perspective, any dream where water is involved suggests an act of cleansing or initiation. Communal bathing depicts innocence and sensuality combined.

When we dream of bathing someone, it shows the need to nurture or to have an intimate connection with another person. We may have knowledge which can help or heal.

When we dream of being in the bath, it may indicate the need for cleansing of some old feelings, the need to relax, to let go. We have an opportunity to contemplate what has occurred in the past and to adopt new attitudes. To be wearing a bathing costume denotes a degree of permitted exposure.

For many women a bath can be a relaxing time of contemplation and can, therefore, have that significance in dreams. For men, it is more likely to be functional and, therefore, a time of planning.

*You might like to read the entries for Swimming, Washing and Water.*

## BATON

Symbolic of spiritual authority and rhythm, the baton is a tool to enable us to proceed in an orderly manner, under the control of a higher authority. A musical conductor's baton suggests this interpretation.

If the dream is of a drum baton or stick, the dream may represent the need for self-expression in a more forceful way than normal. A baton such as those used in relay races is representative of the passing on of information or responsibility. This, of course, returns it to its original meaning, more pertinent to dreams.

If the dream is of a police baton, then it can represent authority or male sexuality and our attitudes to them.

In a woman's dream the baton can suggest perfect timing, whereas in a man's dream it is more likely to suggest authority.

## BATTLE/BATTLEGROUND – *see* ARENA, FIGHTING AND WAR

## BATTERY

A battery symbolizes both power and energy. To dream of a battery running out of power suggests that there may be a health problem as yet unrecognized.

⟁ As there are now so many different types of battery, ranging from tiny transistor types to large cells, the interpretation will vary somewhat. Largely, however, a battery is seen as a source of power.

▦ More mundanely, we may be having a problem in finding the energy to complete a project and need to find a different source of inspiration.

⟐ In both men and women's dreams, since the principle is one of a balance of positive and negative, a battery can suggest the libido or the driving force.

**BAY**

⟁ The wolf baying at the moon shows the overcoming of basic animal instincts. The bay tree or leaves signify victory, eternity and immortality.

⟁ To be keeping something at bay indicates a need to be on our guard – on some level we are feeling threatened.

▦ Traditionally to be conscious of a bay or inlet showed an awareness of a woman's sexuality and receptiveness. Since water signifies emotion, a bay or inlet can also represent a sinificant emotional connection with feminine energy.

⟐ In dreams the mind frequently gives us images that clarify our attitude to ourselves and our everyday lives. For a man, entering a bay or inlet touches on the ancient myth of Jason and the Argonauts and their search for something attainable only with difficulty. For a woman, a bay or inlet suggests her secret and private self.

*Also consult the entry for Laurel/Bay Leaves.*

**BEACH**

⟁ The potential for emotional clarity is present, particularly if the beach is deserted. The sea signifies emotion and the land security or the everyday.

⟁ Depending on our actions and state of mind in the dream, dreaming of a beach usually means relaxation and creativity, and also the need to understand our need for time out.

▦ To be on a beach shows our awareness of the boundary between emotion and reality, our ability to be in touch with the elements and the capacity we have for combining perception and feeling in a relaxed manner.

**BEACON**

⟁ As a source of light, beacons take on the symbolism of illuminating the way to spiritual enlightenment and to sanctuary for the spirit.

⟁ Our emotions may be 'flaring up' and need directness of communication. If the flame is unprotected a beacon may signify passion.

▦ This can show, variously, as a warning, the need for communication or a strongly held principle by which you live.

▣ In a man's dream, without the spiritual connotations, a beacon can be a symbol for sexuality. In a woman's dream it is more likely to suggest passionate feelings.

*You might like to consult the entries for Fire, Light and Torch.*

### BEADS

⚙ Beads made from semi-precious stones are used as spiritual reminders – as in rosaries or votive beads. In many religions prayers are counted by using beads and repeated prayers are notated in order to ensure that the right number are said. In dreams we tend to be more conscious of spiritual discipline.

♥ Psychologically we are looking for perfection. To be counting beads suggests that we are enumerating our talents, blessings or skills (the number may be important).

▦ When we dream of beads strung together – for instance in a rosary – we are becoming aware of continuity or logical progression. To dream of beads breaking indicates the failure of a favourite project.

*You might like to consult the entries for Gems/Jewels, Necklace and Numbers.*

### BEAKER – *see* CUP

### BEAN

⚙ The bean can signify immortality and magical power, containing as it does the potential for life and manifestation.

♥ Psychologically the bean can represent stored potential. We have the ability to tap into it to achieve whatever we want. Traditionally the bean was supposed to be capable of feeding, clothing and providing an object of exchange for barter.

▦ To be storing beans in a dream may show a fear of failure or a lack of confidence in our ability to carry through an objective at this point. We may, however, need to create something in the future. To be planting beans would suggest faith in the future and a wish to create something useful.

▣ In a man's dream the bean suggests the life force, whereas in a woman's dream it will signify her own fertility.

*Consult the entries on Garden, Gardener and Plants.*

### BEAR

⚙ The bear symbolizes spiritual strength and power, both latent – for example, when a bear hibernates – and also apparent. In shamanism the bear is a very powerful totem animal – a form of guardian.

♥ Psychologically, we have recognized the need to meet the force of our own creativity. As a symbol from a play on words, it can also suggest stamina, whether we are able to bear or put up with certain difficulties.

▨ To have a bear appear alive in a dream indicates aggression, or if it is dead, the handling of one's deeper negative instincts. To dream of a toy bear – i.e. a teddy bear – shows a childlike need for security.

▨ As a protective force in both men's and women's dreams, the bear can represent maternal energy.

*Consult the entries on Animals, Archetypes in the Introduction and Mother in Family.*

## BEARD

▨ Spiritually there is a degree of ambivalence in the symbol of the beard and the meaning will depend on the dreamer's own culture. It may mean wisdom and dignity, or alternatively it may mean deceit and deviousness. The bearded Wise Old Man of the archetypes signifies inner wisdom.

▨ We perhaps need to consider more masculine attributes in ourselves or others. To dream of cutting or having a beard cut suggests a loss of power.

▨ To dream of a man with a beard generally means we must guard against cover-up and deceit, though it can also be a sign of good luck.

▨ In a man's dream a beard suggests masculine power but in a woman's dream it suggests that someone is trying to hide information. If a woman is growing a beard in a dream it shows she needs to be more assertive.

## BEAST – *see* MONSTER

## BEATING

▨ Particularly if you yourself are taking a beating, humility, anguish and grief are symbolized, along with the recognition of a degree of cruelty by others.

▨ To be beaten, either physically or in a game, indicates submission on our part to a greater force.

▨ In dreams the act of beating something or someone represents our need for 'power over' whatever is represented. It suggests a need to control.

## BEAVER – *see* ANIMALS

## BED/BEDROOM

▨ Since sleep is a way of leaving the busy world behind, a bed can represent a form of spiritual sanctuary and a sense of purity.

▨ To be going to bed with someone can variously represent either our sexual attraction to that person or indicate that we need have no fear of them – depending on other circumstances within the dream. Such an act may suggest our search for companionship and love.

▨ To be going to bed alone in a dream can indicate a desire for a return to the safety and security of the womb. To dream of a bed made up with fresh linen indicates the need for a fresh approach to those thoughts and ideas that really matter to us.

⚂ For most people, the bed and bedroom signify a private place, though sometimes from different perspectives. For both men and women, dreams about beds can give an insight into our attitude to relationships, not necessarily with the opposite sex.

*Also consult the entries for Buildings, Furniture/Furnishings and House.*

## BEDWETTING

⚙ Bedwetting in dreams can suggest a need for freedom of personal expression. It can signify the need to let go but can also highlight issues of self-control.

♥ We may have worries about correct behaviour in society or of being condemned for improper behaviour.

▦ In dreams, we often regress to a former state, and to dream of wetting the bed indicates anxieties over lack of control. In some cases it may also indicate that we have concerns with sex or sexuality.

⚂ In everyday life control of the bladder during sleep can occur quite late – often later in boys than girls – so dreaming of bed wetting may arise from traumatic experiences, or from issues of self-esteem, which take the dreamer back to childhood.

## BEE/BEEHIVE

⚙ The bee symbolizes immortality, rebirth and order. Through a connection with the Great Mother, a beehive signifies eloquence and direct speech.

♥ To dream of a queen bee registers our need to feel, or be, superior in some way. We may possibly feel the need to be served in our chosen purpose by others. We are also aware of the need for hard work and industry. To dream of tending a beehive alerts us to the need for good management of our resources.

▦ As a symbol of something to be feared, as well as tamed and used, the meaning of bees in dreams can be ambivalent. To be stung by a bee is a warning of the possibility of hurt. Being attacked by a swarm indicates that we are creating a situation which may become uncontrollable. The beehive is said to represent an ordered community and, therefore, the ability to absorb chaos.

*You might also like to consult the entry for Hive.*

## BEETLE

⚙ The scarab beetle was an ancient Egyptian solar symbol – it is said to have rolled the sun across the sky. A beetle thus represents protection from evil. You should look at what, or who, you feels needs to be protected.

❂ The industriousness of the beetle is often taken to represent hard work, efficient planning and use of resources which needs to be undertaken.

▣ Considered by many to be dirty, in a dream the beetle carries the same symbolism as all insects – that is, something which is unclean if not given the correct attention.

*Consult the entry for Insects for further clarification.*

## BEG/BEGGAR

❂ Begging was at one time considered a valid spiritual discipline in that people were expected to share what they had. A beggar can be a hermit and, therefore, a spiritual petitioner, someone who trusts in the universe to provide.

❤ More negatively, emotions, drives and thoughts which have been 'starved' in our waking lives can often appear in dreams personalized as a beggar – that is begging for attention.

▣ To dream of being a beggar represents our own feeling of failure and lack of self-esteem. To dream of someone known to us as a beggar indicates that on some level we are conscious that there is a lack on their part, perhaps that they make too many demands on us, or conversely that we have a resource that they need.

## BEHIND – *see* POSITION

## BELL

❂ The bell is an ancient charm against the powers of destruction and 'bad' spirits and is used to clear an atmosphere. A bell in dreams may forewarn us of approaching spiritual danger.

❤ Bells can indicate the conscience and our need to seek approval from others. It may also indicate that we have a desire to communicate with someone who is distanced or estranged from us.

▣ Traditionally, to hear a bell tolling in a dream was to be warned of disaster or of a death. While that meaning is less prevalent now as there are more efficient ways of communication, a bell in a dream (such as a door bell) does warn us to be on the alert.

## BELLY

❂ The belly is the seat of the solar plexus, a spiritual centre or chakra which carries vitality. It can, therefore, also be a focus for appetite and earthly desires. At times it suggests an initiatory process when it takes on the symbolism of the womb.

❤ If our own belly is distended in our dream, we may be at a point where, psychologically at least, release is necessary either through anger or frank speech. To be aware of someone else's belly draws our attention to their emotions.

🖼 You may need to learn to trust your own instincts and intuition. Equally you may be coming to terms with repressed emotion and pain.

🈁 Often before she knows she is pregnant, a woman may become conscious of her belly in dreams. Body dysmorphia, such as dreaming of becoming fat, is quite common at this time.

*Consult the entries for Abdomen, Stomach and Womb in Body.*

**BELOW –** *see* **POSITION**

**BELT**

🔅 A belt is an insignia of power and can represent either the spiritual power we have, or the power we are able to obtain.

♦ Intellectually we may be 'hide-bound' or constrained in some fashion.

🖼 When we dream of a belt that attracts our attention, we are perhaps being bound by old attitudes, duty and so on. An ornate belt can represent a symbol of power or office (as in regimental or nurses' belts).

🈁 In a woman's dream a belt can have the same significance as a girdle – a symbol of her femininity. In a man's dream it is more likely to be a symbol of security.

**BEND/BENDING**

🔅 The simple explanation of a bend in a path or road is a change in spiritual direction, perhaps to accommodate new information. Whether the change is to the right or left may be important. To bend as in bowing generally acknowledges a higher power or authority.

♦ If you are bending forwards, this suggests submission or adapting to new circumstances, whereas bending backwards would signify a need to please or accommodate others.

🖼 When you are bending an object you are hoping to change – perhaps a project or way of life. When something is bent there is a distortion which needs to be understood. To find yourself bending the rules shows an element of rebellion.

*You might also like to consult the entry for Bow.*

**BERRIES –** *see* **FRUIT**

**BET –** *see* **GAMBLING**

**BIBLE –** *see* **BOOK AND SPIRITUAL IMAGERY IN THE INTRODUCTION**

**BICYCLE**

🔅 Spiritually the bicycle signifies duality or the balance of two aspects of belief.

♦ Psychologically, we could be looking for freedom without responsibility. We probably need to achieve some way of moving forward in a project using balanced judgement.

▦ When we dream of riding a bicycle it shows the need to pay attention to personal effort or motivation. To fall off the bicycle indicates a lack of good judgment.

⌐ A bicycle in a woman's dream represents personal freedom and previously might have suggested rebellion. In a man's dream it is most likely to have links with childhood memories.

*Also consult the entries for Journey and Transport.*

**BIG – *see* SIZE**

**BIGAMY**

✤ Spiritually, bigamy can represent the choices one has to make, possibly between right and wrong. By association it may represent the astrological sign of Gemini or the union of two parts of our personality.

♦ When we dream we are married to a bigamist we need to be aware that we are being deceived by someone very close to us.

▦ To dream of being a bigamist indicates not being able to decide either between two loves, two courses of action or two loyalties. We are being presented with alternatives, both of which have equal validity.

⌐ As customs change we are less likely to dream of bigamy and more likely to dream of multiple liaisons with the opposite sex. For instance, a man might dream of a harem whilst a woman is more likely to dream of serial monogamy.

*You might like to consult the entries for Affair and Marriage.*

**BILL**

✤ To be given a bill (a request for payment) suggests there is a spiritual cost in some of our actions. To be paying a bill signifies that we have accepted such a responsibility.

♦ In everyday life the exchange of payment is constantly taking place. When we find this highlighted in dreams it is necessary to give some thought to our attitude to such transactions.

▦ Often it is the emotion associated with financial transactions that is important and we would be wise to consider whether we want or need whatever is represented in the dream.

*Also consult the entry for Money.*

**BIND/BINDING – *see* BONDS**

**BINGE**

✤ Any excess in spiritual terms is an attempt to change consciousness or awareness. Since bingeing is an intermittent activity it suggests that there are attempts to impose a degree of control without actually having the correct self-discipline.

⬧ Lack of self-discipline in our day-to-day lives can be very wearing. We are being reminded that excess of any sort can be harmful. Remembering that taking in food or liquid is supposed to be nurturing, we need to consider our everyday activities very carefully.

▦ When we dream of 'going on a binge' we may have to be less rigid in our approach to caring for ourselves. Such a dream may be setting the scene for a relaxed approach to problems.

## BIRDS

◉ As far back as pagan times, man has been fascinated by birds and by flight. Birds were believed to be vehicles for the soul and to have the ability to carry the soul to heaven. As a result, birds were very often invested with magical and mystical powers. Birds have come to represent the Soul – both its dark and its enlightened side.

⬧ Psychologically, man often needs to project human qualities onto objects outside himself, and because birds' conduct is entirely instinctive, they can be used in dreams to understand man's behaviour. Different breeds of birds have various meanings in dreams as follows:

**Albatross** – as one of the world's largest birds it can represent a burden or dead weight, but also self-sufficiency and tenacity.

**Buzzard** – *consult the entry for Vulture in this section.*

**Chicken** – the imagination is being used to serve a practical function. There is potential for growth, though this may also come about through belonging to a group. The chicken can also represent stupidity and cowardice.

**Cock** – the cock is the symbol of a new day and of vigilance or watchfulness. It represents the masculine principle and thus the need to be more upfront and courageous.

**Crow** – dreaming of a crow can have two meanings. Traditionally the crow warns of death, although today it is more likely to mean great change. It may also represent wisdom and deviousness.

**Cuckoo** – the meaning of the cuckoo is rather ambivalent. It can represent deviousness or unrequited love, yet as the herald of spring it indicates a change from old, stale energy to newness and freshness.

**Dove** – as the bringer of calm after the storm, in dreams the dove depicts the Soul and the peaceful side of man's nature. It is also a representation of the Anima.

**Duck** – in a dream a duck denote some kind of superficiality or childishness.

**Eagle** – as a bird of prey, in dreams an eagle signifies domination and supremacy. It can also mean perceptiveness and awareness as well as farsightedness and objectivity. If you can identify with or have sympathy for the eagle, your own wish to dominate is becoming apparent, though there may be some difficulty in reconciling other parts of your nature. If you feel threatened, somebody around you may be threatening the status quo.

**Falcon** – the falcon shares much of the symbolism of the eagle. As a bird of prey, it typifies freedom and hope for those who are being restricted in any way. It can represent victory over lust.

**Geese/Goose** – the goose is said to represent watchfulness and love. Like the swan it can denote the dawn or new life. A flock of geese is often taken to represent the powers of intuition and to give warning of misfortune. The wild goose can represent the soul and often depicts the more nature-oriented side of our personality. Geese, in common with cats, are considered to be witches' familiars.

**Hen** – the hen denotes providence, maternal care and procreation. When a hen crows in a dream it is taken to represent feminine domination.

**Ibis** – the ibis, sometimes taken to be the stork, is the symbol of perseverance and of aspiration.

**Jackdaw** – *consult the entry for Magpie in this section.*

**Kingfisher** – to dream of a kingfisher is to dream of dignity and calmness.

**Lark** – a lark traditionally represents the transcendence of the mundane, overcoming the everyday problems to reach a wider viewpoint.

**Magpie** – there is an ancient belief that magpies and jackdaws are thieves, so to dream of one indicates we believe someone will take away, or we may lose, something we value. On a more positive note, the magpie can signify good news.

**Ostrich** – dreaming of an ostrich indicates that we are attempting to run away from responsibility.

**Owl** – sacred to Athena, goddess of strategy and wisdom, in a dream the owl shares these qualities. Because it is also associated with the night-time and, therefore, the underworld, it can sometimes represent death and messages from the hidden realms.

**Peacock** – to see a peacock in a dream indicates a growth of understanding from the plain and unadorned to the beauty of the fully plumed bird. Like the phoenix, it represents rebirth and resurrection.

**Pelican** – there are two meanings to the symbolism of the pelican. One is sacrifice and devotion and the other is careful and maternal love.

**Penguin** – the penguin is thought to represent adaptability, although it can also indicate stupidity or, perhaps more accurately, unwise behaviour.

**Pheasant** – to dream of pheasants generally foretells prosperity and good fortune to come.

**Phoenix** – the phoenix is a universal symbol of rebirth, resurrection and immortality (dying in order to live).

**Quail** – the quail represents amorousness, sometimes courage and often good luck. In its negative form it can also represent witchcraft and sorcery.

**Raven** – the raven can be a symbol of sin. However, if it is seen to be talking it often represents prophecy. Its meaning can be ambivalent since it can represent evil, but also wisdom.

**Seagull** – the seagull is a symbol of freedom and power.

**Sparrow** – the sparrow represents business, industry and hard graft.

**Stork** – the stork is a symbol of new life and new beginnings.

**Swallow** – the swallow seen in a dream represents hope and the coming of spring, a time of new beginnings and fecundity.

**Swan** – as the soul of man, the swan is often taken to be the divine bird. It can sometimes denote a peaceful death or ending as in 'swansong' – at one time swans were believed to sing only at the point of death.

**Turkey** – the turkey is today a food for celebrations and festivals. Dreaming of one can, therefore, denote that there may be good times ahead.

**Vulture** – as scavengers, vultures and buzzards have an association with the feminine aspect in its destructive persona.

**Woodpecker** – the woodpecker is a guardian of both kings and trees in mythology. It is also reputed to have magical powers.

▣ Birds in dreams usually represent freedom, imagination, thoughts and ideas which, by their nature, need freedom to be able to become evident. Dreaming of them in particular scenarios has the following meanings:

**A caged bird** can indicate restraint or entrapment.

**A bird flying freely** represents aspirations and desires and possibly the spirit soaring towards the Divine.

**A display of plumage** indicates our facade – the way we see ourselves and how we present ourselves to the outside world.

**A flock of birds** containing both winged and plucked birds indicates confusion over bodily or material considerations, as opposed to spiritual aspirations. Birds can sometimes denote the feminine, free side of the being. **The golden-winged bird** has the same significance as fire and, therefore, indicates spiritual aspirations. **A high-flying bird** indicates spiritual awareness or that part in us that seeks knowledge.

**Black/White birds** – the two aspects of the Anima or Self may be represented as two opposites; the black bird signifies the dark, neglected or shadowy side; the white the open, clear, free side.

**A pet bird** – personal circumstances, experiences and emotions can have a profound effect on our self-image/expression, and remembered happiness can be experienced in dreams about pet birds.

◈ In a man's dream, a bird can represent the Anima. In a woman's dream, it suggests the Self, in the sense of the spiritual self.

*Consult the Introduction for further information on the Anima and Self.*

## BIRTH

◈ The urge to care, to love and to give birth are all suggested by dreams of birth. It may be both a spiritual – and, therefore, an unselfish – need as well as an emotional one.

◈ Psychologically, we are coming to terms with our own existence and perhaps are recognizing our own validity.

◈ We tend to dream of birth at the beginning of a new way of life, a new attitude, new ability, or a new project – also when we become aware of the death of old ways of being.

◈ A woman will often dream of small animals and fish as she approaches pregnancy and birth. A man is more likely to dream of protecting the child or the mother in some fashion.

## BIRTHDAY

◈ Any celebration is a time for a release of or change in energy, and a birthday gives an opportunity to look back and take stock, from a spiritual perspective, either of the year just past or of the decade.

◈ Dreaming of a birthday signifies that we have the right to celebrate – either an anniversary or a new phase in life.

◈ There may be a sense of anticipation about something which lifts us away from the ordinary. We may have a gift or talent which is now usable.

*You might like to consult the entries for Feast and Party.*

## BITE/BITTEN

◈ In a dream in which we are biting a person or an object, we have returned to very basic drives of anger and aggression, and behind that is the need to protect ourselves or our personal space. Being bitten by a snake often represents some kind of initiation.

◈ To be biting into something such as fruit within a dream indicates that there is literally an idea or a concept which we need to get our teeth into.

Being bitten in a dream may show that we are experiencing aggression from someone else, or conversely that our own aggressive instincts in our waking lives are not under control. We are feeling threatened.

**BIZARRE** – *see* **TYPES OF DREAMS IN THE INTRODUCTION**

**BLACKBIRD** – *see* **BIRDS**

**BLACK HOLE**

In spiritual terms a black hole has the same connotation as the void or the abyss.

There are times when a black hole can warn of depression or of venturing into the unknown.

Experiencing a black hole in dreams can be a little like Alice in Wonderland's rabbit hole – an entry into the bizarre world of dream images. *Consult the entries for Abyss and Void.*

**BLACKMAIL**

Blackmail suggests that there is a part of us that is aware of information that we hold. However, we have difficulty in sharing that information with others. We may also be called upon to account for past actions.

For many people privacy is a very emotive issue and to dream of blackmail suggests that someone has penetrated our defences, probably in an inappropriate way.

When there is conflict between two courses of action, to dream of blackmail suggests that we are being forced in some way to take an action which goes against our natural instincts.

**BLACKSMITH** – *see* **ANVIL AND FORGE**

**BLAZE** – *see* **FIRE**

**BLESS** – *see* **SPIRITUAL IMAGERY IN THE INTRODUCTION**

**BLINDFOLD**

In spiritual terms, being blindfolded is often seen as a rite of passage. It is a transition between two states. It also signifies some kind of initiation.

When we cut ourselves off from visual contact with the external world we are turning inwards in order to know and understand ourselves better. Such an image in dreams suggests that we need to become introverted for a time, perhaps so that we do not try to affect the situation around us.

If we have been blindfolded in a dream, it shows a deliberate attempt is being made to deceive us. If we are blindfolding someone else, we are not being honest in our dealings with other people. This may be through ignorance on our part.

**BLINDNESS**

☀ Spiritually, blindness is a form of ignorance. It can suggest the irrational. It is also a form of initiation.

♡ Intellectually we may be aware of certain facts, but choose not to use that knowledge in the most appropriate way.

▨ If we ourselves are suffering from blindness in a dream, there is an unwillingness to 'see', i.e. perceive something. We have lost sight of a goal or objective or we are seeing qualities in ourselves that we don't like.

**BLOCK**

☀ A block suggests either a preventative measure or a warning to ensure that we do not make a mistake.

♡ Blocks appear in dreams when we need to make a special effort to overcome an obstacle to progress.

▨ In dreams, a block may present itself in many forms. We can experience it as a physical block – that is, something that needs to be climbed over or got round, a mental block – for instance, not being able to speak or hear, or a spiritual block such as the figure of an angel or a demon appearing in our dreams.

▣ A block as in a cube represents the physical material realm in both men's and women's dreams.

*You might also like to consult the entry for Obstacle/Obstruct/Obstruction.*

**BLOOD**

☀ Spiritually, being aware of blood circulating through the body can symbolize the rejuvenating or life force. This is similar to *ch'i* in Chinese medicine.

♡ Emotional abuse and difficulties can translate itself in dreams into bloody wounds and can appear to be either self-inflicted or being inflicted by someone else.

▨ From time immemorial blood has represented the life carrier or the life force. To dream of a violent scene where blood appears indicates that we are being self-destructive in some way. If we are having to deal with blood, we need to be aware of our own strength. If we have been injured and someone else is dealing with the blood, we need to look at what help is necessary to overcome hurt.

▣ For a woman to dream of menstrual blood may alert her to a health problem, but may also draw attention to her essential femininity.

*Also consult the entry in Body.*

**BLUNT** – *see* INSTRUMENT

**BOAR**

🔆 By association with mythology and children's fables a boar can suggest evil, or rather overbearing aggression. It also suggests abundance and vitality.

♥ The boar was once much associated with feasting and festivals and can thus signify lust and gluttony.

🖼 One of the ways in which the dream mind can bring matters to our attention is by a play on words, and since not many people have contact with the animal per se, for this to appear in a dream usually indicates a 'bore'.

*Consult the entries for Wild Boar in Animals and also for Pig.*

**BOAT/SHIP**

🔆 Boats represent our attitude to death and 'The Final Journey'. They can also represent fertility and adventure and in antiquity were seen as the bearers of gods and kings.

♥ To dream of being alone in a small boat means we need to consider how we handle isolation and the ability to be alone. To dream of being on a large ship alerts us to how we handle group relationships. To dream of missing a boat is often the dream of a perfectionist who fears missing chances or opportunities.

🖼 To dream about a boat or a ship very often indicates how we cope with both our own emotions and those of others. It may well represent how we navigate our way through life and whether we feel that we are in control of our lives.

*You may also like to consult the entries for Journey and Transport.*

**BODY**

🔆 The body is a physical manifestation of an inner spirituality, so in theory should be almost perfect. Sometimes, rather than looking to heal the body, it is easier to heal the spirit, and dreams of the body can highlight the areas in which we need to make changes.

♥ Most experience can be translated into bodily feeling – tension or relaxation perhaps – and, therefore, becomes a rich source of symbolism in dreams. When emotions cannot be faced in ordinary everyday life, they very often become distorted dream symbols.

**Abdomen/Belly/Stomach** – when the dream appears to concentrate on the abdomen, there is a need to focus on emotions and repressed feelings.

**Anus** – the young child's first experience of control is as he or she gains control over bodily functions, particularly the anal muscles. In dreams, the mind returns to that experience as a symbol of self-realization and self-reliance and, more negatively, of suppression and defence. Such a dream, therefore, is indicating an aspect of childish behaviour or egotism. *Also consult the entry for Excrement in this section.*

**Arms** – we use our arms in all sorts of different ways. In dreams we may be defending ourselves, fighting or being held. We may also be showing passionate commitment. *You might also like to consult the individual entry for Arms.*

**Back** – dreaming of seeing someone else's back suggests we should identify the more private elements in our characters. We should also be aware that other people may not yet wish to share their thoughts with us. We may also find that we are vulnerable to the unexpected. If we dream of turning our backs, we are rejecting the particular feeling being experienced in the dream. *You might also like to consult the individual entry for Back for further clarification.*

Backbone – if the backbone is particularly noticeable in a dream, we should consider the main support structure in our lives. Intellectually, we need to consider our firmness of character.

**Breasts** – to be conscious of breasts in dreams indicates our connection with the mother figure and our need for nurturing. Such a dream can also indicate a wish to return to being an infant without responsibilities. *Also consult the individual entry for Breasts.*

**Eyes** – any dream in which the eyes play an important part is to do with observation and discrimination. Eyes are indicative of enlightenment and wisdom, protection and stability. They also have a connection with the power of light and, in ancient times, of the sun-gods. Through its connection with Egyptian symbolism, the eye is also a talisman. Loss of eyesight signifies the loss of clarity and, depending on which eye, can be either the loss of logic (right eye) or the loss of intuition (left eye). Regaining the eyesight can indicate a return to the innocence and clear-sightedness of the child.

**Foot/Feet** – for some cultures, to dream of the feet may symbolize divine qualities since the feet are considered the holiest part of the body. They signify taking responsibility and are the anchor or foundation in life, that which roots or grounds you. The foot also represents your whole being and is a reflection of your persona.

**Hair** – hair represents strength and virility. In dreams, to be combing hair is to be attempting to untangle a particular attitude we may have. To be having our hair cut is to be trying to create order in our lives. To be cutting someone else's hair may be to be curtailing an activity (it is possible that there may be some fear or doubt connected with sexuality). To be bald in a dream is to perhaps recognize our own intelligence. *Also consult the entries for Bald and Hairdresser.*

**Hands** – the hands are one of the most expressive parts of the body and signify power and creativity. The right hand is the 'power' hand, while the left is passive and receptive. Sometimes in dreams the left hand can represent cheating. If the hands are contrasted with each other and/or have a different object in each, it indicates there may be some conflict in us between our beliefs and feelings. A hand on the breast signifies submission. Clasped hands indicate union or friendship, while clenched hands suggest a threat. Folded hands suggest deep repose or a state of rest. The hands covering the eyes generally represent shame or horror, while hands crossed at the wrists suggest that we are being bound, perhaps by our own actions. The open hand represents justice whilst the laying on of hands signifies healing and blessing, particularly if the hand is placed on the neck. Hands placed together give an indication of defencelessness; if they are placed in someone else's it suggests a pledge of service or commitment. When the hands are raised this can indicate either adoration, prayer or surrender; if the palms are turned outwards a blessing is being given; when they are raised to the head we should give a great deal of thought and care to our current situation. Washing the hands suggests innocenceor rejection of guilt, while wringing the hands signifies grief. A huge hand, particularly from the sky, suggests that we have been 'specially chosen'. For this reason, advertising that contains such an image has a profound effect.

**Head** – the head is considered to be the principle part of the body. Because it is the seat of the life force, it denotes power and wisdom. Dreaming of the head suggests that we should look very carefully at the way we deal with both intelligence and folly. To dream of the head being bowed suggests supplication. When the head is covered we may be covering up our own intelligence or acknowledging somebody else's superiority. A blow to the head in a dream can indicate that we should reconsider our actions in a particular situation.

**Heart** – the heart is the centre of the being and represents 'feeling' wisdom rather than intellectual wisdom. It is also representative of compassion and understanding.

**Heel** – this suggests the part of ourselves that is strong but, at the same time, vulnerable.

**Jaw** – often representative of our self-expression, on a more esoteric level the jaw suggests the opening to the underworld.

**Kidneys** – the kidneys are organs of elimination, therefore, to dream of them is to be aware of the need for cleansing.

**Knees** – the knees are symbolic of prayer and supplication, and of emotional commitment.

**Legs** – the legs in dreams suggest support and stability, the ability to stand firm and also the capability of moving forward. The calf represents speed and control.

**Limbs** – whether it is partly to do with some kind of cellular memory and the growth process that takes place is uncertain, but in dreams any limb can be taken to mean sexuality and fears associated with gender issues. Being dismembered can be taken in its literal sense – we are being torn apart. Sometimes this can suggest the need to restructure our lives and begin again. At other times it can indicate that there is a way in which we are being threatened to the very core of our existence. *Consult Arms in this section and also the individual entry for Arms.*

**Liver** – the liver is representative of irritability and suppressed anger.

**Lungs** – in Chinese medicine the lungs represent grief. They are also involved in decision making. Spiritually, the lungs are the seat of righteousness and the source of thoughts concerning the Self.

**Mouth** – the mouth represents the devouring, demanding part of ourselves. It can also stand for the receptive side. The circumstances of the dream may give a clue to the correct interpretation. Sometimes the mouth can symbolize the feminine side of our nature.

**Nose** – in dreams the nose indicates curiosity and intuition.

**Penis** – dreaming of a penis, either your own or someone else's, usually highlights the attitude to penetrative sex.

**Skin** – skin in a dream stands for our persona or the facade we create for others. Hard, tough skin shows we have created a tough exterior and are trying to protect ourselves, whereas particularly soft skin indicates we are aware of our vulnerability.

**Stomach** – *consult the entry for Abdomen in this section.*

**Teeth** – popularly, teeth are supposed to stand for aggressive sexuality – although more properly they signify the growth process towards sexual maturity. Teeth falling or coming out easily indicates we are aware of going through a form of transition, similar to that from childhood to maturity, or from maturity to old age and helplessness. If we are anxious about teeth dropping out it suggests there is a fear of getting old and undesirable, or an anxiety about maturing. In a woman's dream, if the teeth are swallowed this can sometimes signify pregnancy, a wish for pregnancy, or an issue with sex.

**Throat** – dreaming of the throat shows we are aware of our vulnerability and also of the need for self-expression.

**Thumb** – dreaming of a thumb suggests awareness of how powerful we are. The thumb pointing upwards represents beneficial energy, whilst pointing downwards indicates a negative response.

**Tongue** – the tongue in dreams often signifies our ability to know when to speak and when to remain silent. It may also be to do with our own understanding of information that we wish to pass on to other people. We may have deeply felt beliefs we wish to share. Another explanation that is much more basic is that of the symbolism of the serpent and the phallus, and hence sexuality.

**Vagina** – most often, dreams of the vagina are to do with self-image. In a woman's dream it highlights her receptivity. In a man's dream it suggests his need to be penetrative, both mentally and physically. *You may also like to consult the entry for Sex/Sexual Images.*

**Womb** – the womb represents a return to the beginning. We all have need of basic security and shelter, and perhaps to do away with responsibility. Dreams of the womb can signify our need to satisfy those requirements. On a slightly more esoteric level the womb represents our connection with the Great Mother or Mother Earth. Dreams of returning to the womb suggest our need to reconnect with the passive, more yielding side of our nature. We may need a period of self-healing and recuperation.

The body represents the individual and is his outward physical projection of all that he is. In dreams, the body often represents the Ego. Since being 'physical' is the baby's first experience of itself, the body forms the prime source of information. The various functions and unusual aspects of the body in dreams have particular symbolic significance:

**Abscess** – an abscess is a localized infection. This appearing anywhere in the body highlights that particular area which is in need of consideration.

**Blood** – dreaming of blood can have one of two meanings. It can signify that we feel that a sacrifice is being made on some level. This links into the ancient belief that the blood somehow contained the life of the spirit and, therefore, spilt blood was sacred. It can also represent renewal of life through its connection with menstruation. Many people fear blood and thus a dream about blood can highlight the need to come to terms with these fears. On a more spiritual level it represents the blood of Christ. *Also consult the individual entry for Blood.*

**Constipation** – retention signifies an inability to let go of the past or of previous patterns of behaviour, literally to be uptight. *Also consult the entry for Anus in this section.*

**Excrement** – you may not have progressed on a subconscious level beyond a feeling that anything to do with bodily functions is dirty and self-centred. There could be an element of rebellion in your waking life. Playing with excrement can represent your attitude to money and value, highlighting fear of responsibility, as well as anxiety about money. If the excrement is transformed into living animals, maybe rats, you are accepting that you are responsible for managing your own impulses. Excrement in its more spiritual meaning belongs to the realm of feelings and you may simply be trying to get rid of bad feelings. Those bad feelings can be turned into something worthwhile. Evacuation of the bowel usually highlights our need to be free of worry and responsibility, or possibly the need to learn how to be uninhibited. It can also signify the sexual act.

**Fat** – dreaming of becoming fat means we are recognizing the need to widen the scope of our activities in some way. More negatively, it suggests the need for protection. If we are uncomfortable with our size it indicates fear, possibly of taking on too much responsibility or of not being adequate for a task.

**Urine** – urine in a dream often indicates our feelings about emotional control. We may either yield to emotion or bottle it up. The way we deal with urine in dreams often also tells us a great deal about our own sexuality, because they are both instinctive behaviours.

To dream of **the upper part of the body** links with the mind and the spiritual aspects of the character, while **the lower part of the body** represents the instincts and emotional aspects. **An adult's head on an immature body, or a child's head on an adult body** is an indication that we need to recognize the differences between mature thought and emotion. If there is conflict between the upper and lower part – for instance the lower half being bigger and the top half smaller – then it indicates that there is disharmony between the mental faculties and instinctive behaviour. **The right side or right hand** being especially noticeable in dreams signifies we should take note of the logical side of our personality, whereas **the left side or left hand** indicates we need to be aware of our intuitive, creative side. *You might like to consult the entries for People and Position for further clarification.*

**BOIL**

✺ The symbolism of fire applied to water to bring about a change in temperature is a strong spiritual image denoting perhaps passion and ferment. Two Elements in juxtaposition esoterically suggests power and energy. A boil as in a skin condition signifies an infection or contamination of a cherished idea.

⚙ Water often signifies emotion, so to boil water suggests an increase in emotional content. To dream of being covered in boils signifies that we have offended a code of ethics and feel that we are 'unclean'.

▦ When we are boiling up – as in running a fever – in dreams we are echoing distress in everyday life. There is nowhere for excess energy to go.

⛨ In a woman's dream, to be boiling a kettle suggests that she is seeking some kind of transformation in herself. For a man to have such a dream indicates he is more likely to be seeking this in someone else.

*Consult the entries for Fire, Kettle and Water.*

## BOLT

⚙ Since there is more than one meaning for bolt, you will need to decide which is appropriate. A bolt on a door may signify that you are feeling imprisoned in a situation, perhaps by your own beliefs. A bolt as in nuts and bolts suggests the masculine principle or drive, while the bolt from a crossbow signifies direct action or speech.

♥ Psychologically, dream images can highlight a state of mind, and seeing nuts and bolts is often a way of alerting us to basic ideas or how things work, so that we understand better. The idea of a bolt from the blue suggests sudden comprehension.

▦ When we are bolting a door we may be trying to shut something in or out – often a feeling or emotion. When a plant has bolted or gone to seed, circumstances around us have gone past their best.

⛨ In engineering terms a nut represents the feminine and the bolt the masculine. In both men's and women's dreams the bolt can thus signify sex or the sexual act, but is more often to do with intimate relationships – perhaps where two people have an innate understanding of one another.

*You might like to consult the entries for Bow, Key, Keyhole and Nut for further clarity.*

## BOMB

⚙ A bomb exploding in dreams often forecasts an unexpected event. Dreaming of a bomb would appear to suggest a fear of sudden death or a cataclysmic event.

♥ Psychologically, we need to be aware that our own emotions are likely to get the better of us. Anger, for instance, can be a particularly destructive force.

▦ Bombs appearing in a dream usually indicate some form of explosive situation with which we need to deal. Exploding a bomb indicates the need for positive action, while defusing a bomb suggests taking care not to make a situation worse.

*Also consult the entry for Atom Bomb, Explode/Explosion, Nuclear Explosion and War.*

**BONDS**

There are two meanings for bonds in dreams. One is as in savings bonds (promissory notes) and the second as in bindings and cords. Spiritually, the significance is that of an undertaking, the changing of conflict into law and order, of chaos into cosmic order. Evil can traditionally be contained by binding it, whether by magical technique, symbolism or visualization. Depending on whether the dreamer is being bound or doing the binding, it shows submission to a greater force.

Depending on whether we are giving or receiving promissory bonds, we need to consider our emotional commitment to ourselves and our own concerns. To be aware of being fettered, snared or held fast by chains or other such bonds indicates the possibility that our emotional selves may be out of control.

To dream of promissory notes indicates that we have a sense of commitment to a person or a principle – that we are capable of making promises which we can keep. To dream of other bonds deals with the binding or holding that can occur in situations and relationships.

*You might like to consult the entries for Chains, Chaos and Halter.*

**BONES**

Bones are one of the integral parts of man, or indeed of most creatures. Spiritually, they represent structure and the basic building material of the physical realm. They often hold the key to our ideas of death and resurrection.

To dream of a full skeleton indicates that we need to reconsider the structure of our lives. To be conscious of particular bones in the skeleton, particularly the joints, highlights the way we move or create.

Bones appearing in a dream usually indicate that we need to be aware of fundamental material. We need to 'go back to basics'. To dream of a dog eating a bone means we need to consider our natural instincts. To dream of finding bones indicates that there is something essential we have not considered in a situation.

*You might like to consult the entries for Limbs in Body as well as the entry for Skeleton/Skull.*

**BONFIRE**

Spiritually, a bonfire reflects the power of the sun and encourages the power of good. It also represents solar festivals, where the life-giving power of the sun is acknowledged and renewal is celebrated.

🜊 When we are conscious of feeding a bonfire, the passionate side of our emotional selves needs to be allowed freedom of expression. Old, outdated concepts and beliefs can be let go in order to create something new.

🜊 To be lighting or tending a bonfire in a dream indicates a need for cleansing some aspect of our lives. In past times, old bedding and litter was burnt with some ceremony to mark the beginning of a fresh cycle of existence. Such a fire can also represent passions that are not confined by rigidity and custom.

*Also consult the entries for Fire and Smoke/Smoking.*

**BONUS**

🜊 A bonus signifies a spiritual benefit earned through hard work and application.

🜊 This is a 'just reward' usually given by a higher authority, often that part of us which knows what is best for us.

🜊 On a purely mundane level dreaming of a bonus, either giving or receiving it, signifies approval of some sort, which is considered to be of benefit.

**BOOK**

🜊 A book, particularly a sacred one such as the Bible or Koran, signifies hidden or sacred knowledge. Any religious book in dreams presupposes some kind of spiritual realization or some knowledge gained. It represents our need to look into the realms of sacred or arcane knowledge or for reassurance that we are going in the right direction.

🜊 Intellectually, we are searching in our dreams for ways which will help us to handle what happens in our lives. We will need to look very carefully at our religious beliefs, myths and legends, and decide what relevance they have for us. Many systems of belief have long held to there being a book in which all our deeds are recorded, and for which we are accountable.

🜊 Our search for knowledge and the ability to learn from other people's experience and opinions is symbolized in dreams by books and libraries. To dream of old books represents inherited wisdom and spiritual awareness. If we dream of a Bible or other religious book it usually means that we are aware of traditional moral standards. We need a code of conduct that helps us to survive. To dream of account books indicates the need or ability to look after our own resources, practical and otherwise.

*You may also like to consult the entry for Reading for further clarity.*

**BOOT**

🜊 In many ways a car boot has the same meaning as any empty vessel, a container or repository for goods. However, spiritually, it signifies a mechanized way of carrying material and perhaps the need to be aware of how much baggage we carry. Boots as in footwear suggests protection and proper grounding, the spiritual functioning within the physical realm.

It will depend on whether the boot is packed in an orderly fashion or not, but a car boot can represent the mind and all it contains: ideas, concepts thoughts and beliefs. When our attention is being drawn to footwear we should consider our hold on reality.

From an everyday perspective protective footwear highlights our need to be practical and pragmatic while also being protected. To be unloading a car boot suggests the completion of a task or project. To be packing a boot signifies the need to ensure we have sufficient resources for the task in hand.

**BORDER**

This signifies meeting a different aspect of the Self and through this a new experience in life. We need to decide if the time is right to make a transition.

Psychologically we may need to make decisive changes in the way we think and feel.

A border can appear in many different ways in a dream. To have our attention drawn to the edge or border of material can indicate changes we will make in the material world. To be standing on a border between two countries would show the need to be making great changes in life.

*Also consult the entry for Frontier.*

**BORROW**

To borrow something implies having to give it back at some point. So, when we use energy or resources from a spiritual perspective, we also have to give something – usually effort – back.

The transaction of borrowing suggests not yet being in the position of 'owning' ideas and concepts but being prepared to make use of them.

On a purely mundane level, when we dream of borrowing articles we perhaps cannot use knowledge or information without having acknowledged that they are someone else's ideas. We must admit that we owe them a debt.

**BOTTLE**

This is a womb symbol: the principle of containing and enclosure and, therefore, an aspect of femininity, fertility and intuition.

Opening a bottle could mean making available resources you have but may have suppressed. A broken bottle could indicate either aggression or failure.

To a certain extent it depends on which type of bottle is perceived in the dream. When the image is of a baby's feeding bottle, it would indicate the need to be successfully nurtured and helped to grow. A bottle of alcohol would show the need to celebrate, or to curb an excess, while a medicine bottle might symbolize the need to look at one's own health.

In a woman's dream, given the above significances, the image of a bottle is probably to do with her own intimate feelings about herself as a woman. In a man's dream such an image will be more to do with his perception of women.

**BOTTOM** – *see* **BODY AND POSITION**

**BOUQUET** – *see* **FLOWERS**

**BOW**

Variously a bow can indicate superiority, the union of masculine and feminine and celebration.

While intellectually we may not feel inferior, bowing in a dream shows that on an unconscious level we may actually sense someone else's need to feel superior and acknowledge that in the dream state. Such a dream could also indicate our own sense of inferiority.

To perceive a bow, as in Cupid's bow, can indicate the need to be loved – the union of masculine and feminine. To see a bow made of ribbon is making a connection to the feminine principle and beauty. An archery bow represents a compulsive force.

When the arrow is taken to represent masculine energy, in a man's dream the bow – the actual means of propulsion – signifies his need to succeed. In a woman's dream it will suggest her need to procreate.

*You might like to consult the entries for Arrow and Bend/Bending.*

**BOWL**

As with many other symbols of receptivity, a bowl represents ultimate feminine wisdom and instinctive feeling as well as fertility. It thus becomes a symbol of the Great Mother.

Because of its connection with instinctive feeling and intuition, a bowl can represent the ability to see the bigger picture. In ordinary life, scrying (technically, divining the future) uses the focus of intuition through the medium of a bowl of water. In dreams, such a bowl would indicate the possible development of clairvoyance.

A bowl of food in a dream represents our ability to nurture and sustain others. A bowl of flowers can represent a gift or a talent, while on a more mundane level a bowl of water represents our emotional capacity.

**BOX**

Any enclosed space tends to signify the feminine containing principle. A box also represents the material world. A box also implies a degree of rigidity in our thinking.

❧ Various types of boxes perceived in a dream may represent different aspects of the feminine personality. Thus a decorated box can represent a flamboyant personality, whereas a plain cardboard box might suggest ordinary everyday concerns.

❧ When we feel boxed in we are being prevented from expanding in an appropriate way. To dream of packing things in a box indicates that we are trying to get rid of feelings or thoughts with which we cannot cope.

**BOY** – *see* **PEOPLE**

**BOYFRIEND** – *see* **PEOPLE**

**BRAIN**

❧ The brain is considered to be the seat of the soul. Spiritually it represents the coming together of power and intellect.

❧ It is unlikely that anyone will dream of a brain *per se,* however, since the brain is also the seat of learning, we may need to consider our beliefs and ideals in the light of experience.

❧ When attention is drawn to the brain in a dream, we are expected to consider our own or others' intellect. To dream of the brain being preserved indicates the need to take care in intellectual pursuits. We may be pushing ourselves too hard.

**BREAD**

❧ Bread has always been symbolic of life itself. In its highest aspect it is considered to be spiritual nourishment – manna. It can also represent the need to share spiritual knowledge.

❧ If the bread is out of the ordinary or has an unusual taste, we may be unsure of what we really need out of life. We may not be following the most productive course of action in our lives.

❧ Dreaming of bread connects us with our need for basic emotional and physical or material needs. To be sharing bread in a dream represents our ability to share our experience with others so that they may learn.

*You might like to consult the entries for Eating, Food and Nourishment.*

**BREAK**

❧ There are two spiritual interpretations for break. One is shattered idealism, hope and faith, while the other much more positive interpretation is a holiday, or 'holy day', to enable us to recharge our spiritual batteries.

❧ If we dream of breaking something, we need to decide whether it is worth mending or repairing what is represented. A favourite gift might suggest a lack of appreciation of that particular association.

❧ To dream of something being broken symbolizes loss or damage. On a mundane level, if a favourite object or childhood toy is broken we need to make changes and break from the past. If a limb is broken we may be prevented from moving forward or carrying out a certain action.

## BREASTS

⚙ Almost inevitably from a spiritual perspective breasts represent motherhood, protection and love. Considered to be one of the most often dreamed about parts of the body, it is the symbolism of the nourishment and love belonging to motherhood that is most often understood.

◈ While intellectually we may deny the need for mothering or 'smother-love', this need surfaces when we are under stress. It often appears as the dream image of breasts.

▦ Representing femininity, breasts are an important part of the anatomy. Dreaming of losing a breast may alert us to health matters, or indicate that we are withholding love and affection from someone.

⊞ For a man to dream of breasts usually indicates his unconscious connection with his mother or the nurturing principle. For a woman, changes in size may suggest that she uses her feminine attributes in a different way.

*You might like to consult the entry for Body for further clarification.*

## BREATH/BREATHE – see WIND

## BREEZE

⚙ As a soft wind, a breeze suggests unconditional love and the presence of the divine spirit. In some senses, it can also represent purity.

◈ Psychologically, for most people a breeze indicates happy times to be savoured and remembered.

▦ To dream of a breeze being meaningful indicates a contented state of mind. Wind and anything to do with air is usually considered to belong to the intellect, so by association a gentle breeze indicates love, while a stiff breeze indicates a degree of abrasiveness.

*Consult the entry for Wind for further information.*

## BRIDE

⚙ A bride represents a change of status from the innocent maiden to a woman with responsibilities. In dreams she represents the spiritual need for, and recognition of, love, receptivity and fertility.

◈ To dream of being at a wedding, especially your own, indicates the integration of inner feeling and outer reality. We are seeking union of the unintegrated part of ourselves. We may be looking for the innocent feminine within.

▦ As marriage itself becomes less important for many, a sense of commitment is not. To dream of a bride suggests that, at some level, a commitment has been made to another human being.

⊡ When a woman dreams of being a bride, she is often trying to reconcile her need for relationship and her need for independence. She needs to have an understanding of the changes in responsibility. In a man's dream, a bride indicates his understanding of the feminine, innocent part of himself.

*Also consult the entries for Bridegroom and Wedding/Wedding Dress/Wedding Ring.*

## BRIDEGROOM

✾ A bridegroom can represent the need to take care of another person, maybe to exert a degree of control and, in spiritual terms, to commit to the continuance of the human race.

♡ The need for partnership can sometimes be more intellectual than emotional. In connecting with the drive of the masculine we can become creative in many different ways.

▦ To dream of a bridegroom usually indicates the desire to be married or to find a partner. It often shows a willingness to be more responsible or to take on responsibility for someone else, thereby becoming more mature. It is a connection with, and an understanding of, the 'romantic' side of our nature and indicates the need for integration of the intellect and the real world.

⊡ In a woman's dream a bridegroom may be something of a fantasy figure, allowing her to understand the qualities she needs in a partner on a mundane level. In a man's dream, he is perhaps putting himself in touch with his finer aspects.

*Also consult the entries for Bride and Wedding/Wedding Dress/Wedding Ring.*

## BRIDGE

✾ The bridge is one of the most commonly found images in dreams. It signifies crossing from one state of being to another, spanning the River of Life. The ancient image of crossing the River Styx accompanied by the ferryman Charon has been largely superceded by the symbol of a bridge.

♡ The symbol of a bridge signifies the emotional connection between us and other people or aspects of our lives.

▦ This almost invariably indicates the crossing from one phase of life to another, perhaps a rite of passage. The bridge may be depicted as weak or strong, sturdy or otherwise, which gives an indication of the strength of connection necessary to make changes in our lives.

## BRIDLE

✾ Spiritually, the bridle has the same connotation as a halter and suggests a degree of spiritual restraint or control.

♡ The bridle, in reining us in and keeping us focussed, can indicate the need for attention to various aspects of our lives.

To be bridled in a dream indicates the need for restraint and the ability to curb an excess of energy. Being yoked suggests the need to consider more than one aspect of everyday life. We may need to work in partnership or as a team.

If the bridle is made of flowers it indicates a feminine, gentle way of imposing control. If the bridling is more austere – such as one of metal and/or leather – we perhaps need to use firmness and restraint (more masculine qualities). There may also, of course, be wordplay here with the word 'bridal'. *You might like to consult the entries for Halter and Harness.*

**BRIGHT** – *see* LIGHT

**BROADCAST** – *see* AUDIENCE

**BROKEN** – *see* BREAK

**BROOM/BRUSH**

Magically, a broom is a witch's implement. In dreams, brooms and brushes can have a similar meaning in that they clear a spiritual space of negativity in preparation for changes to be made.

The idea of clearing or cleansing is as important on a psychological level as it is on the spiritual. Clearing away outmoded beliefs or habits is an important part of progression.

On a mundane level, the proverbs associated with brooms and brushes – 'a new broom sweeps clean' etc. – show us the actions that are necessary to make workaday life easier.

Brooms and brushes have largely given way to technological advances. In dreams, however, they still retain their old significance. In a man's dream, a broom may suggest ordinary, mundane tasks, whereas in a woman's dream it may suggest control over her environment.

**BROTHEL**

In a bastardization of the original meaning of brothel, such an image suggests the darker, more frightening side of femininity. In fact, women as priestesses seeking union with the Divine were a potent force for life. Hence a brothel may also represent awareness of man's spiritual debt to woman.

To dream of a brothel indicates the wish for sexual liberation and freedom without responsibility.

Visiting a brothel suggests the need for comfort and reassurance in a somewhat unorthodox manner. Working at a brothel suggests an appreciation of how women can use their sexuality as a tool.

If a woman dreams of being in a brothel, she has not yet come to terms with the sexually active side of herself. If a man dreams of being in a brothel it may show a fear of the feminine.

*You might like to consult the entries for Prostitute and Sex/Sexual Images.*

**BROTHER** – *see* FAMILY

**BROTHERHOOD** – *see* FREEMASONRY

**BRUTALITY** – *see* ANGER

**BUBBLE**

A bubble being spherical suggests perfection, in this case temporary, and, therefore, represents the illusory elements of everyday life. More specifically, it suggests the daydream in that it comes and goes.

Bubbles as beautiful but fragile objects remind us of the transitory nature of human existence – that nothing is permanent.

We may dream of bubbles as part of our need to have fun in a childlike way. We often become aware of the temporary nature of happiness and our need for illusion.

*For further clarification consult the entry for Sphere in Shapes/Patterns.*

**BUCKET**

The bucket as a hollow object has all the symbolism of the womb and the feminine principle. In its guise as a household tool it suggests pragmatism and a down-to-earth approach to spirituality.

A bucket with a hole in it signifies we are losing energy more quickly than we can replace it. An overflowing bucket suggests an excess of emotion, whereas a completely empty bucket depicts a lack of something essential in our lives.

When a bucket appears in our dreams, we should be considering down-to-earth, practical ways of dealing with problems. We perhaps need to consider somewhat old fashioned methods. To knock over a bucket means to put an end to previous good work and the slang phrase 'to kick the bucket' denotes losing our essential life force.

**BUCKLE**

A buckle can have a double meaning in spiritual terms. It can represent a protective element against the forces of evil; it can also help us to take the strain and not 'buckle' under pressure.

To be fastening a buckle in a dream shows that we accept responsibility for what we do. It can also suggest 'locking in' a specific type of energy.

Dreaming of an ornate buckle has the same symbolism as that of a belt, in that it can represent the holding of high office or status. It can also indicate honour and can be a symbol of loyalty or membership of a particular group of people.

*You might like to consult the entries for Belt and Girdle.*

**BUD**

🌸 How the world unfolds before us – and how we can influence that – is symbolized in spiritual terms. Unfolding gently and without force is one way of developing spiritual awareness.

💮 A new idea or way of thinking holds a great deal of potential, as yet untapped. At an early stage we can only hope that it will fulfil its promise.

🔲 To dream of a bud is to recognize the unfolding of a new way of life, new experiences or new emotions. To dream of a bud dying or shrivelling up indicates the failure of a project.

*Also consult the entry for Flowers.*

**BUDDHA, BUDDHIST –** *see* **SPIRITUAL IMAGERY IN THE INTRODUCTION**

**BUILDINGS**

🌸 Buildings in dreams represent the constructions we make in our lives. They are attitudes and beliefs we have built from our experience, perception and often from our family habits and customs. From a spiritual perspective, buildings in dreams allow us to see clearly the constructs we put in place to keep us safe.

💮 Where in real life we can learn a lot about a person from his personal environment, so in dreams a building can also reflect the dreamer's character hopes and concerns. The environment we put ourselves in reflects our state of mind or the emotions we have about a particular situation. We all have the ability within us to construct successful lives and equally an ability to self-destruct. A dream that highlights construction or demolition gives us access to those qualities and abilities within ourselves.

There are many different types of buildings and we have included here the ones that have particular meanings in dreams:

**Castle/Citadel/Fortress** – the castle or fortress has been seen as a defended space since medieval times and, therefore, can be taken to represent the protected feminine. Its connection with the Great Mother and her attribute of Wisdom arises from this concept. *Also consult the individual entry for Castle.*

**Church** – *see Religious Buildings below and in Spiritual Imagery in the Introduction.*

**Courtyard** – in dreams, the courtyard is a place of refuge, if only transitory at times, and often the shape will be relevant. A square courtyard would focus on physical or material concerns for instance – perhaps the manifestation of spiritual energy in a difficult situation *(see Shapes/Patterns).*

**Hotel** – to dream of a hotel or any establishment that is temporary accommodation indicates that we may not feel secure within our present living conditions. The type of accommodation often gives clues as to the insecurity we are experiencing. A bed and breakfast place could be interpreted as basic but comfortable whereas a five-star hotel might suggest expensive luxury.

**House (or any place of residence)** – if we are aware that the house is not empty – that it is furnished in some way – those articles will mirror some aspect of our character or day-to-day concerns. *Also consult the individual entry for Furniture/Furnishings.* Being aware of someone else in the house suggests that we may be feeling threatened by an aspect of our own personality. If there are different activities going on it indicates that there is a conflict between two parts of our personality, possibly the creative and the intellectual. Being especially aware of the front of the house portrays the facade we show to the outside world, whereas going into/out of the house indicates we need to decide whether to be more introverted or more extroverted in our dealings with other people. An impressive, awe-inspiring house indicates that we are conscious of the Self or the Soul. Dreaming of moving to a larger house shows there is need for a change in our lives, perhaps to achieve a more open way of life, or even for more space. Being outside a house depicts our more public side and how we relate to external interests. Dreaming of a small house, or the house where we were born or grew up, means we are seeking security, or perhaps the safeguards of childhood, when we had little responsibility. If we find the smallness of the house constricting, we feel we are being trapped by our responsibilities. If we are aware of work being carried out on the house (cementing, repairing etc.) it implies that relationships may need to be worked on or repaired, or perhaps we need to look at health matters. We should take note of any damage, decay or difficulty that has occurred in our lives.

**Igloo** – an igloo is warm on the inside and cold on the outside and, therefore, signifies the difference between the internal and the external. Because of its shape, based on the sphere, the igloo stands for wholeness and protection. *You may wish to consult the individual entry for further clarity.*

**Mosque** – *see Religious Buildings below and Spiritual Imagery in the Introduction.*

**Pyramid** – considered to be a focus for power, if a pyramid appears in a dream it shows we are concentrating on the inherent power within us. *You may also like to consult the individual entry for Pyramid for more detailed information.*

**Religious buildings (such as a church, mosque or temple)** – as an environment for us to consider our system of belief, any religious building will suggest a place of sanctuary and refuge and a place where we can be closer to whatever concept we have of the Divine or Ultimate Power. Although we may not consciously adhere to any particular religion, most of us have principles by which we live, which will surface in dreams in recognisable images. *Also consult the information about Religious Buildings in Spiritual Imagery in the Introduction.*

**Temple** – *consult the individual entry, Religious Buildings above and also Spiritual Imagery in the Introduction.*

**Temporary buildings** – any temporary building, such as a caravan, tent or site office, suggests some degree of impermanence. In a dream, such a structure indicates a transition between two states of being.

**Tower (or any similar image such as a lighthouse, obelisk, steeple etc.)** – the image of a tower represents the personality (the outside walls) and the Soul within (the inner space). While there are obvious connotations that connect it with masculinity, the tower is more correctly perceived as the individual being within the wider global or cosmic context. When thought of in this way our attention can focus on other aspects of the tower, such as where windows, doors and staircases are placed. This helps us to understand the Spiritual Self and how we function in the everyday world. *You may also like to consult the individual entry for further information.*

■ The features of the building often mirror aspects of the dreamer's personality or what is going on on a mundane level. Sometimes buildings in dreams can become composite and, therefore, confusing. In understanding the dream we should interpret the main appearance of the building first, as its main function, and the secondary appearance as qualities to be recognized. As well as buildings themselves, the various components also have a great deal of relevance in dreams.

**Balcony (or ledge, sill etc.)** – we all have need for support within our lives and a balcony indicates both support and protectiveness. Being raised from the ground it can also represent the Mother in her protective guise.

**Ceiling** – a ceiling will often represent the division between the spiritual and mundane worlds.

**Doors** – doors often refer to the openings of the body and, therefore, by default, one's sexuality. The front door and back door signifies the vagina and the anus respectively. Breaking down such a door can be taken to indicate the need to deal with some kind of inhibition over privacy or sex; there can be an unwillingness to face whatever issues this may bring up. Barring the door highlights our need for self-protection, not just in matters of relationship. Opening and closing the door can show an ambivalent attitude to sex, whereas refusing to open the door represents an innocent approach to our own sexuality; we may have a virginal mentality. A door between the outer and inner rooms shows there may be a conflict between the conscious and the unconscious. If an animal or person forces his way in and destroys the lock, it shows our own protective mechanisms have let us down. Escaping by another door indicates we need to find a new solution to the one we originally thought of to solve a problem. Someone knocking on the door signifies that our attention is being drawn to an external situation. *You might like to consult the individual entry for Door.*

**Hall/Passages** – any passage can represent the passages within the body, for instance the vagina or the anus. Equally, on a psychological level, it signifies how we allow our personal space to be penetrated. Passages or corridors also represent the transitions between the various stages of our lives and how we handle the growth to maturity.

**Lifts** – these usually indicate how we deal with information. For instance, a lift going down would suggest going down into the subconscious, while a lift going up would be moving towards the spiritual or cosmic concerns. In the sleep state we are thought to leave our physical bodies behind, so, descending in a lift and getting stuck suggests the potential to lose touch with spirituality, concentrating only on the mundane.

**Rooms** – in a dream, these can describe various parts of our personalities or levels of understanding, but often signify either the womb or the Mother Figure. Thus the kitchen would be the home-making part of us, whereas a sitting room would be the more relaxed, comfortable side. A small room with only one door or a basement with water in it is a direct representation of the womb and may indicate a wish to return to the womb-like state of innocence, where everything is taken care of for us. A series of rooms refers to the various aspects of femininity and often to the whole soul. An upstairs room usually signifies mental or spiritual attributes, so any object within such a room will represent an idea or concept. The meaning for a basement or cellar can be ambivalent, since a cellar can represent the parts of ourselves that we have chosen to suppress. It can also represent family beliefs and habits, particularly if the basement is one that belongs to our parents. If we deliberately leave one room and go into another then it represents a change of state and of leaving something behind. Empty rooms signify that something, such as comfort or support, is lacking in our lives.

**Stairs** – stairs are often an indication of the steps we must take in order to achieve a goal. Climbing the stairs is indicative of the effort that we must make in order to have access to the more mystical, spiritual side of our being. More simply, it is the exertion we practise in our everyday life – the effort to be ourselves. Conversely, in order to have access to the hidden, unconscious side of ourselves, we need to 'go downstairs' into the unconscious. A golden staircase is such a basic image, with so many interpretations, that particular attention needs to be paid both to other aspects of the dream, and also our spiritual state at that specific time. Largely it represents a 'death', but not necessarily a physical death. It is more the realization that we no longer need to function solely within the physical or material realms but can move towards a more fulfilling life. It is a way out of the mundane.

**Walls** – walls signify a block to progress, a difficulty we have or will come up against. Often the nature of the wall will give some clue as to what the block is. For instance, a wall which looks old will signify an old problem, whereas a glass wall would indicate some difficulties with perception. Walls closing in could describe the remembered feelings of birth, but is more likely to represent a feeling of being trapped by the lifestyle we have. A brick wall, rampart or dividing wall all signify the difference between two states of reality – often the inner psychological state and the exterior, everyday world.

**Windows** – windows describe the means by which we appreciate the world we live in, the way we perceive reality. Dreaming that we are looking outwards through a window can suggest that we have a more extrovert view of ourselves and will tend to look at external circumstances. Looking inwards through a window indicates we are looking inwards at our own personality, and perhaps at our own motivation. The interpretation for opening a window depends on whether we are opening the window from the inside or the outside. If the former, we are dealing with our inner feelings which we may need to escape; the latter shows our attitude to outside opinion. Breaking through a window (or glass door) can suggest the first sexual experience, or the shattering of illusions. Because of the connection with religious buildings, stained glass can be accepted as picturing religious belief and ideals.

## BULL

🌑 The bull is connected with the moon goddesses and also represents Taurus in the Zodiac.

♡ The bull appearing in a dream can point to the dreamer's own stubbornness and tenacity.

▥ In dreams, the bull represents the masculine principle and fertility. It also can indicate the way we handle male sexuality.

*You might also like to consult the entry for Animals.*

## BULLET

🌑 Spiritually, a bullet suggests fast, decisive action, hitting a target. The symbol is a potent one as we learn to use our energies more successfully.

♡ There is a need to understand what 'ammunition' we have available – that is, in the sense of resources to be used.

▦ To dream of bullets is often to be aware of aggression and a desire to hurt. If the bullet is being fired at us, it may be considered to be a warning of danger. If, however, we are firing the bullet, it shows we have become aware of our own vulnerability and, perhaps, lack of control.

⊞ A bullet can represent the need for, and control of, sexual impregnation. The differences in a man's and a woman's dream are self-explanatory.

*You might like to consider the entry for Shot/Shooting.*

## BURGLAR

☼ Intrusion – either on a physical or material level – is intrinsic to the idea of a burglar. Spiritually, there is a violation of our sacred space.

♡ A part of our psyche may have been neglected and left to fend for itself. It then intrudes on our awareness seeking attention.

▦ When we become aware of a burglar or intruder in our dreams we are experiencing some form of unwelcome attention. This may be from external sources or from our own inner fears and difficult emotions.

⊞ Since traditionally a burglar is perceived to be masculine, in a woman's dream he may represent the wayward antisocial aspect of the men around her. In a man's dream, a burglar is more likely to represent his need to control his own sense of impropriety.

*Also consult the entries for Intruder and Offence/Offend as well as the People section.*

## BURIAL

☼ The obvious spiritual symbols of death, loss and pain are relevant here. Equally, burial has the connotation of transmutation – an object buried may or may not be changed. In magical practice, it is the habit to bury or return to the earth anything which has negativity attached to it.

♡ To be attending a burial in our dreams shows the need to come to terms with loss. To be burying something suggests that we are hiding an emotion or feeling even from ourselves.

▦ To have a dream about being buried indicates a fear of being overcome, possibly by responsibility or by someone else's ill-feeling.

*Consult the entries for Coffin, Death and Grave for further clarification.*

## BURN

☼ Sacrificial fire and its attendant pain has many spiritual connotations. A funeral pyre suggests burning up or consuming that which is no longer spiritually necessary to us. A burning bush signifies divine knowledge imparted with passion.

♡ To be burning rubbish signifies getting rid of concepts and ideas for which we no longer have any use. When we are burning books, we are perhaps being judgemental in our appreciation of knowledge and information.

▦ A burning building signifies that we are putting an end to a particular way of life. To burn a boat suggests cutting off a means of escape.

*You might like to consult the entries for Fire and Light.*

**BUS**

☼ To be travelling by bus can be interpreted in more than one way. Literally the omnibus is for all and, therefore, signifies the Greater Good. Also a bus suggests a spiritual journey which must be paid for in some way.

♥ We may be experiencing the need to act as an individual, undertaking our own 'journey' while at the same time belonging to a group with a common purpose.

▦ Travelling on a bus suggests that we are coming to terms with the way we handle group relationships, and the new directions we need to take in company with others.

*You might like to consult the entry for Transport.*

**BUTCHER**

☼ The butcher has spiritual connotations with the Grim Reaper and death. The meat cleaver can be taken to represent the scythe. As people become less accustomed to seeing a traditional butcher, such an image has not so much relevance.

♥ We may need to become aware of a destructive – or rather divisive – streak in ourselves, one which at the same time has particular skills.

▦ We see the butcher as one who mutilates, but provides for us at the same time, and this is reflected in dreams when he appears as someone who separates the good from the bad. He may also be a destroyer.

**BUTTERFLY**

☼ When seen in dreams or even meditation, the butterfly represents the freed soul and immortality. There is no need for the soul to be trapped by the physical body.

♥ Psychologically, the butterfly indicates a lack of ability to settle down or to undertake a protracted task. In growing from a chrysalis, however, it has transmuted into a thing of beauty and simply is itself.

▦ On a practical level, the butterfly represents light-heartedness and freedom. As a symbol of conservation we are aware that our energy needs to be used in the best, most efficient way.

**BUTTONS/BUTTONHOLES**

☼ Buttons and buttonholes were simple fastenings holding two different pieces of material together. Spiritually this can represent uniting the physical and spiritual realms into one coherent whole.

♦ Buttons were originally a form of insignia, allowing easy identification of friend or foe. If our attention is drawn to buttons in a dream, it is usually to bring about such recognition.

▦ The size, shape and configuration of the button and buttonholes may be important. An ornate button will have a different relevance to a simple one; more work or effort is required for the former. A particularly decorative buttonhole suggests that more energy needs to be put into 'fastening down' a project – it perhaps needs to be more upfront.

**CABLE**

&#9881; In the sense of a rope, a cable will represent strength and security, and may have the same connotation as any binding image. However, in this technological age, from cables associated with television and computers, they also suggest efficient communication from a remote source.

&#9826; A cable without a plug implies that we have not yet made proper connections whereas a broken cable that we have lost contact.

&#9632; In joining two objects together a cable highlights the added efficiency obtained by linking two thoughts, ideas or ways of working.

&#9839; In a woman's dream a cable may highlight the strength of her bonds with someone else whereas in a man's dream it can suggest restrictions within his closest relationships.

**CADUCEUS**

&#9881; The Caduceus, or double-headed snake entwined round a central staff, is an ancient spiritual symbol which signifies that there is power in uniting the opposite polarities of the spiritual and the physical realms. Once we reconcile these opposing sides, this creates healing, rebirth and renewal, universally represented as two snakes. This is a symbolic representation of the basic form of DNA, the 'building blocks' of life.

&#9826; The body recognizes and communicates in dream images its need and expectation of good health. To dream of the Caduceus can mean that we need to create better conditions for achieving this. This symbol often appears as we learn of our own ability to heal others.

&#9632; The Caduceus is the sign that is used by doctors and medical establishments as the sign of healing. Initially it was the staff carried by the Greek god Hermes. Wellbeing, our own or other people's, needs consideration.

**CAGE/CELL**

&#9881; We need to examine and reconsider ideas and beliefs, particularly about religion and spirituality, which restrict and restrain us.

&#9826; We are being warned that we are enforcing too much restraint on our hidden abilities. We could be allowing others to hold us back.

&#9632; The cage normally represents a form of trap or jail. To dream of caging a wild animal alerts us to our need to restrain our wilder instincts. To dream that we are in a cage indicates a sense of frustration and perhaps of being trapped by the past.

*You may also like to look at the entries for Jailer and Prison.*

## CAKES

❂ Cakes or buns used in religious and magical rites and marked with the cross originally symbolized the round of the moon and its four quarters. Such cakes later became Eastertime Hot Cross buns and in dreams suggest spiritual celebrations.

♥ Baking cakes indicates our need to care for others or to nurture an inner need.

▦ When we dream of celebration cakes – such as a wedding or birthday cake – we are being shown that there is cause for celebration in our lives.

⊡ Traditionally, baking cakes was a particularly feminine activity, and therefore such dreams had more relevance to nurturing. As men develop their more caring side, cakes take on this meaning in their dreams.

*To interpret the meaning of candles on a cake consult the entries for Candle and Numbers.*

## CALCULATOR

❂ As a modern day counting device the calculator can signify the complexities of the choices we make as we undertake spiritual development.

♥ The symbol of a calculator alerts us to the possibility of risk. It is wise for us to be able to weigh up the risks or to be able to assess what the outcome of a situation might be.

▦ In more mundane terms the presence of a calculator in dreams may signify that the focus of the dream is work related. The numbers and totals may be significant.

*You may like to consult the entry for Numbers for further information.*

## CALENDAR

❂ A calendar is initially a way of naming periods of time, usually days, though also of particular cycles such as the seasons. Cycles in a calendar are often measured by the motion of planets and stars. This allows celebrations and festivals to be calculated. We should become more aware of these timetables.

♥ Because time is a self-imposed constraint, when anything that marks time appears in a dream we are being warned of the potential for limitation.

▦ If a calendar appears in a dream there can be more than one meaning. Our attention may be being drawn to the past, present or future and something significant in our lives, or we may be being warned of the passage of time in an important scheme.

**CALF –** *see* **BABY ANIMALS IN ANIMALS AND LEG IN BODY**

**CAMCORDER/CAMERA**

⚙️ There is a need to be watchful and perhaps to preserve an image. Tribal cultures believed that the camera captured the soul or essential being, and may have this significance in dreams. The camcorder with its greater technological abilities has a similar meaning.

♥ There is a necessity to retain a mental picture of what is important to us. A broken camera or camcorder immediately suggests a faulty memory or distorted perception.

▦ To be using a camera or camcorder in a dream means that we should record events or occasions in such a way that they are preserved, perhaps for posterity or as evidence. Being filmed indicates that we need to look more carefully at our actions and reactions to certain situations.

**CAMEL**

⚙️ The spiritual significance of animals harks back to ancient times. The camel suggests dignity as the bearer of royalty.

♥ Psychologically the camel can represent stamina and self-sufficiency.

▦ Depending on the environment in the dream the camel can represent the unusual or bizarre. It also represents available resources and obedience to a basic principle.

**CAMELOT**

⚙️ Fairy tales and myths often seem to have arisen from dreams and vice versa, so the stereotypical vision of a place such as Camelot highlights the qualities of spirituality, chivalry and adventure inherent in each of us.

♥ Camelot is a representation of a perfect society even up to and including its downfall and ending, so such a dream will put into perspective areas in life we feel we have not reached our potential.

▦ As legends and myths take on a life of their own, sometimes bearing little relationship to the original occurrence, they become somewhat sanitized and personalized to fit with the patterns of society, at any particular time. Archetypal images, such as the authoritative king (Arthur), the young knight (Lancelot) setting out on a journey, or Merlin the magician, thus become available through these dream characters to help us understand ourselves.

▤ It will depend upon the dreamer's own personal development how such a dream is interpreted. In a woman's dream, for instance, it can help her come to terms with her treatment by, or of, the men in her life; whereas in a man's dream he may be dealing with his own personal journey to maturity.

*You might like to consult the entry for Archetypes in the Introduction, the individual entry for Hero/Heroine, Hero in the People section, Magic/Magician and Round Table.*

**CAMOUFLAGE**

🔅 Camouflage has the effect of making an object disappear or appear to be something else. The symbolism is therefore of information deliberately hidden or occluded.

💚 We hide – both from ourselves and others – those aspects of our personalities with which we cannot deal. This is a defensive mechanism which when highlighted in dreams, needs to be considered very carefully.

🎴 Whereas camouflage in nature is a spontaneous occurrence, in Man it is a more deliberate act and for many is associated with war or dangerous situations. There may be a threat to our integrity or sense of control.

**CAMP**

*See Temporary Buildings in Buildings and also the entry for Tent.*

**CANAL**

🔅 Because a canal is a man-made structure it suggests an imposed structure, definition of boundaries or rigid belief.

💚 We need to structure our knowledge of ourselves to create a workable system.

🎴 A dream about a canal usually indicates that we are inclined to be rigid insofar as the control of our emotions is concerned. We may be introducing too much structure into our lives at the expense of our creativity.

*Also consult the entry for Water.*

**CANCER**

🔅 Symbolically Cancer represents the Moon, the Eternal Mother and the astrological sign of Cancer.

💚 Intellectually we may have worked through our fears but still be left with attitudes and beliefs that cannot be cleared away. Very often this appears as cancer or illness in dreams and equally can represent something 'eating away' at us – usually a negative idea or concept.

🎴 Cancer is one of the prime fears that a human being has to deal with, so to dream of a cancer indicates we are out of harmony with our body. It also indicates fear of illness.

🔯 Since the astrological sign of Cancer represents a feminine attribute, in a woman's dream she may be considering her ability to nurture. In a man's dream his focus may be on his attitude to his mother or mothering.

## CANDLE

✹ The symbolism of candles has recently taken on a whole added significance as people re-explore religion and belief more thoroughly. They have always signified illumination, wisdom, strength, beauty and now signal the end of darkness or ignorance. Lit, they suggest the enduring flame of life and the use of power. Unlit, they signify potential held in reserve.

♥ Psychologically candles can represent knowledge or wisdom that has not yet fully crystallized. Used as tools, they mark our control of personal magic and dreams will often give information as to their best use. Lighting a candle to Bridget to welcome her in was transposed in the Christian church to the celebration of Candlemas on 2 February when new candles were placed in churches signifying the end of winter.

▦ In Pagan times, the candle or taper represented the ritualistic dispersing of darkness and a way of worshipping power. To dream of candles indicates that we are trying to clarify something that we do not understand. Candles on a birthday cake can therefore indicate that we are marking a transition from the old to the new. Lighting a candle represents using courage and fortitude or asking for something which we need.

⛨ It has been suggested that the candle epitomizes masculine power (candle) and feminine passion (flame), the one being useless without the other. In a woman's dream, therefore, extinguishing a candle might suggest control of a perceived power, whereas in a man's dream it will suggest control of external factors.

*You might like to consult the entries for Fire, Light and Wax as well as the information on Phallus in Sex/Sexual Images.*

## CANE

✹ Probably used first as a weapon, the cane took on the symbolism of strength and power and eventually authority and social prestige. Spiritually, it also came to signify self-flagellation.

♥ Because a cane also represents pliability, we may be trying to achieve a balance between our willingness and our unwillingness to accept a situation.

▦ Because many people associate the cane with some form of punishment or sadism, it can represent self-punishment or masochism. It is more likely, however, that we are trying to come to terms with some form of childhood trauma.

*Also consult the entry for Staff.*

## CANNIBALISM

✹ From a spiritual perspective the act of cannibalism is absorbing powers or qualities belonging to someone else.

◈ Eating human flesh in a dream can mean that we are taking in wrong information in everyday life.

▦ To dream of cannibalism usually represents unsophisticated or inappropriate behaviour. To be aware of eating human flesh may indicate our dislike of unsuitable foods or actions. There is often a part of ourselves we have not 'internalized' which we need to absorb.

## CANOE

❀ In Polynesia the port hull of the canoe is the 'wahine' hull and the starboard is the 'Kane' hull. The spiritual symbolism is that the male and the female forces give us life and balance each other. The older symbolism is that of a lunar barque, and the crescent moon.

◈ We may be protected from our emotions, but also at risk. A degree of skill is necessary to enable us to handle what might happen and achieve the correct balance.

▦ To dream of a canoe suggests that we can only handle our emotions by becoming immersed in them. We are possibly making efforts to control or tame the flow of our emotion. We are aware that we are capable of making changes but only by our own efforts.

⬥ By its association with the feminine, in a woman's dream the canoe represents her place within the world. In a man's dream it signifies the hunter and protector.

## CANOPY

❀ Royalty or powerful people often used a canopy with a special symbol either for spiritual protection or to signify their rank. We still acknowledge this privilege on a deep internal level.

◈ A canopy protects the head which is the seat of intellect. We have a need to draw attention (or have our attention drawn) to higher ideals or aspirations.

▦ When we dream of a canopy we are looking to be protected, sheltered or loved. In olden times a canopy was used to shelter those with special duties or powers, such as kings and queens or priests and priestesses. If we ourselves are being sheltered we recognize our own abilities and potential for greatness.

## CAP

❀ A cap signifies nobility and freedom. The jester's cap was said to be a parody of the king's crown demonstrating how transient power really is.

◈ The cap shows the need for respect for a person's beliefs and wisdom or knowledge.

▦ The cap has the same significance as the hat in dreams and draws attention to status or spiritual powers. If we are wearing a cap in a dream, we may be covering up our creative abilities.

*Consult the entries for Hat in Clothes and Joke/Joker.*

**CAPITAL –** *see* **MONEY**

**CAR**

🌸 The car is very often representative of our own personal space, an extension of our being. It also stands for spiritual direction and motivation.

♥ Dream scenarios involving cars are often much to do with what we are doing to ourselves on a psychological or emotional level. Being alone in a vehicle indicates independence, while dreaming of the brakes shows our ability to be in control. The car engine indicates the essential drives with which we have to deal. A crashing vehicle suggests fear of failure in life, while a car on fire denotes stress of some sort, either physically or emotionally. To be in a car which is driven carelessly, either by us or someone else, marks a lack of responsibility, while a feeling of being left behind would be shown by your car being overtaken. To dream of reversing a car registers a feeling that we are slipping backwards into old patterns of behaviour or are having to reverse a decision.

▦ To dream of being in a car usually alerts us to our own motivation, thus driving the car can indicate our need to achieve a goal, while being a passenger could indicate that we have handed over responsibility for our lives to someone else.

*You may find it helpful to read the entries for Journey and Transport.*

**CARAVAN –** *see* **TRANSPORT**

**CARDS**

🌸 Cards of any type signify visual communication and the ability to convey a message spiritually. The Tarot – our Inner Truth – can be used as images in dream work. To dream of giving or receiving a card such as a birthday card alerts us to the need for a specific kind of communication, perhaps celebrating our own or others' good fortune and luck.

♥ On a psychological level, card playing in a dream can be seen as taking calculated risks and alerting us to potential danger. Generally, our subconscious may be registering concern, either about ourselves or others. Business cards convey the idea that we are happy to give other people information about ourselves, or to receive such information from others.

▦ Greeting cards are quite literally an acknowledgement of a special occasion. In a dream, playing cards highlight our ability to be open to opportunity or to take chances. The cards that one deals, or is dealt, in a dream may have significance as to number or suit: Hearts indicate emotion and relationship. Diamonds represent material wealth. Spades represent conflict, difficulties and obstacles. Clubs represent action, work and intelligence. The King portrays human success and mastery. The Queen indicates emotional depth, sensitivity and understanding whereas the Jack represents impetuosity, creativity or an adolescent energy.

*Also consult the entry for Numbers.*

## CARETAKER – *see* SECURITY PERSONNEL IN PEOPLE

## CARGO

🔅 In the sense that cargo is goods which require transportation, in dreams it represents thoughts, ideas and concepts which need to be considered in a different context to their original purpose.

♥ When goods are packed for cargo they are carefully protected and often stowed away, so when such articles appear in dreams it is time to become aware of forgotten dreams and ideals – of creativity 'stowed away' to be used in different circumstances.

▦ Cargo has the same significance as luggage and baggage. Unpacking cargo suggests looking hard at what assets and talents you have. Packing cargo indicates that the time may not be right for a particular plan.

⊡ In a woman's dream bearing cargo may suggest pregnancy or her feelings about this. In a man's dream it suggests responsibility.

*Consult the entries for Baggage and Luggage for further clarification.*

## CARPET – *see* FURNITURE/FURNISHINGS

## CARRIAGE/CART/CHARIOT

🔅 The carriage is a symbol of majesty and power, and a chariot also represents the Sun and the Divine. The cart is a more mundane symbol signifying down-to-earth hard work.

♥ Any symbol which signifies our being moved in some way draws attention to our ability to make progressive changes in our lives. We may have to explore archetypal images for an understanding of our own motivations. The chariot in the sense of a gladiatorial vehicle can represent basic urges before they have been honed by conditioning and knowledge. Again a cart is representative of workaday concerns.

▦ In modern times most people will dream about the car or other similar forms of transport. Dreaming of a carriage, such as a horse-drawn one, could be suggestive of old-fashioned attitudes to modern thinking, and a chariot means we have to accept a very basic kind of control. A train carriage would indicate that we are taking a 'journey' that is slightly more public than a car journey.

*Also consult the entry for Car and the Journey and Transport sections.*

**CARRY**

🔆 When we are prepared to 'carry' something we are taking Spiritual Responsibility – being aware of our responsibility for the world we live in perhaps. This may be either in the long-term or a short-term project.

♥ To dream of carrying someone registers the fact that we may be accepting responsibility for someone else. It is for us to decide if this responsibility is a burden or not.

🔲 When we are aware of carrying an object we need to decide how we perceive our particular relationship to that object or its symbolism. If we dream of being carried, we may feel that we are in need of support.

**CASH** – *see* **MONEY**

**CASK**

🔆 Like most containers, a cask represents the feminine principle. An apparently bottomless cask represents needless effort.

♥ It is more likely to be the content of the cask which has meaning on a psychological level and such a dream indicates our ability to be creative with raw materials – to fashion something of value.

🔲 Since a cask or barrel is often hand-made, to dream of one indicates the care taken in dealing with our own emotional make-up. This is because a cask was, and is, mostly used for storage.

⛏ For a woman a cask will represent her ability to preserve her culture or ideas, but for a man it is more likely that he feels he has the opportunity to enjoy the fruits of his labours.

*Consult the entry for Keg for more information.*

**CASTLE**

🔆 Dreaming of a castle links us to the principle of an enclosed and defended private space. Spiritually it suggests some kind of test or challenge or overcoming obstacles in order to gain greater understanding.

♥ Before we can be fully open to other people, we normally have to let down our barriers, and being trapped in a castle may highlight our difficulty in freeing ourselves from old attitudes. Trying to enter a castle signifies that we recognize that we ourselves create difficulties which have to be overcome.

🔲 A castle can represent the fantastic, the unattainable or perhaps difficulty in obtaining our objectives.

⛏ The castle represents the essential feminine wisdom so a woman is more likely to dream of being in a castle. A man will tend to dream of trying to enter one.

*You might like to consult the entries for Buildings, Camelot and Tower.*

## CASTRATION

☀ Dreaming of castration means we are prepared to make a life sacrifice, to give up or control the sexual act in favour of celibacy and perhaps a more ascetic lifestyle.

♥ Conventionally, there may be some difficulty in coming to terms with the conflict between the masculine and feminine within ourselves.

▦ In any dream that contains sexual trauma, we are being alerted to our inner fears, not necessarily associated with the sexual act. The violent act of castration in a dream indicates the damage we are doing to ourselves in denying such fears, or in denying natural urges.

⊞ Castration in a man's dream suggests that his sense of self is being attacked. In a woman's dream she should take care that she is not emasculating her partner or colleagues.

## CAT – *see* ANIMALS

## CATACOMB/CRYPT

☀ As a place of hidden forces and occult power, in dreams the catacomb will represent the unconscious. Catacombs suggest interlinking ideas or principles while a crypt is complete within itself.

♥ Our subconscious fears or feelings connected with death can show in a dream as a catacomb or crypt. Inherent in both is the idea of sanctuary for the soul.

▦ Many dreams contain images which are to do with a space underground, and to dream of a crypt or a catacomb signifies a need to come to terms with subconscious religious beliefs or training.

*You might like to consult the entry for Tomb.*

## CATERPILLAR

☀ The symbol of a caterpillar is of metamorphosis or the spiritual potential, largely unrecognized, which must transmute into something more beautiful. We must change and grow from what we are now into a different way of being.

♥ To dream of caterpillars would indicate that we need to remain flexible in our attitude to change. Also, because of the caterpillar's association with creeping things, it may represent evil or difficulty.

▦ The caterpillar appearing in a dream usually indicates that we are undergoing some form of major change. We may be being warned that we must undergo a complete upheaval before we can achieve our goal. There may well then be a period of transition or apparent stasis.

⊞ The caterpillar is a recognizable first symbol of the growth process. In a woman's dream it may represent an awareness of a potential pregnancy whereas for a boy such an image suggests his emerging sexuality. In a man's dream a caterpillar signifies the commencement of a journey of discovery about his spirituality.

## CAULDRON

☼ Spiritually the cauldron symbolizes renewal and rebirth. Many folk tales use the symbolism of cooking to represent the making of mankind. A cauldron can also represent the womb.

♥ Psychologically, when a cauldron appears in a dream we may need to take note of our intuitive abilities, or of our ability to create new things from simple ingredients.

▦ Almost universally the cauldron represents abundance, sustenance and nourishment. By association, the magic cauldron suggests fertility and the feminine power of transformation. To dream of a cauldron, therefore, reconnects us with our basic principles.

▸ Originally the cauldron was round-bottomed, thus reinforcing the symbolism of the womb. In a woman's dream it therefore suggests transformation often brought about by her own power. In a man's dream he is more likely to use power beyond himself.

*You might also like to consult the entry for Kettle.*

## CAVE

☼ In common with many underground symbols, the cave represents spiritual shelter or sanctuary, initiation and rebirth. Meditating on the image of an inner cave gives insight into how we tackle life events.

♥ Passing through a cave signifies a change of state, transition and a deeper understanding of our own negative impulses.

▦ As with the catacombs, the cave represents a doorway into the unconscious. While initially the cave may be frightening, an exploration can reveal strong contact with our own inner selves.

▸ In both men's and women's dreams a cave will represent exploring the subconscious, but in a woman's dream she is more likely to sense something greater than herself whereas initially a man will begin to appreciate his own intuitive senses.

*Consulting the entries for Catacomb and Door will enhance your understanding.*

## CEILING – *see* BUILDINGS

## CELEBRATION – *see* PARTY

## CELEBRITY

☼ Spiritually, as we reach for perfection we need to 'work through' various aspects of our personality. Sometimes we are able to reject such aspects as not being appropriate for the life we live. For instance, we may realize that the destructiveness of a celebrity's public life would take its toll within our own lives.

🜚 Celebrities, pop, film and sports stars may also serve in dreams as a projection of the type of person we would like to be. We may, for instance, in real life be shy and withdrawn, but deep down need to be admired and loved.

▨ Most of us are capable of creating an ideal person on whom to project our fantasies and wishes. We are not at this stage particularly in touch with reality. In dreams a celebrity, or any public figure will represent the Animus or Anima. A young person dreaming of a celebrity may not be ready for the responsibility of a real relationship.

▨ In a woman's dream a male celebrity may allow her to experiment with the type of person she considers worth her attention. In a man's dream the reverse will be the case.

*Consult the information on Anima/Animus in the Introduction as well as the entries for Fame and Media for clarification.*

**CELLAR – *see* BUILDINGS**

**CEMETERY**

🜚 A cemetery is the place of the Dead but also of spiritual regeneration. As a place where we put aside the physical but can allow ourselves to mourn, it becomes an area of transition to something better.

🜚 In dreams we can often allow our fears to come to the surface in an acceptable way. The cemetery in dreams is a place set apart, where we can confront our fears of death and dying.

▨ The cemetery and its association with death can have a double meaning. It can represent the parts of ourselves that we have 'killed off' or stopped using. It can also depict our thoughts and feelings about death and the attitudes and traditions surrounding it.

*The entries for Catacomb/Crypt, Coffin, Grave, Sarcophagus and Tomb should clarify your understanding.*

**CENTAUR**

🜚 Traditionally, the Centaur was half-man and half-beast, and this creature is associated with the Zodiac sign of Sagittarius. It signifies vision and wisdom.

🜚 The symbol of a Centaur in a dream represents our ability to unite two complete opposites in an acceptable way.

▨ To have a Centaur appear in a dream demonstrates the unification of man's animal nature with his qualities of human virtue and judgement.

*Also consult the entry for Fabulous Beasts.*

## CENTRE

🔆 In spiritual geometry, the centre of anything represents totality and wholeness. It is the origin or beginning of everything. At this centre is 'sacred space'.

♥ Psychologically, to be at the centre, or in the middle of a situation, shows we need to be aware of both our ability to control that situation and our ability to be flexible. Moving towards the centre shows our need for integrity in our day-to-day life.

🎴 To dream of being at the centre of something, such as in the centre of a group of people, highlights our awareness of our ability to be powerful within a situation; that everything revolves around us. To be moving away from the centre indicates that part of our lives may be off balance.

*You might like to consult the entries for Point and Position.*

## CEREMONY

🔆 Ceremonies and rituals are used for initiation – to be accepted by a group – to achieve deeper awareness and to establish new order.

♥ Any major life change has a profound effect on the dreamer and this is very often shown in dream form as a ceremony or some kind of rite of passage.

🎴 When we dream of taking part in a ceremony or religious ritual we are conscious of a new attitude or skill that is needed or an important change which is taking place in our lives, perhaps a promotion at work or acceptance by our peer group.

*You might like to consult the entries for Altar and Rite/Ritual as well as the information on Spiritual Imagery in the Introduction for further clarification.*

## CERTIFICATE

🔆 As a paper acknowledgement of a learnt skill, a certificate suggests awareness of the long-term benefit of spiritual knowledge – perhaps an initiation into a particular type of this knowledge.

♥ Being given a certificate or diploma suggests our efforts have been acknowledged by others. Giving someone such a document signifies that we have successfully passed on our own knowledge.

🎴 Since it confers status, we may dream of a certificate when we feel we have developed a degree of competence in our everyday life.

## CHAIN

🔆 In religious art bondage and slavery, dignity and unity are all symbolized by chains. The links in a chain suggest that we cannot exist in isolation.

♥ In dreams, we can become conscious of beliefs or mental attitudes – both in ourselves and others – which can create problems and hold us down. The links in a chain can very often symbolize the communication that we need to free ourselves.

🔲 To dream of chains in any form indicates a type of restriction or dependency. Just as we need strength to break out of chains, this is also needed for chains which support. In becoming aware of what is holding us back, we also become appreciative of how to break free.

**CHAIR** – *see* **FURNITURE**

**CHALICE**

🔅 The chalice is symbolic of the source of inexhaustible sustenance, abundance and the Holy Grail. Because of this religious significance, the chalice usually represents something that may seem to be unattainable except without a great deal of effort.

💠 From medieval times the chalice has been associated with the symbolism of the heart, containing the life-force. In the full chalice this is represented by wine – wine and blood sharing the same meaning.

🔲 In dreams the chalice represents the feminine. It can also represent an important event or ceremony.

🔀 In a woman's dream the chalice tends to represent her sense of Self and her connection to the ultimate. In a man's dream it is more likely to be symbolic of his quest for autonomy.

*To enhance your understanding consult the entries for Blood, Cup, Goblet and Quest.*

**CHALLENGE**

🔅 A spiritual challenge in dreams is one which takes us outside our comfort zone. This could show as a dream about a difficult journey for instance, an apparently insurmountable object or a descent into the underground. Ultimately we may find that it is not as difficult as we first thought.

💠 We are forced to reassess our attitudes to our own concepts, ideals or deeply held beliefs when we are challenged in any way in dreams.

🔲 To be challenged in dreams perhaps by someone barring our way or having an argument suggests that we need to know and understand our skills and talents.

**CHAMPION** – *see* **WIN/WINNER**

**CHANT** – *see* **CHARM, MUSIC AND SING**

**CHAOS**

🔅 Before the universe began it was thought there existed a disordered state of unformed matter and infinite space. Spiritually therefore in dreams chaos is a representation of Source and the beginning of all things. There is, though, an underlying pattern, which may not be immediately apparent.

◈ A disorderly mass or jumble of thoughts and ideas which have not yet crystallized is experienced as chaos. They appear erratic and unpredictable.

▦ Chaos and confusion in dreams represent the changes over which we have no control. If we find ourselves trying to establish order then we are usually gaining insight into either our own state of mind or difficult situations around us.

*Consult the entry for Churning for further clarification.*

## CHAPEL – *see* RELIGIOUS BUILDINGS IN BUILDINGS

## CHARITY

✹ Charity comes from the word *caritas* which means 'caring from the heart'. Since the heart is the seat of self awareness this caring has a very special spiritual quality about it.

◈ Charity has implications in our ability to care for and about others. Apparently altruistic acts frequently have an ulterior self-interested motive. When we dream of a charitable act it often alerts us to the wider issues that are important in our lives.

▦ To dream of giving or receiving charity has a lot to do with our ability to give and receive love. A charity box or donation in a dream usually indicates an awareness of our own needs.

## CHARM

✹ Technically, a charm is a spell or object possessing magic power, and was initially empowered by chanting (rhythmic singing). In dreams, it can have any of these resonances and suggests the idea of using power beyond the norm.

◈ Continuing the idea of magic, to perceive such an object in dreams alerts us to any special powers or talents we might have and our ability to use them. A charm bracelet was initially worn for protection and to attract good fortune.

▦ One of the magical techniques is to 'charm' someone – i.e. make them do something they would not normally do. In dreams we may find ourselves using such techniques as a way of alerting us to abilities and skills we have that we might not normally use. When someone else is being charming or attempting to charm us the opposite applies – we are being expected to do something which goes against the grain.

## CHASE/CHASED

✹ Spiritually the image of being chased or pursued suggests either fear of our own actions, or is a play on words, as in 'chaste', i.e. trying to preserve our innocence.

♥ Being chased by shadows shows the need to escape from something previously repressed, such as past childhood trauma or difficulty. To be chased by an animal generally indicates we have not come to terms with our own passion.

▦ Dreaming of being chased or of trying to escape is perhaps one of the most common dreams; usually we are trying to escape responsibility, our own sense of failure, fear or emotions we can't handle.

⌘ It is not unusual for a woman to dream that she is being pursued in dreams. The implication is that she has something special which she does not wish to relinquish. If a man is being chased by a woman or that which he cannot identify then it is usually in response to his fear of being 'consumed.'
*Consult the section on Animals and the entry for Hunt/Hunting/Huntsman for more information.*

## CHASM

☀ We are faced by the Unconscious, the Void. In developing spiritually there is often a sense of having to go down into the depths to reach understanding.

♥ We are being confronted by unknown or perhaps unrecognized negative elements in our own make-up; we have no previous experience by which to judge our actions or reactions.

▦ When we dream of a chasm or large hole, we are usually being made conscious of situations that contain an element of the unknown, or are in some way risky. We are going to have to make decisions as to whether to face the risk or withdraw.
*You might like to consult the entries for Cave, Cliff, Hole and Void.*

## CHEMIST/CHEMISTRY

☀ The alchemist is one who changes base material into spiritual gold. Each of us has the potential to turn a very basic spiritual knowledge into a tool to help us live fulfilling lives.

♥ On a psychological level the chemist in the sense of an apothecary is the part of us which looks after health concerns and self-healing. He has access to knowledge that we need in order to stay in good health. In today's technological age a chemist in a dream signifies someone who has the ability to break down complex structures into their various components.

▦ To dream of a chemist is to link with that part of ourselves that is capable of altering the way we behave in our work-a-day lives, We are in touch with the wisdom – which is inherent in us all – concerning the Self.
*You might also like to consult the entry for Alchemy.*

**CHERUB** – *see* ANGELS AND SPIRITUAL IMAGERY

**CHESS**

🕮 Based as it is on a battle, chess highlights the conflict between the spiritual powers of light and darkness. The white pieces and squares represent the light, and the black, darkness.

♡ Playing chess and losing indicates that we have undertaken an activity in our waking lives which cannot be successful. We have not got the wherewithal, or perhaps the knowledge, to pit ourselves against greater forces.

▦ In dreams, chess can express any internal conflict. It may also indicate the need for strategy in our lives.

*Also consult the entry for Games.*

**CHEST/BOX**

🕮 Pandora's Box and the story of how negativity was released into the world is the best example of a box image on a spiritual level. A chest or box represents all those things we suppress or want to keep hidden, sometimes the darker side of ourselves, sometimes aspects that we have not yet explored. We need to be aware that care must be taken when first exploring the spiritual.

♡ Emotionally, we need to give some limitation to our feelings and secret desires. In dreams a box – whether plain or otherwise – will show how we handle life. When the chest area is highlighted in the body our attention is being drawn to our ability to love and care for others.

▦ A chest or box appearing in a dream delineates the way we keep hidden or store our emotions. Additionally, our most important ideals and hopes may need to be kept secret. It may also show the best in us; our best insights. A jewel box signifies that which needs to be kept safe and only made use of when appropriate.

**CHILD/CHILDREN** – *see* PEOPLE

**CHIMNEY**

🕮 Any opening in a roof of a temple, tepee, tent, etc. represents the awareness of a change of state that may be an important part of spiritual growth. Dreaming of a chimney indicates that escape to the heavens through the solar gateway – that is, access to the gods – is possible. Rising smoke, such as that seen with incense, is also a symbol for prayer.

♡ Psychologically, a chimney and the passage of smoke portrays the channelling of energy in a more productive way than is presently occurring.

▦ When we dream of chimneys we are linking with a very old concept, that of escape from the mundane and ordinary into freedom.

⚡ In a man's dream the chimney may symbolize his sense of his own potency. In a woman's dream it will suggest her drive and desires.

**CHISEL**

✦ In sacred architecture the chisel is the active, masculine principle in relationship with the passive and feminine. In spiritual terms, therefore, the chisel signifies activity as opposed to waiting.

♥ Our intellectual need to succeed may put us in a position of trying to break through a barrier in order to complete a favourite project.

▣ The meaning of a chisel in a dream would depend on whether or not you are a craftsman in waking life. In such a case it will depict pride in achievement and specialist knowledge. If you have no such skill it will depend on other symbolism in the dream, but will probably indicate the need to use some force in a situation recognizable to you – literally to chip away at the structure.

⚡ In modern times the use of tools is not so gender specific as it used to be so in both men and women's dreams using a chisel suggests properly applied energy.

**CHOCOLATE**

✦ In the Mayan culture chocolate was food fit for the gods. This puts it in the framework of food for the soul and the release of our best efforts.

♥ Emotionally comforting, chocolate in a dream has a soothing effect. If we are eating or being given chocolate we need such soothing. If giving to someone else we are capable of soothing hurt and distress. The quality of the chocolate may be important.

▣ It is now well known that chocolate contains an essential amino acid called tryptophan which is essential to our wellbeing. Dreaming of chocolate may highlight a very real need for the beneficial effects of such a food.

⚡ Often highlighted as a suitable gift for lovers, in a woman's dream such a gift may signify an unrecognized potential in a relationship. In a man's dream he may recognize in himself the need to care for and appreciate others.

**CHOICE/CHOOSE**

✦ Choice in dreams suggests that we must weigh up two alternatives – right or wrong, spiritual or material, good or bad, individual or community.

♥ Decision-making can be difficult for many people. Being forced to choose in a dream suggests that we are not yet emotionally ready to make choices.

▣ When in our working or personal life we choose a particular course of action, yet are aware that we are unsure, this can present itself in dreams as confusion or dual images.

⊟ Most women will make choices from an emotional perspective and most men from a logical one. In dreams this is often reversed.

## CHOKE

❀ Choking can indicate spiritual conflict and restraint. Choking in a dream highlights that we need to learn wisdom – when to speak and when to remain silent.

♡ Being choked suggests that we are being stifled by people or circumstances and are not in control of either. Choking on food suggests that there is something unpalatable in our lives.

▣ When we find ourselves choking in a dream we are coming up against our inability to express ourselves appropriately. There is some conflict between our inner and outer selves, perhaps some indecision over whether we should speak out or remain silent.

## CHOP – see AXE AND TREE

## CHRYSALIS

❀ Metamorphosis and Magical Powers are symbolized by the chrysalis. That which is intrinsically ugly and therefore apparently spiritually unacceptable goes through a process of inactivity to become something new.

♡ Change is taking place within us, but on a very subtle level which is not immediately recognizable.

▣ There are two ways in which a chrysalis can be interpreted within a dream. Firstly, as potential for action, which has not yet been realised, and secondly protection in a situation that must wait until the time is right.

⊟ As a period of gestation, the chrysalis may appear in women's dreams to alert her to the possibility of pregnancy.

*You might also like to consult the entry for Butterfly.*

## CHURCH – see RELIGIOUS BUILDINGS IN BUILDINGS

## CHURNING

❀ Ultimately, chaos must give way to order. One school of thought is that form arose out of churning the Chaos. In dreams such an idea has some merit, since many dream images appear to arrive from nowhere.

♡ We very often need to become conscious of a very deep-rooted sense of churning or movement within ourselves in order to become appreciative of our capacity for order.

▣ Most dreams in which there is a liquid being churned, boiled or made to move in some way link back to a very primitive sense of chaos (lack of order). This indicates we may need to reassess our creative abilities to make use of the energy available to us.

*You might like to consult the entry for Chaos.*

**CIRCLE** – *see* SHAPES/PATTERNS

**CIRCUMAMBULATION**

🔆 We symbolize creating the centre of our universe by circumambulation. Many religions use walking around an area in a circle more than once to signify a magical or sacred space.

💗 Psychologically we all need to have a place which is ours alone. To dream of circumambulation signifies taking responsibility for ourselves and our actions.

🔲 To be walking around a building or a particular spot in a dream is to be creating a 'universe' in which action can take place. It is to be designating that place as having a particular significance.

**CIRCUMCISION** – *see* SEX/SEXUAL IMAGES

**CIRCUMFERENCE**

🔆 Spiritually the circumference of a circle delineates a dividing line between two worlds. It suggests limitation and is a line between the spiritual realms and the physical material world.

💗 We are on the edge of new knowledge or information and could move in either direction.

🔲 To be held within the circumference of a circle is to be made aware through dream images of the limitations we may have set ourselves. To be shut out of the circumference of a circle is to be unworthy, or perhaps unknowing.

*Also consult the entry for Circle in Shapes/Patterns.*

**CITY**

🔆 A spiritual community to which we belong can be represented in dreams by a city, since a city was originally given status because it had a cathedral.

💗 A city usually has a core community, and we sometimes represent the place of work or opportunity in this way.

🔲 Dreaming of a city, particularly one known to us, is to be trying to understand our sense of community; of belonging to groups. We will often, through dreams, give ourselves clues as to what we require in the mental and emotional environment in which we live, and a bustling city may show our need for social interaction. A deserted city may portray our feelings of having been neglected by others.

*Also consult Religious Buildings in Buildings and Spiritual Imagery in the Introduction.*

**CLAMP**

🔆 Any kind of clamp implies restraint – to dream of one indicates we are being prevented from making progress in our spiritual aims.

To find ourselves using a clamp such as a woodworking tool suggests having to make an extra effort to hold a situation stable.

A car being clamped in dreams suggests a deliberate bar to movement. This may be because a particular task has taken too long, because authority has stepped in or because we have not paid enough attention to detail.

## CLEAN/CLEAR

Cleanness or clarity represent spiritual purity. Cleanliness, in the sense of having been cleansed, signifies one way of getting to that state. Baptism is a ceremony indicative of this.

To be cleaning an article suggests that we are not satisfied with its original state. Making a clear statement suggests a deeply held belief.

When dirty water runs clear or we have a sense of clarity we have an opportunity to clarify misunderstandings and difficulties in everyday life.

## CLIFF

The cliff edge denotes a step off into the Unknown. A cliff equally can suggest an obstacle to be scaled.

There may be a step we need to take which will psychologically put us either on edge or on the edge in such a way that we must overcome our own fears in order to proceed through our own limitations.

To be on the edge of a cliff in a dream indicates the dreamer is facing danger. It shows the need to make a decision as to how to deal with a situation, and possibly be open to taking a risk. We are often facing the unknown.

*Consult the entries for Edge and Mountain for further clarification.*

## CLIMATE

Nature and natural occurrences have always played an important part in man's spiritual understanding. Changes which were previously attributed to the gods, such as thunderstorms and floods, tend to have a more prosaic explanation in the present day. In dreams they represent disturbances.

Climate changes in dreams can often reflect our own emotions and moods.

As the world is seen to undergo climate change through human intervention, dreams can take on a more apocalyptic feel. We seem to be less in touch with the effect we have on the world we live in.

## CLIMB

Ascension, in the sense of climbing to achieve enlightenment, is an often perceived spiritual symbol.

Climbing upwards suggests we are trying to reach new heights in our lives, and are possibly having to make greater efforts than before to succeed.

Climbing down, in the sense that it uses a different technique, suggests having to assess the risks of a change in position.

🔲 To dream of climbing is to dream of getting away from something, possibly to escape. We may be avoiding trouble.

**CLOAK** – *see* **CLOTHES**

**CLOCK** – *see* **TIME**

**CLOSE/CLOSED**

🔆 Spiritually to be close to someone is to have empathy with them. A closed door suggests that an opportunity has passed.

♡ We can indicate to ourselves in dreams the fact that we are emotionally closed within a situation. This often manifests as a sense of being closed in.

🔲 To be close to someone in a dream can mean we are looking for intimacy, or perhaps protection. To close a door acknowledges the fact that we must make a decision to put the past behind us.

*Consult the entries for Door and Trap/Trapped for further clarification.*

**CLOTHES**

🔆 Clothes can suggest spiritual protection. For instance, certain types of clothes will highlight roles and status. The priest's habit or judges robes are two such examples.

♡ Clothes often act as a form of protection, particularly against being touched. This protection may also be against having our real self violated. Clothes can also conceal or reveal: in covering up nudity they conceal our perceived imperfections and, by implication, disguise our sexuality. In revealing certain parts of our bodies our dreams may show in what ways we are vulnerable.

Various articles of clothing have certain symbolic meanings in dreams:

**Coat/cloak/shawl** – any type of coat can suggest warmth and love, but also protection. This protection can be either physical or emotional, and particularly in the case of a cloak, can be the spiritual protection of Faith. A sheepskin coat may emphasize this significance Fear of losing the coat can suggest the fear of losing faith and belief. If the coat is too short or not thick enough it shows we may be fearful that our love, or the protection we have, is not adequate for our needs. *Also consult the entry for Sheep in Animals.*

**Gloves** – the meaning of gloves can be ambivalent in dreams. They can represent covering and protection, but also 'showing one's hand' and challenging the status quo. *Also consult the individual entry for Gloves.*

**Hat/cap** – a hat or cap is a symbol of wisdom and the intellect and also of protection. It can also signify both spirituality and sexuality, depending on the other aspects of the dream.

**Pyjamas/nightclothes** – pyjamas or any type of nightclothes suggest relaxation and hence openness.

**Raincoat** – in common with other types of coat, a raincoat holds the symbolism of protection, but more specifically this time against other people's emotional onslaught. Very occasionally it may suggest some kind of wish to return to a womb-like state.

**Shirt** – a shirt can suggest appropriate action; correct for the occasion or casual, more relaxed. Wearing a hair shirt denotes grief and penitence.

**Shoes** – our ability, or otherwise, to be grounded and in touch with everyday life is symbolized in dreams by shoes. Shoes that we, or others, are wearing in a dream are there to alert us to an adjustment that needs to be made in our attitude to life. Lacing up shoes in a dream was once thought to be a well-known symbol of death as were shoes on a table. Today, these images are much more likely to indicate change is necessary.

**Tie** – a tie has two main significances in dreams. For some it can represent correctness and good behaviour, whereas for others, presumably because of its shape, it will signify the phallus and thus masculine power.

**Underclothes** – when we dream of underclothes – whether our own or other people's – we are considering hidden attitudes to self-image or sexuality.

**Veil or veil-like garments** – when we, or others, are wearing a veil we are either trying to hide something, or are only partially accepting knowledge about ourselves or our relationship to others. *Also consult the individual entry for Veil.*

▣ The clothes we wear in a dream can often depict the facade, or persona, we create for other people. We have certain roles that we adopt in response to others' reactions. Clothes which others are wearing in our dreams can also set the scene for an acting out of some of the confrontations which take place. Some common images which have particular relevance are:

**Getting undressed** can suggest the shedding of old beliefs and inhibitions whereas losing one's clothes or being naked highlights our vulnerability and fears.

**Dressing inappropriately**, perhaps wearing formal clothes on a casual occasion and vice versa, shows we are conscious of our own difficulty in 'fitting in' with other people. It will depend on the dream scenario whether we are surprised or distressed, and it is often the emotion that we experience which gives us the correct interpretation. We may be deliberately not conforming to others' perception of us, or trying to conform too much in adopting a certain role. The colour of the clothing is often significant.

**Clothes being worn by someone to whom they do not belong** indicate there is confusion in the our mind as to which roles are appropriate for each character. If a man is wearing woman's clothing it shows that we need to be more conscious of our feminine side. A uniform on a woman highlights the need to be aware of the more disciplined and masculine side of our personality. If we are changing clothes we are attempting, or perhaps need to consider how, to change our image. Clothes that have been cut short indicate that we may be outgrowing former pleasures and need to look to pastures new for our entertainment, whereas particularly pretty clothes show we have much to appreciate in our lives. If we are aware that clothes belonging to a particular person then we are being reminded of that person, even though we are aware that they cannot necessarily be with us.

## CLOUDS

Being unreachable, clouds symbolized the potency of the Ultimate. Similar to smoke, they were previously considered to be the vehicle for Divine Power. They retain this significance in dreams today.

We may have a hidden depression, shown by dark clouds, which can be dealt with only after it has been given form in a dream. White clouds suggest contentment, but may also suggest a transitory awareness of an idea.

Dreaming of clouds can have two meanings, depending on the other circumstances in the dream. It can either indicate uplifting or religious feelings, or can show that we are feeling overshadowed by someone or something. It can also warn of the possibility of difficulty or danger to come.

## CLOVER

The three-leaved clover is an example of body, soul and spirit, or any representation of the triad of divinity such as Father, Son and Holy Spirit. The four-leaved clover includes the feminine principle, and therefore the quaternity which predates the Christian religion.

We need to look at our ability to bring the various parts of our personality back into harmony with one another. The four-leaved clover symbolizes the balance of the Ego functions: thinking, sensing, feeling and intuition.

Traditionally the clover plant is considered to be lucky, so to find clover in a dream denotes good fortune is on its way. The three-leaved clover suggests the past, the present and the future.

In a woman's dream clover generally highlights the psyche and her intuitive abilities. In a man's dream the focus will be on his ability to use his talents to the full.

## CLOWN

🜚 Spiritually the figure of the clown has the same significance as the jester, that being the ability to laugh at our foibles and idiosyncrasies.

♥ The clown will often suggest the ability to see and sense the ridiculous in life. Often there is a tinge of sadness in this, however.

▣ In life a true clown must register his mask after which no-one else can use the same make-up and a clown can have this same significance in dreams. We must 'register' the performance we put on for the world.

## CLUB (PEOPLE)

🜚 Organized Ritual and dance as an expression of an inner rhythm is an important part of the progression to spiritual awareness

♥ It requires a certain level of maturity to be at ease being part of a group, so to dream of being with a crowd and enjoying the interaction, particularly in a public place, can indicate our awareness of ourselves.

▣ When we dream of being in a club such as a night-spot or sports club, we are highlighting the right of every human being to belong to a group with common aims and beliefs.

## CLUB (WEAPON)

🜚 The club as a weapon is a stereotype of masculinity, although rather crudely expressed in this instance. The type of club used in the game of golf for instance suggests the ability to use masculinity in a more refined way.

♥ We have great strength at our disposal, for which we need to find an outlet.

▣ To dream of using a weapon to club someone denotes an inner turmoil that has remained unexpressed. It may also depict our feelings of violence against ourselves.

⬧ Rather obviously, a club can be taken as a symbol of the penis in both male and female dreams.

*You might also like to consult the entry for Weapons.*

## COBWEB

🜚 It will depend on the state of the cobweb as to the spiritual interpretation. A spider's web can suggest the symbol of the eight pointed star, the mandala – an aid to meditation – and hence the Buddhist eightfold path to spiritual enlightenment. A dirty cobweb, however, denotes that spirituality is contaminated in some fashion.

♥ The cobweb, because it is easily damaged, signifies indecision, perhaps an idea that has not quite crystallized yet.

▣ On a purely practical level the cobweb symbolizes unused talents and potential which has been allowed to go stale.

*You might like to consult the entries for Spider and Star in Shapes/Patterns for further clarification.*

## COCK

❂ The masculine principle, the spiritual Bird of Fame and the dawn are all part of the significance of this bird.

♡ We may need to be more up front and courageous in what we are doing.

▦ The cock has always been a symbol of a new day, and of vigilance or watchfulness, so to have one appear in a dream forecasts a new beginning or warning to be vigilant in one's daily work.

⊡ There is obvious significance in the slang word for the penis in a man's dream and there may be a similar word-play in women's dreams.

*The section on Birds will give you additional information.*

## COCOON – *see* CHRYSALIS

## CODE

❂ A spiritual code may appear in dreams as an unrecognizable language which requires deciphering. It can also be a code of behaviour by which one must live.

♡ To be deciphering a code in dreams suggests that we need some understanding of the 'key' to our own or others' behaviour or that there is knowledge at present hidden from us.

▦ To be using a door code or some kind of numerical combination suggests that we have the necessary information to gain access. Not to know the code or to have forgotten it indicates that we must be more careful in future. This meaning holds good if we do not know the correct code of behaviour.

## COFFIN

❂ Redemption, resurrection and salvation are all symbolized by the coffin. Contemplation of the death experience can lead to dreams of a coffin, in this case symbolizing the physical body, though we may be attuned to the unseen spiritual world.

♡ We are perhaps shutting our own feelings away and therefore causing a part of ourselves to die. There may be a dull, unaware state of consciousness which is lacking in spiritual insight.

▦ When we dream of a coffin, we are reminding ourselves of our own mortality. We may also be coming to terms with the death of a relationship and feelings of loss. This may also be the first warning of a weakened state, a total lack of vitality.

*Consult the entries for Catacomb/Crypt, Cemetery, Dead People, Death and Hearse for more information.*

**COINS** – *see* MONEY

**COLD**

⚙ The loss of our connection to the spirit realms can be felt in dreams as extreme cold. Equally, this can signify the presence of a spiritual energy.

♡ A physical feeling in dreams often reflects our inner feelings or our emotions. To feel cold is one such way of highlighting a state of mind.

▦ To be conscious of cold in a dream is to be aware of feeling neglected, or of being left out of things.

**COLLAPSE**

⚙ Anything which collapses suggests there is not enough energy to hold a structure together – in this case spiritual energy.

♡ When an object in dreams collapses we need to be aware of situations in our lives which are damaged or under threat if we do not take care. Seeing a person collapse suggests that there may be a health issue around which needs attention.

▦ If a barrier or wall is seen to collapse without assistance it signifies that two aspects of life are coming together and there is no longer need for division.

**COLOURS**

⚙ Colour affirms the existence of light. In spiritual terms, red is the colour of self-image and sexuality, orange is relationship – both with ourselves and others. Yellow is the emotional self, green is self-awareness and blue is self-expression and wisdom. Indigo is the colour of creativity, while violet depicts cosmic responsibility. Pure white suggests absolute spirituality.

♡ The symbolism of colour is very relevant in dreams since we know that these colours are not physically produced, but are a mental image. Some meanings given to colours are:

**Black** – holds within it all colour in potential. It suggests manifestation, negativity and judgement.

**Blue** – the colour of the clear blue sky and is the prime healing colour. It suggests relaxation, sleep and peacefulness.

**Brown** – the colour of the earth and of commitment. It also symbolizes death.

**Green** – the colour of nature and of plant life. It signifies balance and harmony.

**Grey** – there is probably no true grey, it being a combination of black and white. Sometimes the colour of nuns' habits, it means devotion and ministration.

**Magenta** – in some ways a colour which links both the physical and spiritual. It signifies relinquishment, selflessness, perfection and meditative practice.

**Orange** – an essentially cheerful uplifting colour. The qualities associated with it are happiness and independence.

**Red** – vigour, strength, energy, life, sexuality and power are all connected with this colour. A beautiful clear mid-red is the correct one for these qualities; if there is any other red in dreams, its attributes may not be totally uncontaminated.

**Turquoise** – clear greeny blue. In some religions it is taken to be the colour of the freed soul. It means calmness and purity.

**Violet** – while found by some to be too strong, means nobility, respect and hope. Its purpose is to uplift.

**White** – contains within it all colours. It suggests innocence, spiritual purity and wisdom.

**Yellow** – the colour that is closest to daylight. Connected with the emotional self, the attributes are thinking, detachment and judgement.

🔲 Colour is a vital part of symbolism, dream and otherwise. By learning to work with our own colour spectrum, particularly in the dream state, we can maintain and enhance our physical wellbeing. This is partly to do with the vibratory frequency which each individual colour has, and partly to do with tradition. Experiments have been carried out to ascertain what effect colour has, and have proved what occultists and healers have always known. In working with the colours of the rainbow, we discover that the warm, lively colours – which give back light – are yellow, orange and red. Cold passive colours are blue, indigo and violet. Green is a synthesis of both warmth and cold. White light holds within it the whole colour spectrum and its potential.

**COLUMN**

🔯 Spiritually a single column has the same significance as a tower, a structure to enable us to reach the heavens or the Divine. It may be an object of worship or a memorial. A column of light denotes an awareness of spirit or spiritual energy. Boaz (strength) and Joachim (beauty) are the two columns which stood at the entrance to King Solomon's temple in Jerusalem.

♡ Single columns could represent strength or single mindedness. Two stone columns in the distance indicate a doorway to the future or a way into the unknown.

🔲 A column will suggest the penis but also masculinity. It is also structural or emotional support.

*You might like to consult the entry for Pillar for further clarification.*

**COMB**

🔯 Fertility, the rays of the sun, entanglement and music are all represented by the comb.

♥ We may be conscious of the fact that we need to work with our self-image.

▦ A comb is a many-toothed implement and often emphasizes the need to neaten or tidy something up in our lives. We need to tidy up our thoughts.

▯ In a man's dream, a comb can indicate seduction or sensuality. In a woman's dream it perhaps has more to do with her devouring nature – the ability to destroy.

**COMBAT** – *see* ARGUE/ARGUMENTS, CONFLICT, FIGHT AND WAR

**COMBINE** – *see* CONNECT

**COMET**

✹ The coming of calamity, war, fire or danger can be seen in dreams as the comet. Comets were once thought to be divine messengers.

♥ As an intense, rare occurrence when we are most under pressure, a comet appearing in a dream indicates the answer to a problem may be about to appear to us at the speed of light.

▦ To dream of seeing a comet is to recognize the possibility of circumstances very quickly arising over which we have no control. The outcome may be unavoidable.

**COMMITTEE**

✹ A committee is a group of people brought together for a specific purpose. Dreams often produce such an image when our commitment is required for a particular spiritual task.

♥ When a consensus of opinion or a concerted effort needs to be made we will often dream of a committee in order to highlight the issue.

▦ In working life, a committee in dreams signifies a shared responsibility. Discussion and good management rather than personal concerns will carry the day.

**COMMUNE**

✹ A commune suggests a group of like-minded people who have chosen to live together to achieve a particular spiritual objective.

♥ Finding ourselves living in a commune in dreams signifies our understanding that a group of people with a common purpose are exponentially more powerful than the sum of the individuals.

▦ In dreams a commune may represent any 'family' to which we belong – a religion, our work colleagues, a hobby group. It is the shared passion that is important.

**COMMUNICATION**

✹ Any tool of communication – telephone, mobile or cellphone, email, fax machine, computer, internet, television – suggests that the veil between the spiritual and physical worlds can be penetrated. We are capable of better and wider communication than previously.

◈ The computer can symbolize spiritual records and the past, present and future. A database would, for instance, suggest the ordering of information. Text messaging might suggest brief but necessary information, whereas a fax, being slightly outdated, requires us to bring what we know up to date. The telephone signifies communication with unseen people and might therefore highlight communication with the spirit world. The television is, quite literally, a medium through which information is passed. The internet will tend to signify wider, more global, communication and available information.

▨ Communication occurs on so many levels that images of modern technology can now accurately mimic in dreams the way we communicate. A stored document suggests that we are making a link with past memories or stored information which we may need to access in order to progress. The computer and other high technology images are now such a part of people's lives that it very much depends on other circumstances in the dream as to the correct interpretation of the image. A computer crashing, for instance, suggests that there is a problem with the means of communication rather than communication itself.

As modern day technology spreads, such an image may simply be a means of conveying a message from the unconscious to the conscious mind, whereas in other cases it will be a reminder of personal potential or abilities. A keyboard, requiring a certain degree of skill, can suggest the stages of proficiency we need to acquire in order to communicate our ideas efficiently.

*Also consult the entries for Email, Telephone, Text and Web.*

## COMMUTE

❀ Since commuting implies changing – perhaps moving from personal concerns to work-orientated matters – the significance is shifting from a relaxed to a more focused state.

◈ Just as our mindset must change as we travel to and from work from personal to work concerns, substituting one way of thinking for another, in essence changing perspective, can lead to radical changes in lifestyle.

▨ In modern-day life commuting has turned into a time of transition, a way of covering distance and a time for planning. Dreaming of such an occurrence can highlight any of these activities.

*For further clarity see Journey and Transport.*

## COMPASS

❀ When we are trying to find direction, and overcome our own spiritual limitations and boundaries, we will dream of a compass.

♥ Often having the same significance as the circle, the compass can represent the source of life, or sometimes justice. Instinctively, compass directions suggest certain states of being such as north suggesting coldness and south suggesting warmth.

▦ Dreaming of a compass is often an attempt to find a new direction or activity. We need to be able to understand the differing opportunities offered to us, and to follow the one that is right for us.

▤ In magical work the compass is used to help define the four most powerful directions. In both men's and women's dreams a compass may suggest the search for magical power.

*You might like to consult the entries for Position and Map.*

## COMPETE /COMPETITION

✺ Any competition suggests a struggle between two polarities, though in the spiritual sense it is actually a joint effort to overcome a challenge.

♥ To be competing in a dream is to perhaps look for a better performance from ourselves than we have managed hitherto.

▦ As today's world is highly competitive our dreams may highlight competitiveness in ways that we do not consciously recognize. Dreaming of running a race might highlight such competition in the workplace.

▤ Competition in both men's and women's dreams will highlight their area of competitiveness. A woman for instance might find herself competing against another woman for recognition, whereas a man may simply find himself in competition with all and sundry.

**COMPUTER** – *see* COMMUNICATION, EMAIL AND MICROCHIP.

**CONCH** – *see* SHELL

**CONCUBINE** – *see* SIRENS IN ARCHETYPES IN THE INTRODUCTION

**CONDEMN** – *see* JUDGE/JUDGEMENT AND JUSTICE

## CONFER/CONFERENCE

✺ A conference holds the symbolism of a group meeting together to achieve a consensus either of opinion or action.

♥ To find ourselves at a conference suggests that we need to ensure that all aspects of our personality are in agreement.

▦ Conferring signifies a bringing together of perhaps differing opinions to reach a sense of common ownership. In everyday terms this image will arise when such a consensus is important to progress. The image of a conference can also come up when we find ourselves at odds with the majority.

## CONFESS/CONFESSION

✺ Confession is a recognition of those aspects of our lives which are not within a particular code of conduct, whether spiritual or otherwise.

To be confessing to someone else signifies that we have not been acting with integrity. To have someone make a confession suggests that we are judging a particular behaviour – our own or people around us.

We feel that we are carrying a responsibility which we need to share with someone else more competent.

When the other person is known in dreams or of the opposite gender both men and women will need to monitor their own integrity. This is an aspect of the Animus or Anima and suggests that the physical being is not in alignment with the spiritual self.

## CONFLICT

When two opposing forces meet, particularly in the spiritual sense, this is pictured in dreams as conflict.

Conflict suggests that two aspects of our personality are having difficulty in reconciling their needs and requirements. Conflict arises when the conscious self needs to make a choice between their differing needs.

The dream image of conflict arises when we are at odds with others in our everyday life. Sometimes a resolution can be reached in dreams which points the way to managing the external conflict.

It is supposed that men are more logical in their thought processes and women more intuitive. However, when a woman dreams of a strategic response to a conflict she is accessing her more logical side. Conversely, when a man follows his own instincts he will be seeking an intuitive answer.

*You might like to consult the entries for Argue/Arguments, Fight and War.*

## CONNECT/COMBINE

Part of the process of spiritual development is integration – making connections between various aspects of our personality and combining them to make a more coherent whole. We tend to search for how things fit together, how they interact, how they contribute to the whole.

When we dream of connecting or combining two articles, for instance two opposing forces, we are attempting to dispense with duality and perhaps achieve a better use of energy.

Making connections in dreams can signify forming relationships. Missing a connection when travelling suggests that we have not linked timing and effort. Dreaming of combinations of things creates a composite, combining qualities from each of them.

*For further clarity read the information on Composite Animals in Animals, as well as the entries for Journey and Transport.*

**CONSECRATE** – *see* **SPIRITUAL IMAGERY IN THE INTRODUCTION**

**CONSERVATION**

   🕉 Conservation suggests that we are aware of global issues and spiritual responsibilities.

   ♡ Conservation implies the best usage of the resources available to us. By looking at symbols of resources which appear in dreams we are given the opportunity to become more efficient.

   ▦ As the issue becomes more noticeable in everyday life conservation can have two meanings. On a personal level it can represent the best use of our talents and abilities. In a wider sense it will suggest our responsibilities towards others – family, colleagues and others. To dream of working for an organization dealing with conservation may mean that we should seek out others of a like mind.

**CONTAGION/CONTAGIOUS** – *see* **INFECTION**

**CONTAMINATE/CONTAMINATION** – *see* **DIRTY**

**CONTRACEPTIVE** – *see* **SEX/SEXUAL IMAGES**

**CONTRACT**

   🕉 A contract suggests a spiritual commitment.

   ♡ In that a contract is a binding agreement between two parties it signifies having made a promise to carry out a particular task, which should be easily identifiable after a little thought.

   ▦ A work contract denotes a commitment of our working life. A contract to buy signifies a long-term commitment, whereas an unsigned contract suggests that we are unable to make any commitment at this stage.

   ⊞ As women are able to exercise more autonomy over their lives, signing a contract such as a prenuptial agreement suggests the making of a deeper commitment to themselves. In a man's dream a contract can have a more workaday connotation.

**CONVENT** – *see* **SPIRITUAL IMAGERY IN THE INTRODUCTION**

**CONVICT/CONVICTION/CONVINCE**

   🕉 A conviction in the sense of a firm belief is a necessary part of spiritual commitment. A convict on the other hand is someone who has offended against others' deeply held beliefs.

   ♡ All three aspects (convict, conviction and convince) presuppose an emotional connection with our own beliefs. To be convinced in a dream means that we have been deeply impressed and to have a conviction follows this same idea. To convict someone, however, suggests that we have a deeply held belief that that person has committed some wrongdoing.

🔲 To receive a conviction, therefore, means to be at the mercy of other people's opinions, whereas convincing someone means that we have converted them to our way of thinking.

## CONVOLVULUS – *see* BINDING AND FLOWERS

## COOKING

🌀 Cooking can symbolize creativity. There is a delightful fable which tells how God baked the various ethnic races into being.

💚 To be able to move forward in our lives we may need to blend certain parts of our existence in new and original ways in order to succeed. We may need to nurture a new ability. This is often brought to our attention by dreams of cooking.

🔲 To be cooking in a dream is to be preparing nourishment or to be satisfying a hunger, whether our own or other people's. This may not simply be a physical hunger, but something more subtle such as a need to make use of the varied opportunities available to us.

🔳 In a woman's dream cooking may suggest work-a-day activities as well as domestic ones, a metaphor for the way she constructs a project. A man's dream may be a way of refocusing on a creative problem.

*You might like to consult the entries for Bake/Baker/Bakery, Food and Hunger.*

## COPY

🌀 Copying in spiritual terms signifies reproducing the perfect, producing duality where there was previously only one. It represents emanation, flowing out from the Divine.

💚 To be copying an action in dreams suggests we need to learn from others.

🔲 When we find ourselves making copies we are aware that we need to retain information for ourselves. Such a dream can suggest the idea of reproduction.

*Consult the entry for Forge for further clarification.*

## CORD

🌀 The Silver Cord – that subtle energy which holds the life force within the body – is an image which manifests in dreams as we begin to recognize spiritual progression.

💚 There is a need to be appreciative of the ties of duty and affection.

🔲 Within any relationship there are certain restrictions or dependencies that become apparent, and these may be depicted in dreams as cords or ties. These emotional bonds can be both limiting and freedom-giving.

*Also consult the entries for Bonds, Chains and Umbilical Cord.*

## CORN

🔆 The Great Mother, or Mother Nature, in her nurturing aspect is always shown with corn representing fertility and fecundity.

♡ To be harvesting corn is to be reaping the rewards of hard work. We may be linking with some very primeval needs and requirements.

▦ Most dreams containing images of corn or wheat symbolize fertility or fruitfulness. They may also represent new life – either pregnancy or new developments in other ways.

⊞ Women are much more in touch with the natural forces so tend to dream of goddesses and their attributes.

*You might also like to consult the entries for Harvest and Mill/Millstone.*

## CORNER

🔆 To turn the corner spiritually is to gain a new perspective on our own spiritual indecision.

♡ We are making available a hidden or little admitted aspect of ourselves. We no longer need to feel trapped or restricted. We can handle the unexpected or the new experience.

▦ To turn a corner in a dream indicates that we have succeeded in moving forward into new experiences, despite what may have seemed to be obstacles in front of us. Turning a right-handed corner indicates a logical course of action, to turn a left-handed one indicates a more intuitive approach.

## CORNUCOPIA

🔆 The Horn of Plenty is an image common in one form or another in all spiritual work. The abundance may be for us or the rest of the world.

♡ Within ourselves we have unlimited potential to create both an acceptable present and a sustainable future.

▦ Like the conch shell, to dream of a cornucopia can denote abundance, endless bounty, fertility and fruitfulness. It may be more than we are used to or can handle.

*Also consult the entry for Horns for further information.*

## CORPORATE

🔆 A corporate environment in dreams will suggest a diverse group of people who are brought together for a common purpose – a perhaps bureaucratic approach to spirituality.

♡ A corporate environment will not necessarily have visible within it a passion for overall success and therefore suggests a competitive spirit which may or may not be in line with our own aims as individuals.

▨ This can simply represent our everyday workplace or a task which we have undertaken.

*You might like to consult the entry for Work.*

**CORRIDOR** – *see* **BUILDINGS**

**CORRUPTION**

✹ Any kind of corruption suggests deliberate interference in a negative way. Morally, we have moved beyond acceptable behaviour.

♥ Corruption denotes a tainting or spoiling, particularly of our integrity, so any such image signifies something which is imperfect or has been made so by a negative influence.

▨ An article which is decaying or corrupted is now no longer useful so from a mundane perspective we may need to look at aspects of our lives which have outlived their usefulness.

**COSMETICS**

✹ The personality can and does show itself in many guises. From a spiritual perspective we find a need to cover up or disguise blemishes in our character.

♥ Psychologically we may feel that we have a problem with our public image, and need to put on some sort of front before we can be seen by others.

▨ To be using cosmetics in a dream can have two meanings. We register the fact that we are covering up our features or that, conversely, we are enhancing our natural beauty. If we are using cosmetics on someone else, we literally need to 'make up' with that person.

*You might like to enhance your understanding by consulting the entry for Make-Up.*

**COUNT** – *see* **ABACUS AND NUMBERS**

**COUNTERFEIT** – *see* **FAKE/FALSE**

**COUNTRYSIDE**

✹ The forces of nature in us can be symbolized by scenes of the countryside. We can return, without feeling guilty, to a very relaxed state. As our lives become more frenetic we need an image which induces good feelings.

♥ There is, in most people's minds, a type of freedom and openness about the countryside which is not necessarily available in towns and cities. Such an image appears shows we may need to clarify our own feelings about our lifestyle.

▨ When we dream of the countryside we are putting ourselves in touch with our own natural spontaneous feelings. We may have memories of the countryside that invoke a particular mood state or way of being.

*Also consult Places.*

**COUP –** *see* **WAR**

**COURT**

⚙ A court in the sense of a legal arena suggests judgement by a higher authority. This implies that we are not necessarily acting with integrity. A games court represents a degree of team spirit.

♡ Appearing in court suggests that we have committed a misdemeanour of some sort and must expect to be judged or held to account by our peers.

▦ Taking someone to court for a debt or a minor offence is a way of dealing through dreams with a perceived hurt or indiscretion. A court such as a tennis or squash court suggests an acceptable way of acting out our competitive instincts.

*Consult Authority Figures in People, Crime/Criminal, Debt, Games, Judge/Judgement and Justice for any further information you might need,*

**COUSIN –** *see* **EXTENDED FAMILY IN FAMILY**

**COVEN**

⚙ A coven is a gathering of a group of people with a common belief, particularly Wiccan. Capable of calling on natural forces for either good or bad, it gathers to enhance the vibration of both the individual and the group.

♡ When we dream of belonging to a coven we are becoming aware of the 'power of the many' and thus share our knowledge with others.

▦ The popular image of a coven of witches can appear in dreams when relationships with work colleagues or family require a common focus.

⊡ Since coven also means a religious assembly in both men's and women's dreams it will depict a heightening of both emotional and spiritual vibrations.

*Consulting the entries for Magic/Magician and Witch as well as Spiritual Imagery in the Introduction will enhance your understanding.*

**COVER**

⚙ Covering something suggests obliterating it or hiding that which we do not want others to know about us. Burying something in the earth in a dream suggests hiding a misdeed of some sort.

♡ Covering over anything signifies making the best of or preserving what we have, perhaps ensuring that shortcomings are not recognized.

▦ It will depend what and how we are covering in dreams. Covering an article in brown paper portrays the need to be pragmatic while covering an altar signifies an act of devotion. Covering a chair suggests added comfort while covering up our actions suggests we are aware of opprobrium.

*Consulting the entries for Altar, Canopy and Paper will assist in your interpretation.*

**COW** – *see* ANIMALS

**COYOTE** – *see* WOLF IN ANIMALS

**CRAB**

🔅 The astrological sign of Cancer and the Great Mother are both represented by the crab.

❤ Because the crab has a hard shell and is thus self-protective, in dreams this quality can be highlighted. When someone is 'crabby' they are irritable or morose. The crab apple is small and sour and therefore has this same connotation.

▦ A crab appearing in a dream can indicate mothering, particularly of the 'smother love' type, but can also be the qualities of unreliability and self-interest. The crab can also, because of the way it moves, denote deviousness.

⦂ In a woman's dream the crab will often represent the different aspects of the three-faceted Moon goddess, maid, mother and crone. In a man's dream it is more likely to suggest the 'smother mother'.

**CRACK**

🔅 There may be a spiritual flaw in our make-up. A little thought should reveal what it might be.

❤ Psychologically a crack may represent the irrational or the unexpected. It may indicate our inability to hold things together mentally. Dreaming of the street drug crack will have this connotation.

▦ Dreaming of an article which is cracked indicates our recognition of something which is flawed in our lives. There may be a weakness or difficulty in the attitudes and defences we use to meet life's problems.

**CRADLE/CRIB**

🔅 The physical as opposed to the spiritual body is sometimes represented as a cradle or baby's crib.

❤ An empty cradle can represent a woman's fear of childlessness or her fears of motherhood, depending on the other aspects of the dream. It may also suggest a lack of creativity or new ideas. A crib was initially a food receptacle, although today it can suggest a new life.

▦ To dream of a cradle or crib can represent new life or new beginnings.

⦂ As a precognitive dream a cradle can represent pregnancy, while in a man's dream it can represent the need to return to a womblike, protected state.

**CRANE**

🔅 As a bird, the crane is a messenger of the gods. It allows communion with the gods and the ability to enter into higher states of consciousness.

*T'ai chi*, a form of spiritual discipline, is said to symbolize a fight between a crane and a snake.

♥ We are capable of gaining control or status within a situation so we can build on it to our advantage.

▦ When we dream of a building crane we are often being told of the need to raise our level of awareness in some matter. We need to make an attempt to understand the overall or universal implications of our actions.

## CRASH

☀ Crashing actually suggests breaking up and signifies, therefore, a difficulty in remaining whole or complete in a spiritual sense.

♥ A crash as in a collision suggests a traumatic occurrence, perhaps by not paying attention to detail. Crashing out would suggest losing a hold on reality.

▦ A computer crashing in dreams signifies a loss of information or power. To hear a crash is to be alerted to an imminent problem.

*Also consult the entries for Car and Journey.*

## CREDIT

☀ To be given credit, whether financial or otherwise, is to receive the correct recognition or approval. We are valued for who we are.

♥ To dream about credit cards relates to our worth, value or status. Receiving a credit note suggests we have not received the correct value or have not received it at the right time.

▦ Financial transactions of any sort in dreams highlight our attitude to money, value and authority. We may need to look at who we feel either owes us or to whom we owe value.

*You might also like to consult the entries for Debt and Money.*

## CRESCENT – *see* SHAPES/PATTERNS AND MOON

## CRICKET – *see* GAMES AND INSECTS

## CRIME/CRIMINAL

☀ A crime or criminal in spiritual terms signifies an offence against spiritual law.

♥ We all have a part of ourselves which dislikes external control. Committing a crime in dreams may be a form of rebellion. To observe a criminal at work is to recognize the potential for wrong-doing.

▦ Criminal activity offends against both personal integrity and the laws of society. When we consider the other aspects of the dream scenario we will appreciate any adjustments which need to be made in our everyday activities.

*Consult the entries for Court and Justice to enhance your understanding.*

## CROCODILE

❀ Liberation from the limitations of the world is symbolized by the crocodile. Though we are consumed by our fear of death, or perhaps the death process. we must work through this fear in order to come to terms with physical death. Understanding brings liberation.

♡ To see a crocodile in dreams forewarns of hidden danger. We should beware of poor decision-making.

▦ To dream of crocodiles, or indeed any reptile, indicates we are looking at the frightening lower aspects of our nature. We may feel we have no control over these, and it would therefore be very easy to be devoured by them.

⊡ In the Egyptian story of Isis and Osiris the crocodile god is said to have swallowed Osiris' manhood. In a man's dream, therefore, the crocodile can symbolize emasculation. In a woman's dream it is more likely to represent an aspect of negative masculinity.

*Also consult the entry for Reptiles in Animals.*

## CROSS – *see* ANGER, SHAPES/PATTERNS AND SPIRITUAL IMAGERY IN THE INTRODUCTION

## CROSSING

❀ Crossing a river or chasm often depicts death. This is not necessarily a physical death but possibly spiritual change of some kind.

♡ We may encounter something we cannot control, and which may control us. To be crossing a field shows we could have a false sense of security, or may need to bring our feelings out into the open.

▦ To dream of crossing a road is recognizing the possibility of danger, fear or uncertainty. We are perhaps pitting ourselves against something that is bigger than us. Crossing someone suggests getting on the wrong side of them.

## CROSSROADS

❀ A crossroads is a magical but dangerous space, full of spiritual potential, since we can go in any direction which seems appropriate. In times gone by shrines were erected at crossroads.

♡ We are in a situation where two opposing forces are coming together, not in conflict but in harmony. Many magical spells are dissipated at crossroads when they are thrown to the four winds. This image in dreams is therefore very powerful.

▦ Dreaming of crossroads indicates that we are going to have to make choices in our lives, often to do with career or life changes. We perhaps need to be aware of where we have come from in order to make intelligent decisions. Often, to turn left at crossroads can indicate taking the wrong route, though it can indicate the more intuitive path. To turn right can obviously mean taking the correct path, but can also mean making logical decisions.

*You might also like to consult the entries for Journey and Position.*

**CROW – *see* BIRDS**

**CROWD**

    ⚜ A crowd suggests a group with a popular belief, or common religious feelings. More negatively a mob has a common belief, but of a more fanatical nature.

    ♥ Dreaming of being in a crowd could be indicative of the fact that we do not wish to stand out, or that we do not have a personal sense of direction at present. The type of people in the crowd may also be relevant.

    ▦ We may wish to camouflage our feelings from others, to get lost or even to hide our opinions. In everyday life we need to retain our anonymity, to create a facade for ourselves. Conversely, there may be safety in numbers if we join a group of like-minded people.

*You might also like to consult the entry for Group.*

**CROWN**

    ⚜ A crown signifies a change into a different level of awareness, victory over death and a recognition of status. The diadem, the forerunner of the crown, was initially a simple white ribbon, ending in a knot and two stripes that were placed on the shoulders, that surrounded the head of the king to denote his authority. It signified being bound to his spiritual task.

    ♥ We may have striven for something and our greatest victory has been against our own inertia. The crown can represent dedication, particularly to duty. It suggests the attainment of knowledge. When a crown is highly decorated we acknowledge our past attainments.

    ▦ To dream of a crown is to acknowledge our own success, and to recognize that we have opportunities that will expand our knowledge and awareness. We may be about to receive recognition or a reward of some sort.

*Consult the entry for Diadem for further clarity.*

**CRUCIBLE – *see* SPIRITUAL IMAGERY IN THE INTRODUCTION**

**CRUCIFIXION – *see* SPIRITUAL IMAGERY IN THE INTRODUCTION**

**CRUDE**

    ⚜ Crude signifies the rough or unworked part of creation. It has been given form but is as yet unrefined and has not been differentiated.

    ♥ Crudeness suggests the rawness of emotion which has not yet been allowed proper expression. It also suggests instinct as opposed to intelligence.

▨ In terms of everyday life, if an article seems crude in a dream, a plan or idea has not yet reached fruition or been properly considered.

**CRY** – *see* **EMOTIONS AND WEEPING**

**CRYSTAL** – *see* **GEMS/JEWELS**

**CUBE** – *see* **SHAPES/PATTERNS**

**CUCKOO** – *see* **BIRDS**

**CUL-DE-SAC**

🔆 A cul-de-sac in spiritual terms suggests futility and sometimes lack of foresight.

♡ We are stuck in patterns of behaviour which give us no way out. We are being threatened by past mistakes.

▨ When we find ourselves trapped in a cul-de-sac it symbolizes wasted action, but perhaps also a state of inertia. Circumstance may be preventing a forward movement, and it may be necessary to retrace our steps in order to succeed.

**CUP**

🔆 The feminine awareness of the draught of life, immortality and plenty is intuitively and sensitively used. The cup has much of the symbolism of the chalice, indicating a receptive state which accepts intuitive information.

♡ If we are open to the more feminine side, we are able to both give and receive help and assistance. The cup often signifies happiness or joy.

▨ An offering or opportunity is being offered in everyday matters which we would do well to identify. Often the feminine is offering an opportunity from the unconscious.

⊡ To some extent the interpretation depends on what kind of cup is depicted. An ordinary teacup or mug for instance focuses on mundane matters and – for a woman – her feelings about domestic concerns. In a man's dream the emphasis is more likely to be on his feelings about his wife, family and happiness.

*Consult the entries for Chalice, Trophy and Win/Winning for further clarification.*

**CUPBOARD**

🔆 A cupboard was initially just that, a place to store utensils. Now it often represents a repository, perhaps in the spiritual sense, for skills or for hidden talents.

♡ Various types of cupboard can appear in dreams. A wardrobe suggests a period of transition and, because it houses our clothes, how we deal with our self-image, whereas a larder represents our ability to preserve or conserve our stores of energy. Finding a hidden cupboard suggests rediscovering something we may have forgotten. Opening a cupboard and finding it bigger than expected suggests available opportunities.

🔲 Clearing out a cupboard indicates that we may have to put our lives in order. Articles falling out of a cupboard suggest that we may be overstretched and/or overstretching ourselves.

**CURE** – *see* **HEAL/HEALING**

**CUSHION** – *see* **FURNITURE/FURNISHINGS**

**CUT** – *see* **KNIFE, OPERATION AND WOUND**

**CYMBALS**

☀ Spiritually cymbals signify two inter-dependent halves – one cannot normally operate without the other. Thus they can symbolize marriage or partnership of some sort. They may also suggest the interdependency of the sacred and the secular, the spiritual and the physical.

♥ We are reconciling passion and desire.

🔲 Cymbals are connected with rhythm and sound, so for them to appear in a dream is an indication of the need for and return to a basic vibration. In some cultures, along with the drum and tambourine, they are used to induce an ecstatic state, suggesting a need for relaxation.

⬛ Any instrument which is struck in a woman's dream suggests the coming together of her two aspects, Lilith and Eve, harlot and mother. For a man such a note signifies his life force.

## DAGGER

⚙ In dreams the dagger represents an age-old instrument of blood sacrifice. Spiritually, of course, such sacrifice is no longer valid under any circumstances. If we find the dagger is turned on us in a dream we need to beware of the likelihood of self-sacrifice.

♡ Psychologically, to be penetrated by any sharp instrument in a dream is usually to do with our masculine energy and at the same time often refers to our feelings about sexuality.

▦ When a dagger appears in a dream, the meaning can either be aggressive or defensive. If you are using the dagger to attack someone then you may be trying to cut out a part of yourself or trying to get rid of something you do not like. Being stabbed highlights our vulnerability.

⊟ As with any weapon in a man's dream, the dagger represents his developing assertive behaviour, whereas in a woman's dream it will be more to do with her drives or her Animus.

*Consult the entries for Knife and Weapons for further information.*

## DAISY – *see* FLOWERS

## DAM

⚙ The image of a dam presupposes that there is a block to progress. However, one interpretation suggests that it is the conservation of a scarce resource (perhaps our spiritual awareness), until it is available in sufficient quantity. By word association the image can suggest to be damned or rendered powerless.

♡ While consciously we may need to exercise control over our emotions, in a dream sequence we will often demonstrate a natural expression of difficulty or frustration by an overflow of water or the blocking of a natural channel.

▦ When we dream of a dam its significance may vary. We may be bottling up our own emotions and drive, or conversely we could be trying to stop somebody else's emotional outburst from happening. To be building a dam indicates we are likely to be putting up defences, whereas if a dam is bursting we may feel we have no control over emotional situations around us.

*For further clarity consult the entry for Water.*

## DAMAGE

⚙ Damage from a spiritual perspective can be very subtle, so to dream of an article, which is damaged, suggests some kind of difficulty or misperception.

A chipped vase, for instance, might signify a difficulty in perceiving the feminine correctly.

🜔 To be damaging an object in dreams suggests a strong sense of perhaps misplaced aggression. Other images in your dream should help to clarify the interpretation.

▨ If we dream of damaged articles it may be worthwhile exploring our self-esteem in waking life. A broken bone may suggest we need to look at the way we create structure in our lives, whereas a damaged door might signify a lack of self-respect.

⊞ Damage to the self, as in self-harm, in both men's and women's dreams, signifies a lack of self-appreciation. For a man, losing a limb highlights his sense of emasculation, whereas cutting into the flesh, particularly for a woman, signifies a release from pain.

## DANCE/DANCING

🜨 Spiritually, dancing has always been taken to represent the rhythm of life. The patterns created are reputed to mirror the patterns of creativity. If space and time are part of one continuum, movement and the flow of dance link the two together.

🜔 Psychologically, dance can be a reinforcement of freedom of movement, strength and emotion. Ballet in particular portrays an ethereal appreciation of mood; flamenco and other such energetic dancing reflect passion.

▨ Dance has always represented freedom and been symbolic of other actions which were necessary for survival. To be dancing in a dream portrays the creation of happiness, feeling at one with the surroundings and possibly getting closer or more intimate with a partner.

*You might also like to consult the entry for Ballerina/Ballet Dancer.*

## DANGER

🜨 Dreaming of being in a dangerous or precarious position can indicate a spiritual insecurity.

🜔 Dreams can often point to a danger in symbolic form, such as conflict, fire or flood. We may need to have pitfalls represented in such a way in order to recognize them on a conscious level.

▨ When we find ourselves in dangerous circumstances in dreams, we are often reflecting the anxieties and dilemmas of everyday life. We may be conscious that our activities could be harmful to us if we carry on in the same way.

⊞ Men and women perceive danger differently in dreams. Men often confront the difficulty, whereas women may attempt to placate or work round it. Interestingly, as the differences between the genders become blurred in everyday life, these natural responses are also modified.

*Consult the entry for Threat/Threaten for further clarification.*

**DARE** – *see* **RISK**

**DARK/DARKNESS**

🔆 That side of the personality where chaos may reign, and where, unless some spiritual understanding can be attained, is seen as dark. Also darkness is full of mystery and part of the unknown, the obscurity which hides the Divine.

♥ Intellectually, we are in touch with the hidden side – the Shadow – and may need to deal with the darker suppressed aspects of ourselves. To be surrounded by darkness suggests that there is potential for failure in some scheme or a sense of being lost.

▦ To dream of being in the dark usually represents a state of confusion or being in unknown and difficult territory. It may point to a secret part of ourselves or a part that we do not yet know.

**DART(S)**

🔆 As with any penetrative weapon, a dart is seen as strength, control and capability. In a spiritual sense it also suggests focus.

♥ Since it requires expertise and practice to throw darts successfully, in dreams playing darts also suggests discipline and concentration. It is thought that the game arose in the Middle Ages when bored soldiers took to hurling arrows at the upturned covers of wine barrels, perhaps seeing who could come closest to the cork bung. The shortened form of arrow became the dart, and a slice of tree trunk the target.

▦ Darts can symbolize harsh words deliberately intended to hurt or a way of bringing something to our notice which needs understanding.

⦂ In a woman's dream a dart may be seen as a direct approach from the masculine or perhaps her own attitude to achievement. In a man's dream it is more likely to be seen as a recreational pastime, or his ability to get straight to the point.

*You might also like to consult the entry for Arrow.*

**DATE (FRUIT)**

🔆 Fruit, and particularly the date, is often associated with fertility and fertility rites. In Roman times dates, because of their luscious taste and spiritual connections, were often used as an aphrodisiac during pre-nuptial activities. They are also considered to enhance the psychic senses.

♥ Our deepest emotional needs need to be cared for and looked after in a way that is different from normal.

■ Because dates are rather an exotic fruit, when we dream of them we are becoming conscious of the need for the rare or exotic in our lives. Equally, we may need sweetness and nurturing.

**DAUGHTER** – *see* **FAMILY**

**DAWN/DAY AND NIGHT**

☀ A form of spiritual illumination is quite often felt within this type of dream. There is a gradual awareness rather than a blinding flash of illumination. A new dawn can bring a great sense of hope. Day and night can represent opposites, as in black and white, boy and girl etc. Indeed, any two opposites may have relevance, and it is up to us to decide what opposition there is in our lives.

♥ Psychologically we are aware of the passage of time, of darkness or difficulty passing and perhaps the need to mark or celebrate this in some way. We often differentiate between two states in dreams, and the contrast between day and night highlights this.

■ To dream of a dawn or a new day represents a new beginning or a new awareness in circumstances around us. We are looking for different ways of dealing with old situations. Dreaming of both day and night indicates the cycle of time or of changes that will inevitably take place. Sometimes indication is given of the nature of a period of time.

**DAY/DATE**

☀ A certain date or day could point to information about a spiritual festival or anniversary that we have subconsciously retained and that may have relevance for us. When we dream of a day passing, or register that time has passed, we are alerting ourselves to the fact that we need to gauge time in some activity, or that action needs to be taken first before a second thing can happen.

♥ Very often the psyche gives us information in dreams which is precognitive and it is possible to be alerted to particularly important events in dream form. Time has no real meaning in dreams, so to note that time is measurable suggests that we are contemplating the validity of our lives.

■ In dreams, a day may also represent a much longer period of time than first thought. When a particular date is highlighted in a dream, we are either being reminded of something particularly significant – or possibly traumatic – in our lives or perhaps to consider the symbolism of the numbers contained in the date itself.

*Consult the entries for Numbers and Time for more information.*

**DEAD PEOPLE**

☼ To dream of dead people may suggest a link of a spiritual nature to our long-forgotten ancestors, and may deal with family patterns of belief. Loved ones who have died appearing in dreams show that the veil between this world and the next is very thin.

♡ Memories can remain buried for years and often when people who have died appear in dreams, we are being reminded of different times, places or relationships which will help us to deal with present situations.

▦ Dead people we have known appearing in dreams usually refer back to strong emotions we have had about those people, whether they are negative or positive. For instance, there may be unresolved anger or guilt we still hold and the only way we can deal with it is within a dream sequence.

*Also consult the entries for Death and Hearse.*

**DEAL**

☼ A deal in spiritual terms is a negotiation between two aspects of Self: the 'higher' part, which knows what is right from a cosmic perspective, and the lower part, which is more concerned with everyday matters.

♡ When there is some difficulty in integrating all parts of the personality we will often dream of a deal in order to clarify what action we need to take.

▦ As so much of everyday life is taken up with deals and negotiations we will often mirror such situations in dreams. To be dealing cards may suggest taking a gamble or a calculated risk.

⊞ In a woman's dream a deal is likely to highlight aspects of her masculine, more driven side but in a man's dream it may be the more intuitive skills which come to prominence. Both, of course, are skills required in efficient negotiation in the ordinary world.

**DEATH**

☼ Death is a transition from an awareness of the gross physical to the more spiritual self. It signifies the unseen aspect of life; omniscience, spiritual rebirth; resurrection and reintegration. To dream of our own death suggests that we are exploring our own feelings about death or our retreat from the challenge of life. The sensation of leaving the body is an aspect of the changes in consciousness necessary for a fuller understanding of the spiritual dimension.

♡ On an intellectual level we are becoming conscious of potentials we may have missed or not expressed fully and because of this we are no longer able to make use of them. We need to be sensitive to our ability to resurrect these talents. A change of awareness is taking place, and we may be going through some 'rite of passage' such as puberty to adulthood, maturity to old age and so on. Our own death can often be used in dreams to explore our perception of others' feelings about us.

🖫 Traditionally to dream of death indicated the possibility of a birth or a change in circumstances in one's own life or that of people around. Because in the past death held great fear, it also represented calamity, in the sense that nothing would ever be the same again. It was something that had to be experienced and endured rather than understood. In these present times, as peoples' attitudes change, death in a dream indicates a challenge we must confront. We need to adjust our approach to life and to accept that there can be a new beginning if we have courage.

*Also consult the entries for Coffin, Dead People and Grave.*

### DEBATE

✹ The spiritual implications of a debate within a dream are to do with ascertaining the merits of a positive versus a negative argument, where both are given an equal hearing.

♦ When we find that we are in a debate, it symbolizes some inner turmoil or conflict that is as yet unresolved. It also means that you will find closure to those unresolved issues.

🖫 Listening to a debate suggests that there are things going on that need careful consideration. Taking part in a debate signifies a more 'hands-on' approach is required in some areas of our life.

⚲ Since debate often contains both logic (a masculine trait) and emotion (a feminine one), men and women will weigh up the merits of the opposite perspective in a debate in dreams.

*You might like to consult the entry for Argue/Arguments.*

### DEBRIS – *see* DEMOLITION

### DEBT

✹ Power or energy that we feel we owe to a force other than ourselves may be depicted as a debt in dreams.

♦ Being unable to pay a debt suggests that we have run out of emotional or mental resources. Paying off a debt suggests that we have fulfilled our obligations.

🖫 As debt becomes more prevalent in everyday life, the anxieties associated with it will reflect in dreams as being chased or hounded. Figures of authority will also figure quite prominently. Dreaming of lost credit cards or cash can also symbolize debt.

*You might like to consult the entries for Credit and Money for further clarity.*

## DECADENCE

🔆 Decadence suggests a fall from grace or a debasement of the natural laws. It describes self-indulgence rather than a concern for global matters.

💗 Decadence suggests self interest and a profligate use of the resources we have. If we are content with the sense of decadence in a dream scenario we are learning to value ourselves better. If it distresses us then we need to assess how far and how much we are moving away from our own sense of self.

🔳 As poverty becomes more of a global issue, we become more conscious of the differences between lifestyles and just how decadent, materialistic and wasteful those who have enough can be. When this is highlighted in dreams, we would do well to pay attention to such matters in everyday life.

## DECAY

🔆 Decay in dreams is evidence of the natural cycle of life: growth, decline and regeneration. Out of decay comes new growth and knowledge.

💗 When something is decaying it is running out of energy. For it to appear in dreams indicates we must be prepared to allow things to run their natural course. Putrefaction is when the process of decay has gone past the point of no return.

🔳 In mundane terms, we have a situation in our lives – perhaps a work project or a relationship – that has come to a natural conclusion and does not need to be nurtured. The experience we have gained, however, can be put to good use.

*You might also like to consult the entry for Mould/Mouldy.*

## DECEIVE – *see* LIE

## DECIDE/DECISION

🔆 Decisions are an integral part of spiritual progression, and to be conscious of deciding on a particular course of action, for instance, suggests choosing between right and wrong or any other two polarities.

💗 Fear and doubt can prevent us from making the correct decisions or choices for us. Dreams will highlight these fears when often we are not even aware that they exist.

🔳 Often when we are unable to make a decision in waking life, dreams provide us with an answer to our dilemma by presenting answers in symbolic form and allowing us to observe the effect of our actions.

## DECORATE/DECORATION

🔆 Decoration is a way of honouring the divine and there is much symbolism attached to this from the altar cloths in Christian and Wiccan religions to food for the spirits in Thai Buddhist spirit houses. Dreams often access such spiritual knowledge.

◉ When we dream of decorating a room or dwelling place we are aware that changes need to be made in our environment, perhaps to utilize a particular vibration.

▦ Colour may be important in the way we decorate our dream rooms, as may be the articles we choose to have in our environment. When such an article is highlighted it suggests ways of enhancing our day-to-day lives by what it represents.

⊡ Men's and women's dreams may be very different in terms of the way they adorn their rooms. Traditionally it was thought that women were more drawn to frills and men to sleeker lines. If the decoration seems out of character we probably need to develop some aspect of creativity.

*You might like to consult the entries for Colour and Furniture/Furnishings for further information.*

## DEEP

◉ The Unknown, and therefore the unfathomable, is often symbolized by depth in some way – deep water, deep underground etc.

◈ We may be trying to understand archetypal patterns that have not been recognizable in the past. There is information available to us which we can only understand through being able to appreciate our own emotional depths.

▦ When we dream of the deep we are usually considering past family influences of which we may not be consciously aware. Patterns of behaviour are often repeated in families and it takes some dredging through family stories and myths to have us recognize such patterns.

*You might like to consult the entries for Abyss and Descent/Descending.*

## DEER – *see* ANIMALS

## DEFEAT

◉ To suffer defeat in a spiritual sense is to be overcome by negativity.

◈ To feel defeated is to recognize that opposing forces are too strong for us.

▦ To be defeated signifies that there are situations around us in the everyday in which we cannot achieve an advantage.

*You might also like to consult the entries for Argue/Arguments, Conflict, Fight and War for more information.*

## DEFECATE – *see* EXCREMENT IN BODY

## DEFEND/DEFENCE

◉ Defending anything in a dream is protecting it spiritually, perhaps from contamination or from penetration. Defending any type of sacred space would have this meaning.

◈ Defending our position suggests that there is a conflict of some sort in us, maybe of ideas or principles.

▨ Putting up a defence, perhaps a wall or barrier, signifies that we feel threatened in some way. We may have to justify our position over a situation in our waking lives.

⬛ If a woman is defending herself in a dream she is guarding against some kind of 'assault', often of her own private space. If a man has such a dream, it shows he will defend against his own vulnerability.

## DEFY/DEFIANT

☀ Originally 'to defy' meant to renounce our faith, but its more modern day meaning is to challenge belief or given wisdom.

♡ To be defiant suggests that we cannot accept and act on information we have been given.

▨ When we defy authority in dreams it is often because intrinsically we are aware that something is not right in our waking life.

## DELAY

☀ Delay from a spiritual perspective suggests that the time is not right for a particular event or course of action.

♡ If we are causing delay then we are not yet ready to take action: if someone else is the cause then we must wait for outside circumstances to be right.

▨ Delay can signify a lack of organization and can also, through dreams, allow the expression of frustration.

*You might like to consult the entry for Time.*

## DEMOLITION

☀ Fanaticism and anarchy (a need to break down or destroy an old order) can be demonstrated by demolition in a dream. Spiritually the idea of using the old debris as a foundation for the new is seen in the image of the Tower in the Tarot.

♡ We may be conscious of a build-up of emotional energy within us, which can only be handled by a breakdown of old attitudes and approaches. The 'debris' left behind after such a breakdown needs sorting through to discover what needs to be retained and what discarded.

▨ It rather depends on the circumstances in the dream whether demolition highlights major changes in the dreamer's life, or a self-inflicted trauma. If we are deliberately destroying something or carrying out the demolition we need to be in control, but if someone else is in charge we may feel powerless in the face of change. The debris in this case symbolizes the fall-out from such changes. Large amounts signify major adjustments are necessary.

*Consult the entry for Ruin/Ruins for further information.*

**DEMON**

☀ Although the word 'demon' originally came from the Greek word for 'deity', for many hundreds of years it was taken simply to mean spirit. In the modern day it is taken to be an evil spirit, one at odds with God, and has this meaning in dreams.

♥ Psychologists now believe that demons in dreams are often personifications of deeply held or ingrained fears. The colour of the demons will often give information as to their relevance. Red indicates extreme and black might represent fear.

▦ Passionate beings with their own agenda, demons may represent a particular type of personality that will not allow itself to rest until a task is completed.

*You might like to consult the entries for Colour, Devil, Fiend and Imp.*

**DEMONSTRATE/DEMONSTRATION**

☀ When we take part in a public demonstration we are declaring our allegiance to a belief or ideal.

♥ To demonstrate is to prove conclusively that something is possible. Often we will dream of a solution to a problem that proves to be workable.

▦ When we find ourselves demonstrating a skill that we did not know we have, it suggests a strand of creativity that needs to be explored.

*You might also like to consult the entry for Procession.*

**DENTIST**

☀ Dreaming of a dentist, since the emphasis is on the mouth, may signify that we are having difficulty in articulating our own Spiritual truth – that in which we believe.

♥ Because of its association with pain, a visit to the dentist in dreams may highlight fears or hurt that we have hidden. A dentist may signify that a particular type of healing is appropriate, such as the removal of 'decaying' information.

▦ In everyday life the development of teeth is thought to be a step towards speech and, therefore, correct communication. A dentist in dreams suggests that a degree of care is needed in what we are saying to others.

**DEPARTING –** *see* **JOURNEY AND LEAVE/LEAVING**

**DEPRESSION –** *see* **EMOTION AND WEEPING**

**DERELICT**

☀ A derelict building or person signifies a lack of hope, a 'lost sheep'.

♥ Since hope and faith are two prime motivators, anything that appears derelict suggests that we have lost the ability to move away from difficult circumstances.

🎖 When the energy has gone from a project or, for instance, a relationship, and it has lost focus, we may dream of dereliction. This is when there is no hope of re-energizing the project or relationship.

*Also consult the entry for Demolition.*

## DESCENT/DESCENDING

🌣 Going down into the underworld, the quest for mystic wisdom, rebirth and immortality are all shown in dreams by descent. It is a symbol for exploring the unconscious.

♡ Descent often signifies applying practical solutions to problems. We may fear a loss of status, and yet be aware of the positive aspects of such loss which include not having to have such high expectations of ourselves and others.

🎖 When we dream of a descent, such as coming down a mountain or steps, we are often searching for an answer to a particular problem. We need to be conscious of past trauma or something we have left behind and decide what we can learn from the experience.

*You may also wish to consult the entries for Deep and Fall/Falling*

## DESERT

🌣 A desert can symbolize desolation and abandonment, but also a place of contemplation, quiet and divine revelation.

♡ Desertion implies that all support has been removed or rejected so the idea of deserting a post, task or friend suggests a sense of inadequacy. Experiencing ourselves as having been deserted signifies being left to our own devices.

🎖 To dream of being alone in a desert signifies a lack of emotional satisfaction, loneliness or perhaps isolation. Dreaming of being in a desert with someone else may show that particular relationship is sterile, or going nowhere.

*You might also like to consult the entry for Abandoned.*

## DESERT ISLAND – *see* ISLAND

## DESK – *see* ALTAR AND TABLE

## DESTINATION

🌣 A Spiritual goal or aspiration is signified in dreams by knowing what our destination is.

♡ Destinations such as exotic and faraway places could signify our need for excitement and stimulation, or hopes we may have for the future.

🎖 Dreaming of trying to get to a particular destination would normally indicate a conscious ambition and desire. If the destination is not known to us, we may be moving into unknown territory, or be attempting something new and different. If we have difficulty in reaching our destination there may be difficulties associated with our aspirations.

*Also consult the entry for Journey.*

**DESTROY** – *see* DEMOLITION

**DEVIL**

The Devil tends to be seen as the personification of Evil, or Lucifer, who, incidentally, was originally supposed to bring enlightenment to the world. It does need to be borne in mind, however, that the Devil also represents the Ego, or part of us that refuses to 'return to the light'.

In order to deal with the out-of-control side of ourselves, we often need to have an object or image to confront. In dreams, as in fantasies, the Devil allows us to do this. If we fear our own wrongdoing, that fear can also manifest as the Devil.

In previous times, the figure of the Devil was one to be feared and hated. Our wilder, more instinctive side will often appear in dreams as the conventional figure with horns and a tail. Once it is understood as something to be confronted, as something belonging to all of us, the Devil loses its potency.

The Devil as Satan used to appear with some frequency in both men's and women's dreams. Now the image is more likely to be that of one of the Nature Gods such as Pan, and represents basic instincts and urges.

*You may also wish to consult the entries for Demon, Fiend and Imp.*

**DEVOUR**

Clearing evil or decay, or taking in good, is symbolized as devouring it – that is, eating it greedily. Kali, the Hindu mother goddess, as the keeper of the graveyard, demonstrates this, as do the devouring Gods such as Dionysus. Such clearing is a way of returning to source and receiving spiritual upliftment. Shamanic belief puts forward the theory that we take on the power of that which we eat. We are not allowed to eat our own totem animal, however.

If we ourselves are devouring something in a dream we may need to consider the way we nurture ourselves. We perhaps are not paying attention or giving enough respect to what we are doing.

When we dream of being devoured we are facing our fear of losing our sense of identity; of being consumed by something such as an obsession, an overwhelming emotion or drive, or of having to deal with something we cannot control.

*Also consult the entry for Eat/Eating.*

**DEW**

Spiritual refreshment, benediction and blessing are all symbols connected to dew.

We may need to accept that gentle, and not forceful or overpowering, emotion can cleanse us of whatever is troubling us.

▦ Dew or gentle rain falling in a dream can represent a sense of newness and refreshment we have perhaps not been able to obtain, except from an external source.

## DIADEM

✴ The diadem or tiara is perceived as an emblem of the Queen of Heaven and the circle of continuity. It often has 12 jewels, which are said to represent the 12 Tribes of Israel.

♡ There is always a magical feeling or sense of wonder associated with the diadem or tiara, and it can be taken to represent the magical and unknown. In dreams as in real life it is felt to confer status.

▦ The diadem or tiara in a dream often acknowledges the power of the feminine, or the ability to use the mental or intellectual abilities to obtain supremacy.

⊡ In a woman's dream she is more likely to be wearing a tiara, this being a feminine image. In a man's dream he is more likely to wear a crown or coronet – a less elaborate form of crown.

*You might like to consult the entry for Crown.*

## DIAMOND – *see* GEMS/JEWELS

## DICE/DIE

✴ Dice or a die, through the play on words, is a way of taking chances, which, in the spiritual sense, may be irrevocable and may lead to a 'death' – perhaps of an opportunity, for instance.

♡ If someone else is rolling the dice, we are leaving our fate in the hands of other people and must, therefore, consider whether we should run our lives according to their rules.

▦ To be playing with dice in a dream emphasizes the fact that we are playing with fate or taking chances in life, which we really ought to be considering more carefully.

*You may also like to consult the entries for Games and Gambling.*

## DICTATOR – *see* PEOPLE

## DIGGING/EXCAVATION

✴ Spiritually we need to have access to the characteristics of the unconscious. It will always take effort to uncover such aspects and this is symbolized by digging. Excavating, perhaps in the form of an archaeological or other professional type of digging, would suggest a more structured approach.

♡ On a creative level we may have realizations that are hard to access and must be dug out. Excavating objects can also imply that there is 'buried treasure' which belongs to the past.

🔲 Often when we begin the process of learning about ourselves we need to uncover those parts we have kept hidden, and this is shown in dreams as excavating a hole or digging up an object. If the act of digging is important then we are required to make an effort rather than simply wait for information to come to the surface.

*Also consult the entry for Mine/Miner.*

## DINOSAURS

🔆 We all have within us a chaotic past which has been a huge part of our lives. Spiritual progress, however, dictates that we understand that this part can be changed and our present selves can grow from that ability to change. Old standards are now extinct and will no longer stand up to scrutiny.

💗 We are in touch with an archaic or outmoded part of ourselves. Remembering that dinosaurs are extinct, and that for most people they are perceived as fossils, such a dream can recognize the part of ourselves that has become set in stone.

🔲 When we dream of monsters or prehistoric animals we are touching into very basic images which have the power to frighten and amaze us. Because they are considered to be so large, we need to be aware of whether it is their size or their power which is frightening. Urges as basic as this can threaten our existence, by either their size or power.

*You might also like to consult the entry for Prehistoric.*

## DIRECTION – *see* POSITION

## DIRTY

🔆 Evil or negative impulses are often represented in dreams as things or people being dirty. In the search for spirituality we may often feel dirty or contaminated by such negativity.

💗 To be dirty in a dream may indicate that we are not at ease with our own bodily functions. If someone we know has made us dirty or contaminated us it is an indication not to trust that person.

🔲 We will dream of being dirty when we are not operating within our own principles or when someone else's action has put us in a situation which we find compromises us.

## DISAGREE – *see* ARGUE/ARGUMENTS, CONFLICT AND WAR

## DISASTER

🔆 A disaster in dreams is any negative event that tests our beliefs and finer feelings. We do need to remember that the heightened sensations take us into areas within our psyche where we have perhaps not ventured before.

◈ Disasters such as crashing aeroplanes, falling buildings or other such images are presented to highlight extreme emotions such as fear, anger and anxiety.

▦ Many disasters in dreams echo difficulties in everyday life, pictured in such a way that they allow us to work through the problems. An exploding mine, for instance, depicts undue pressure or stress placed on an individual.

*You might like to consult the entries for Aeroplane, Buildings and Mines for additional clarification.*

## DISCIPLE – *see* PEOPLE

## DISCRIMINATION

◈ Being able to discriminate suggests that we have sufficient vision to be able to make spiritually correct choices, of choosing right rather than wrong, for instance.

◈ If we find we are being discriminated against in dreams we need to recognize and honour our own uniqueness.

▦ The need to discriminate and take the best option often comes up on a day-to-day basis. We often have to compare and contrast our alternatives. This reflects in dreams perhaps more vividly than in real life and allows us to discriminate in our choices.

*You might also like to consult the entry for Choice/Choose.*

## DISCOVER

◈ There is much spiritual information that is revealed only when we are ready for it; the sense of discovering our own truth is part of progress.

◈ Discovering the unexpected in dreams highlights information that is needed. The symbolism of the object or the idea will be important. Discovering a jewel, for instance, suggests something that is precious from an emotional perspective.

▦ When the correct method or information needed for carrying out a task on a work-a-day basis is not forthcoming it is possible that dreams will offer information that points us in the right direction and allows us to discover the answer.

## DISEASE – *see* ILL/ILLNESS

## DISK

◈ Divinity and power are represented spiritually by the disk, through its connection with the sun. It represents perfection and the renewal of life.

◈ The disk in a dream has emotionally the same significance as the sun, and can be considered both as a powerful source of information and initially of life itself.

🔲 A computer disk suggests that there is a great deal of information and knowledge available to us. As other forms of storage become available such knowledge enters the realms of the everyday.

## DISMEMBERMENT

🔆 Dismemberment of the body, or indeed any dream where some type of fragmentation takes place, is largely to do with being rendered powerless. It is the death, or rather dissolution, of the Self before reintegration and rebirth take place.

♥ Psychologically we need to take our old feelings and ideas apart to make sense of what is going on. This process has to take place before we can rebuild our lives.

🔲 A situation may be tearing us apart and drastic action may be necessary before we can recover our equilibrium.

*You may also like to consult the entries for Amputation and Limbs in the Body section.*

## DISSECT/DIVIDE

🔆 Any division or deliberate dissection into two parts or more suggests a movement away from unity, from a state of perfection.

♥ To divide into parts signifies creating manageable portions, perhaps breaking down a series of actions to understand them better. Crossing a divide is similar to crossing a chasm: we must face our own fears.

🔲 When we are dissecting a body or animal we are trying to learn how something works or what relationships the various parts might have with one another. This might apply to a task or project in waking life.

*You might like to consult the entries for Chasm and Half.*

## DIVING

🔆 Diving suggests the taking of spiritual risk. Skydiving suggests pitting ourselves against natural forces.

♥ We need to be extremely focused and attentive to dive successfully and must bring these qualities into play in a situation we are in in our waking lives.

🔲 To dream of diving can represent the need for freedom within our lives, although we may associate freedom with taking risks. We may need to burrow into our unconscious to find the ability to face anxiety.

*Also consult the entry for Water.*

## DIVORCE

🔆 To dream of divorce would suggest that there is a loss of integration in our personality and a potential difficulty in understanding spiritual matters.

♥ Divorce – that is, a sense of the severance of some kind of link – may also indicate the necessity to clarify our own relationship between the various facets of our personality. We are becoming conscious of the need to express emotion if we are to maintain our own integrity. We are moving into a new way of life, perhaps without the old support systems we have used.

▦ Dreaming of divorce may actually refer to our feelings about the other person in the dream, and perhaps our need to be free of responsibilities. It may simply highlight the need for a change in the relationship structure.

⊞ In any dream where the differences between male and female are highlighted, both men and women may be struggling with the conflict between logic and intuition.

## DOCTOR

❀ The presence of a doctor in dreams suggests the appearance of the healer within. We each have within us an aspect of spiritual knowledge, which is capable of reminding the physical body of its right to be well.

♥ It will depend what sort of doctor appears in our dream as to the correct interpretation. A surgeon would suggest the need to cut something out of our lives. A physician would indicate that careful consideration should be given to our general state, whereas a psychiatrist or psychologist signifies the need to look at our mental state. If the doctor is known to us he may stand as an authority figure.

▦ When we dream of a doctor we are aware that we need to give way to a higher authority in health matters. For older people the doctor may also represent the professional classes.

⊞ By and large a woman will tend to dream of the doctor as masculine, and a man the opposite. Only when the Shadow – the repressed parts of our personality – is understood will true healing take place.

*You might like to consult the entries for Analyst and Medication/Medicine as well as the information on Authority Figures in the People section.*

## DOG

❀ A dog symbolizes the guardian of the underworld. In Egyptian mythology this is depicted by Anubis, the dog-headed god, who guided the souls of the dead to the underworld – our most secret part.

♥ To dream of a pack of wild dogs portrays emotions and feelings of which we are afraid. To be chased by a black dog suggests a fear of depression.

▦ Dreaming of a dog depends on whether it is one known to us (such as a childhood pet), when it then may represent happy memories; if unknown it may signify the qualities of loyalty and unconditional love associated with dogs.

*Also consult the entry for Dog in Animals.*

## DOLL

The doll can be a representation of the soul of a particular person who can be helped, or harmed, by sympathetic magic or witchcraft. The puppet, far from being malign, is a doll that is fashioned for a particular purpose. In dreams it serves as a focus of energy.

We tend to learn through play, and for a doll to appear in a dream usually indicates the need to relearn some childhood lessons that we have forgotten. A puppet rather than a poppet can suggest that we are being manipulated.

A doll can depict either how we felt as a child, or a need for comfort. It may also express an undeveloped part of our personality.

*Consult the entry for Puppet for additional information.*

## DOLPHIN

In dreams the dolphin represents spiritual sensitivity and safety. They are known to be highly intelligent and to act instinctively in a supportive way.

The dolphin may portray the more playful side of our personality, but at the same time may make us aware of the trickster and behaviour that is unexpected. Dreaming of swimming with dolphins suggests putting ourselves in touch with, and appreciating, our own basic emotional nature. Coming from the depths – the unconscious – the dolphin represents the hidden side of ourselves that needs to be understood.

Dolphins are perceived by sailors as saviours and guides, as having special knowledge and awareness, and this is the image that surfaces in dreams.

## DONKEY – *see* HORSE IN ANIMALS

## DOOR

Spiritually a door represents the sheltering aspect of the Great Mother.

If the door in the dream is shut or difficult to open, it indicates we are creating obstacles for ourselves, whereas if the door is open we can have the confidence to move forward.

A door in a dream signifies a movement between two states of being. It can represent entry into a new phase of life, such as puberty or middle age. There may be opportunities available to us about which we must make deliberate decisions.

*You might like to consult the entry for Door in Buildings and to re-read the section on Archetypes in the Introduction*

## DOVE – *see* BIRDS

## DRAGON

The dragon is traditionally the Guardian of Power. The original of all dragons was a version of the serpent Tiamat Goddess of Chaos and

Darkness. In conquering the dragon, spiritually we become custodians of our own future.

◈ There is a heroic part in each of us which must face dangerous conflict in order to overcome the lower side of our natures and reach our inner resources. Dreaming of a dragon allows us that conflict.

▦ The dragon is a complex and universal symbol. Seen as both frightening and yet manageable, under certain circumstances it will represent in us our own untamed nature. We must come to terms with our own passions and chaotic beliefs. Often we can only achieve this through dreams, in an environment that has been suitably created.

*You might like to consult the entries for Fabulous Beasts and Monster.*

## DRAGONFLY

◈ Though the dragonfly's physical existence is short, it symbolizes immortality and regeneration.

◈ We may be pursuing a dream, but without any real focus as to what we actually want out of life. Our reactions are instinctive rather than logical.

▦ To dream of a dragonfly is to appreciate the need for freedom, but equally to recognize that freedom can be short-lived.

## DRAUGHT

◈ The Holy Spirit manifested as a rushing wind to enable the disciples to spread the Gospel. A draught suggests an unseen force or current, which creates almost imperceptible movement.

◈ Traditionally, a cold draught when working psychically indicates a visitation by Spirit. In dreams it suggests a communication from a hidden part of ourselves.

▦ To feel a draught in a dream is to be aware of an external force which could affect us or a situation we are in. To create a draught is literally to be attempting to clear the atmosphere.

*Also consult the entry for Wind.*

## DRAUGHTS/CHEQUERS – *see* GAMES

## DRINK

◈ Spiritually there is a belief that the drinking of wine is, or symbolizes, the imbibing of Divine life and power.

◈ Drinking, not necessarily of wine, in a dream may indicate our need for comfort and sustenance. Drinking – the taking in of liquid – symbolizes the interplay between the inner need to sustain life and external availability of nourishment. It also suggests our requirement for emotions that flow rather than getting stuck.

▦ To be drinking in a dream is to be absorbing or taking something in.

What we are drinking is also important, e.g. fruit juice would indicate we are aware of the need for cleansing and purity. The colour of what is being drunk is also important.

*Consult the entries for Alcohol/Alcoholic and Colours for further information.*

**DRIVE – *see* JOURNEY**

**DROWNING**

🜨 Drowning symbolizes an immersion in the Sea of Life, and therefore a loss of ego. We seem to have nothing to support our efforts.

🜨 When we are drowning in a dream this usually indicates we are in danger of being overwhelmed by emotions we cannot handle. We are fearful of allowing our emotions free expression.

🜨 Drowning may also indicate a perceived inability to handle a stressful situation around us at the time of the dream. We have been put in a situation over which we have no control. We may be 'floundering around' with no way of being able to escape from the difficulty.

*Also consult the entries for Swimming and Water.*

**DRUGS**

🜨 It has long been known that ingesting certain substances, particularly herbal derivatives, can alter perception. These can induce anything from a state of euphoria to a distortion of reality. This, however, can be dangerous – without knowledgeable supervision – since it is like using a crowbar rather than a key to open a door to the psyche.

🜨 We may be attempting to avoid reality and drugs can enable us to do this. They can also be a healing agent in restoring balance. In dreams, to be given drugs by a qualified person signifies that we have accepted someone else's greater knowledge. To be sold drugs illegally indicates that we are prepared to take unnecessary risks.

🜨 When drugs appear in a dream – whether self-administered or not – this suggests that we may need external help to enable us to change our inner perceptions. To be taking drugs suggests we feel we have relinquished control of a situation in our waking lives and are having to rely on external stimuli. To have an adverse drug reaction in dreams could mean that we fear madness. To be given drugs against our will indicates that we are being forced to accept an unpalatable truth.

*You might like to consult the entries for Alcohol/Alcoholic, Drunk and Medication/Medicine.*

**DRUM**

🜨 The drum is an instrument that beats a rhythm. Thus it comes to represent the sound of Creation, Divine Truth and Revelation.

◈ We may be seeking a more natural form of expression or a change of consciousness from the normal, everyday methods we use.

▦ To hear a drum in a dream indicates the basic rhythm needed to keep us sane and healthy. We need to be more in touch with our natural rhythms and primitive urges. To be playing a drum is taking responsibility for the rhythm of our own lives.

*You may also wish to consult the entries for Music/Rhythm and Musical Instruments.*

## DRUNK

◉ In previous societies it was an accepted part of life that, at certain times, drunkenness was allowed as a way of celebration or as a release of tension – hence the term a 'Bacchanalian revel'.

◈ Being drunk indicates the need to reconnect with a part of ourselves that can tolerate inappropriate behaviour. Ecstasy or extreme joy is reputedly achieved after inhibitions have been removed through getting drunk.

▦ To be drunk in a dream means that we are abandoning ourselves to irrational forces. We want to be free from responsibility and from having inhibitions. To make someone else drunk is to be forcing our irresponsibility on to someone else.

*Also consult the entries for Alcohol/Alcoholic and Drugs.*

## DUCK

◉ The duck as a bird is said to be a symbol of superficiality, presumably because it floats on the water rather than in it. In former times religious belief was tested by the ducking stool.

◈ We may need to allow the current of life to move us rather than taking action ourselves. Knowing when to go with the flow suggests a kind of innate wisdom. In dreams, ducking to avoid an obstacle demonstrates the need to be careful.

▦ As always, other circumstances in the dream may indicate the true relevance of the symbol. A toy duck may denote the childlike part of ourselves. To be feeding the ducks may show some kind of therapeutic or calming activity is important. To be eating duck suggests a treat or celebration in store.

*Also consult the entry for Birds.*

## EAGER

⚜ Eagerness signifies a passionate commitment to a cause or principle.

♥ To be eager in dreams, for instance for a particular outcome, highlights our need for emotional support.

▦ When we feel deeply about a subject we become focused on the matter in hand, and able to apply concentration. Eagerness is a component of the passion we feel.

## EAGLE

⚜ The eagle represents a form of spiritual victory and the ability to be dispassionate.

♥ We can take authority for our own lives and have the ability to use our intellect to succeed. Using the image of an eagle as a starting point, we can become objective and take a wider viewpoint than we have done previously. This will help us to release ourselves from old ideas or attitudes.

▦ An eagle signifies inspiration and strength. As a bird of prey, the eagle is capable of making use of all the opportunities available to it, the implication being that we can learn to do the same.

*Also consult the entry for Birds for further information.*

## EARLY – *see* TIME

## EARN/EARNINGS – *see* WAGES

## EARTH/EARTHQUAKE

⚜ Earth is the Great Mother and is synonymous with fertility. An earthquake represents Spiritual upheaval.

♥ We all have the need to be grounded and practical but need support to be so. If we find ourselves under or trapped by earth in dreams it shows we need to be more aware of, and understand, our unconscious drives and habits. Old opinions, attitudes and relationships may be breaking up and causing concern. When we are conscious of an earthquake, our basic emotional stability will have been called into question.

▦ Dreaming of an earthquake alerts us to an inner insecurity with which we must deal before it overwhelms us. There is great inner change and growth taking place, which could cause upheaval. To dream of the planet Earth is to take account of the supportive network we have in place and those attitudes and relationships we take for granted. We are searching for some kind of parental love or social order. Soft earth particularly links with the need for mothering or tactile contact.

⚐ Symbols and images relating to earthiness and the nurturing of others will be more likely to appear in a woman's dream than in a man's. Equally, as the earth is put more at risk, men will be likely to recognize the destructive element within themselves.

*Consult Archetypes in the Introduction for fuller information on the Great Mother.*

## EAST

☀ The East in spiritual terms has from ancient time suggested the spring, a time for hope and youth. The archangel for the East is Raphael, Healer of the world.

♡ We may be looking towards new life or a new beginning. The magical element associated with the East is Air and the colour is yellow; these significances often reveal themselves in dreams.

▨ Specifically dreaming of the East indicates we are looking at the mysterious and religious side of ourselves. We link with instinctual belief as opposed to logical reasoning.

*You might also like to consult the entries for Dawn/Day and Night, Elements and Position.*

## EASTER EGG

☀ An Easter egg is associated with spring, rebirth and resurrection.

♡ Dreaming of an Easter egg indicates there is a great deal of potential available to us on a mental level that needs releasing. There is an element of celebration about life that needs to be maintained.

▨ The Easter egg is a pagan symbol of renewal and in dreams often takes us back to childhood feelings of promise and wonder. It may also alert us to the passage of time, since the mind will often produce symbols of times and seasons rather than actual dates.

⚐ Arising from the symbolic meaning of eggs, when a woman dreams specifically of an Easter egg her attention may be being drawn in a non-threatening way to her own fertility. For a man such a dream is more likely to be to do with his innate sense of timing.

*Also consult the entry for Egg.*

## EAT/EATING

☀ There is a belief that we are reputed to become what we eat, so to feed ourselves spiritually we perhaps should eat the best food possible, putting ourselves as much in touch with nature as possible. This can have a holistic effect on us, putting us more closely in touch with our own spirituality, often through dreams.

♥ Dreaming of eating may denote that we lack some basic nutrient or feedback in our lives. To not eat or refuse food indicates an avoidance of growth and change. We may be attempting to isolate ourselves from others or be in conflict with ourselves over our body image. Being eaten in a dream signifies we are aware of being attacked by our own – or possibly other people's – emotions and fears or by our internal drives. Being eaten by a wild animal shows the likelihood of us being consumed by our more basic, animal nature.

▨ To be eating in a dream shows that one is attempting to satisfy one's needs or hunger. Hunger is a basic drive and we need to realize that only once such a drive is met can we move forward to satisfying our more aesthetic needs.

*Consult the entries for Devour, Food and Nourishment for further information.*

### ECLIPSE

☀ On a spiritual level, an eclipse can represent a loss of faith, a darkening of the light which guides us.

♥ We are about to go through a period of difficulty when we could find ourselves unable to maintain our usual cheerfulness. Covering up a source of illumination and enlightenment, an eclipse can also represent being forced to cover our emotions through external circumstances.

▨ Dreaming of an eclipse signifies our fears and doubts about our own success. Others around us seem to be more important or able than we are, which does not allow us to shine or excel at what we are doing.

*Consult the entries for Moon and Planets for further information*

### ECOLOGY

☀ As ecology is the branch of science that deals with relationship and interaction, in a spiritual sense it signifies the action between the spiritual and physical realms.

♥ As the Earth becomes more threatened, issues of climate change, conservation and preservation will become part of our everyday concerns and, therefore, part of our dreams. Any of these issues – particularly climate change – can represent a change in emotional focus.

▨ Dreams to do with ecological concerns usually focus on the efficient use of resources and it is this meaning which will often arise in dreams whether those resources are personal, work-related or of more global impact.

*Also consult the entries for Climate, Conservation and Earth/Earthquake.*

### EDEN – *see* PARADISE

### EDGE

☀ An edge suggests a changeover from one state of awareness to another, being on the brink, or about to begin a new spiritual phase.

◈ An edge signifies a lip or rim that may seem like an obstacle or difficulty initially. The kerb on a pavement marks its edge, but can also be a hazard. To be on edge in a dream suggests we are under some emotional pressure that may not yet have surfaced in waking life.

▦ To actually be on the edge of something in dreams may mean that we have to change our perspective about our lives.

*Consult the entries for Cliff and Threshold for further information.*

## EDUCATION

❀ Education can be taken as a symbol of Spiritual Awareness.

◈ Since dreaming of education usually takes us back to a former, less responsible state, we need to apply knowledge from the experiences we have had to enable us to deal with a present situation.

▦ To dream of a place of education, such as a school or college, indicates that we should be considering our own need for discipline or disciplined action. We are perhaps inadequately prepared for a task we are to perform, and need to access more knowledge.

*Also consult the entries for School, Teacher and University.*

**EEL** – *see* SERPENT AND SNAKE IN ANIMALS

**EFFIGY** – *see* STATUE

## EGG

❀ The life principle and the germ of all things are said to be contained in the Cosmic Egg, which spiritually represents our potential and power to be perfect.

◈ We have a sense of wonder to do with the miracle of life, and a realization that there is much to plan – a gestation period – before we can enjoy life to the full. We may have to withdraw and contemplate before we can undertake new learning experiences.

▦ The egg is the symbol of unrealized potential, of possibilities yet to come, so to dream of an egg indicates that we have not made ourselves fully conscious of our natural abilities. To be eating an egg shows the need to take in certain aspects of newness before we can fully explore a different way of life.

⊡ For a woman, an egg will usually have links with fertility, whether her own or someone else's. In a man's dream an egg more often suggests potential.

*Also consult the entry for Easter Egg.*

**EIGHT** – *see* NUMBERS

## EJACULATION

❀ From a spiritual viewpoint, ejaculation may signify a loss of power or 'the little death'.

◊ The act of ejaculation in dreams may be the giving up of old fears and doubts about ourselves and our sexual prowess.

▦ Our instinctive attitude to sex often becomes apparent in dreams through the sexual act, and to ejaculate in a dream may be an effort to understand negative feelings. It could also simply be indicative of the need for release, and the satisfaction of sexual needs.

⊡ Most teenage boys have what are called 'wet' dreams – or more properly nocturnal emissions – when they do actually ejaculate in sleep. These usually occur before the youngster has fully come to terms with the changes occurring in his body.

*Also consult the entry for Sex/Sexual Images for further information.*

## EJECT

☼ To be ejected means to be thrown out and in a spiritual sense suggests being punished for a misdemeanour.

◊ To eject an object in dreams is to signify getting rid of a feeling or emotion – whatever is symbolized by the object – in a forcible fashion.

▦ From a purely pragmatic viewpoint, any ejection signifies complete out-of-hand rejection of a principle or idea.

⊡ The act of ejection implies the use of force. In a woman's dream such an image may imply that she must become more forceful. In a man's dream it may mean that he needs to be more focussed.

## ELDER/ELDERLY

☼ The elders in a tribal society traditionally had the wisdom of age and experience. Spiritually, therefore, they had the right to guide others. This gives a similar significance to them as authority figures today. It is in this sense that the Wise Old Man represents an inner wisdom.

◊ From an emotional perspective, in dreams the elderly can be accorded respect and may represent knowledge, power and understanding.

▦ The elderly in dreams can symbolize old fashioned or outdated values and methods of operating, as well as those that are to be honoured.

⊡ In a woman's dream the elders or the elderly may suggest a more matriarchal aspect. In a man's dream this may be more paternalistic. It will, of course, depend on whether the gender of the dream figures is recognized.

*You might also like to consult the entry for People.*

## ELECTION – *see* VOTE

## ELECTRICITY

☼ Electricity symbolizes the greater Spiritual Power. Without an efficient, well-understood method of using this power, however, it can be dangerous or harmful.

◈ If in a dream we receive what seems to be an electric shock it shows we are not protecting ourselves from danger and need to be more aware of external events. A sudden jolt can either be destructive or bring us back in line. The muscle jerk as we fall asleep might be interpreted by the dreaming mind as an electric shock.

▦ Electricity often represents power and it will depend on the context of the dream which aspect of power is being highlighted. To dream of electrical wires is to be aware of our capability and perhaps our use of energy, while to dream of switches is to be aware of the ability to control situations around us.

## ELEMENT/S

☀ Since the word 'element' means first principle, spiritually this can mean the Creator. The elements Fire, Air, Water and Earth are the first principles of creation. The Chinese way of thought includes Metal as the fifth element. It is these core meanings that come across in dreams.

◈ Water is the element most strongly associated with emotion and tends to have this significance in dreams. Air represents intellect. In magical terms each element has its own significance and direction. It is these correspondences that may first appear in dreams.

▦ Fire represents energy and power and Earth represents stability. In dreams, therefore, where these elements are prominent, we are often considering how best to use these qualities within a particular situation.

*Consult the entries for Earth/Earthquake, East, Fire, North, South, Water and West.*

## ELEPHANT – *see* ANIMALS

## ELEVEN – *see* NUMBERS

## ELIXIR

☀ In alchemy an elixir is capable of prolonging life and of transmuting base metal into gold. In spiritual terms, therefore, it is the power of transformation.

◈ A substance such as an elixir, which has undergone several processes to reach a state of purity, symbolizes a process of psychological change which many people go through, bringing understanding of ourselves and others.

▦ In mundane terms an elixir is a distillation of the essence of things, so can signify the need to return to basics and simplify matters in order to find the most efficient solution.

*You might also like to consult the entry for Alchemy.*

## ELOPING/ELOPEMENT

☀ Elopement signifies a union – spiritual or otherwise – particularly in adversity.

◈ In a dream, planning an elopement is trying to create conditions where some sort of integration within aspects of our personalities can take place. Such changes may upset and disturb others in the meantime.

▦ Dreaming of eloping, particularly with someone you know, is trying to escape from a situation that could ultimately be painful. We must maintain a balance between the need for emotional and/or material security.

▐ Since men and women would in waking life view eloping from different perspectives – for men the 'rescuing' of the maiden and for women being rescued – such dreams can allow us to explore the need to escape from different perspectives.

### EMAIL

◈ Spiritually, an email signifies fast, efficient communication.

◈ As the email – mail by electronic transfer – takes over from the letter in ordinary life, in dreams it becomes both a more immediate source and purveyor of necessary information.

▦ In dreams, a message by email has for most people moved beyond its initial use as communication in business and become, as in waking life, a way of expressing immediate thoughts and ideas. If we are sending an email in dreams we have information which others may need.

*Also consult the entries for Communication and Letter for further information.*

### EMBERS

◈ The embers of a fire will symbolize a spiritual energy that is beginning to die down, to lose its potency.

◈ Embers suggest emotions that have moved beyond a clear expression. Whatever has been our passion is beginning to wane.

▦ As embers are what is left when material has been consumed by fire, we may need to decide whether or not a project or idea needs reviving with new input or allowed to die away quietly.

*You might also like to consult the entries for Ashes and Fire.*

### EMBEZZLE – *see* STEALING

### EMBLEM

◈ An emblem is a symbol, a pictorial representation of something that allows the mind to make a connection. Spiritually, therefore, it is a way of changing our perception.

◈ In a more technological age an emblem will have less connection with heraldry, a former source of emblems, and more to do with commercial concerns. A particular emblem or logo in dreams usually has some kind of personal resonance for us.

▣ An emblem, much like the knight's standard of old, is a rallying point or a call for loyalty. It is also an easily recognized instruction as in road signs. In dreams, once we have sorted out the symbolism, it often performs this function.

*Also consult the entry for Badge/Brooch.*

**EMBRYO**

✺ The core of physical being is the embryo, a union of masculine and feminine principles. This therefore symbolizes the centre of Creation.

♥ We are linking back to conception, to a point where life begins and takes on meaning. We may need to look at the process of becoming consciously knowledgeable of all that we are or can be.

▣ To dream of an embryo or foetus is to become aware of an extremely vulnerable part of ourselves. We may also be making ourselves aware of a new situation in our lives, one which has not got beyond a germ of an idea.

⟦⟧ Since a woman is more intimately concerned with the formation of an embryo, her dreams may be more connected with the processes of development rather than the existence of a child. In a man's dream an embryo need not have the symbolism of a foetus, but rather the rudiments of an idea.

*Also consult the entry for Baby in People.*

**EMERALD – *see* GEMS/JEWELS**

**EMERGENCY**

✺ Experiencing an emergency in a spiritual sense is having to deal with the unexpected, which may test our perceived limitations.

♥ Any emergency puts our emotions under stress and so it is in dreams. If we are under stress in waking life we may dream of an emergency and equally if there is an emergency in real life we may dream of explosions and other such images.

▣ What seems like an emergency to one person may not be so to another. Anxiety dreams often contain some element of the necessity for immediate action.

*You might also like to consult Accident and Explode/Explosion.*

**EMIGRATE**

✺ Emigration symbolizes moving away from our perceived comfort zone.

♥ When we dream of emigrating we are leaving behind the known for the unknown. Implicit in this is the idea of new experiences, new ways of thought and new friends. The method of emigration – train, plane or other means – may be important.

▣ In the ordinary everyday world we do not often have the opportunity to make radical changes. Dreaming of emigration alerts us to the possibility of leaving a situation we are in and doing something completely different.

*Consult the entries for Aeroplane, Boat/Ship, Journey, Train and Transport for further information.*

## EMOTIONS

✵ Our emotional requirement, particularly responsiveness to the more subtle energy of spirituality, allows us to begin the process of self-development. A 'lifting of the spirits' is indeed a change in consciousness and perhaps a reaching towards something beyond ourselves.

◈ Occasionally, in order to understand a dream, it is easier to ignore the symbolisms and concentrate on the moods, feelings and emotions that have surfaced. This will often give us a clearer interpretation of our state of mind, rather than confusing ourselves by trying to interpret myriad symbols.

▦ Within the framework of a dream our emotions can seem very different to those we have in everyday life. They may be more extreme, for instance, almost as though we have given ourselves freedom of expression, or we may be able to notice that there are strange swings of mood. Thus joy is extreme pleasure and despair a lack of hope. Negative emotions such as the latter are often easier to acknowledge within dreams rather than in real life.

*You might also wish to consult the entries for Anger, Hysterics and Weeping.*

## EMPLOYMENT

✵ Spiritual employment suggests using our talents and gifts effectively for the Greater Good.

◈ When we are fully employed and properly rewarded our attention is very focused on what we are doing. To dream of being employed in a job other than our own can suggest that we have issues about satisfaction and lifestyle choices.

▦ Dreams about employment are often more to do with issues of personal satisfaction. Since employment can also represent the way that other people think and feel about us, such dreams will contain an element of self- assessment.

*You might also like to consult the entries for Unemployment and Work.*

## EMPTY

✵ Spiritually, any sort of experience that brings about a sense of emptiness signifies the Void.

◈ We may need space to be ourselves in order to come to terms with what is occurring in our lives. To be in an empty house or building denotes the fact that we have left behind old attitudes and habits.

◼ To experience emptiness in a dream indicates there is a lack of pleasure and enthusiasm. We could be suffering from a sense of isolation, or perhaps of not having anything to hold on to. We may have had expectations that cannot be realized.

*You might like to consult the entries for Abyss and Void.*

## ENCHANTRESS

◈ An enchantress exudes the destructive side of the Feminine, represented by, for instance, Lilith, the first wife of Adam, who created demons in anger, or the Hindu goddess Mohini.

◈ The enchantress can appear in dreams when a woman begins to come to terms with her self-destructive side. She is to be understood rather than feared.

◼ The enchantress is such a strong image within both the masculine and feminine psyches that she can appear in dreams in many guises. She is the feminine principle in its binding and destroying aspect; the evil witch or the beautiful seductress. She has the power to create illusion and the ability to delude others.

*You might like to consult Archetypes in the Introduction as well as the entry for Siren for further clarification.*

## ENCLOSED/ENCLOSURE

◈ Spiritually, any enclosure represents the protective aspect of the Great Mother.

◈ Aspects of ourselves that are too frightening, disturbing or private to be allowed full expression are often perceived as enclosed spaces. To be in an enclosed space suggests an exploration of these aspects. To be outside this space signifies a fear of them.

◼ In dreams, the defence mechanisms we put in place to prevent ourselves from deeply feeling the impact of such things as relationships, love, anxiety or pain can often manifest as an enclosed space. Restraints and constraints can appear as actual walls and barriers.

*Consulting the Introduction for information on the Great Mother and also the entries for Barrier and Walls will further help in interpreting your dream.*

## ENCOURAGE

◈ Encouragement in dreams is often symbolized by a parental, authority type of figure or an easily recognized spiritual being.

◈ There is an inner aspect of our personality that knows what is right for us. This will often appear in dreams, albeit as differing characters, to encourage us when we cannot consciously make a decision.

◼ To encourage is to 'give heart to' and from a practical perspective any positive dream images can do just that. Waking from a dream with a sense of being able to move on successfully or to take positive action comes from that sense of inner encouragement.

## END/ENDING

🔅 An ending from a spiritual viewpoint indicates a successful conclusion. To be at the end can mean exploring the subconscious and sometimes the consideration of death.

◈ A situation that may have given us problems is coming to a natural end. There need no longer be such concern.

🔳 To dream of there being an end or an ending to something signifies the reaching of a goal, or a point at which things must inevitably change. We need to decide what we can leave behind, and what must be taken forward. We must decide what we value most.

## ENEMY

🔅 Any spiritual conflict may have us cast a dream character as an enemy. An enemy is 'not a friend', someone who does not have our welfare at heart.

◈ By definition, an enemy is someone who is a threat to us, perhaps emotionally, perhaps from the point of view of integrity. Dreaming of such a figure highlights such a situation.

🔳 When we are in a confrontational situation the opponent will become the enemy, particularly in dreams. By working through the dream scenario we are able to deal with the actual situation in waking life.

*You might also like to consult the entry for Oppose/Opponent.*

## ENGINE

🔅 An engine is symbolic of our own Spiritual inner motivations and drives.

◈ To perceive a diesel or railway engine may be putting us in touch with our own inner power or principles. Depending on the type, the engine can sometimes represent the sexual act.

🔳 The motivating drive or energy that we need within a situation can be perceived in dreams as an engine. When the dream seems to concentrate on the mechanical action of the engine, we may need to be looking at the more dynamic pragmatic ways of dealing with our lives. To be removing the engine could indicate a health problem, perhaps putting our health at risk by overdoing it.

*You might also wish to consult the entries for Car, Engine, Piston and Transport.*

## ENGINEERING

🔅 Spiritual engineering signifies gaining control of our own inner power and being able to make use of it.

◈ Engineering suggests the ability, through techniques and mechanical means, to use forces that are not normally available to us. To dream of engineering in this way highlights our ability to take control of power that is external to us. We are able to manipulate (influence) events in order to achieve our goals.

To dream of engineering is to link with our ability to construct. This is our ability to create a structure that will either allow us to move forward or will make life easier for us. To dream of engineering works – as in roadworks – is to recognize the need for some adjustment in part of our lives. *Also consult the entry for Machine for further information.*

## ENGRAVE/ENGRAVING

An engraving is a carving of special meaning, either because of its content or its craftsmanship. In dreams the spiritual relevance will be particularly highlighted.

When we dream of engraving an article, we are creating an object that has personal meaning. We may be recording information or marking a special event.

If we dream of finding an engraved article we might consider it as a message from the past. There is the potential for it to hold secret information. Following the fashion of engraving an article to mark an achievement or special event, it will have the same meaning as an accolade. *You might like to consult the entry for Inscription for further clarity.*

## ENORMOUS – *see* SIZE

## ENTER/ENTRANCE

Because of the symbolism of moving from the external to an inner enclosed space, an entrance signifies the Eternal Feminine. It can also symbolize a new beginning.

When we need to be in touch with the hidden side of ourselves, the intuitive or more 'knowing' side, and have the knowledge and ability to experience ourselves in new ways, we will often dream of a secret entrance, usually opening inwards.

An entrance in a dream has the same significance as a door, representing a new area of experience, or the new experience itself. Such a dream often signifies the need to make changes, to create new opportunities, perhaps to explore the unknown. The entrance, often a door, gate or similar, will often open outwards. *You might also consult the entries for Door and Gate.*

## ENVIRONMENT – *see* THE INTRODUCTION AND LANDSCAPES

## EPIDEMIC/PLAGUE

Spiritually an epidemic constitutes a generalized plague, infection or contamination of ideas and concepts.

For an epidemic/plague to take hold people would need to be capable of being contaminated. From an emotional perspective in dreams an epidemic might suggest some kind of group hysteria.

To dream of an epidemic suggests that we are under some pressure, perhaps to maintain our own viewpoint or integrity in the light of group pressure.

## EQUAL/EQUALITY

Any image that portrays things as being equal suggests that there is an intrinsic state of balance; spiritually, matters are as they should be.

Equal suggests 'the same as' and also implies that a comparison has been made. This may be whether a particular dream emotion is valid or not, or even if we have come across similar circumstances before.

Any dream of equality can highlight our relationships with siblings or with work colleagues. We may have issues that cannot be properly dealt with in waking life, and therefore our mind will try to resolve these concerns through dreams.

As women's equality has become more important, women may dream of perceived unfairness, whereas men may feel themselves to be threatened or under pressure. As equality is established, both may dream of the right to self-expression.

## EROSION

Erosion being the wearing down of a hard substance, it symbolizes submission to higher spiritual forces or principles.

Extreme emotion can be very wearing, so often when we are under stress we can dream, for instance, of a river eroding its banks or of the sea wearing away a cliff.

Such an image can suggest that, by perseverance, we are able to overcome difficulties. There may not be an immediate solution to a problem, but by working away at it, it can be solved.

*You might also like to consult the entry for Cliff.*

## ERUPTION – *see* EXPLODE/EXPLOSION AND VOLCANO

## ESCAPE

Escape represents our own need for spiritual freedom and the ability to consciously move on.

Trying to escape from someone signifies that we are feeling threatened. It is possible that anxiety or past trauma means we are unable to do anything other than try to escape from the situation itself.

When we dream of escape we are trying to move beyond – or to avoid –

difficult feelings. We may be trying to run away from responsibility or from duty.

🔰 Broadly, escape in a woman's dream will have an emotional content perhaps triggered by fear. In a man's dream the reason is likely to be more considered.

**ESTIMATE** – *see* **QUOTE/QUOTATION**

**EVAPORATION**

☀ Fire and water combined is an alchemical symbol for the transformative power of the Spirit.

☯ By raising one's consciousness, the energy within a situation can be changed for the better. We have it within our power to create opportunities for transformation.

▦ To be aware of water in a dream and then realize that it has evaporated is to recognize the transformation that can take place, once emotion is dealt with properly.

**EVENING**

☀ Evening signifies old age, wisdom and many years of Spiritual experience.

☯ The evening can be a synonym for twilight and the boundaries of our conscious mind. At this time there may be 'apparitions' around, of which we do not become aware until we start working with the unconscious.

▦ When we are aware of it being evening in a dream, we need to recognize the fact that we need time for ourselves – perhaps relaxation and quiet peace.

*Also consult the entries for Dawn/Day and Night and Time.*

**EVIL**

☀ Evil in the sense of moral wickedness is often personified in dreams by the figure of the Devil – itself a corruption of Lucifer the light bearer.

☯ Evil is an expression of disapproval of that which cannot be explained away. Any violent action might be interpreted as evil – against the norm. Any darkness can also be seen as evil since for some time the colour black has been associated with it.

▦ To experience evil in a dream is usually to be conscious of our own urges, which we have judged to be wrong. Other aspects of evil, such as inappropriate action by others, may be experienced as dread and disgust.

*You might like to consult the entries for Dark/Darkness, Demon and Devil.*

**EVOLUTION**

☀ Evolution in the spiritual sense is the opening out to a new and better state of being.

⟡ To experience evolution in dreams is to be part of a process of growth. To evolve is to progress from one stage of existence to another. The whole process of dreaming could in itself be said to be a process of evolution, particularly when we dream in series.

▦ Dreaming of evolution and its associated issues such as the natural development of flora and fauna can be a way of reminding ourselves of the steps needed to develop a project from start to finish.

## EXAM/BEING EXAMINED

✸ There is recognition of the need for spiritual examination and a degree of objectivity in the way we deal with problems.

⟡ We may be in the habit of setting ourselves tests of self-value, or habitually be concerned with our accomplishments. To be late for an examination or to be unable to take it suggests fears and doubts about our own competence. There are many instances recorded of people having been abducted by 'aliens,' of having been examined, and then returned to earth. Opinions vary as to whether these were dreams or not.

▦ Dreaming of examinations (particularly educational ones) is usually connected with self-criticism and the need for high achievement. We may be allowing others to set our standards of morality and success for us. Being examined by a doctor indicates concerns over our own health.

*Also consult the entries for Aliens/Alienated and Tests.*

## EXCHANGE

✸ Spiritually any exchange signifies the idea of give and take.

⟡ In dreams, as in real life, to be making an exchange suggests we are not satisfied with what we had originally. Dreaming of the stock exchange signifies the excitement of taking a calculated risk.

▦ An exchange suggests that someone or some circumstance has initiated the need for change. To be exchanging clothes with someone signifies our need for a new persona.

## EXCOMMUNICATE

✸ Technically, to be excommunicated is to be denied access to the sacraments, so in dreams signifies being prevented from communicating with the Divine

⟡ Emotionally, to find ourselves excommunicated in dreams suggests being cut off from a source of comfort.

▦ As humans we have a strong need at times to belong to groups. When we dream of being excommunicated we must cope with feelings of rejection, and perhaps of disapproval.

**EXCREMENT**

🔆 In ancient times the power of the person was said to be contained in his excrement. Now, dreaming of it is more likely to indicate a sense of relief, a letting go of old beliefs.

♡ Dreams of excrement suggest that there are certain aspects of our lives which we have used up and need to expel. Large quantities of excrement indicate that we may be feeling overwhelmed.

▥ When we dream of faeces or excrement we are returning to an infant level of expression and pleasure in bodily functions. Experiences we have had may have been relevant at the time but we now need to let them go. More negatively, we may feel that we have to process other peoples' negativity.

*You might like to consult the entries for Excrement in Body and for Toilet.*

**EXECUTE**

🔆 An execution often suggests a violent conclusion. Its secondary meaning (completing a duty or task) has more resonance with the spiritual significance of such a dream.

♡ There is a sense of coercion – of having to – in the idea of execution of a task. If we tend to be driven by our emotions this will come across in dreams

▥ Violence of any sort in dreams usually signifies that something is badly out of balance, so to dream of an execution may signify that we are acting (wrongly) more from an intellectual viewpoint than from a feeling perspective.

*You might also like to consult the entries for Guillotine, Punish/Punishment and Violence.*

**EXHIBIT/EXHIBITION**

🔆 To dream that we are being exhibited probably means that our spiritual identity is being questioned. When we are at an exhibition we are being presented with new ideas.

♡ Psychologically we do not appreciate being inspected like an exhibit, so this type of dream may show some disquiet about the way people regard us.

▥ An exhibition hall tends to be a place where similar objects are grouped together, so from a mundane perspective would denote such a situation in working life, possibly uncovering a difficulty with being managed too closely.

*Consult the entry for Exam/Being Examined for further clarification.*

**EXIT**

🔆 Spiritually an exit can suggest that we must consider leaving a situation that is not giving us the sanctuary we need. This may mean that we must consider our concept of death. This does not suggest death itself, merely the concept.

❧ An exit is a way out, so for this to be highlighted suggests that we need to be aware of the ability to bring an end to an emotional problem.

❧ If an exit is barred, there is little that we can do except find another way out. If in dreams we seem to have a choice of exits then we have a number of possibilities that will move us into a different space. If we cannot see the exit, we need to consider our options in a workaday situation.

*You might also like to consult the entries for Death, Door and Leave/Leaving.*

## EXORCISE/EXORCISM

❧ Spiritually exorcism depicts a rite or ceremony deliberately designed to get rid of negativity and evil. It was specifically designed to expel evil spirits, but now has the symbolism of getting rid of negativity.

❧ When emotion becomes unbearable, specific action needs to be taken to exorcise the bad feeling. In dreams we can find ourselves banishing evil, which gives us the clarity to function properly.

❧ Dreaming of exorcism suggests that there is a situation or occurrence in waking life that needs dealing with promptly. Whether we choose to use dramatic methods is a choice we must make.

*You might also like to consult the entries for Ceremony, Evil, Rite/Ritual and Spiritual Imagery in the Introduction.*

## EXPLODE/EXPLOSION

❧ An explosion in a spiritual sense would suggest a revelation of some sort, a welling up from the depths rather than caused by external factors.

❧ A forceful explosion of an emotion – anger, fear or sexual release for instance – can accomplish a cleansing. A dream may be a safe space in which to accomplish this, the emotion having been suppressed for some time.

❧ An explosion in a dream usually indicates a release of energy in a forceful way, which will allow us to make changes in the way we express ourselves or in the life we live. Apparently destructive, the outcome may be positive in that the debris has to be cleared away.

*You might like to consult the entries for Atom Bomb, Bomb, Demolition, Earth/ Earthquake and Nuclear Explosion.*

## EXPOSE/EXPOSURE

❧ Exposure has two connotations spiritually. The first suggests vulnerability and the second the ability to reveal – for instance, a truth.

❧ When we feel exposed in dreams it suggests that we have been made emotionally vulnerable, that the defences we put up have been stripped away. To expose an object or information ourselves suggests that something is hidden that will be revealed.

▣ When a particular task or project is not going well, we may find our self doubts prevent us from making progress. A dream that helps us deal with these doubts and fears often has elements of exposure in them, such as digging for treasure or emptying a cupboard.

▣ Of necessity in relationships, we have to open up to someone else. In both men and women this may lead to dreams of exposure.

## EXTINCT

▦ When energy is perceived as extinct it has been deadened for some time.

♥ An extinct volcano suggests that we have become aware of old feelings and emotions that are not relevant in the present circumstances.

▣ Dreaming of extinct animals such as dinosaurs suggests that we are aware of attitudes and behaviours that are no longer relevant.

*You might also like to consult the entries for Dinosaur and Volcano.*

## EXTINGUISH

▦ Extreme suffering – spiritual, emotional or physical – may be perceived as having extinguished or sapped spiritual passion.

♥ Usually extinguishing suggests putting out a fire or a light, having the symbolism of smothering emotions or covering up deeper feelings.

▣ When we dream of extinguishing fire or light it is often worthwhile to look at how this is done. Dreaming of switching off a light suggests that we have cut off a source of energy, with the potential for it to be reinstated. For instance dousing a fire with a blanket suggests suppressing a powerful energy.

*You might like to consult the entries for Fire, Embers and Light for further clarification.*

## EXTRA-TERRESTRIAL

▦ Extra-terrestrial beings in spiritual terms are those that do not have the same qualities as human beings. They are not 'of the ordinary'. Such images suggest that we have access to other realms of being in the dream state.

♥ Emotionally, anything that is beyond our normal experience may be depicted as extra-terrestrial. We need to give such emotions some kind of form in order to be able to deal with them. It is possible that in feeling different to others we sense ourselves to be alien and not of this world.

▣ From a practical perspective, there is no reason to suppose that extra-terrestrial beings do not exist, or that there is no such things as UFOs (Unidentified Flying Objects). However, opinions vary as to whether the objects and beings we encounter in dreams are figments of the dreaming mind or aspects of our own personality, or are indeed extra-terrestrial.

*You might also like to consult the entry for Alien/Alienated.*

## EYES – *see* BODY

## FABRIC

⚜ Material or fabric in spiritual terms is that which has become tangible or has a reality of its own. Fabrication in the sense of lying is making something up, creating a Spiritual untruth.

♥ Originally simply any manufactured substance – and only later specifically textile – fabric in dreams is symbolic of the physical world. The colour and texture may be important in interpretation.

▦ In mundane parlance, fabric in dreams is a tactile representation of something we need to know or remember. A rough fabric might denote a difficulty and a smooth fabric or material a carefully crafted project. Seeing fabric which has been mended or patched suggests that our original thoughts perhaps had an inherent flaw. A patch of the same colour may be an attempt to cover this up, whereas one of a different fabric or texture highlights a perhaps innovative solution.

*You might like to consult the entry for Colour for further information.*

## FABULOUS BEASTS
### (SUCH AS CENTAURS, GRIFFINS, MINOTAURS AND UNICORNS)

⚜ Fearsome and terrifying powers of nature were often previously represented as fabulous creatures. In addition, they were given animalistic qualities. Learning to control these qualities within ourselves is a large part of the spiritual development which can take place through dreams.

♥ Given the freedom to create, the mind can produce both the fantastic and the grotesque, particularly in dreams. There are many combinations which are possible and we, therefore, have an almost unlimited potential to use our creative abilities. By and large, the appearance of fabulous beasts is the result of trying to reconcile two apparently diverse polarities.

▦ In dream imagery, in order to draw the dreamer's attention to certain qualities, fabulous beasts are shown as having dual characteristics. The centaur represents the combination of man with beast whilst the minotaur does the reverse – that of beast with man. These combinations are intended to show that we are able to combine two basic principles.

⊞ The unicorn has its horn representing mysticism, the griffin has the qualities of both the lion and the eagle. These representations are of the best qualities of masculinity and femininity. Only the purest of women (the virgin) can tame the unicorn and only the bravest of men can tame the griffin. (It is sometimes said that only the female griffin has wings, yet the griffin is also said to draw the chariot of Nemesis, goddess of justice, across the sky.)

**FACE**

🔆 Traditionally the face represented, or rather symbolized, the basic powers of the Soul; the eyes are the mirror, the mouth represents expression, the forehead knowledge.

🛡 We learn most about people from their faces, so to be particularly conscious of faces in dreams suggests that we may be seeking knowledge or information not otherwise available to us. If any part of the face seems particularly prominent or outstanding that should be interpreted separately.

🎴 To concentrate on somebody else's face in a dream is an attempt to understand the outward personality. To be looking at our own face reflected in a mirror means that we may be trying to come to terms with the way we express ourselves in the ordinary, everyday world. We may also be attempting to understand our own ulterior motives. When the face is hidden or has no features, we are hiding our own power, or refusing to acknowledge our own abilities.

*Consult the entries for Eyes, Hair, Head and Mouth in Body for further clarification.*

**FACTORY**

🔆 Being a commercial building a factory suggests manifestation from the spiritual to the ordinary mundane world.

🛡 A factory is often a large, busy space, so it is often representative of our own lives and the way we fill our inner space.

🎴 Depending on what seems to be happening in a dream a factory can actually represent the workplace and our attitude to our employment. An assembly line might suggest a sense of boredom for instance.

**FAIL/FAILURE**

🔆 When we have a sense of failure in dreams this may be highlighting depression or spiritual frustration. Such a feeling may indicate, before we are consciously aware of it, that we have not come up to our own expectations and feel we have let others down.

🛡 The fear of failure is almost universally present in one form or another. To dream of failure at least gives us the opportunity to face that fear in a manageable fashion.

🎴 Personal failure in a dream indicates a degree of competitiveness and will also highlight different ways of operating in everyday life. Failure in a dream is not necessarily personal. If, for instance, lights fail or refuse to work, we need to be aware of a lack of energy, power or enthusiasm around us.

## FAIR/FAIRGROUND

✹ A metaphor for life itself, with its merry-go-round and its spiritual 'ups and downs', is the image of a fairground.

♡ The fairground has a dreamlike quality of its own. It is a sort of enclosed world, a place where the trials and tribulations of the external world can be forgotten for a time. When we dream of such a place we are becoming more aware of the more hedonistic side of our nature. We are more wrapped up in our own pleasures.

▦ To dream of being in a fairground may represent a reconnection with our light-hearted childlike nature. We can afford to be less inhibited in public. To be attending a carnival or fiesta means we can drop whatever constraints or restraints we may impose on ourselves or others.

## FAIRY

✹ Fairies are a specific group of otherworldly beings with mystical abilities found in most folklore, particularly in Celtic and Teutonic tales. Usually known for being mischievous, it is this aspect that becomes important for us in dreams. As a branch of Neopaganism the increase of belief in fairies may well lead to a greater awareness and appreciation of these nature spirits and their qualities. As archetypal figures they may appear more frequently in dreams.

♡ Fairies are known to be capricious, and on a psychological level they may represent the side of our being that does not wish to be controlled, and wishes to have the freedom to react and be spontaneous.

▦ Because fairies are representations of the elemental forces of nature, for them to appear in a dream signifies our connection with those forces within ourselves. There is a need for control, otherwise the mischievous side in us can run riot.

*Consult the entry for Nymph for additional information.*

## FAKE/FALSE

✹ Anything that is fake or false is counterfeit (made in imitation of the original). This echoes the idea that man was made in the image of God, a spiritual concept. In dreams we can become acutely aware of humanity as opposed to divinity.

♡ When we become aware that something is a fake or is false in dreams it is time for us to assess our own integrity. There are flaws or misperceptions in the way we regard ourselves.

▦ A counterfeit object is one that in comparison with the original is seen to have flaws. We can admire the fake for its own intrinsic beauty while accepting the flaws. Actually fashioning fake objects suggests that we are conscious that our creativity is not being best used. Projects and tasks all have flaws that can be improved upon, and dreaming of fakes and false objects give us the opportunity to iron out difficulties before they develop into problems.

**FALCON**

🌖 Ascension and freedom from Spiritual Bondage are represented by the falcon, a bird of prey.

♥ To dream of a falcon or any trained bird can represent energy fully focused on a particular project with complete freedom to act. Such a dream may allow us to concentrate on our aspirations, hopes and desires.

🖼 The power that we have to succeed must be used in a contained, directed way. A falcon – as a trained bird and one of the fastest fliers – can depict this. *Consult the entry for Birds for more information.*

**FALL/FALLING**

🌖 Spiritual fear or forgetfulness is symbolized here, particularly the Fall from Grace, from a state of innocent bliss to a state of sinful understanding, with its attendant consequences We may feel we are slipping away from a situation, essentially we are losing our place. This can be because of others' negative influence.

♥ Falling has come to be interpreted as surrender (particularly sexual) and with moral failure, of not being as one should. Statistically, dreams of falling are one of the most common types of dream. They tend to occur during the first stage of sleep and are often accompanied by muscle contractions of the arms and legs, sometimes the whole body. These are known as myoclonic jerks.

🖼 A fall in a dream outlines the need to be grounded, to take care within a known situation. We may be harmed by being too pedestrian. To dream of falling shows a lack of confidence in our own ability. We may feel threatened by a lack of security, whether real or imagined. We fear being dropped by friends or colleagues.

**FALSE** – *see* **FAKE**

**FAME**

🌖 Spiritually, fame suggests the need to accept our own integrity, our ability to be ourselves under all conditions.

♥ The Ego – our sense of individual existence – is a very powerful tool and the human being's need for recognition arises from this. If we are trying to make decisions as to how to move forward within our lives, we have to recognize our potential to stand out in a crowd – or not as the case may be. To dream of fame allows us to crystallize our attitude to our own unique sense of being.

⬛ Dreaming of being famous, or of achieving fame within a chosen field, signifies that we ourselves need to recognize and give ourselves credit for our own abilities. In waking life we may be relatively shy, but in dreams we can often achieve things we would not believe we were capable of. Often such a dream gives us the courage to attempt what seems impossible.

*You might also like to consult the entries for Celebrity and Famous People.*

## FAMILY

⚜ The family symbolizes the Spiritual Triangle, the unification of Love and Wisdom from which arises Power. It is also a group in which we feel safe.

♦ Psychologically the struggle for individuality should take place within the safety of the family unit. This, however, does not always happen. In dreams we are able to 'manipulate' the images of our family members, so that we can work through our difficulties without harming anyone else (it is interesting to note that one person working on his own dreams can have a profound noticeable effect on the interactions and unconscious bondings between other members of his family). Almost all of the problems we encounter in life are reflected within the family, so in times of stress we will dream of previous problems and difficulties that the family has experienced. Dreams about the family figure so prominently because most of the conflicts and problems in life are experienced first within that environment. It is as though a pattern is laid down which, until it is broken willingly, will continue to appear. Individual members and their position within the family can also symbolize the various archetypes – father can represent the masculine principle and authority, whereas mother represents the nurturing, protective principle. For ease of reference the relevance of each figure in men's and women's dreams is included under each heading. Because we have had an intimate connection with members of the family they become easy targets for projection as dream images. We do have to decide whether they are in our dreams as themselves or whether they are there in a symbolic capacity.

The family relationships in more detail can be interpreted thus:

**Brother** – a brother can represent both feelings of kinship and of rivalry. In a man's dream an older brother can represent experience and authority, while a younger brother suggests vulnerability and possibly lack of maturity. In a woman's dream, a younger brother can represent a sense of rivalry, but also of vulnerability, whether her own or her brother's. An older brother can signify her extrovert self.

**Daughter** – when the relationship with a daughter is highlighted in dreams, it often represents the outcome of the relationship between the dreamer and their partner. In a woman's dream, the relationship with the daughter usually suggests a mutually supportive one – although rivalry and jealousy can arise and needs to be dealt with. Sometimes this can safely be done in dreams. In a man's dream his daughter may represent his fears and doubts about his own ability to handle his vulnerability.

**Extended family (such as cousins, aunts, uncles)** – members of the extended family usually appear in dreams either as themselves, highlighting our relationship with them, or typifying various aspects of our own personality that are recognizable.

**Father** – if the relationship with father has been successful in waking life, the dream image will tend to be a positive one. Father represents authority and the conventional forms of law and order. If the relationship with father has been a difficult or negative one, there may be some resistance in waking life to resolving the various conflicts that will have arisen. Often this can be accomplished spontaneously in dreams. In a man's life father becomes a role model, whether appropriate or not. It is often only when the individual realizes that he is not being true to his own nature that dreams can point the way to a more successful life and perhaps an understanding of his father. In a woman's life, father is the 'pattern' on whom she bases all later relationships with men. When she appreciates that she longer need use this pattern, she is often able to work out in dreams a more appropriate way to have a mature relationship. This can lead to dreams of her perhaps walking away from her father or leaving him behind.

**Grandparents** – if grandparents appear in dreams it can highlight our attitude to them, but also to the traditions and beliefs handed down by them. It is often said that grandparents do not know whether they have done a good job of raising their children until their sons and daughters have children of their own. In dreams grandparents can offer security, but this will often depend on the relationship our parents have had with them.

**Husband/Live-in partner** – crucial within the husband/wife relationship are the wife's feelings about her own sexuality and intimacy of body, mind and spirit. Her view of herself will have been formed by her connection with her father and any subsequent partnering may well be coloured by that attachment. If her doubts and fears about validity are not properly expressed, they will surface in dreams about the loss, or death, of her husband. Such fears may also be projected onto other women's husbands, almost as though her own husband is too close to her.

**Mother** – our relationship with mother is pivotal in our development and will often give rise to her appearance in dreams. Largely it is the first relationship we develop, probably should be perceived as a nurturing, caring one, and allows us to develop such relationships with other people. If this does not happen, fears and doubts may arise. In a man's life this may result in continually developing dependent relationships with older women, or denying his right to a relationship completely. His dreams may highlight this difficulty until such times as he is prepared to address the problem. As he grows to maturity he may experience dreams that highlight the loss of his mother. In a woman's life, her relationship with her mother will colour all other relationships. Negatively, she may find herself pushed into nurturing the needy male, or in forming relationships with both men and women that do not satisfy her basic needs. There are many ways through dreams of working through relationships with mother, both symbolically and otherwise, and much can be gained by daring to take this step. Provided we have come to terms with and understood this relationship, much material and spiritual success can be achieved. Positive images of mothering and motherhood may also give us access to archetypal material that is connected with Mother Earth and our place in the world.

**Sister** – the sister in dreams usually represents the feeling side of ourselves. We have the ability to make links with that side of ourselves through being able to understand our sister's personality. In a man's dream if she is older, the sister can represent the potential for persecution, but also of caring. If she is younger then she can epitomize the more vulnerable side of him. In a woman's dream if the sister is younger, she can represent rivalry. If older she stands for capability.

**Son** – in dreams the son can signify our need for self-expression and for extroversion. He can also signify parental responsibility. In a mother's dream he may represent our ambitions, hope and potential. In a father's dream he can highlight unfulfilled hopes and dreams.

**Wife/Live-in partner** – the relationship between husband and wife is often based on how the man perceives himself to be, and can be enhanced through his dreams. Dreaming of a partner sometimes signifies the part of our personality that we cannot quite make full use of without help. A man will often attempt to prove himself a good husband through his dreams. He may experience in dreams the potential loss and death of his partner with the same intensity as he experienced the first 'loss' of his mother.

▦ The family is the first basic security image that we have. Often, through circumstances not within our control, that image becomes distorted, and dreams will either attempt to put this image right or will confirm the distortion. Thus we may dream of an argument with a family member, but the interpretation will depend on both the circumstances of the dream and our everyday relationship with that person. All future relationships are influenced by the ones we first develop within the family.

Since relationships in the family are so important, dreams containing family members can have extra significance. Some typical dreams are:

**A man's mother being transformed into another woman** – a man's first close relationship with a woman is with his mother or mother figure. This transformation indicates some change in his perception of women. Depending on the circumstances of the dream, such a transformation can be either positive or negative. For instance he may dream of his mother turning into his boss. This suggests he may have certain expectations as to how he should be treated. It can be a sign of growth for him to realize, through dreams, that he can let mother go.

**A woman's father, brother or lover turning into someone else** – similarly, a woman's first relationship with the male is usually with her father or father figure. She must learn to walk away from that relationship in order to progress onto fuller relationships. When she can handle her Animus she is ready for that transformation.

**A man's brother or a woman's sister appearing in a dream** – this often represents the Shadow. Often it is easier to project the negative side of our personalities onto members of the family. If this projection is allowed to continue, and not understood, it can cause difficulty with family relationships. Often the solution will present itself in dreams to enable us to come to terms with our own projections. The pattern of aggressions between family members is fairly typical, but oddly is often easier to work through in dreams than in everyday life.

**Confusion of family members (e.g. mother's face on father's body)** – this suggests that we may be having problems in deciding which parent or person is most important to us.

**Family members suffering from injury or trauma or appearing to be distorted in some way** – may reflect our fear for, or about, that person.

**A family member continually appearing in dreams or, conversely, not appearing when expected** – shows that the relationship with that person (or our concept of them) needs to be better understood.

**Dreaming of an incestuous relationship** – may indicate that we have become obsessed in some way with the other person. We are searching for integration of their qualities within ourselves.

**Parents crushing us and thus forcing rebellion** – this suggests that we need to break away from learnt childhood behaviour and develop as an individual. Dreaming of a parent's death can also have the same significance. When a parent appears in our own environment, we will have learnt to change roles within the parent/child relationship and perhaps will accept our parents as friends. Parents behaving inappropriately in dreams can indicate our need to recognize that they are only human, and not as perfect as we had first perceived. In tribal societies the rite of passage between childhood and adulthood is clearly marked, by initiation. Rivalry with one or both parents is highlighted in dreams when such a transformation is not properly handled and our feelings and emotions have not been given due validity.

**Dreaming of conflict between a loved one and a member of our family** – this shows we have not fully differentiated between our needs and desire for each person. Learning how to love outside the family is a sign of maturity. The figure of a family member intruding in dreams suggests that family loyalties can get in the way within our everyday life. Rivalry between siblings in dreams usually harks back to a feeling of insecurity and doubt, possibly as to whether we are loved enough within the family framework.

**Dreaming of being adopted** – suggests that we feel out of place and in some way different to other members of the family. This dream often occurs as teenagers are growing towards maturity.

**Dreaming of having any family member** – e.g. a brother – when we do not have one in waking life denotes our search for completion and 'missing' parts of our personality.

## FAMINE

A famine symbolizes a lack of Spiritual sustenance, which should give us enough energy to remain active within the physical.

Famine from an emotional perspective signifies a lack of love or appreciation. In waking life those in authority may seem to withhold approval or approbation.

In the Western world famine is not so prevalent but as a dream image it may signify a concern over global matters. On a more personal note, such an image suggests that a project or task is no longer receiving the attention it deserves and, therefore, lacks nurturing.

In both men's and women's dreams famine suggests a lack of resources, though which particular ones will depend on everyday circumstances.

*You might also like to consult the entries for Eat/Eating, Fasting, Food and Nourishment.*

## FAMOUS PEOPLE

Spiritually, as we reach for perfection we need to 'work through' various aspects of our personality. Sometimes we are able to reject such aspects as not being appropriate for the life we live. For instance, we may realize that the destructiveness of a public life would take its toll within our own lives.

⬥ Famous people, pop and film stars and sporting celebrities may also serve in dreams as a projection of the type of person we would like to be. We may, for instance, in real life be shy and withdrawn, but need to be admired and loved. In today's climate of media celebrities, both minor and otherwise, such figures can also be targets for opprobrium.

▦ Most of us are capable of creating an ideal person on whom to project our fantasies and wishes. We are not at this stage particularly in touch with reality. In dreams a film, pop star or public figure will represent the Animus or Anima. A young person dreaming of a film star may not be ready for the responsibility of a real relationship.

⬩ In a woman's dream a male pop star or famous person will most likely represent the 'knight in shining armour' destined to take her away from her mundane life. In a man's dream a female star is more likely to represent a desired type of femininity.

*Consult the information on the Animus/Anima in the Introduction and also the entries for Celebrity and Fame for more information.*

## FANATIC

⬥ A fanatic was initially 'one who was inspired by God', zealous in all he did in the service of his god. Only later did this become debased into the more negative meaning of someone who has no sense of respect for physical life. It is, unfortunately, this latter interpretation that surfaces in many of today's dreams.

⬥ When we find ourselves in dreams being totally focused to the point of fanaticism on a particular outcome it is perhaps wise to consider and appraise our commitments.

▦ Without determination and tenacity many tasks cannot be completed. Dreaming of a known fanatic or act of fanaticism can help us to complete our projects.

*You might also like to consult the entry for Martyr.*

## FARE

⬥ A fare-paying dream often occurs when one feels that past actions have not been paid for or taken into account. Before we can move on we must pay our dues and come to terms with them.

⬥ Demands may be being made on us and we have to decide on their appropriateness. To be paying a fare suggests acknowledgement of help we have received on our 'journey' through life. To be receiving a fare indicates that we have facilitated someone else's passage.

⊞ To be paying a fare in a dream is acknowledging the price that is paid in order to succeed. A taxi-fare would imply a more private process than a bus fare. From a mundane perspective, wordplay suggests that a transaction that we have undertaken is 'fair'.

## FARM/FARMYARD

⟐ A farmyard is an enclosure in which we may feel safe and, to some extent, looked after. Dreaming of such a place shows that we are within safe Spiritual boundaries.

♡ Our natural drives such as a need for physical comfort, herd behaviour and territorial rights are best expressed in a safe, conserving environment, symbolized by the rural idyll of a farm. As time goes on the image of a farm or farmyard is superceded by the commercial requirements of a working farm, analogous with our own working environment.

⊞ To be in a farmyard in a dream (if it is not a memory) shows us as being in touch with the down-to-earth side of ourselves. There are many facets of behaviour that can be interpreted in animal terms and often this type of dream has more much impact than one including people.

⊟ The agricultural environment is an easy way to learn about procreation and conservation. In both men's and women's dreams a farm or farmyard may symbolize such issues.

*You might like to consult the entry for Animals for further qualification.*

## FAST – *see* SPEED

## FASTING

⟐ Fasting is a very old way of bringing about a change in consciousness, and also a move towards self-realization through resistance to temptation. It is considered to be the most powerful spiritual discipline there is, but should not be indulged in in everyday life without properly qualified support. Dreaming of fasting suggests that some kind of spiritual discipline may be required.

♡ Dreams while actively fasting can be particularly vivid or lurid. If we have what we consider to be a grievance, self-denial may manifest as the image of fasting (doing without sustenance). This may be the psyche's way of making this grievance known.

⊞ Deliberately depriving the body of sustenance in a dream may be an attempt to come to terms with some perceived trauma, such as a lack of love, or to draw attention to the need for cleansing in some way.

*You might like to consult the entries for Eat/Eating, Famine, Food and Nourishment for additional clarification.*

**FAT**

    ✦ Pharaoh's dream of seven fat cows being devoured by seven lean ones is a perfect illustration of fat representing a surplus or surfeit of anything. The spiritual significance can be of energy, power or knowledge.

    ♦ Depending on how we think of our bodies in the waking state, we can often use the dream image of ourselves to change the way we feel. Body dysmorphia (distortion) in dreams is not uncommon, particularly in lucid dreaming. Dreaming of being fat can also suggest the carrying of a weighty burden.

    ▦ To dream of being fat alerts us to the defences we use against inadequacy. Equally, we may also be conscious of the sensual and fun side of ourselves we have not used before.

    ▤ A woman will sometimes dream of becoming fat before she is consciously aware of being pregnant.

**FATHER** – *see* FAMILY

**FAX MACHINE/FAX** – *see* COMMUNICATION

**FEAST** – *see* FESTIVAL

**FEATHER**

    ✦ Feathers, particularly white ones, are said to symbolize the Heavens and messages from the Angelic realms and the Soul. Spiritual triumph is shown by a display of plumage.

    ♦ Feathers often represent flight to other parts of the Self, and because of their connection with the wind and the air, can represent our more spiritual side. A bird's plumage is its protection, but it is also its power and strength. Used in this sense, it is alerting us to the fact that we can use our own strength and ability to achieve what we want to do in the future.

    ▦ Feathers in a dream could denote softness and lightness, perhaps a more gentle approach to a situation. We may need to look at the truth within the particular situation and to recognize that we need to be calmer in what we are doing. In a dream, plumage being drawn to our attention can often stand for a display of power and strength. It may also be a signal of defiance; we need to stand firm and show our colours.

**FEED/FEEDING** – *see* EAT/EATING

**FEET/FOOT** – *see* BODY

**FENCE**

    ✦ A fence can represent spiritual boundaries. We need to be aware of what checks and limitations there are to our spiritual progress.

    ♦ When we come up against a fence or a barrier there is extra effort needed for us to overcome whatever that barrier represents.

▨ When we dream of fences we are dreaming of social or class barriers or perhaps our own need for privacy. We may be aware of boundaries in relationships that can prevent us from achieving the proper type of connection we need. We may have difficulty in expressing ourselves in some way.

*You might like to consult the entries for Barrier and Edge.*

## FERMENTATION

❀ Fermentation in alchemy symbolizes spiritual transformation and transmutation. It has this same symbolism in dreams and we become aware of changes that are both necessary and are taking place. Fermentation is living inspiration.

♥ A process of fermentation shows the ways in which we can transform and transmute aspects of our personality that do not necessarily serve us well into new and outstanding characteristics.

▨ To dream of the process of fermentation indicates that events are occurring in the background, of which we are aware but we must wait for them to develop. Often a project will lose energy before it takes on a new lease of life.

## FERRY

❀ The ferry is one of the oldest symbols associated with death. It signifies transition, often from the physical realm to the spiritual. We may be undergoing a spiritual 'death' or change of some kind, moving on from present knowledge.

♥ The old idea of being ferried across the River Styx, the boundary between life and death, gives an image of making major change, when we may have to leave behind all that we have known.

▨ To dream of being on a ferry indicates that we are making some movement towards change. Because the ferry carries large numbers of people it may also represent a group to which we belong needing to make changes, needing to change its way of working and take responsibility for moving as a group rather than as individuals.

*You might like to consult the entries for Boat/Ship and Death.*

## FESTIVAL

❀ A festival is a church or religious feast, as in harvest festival. This was originally a pagan feast to honour the fertility gods and give thanks for a good harvest. It signifies a spiritual celebration.

♥ Festivals are very specific for a number of cultures. While in many cases they have become somewhat secularized, in dreams they mark the need for family or group gathering in order to celebrate an event or happening. Such rituals and occasions help to cement both individual and community relationships.

▦ Nowadays music and art festivals take the place of religious festivals. When we dream of such a festival it is the common bond and how we fit in which is important.

*Also consult the entry for Meal and Party.*

**FIEND**

◉ Technically the opposite of friend, a fiend is a manifestation of Satan as the enemy of mankind. In dreams a fiend can symbolize the enemy within, that part of us that resists spiritual development.

♡ We may be afraid of our own passions, anger and fear. As a fiery creature and initially a symbol for evil, the fiend is a manifestation of those emotions. It is possible in dreams to confront such a creature.

▦ To dream of a fiend or devil usually means that we have got to come to terms with a part of ourselves that is frightening and unknown. We need to confront this part and make it work for us rather than against us.

⊡ In a woman's dream a fiend may manifest as all the unexpressed frustration that she is experiencing. In a man's dream such a figure will be more overtly aggressive.

*Also consult the entries for Demon, Devil and Imp.*

**FIG/FIG TREE**

◉ The fig is known to enhance psychic ability and also has a direct connection with the beginning of physical life. The Sacred fig is the Bo tree and is revered by Buddhists and Hindus alike. It was beneath this tree that Guatama Buddha received enlightenment. Jesus is said to have blasted the fig tree, when it would not provide him with nourishment. The fig tree in dreams usually suggests that we are in touch with a deeper spiritual awareness of which we have previously had no conscious knowledge.

♡ Because the 'fruit' of a fig is actually a specialized structure, an involuted (nearly closed) receptacle with many small flowers arranged on the inner surface, it has come to represent intuition and wisdom and their application in the ordinary world. This gives it an association with the Tree of Knowledge, the beginning of duality, and ultimately with masculinity and femininity.

▦ Often because of its shape, the fig is associated with sexuality, fertility, masculinity and prosperity. To dream of eating figs may well be a recognition that some kind of celebration is necessary although equally that a situation holds more potential than at first thought.

⊡ Because it holds many seeds, the fig is seen as a potent fertility symbol. In a woman's dream this image may represent her partner's fertility and, therefore, his ability to father children. In a man's dream it is more likely to suggest his virility.

## FIGHT

⚜ A fight in dreams is quite literally a spiritual conflict. We need to work out where and why there is a conflict and perhaps deal with it in a subtle way. ⚜ If we dream that we are in a fight, it usually indicates that we are confronting our need for independence. We may also need to express our anger and frustration and the subconscious desire to hurt a part of ourselves. We also may wish to hurt someone else, although this would be unacceptable in the waking state.

▣ To fight back is a natural defence mechanism, so when we are feeling threatened in our everyday lives, we will often dream of taking that situation one stage further and fighting it out. To throw a punch in a dream is to recognize our own distress or aggression. To be punched is often to have invited such aggression.

⊞ Fighting tends to be a masculine response to a problem so in a man's dream he may well be attempting to deal with his own reactions. In a woman's dream she will be developing her own assertiveness and must decide whether her actions are appropriate.

*You might like to consult the entry for Conflict for further clarification.*

## FILM

⚜ Film in dreams symbolizes the spiritual Akashic Records, which are understood to have existed since the beginning of Creation. Being able to access these gives us more understanding of Divine Will.

⚜ Film as recording images is an important part of modern man's make up and to be viewing film within a dream is to be creating a different reality from the one we presently have. This usually applies to the waking self, rather than to the sleeping self. If we are making a film, when this is not our normal occupation, we may need to question the reality we are creating, but may also be being warned not to try to create too many realities.

▣ To dream of being at a film – as in the cinema – indicates we are viewing an aspect of our own past or character that needs to be acknowledged in a different way. We are attempting to view ourselves objectively or perhaps we may be escaping from reality.

## FIN – *see* FISH

## FIND

⚜ Finding something after a deliberate search in a dream signifies that we have enough spiritual awareness to move forward. Finding something by chance suggests an element of spiritual assistance. A found object is something to be treasured.

🜨 The mind has an uncanny knack of drawing our attention to what needs to be done to enable us to achieve our aims. It will use hiding, searching and finding as metaphors for effort we must make in the waking state. So to find something without having to make too much effort would show that events will take place that will reveal what we need to know.

🔲 If we dream of finding a precious object, we are becoming aware of some part of ourselves that is, or will be, of use to us. We are making a discovery or a realization, which may be about us or about others.

## FINGER

⚜ A hand with a finger pointing the way signifies the spiritual direction to be taken. When the thumb and middle finger are held together it suggests suppression of the Ego (the conscious self).

🜨 When we become conscious in dreams of the fingers on a hand we are often being given important information. A beckoning finger is encouragement, whereas if the fourth or ring finger is more noticeable, love of a selfless kind is suggested. If the little finger is crooked traditionally there may be some deviousness around.

🔲 When the fingers are splayed, this can suggest openness and honesty; when curled towards the palm, information is being hidden. If bunched into a fist there is aggression against us. If the fingers on both hands are interlaced, some self-control is necessary.

*You might also like to consult the entry for Hand in Body.*

## FIRE

⚜ Being aware of the heat of a fire is to be aware of someone else's strong feelings. Baptism by fire signifies a new awareness and awakening of spiritual power and transformation created sometimes through extremes of emotion. Fire is a valid Western symbol of the spiritual energy known as Kundalini, which rises from the base of the spine to the crown of the head and brings with it a shift in perception. A fire bucket, as with any hollow vessel, can represent the feminine principle.

🜨 Psychologically, fire often appears in dreams as a symbol of cleansing and purification. We can use the life-giving and generative power to change our lives. Sometimes fire indicates the need to use our sexual power to good effect. To dream of being burnt alive may express our fears of a new relationship or phase of life. We may also be conscious that we could suffer for our beliefs. As a symbol, the fire bucket indicates that we may have a situation around us that is out of control. The interpretation will depend on whether the bucket is full or empty for it is often only by a display of 'dampening' emotion that there can be any progress.

Fire in a dream can suggest passion and desire in its more positive sense, and frustration, anger, resentment and destructiveness in its more negative. It will depend on whether the fire is controlled or otherwise on the exact interpretation. To be more conscious of the flame of the fire would be to be aware of the energy and strength that is available to us. A fire basket draws our attention to the fact that these energies can be contained; whereas a fire bucket, particularly if it is filled with sand, suggests such energies should be smothered.

## FIREWORKS

There is an excess of spiritual emotion, which needs to be channelled properly in order to prevent it shooting off in all directions. Various fireworks may have specific significances. The Catherine wheel signifies the martyrdom of St Catherine of Sienna, so in dreams could represent oppression of the feminine, while the rocket suggests aiming for the unknown.

Fireworks can have the same significance as an explosion. Such a release of energy or emotion can have quite a spectacular effect on us, or on people around us.

Fireworks are generally accepted as belonging to a happy occasion or celebration, though they may also be frightening. When we dream of fireworks we are hoping to be able to celebrate good fortune, although there may be a secondary emotion associated with that celebration.

## FISH

Fish signify temporal and spiritual power. When pictured as two fish swimming in opposite directions, it is recognized as the sign of Pisces. The Collective Unconscious as Jung has called it – that part of life everyone shares, the common experience, awareness and knowledge that we all have – is becoming available to us.

Dreaming of fish connects with the emotional side of ourselves, but more our ability to be wise without being strategic. We can often simply respond instinctively to what is going on, without needing to analyze it. The salmon symbolizes wisdom; a cooked fish is a completed task and other fish represent prosperity. The fin of a fish signifies positive movement and 'going with the flow'.

In dreams the fish tends to represent anything – an idea or project – that is taking on form but at this point has not yet become conscious. Catching a fish is to get hold of such an idea. The fish and fishing can also represent the actual process of dreaming itself.

It has been thought that small fish represent semen in a woman's dream and larger fish suggest children. In a man's dream, small 'fry' suggest problems with self-image – he has not yet integrated certain aspects of his personality. The rod probably represents the penis.

**FISHERMAN**

🎐 Because of its Christian connection a fisherman can symbolize a priest or holy man in dreams. Equally, he is one who has the patience to sit out a situation without anticipating any particular outcome.

🜨 We may be trying to 'catch' something, such as a job or a partner.

🜳 Whenever one of our dream figures is carrying out a specific action we need to look at what is represented by that action. Often a fisherman will represent a provider, or perhaps bravery, as with a deep-sea fisherman, whilst a fresh water fisherman may indicate the need for rest and recuperation.

*You might like to consult the entry for Occupation.*

**FLAG**

🎐 Spiritual crusades and journeys often require certain standards of behaviour and flags in dreams will often symbolize an idea or principle.

🜨 Any national flag will signify a degree of patriotism that may be necessary, or possibly the need to be more militant. Now with its connection to international sport, a flag can suggest an opportunity for exhibitionism.

🜳 A flag in a dream will have the same meaning as a banner – that is a standard or a place round which people with common aims and beliefs can gather. It may represent old-fashioned principles and beliefs.

*You might like to consult the entry for Banner for further clarification.*

**FLAME – see FIRE**

**FLASH**

🎐 The lightning flash is a function within Jewish Kabbalist belief when something to be manifested is drawn very quickly through the Sephiroth (spheres of existence) to become real in the physical world. As we become more aware of spiritual matters this symbol becomes part of our vocabulary.

🜨 A flash in dreams signifies a build up of energy, which may be emotional, warning us that such energy, while potentially destructive, can be used positively.

🜳 Concentrated light is significant on the mundane level as a flash of inspiration in a particular project or a moment of clarity when circumstances are particularly obscure.

*You might like to consult the entry for Lightning for further information.*

**FLEAS – see INSECTS**

**FLIES – see INSECTS**

## FLOAT/FLOATING

⚜ From a spiritual perspective floating in dreams is often a precursor to out of body experiences. In lucid dreaming we can learn to control flight, and to Astral travel (deliberately change consciousness).

♡ Because we are not taking charge of our own direction, we are being indecisive and perhaps need to think more carefully about our actions and involvements with other people.

▦ Floating in a dream was considered by Freud to be connected with sexuality, but is probably much more to do with the inherent need for freedom. Generally we are opening to power beyond our conscious self, when we are carried along apparently without our consent. We are in a state of extreme relaxation and are simply allowing events to carry us along.

## FLOCK – *see* GROUP

## FLOGGING

⚜ Flogging with a whip or scourge suggests punishment and the atonement of sins.

♡ Flogging someone else means we have to be careful that we are not attempting to impose our will on or torture the dream figure. Flogging in the sense of selling something suggests that we have to be aggressive in promoting our ideas.

▦ Any violent act against the person usually indicates some form of punishment. To dream of being flogged would indicate that we are aware that someone is driving us beyond our limits, often in an inappropriate manner. Flogging ourselves would highlight a type of masochism in our own personality, which may be inappropriate and suggest self harm.

## FLOOD

⚜ A flood signifies the end of one cycle and the beginning of another. Old grievances and emotional difficulties are washed away, leaving a clear head and a clear way forward.

♡ If we are not good at expressing ourselves verbally, dreaming of a flood may allow us to come to terms with our anxieties and worries in an appropriate way. An overflow of repressed or unconscious feelings needs to be got out of the way before progress can be made.

▦ Flood dreams are fascinating, because while frightening, they often indicate a release of positive energy. To be in the middle of a flood indicates we may feel we are being overwhelmed by feelings or circumstances, while watching a flood suggests we are simply watching ourselves. Sometimes a flood dream can indicate depression.

*You might also like to consult the entry for Water.*

## FLOWERS

☀ Spiritually flowers signify love and compassion, both that which we may receive and that which we give to others.

♡ The feminine principle is often represented in dreams by flowers, as is childhood. The bud represents the potential available, while the opening flower indicates development. To be given a bouquet – and the colour of the flowers may be important – means that we are being rewarded for an action, perhaps a spiritual offering of some sort.

Each individual flower has a particular symbolism in dreams and below are just a few. These meanings arise from often ancient symbolism.

**Anenome** – forsaken by love. **Arum Lily** – intensity of love and nowadays also mourning. **Bluebell** – humility. **Buttercup** – childishness, innocent action. **Carnation** – fascination. **Clover** – the Holy Trinity, completion. **Chrysanthemum** – cheerfulness and friendship. **Daffodil** – deceitful in love. **Daisy** – wakefulness and awareness. **Forget-me-not** – memories of true love. **Forsythia** – anticipation of good times. **Geranium** – foolishness. **Honeysuckle** – affectionate ties. **Iris** – courage, faith and hope. **Jasmine** – charming and loveable. **Lime/Linden** – married love. **Marigold** – trouble and jealousy. **Mistletoe** – clinging affection. **Myrtle** – love and marriage. **Narcissus** – selfishness and egotism. **Peony** – shame and distress. **Poppy** – sleep and sweet oblivion. **Primrose** – total devotion. **Rose** – love, and perhaps a wedding. **Snowdrop** – consolation. **Tulip** – the perfect lover. **Violet** – modesty and faithfulness.

▦ Flowers in a dream usually give us the opportunity to link to feelings of pleasure and beauty. We are aware that something new, perhaps a feeling or ability, is beginning to come into being and that there is a freshness about what we are doing.

*Also consult the entry for Colour and Garden.*

## FLUTE

☀ The flute generally signifies celestial music. In many cultures, ceramic instruments express the desire to unite earth and music in order to supplicate the benevolent spirits and elicit their favour. Bamboo or wooden flutes call forth the sounds of the wind or spirit.

♡ As a way of expressing the sound of the spirit, and therefore harmony, the flute can be seen in dreams as a symbol of happiness and joy. A further aspect of the flute's symbolism is its portrayal of nature and rural life.

▦ Many musical instruments – particularly wind instruments – indicate extremes of emotion, enticement and flattery. Because of its shape the flute is often taken as a symbol of masculine virility, but could also be taken to stand for anguish since its music is somewhat plaintive.

*Also consult the entry for Musical Instruments.*

## FLYING/FLIGHT

✵ Flight is a common image when seeking spiritual freedom. To be flying upwards is to be moving towards a more spiritual appreciation of our lives, while to be flying downwards is to be making an attempt to understand the subconscious and all that entails.

♥ Flying in dreams denotes freedom from physical inhibitions and is a recognized aspect of astral travel – the soul's ability to transcend its physical existence – and of lucid dreaming. In the latter, until proficiency is gained, the realization that we are flying is enough to have us lose the ability.

▦ Conventionally to dream of flying is to do with sex and sexuality, but it would probably be more accurate to look at it in terms of lack of inhibition and freedom. We are releasing ourselves from limitations that we may impose on ourselves.

*Consult the entries for Aeroplane and Wings as well as the sections on Journey and Transport for further information.*

## FOG – *see* WEATHER

## FOLLOW/FOLLOWER

✵ We are aware of either the need for, or the recognition of, 'discipleship' in life. In undertaking our own spiritual development there is a path that we must follow.

♥ When we dream of being followed we need to identify if what is following us is negative or positive. If it is negative, we need to deal with past fears, doubts or memories. If positive, we must recognize our need to take the initiative, or to identify what drives us.

▦ If we are following someone or something in a dream we may need a cause or crusade to help give us a sense of identity. We are looking for leadership or are aware that we can be influenced by other people. It also indicates that, particularly in a work situation, we are perhaps more comfortable in a secondary position rather than out in front.

⊞ In previous times and in many cultures the woman generally followed the man. When this image surfaces in a woman's dream she must look at how she feels subservient. In a man's dream he will become aware that he is adopting a protective, more assertive role.

## FONT

✵ A baptismal font is a symbol both of acceptance into a spiritual life and of a washing away of the past and of initiation into a new way of being.

◈ The two meanings of font come together on an emotional level. As a font is a receptacle for water it suggests feeling and security, as a typeface used in printing it suggests knowledge.

▦ The commercial meaning of font as a form of lettering can give rise to images in dreams particularly in relation to the workplace. To be changing a font would suggest doing things differently, whereas not being able to load the correct font suggests a difficulty in getting matters into perspective.

## FOOD

✺ Food in dreams always symbolizes spiritual sustenance – what we need to continue on our journey through life.

◈ Our need – or enjoyment – of food fulfils certain psychological needs. The meanings of various foods are as follows:

**Bread** – we are looking at our experiences and our basic needs. Unleavened breads, such as chappatis, matzos, pancakes and tortillas, have symbolic importance in a number of religions. Fancy breads can show a recognition of cultural diversity.

**Cake** – sensual enjoyment and celebration is represented in dreams by cakes.

**Chocolate** – as something considered to be the food of the gods and of the spirits, chocolate suggests sensuality and enjoyment and freedom from the mundane.

**Fruits** – the potential for prosperity is shown in dreams as ripe fruit. The results of our efforts and experiences – the fruits of our labour – can be represented in dream form by fruit. The colour can also be significant.

**Ham/Cured Meat** – our need for preservation of the status quo is represented by cured meats.

**Meals** – depending on whether we are eating in a group or alone, meals can indicate the desire for acceptance by our peers, sociability, a fear of not being part of a greater whole, or a need to be alone.

**Meat** – physical or worldly satisfaction or needs are shown often in dreams as meat. At one time raw meat supposedly signified impending misfortune, although today it is more likely to represent the need to make sure we are fully prepared for impending activities.

**Milk** – as a basic food, milk will always signify simple nurturing and giving to oneself.

**Onion** – that we all have different levels, or layers, to our personalities is often shown in dreams as an onion. If we are peeling an onion we perhaps need to examine each part of our personality.

**Picnic** – the informal nature of a picnic tends to represent freedom, connection with nature and choice.

**Sweets** – these tend to represent sensual pleasure, cosseting and the sweetness of life.

**Vegetables** – our basic needs and material satisfaction are represented in dreams by vegetables. They also suggest the goodness we can take from the Earth and situations around us. The colour may also be important.

🔲 Food signifies a satisfaction of our needs whether those are physical, mental or spiritual. It is something we might take or are taking into ourselves. Frequent dreams about eating suggest a great hunger for something, not necessarily food. Food that is mouldy suggests that we are seeking sustenance in the wrong fashion or from the wrong direction.

*Consult the entries for Bread, Cakes, Colour, Eat/Eating, Fruit, Nourishment and Onion for further clarification.*

## FOOTPRINTS

🔆 We may be aware, on a subconscious level, of a Divine presence. This we may follow or perhaps feel supported by. Interestingly if the footprints are of bare feet we need simplicity, if the feet are shod then a more sophisticated approach is called for.

♥ In dreams, if we see footprints going in opposite directions, we need to consider carefully what has happened in the past and what is going to happen in the future. We are standing in the here and now and must consider the confusion of the present, how it may affect our future and what choices we must make. We also need to consider what actions we have initiated in the past that will enable us to move into the future.

🔲 To see footprints in a dream indicates that we need to follow someone or their way of being. If those footprints are stretching in front of us, there is help available to us in the future, in the sense that someone has experienced similar circumstances. If the footsteps are behind us or seem to be our own then perhaps we need to look at the way we have acted in the past, who we have affected and what we still need to be responsible for.

*Also consult the entry for Foot/Feet in Body.*

## FORCE

🔆 Force implies strength greater than our own, in this context spiritual strength and awareness. Psychic disturbance and spiritual presence is often felt by many sensitives as an inexorable force.

♥ Often in dreams we become aware of energies and forces that seem to be beyond our control. These may often be potentials that we can understand and manage with greater understanding.

🔲 Pressure and stress in day-to-day living may show itself in dreams as a force that needs to be controlled.

**FOREST**

The forest symbolizes the psyche and the hidden realms, the place of original experience. The dark or enchanted forest that very often appears as an image in fairy tales and dreams is a threshold symbol. It is the soul entering the areas it has never explored before, working with intuition and with our own ability to sense and feel what is going on around us.

Dreaming of forests or a group of trees usually means entering the realms of the feminine. A forest is often a place of testing and initiation. It is always to do with coming to terms with our emotional self, of understanding the secrets of our own nature or of our own spiritual world.

We may find that a dream of forests can be interpreted as being lost and unable to find direction. As conservation of the earth's resources becomes more of an issue, the forest becomes synonymous with our care of the land.

Traditionally women tend to be more in touch with their own inner resources so a forest in a woman's dream suggests her exploration of these resources. In a man's dream, dreaming of a forest suggests an aspect of his hero's journey through his own hidden and perhaps more frightening sensitivities.

*You might also like to consult the entries for Trees and Wood.*

**FORGE**

The forge represents the Sacred Fire or Spirit that resides in all of us. This is an idea common in many cultures, the power or ability to transmute that which is base and unformed into something sacred.

The forge represents the masculine and active force. To dream of a forge indicates that we are changing internally and allowing our finer abilities to be shown. The forge Gods such as Thor and Vulcan were an important aspect of ancient belief and often represented the ability to change.

When the forge and the blacksmith were a part of normal, everyday life this particular dream would indicate some aspect of hard work or desire to reach a goal. Now it is more likely to mean a ritual action. Forging in the sense of counterfeiting an object in dreams suggests we do not trust our own creativity.

**FORK**

We may have come to a fork – a divergence – on our spiritual path and development and need guidance as to which direction to take. A fork, particularly a three-pronged one, is often considered to be the symbol of the Devil and, therefore, can symbolize evil and trickery.

Psychologically the fork can signify the same as a barb or a goad – something that is driving us, often to our own detriment.

In dreams, a fork denotes duality and indecision. A garden fork suggests hard work coupled with responsibility, whereas a kitchen fork signifies perhaps nurturing and management of assets.

**FORTRESS – see BUILDINGS, CASTLE AND TOWER**

**FORWARD – see POSITION**

**FOSSIL**

A fossil, from a spiritual perspective, represents the need to preserve perfect form.

When emotion becomes too rigid and reflective of the past, we may dream of fossils.

If an idea or project has got stuck in outmoded ideas, we may dream of fossils. We need to be able to take the best of the old and incorporate it in different ways.

*You might also like to consult the entries for Dinosaur and Prehistoric.*

**FOUND – see FIND**

**FOUNDATIONS**

When we become conscious of the foundations of buildings, we become aware that spiritual practice needs a good basis from which to start.

Foundations are often formed from the rubble of previous building and when this image appears we need to remember that we have available all our previous experience on which to draw.

In everyday life strategy and planning are good foundations from which to start. When we become aware that there is something wrong with the foundations of our dream building, we may need to go back to the planning stage.

*You might also like to consult the entry for Buildings.*

**FOUNTAIN**

Spiritually a fountain symbolizes Eternal Life and is a direct reference to the Fountain of Immortality, an image seen in many systems of belief.

In dreams, the fountain, by its association with water, often represents the mother figure or perhaps the source of our emotions.

To dream of a fountain means that we are aware of the generative principle, the process of life and 'flow' of our own consciousness. Because of its connection with water, it also represents the surge of our emotions, and often our ability to express this. The fountain can also represent an element of play in our lives and the need to be free-flowing and untroubled.

⊡ To some extent it will depend which part of the fountain is more noticeable in dreams as to its relevance. The bowl or pool usually represents the feminine and the fountain itself the masculine.

*Consult the entry for Water for further clarification.*

## FOX – *see* ANIMALS

## FRACTION/FRAGMENT

⚜ Any fragmentation perceived from a spiritual perspective suggests that integration has not yet taken place or has broken down. We have only partial information available to us.

♥ When we recognize that we can see only a fraction or fragment of a dream object we need to take further action to gain control of emotions and feelings associated with whatever is represented. The shape of the fragment might be relevant.

▦ It may be unusual to be aware of fractions in dreams except in the sense of 'things half-done' However, when allowing dreams to help us work through our problems fractions and fragments become much more relevant. A dream in three parts may give us the information we need.

*Also consult the entry for Shapes/Patterns.*

## FRAME

⚜ When an object such as a picture is framed, our attention may be being focused with intensity or we may have to become aware of some spiritual limitation.

♥ If the frame is somewhat ornate, we are perhaps being somewhat neurotic in our approach; if it strikes us as very simple then we need to simplify our way of thinking.

▦ Frames give a defined border to objects, making us aware of limitations and restrictions. Within the workaday world these are often not of our own making but put in place by others. An inappropriate frame will highlight a restriction on our creativity. Being 'framed' for an activity we have not done suggests that we are conscious of an injustice in waking life.

*Consult the entries for Border and Edge for more ideas.*

## FRAUD

⚜ We should look at our true spiritual aims and be true to them. Pious fraud – which is deception as a means to a good end – may reveal itself in dreams.

♥ If we accept that the various figures appearing in a dream are parts of our personality, a person who is fraudulent means that we should guard against being dishonest with ourselves and, therefore, deceiving others.

▦ When fraud appears in a dream, particularly if the dreamer is being defrauded, there is the potential to be too trusting of people. If the dreamer is the one committing fraud, he or she runs the real risk of losing a good friend.

## FREEMASON

Spiritually we gain support by belonging to a group of people who think and feel the same way as us. Freemasonry is not a religion as such but it is rich in symbolism, much of which is perceived in dreams as archetypal images. Truly holy men seek harmony and balance in the universe and as Freemasons are self-initiated, they will symbolize this quality in dreams. They may also symbolize esoteric knowledge.

Any grouping of the masculine usually alerts us to the many sides and aspects of the masculine personality. The four prime beliefs of Freemasonry are: the Fatherhood of God; the brotherhood of man; relief to others; and the search for truth. When these qualities are required in our lives we may dream of Freemasonry or of someone of this belief.

Dreaming of belonging to a brotherhood, a mystery school or a closed (secret) society indicates our need to belong to a group of like-minded people. We all need approval from our peers, and such a dream indicates the way we handle ritualized group behaviour.

*For further clarification you might like to consult Spiritual Imagery in the Introduction.*

## FREEZE/FROZEN

When something appears frozen in dreams it has been rendered immobile and usually requires some spiritual effort to free it from its rigidity.

To be freezing something – for instance food – suggests that we are attempting to preserve an emotion or feeling, perhaps to keep a memory pure. It may not be appropriate to do this, however.

In the mundane world a project may be 'frozen' either because of time constraints or to prevent it degenerating. This may translate itself in dreams as something being frozen.

*Consult the entry for Ice/Icebergs/Icicles for further help in interpretation.*

## FRIEND/FRIENDSHIP

A friend is someone we have special feelings for; friendship is much valued in spiritual work. We can continue on our spiritual search in the knowledge that we are being supported.

In dreams friends often highlight a particular part of our own personality that we need to look at, and perhaps understand or come to terms with, in a different way. The concept of friendship appearing in dreams clarifies how we relate to other people.

Friends appearing in our dreams can signify one of two things: firstly we need to look at our relationship with that particular person, and secondly we need to decide what that friend represents for us (for instance security, support and love). Childhood friends may signify innocence, whereas a best friend might be an identification of the best in us.

⚡ Often in male/female relationships we will dream that lovers have changed to loving friends and vice versa before this has actually occurred in waking life.

*Also consult the entry for People.*

## FRINGE – *see* EDGE

## FROG

⚜ The frog is a well-known symbol of transformation and transmutation. The Chinese money frog in *feng shui* (literally the science of wind and water) is a mythical creature, which is said to appear every full moon near homes that will receive good news of increased wealth or monetary gain. For this reason many homes will have a figurine depicting Chan Chu, as it is known, and this will appear as a dream image.

♡ The frog is a symbol of fertility and eroticism. In dreams it is also representative of a perhaps slightly unpleasant aspect of character that can be changed. This image is seen in myths and legends where the frog becomes a prince.

▦ Many people associate the frog with a visible growth pattern, which mirrors the growth to maturity of the human being. In dreams, to see a frog at a particular stage of its growth depicts the feeling we have about ourselves. For instance, to see it at the stage where it has grown its back legs would suggest that we capable of moving forward in leaps and bounds

*You might like to consult the entries for Frog and Reptiles in Animals.*

## FRONT – *see* POSITION

## FRONTIER

⚜ Spiritually, as a frontier is a borderland, we have a new experiences and explorations of the unknown ahead of us. This may lead to new ways of living and being.

♡ Psychologically when we cross from one way of life to another – such as changing from puberty to adulthood or from middle age to old age – we need to depict this by creating an actual marker. In dreams, for a frontier to appear it means crossing a barrier within ourselves. Initially a frontier was a military term signifying the front line of foot soldiers, so the idea of strategy and planning is appropriate.

▦ To dream of crossing a border or frontier from one place to another represents making great changes in life, actively instigating a change from one state to another, into unknown territory. Perhaps we are taking ourselves from the past to the future, or causing other people round us to make those changes.

*You might also like to consult the entry for Border.*

**FRUIT**

✦ Almost inevitably fruit suggests creativity and a natural growth process towards the spiritual.

♥ Psychologically, when we have worked hard we ought to be able to recognize the fruits of our labour. Dreaming of fruit in this way indicates that we have succeeded in what we set out to do. Below are some symbolisms of various fruits.

**The apple** is a symbol of nourishment and growth to maturity of the intuitive Self.

**The apricot** symbolizes self-fertilization and, therefore, the androgynous.

**Berries** in general signify a good harvest and also peace.

**Blackberries** denote sorrow and arrogance, said to date from when Lucifer fell into a bush when he was sent to Earth from Heaven.

**Cherries** are thought to represent youth and innocence and sometimes even virginity.

**Cranberries** stand for the earth's abundance, yet tinged with bitterness and responsibility.

**The orange** is a wish for good fortune.

**The pineapple** is known in some societies as 'anana' or 'excellent fruit', and displays wealth.

**The pomegranate** symbolizes fertility; it was the fruit offered to Persephone to tempt her to remain as Queen of the Underworld.

**Quince** is a symbol of love and happiness.

**Raspberries** denote kindness.

**The strawberry**, as the only fruit to carry its seeds on the surface, signifies honesty and love.

▣ To dream of fruit, particularly in a bowl, very often indicates the culmination of actions that we have taken in the past. We have been able to 'harvest' the past and to make a new beginning for ourselves. Unripe fruit suggests that a plan or project has not yet reached a point where it can be used. Rotting fruit suggests that we have missed an opportunity.

*You might also like to consult the entry for Food.*

**FUNERAL**

✦ As a ritual that marks the end of life, a funeral is a Rite of Passage. Spiritually in dreams it signifies that we can put behind us matters that belong to the material world and can move into a more spiritual life. In allowing others the opportunity to honour their memories, they may make their own adjustments to a change of status. When we appreciate that the funeral is a wake, the symbolism is literally of coming awake to the validity of other realms.

 Dreaming of our parents' funeral indicates a move towards independence, or of letting go of the past, which may be painful. We may need to let our childhood – or childhood experiences – go, and mark that by some ritual or ceremony, being prepared to take responsibility for our own lives. A teenager will often dream of a parent's funeral, as they themselves pass into adulthood.

 To dream of being at a funeral indicates that we need to come to terms with our feelings about death and our attitude to loss. This may not simply be our own death but our issues over the death of others. It may also indicate a time of mourning for something that has happened in the past. This ritual perceived in dreams can allow us to move forward into the future. To dream of our own funeral can indicate a desire for sympathy. It may also indicate that a part of us is dead and we have to let it go.

 In a woman's dream when a relationship ends she may need the finality of such a dream image to allow her to come to terms with the break-up. In a man's dream a funeral may highlight his own emotional make-up and perhaps his feelings of inadequacy in such a situation.

*For further clarification consult the entries for Coffin, Death, Hearse, Mourning and Wake.*

**FUNNEL**

 The symbol of a funnel suggests energy and power running from the upper realms (the spiritual) to the lower (the physical).

 As a funnel channels material placed within it in a controllable way, this image can suggest control of spiritual or creative energy, for instance in healing, but also control of the emotions in certain situations.

 From a mundane perspective, a funnel suggests focusing your energies in a specific way in order to get the best out of any circumstances. A blocked funnel signifies either a lack of receptivity or too much information being given at one time.

 In dreams, material placed in the funnel may be seen as the power available for a particular project, whereas the flow from the bottom is more the power to take action.

The former is a more feminine attribute, the latter masculine.

## FURNITURE/FURNISHINGS

Furniture usually symbolizes our inheritance or revered objects. It also reflects our 'inner landscape', that part of ourselves to which we retire when seeking sanctuary.

Sometimes the furniture that appears in a dream can highlight our need for security or stability, particularly if it is recognizable from the past.

Different articles of furniture have various meanings:

**Bed/mattress** – this can show exactly what is happening in the subtle areas of our close relationships. We can get an insight into how we really feel about intimacy and sexual pleasure. For some people the bed is a place of sanctuary and rest, where they can be totally alone.

**Carpet** – often when carpets appear in a dream we are looking at our emotional links with finance. The colour of the carpet should also be noted.

**Chair** – a chair can indicate that we need a period of rest and recuperation. We may need to deliberately take time out, to be open to other opportunities and openings.

**Cupboard/Wardrobe** – cupboards and wardrobes may depict those things we wish to keep hidden, but may also depict how we deal with the different roles we must play in life.

**Cushion** – this suggests support and comfort.

**Table** – for a table to appear in a dream is often to do with communal activity and with our social affiliations.

**Rugs and other soft furnishings** may show what we need in the way of cosseting, and may reflect our tactile nature.

The furniture that appears in our dreams, particularly if it is drawn to our attention, often shows how we feel about our family and home life, and what attitudes or habits we have developed. It also can give an indication as to how we feel about ourselves. For instance, dark, heavy material would suggest the possibility of depression, whereas brightly painted objects could testify to an upbeat mentality. Broken furniture or that which breaks as we use it can indicate a lack of security and support, or fears about the future.

*You might also like to consult the entries for Altar, Colour and Table.*

## FUTURE

When we are aware of dreaming of the future we begin to understand the process of Spiritual Manifestation – that the past creates the present and the present is the foundation for the future.

Psychologically, if we are to be in control of our lives, we often need to feel that we have to be aware of the future, and dreams can give an insight into best courses of possible action. Dreams allow us to play out certain scenarios, to explore possibilities without coming to any harm.

There are several aspects to dreaming about the future. We may be aware within the dream itself that the events will take place in the future and are usually to do with actions we need to take in waking life. We also may have precognitive dreams, which is when we dream of events – sometimes symbolically – before they take place, and then recognize that we already have the information: we 'knew' about it. The past, present and future co-exist side by side, as it were, and it is possible to 'read' these records in the dream state. Our experience of them is subjective, although we are in the position of observers.

## FUZZY

When an image is indistinct or fuzzy, from a spiritual perspective this can mean that an aspect of knowledge or awareness has not yet become clear. The 'third eye', which is the ability to perceive the truth, will sometimes operate in dreams before we are aware of this faculty in waking life.

Emotional difficulties can make our thought processes confused, symbolized in dreams by a fuzziness in the images we perceive.

As a reflection of real life, when projects or concepts and ideas have not been properly clarified, dream images will appear fuzzy and indistinct in an effort to make us aware of a problem.

## GAG

◉ From a spiritual perspective a gag is anything that stops us from communicating effectively. This will encompass both negative and positive aspects; that is, when prudence dictates that we say nothing or when an external condition forcibly restrains us.

◈ Many people have difficulty in expressing their emotions, so a gag in dreams may symbolize the underlying emotional difficulty that prevents us from doing so. This might, for instance, be childhood trauma or the feeling that we will not be listened to. To gag, as in experiencing nausea, suggests we are trying to get rid of negative feelings.

▦ If we are being gagged in a dream then there is a strong possibility that in waking life we are being prevented from expressing an opinion over something we feel to be important. If we are doing the gagging then we will be suppressing our ability to speak clearly or honestly.

*You might also like to consult the entries for Talking and Vomit.*

## GALAXY

◉ The term 'a galaxy of stars' originally applied to what we now call the Milky Way. In that sense, it symbolizes a potent part of our own universe, and a concept the magnitude of which is not easily grasped.

◈ A galaxy is a huge collection and thus symbolizes vastness and depth in dreams, and not only one emotional response but many. Since we in dreams are usually observing the phenomena, there is an element of objectivity in being able to view our emotions in this way.

▦ A galaxy of celebrities, in the sense of a group of people, most of whom have some importance in their own field, are perceived as powerful. In dreams, if this image is present we perhaps need to decide what the common factor is between them and how this might relate to our lives.

*You might like to consult the entries for Celebrity, Crowd, Group, Planets and Shapes/Patterns.*

## GALE – *see* WIND

## GAMBLING

◉ Man has, since time began, attempted to discover the will of the Divine. Spiritually, therefore, to dream of gambling offers us an opportunity to do just that. It represents taking a risk that has been assessed as far as we are able.

⚕ To dream of gambling indicates that we may need to look at something in our lives that is figuratively a gamble; we may need to take risks, but in such a way that we have calculated them as best we can.

▣ From a practical perspective, gambling dreams can represent not taking life seriously. They can show how we work within the competitive field and give us some kind of insight into our own sense of winning or losing.

*Consult the entries for Dice/Die, Games, Lottery and Win/Winning for further information.*

## GAMES

✸ Spiritually, games are a form of ritualized conflict between two opposing forces. Wars and tribal localized fights were used previously by elders and priests to channel aggression. In the same way, because they are mock fights, games in dreams can be used as expressions of aggression against other people.

⚕ Specific games such as football, baseball, rugby and cricket (which are team games) represent for many the strong ability to identify with a 'tribe' or a group of people. They indicate the way in which we gain identity and how we connect with people. A referee in such a game signifies the monitoring of our behaviour. In dreams, games that require the power of thought and strategy – such as chess or draughts – often give some idea of how we should be taking a situation forward. Decisions may need to be made where we have to gauge the result of our action and take into account our opponent's reaction.

▣ Playing a game such as golf in our dream indicates that we are taking note of how we play the game of life. If we are playing well we may take it that we are coping well with circumstances in our lives. If we are playing badly we may need to reassess our abilities and identify which skills we need to improve in order to do things better.

*Consult the entries for Chess, Gambling and Win/Winning for further information.*

## GANG – *see* GROUP

## GARAGE

✸ We all have certain spiritual tools, such as compassion, empathy and perception, which we can call upon at certain times; they are part of our motivation. A garage is a symbolic reminder that we have them in storage and they can be utilized at any time.

⚕ A car repair garage – remembering that a car represents the way we handle our external life – can indicate the need for personal attention and perhaps bodily maintenance.

▣ A garage appearing in a dream may indicate how we store our own personal abilities. It is the workshop from which we need to move out into the world in order to show what we have done. We are looking at our reserves of drive and motivation and possibly at our abilities.

*You might also like to consult the entries for Car, Engine, Transport and Workshop.*

**GARBAGE –** *see* **RUBBISH**

**GARDEN**

⚙ A garden can represent a form of paradise, as in the Garden of Eden. We are able to allow ourselves some spiritual relaxation and life need not be too much of a trial. Dreaming of herbs in a garden is often to do with the magical and mystical.

♡ The garden is often a symbol of the wilder feminine attributes, which need to be cultivated and tamed in order to create clarity. Enclosed gardens particularly have this significance and traditionally have represented virginity.

▦ Dreaming of a garden can be fascinating because it may indicate the area of growth in our own lives, or it can be that which we are trying to cultivate in ourselves. It often represents our inner life and that which we totally appreciate about our own being.

◲ In a woman's dream a garden signifies her own personal space or territory, whereas for a man it will suggest a shared space.

*You might also like to consult the entries for Flowers, Gardener, Magic/Magician, Paradise, Plants and Weeds.*

**GARDENER**

⚙ A gardener helps us identify with our wiser aspects such as correct speech and careful thought. We need to tend to these gifts of wisdom and not let them become stagnant.

♡ If we find ourselves looking after a garden within a dream, we are nurturing those aspects of ourselves that we have carefully cultivated and that we need to keep 'tidy', in order to get the best out of ourselves.

▦ Whenever a person appears in our dream in a certain role it is important to look at what he is actually doing. The gardener can represent the insights that we have gathered through our experience in life and can equally represent wisdom, but of a particular sort. Often the gardener indicates someone on whom we can rely, who will take care of those things with which we do not feel capable of dealing.

*You might also like to consult the entries for Flowers, Garden, Plants and Weeds.*

**GARLAND**

⚙ A garland is symbolic of the need for dedication, either spiritually or physically. It may also represent an element of our subconscious Holiness, or rather undeveloped spirituality, which we need to acknowledge.

♥ Psychologically, a garland can represent honour and recognition and can form a link or bond with the people who honoured us. In dreams, it will be important to interpret what the garlands are made of, since this may help us to identify our best abilities; for instance, garlands of bay laurel were used to honour Apollo and his many attributes.

▦ Depending on the type of garland in the dream, we are recognizing some distinction or honour for ourselves. If we are wearing the garland, such as a Hawaiian flower garland, we are looking at various ways of making ourselves happy. We are looking at dedication, and at some way of setting ourselves apart from others. Winners in sports contests are often honoured by garlands, so in dreams these would signify competition.

*Consult the entries for Bridle, Flowers, Laurel/Bay Leaves and Wreath for further information.*

## GARLIC

❀ Garlic is considered a herb of Magic. As a protective amulet, particularly against the evil eye, it is of significance against negativity. In Chinese lore it also symbolizes luck, health and many children, so in dreams may signify all of these.

♥ Garlic is now known to help all sorts of physical conditions – including strengthening the heart – and therefore protects one against fear. Dreaming of garlic may be a way of our body alerting us to a need for such protection from infection.

▦ Garlic in olden times had much significance. Because of its shape and its many parts it was often seen as a symbol of fertility; because of its smell it was seen as protection. Dreaming of garlic may, therefore, link back to either of these meanings. In practical magic, garlic is a specific against witches.

⊡ As a fertility symbol a full head of garlic in a woman's dream may symbolize the testicles. In a man's case such a dream is more about essential masculinity.

*You might also like to consult the entries for Magic/Magician, Protect/Protection and Witch.*

## GARTER – *see* WEDDING/WEDDING DRESS/WEDDING RING

## GATE

❀ The gate in dreams is a potent image of the transition between the physical and spiritual realms, not just in the sense of death, but also as we learn more about spirituality. It is used as a 'gateway' for communication, and as a visualization before sleep can help us to access much information. It will sometimes signify the half-aware hypnogogic and hynopompic states between sleeping and waking.

🏵 Dreaming of a gate usually signifies some kind of change, often in awareness. We are passing a threshold in our lives, perhaps trying something different or moving from one phase of life to another. Often the awareness of change is highlighted by the type of gate. For instance, a farm gate would tend to indicate a work change, whereas a garden gate might represent pleasure.

🔲 In everyday life the image of passing through some kind of barrier appears often in dreams. An ornate gate might suggest a somewhat structured change, whereas an old gate, particularly if it is broken, suggests a well-worn way of working, which may need updating.

*Also consult the entries for Barrier and Door.*

**GATHERING** – *see* **MEET/MEETING**

**GAUGE** – *see* **MEASURE AND WEIGHING/WEIGHT**

**GAZELLE** – *see* **DEER IN ANIMALS**

**GEAR**

🏵 In spiritual terms a gear signifies a change of consciousness. Moving up a gear suggests moving towards the spiritual and moving down, towards the physical or material.

🏵 Psychologically we sometimes need to change perspective. This can be seen as changing gear in a vehicle, to alert us to changes that need to be made.

🔲 In the vernacular, gear can represent both the paraphernalia associated with drug-taking and also clothes. We shall need to make some kind of link with the circumstances in our everyday lives. For instance, if in the drug-taking 'gear' a component is missing, we may be creating difficulties for ourselves. Insofar as clothes are concerned, we probably need to act more appropriately.

*You might like to consult the entries for Clothes, Drugs and Transport.*

**GEMS/JEWELS**

🏵 From a spiritual point of view, gems and jewels have always had esoteric significance. The understanding and use of gems and jewels can greatly enhance personal development. In most dreams it is the better-known stones which appear, but when the lesser-known ones are seen, there is much benefit to be gained by learning more on a conscious level. Many stones have healing properties.

🏵 If, in dreams, the jewels are set – made up into wearable articles – we are aware of some of the uses of whatever the jewel signifies. For instance, to find an emerald ring might suggest that we have completed one of the stages of growth towards immortality. There are different interpretations for each gemstone, and opinions do vary. The significances of some well-known jewels and gems that have particular relevance in dreams are:

**Agate** (black) symbolizes wealth, courage, assurance and vigour; (red) peace, spiritual love of good, health, prosperity and longevity.

**Amber** represents crystallized light. There is an element of magnetism in it.

**Amethyst** is the healing gem. Connecting us with the spiritual, it represents the influence of dreams and also humility, peace of mind, faith, self-restraint and acceptance.

**Aquamarine** embodies the qualities of hope, youth and health.

**Beryl** is believed to hold within it happiness, hope and eternal youthfulness.

**Bloodstone** holds the qualities of peace and understanding. It is also reputed to grant all wishes.

**Carnelian** highlights friendship, courage, self-confidence and health.

**Chrysolite** represents wisdom, discretion, tact and prudence.

**Chrysoprase** symbolizes gaiety and unconditional happiness. It is also the symbol of joy.

**Crystal** symbolizes purity, simplicity and magical power.

**Diamond** has a number of influences: light, life, the sun, durability, incorruptibility, loyalty, sincerity and innocence.

**Emerald** embraces immortality, hope, youth, faithfulness and also the beauty of spring.

**Garnet** can help energy levels and indicates devotion, loyalty and grace.

**Jade** represents 'all that is supremely excellent', the yang power of the joyful heavens.

**Jasper** holds the qualities of joy and happiness.

**Jet** is usually associated with darker emotions such as grief and mourning, although it also controls safety within a journey.

**Lapis Lazuli** is a favourable stone said to evoke divine favour, success and the ability to show perseverance.

**Lodestone** holds within it the qualities of integrity and honesty; and is also said to influence virility.

**Moonstone/Selenite** symbolizes the moon and its magical qualities, tenderness and the romantic lovers.

**Onyx** is for perspicacity, sincerity, spiritual strength and conjugal happiness.

**Opal** not only represents fidelity, but also religious fervour, prayers and assurance of spiritual beliefs.

**Pearl** symbolizes the feminine principles of chastity and purity, and also the moon and the flow of water.

**Ruby** represents all that is traditionally associated with royalty; dignity, zeal, power, love, passion, beauty, longevity and invulnerability.

**Sapphire** holds within it worldly truth, contemplation of the universe, heavenly virtues and chastity.

**Topaz** holds the beauty of the Divine: goodness, faithfulness, friendship, love, sagacity. Topaz also symbolizes the sun.

**Tourmaline** represents inspiration and imagination as well as friendship.

**Turquoise** symbolizes courage – physical and spiritual – fulfilment and also success.

**Zircon** holds within it much worldly wisdom as well as the virtues of honour and the prestige (or otherwise) of riches.

▨ Jewels appearing in dreams almost invariably symbolize those things that we value. These may be personal qualities, our sense of integrity, our ability to be ourselves, or even our very essential being. When we feel we know what we are looking for, we are aware on some level of its value to us or others. When we simply register that we are looking for jewels, sometimes up a mountain, otherwise in a cave, we are attempting to find those parts of ourselves that we know will be of value in the future. Counting or in some way assessing them would suggest a time of reflection is needed. One system of belief suggests the following practical meanings:

**Amethyst** promotes healing and influences dreams.

**Diamond** signifies human greed, hardness of nature and what we value from a cosmic perspective.

**Emerald** highlights personal growth.

**Opal** suggests the inner world of fantasies, dreams and psychic awareness.

**Pearl** signifies inner beauty and value.

**Ruby** informs on emotions, passion and sympathies.

**Sapphire** highlights religious feelings.

*You might also like to consult the entry for Jewellery.*

**GERMS –** *see* **DIRTY AND INFECTION**

**GHOST**

✺ If a ghost – i.e. a shadowy shape – appears in a dream we may be alerted to our past states of being and ways of behaviour. We need to identify these and acknowledge that we have moved on.

◈ We may be resurrecting old memories or feelings in order to understand our own actions. By putting ourselves in touch with what is dead and gone we can take appropriate action in the here and now. If we dream of being haunted by a ghost we have probably not handled an emotional trauma well.

🔲 Actually dreaming of a ghost links us to old habit patterns, or buried hopes and longings. There is something insubstantial in these, possibly because we have not put enough energy into them.

*You might like to consult the entry for Spirit for further information.*

## GIANT

✹ A giant represents primordial power, somewhat overwhelming in its force.

♡ Giants and ogres often represent the emotion of anger, particularly masculine anger. This can be confronted in dreams where perhaps we cannot do this in waking life.

🔲 Dreaming about giants may mean we are coming to terms with some of the repressed feelings we had about adults when we were children. They may have seemed larger than life or frightening in some way.

*You might also like to consult the entries for Anger, Monster and Size.*

## GIFT/GIVE/GIVING

✹ In a spiritual sense, dreaming of a gift may be pointing us towards our creative talents, of which we may not yet be aware. We need to acknowledge the gifts and talents we have and use them appropriately. In a spiritual sense giving in is submitting to a higher authority.

♡ Each of us has a store of unconscious knowledge, which from time to time becomes available to us and may appear in dreams as gifts. Some of these gifts we are able to share with others. This satisfies one of the fundamental needs of the human being: to be able to give to others. Psychologically this represents our ability to belong to a community, to have others belong within our lives and to assume responsibility for other people.

🔲 Giving is all about the relationships we have with ourselves, the environment and with others. So to dream of giving somebody something in a dream indicates our need to give and take within a relationship – our need to give of ourselves, perhaps to share with others what we have, and to create an environment that allows for give and take. To receive a gift within a dream is to recognize our talents and abilities.

*You might also like to consult the entries for Present/Presents for further information.*

## GIG – *see* DANCE/DANCING, MOVEMENT AND MUSIC/RHYTHM

## GIGGLE – *see* LAUGH

## GIRDLE

✹ A girdle represents spiritual wisdom, strength and power. Its appearance in dreams indicates we are progressing in the right direction, with some degree of protection. The girdle is a length of material which symbolizes time, yet, because it encircles the body, it also symbolizes completeness. It thus represents the inevitability of life and death.

♥ Like a belt, in dreams a girdle can represent an insignia of honour or of power, but perhaps of a more intuitive feminine kind. Mythologically, the magical girdle of Aphrodite had the power to influence desire.

▦ For those who have an interest in magic and magical practices, the cingulum or witch's girdle – in itself a magical tool – will often appear in dreams.

⊞ In a woman's dream the girdle may depict her sense of her own femininity, for instance when she feels bound or constricted by it. In a man's dream it is more likely to show his understanding of his power over his own life.

*You might also like to consult the entries for Belt, Magic/Magician, Witch and Wizard.*

**GIRL – *see* PEOPLE**

**GIRLFRIEND – *see* PEOPLE**

**GLACIER – *see* ICE/ICEBERG/ICICLES**

**GLASS**

⚘ Glass, being transparent, symbolizes the barrier between ordinary life and the life hereafter and between the physical and spiritual realms. It can also suggest the transparency of truth as we understand it.

♥ To dream of breaking glass is to be breaking through barriers. We are shattering the emotions that keep us trapped and moving into a clearer space where we do not allow barriers to build. Frosted or smoked glass can indicate a desire for privacy, or our obscured view of a particular situation within our lives.

▦ Dreaming of glass indicates the invisible but very tangible barriers we may erect around ourselves in order to protect ourselves from meaningful relationship with other people. They may also represent the barriers that other people put up and also be those aspects of ourselves that we have built up in our own defence.

*Also consult the entries for Barrier, Break, Mirror and Reflection as well as Windows in the Buildings entry.*

**GLASSES/SPECTACLES**

⚘ Spiritually, a dream of glasses or spectacles may be urging us to take a different viewpoint – on a physical as well as spiritual level.

♥ Psychologically, when we are able to wear glasses we are more able to look at that which is external to ourselves rather than turning inwards and becoming introspective. So, in dreams, glasses can represent the need for extroversion within a situation.

🔲 For glasses or spectacles to stand out in a dream indicates a connection with our ability to see or to understand. Equally, if someone is unexpectedly wearing glasses, it is to do either with our lack of understanding or perhaps their inability to see where we are coming from.

*Also consult the entry for Goggles and Lens.*

## GLOBAL WARMING – *see* CLIMATE

## GLOBE

🌑 Dreaming of a globe or sphere is to dream of power and of dignity and symbolizes our need for wholeness. It also suggests concern for global matters such as conservation or global warming. Spiritually a globe suggests completion.

💙 It is a representation of the wholeness of life We have certain powers within us that will enable us to create a sustainable future, and for this we need to be able to understand and take an objective world view.

🔲 To dream of looking at a globe, particularly in the sense of a world globe, indicates our appreciation of a wider viewpoint. We can cultivate the ability not only not to be narrow-minded but to be more globally aware. If we are looking at, for instance, a glass globe we may be looking at a lifestyle that is complete in itself.

*You might also like to consult the entry for World.*

## GLOOM

🌑 Gloom usually indicates the presence of negative feelings, which will be dissipated as we become more spiritually aware. Light and lightness are symbolic of spirituality, so the opposite can suggest a movement – whether involuntary or otherwise – towards emotional distress.

💙 If in dreams we find ourselves enclosed in gloom while others appear to be in the light, we may be being warned of an aspect of depression that is affecting us, but not affecting them. Conversely if we are in light while other people are in shadow we may have information that will help them to enhance their lives.

🔲 Gloom is less pervasive than darkness, so if it is around in a dream, it can indicate difficulty in being able to see or comprehend things from an external viewpoint. There may be negativity around in waking life of which we have to be aware in order to be able to dispel it – to create light and clarity – so that we can make progress.

*Also consult the entries for Dark/Darkness and Light.*

## GLOVES

Spiritually, since hands are symbolic of our innate creativity, gloves can symbolize the need to protect our creative ability. In dreams, they may also signify an impediment to full creative expression, our ability to give form to our ideas.

To some extent it will depend what sort of gloves are represented. Working gloves will suggest protection from harm, whereas dress gloves denote enhancement of our abilities. Surgical gloves signify a degree of sterility in our dealings with other people. Throwing down a gauntlet or glove means we are challenging belief.

Often in previous times the glove had greater significance than it does nowadays. Because it was so much part of social etiquette it represented honour, purity and evidence of good faith. Now being aware of gloves in a dream often represents some way in which we are hiding our abilities from people around us. To take off the glove signifies respect and an act of sincerity. To dream of boxing gloves could indicate that we are trying too hard to succeed in a situation where there is aggression.

*Consulting the entries for Clothes and also Hands in Body will give further information.*

## GNAW – *see* BITE/BITTEN

## GNOME/GOBLIN

The name 'gnome' was given by the medieval scholar Paracelsus to describe the most important of the earth spirits. Goblins are a different, more grotesque, malicious variety of gnome. Visible to some who have developed clairvoyance, they are manifestations of nature's power.

Gnomes are said to guard the treasures of the earth, living underground, whereas goblins have no real home. In dreams, therefore, the former will signify contentment but the latter stands for discontent.

When gnomes or goblins appear in dreams we are linking with the inherent powers of nature and perhaps the personalization of parts of our own psyche. The hidden instinctive aspect is seen in the gnome and the well-buried malicious persona in the goblin. We perhaps should look at how our actions are affecting others.

*You might also like to consult the entries for Fairies and Nymphs.*

## GOAD

Power and Spiritual authority often act as a goad so we can improve our knowledge. The trident depicted in images of the God Neptune is a goad and represents illusion, intuition and inspiration – a threefold spur towards understanding.

◈ Psychologically, we are all goaded by our own more aggressive and negative parts. Often a dream can reveal how we are making things difficult for ourselves and indicate which part is becoming too aggressive.

▦ The goad can be shown in many ways, not just as the conventional spiked stick. Often if we are goading somebody to do something they do not want to do, we must take care that we are not creating circumstances that could rebound on us. We may be trying to force people to take action to move forward but we must also be aware that we need to be in control of that particular movement.

## GOAL

❂ Our spiritual aspirations are being highlighted. If we are aware of our goal then we can make tremendous inroads towards attainment. The dream image is not then just a pictorial representation, but can be used as a visualization of our success.

◈ To set life goals – or to be conscious of doing this in a dream – indicates that we are in touch with our own internal sense of our ability to achieve. The external is often a reflection of the internal, and goals can indicate that we instinctively know how much – and what – we are capable of doing.

▦ To dream of scoring a goal may indicate that we have set ourselves external targets. In achieving those targets we may also recognize that the goals we have set ourselves in life are either short-term or long-term and we may need to adjust them in some way. To miss a goal or target indicates that we have not taken all the circumstances within a situation into account and need, perhaps, to reassess our abilities to achieve.

*You might like to consult the entry for Target for additional clarification.*

## GOAT – *see* ANIMALS

## GOBLET

❂ In dreams the goblet has similar significance to the chalice. It represents the feminine, receptive principal and our ability to achieve enjoyment in different ways. As with all hollow vessels, spiritually it suggests also the Cup of Life.

◈ To dream of a set of goblets (as in wine glasses) rather than just a single one signifies the diversity of our own emotions and the value to us of social occasion. If a goblet is broken we may have made an error of judgement.

▦ We may be able to make a celebration out of something that is quite ordinary. To be drinking from a goblet indicates allowing ourselves the freedom to enjoy life to the full. If the goblet is decorated we may find that it signifies a particular skill or ability.

*Consult the entries for Chalice and Cup for further clarification.*

**GOBLIN** – *see* GNOME/GOBLIN

**GOD/GODS**

⚛ Spiritually, we are aware of a greater power (the Divine). Christian belief holds to one God, although manifesting in three forms – Father, Son and Holy Ghost. Other religions attribute the powers to various Gods. As we grow in understanding, we can appreciate the relevance of both monotheistic and polytheistic beliefs and can begin to understand God as an all-pervading energy.

♥ The powerful emotions we sometimes experience may be connected with our tremendous childhood need for love and parental approval. Often these emotions can be personalized and recognized in the figures of gods from the numerous belief systems around the world.

▦ When we dream of God we are acknowledging to ourselves that there is a higher power in charge. We connect with all humanity and, therefore, have a right to a certain set of moral beliefs. We all have needs for love and approval, which can only be met through our understanding of our childhood.

⬒ In a woman's dream, dreaming of the gods will help her to understand various aspects of her own personality. In a man's dream he is linking with his own masculinity and his sense of belonging to himself, and therefore to the rest of humanity.

*For further clarification consult the information on Archetypes and Spiritual Imagery in the Introduction.*

**GODDESS/GODDESSES**

⚛ Spiritually, a woman is able to make intuitive links with the essential aspects of her own personality. She then achieves a greater understanding of her own make-up, and is able to use all facets of her being within her normal everyday life. Sophia (meaning 'Wisdom') is a personalization of an aspect of the Divine.

♥ There are many goddess figures in all cultures. There are those perceived as being destructive, such as Kali, Bast and Lilith, and also beneficent ones such as Athena and Hermia.

▦ Dreaming of goddesses from various cultures connects us with our archetypal images of femininity. In the waking state, it is the sense of mystery – of a shared secret – which is such an intangible force within the woman's psyche. This enables women to create a sisterhood or network among themselves in order to bring about a common aim. To dream about goddesses, therefore, is to accept our right to initiation into this group.

In a woman's dream a goddess will clarify both the connection through the unconscious that exists between all women and female creatures and which particular archetypal aspect of femininity she favours. In a man's dream the goddess figure signifies all that a man fears in the concept of female power. It usually also gives an insight into his earliest view of femininity through his experience of his mother.

*For further clarification consult the information on Archetypes and Spiritual Imagery in the Introduction.*

## GOGGLES

We may be covering up, or denying, the existence of negativity. The eyes are believed to be the seat of the soul and to reflect our inner feelings.

In today's climate of androgynous dressing, goggles and sunglasses in dreams can appear both menacing and in some cases reflective. We must therefore decide whether we are intimidated or intrigued. If we are wearing goggles our vision of the future may be impaired in some way.

Goggles in a dream can have the same significance as spectacles and a mask. The meaning can be ambivalent since goggles can be used either to cover up the eyes or to enable us to see events occurring around us better. Under most circumstances it can be taken as the latter, but the dream image of goggles may indicate the protective shield that we may need in real life.

For a woman to dream that she meets a man with goggles formerly meant that she could not trust that man to be honest with her. It can still have the same significance today. In a man's dream, to be wearing goggles suggests that some important matter is being hidden.

*You might also like to consult the entries for Glasses/Spectacles and Mask.*

## GOLD

Gold in dreams can represent our sacred, dedicated side thus symbolizing Spirituality on a supreme level. The old saying of 'everything that glitters isn't gold' certainly doesn't apply in the spiritual sense.

In an emotional context, gold seldom stands for material wealth. It is more the spiritual assets that we have, such as incorruptibility and wisdom, love, patience and care. These enable us to apply the principles of alchemy and turn base emotional dross into 'gold' and finer feelings.

Gold in dreams suggests our best, most valuable practical aspects, such as integrity and honesty. Finding gold indicates that we can discover those aspects in ourselves or others. Burying gold shows that we are trying to hide something – perhaps information or knowledge – that we have.

*Also consult the entries for Alchemy, Metal and Treasure.*

**GOLF** – *see* **GAMES**

**GOOSE** – *see* **BIRDS**

**GOSSIP**

⚜ Gossip, in the sense of needless chatter might be called spiritual 'static'. When we are developing spiritually we can become rather like badly tuned radios and can pick up needless information.

♥ Within the framework of personal development there is often what could be called the 'gossip' in the background – the chatterbox – that which is part of our personality but which prevents us from moving away from previously held ideas and behaviour. Thus, to be gossiping in a dream may mean that we have to complete certain actions before moving on.

▦ To be gossiping in a dream can mean that we are spreading information, but in a way that is not necessarily appropriate. To be in a group of people and listening to gossip generally means that we are looking for some kind of information, but perhaps do not have the ability to achieve it for ourselves. We have to use other people to enable us to achieve the correct level of information.

*Consult the entry for Talking for further information.*

**GOUGE** – *see* **INJURE/INJURY AND WOUND**

**GRADUATE/GRADUATION**

⚜ Dreaming of graduating has the same spiritual significance as winning an accolade and of initiation.

♥ To graduate is to have reached a certain stage of knowledge or proficiency and in dreams, particularly on an emotional or psychological level suggests an element of self-control.

▦ Taking part in a graduation ceremony means we are receiving acknowledgement for our proficiency in having completed a project or task. We are now ready to move on to the next stage.

*You might like to consult the entries for Initiation and Win/Winning.*

**GRAFFITI**

⚜ Graffiti in dreams may be one way of the unconscious trying to get a message across. It may also suggest that some information we have received is inappropriate.

♥ As a means of self-expression, the liveliness of graffiti may suggest a need to 'lighten up' and show a creative streak.

▦ Graffiti in dreams is something 'writ large', albeit in an inappropriate place. This means we have to consider more than one aspect of a task or project, before committing it to paper.

## GRAIL

🔆 The Holy Grail was thought to be the cup used at The Last Supper and to have contained the blood of Christ. The search for it has, from a spiritual perspective, become part of the Hero's Quest on his journey of self-discovery. Often in dreams it represents the achievement of spiritual success, but can also represent the cup of happiness or fulfilment.

♥ The Holy Grail, as a chalice or goblet, is such a strong mythical image that in dreams it can appear as something miraculous, something that fulfils our wish and allows us to move forward into our full potential. We are searching for something that we may feel at this particular moment is unattainable, but that, by putting ourselves through various tests, we may eventually reach.

▦ The Grail appearing in a dream would indicate that we can expect some form of satisfaction and change to occur within our lives. For our own peace of mind we need to sort out truth from fiction for ourselves and use such an image to help us toward success.

*Consulting the entries for Camelot, Chalice, Goblet, Knight and Quest will enhance your understanding.*

## GRAIN

🔆 Grain can represent the very seeds of life and our need to discover the Hidden Truth. As an offering to Nature it honours the abundance of Mother Earth.

♥ To dream of grain growing in a field can indicate that we are more or less on the point of success, that we have tended our lives sufficiently to be able to achieve growth.

▦ Dreaming of grains such as wheat, oats, barley, etc. can indicate some kind of a harvest. We have created opportunities for ourselves which can now come to fruition. Provided we look after the outcome of these opportunities, we can take that success forward and create even more abundance.

⊡ Grain and the sheaf of corn are old symbols for fertility and for nurturing. In a woman's dream she will recognize her essential nature through these symbols. In a man's dream, he will appreciate Nature and nurturing.

*You might also like to consult the entries for Bread, Food and Harvest.*

## GRANDPARENTS – *see* FAMILY

## GRAPES

🔆 Grapes, representing the food of the Gods, can symbolize Spiritual wisdom and the search for immortality.

♥ Grapes appearing in a dream can represent sacrifice, in the sense of making something sacred. We need to give something up in order to achieve what we are really looking for. Wine is often taken to represent such sacrifice because it has a close religious affiliation with blood and, because of its colour, with blood sacrifice.

To see grapes in a dream generally indicates that there is a need for celebration. The grape is the fruit most closely associated with the Roman god Bacchus or, in his Greek form, Dionysus who was the god of conviviality. To dream of grapes indicates we are searching for fun, laughter and creativity in our lives.

*You might also like to consult the entries for Fruit and Wine.*

## GRASS

Changes of Spiritual awareness can be indicated by grass appearing in a dream. Sacred, hallowed or consecrated ground might be represented by turf.

Grass can often denote our native land, and dreaming of our association with a particular piece of ground can activate memories and feelings connected with happy times. It can also suggest that we need to surrender deeply held beliefs, and thus will clarify a particular problem or situation.

Grass is often a symbol of new growth and of victory over barrenness. In old dream interpretations it could represent pregnancy, but is now more likely to signify new ideas and projects. To dream of being on 'sacred' turf – ground that is revered because of its association, such as particular sports grounds – is to wish for supreme success.

*You might also like to consult the entry for Harvest.*

## GRASSHOPPER

In Chinese history the grasshopper is often associated with enlightenment. Thus, it represents some form of Spiritual freedom.

A grasshopper mind (one which flits all over the place) shows an inability to settle to anything and can actually be seen in dreams as a grasshopper. We should perhaps concentrate more on important matters so we can achieve our aims.

The grasshopper is a symbol of freedom and capriciousness, and in dreams it can often indicate a bid, or our need, for freedom.

*You might also like to consult the entry for Insects.*

## GRAVE

Spiritually, we may fear not just physical death but also its consequences, particularly if we have no particular belief in the after-life. Dreaming of a grave is an indication that we must have regard for our feelings about, or our concept of, death.

A grave may signify the loss of emotion or of feeling. Part of our personality may, quite literally, have been killed off, or is dead and buried to the outside world.

🖼 Such a dream may also be attempting to deal with our feelings about someone who has died. Falling into a grave is an old symbol for initiation. Digging a grave suggests that we need closure over an aspect of everyday life; it may mean that we can go no further with a particular task. Pushing someone into a grave signifies some very negative feelings, which need to be consciously dealt with and not buried.

*You might also like to consult the entries for Burial, Coffin, Dead People, Death, Funeral and Initiation.*

## GRAVITY

☀ In dreams, gravity is a force that draws us towards the physical or material realms, rather than the spiritual, almost despite ourselves. As we wake up to the ordinary, everyday world, we can experience gravity as a tangible physical pressure.

♥ Emotionally, gravity symbolizes a lowering of emotion in dreams towards the more negative feelings of fear and depression. In such dreams there can seem to be an actual physical force present.

🖼 A sense of gravity can inject an aspect of seriousness into our dreams if there are problems or difficulties in waking life. These can be experienced as heavy or weighted objects.

*Also consult the entry for Weighing/Weight.*

## GREENHOUSE EFFECT – *see* CLIMATE

## GREYHOUND – *see* DOG IN ANIMALS

## GRIEF – *see* MOURNING

## GRIFFIN

☀ In antiquity the griffin was a mythical beast with the body of a lion and the head and wings of an eagle. In dreams it is an archetypal symbol and guardian of divine power.

♥ Combining the qualities of wisdom and bravery, emotionally in dreams the griffin advocates right speech and correct action.

🖼 Symbolic of fire and air combined, the griffin is used in everyday life as an emblem, so can appear in dreams in the form of a logo. It will represent the need for intelligent communication.

*You might like to consult the entry for Fabulous Beasts for further clarification.*

## GRIP – *see* HOLD

## GROOM – *see* BRIDEGROOM

## GROUP

☀ A group – usually of people – is a number of different individuals often from different backgrounds with a common aim. Spiritually it is usually this aim that will bind them together. Gangs will develop signs and language peculiar to themselves and will tend to anarchic or criminal behaviour. In dreams, therefore, a group will largely be peaceable and a gang noisier.

❤ Emotionally in dreams a group will tend to be supportive while a gang will be confrontational. Either can appear if we have problems in fitting in socially, and how we deal with them will provide information useful to us in everyday life.

▦ At some point in our lives, social skills become important to us. Groups and gangs in dreams show us how good we are at handling ourselves and others. If we are members of either then we have passed some kind of personal test; in the case of gangs we may feel we have passed through some kind of initiation ceremony. If we are rejected in dreams we ourselves may not yet be ready to belong.

## GROW/GROWTH

❀ Growth in a dream can be the recognition of a new Spiritual maturity, from which we can take heart.

❤ Often when we dream of childhood we are able to put ourselves in touch with the growth process, and can have a sense of growing, usually larger, but sometimes smaller. This can give a strong sense of being very small within the Universe or very large and giant-like within the everyday world.

▦ The changes in us that bring about new ways of relating to other people, who we ourselves are or situations around us, are all stages of growth. They can be pictured in dreams as the growth of a plant or something similar.

*You might also like to consult the entries for Giant and Size.*

## GUARD/GUARDIAN

❀ A guardian is one who watches over us and spiritually this usually means a guardian angel. This belief in guardian angels can be traced throughout all antiquity and as we become more aware of the existence of the spiritual realms we become able to sense their presence in dreams. As we progress it is natural to meet our own guardian spirits and those who are the guardian spirits of Nature.

❤ In dreams, when we become conscious of someone standing guard or guarding an object we perhaps need to be careful of our actions. If it seems that we are being guarded, then we are being protected from harm. If we are the guardian then we should consider our responsibilities.

▦ To be a guard in dreams suggests a sense of duty or obligation, either towards someone or to whatever the object is that we are charged with looking after. This also suggests a particular code of conduct or behaviour.

*You might also like to consult the entry for Angel.*

**GUERRILLA** – *see* **TERROR/TERRORIST**

**GUILLOTINE**

A guillotine represents a severance of some kind in dreams. Since it severs the head from the body, it suggests that we may have become severed from our spiritual sources.

From an emotional perspective, a guillotine indicates that there is the potential for us to lose contact with the part of ourselves that is capable of love, or, in reality, with someone we love. A short, sharp shock in our lives may cause severe disruption.

A guillotine in a dream indicates an irrational aspect in our personality, which is trying to queer our pitch. We may be afraid of losing self-control in an everyday situation, or of having part of our personality amputated. We could be aware of an injury to our person or to our dignity.

*You might like to consult the entries for Amputation, Execute, Injure/Injury Weapon and Wound for further clarification.*

**GUILT**

Spiritual guilt is self-reproach for inadequacy or wrongdoing and arises out of an internal struggle between what we perceive to be right and wrong. In dreams the feeling can be more powerful than in everyday life.

The emotion of guilt is such that, rather than blame others, we will often take the feeling to a very profound level. This can disturb our dreams until we have had the courage to truly forgive ourselves.

When guilt arises in dreams it is usually because our instincts tell us that we have not been true to our own principles of truth and integrity. When we have done something that may result in us being judged, or committed some minor misdemeanour, in waking life we will experience guilt in dreams.

*You might also like to consult the entry for Judge/Judgement.*

**GUITAR** – *see* **MUSIC/RHYTHM AND MUSICAL INSTRUMENTS**

**GULLS** – *see* **SEAGULL IN BIRDS**

**GUN**

The symbolism here reverts to a basic attribute – that of overt masculinity and a strong degree of aggression. Such an attribute can be a positively spiritual one in that Truth is incontrovertible and has to be dealt with.

It will depend on the other circumstances in the dream how we interpret the use of a gun. We may be using it to protect those things we feel are important to us. Particularly in today's climate of criminal culture, a gun can be seen as a badge of honour and in dreams may signify arrogance and power.

When under pressure in waking life, the gun in dreams can signify a particularly aggressive action and the result of that aggression. Obviously it can also signify both the actual sexual act and the result.

If a woman is firing a gun she is aware of the masculine, aggressive side of her personality. If she is being shot at she perhaps feels threatened by overt signs of aggression or sexuality. For a man to be being shot suggests conflict which may, in fact, be territorial.

*You might also like to consult the entries for Injure/Injury, Shot, Wound and Weapons.*

## GURU

For many of us, God is too remote for us to be able to have a personal relationship with him. A guru therefore becomes the personification of all wisdom made available to us through his perception and is a representation of the wisdom of the unconscious. He will help us to access our own innate wisdom.

Psychologically, we all need a symbol for a father or authority figure (a Wise Old Man) and this is one such representation. In searching for knowledge of a specific sort, we need an external figure with whom to relate. In Eastern religions, this is the guru – who performs the same function as the priest in Western religion.

A guru appearing in a dream nowadays need not only be a holy figure, but more a person whose words can be heeded. Thus, someone who is considered to be knowledgeable in the field of business might be seen as a guru.

*Consult the information on Archetypes and also Religious Leaders in Spiritual Imagery in the Introduction for further clarification.*

## GYM

In dreams, from a spiritual perspective the gym is a place where we face ourselves and our own foibles; its original meaning was a place where one trained naked. Today this can be translated as hard work with honest effort.

The gym is an environment where emotions can become raw and we are able to work out our problems, both from a physical perspective and from many others. In dreams, it will therefore represent a safe space, but also one of focused power.

In dreams the gym represents a place that is not work-oriented and yet requires effort, so may identify what needs to be tackled from a social perspective. These need not be problems, but perhaps a structured series of actions that can enhance our lives.

## HAG

⚜ The hag or crone is a representation of the Wise Woman, someone who has with age achieved wisdom through understanding her own feminine traits.

♥ In dreams, the hag is variously the cantankerous old woman or that aspect of femininity that aspires to use intuition and understanding for the benefit of her community. If the former, we need to come to terms with what appears to make her cantankerous in the dream – pain or disillusionment perhaps. If the latter, then the Greek goddess Hecate, as keeper of the crossroads, is worth studying.

▦ In the everyday world when we are struggling to come to terms with what appears to be interference in our affairs, the hag will appear in dreams.

⊟ In a woman's dream the hag will manifest either as mentor and friend or as a judgemental personality. In a man's dream she will tend to be more of a figure of fear. In the Hero's journey he must overcome his fear and gain her blessing.

*Consult the entries for Goddess/Goddesses and Witch for further clarification.*

## HAIR – *see* BALD AND BODY

## HAIRDRESSER

⚜ In terms of spirituality there is an obvious connection between self-image and beauty; we cannot grow spiritually unless we like ourselves. A hairdresser in dreams may also signify that our ego needs some attention.

♥ Psychologically and intellectually, the hairdresser can represent the healer within us. Developing an intimate yet objective relationship, with ourselves or others, can be valuable and a hairdresser appearing in dreams would signify this.

▦ In dreams the hairdresser may appear as the part of ourselves that deals with self-image and the way we feel about ourselves. We perhaps need to consider ways in which we can change our image or how we look at things.

⊟ For many women, her hairdresser is someone with whom she can communicate freely. In her dreams, therefore, this will represent freedom of speech. In a man's dream, as grooming becomes more important, his hairdresser will suggest a feel-good factor.

## HALF

⚜ When we look at what our expectations are, there is a degree of spiritual indecision around. There is an incompleteness in us, a sort of in-between state, which means that we have to make decisions – perhaps either looking forward into the future or back into the past: completion or non-completion.

♥ To have only half of what we feel we should have – for instance, perhaps only to have half of the food or drink we had expected – indicates that we are selling ourselves short. We are not allowing ourselves to have what we need. To dream of being half way up a hill or a mountain or halfway down a river would indicate that there is some lack of motivation. We have made an initial effort but more is needed in order for us to be where we want to be. To continually dream of slipping back, until we are only halfway through our task, to be repeating it over and over again, would indicate that we do not have the ability to complete it. There is perhaps an extra skill that we need to enable us to achieve success.

▦ Dreams can often have a very peculiar quality in that our image may only be half there or we perhaps only experience half an action. For instance, in waking life we may be aware of having only half-completed a task, but do not know how to finish it. Often the dream images that appear can show us how to do this. Conversely, if in a dream we have only partially completed a task and are left feeling dissatisfied with what has happened, we perhaps need to consider in waking life what needs to be done to enable us to complete the action in the dream.

*Also consult the entry for Pair/Pairs.*

**HALLOWEEN** – *see* **SPIRITUAL IMAGERY IN THE INTRODUCTION**
**HALLUCINATIONS** – *see* **INTRODUCTION**
**HALO**

🌞 The force field – or electro-magnetic energy – that emanates from each of us has a particular quality in those who have undertaken to develop themselves spiritually. To the clairvoyant eye it can appear as a type of mother-of-pearl radiance, which seems to be brightest around the head and forms a halo.

♥ The charisma that many world and spiritual leaders have is felt by many, and can be experienced as a sort of cloudy radiance. This 'nimbus' is usually slightly more subtle – and therefore more far-reaching – than the ordinary person's aura; the halo, particularly when it is seen in dreams, is an intensification of this energy.

▦ In religious pictures it is the convention to picture this divine radiance around Christ-like or saintly people as the halo. As an archetypal image, therefore, when seen in dreams we can accept the presence of a spiritual power. *You might also like to consult the entries for Angel and Mystic to enhance your understanding.*

**HALTER**

⚙ We may be experiencing some spiritual restraint and should take time consciously to consider what it is that we require spiritually.

♥ When we are moving into new areas of growth we sometimes need to be shown the way, and the halter is a symbol of this leading forward into new creativity. We are, as it were, being led and shown what we need to see.

▦ The halter shares the symbolism of bonds, since under normal circumstances it often controls the head. We are dreaming about reining back on the intellect, instead of allowing our creative energy to flow freely. We are not allowing ourselves the freedom to create to the best of our ability. The halter usually represents restriction of one form or another, although interestingly enough it may indicate restriction that is tolerated by the wearer. *You might also like to consult the entries for Bonds, Bridle, Chains and Harness for further information.*

**HAM** – *see* **FOOD**

**HAMMER**

⚙ The hammer is a symbol of the old Forge gods such as Thor and Vulcan and with a head of iron is a symbol of craftsmanship and good work. When the hammer is a double-sided one known as the labrys it signifies justice and vengeance. It was used by the Amazons, a race of warrior women, and has been adopted as a symbol by some gay women.

♥ In dreams the hammer will signify the judicial application of force rather than out-and-out aggression. Haephestos, a Greek Forge god, crafted beautiful artefacts for his fellow gods with the use of the hammer.

▦ Dreaming of hammers or blunt instruments highlights the more aggressive and masculine side of our nature. There may be the feeling that there is an aspect of our personality that needs crafting or shaping if we are to function effectively.

▣ In a woman's dream the hammer may signify masculine authority, though in a man's dream it will be more to do with his creativity. The labrys may appear when we are attempting to balance the various drives and motivations we have. *Consult the entries for Labyrinth and Mallet for additional information.*

**HAND** – *see* **BODY**

**HANDCUFFS**

⚙ Handcuffs are a binding symbol and spiritually would suggest that we are being hampered, probably by our own doubts and fears.

♥ If we are putting handcuffs on someone, we may be attempting to bind that person to us and assert our supremacy over them or what they represent in the dream. We may be being overly possessive.

⊞ Dreaming of being in handcuffs denotes that we have been restrained in some way, possibly by an authority figure. We may ourselves feel that we need to be more circumspect. 'Joke' handcuffs are often taken as symbols of marriage or committed partnership. In dreams their deeper meaning may signal some doubts about the relationship.

*Also consult the entries for Authority Figures and Police in People as well as Hands in the entry for Body.*

## HANDSHAKE

🌣 Traditionally a handshake symbolizes a welcome into heaven and a farewell to earthly existence. Our spiritual journey contains many welcomes and goodbyes, and today the handshake symbolizes the transitions we make. Equally the handshake can suggest the touch of healers and is also a sign of good faith.

♡ A handshake is a mark of appreciation and of acknowledgement. In dreams it suggests that an emotional bond has been forged, which cannot easily be broken.

⊞ Agreements are often sealed by a handshake, the idea being that we are not going to attack our opposite number if we have shaken hands. In dreams, shaking hands will represent at least a partial bond with the other person since, from the times of chivalry, we remove our gloves in order to do so.

⊟ If the sleeves of the two hands are masculine and feminine in the dream, or the hands are bound by cords, the handshake may symbolize matrimony, the latter by pagan rites.

*You might like to consult the entries for Bonds, Cord, Gloves and Wedding/Wedding Dress/Wedding Ring for further information.*

## HANG/HANGING

🌣 Suppression of an inclination towards the spiritual may be evident. This will prevent us from moving forward, so it will be as well to find the root cause of our difficulty. It may originate in a bad religious experience or from family pressure.

♡ If we are conscious in our dream of something hanging up, there may be word association, in that literally there is a 'hang up' in our lives. If something is hanging over us, then we are feeling threatened by circumstances around us. To be watching a hanging suggests a sense of insecurity. If there are a large number of people present, our reputation may be at stake.

⊞ Hanging is a violent act against a person, therefore if we are present at a hanging we are being party to some kind of unpleasantness and perhaps should reconsider our actions. If we ourselves are being hanged, we are being warned of some difficulty ahead.

*Consult the entries for Knot, Noose and Rope.*

## HAPPY – *see* EMOTIONS

## HARASS/HARASSMENT

🔅 A sense of harassment from a spiritual perspective suggests some kind of compulsion. The drive will come from external sources rather than internal.

💠 When pressure is put on us emotionally, the feeling may be exaggerated in dreams to a sense of harassment, behaviour which is offensive to us. We may dream of stalkers or being hunted.

▦ Stress is one of the biggest disturbers of dreams and sleep. It can translate into dreams of harassment, for instance being worried or jumped on by a dog. Once the cause is identified it can be dealt with by confronting the dog image either in the dream or in a waking visualization.

⬚ To be harassed in a dream by the opposite sex suggests that a man must pay attention to his softer side and a woman to her more assertive aspects. By a figure of the same sex suggests that a better balance needs to be established between the Archetypes. The dream character will usually indicate what needs attention.

*Consult the entry for Hunt/Hunting/Huntsman as well as the information on Archetypes in the Introduction for further clarification.*

## HARBOUR – *see* BAY

## HARE – *see* ANIMALS

## HAREM

🔅 Any group of women appearing in dreams will signify femininity in one form or another and often the many facets of femininity. A harem will therefore symbolize the Great Mother in her more playful aspects.

💠 It will depend on whether we can relate to a particular person in the scenario for a deeper interpretation. The harem may be representative of the feminine aspects of our personality and one dream character may come to the fore more than the others.

▦ In a work situation a group of female colleagues can bond in a way that gives the appearance of a harem. While bowing to authority, there is also a connection between the women that gives a degree of solidarity. Dreaming of a harem can give information that helps to deal with the dynamics of the relationships.

⬚ For a man to dream that he is in a harem shows that he is struggling to come to terms with the complexities of the feminine nature. For a woman to have the same dream shows that she is understanding her own flamboyant and sensual nature. On a different level, she is recognizing her need to belong to a group of women – a sisterhood.

*Also consult the Female Archetypes and Great Mother in the Introduction.*

## HARNESS

☀ Spiritually, we need to harness our energy. This means using what we have available in the most efficient way possible. When we have done this, we are then able to control the more wayward side of our personality.

♡ To harness something is to make it usable in a controlled fashion, so in dreams to be aware of this type of control implies that emotional restraint is necessary to enable the correct things to happen. As a horse is controlled by a harness, so our emotions can be used constructively.

▦ Like the halter, the harness indicates some form of control or restraint. It may be that we are actually being restrained by our own limitations, or that we are being controlled by external circumstances. To be wearing a harness often takes us back to periods in childhood when we were not allowed the freedom we would have liked.

*You might also like to consult the entries for Bridle, Bonds, Chains, Halter and Horse in Animals for further information.*

## HARP

☀ The harp as 'the ladder to the next world' is an image that can be used both in dreams and meditation. It is one that often appears as we explore our spirituality and signifies harmony and healing.

♡ To harp on about something in a dream – that is, to keep repeating what is going on – recognizes that we have a need for acknowledgement or praise in our waking life, and also need to be noticed, perhaps in some activity we are undertaking.

▦ The harp as a musical instrument indicates the correct vibration that we need in order to create harmony within our lives. We ourselves are very much in control of this and since the harp is also a national symbol of music, rhythm and harmony we often link back to our own basic selves.

*Consult the entries for Music/Rhythm and Musical Instruments for further information.*

## HARVEST

☀ Any kind of a harvest represents fruitfulness and fertility, particularly spiritual, and most systems of belief choose to acknowledge the gathering of a harvest. Summer and the feeling of warmth and happiness it generates are connected with spiritual progress.

♡ As harvesting become more mechanized we lose our connection with the community spirit it once engendered. To be taking part in a harvest, or perhaps a harvest festival, indicates that we are celebrating our own life energy – that energy we all have available to us. Happy memories and good feelings may be represented in dreams by stereotyped romantic scenarios such as the hayfield when those feelings need to be reproduced.

To be dreaming about a harvest indicates that we will reap the rewards of previous care we have taken. We are able to work hard, and in working hard we take care of the future. So, to dream of a harvest can actually have two meanings. It can mean looking back into the past and reaping the rewards, or it can mean looking towards the future in order to use what has happened previously. In previous times, for many the hayfield represented fun, relaxation and irresponsibility. Nowadays it is more likely to represent irritation – as in hay fever – and an unknown quality.

In a woman's dream harvest time suggests the realization of a dream. For a man it may suggest prosperity, though not without hard work and some element of sacrifice.

*You might also like to consult the entries for Countryside, Food, Grass and Places.*

**HAT** – *see* **CLOTHES**

**HAUNT** – *see* **GHOST**

**HAWK** – *see* **FALCON IN BIRDS**

**HEAD** – *see* **BODY**

**HEAL/HEALING**

Healing from spirit can take many forms. A dream may give information that allows us to take action. We may dream, among other things, of a laying-on of hands or of a strange light or spiritual figure which brings us comfort.

Emotional hurt can often be healed through dreams when it seems that another part of our being takes over to bring us understanding. If we ourselves are giving healing and easement to someone else in dreams we perhaps need to explore such abilities in waking life.

Dreams of any healing environment, such as a hospital or doctor's surgery, can start a process of healing, as can a character such as a nurse or therapist linked with such places.

*You might also like to consult the entries for Analyst, Doctor, Hand in Body, Hospital and Nurse/Nursing for further information.*

**HEAR/HEARING**

Spiritually, hearing clearly suggests being able to understand what is being said or conveyed to us. To be able to hear is somewhat different to listening, which suggests assimilating information at the same time.

❦ Sound suggests a particular vibration is created and hearing that we have responded to that vibration. In dreams this can occur on a psychic level when we are conscious on waking that our perception has altered.

▦ In practical terms a hearing in a legal sense suggests that we will be listened to and understood. Not to be able to hear in dreams suggests an unwillingness to listen, whereas someone not hearing us suggests that we need to alter the way we are communicating.

## HEARSE

❂ A hearse will always symbolize an ending of some sort, not necessarily death itself but the carrying away of material or physical aspects of life for we no longer need them. We may be aware that a part of ourselves is no longer 'alive' and it is better to let it go rather than resurrect it.

❦ In an emotional sense a hearse signifies a legitimate period of mourning for something that is dead and gone. A relationship may have come to an end, or we need closure in a matter that could affect our future.

▦ To dream of a hearse indicates that we recognize that a time limit has been imposed, either on ourselves or on a project we are connected with. It is coming to a natural conclusion and we need to have regard to our feelings about such finality in order to understand ourselves.

⊟ In that following the hearse was once a man's prerogative, such a dream will signify his acceptance of death or change. For a woman, a hearse may signify her innate and intimate connection with the processes of death itself.

*Consult the entries for Coffin, Dead People, Death, Funeral, Mourning and Wake for further clarification.*

## HEART – *see* BODY AND MACHINE

## HEARTH

❂ The hearth is considered to be the centre, or heart, of the home. Hestia, goddess of the hearth and the sacred fire, was a virgin goddess so spiritually her domain signifies the Anima, that part of ourselves which guards the feminine spirit.

❦ We may be, or need to be, linking with our passionate wilder nature – the seat of our passions. This is not in a confrontational way, however, but gently, as a hearth needs to be tended properly in order for the fire to burn brightly but safely.

▦ To dream of a hearth or fireplace is to recognize the need for security and nurturing. This may be of two different types. One is knowing that the home, our place of existence, is secure. The other is recognizing the security of the inner self, the interior feminine which gives warmth and stability.

The hearth in a woman's dream will suggest her own domesticity and gentleness, whereas in a man's dream it will be more to do with the feminine in his life and his motivation to provide security.

*Consult the entries for Fire, Goddess/Goddesses and Home for further clarification.*

**HEAVEN** – *see* **SPIRITUAL IMAGERY IN THE INTRODUCTION**

**HEAVY** – *see* **WEIGH/WEIGHING**

**HEDGEHOG** – *see* **ANIMALS**

**HEEL** – *see* **BODY**

**HELICOPTER** – *see* **TRANSPORT**

**HELL** – *see* **SPIRITUAL IMAGERY IN THE INTRODUCTION**

**HELMET**

As a heraldic device, the helmet denotes wisdom and security in defence, and will have this significance in dreams. It symbolizes both protection by, and of, the Spiritual Self.

In olden times, the helmet was the attribute of the warrior or hero. Whilst it covered the face, it often had the eye pieces highlighted in order to scare the enemy. Even today – as with the motorcycle helmet – it is still in dreams largely a representation of the masculine.

In dreams, it will depend on whether the helmet is being worn by someone else or by the dreamer. If the former, it may have the same symbolism as the mask in that it prevents the wearer being seen. If the latter, then it is a symbol of protection and preservation.

In a man's dream the helmet will represent his own virility. In a woman's dream it will symbolize her attitude to the masculine. The type of helmet will be relevant, since there are now cycle and sports helmets – among others – which do not cover the face, but do protect the head, the seat of the intellect.

*You might also like to consult the entries for Head in Body, Hat in Clothes, Goggles, Hide/Hidden and Mask.*

**HEN** – *see* **BIRDS**

**HERB** – *see* **GARDEN AND PLANT**

**HERMAPHRODITE**

Spiritually this represents the Divine union or sacred marriage and suggests the masculine and feminine aspects of God united in perfect balance. It is the balance sought by all alchemists, and is an image that occurs in dreams as we become more spiritually proficient.

As we grow and mature, we begin to understand that certain behaviour is appropriate or acceptable. This may mean that other natural emotions, reactions and sensitivities are suppressed and can surface as difficulties later on in life as we search for autonomy. These may cause us a great deal of confusion and can be perceived in dreams as hermaphrodism, with either the masculine or feminine attributes becoming noticeable.

When we dream of a hermaphrodite, we may be having uncertainties about our ability to adjust to the roles usually played by our own sex or about our own individual gender profile. Interestingly, as we learn and understand more about ourselves, we attempt to achieve a balance between the logical and the sensitive sides of our nature. This can appear as hermaphrodism in a dream as we sort ourselves out.

*You might also like to consult the entries for Alchemy, Balance and Sex.*

## HERMIT

A holy man, or the Wise Old Man, will often appear in dreams as the hermit, suggesting that we are discovering the dimension in ourselves which has a spiritual awareness.

There are two types of hermit: one withdraws from life in order to live an entirely spiritual existence and knows that others will care for his bodily needs, whereas the other travels throughout the world using his knowledge and expertise to help others.

There is a kind of loneliness and singularity within many people, which prevents us from making relationships on a one-to-one basis. This may manifest in dreams as the figure of the hermit.

In a woman's dream the hermit may represent one of her links with the Divine in the same way as a priest does. In a man's dream the hermit will often highlight his own links with his god, whatever form that takes.

*Also consult the entries for Ascetic, Monk and Wanderer/Wandering.*

## HERO/HEROINE

The hero is the spiritual archetype who shows courage in adversity and determination in the carrying out of his duties. He was initially a defender or protector.

The hero sets out on his quest or journey knowing that he will undergo trials and tribulations that will have him mature from a youth to a man. In dreams, aspects of that process – such as the knight's conflict with the dragon or the witch – will often appear. The heroine or princess is the counterpart of the hero and has a similar journey to under go albeit in a somewhat more emotional way.

In today's world a hero is considered to be anyone who is held up to public acclaim. This would suggest that it is the quality of determination that has become important and would, therefore, have him become an icon to others.

In a woman's dream a hero will largely appear as a protector and as an aspect of her Animus. As she herself moves towards autonomy she will develop the qualities of bravery required by the heroine. The Princess will appear in a man's dream as an aspect of his Anima, whereas the hero will allow him to acknowledge his maturity.

*Consult the entries for Animus and Anima in the Introduction, Celebrity, Icon, Knight and Quest for further clarification.*

## HEX

�€‹ To hex someone is to cast a malicious spell and is not within the correct use of spiritual energy. It is a deliberately conscious direction of negative energy and is said to rebound upon the perpetrator threefold.

♥ When we dream of being hexed we are probably being coerced in waking life to do something which goes against our own personal code of conduct.

▦ To hex someone is to unduly influence a person or result. Usually this has negative connotations so to dream of having a hex put on us will signify an instinctive dislike of someone, which may or may not be reciprocated. If we are performing such an action in dreams we probably need to take a long hard look at our motivation.

## HEXAGON – *see* SHAPES/PATTERNS

## HEXAGRAM

�€‹ When spiritually we attempt to reconcile two energies – the spiritual and the physical, or the active and the passive – we may experience that union in dreams in the form of patterns. One significant group of patterns are the hexagrams, said to have been discovered on a tortoise shell by an ancient Chinese sage. A hexagram consists of six lines and symbolizes the union of the spiritual and physical worlds.

♥ Technically, according to the Chinese system of I-Ching, the hexagram is a figure of six lines on top of one another. Broadly, the three at the top represent the spiritual world and the three at the bottom the physical. These two forces unite together and seem to exert a profound influence in the ordinary world. In dreams the hexagram provides a diagram of how the two forces come together and with study can help us to live our lives successfully.

▦ In the ordinary world we frequently become aware that two energies combined are far more powerful than each individually. When we need a boost in energy our dreams will often give directives as to how to do this. The hexagrams are a potent image both in dreams and for meditation.

▧ Yang is the masculine or active principle that controls Heaven, the day's activities, the Sun's heat, action and hardness. Yin is the feminine more passive aspect that controls the Earth, the night's mystery, the cool Moon, softness and stillness. In both men's and women's dreams, when a hexagram appears some kind of balance is being established.

## HIDE/HIDDEN

🔅 When information is hidden in a dream it is most likely that at this stage we have not progressed enough spiritually to be able to handle it.

🟡 In waking life we become very good at hiding our emotions. A dream in which we must make an effort to uncover something suggests we perhaps need to understand why we do this. When an object is hidden in dreams we may have to first give ourselves permission to reveal whatever it represents. To find a hidden jewel perhaps suggests a hidden talent.

🔲 To be hiding something suggests we have issues over our own personal privacy or sense of value. If we dream that someone is hiding something from us it may suggest a lack of trust in either direction.

## HIEROGLYPHICS

🔅 True hieroglyphics in dreams are symbols and pictorial representations with hidden meanings, which connect us with a particular stream of knowledge that belongs to the Egyptians. Egyptian magic is a system of belief that gave access to the will of the divine and, once the symbology is understood, can greatly enhance our knowledge. The name originally meant sacred carvings.

🟡 In dreams we will often register a symbol as being a hieroglyphic because it is an idea presented in pictorial form. It is only after conscious thought that the meaning becomes clear and is retained in memory. Hieroglyphics were developed before the written word and, therefore, often represent basic ideas.

🔲 Practically, when a dream contains symbols it helps to work out what it looks like. We can then apply the relevance in everyday life. When we have a definite sense of Egypt about these symbols we probably need to access old knowledge to help us in waking life. Whether we choose to use ancient magic then is our choice.

*Also consult the entries for Mummy (Egyptian) and Magic/Magician.*

## HIGH – *see* POSITION

## HIJACK

🔅 To hijack or steal while in transit has the spiritual meaning of taking over without permission. If we do not have a good life/work balance we may feel we have been hijacked.

🟡 When we are heavily involved with someone, both professionally and personally, we may dream of our emotions being hijacked. We may feel that our motivation or emotions have been sapped and this manifests in dreams as a hijacking.

🔲 When a task or project is taken away from us in waking life there is often a sense of resentment that may lead to dreams of being hijacked. If we ourselves are the hijacker in dreams then we need to take care that we are not being unnecessarily overbearing.

*Also consult the entries for Abduct, Hostage and Kidnap.*

## HILL

A hill in dreams suggests that extra effort is needed in order to achieve the perception necessary for us to continue to progress spiritually.

To be climbing a hill in the company of others often indicates that we have a common goal, that a journey we possibly thought was ours alone is actually connected with other people. We can use their knowledge and comradeship to enable us to reach where we are the best we can be. To dream that we are going downhill would indicate we feel that circumstances are pushing us in a certain direction. We may be moving from a level of attainment and now feel that – with relaxation of effort – we are not so much in control of our own abilities.

To be on top of a hill in dreams – and therefore high up – indicates that we have become aware of our own expanded perception. We have made an effort to achieve something and are able to survey the results of what we have done, to assess the effect on our environment and the people around us. We have achieved those things that we previously thought impossible and are able to undertake further tasks in the light of the knowledge we have attained.

*You might also like to consult the entry for Mountain.*

## HINGE

A hinge initially meant the Axis of the Earth – that which kept everything stable. Any object in dreams that has two parts to it tends to represent the links between the spiritual and physical realms; a hinge particularly symbolizes that link. Neither part works efficiently without the other.

From an emotional perspective a hinge signifies our primary emotions upon which everything hang. A broken hinge in dreams suggests that we are quite literally 'unhinged' – not able to function properly emotionally.

In some ways a hinge has the same significance on a practical level as a hook. In dreams if a hinge is prominent we probably need to look at what the transition stages are between tasks. Too small a hinge on a door, for instance, suggests that planning is defective. A large or ornate hinge would suggest that the actual transition itself is an integral part of the process.

In both men's and women's dreams a hinge can represent a relationship with the opposite sex. The left hand side may represent the feminine and the right the masculine.

*Consult the entries for Door and Hook for further clarification.*

# HIT

🌑 Hit initially meant 'to meet with' and it is this meaning that we can apply spiritually. When a revelation occurs or some truth becomes obvious, it can hit with the force of a blow, as in 'it hit me all of a sudden'.

♥ A hit is the application of some force, so to be hit by someone in a dream or to be hitting someone suggests an aggression or emotion that we find difficult to deal with. To be hitting an object suggests frustration and finding an interpretation for the object may be of assistance.

🔲 A hit may have the slang meaning of food, drink or drugs giving a false sense of bonhomie, which is short-lived, so in dreams a blow, hit or thump can suggest such a feeling. Phrases that contain hit, such as 'hit the ground running', suggest short, sharp action.

# HIVE

🌑 The feminine power in Nature is represented by the hive. The symbol of a hollow vessel holding nourishment or sustenance links with Mother Earth.

♥ The old belief that one told one's sorrows to the bees still manifests in dreams today. Any hive may represent the activity that is needed to get ourselves out of a situation.

🔲 The hive usually represents an area of work where there is considerable industry and activity going on, and where the best use is made of all possible resources. To dream of being near a hive can represent the effort that is needed to be made to create fertility – or fertile situations – for ourselves. The hive can also represent protective motherhood within the everyday world.

*Consult the entry for Bee/Beehive to enhance your understanding of your dream.*

# HOAX

🌑 A hoax is a deliberately created illusion and spiritually suggests that we may be fooling ourselves. An action that we consider to be spiritual may actually be self-centred or negative.

♥ In dreams to become conscious of a hoax suggests that we do not trust our ability to sort out the real from the unreal. If we often find ourselves the butt of practical jokes in waking life our dreams may enable us to deal with this with humour.

🔲 In practical terms a hoax is a deliberately engineered set of circumstances, which has no basis in truth. We may dream of such a thing when we are dissatisfied with circumstances in our lives. We may need to make radical changes in order to be true to ourselves.

*You might also like to consult the entry for Joke/Joker.*

**HOG** – *see* **PIG IN ANIMALS**

**HOLD** – *see* **ARMS**

**HOLE**

&#9775; A round hole traditionally represents the Heavens, a square hole represents the Earth. This symbolism arises from the very simple representations developed to present complex ideas. A hole in the roof of any sacred building, or any hole which allows steam or smoke to escape, is the opening upwards to the celestial world and is the door or gateway to other dimensions.

&#9829; A hole in dreams can very often represent the feminine and the emptiness one feels as one moves towards an understanding of the Self. Without access to the vastness of the heavens – and as central heating, living in flats and in conurbations becomes more commonplace – we tend to feel more and more enclosed and less in touch with the natural order of things.

&#9635; A hole usually represents a difficult or tricky situation. It can also be a place where we may hide, or feel protected in. To dream of falling into a hole indicates that we are perhaps getting in touch with our unconscious feelings, urges and fears. To walk round a hole suggests we may need to get round a tricky situation. We may also need to become aware of the other parts of ourselves that are buried beneath our surface awareness.

*Consult Circle in the Shapes/Patterns, Door, Gate and Hollow for more information.*

**HOLIDAY**

&#9775; A holiday is literally a holy day – one dedicated to the Divine – so spiritual replenishment, rest and relaxation are all part of such a time.

&#9829; Our need to be independent and to be responsible only for ourselves often comes across in dreams as a holiday. It is time set apart for our own concerns. We may need to heed the warning that we require time off to create space for ourselves and restore our own emotional balance.

&#9635; To be taking a holiday in a dream indicates a sense of relaxation and of taking a break from responsibilities. In theory we do not have to be concerned about ordinary everyday matters.

**HOLLOW**

&#9775; Any hollow article tends to represent the feminine. Hollowness can indicate a lack of motivation, particularly on our spiritual journey.

&#9829; Hollowness can come across in a dream in several ways. We can be conscious that we are in a hollow state – reaching an understanding of the Abyss or Void, or of being hollow inside – devoid of emotion. We are in a position where nothing is happening, where we do not feel in control and need to reassert our control of the scope we have been given.

🏛 Dreaming of feeling hollow connects with our feelings of emptiness, lack of purpose and inability to find a direction in our lives. To dream of being in a hollow in a field would indicate that we need some kind of protection from what is going on around us in our ordinary everyday life.

⊡ In a woman's dream hollowness may simply be highlighting her ability to be pregnant. In a man's dream hollowness may signify a sense of inadequacy. *You might also like to consult the entries for Abyss, Empty, Hole, Jar and Vase.*

## HOLY COMMUNION – *see* RITE/RITUAL AND SPIRITUAL IMAGERY IN THE INTRODUCTION

## HOME

🌞 Spiritually, home always represents sanctuary – a place where we can feel safe and be ourselves without fear of reprisal. Literally, in dreams we are inside ourselves and home signifies this spiritual state. Spiritualists and those who believe in an afterlife often speak of death as 'going home', but this should not be seen as a precognitive dream.

♥ Dreaming of a safe environment such as our own home, or sometimes a parental one, suggests that we have the opportunity to integrate learned behaviour with primary personality traits – those qualities with which we are born.

🏛 The human being's primary needs of shelter, warmth and nourishment are initially met (or not) within the home, so a dream about a home on a mundane level suggests a known environment or set of standards – comfortable or otherwise.

*To enhance the interpretation of the dream consult the entries for House in Buildings and this section, Parent in Family and Shelter.*

## HOMOSEXUALITY

🌞 Integration of parts of our personality on an internal level moves us towards spiritual maturity. As this integration takes place we may dream of homosexuality.

♥ Very often, to dream of a homosexual affair is an attempt to learn to love a part of our personality that is not much used in waking life. Often when we come to terms with such a part it will enhance our ability to have successful relationships of any sort. For some people it shows an inherent reluctance to relate fully to the opposite sex either through some trauma or fear.

🏛 Dreaming of having intercourse with somebody of the same sex as oneself often indicates a conflict or anxiety about our own gender roles. We may find ourselves attracted to someone of the same sex in dreams because we are looking for either parental love or a depth of mature love. We may also be looking for love of a different sort – a nurturing rather than sexual love.

⊡ In a woman's dream a lesbian affair does not mean the dreamer is gay, simply that she seeks understanding. In a man's dream there may consciously be a degree of homophobia and a fear of his more sensitive side, but it is more likely that he is seeking approval of some sort from his peers.

## HONEY/HONEYCOMB

✿ As a healing substance, honey has the power to regenerate. It symbolizes both immortality and rebirth. The honeycomb symbolizes the perfect construction.

♥ Honey is thought by some to impart fertility and virility. To be dreaming of honey would indicate that we are perhaps entering a much more productive time on all levels.

▦ Honey almost inevitably represents pleasure and sweetness. To dream of honey – and particularly eating it – can be to recognize that we are needing to give ourselves pleasure. Equally, it can indicate the essence of our feelings, that we have been through some kind of joyful experience, which can now be assimilated and become part of our everyday existence.

*Also consult the entry for Bee/Beehive.*

## HOOD

✿ The hood represented all things hidden and therefore came to represent death and, by association, invisibility. It would now indicate that certain aspects of spiritual knowledge are held invisible until the time is right.

♥ Traditionally, for a woman to be wearing a hood in dreams suggested that she was keeping her motives hidden and may have been being deceitful. It still largely has this symbolism today. If a man is wearing a hood, it suggests that he is withdrawing his energy from a situation. Equally, in its more advanced sense, the hooded figure of a monk can indicate the more reflective side of us as it begins to become more evident in our everyday lives.

▦ A figure wearing a hood in a dream will always appear to be slightly menacing. While not necessarily being evil, there may be a part of us that has been threatened. The hood can also represent that part of ourselves that, if withdrawn, is creating a problem. An aspect of our personality may be invisible to us and may need to be uncovered in order for us to function in an acceptable fashion.

*Consult the entries for Hat in Clothes, Monk and Veil for further information.*

## HOOK

✿ A hook is anything that grabs us and in the spiritual sense suggests that we can become obsessive about our beliefs. At the same time to become hooked is an opportunity to make a commitment to an idea or principle even though it initially feels insecure.

❤ In childhood dreams the hook can represent the hold that a parent or authority figure has over us. This symbolism can continue into adulthood, depicting the way that we allow people to take control within our lives.

▦ When we dream of a hook we are generally understanding that the power to draw things towards us can be either good or bad according to our disposition. As a visualization following such a dream we can use the image to draw positivity and success towards us. It can equally indicate that we are being 'hooked in' or coerced by someone and thus not being allowed the freedom to which we feel we have a right.

## HORIZON

❀ The horizon was once considered to be the edge of the world and in dreams can still have that connotation, though now it is the boundary of the visible physical world. Beyond that is the Abyss or Void.

❤ When a new idea strikes and we become conscious of the narrowness of our viewpoint, we may literally dream of a widening of our horizons. Our perspective changes.

▦ In everyday life when change is the order of the day we will become conscious of changes on the horizon in our dream – perhaps a new building or other object – which may need interpreting, to give us clarity in our prospective actions.

*You might also like to consult the entries for Abyss, Globe and World.*

## HORNS

❀ In a spiritual sense, because horns are associated with the head, they represent intellectual as well as supernatural power. Because they rise above the head, they also symbolize Divinity and the power of the soul. The Horn of Plenty or cornucopia symbolizes gifts from the Gods. The Gate of Horn was a classical concept – dreams that passed through this portal were said to be terrifying but true.

❤ Horns in a dream suggest superiority, either earned or conferred. It is interesting that horns are supposed to bestow the powers of the animal on the wearer. In Pagan times, as well as some tribes today, the donning of horns signifies a particularly senior position within the tribe. Often the wearer is a shaman who, through dreams, can connect with other realms. In Chinese medicine, rhinoceros horn is reputed to be an aphrodisiac. This is possibly because of its association with masculine power. All of these significances, as we become more aware, can appear in dreams.

▦ Horns appearing in dreams hark back to the idea of the animal in the human. The god Pan, who represents sexuality as well as life force, wore horns and will appear in dreams as we become more aware of the power of nature. A musical or hunting horn suggests a call to action or a warning in dreams.

⚏ In both men's and women's dreams a horn can also represent the penis and masculinity. Because it is penetrative, it can also signify the desire to hurt. Protectiveness is also a quality of horns since the male animal will use his horns to protect his territory.

*You might also like to consult the entries for Animals, Antlers, Cornucopia, Gate and Shaman.*

## HORSE – *see* ANIMALS

## HORSESHOE

�',' Spiritually, we can link the horseshoe with a talisman or amulet that protects us and our personal space. The crescent form of the horseshoe links the symbol to pagan Moon goddesses of ancient Europe such as Artemis and Diana, and the protection invoked is that of the goddess herself. The horseshoe is always taken as a lucky symbol and, traditionally, if it is turned upwards it represents the moon and protection from all aspects of evil. When turned downwards, the power is reputed to 'drain out' and therefore be unlucky.

♥ In ordinary everyday life, symbols that have a long history become fixed in, and used by, our unconscious – often to represent other happier times or times when there has been more happening. Nailing an iron horseshoe to a door is said to repel evil spirits, ghosts and witches, iron being a folkloric specific against such things. It will generally have this significance in dreams; each belief system has developed its own particular myths and stories.

▦ The horseshoe is also connected as a lucky symbol to weddings. Traditionally, dreaming of a horseshoe indicated there would shortly be a wedding in your family or peer group. Nowadays it is more likely to signify the commitment of a meaningful relationship.

*You might also like to consult the entries for Iron, Goddess/Goddesses, Moon and Wedding/Wedding Dress/Wedding Ring.*

## HOSPITAL

�',' A healing environment where things can be brought into a state of balance is signified by a hospital. Spiritually it symbolizes a safe environment, where the energy that we need is available to us.

♥ Dreaming of being in a hospital as a patient may be mentally creating a transition period between something that has not gone well, and an improved attitude where things can get better. To dream of visiting someone in hospital indicates that there is an imbalance or depletion in us, is 'dis-eased' and needs attending to in order to give us clarity.

🔲 Depending on our attitude to hospitals, when one appears in a dream it can either represent a place of safety, or a place where our very being is threatened and we become vulnerable. Taken as a place of healing, it represents that aspect within ourselves that knows when respite is necessary from cares and troubles – when we can allow ourselves to be cared for and nurtured and put back into one piece. If we find hospitals threatening, it may be that we are conscious of the fact that we have to 'let go', to put ourselves at the mercy of others and allow things to happen for us, in order that a situation can be improved.

*You might also like to consult the entries for Doctor, Ill/Illness, Nurse/Nursing and Operation.*

## HOSTAGE

🔲 A hostage is a person held as security. Spiritually, therefore, this has the same connotation as kidnap since it would constitute a crime against the right of the individual. Hostages held for religious reasons in dreams suggest that we are unsure of our own beliefs.

🔲 An emotional hostage is that part of us that in dreams recognizes that it has had the ability to think and feel for ourselves taken away, either through trauma or neglect.

🔲 In dreams, to find ourselves taken as hostage suggests that we have put ourselves in the position of being a victim and do not feel that we are able to resist. There may be a higher purpose at stake rather than just our own freedom.

*Consult the entries for Abduct, Hijack, Kidnap and Victim for further information.*

## HOSTILITY

🔲 Spiritual opposition – or rather opposition to our spiritual beliefs – can generate a tremendous amount of hostility. We need to be aware that others may not necessarily agree with our beliefs.

🔲 When we experience hostility within ourselves in a dream, it is often an accurate expression of an emotion we consciously have. It is simply safe to express it in a dream, whereas we may not dare do this in waking life. Hostility is one of those emotions that can be worked through within a dream itself.

🔲 If we can identify what is making us feel hostile in a dream, then we can usually draw a parallel in our waking lives and deal with whatever the problem is. If the feeling is appropriate in a particular situation, and we can justify it, then we can handle it in a conscious state without confrontation. If, however, someone is being hostile towards us, it very often means that we need to be aware that we are not acting appropriately, that others may feel we are putting them in danger.

*Consulting the entries for Anger, Argue/Arguments, Conflict and War should help with clarification.*

## HOT

�_ Spiritual passion is a deeply held feeling. It can be experienced in a dream as a feeling of warmth and can symbolize unconditional love. We can afford to move positively in search of this heat.

♥ Psychologically, feelings of cheerfulness and hopefulness can create an awareness of warmth and can be interchangeable. Occasionally, extreme emotion can be interpreted as a physical feeling – so anger, jealousy or other such feelings can be experienced as heat. Encountering something as hot which should be cold – for example, ice – indicates that we are perhaps having difficulty and experiencing confusion in sorting out our feelings.

▦ Pleasurable feelings can be translated in dreams to a physical feeling of heat or warmth. To dream of being hot indicates warm – or perhaps passionate – feelings. To be conscious of the fact that our surroundings are hot indicates that we are loved and cared for.

*Consult the entries for Emotions and Ice/Icebergs/Icicles for further clarification.*

## HOTEL – *see* BUILDINGS

## HOURGLASS

�_ The hourglass measures time and is a spiritual symbol for the length of our physical lives. In former times, the hourglass was frequently taken as a symbol of death. More properly it is now seen as a measurement of the passage of life.

♥ When we are particularly under stress, we can be overly aware of the running out of time; that it can become an enemy. This is often symbolized in dreams as an hourglass. It is probably from the hourglass that we get the word deadline; when the sand runs out the energy has gone.

▦ In dreams, time is irrelevant. To experience something that measures time is often to alert us to the need for measuring our thoughts and activities. When such a symbol is old-fashioned – as in an hourglass – our perception of time and its management may be old-fashioned. We need to use different, and more precise, ways of measuring those activities.

*You might also like to consult the entries for Sand and Time.*

## HOUSE

🌑 The house is popularly known as the seat of the soul, and in spiritual terms links us to the way we are in the world. A house represents security and safety, and therefore signifies protection and the Great Mother.

♥ In psychological terms, the house also signifies the life we live, the protections we create and the 'structure' we present to other people.

■ In dreams, the different rooms and parts of houses represent the various aspects of our personality and life experiences. There are several interpretations and given below is one such set:

**Attic** – dreaming of being in an attic is to do with past experiences and old memories. Interestingly, it can also highlight family patterns of behaviour and attitudes that have been handed down.

**Basement/cellar** – the cellar most often represents the subconscious and those things we may have suppressed through an inability to handle them. A basement can also highlight the power that is available to us provided we are willing to make use of it. Often associated with self-image and self-confidence, we may not have come to terms with our own charisma and personal power and prefer to keep it hidden.

**Bathroom** – in dreams our attitude to personal cleanliness and our most private thoughts and actions can be shown as the bathroom or toilet. It is the place where we can let go of our negativity in safety.

**Bedroom** – the bedroom portrays a place of safety where we can relax and be as sensual as we wish.

**Chimney** – as a passage from one state to another and a conductor of heat, in dreams the chimney can indicate how we deal with our inner emotions and warmth.

**Hall** – the hallway in a dream is illustrative of how we meet and relate to other people.

**Library** – our minds, and how we store the information we receive, can appear as a library.

*Also consult the entries for Chimney, Home, House in Buildings and Toilet.*

## HUNGER

❀ Hunger in the spiritual sense is a yearning to be filled with spiritual awareness. In dreams this can be experienced as an actual physical feeling of hunger.

♡ Emotionally when we are tired or upset we have the need to be comforted and cherished. There is something lacking and the dreaming mind can translate this into hunger.

■ From a completely practical perspective, if we go to bed hungry our dreams are likely to reflect this fact and register that we need food or sustenance.

*Consult the entries for Emotions, Food and Yearn for clarification.*

## HUNT/HUNTING/HUNTSMAN

❀ An extremely old symbolism of the hunter or huntsman is linked with death, particularly a death containing an aspect of ritual killing or sacrifice.

This 'making sacred' and an understanding of the process of ritualized killing is part of the spiritual journey.

♥ To dream of being a huntsman alerts us to the part of ourselves that can be destructive and vicious. To dream that we are hunting, denotes that we are seeking or pursuing some inner desire, either emotional or physical. We may be looking for a solution to a problem.

▦ Dreaming of being hunted is mostly taken to be to do with our sexuality. To dream of a hunt is to register the necessity for a change of state in everyday life. To be hunting a boar, for instance, could have two interpretations: firstly, to eradicate the boring parts of our lives, and secondly, to root out the uncouth part of our personality. Other animals will have their own symbolism.

⊟ In a man's dream the hunter pursuing his quarry is an image drawn from chivalrous times and epitomizes his struggle for his lady's favour. In a woman's dream she will become the hunted one.

*You might also like to consult the entries for Animals, Chase/Chased, Kill and Sacrifices.*

**HURRICANE – see WIND**

**HUSBAND – see FAMILY**

**HYENA – see ANIMALS**

**HYMN – see MUSIC/RHYTHM AND SING**

**HYPODERMIC – see SYRINGE**

**HYSTERICS**

☼ From a spiritual perspective hysterics signifies the loss of control that can occur when the link to innate wisdom is lost and there is an overemotional reaction.

♥ In dreams emotions can become exaggerated and a hysterical response suggests that we need to consider very carefully what has thrown us so comprehensively off-balance. Often we can express in dreams what we dare not in waking life. While disturbing, such a dream scenario can lead to healing.

▦ When a dream figure appears to be hysterical, we need to identify a situation in everyday life where loss of control, either our own or others', will be detrimental. Since hysterical energy can be highly destructive we may need also to decide what needs to be deconstructed and rebuilt without the highly emotional charge.

*You might also like to consult the entry for Emotions.*

**IBIS** – *see* **BIRDS**

**ICE/ICEBERG/ICICLES**

　🌞 Spiritually, ice symbolizes a part of ourselves that has become frozen and needs to thaw out before we can progress. Ice cream is an image which can be used to signify impermanence. We need to decide if we wish to go for the transitory or permanent. Spiritual isolation – that is, existing in isolation because of the way our lives have gone – can be symbolized by icicles.

　♥ Ice is also a representation of rigidity, of the brittleness that comes from not understanding what is going on around us, of creating circumstances where people cannot get – or be – in touch with us. Depending on how the ice appears in a dream, it can indicate a state of impermanence. To see icicles melting indicates that the troubles that have been around us will literally disappear within a short space of time. Whether the fault is our own or other people's, it would appear that outside circumstances give the ability to overcome whatever has been troubling us.

　🔲 When we dream of ice we are usually looking at the emotions. We are aware that perhaps we are colder than we should be, shutting off any display of warmth and compassion. We are thereby enclosing ourselves in a situation from which it may be difficult to free ourselves. Often in dreams icicles can appear to hang in a certain fashion – it is the pattern that is important as much as the icicle itself. We may be aware that we are having problems with our environment and that it is not supporting it in a way we would expect – thereby creating difficulties.

　*You might also like to consult the entries for Thaw, Water and Winter.*

**ICON**

　🌞 The icon is a small spiritual picture, which symbolizes a greater whole. In dreams it can often represent the threefold aspects of being: body, mind and spirit. For this reason an image received in dreams can often be used as a focus in the use of magic.

　♥ Usually icons are representations of a belief system and, therefore, portray the way we feel about a number of other issues. In a dream, when an icon appears to have a religious picture but in actual fact it contains pictures of our own family, it indicates the ability to idolize the family. Modern day celebrities are often thought of as icons, people who are to be respected for their positions, perhaps with a power they do not have.

▓ Dreaming of any religious symbol usually indicates our very deep connection with old ideas and principles. The icon usually symbolizes the microcosm within the macrocosm – that is, the small world reflecting the larger world. The human being often needs something tangible to represent what is simply a principle or a concept, and the icon performs this purpose. The now popular icon in computer use signifies the gateway to an idea and in dreams suggests that a concept can be expanded.

*Also consult the entries for Celebrity and Magic/Magician as well as the information on Spiritual Imagery in the Introduction.*

**IDOL – *see* RELIGIOUS IMAGERY IN THE INTRODUCTION**

**IGLOO**

✿ The feminine principle, in the sense of sheltering and nurturing, is depicted by the igloo.

♡ The igloo is interesting as a symbol in dreams. It can equally represent a cold exterior containing a very warm interior, or the coldness of the construction itself. It can appear as though someone is uncaring and, therefore, creating an unloving home environment, although in fact there is warmth within that person.

▓ In mundane terms the igloo can represent our own construction, the way in which we fashion our environment in order to work, or rather operate, most effectively.

⦂ The igloo can often represent the feminine and the womb in dreams. Sometimes, in a woman's dream, it represents frigidity, but at other times the ability of a woman to relax and be herself once her barriers have been overcome. In a man's dream it may represent his own domain or space.

*You might also like to consult the entries for Buildings and Ice/Iceberg/Icicles.*

**IGNITE/IGNITION**

✿ The symbol of igniting a light or fire represents the beginning of an exploration of the Spiritual realms. Kundalini – the energy of consciousness or spiritual energy – is perceived as heat at the base of the spine, which may be intensely hot or pleasantly warm. Dreams often picture a spontaneous awakening when the energy, having been ignited, travels up the spine to the top of the head, bringing certain awarenesses along the way.

♡ When the ignition on a car will not fire properly we have not been able to provide the emotional 'spark' that allows us to begin a journey or task. When a huge conflagration, such as a forest fire, is ignited in dreams it symbolizes passion. When we are reigniting a fire we must return to and perhaps adjust our original ideas.

More mundanely, dreaming of igniting or lighting a fire suggests that an initial surge of energy or power is needed to start a project or task. In this case what we use to begin the burning will be important. A match might suggest less effort than a firebrand, for instance.

*Consult the entries for Car, Fire, Light and Spark for further clarification.*

## ILL/ILLNESS

Lack of spiritual clarity can often be experienced in dreams as illness. We are not putting ourselves in touch with a force that can help us to overcome difficulties.

Often when we are ill in a dream we are grappling with part of our personality. Part of us is out of balance and perhaps needs to be dealt with. Often the dream will give the method of dealing with it – perhaps by taking medication, having surgery or a combination of both. Illness also often represents our fears of not being looked after properly, our need to be allowed to heal properly.

Whatever life has to offer, we may be left with painful memories, feelings of anger and difficulties. In a dream these memories and feelings can surface as illness. Most of the time, such a dream image gives us information as to how we should deal with the difficulty. Illness that has manifested on a physical level can trigger vivid or frightening dreams.

*You might also like to consult the entries for Doctor and Hospital.*

## ILLUMINATE/ILLUMINATION – *see* LIGHT

## IMITATE/IMITATION

Spiritually this is a representation of the microcosm of the macrocosm, the small imitating the large.

If we are imitating someone else we are usually conscious that we have the ability to be as they are. To be imitating one's superiors is to recognize their greater knowledge. To be mimicking someone may show that we doubt our own integrity.

To dream of being imitated is ambivalent. It can mean that we are aware that what we have done is the correct thing and that other people can learn from our example. It can equally mean that other people are perceiving us as being leaders.

## IMMERSION

Transformation and rebirth can only be accomplished by a total immersion in spirituality, which is where the symbolism of total immersion in baptism came from, as well as that of being washed clean.

To dream of being totally immersed in water generally indicates the way we handle our own emotions, that we are attempting to find the more innocent part of ourselves that does not need to be affected by external circumstances.

To be totally immersed – totally focused – on something in a dream indicates we need to be able to concentrate entirely on one particular thought or idea to help us understand ourselves We are attempting to clarify situations and to cleanse ourselves, perhaps of ideas and attitudes that have been suggested to us by other people.

*You might also like to consult the entries for Baptism and Water.*

## IMMIGRANT – *see* REFUGEE

## IMMOBILITY

Immobility in the spiritual sense is dynamic stillness. It is The Unconditioned State, or the Self, liberated from the physical. In Sanskrit this is known as *pratyhara* – withdrawal from the external world into the interior self.

To be immobilized in a dream usually indicates that we have created circumstances around us which are now beginning to trap us. Often such a dream comes when we are facing the darker side of ourselves – that which could be called evil. A superhuman effort needs to be made to overcome what is holding us down.

Immobility in a dream can be extremely frightening. A feeling of oppression and of not being able to move usually indicates that we need to sit still and be immobile within our ordinary everyday lives. We need to achieve a kind of stillness which is foreign to most people, and therefore initially frightening, while later on it can be a state of peace and tranquility.

*Also consult the entry for Paralysis.*

## IMP

The Devil as the Tempter can appear in dreams as an imp, or as a manifestation of a particularly irritating type.

The imp can represent the uncontrolled negative part of ourselves, that part that instinctively creates chaos and takes great joy in doing so. It is perhaps an aspect of loss of control.

An imp appearing in a dream usually foretells disorder and difficulty. The imp often has the same significance as the Devil in its aspect of tormenting us, of creating difficulty and harm within our life.

*Also consult the entries for Demon, Devil and Fiend.*

## IMPRISONED

Imprisonment can suggest that we are spiritually too introverted or self-involved. We need to 'open ourselves up' to new influences. We may need assistance in doing this – and have to look to an outside influence to release us.

🕉 When we experience imprisonment in a dream, we are usually becoming conscious of old attitudes and beliefs, which are imprisoning us.

🔲 Being or feeling imprisoned in a dream often means that we are trapped by circumstances, often those we have created through our own fear or ignorance. We feel that other people are creating circumstances around us which will not allow us to move forward. We will often need to negotiate our freedom.

*Consult the entries for Jailer and Prison for further information.*

**INAUGURATION – *see* INITIATION**

**INCA – *see* INDIGENOUS PEOPLES**

**INCENSE**

🕉 Spiritually, incense is used as a vehicle for prayer and as a symbol for the subtle body or soul. In dreams we can become aware of our need to use spiritual symbolism in our work. When we begin to appreciate the use of incense as part of our daily routine we will often intuitively know through dreams what is appropriate for our purpose.

🕉 Incense is used in order to raise consciousness, or to cleanse atmospheres and sacred spaces. In dreams, when we become aware of it being used in this way, we need to consider how best to improve ourselves or our environment.

🔲 Physically, incense is designed to perfume a room. In dreams, it is possible to be aware of the smell of incense, particularly if it has associations for the dreamer. For instance, it may hold childhood memories of church or religious buildings.

*Also consult the entries for Odour and Smell as well as the information on Spiritual Imagery in the Introduction.*

**INCEST**

🕉 In legend and myth, incest among the gods and goddesses was an attempt to maintain the purity of the energy. Spiritually, therefore, when we dream of incest we are attempting to purify or keep clear our own power.

🕉 Since self-image and sexuality are so closely connected, incest in dreams is much more likely to be an effort to sort out our feelings about ourselves than anything else. Dreaming of incest with brothers or sisters may symbolize an attempt to unify the masculine and feminine aspects within us. We are attempting to make a link with the part of our own personality most closely reflected by that person. We can only do this within the safety of a dream.

🔲 Incest is such a taboo subject that to dream of it seldom actually refers to the physical act. It usually represents the need and desire we have to be in control, either of ourselves or of our relationships within the family. It is possible that incest in dreams occurs because the child has not yet been allowed, or had the opportunity to sort out, his or her feelings so far as the family are concerned.

⚕ Dreams of incest with a parent for both men and women may be an attempt to sort out, understand and ultimately be free of the early dependent relationship with that parent.

*Also consult the entry for Sex/Sexual Images.*

## INCOME

⚕ Our income represents reward for our efforts in relating to the world in which we live. Spiritually, this reward will not just be monetary. It will include feedback and a sense of satisfaction.

⚕ Dreaming of receiving a private income – such as a trust fund – suggests we perhaps need to look at our relationships with other people. We are aware of what people have to offer us, and also what we have to do in order to be rewarded for our efforts.

⚕ Any dream connected with the income we earn – an important part of our support structure – will highlight our attitude towards our wants and needs. To dream of an increased income shows we feel we have overcome an obstacle in ourselves and can accept that we have value. A drop in income signifies our neediness, and perhaps our attitude to poverty.

*You might also like to consult the entries for Money and Wages for more information.*

## INCUBATE/INCUBATOR

⚕ Incubation implies bringing something into existence, or rather to a point where it can survive without assistance. Spiritually, therefore, this represents the act of creation.

⚕ An incubator supports life that might not be viable otherwise, so from an emotional perspective will represent a new emotion which needs careful nurturing, such as love for someone else.

⚕ In everyday terms, when we are incubating a new idea or project we may find that our dreams include just such an image.

⚕ As a woman becomes used to becoming pregnant she may have dreams that hold an image such as an incubator. This does not suggest that her baby will be ill, simply that she is aware of herself in that role as the baby grows.

*Consult the entry for Baby in People for further clarification.*

## INCUBUS – *see* DEMON AND DEVIL

## INDIGENOUS PEOPLES

⚕ Indigenous people might be defined as those who belong to a particular area of the Earth and have over many centuries developed their own spiritual practices in order to ensure survival. These practices often resonate in dreams.

⬦ Since everybody has their own view of indigenous people, inevitably dreams will be coloured by our conscious awareness. However, as our knowledge of cultures and customs becomes greater the appearance of indigenous people in dreams take on different shades of meaning. Below are a few possible interpretations:

**Aborigine** – dreams are the soul's journey to another world, where we can enlist the help of spirits and animals. The aboriginal can represent intuitive wisdom, because they experience their dreamtime as the past, present and future co-existing – known as 'all-at-one' time.

**African** – Africa is now thought to be where the human race began, so dreams of Africa and the Africans may refer to our own personal origins.

**Aztec** – because of the Aztecs' emphasis on warfare, the warrior class was highly valued, and often warriors would volunteer for the most important sacrificial rituals. These were needed because they believed the gods had sacrificed themselves for mankind, that their blood had given Man life, and that the Sun was nourished with the blood of human hearts. In dreams, such a figure may signify supreme personal sacrifice.

**Chinese** – traditionally Chinese people often followed a combination of religious beliefs, including Confucianism, Taoism and Buddhism. Practices such as ancestor worship and meditation, together with the worship of gods and magical rituals, still take place and in dreams, as our knowledge increases, can give rich imagery.

**Inca** – politics and religion are forever intertwined and the gods are worshipped as forces of nature. The Sun God is recognized as the supreme civil ruler, so in dreams the figure of an Incan suggests a system where social responsibility is paramount.

**Inuit** – the Inuit traditionally believed in a god-like power that is contained in all of Nature. The Shaman is an important figure in their belief structure, being able to converse with the spirits. In dreams, the Inuit reflect the harshness of life lived as hunters close to Nature.

**Japanese** – many Japanese follow the Shinto religion where tradition and the family, love of nature, physical cleanliness, and *Matsuri* – the worship and honour given to the *Kami* (gods) and ancestral spirits – are important. The oriental woman often appears in dreams as the epitome of feminine, gentle qualities.

**Maori** – three important parts of Maori religion are what they call the life force, spirit (*Wairua*) that can be found in all people and spiritual power or prestige. This means that ancestor worship is important. The Maori stress the importance of growth and change, of working closely with nature, and will signify this in dreams.

**Maya** – many Mayans today believe, as the original Mayans did, in the influence of the Cosmos and the need to pay homage to the gods through rituals of many types. It is this element of ritual that will often surface in dreams today.

**Native American** – the Sun Dance amongst the Plains Native Americans is perceived as a replay of the original Creation. Their religion is Shamanic and as more people become aware of their culture and practices, dreams will reflect the richness of their beliefs and their closeness to nature. Ceremonies such as the sweat lodge give rise to much imagery.

🔲 Becoming aware of other cultures and religious practices has the effect of opening our perception to what Jung called the Collective Unconscious, a library available to all of us. From a mundane perspective, the imagery available to us then becomes useful in remaining close to natural activity and living life mindfully.

*Also consult the entry for Shaman for further clarification.*

**INFECTION**

🌞 In spiritual development, and particularly when dealing with outside influences, we can become contaminated – or infected – by ideology and spurious beliefs. We need to be aware of the possibility that we can be 'taken over' by wrong thought and negativity.

💚 When we are made uncomfortable by external circumstances in waking life, this may appear as an infection in a dream.

🔲 Dreaming of having an infection suggests that there is the possibility of us having internalized negative attitudes from other people. Depending on where in the body the infection appears, there is information as to the type of 'infection'. For example, an infection in the leg may indicate that we feel we are being prevented from moving forward quickly enough in waking life.

*Consult the entries for Injure/Injury and Wound for further information.*

**INFINITY**

🌞 The closest representation to infinity that can be experienced spiritually is the Abyss or Void. In dreams as we progress spiritually we can have a sense of limitlessness.

💚 For most people, infinity is beyond understanding, so when in dreams we have no sense of boundaries or a realization that we are not separate from anything else, this is a sense of infinity.

■ In dreams, the concept of infinity can make us feel very small and insignificant and occasionally without meaning. Conversely, it can make us appreciate how powerful we really are.

*Also consult the entries for Abyss and Void.*

## INHERITANCE

✺ To dream of an inheritance suggests that spiritually we have at our disposal all the knowledge and cultural input that our ancestors have accrued. This includes cultural family and religious knowledge.

♥ Emotionally, our inheritance consists of the influences from the past from members of our family as to how we think and feel. Unless we understand those influences we cannot break free of them.

■ Dreaming of an inheritance suggests that we have been bequeathed something of value, not necessarily monetary. It will be much more to do with strong character traits and perhaps ways of tackling problems.

## INITIATION

✺ Initiation is a rite of passage ceremony marking entrance or acceptance into a group or society. An initiation or inauguration ceremony in a spiritual sense can mark a new beginning, the taking of new spirituality, perhaps Cosmic Responsibility.

♥ Often a ceremony is necessary to mark the fact that we have succeeded in one thing and can now move on, putting that knowledge to the test in the outside world. To be dreaming of such a ceremony indicates that we can be pleased with ourselves and what we have achieved, that we have literally inaugurated a different way of being, and can now move forward into the future.

■ We have many opportunities to make new beginnings, and initiation – in that it indicates a change of status – is one such symbol. This may be important to us in terms of either personal growth or within the work situation. To dream that we are being given such an honour means we can receive acclaim for something that we have done, for our ability to make the transition from the lesser to the greater.

▣ Rites of passage often require a formal acknowledgement and this may well be reflected in dreams. By tradition, initiation for men is more overt and physical, whilst for women it is more intuitive.

## INJECT/INJECTION

✺ Spiritually, to find ourselves accepting an injection indicates that we are prepared to create circumstances within ourselves which will help us to progress. More negatively, an injection can indicate short-term pleasure rather than long-term gain.

◈ An injection may be an attempt to heal, or to make us better. We may feel that we need external help in order to function more successfully. It will depend on our attitude to conventional medicine whether this is seen as co-operation or resistance.

▦ To dream of being given an injection is to be feeling that our personal space has been penetrated. Other people's opinions, needs or desires may be forced on us leaving little option but to co-operate. To dream of giving an injection suggests that we are attempting to force ourselves on other people.

▣ Obviously, because an injection is penetrative by nature, such a dream for both men and women may have sexual connotations.

*You might also like to consult the entries for Needle and Syringe.*

## INJURE/INJURY

❀ Spiritually, an injury or scar may suggest that something negative and harmful has occurred, which is an external force rather than internal. We may not have dealt with it as well as we might.

◈ It will often be significant which area of the body is harmed in the dream. The nervous system can develop ways of giving information without us being conscious of it. This may give some indication of the area of life that is affected by the trauma. To have an arm broken, for instance, might suggest that our ability to hold on is compromised. If we see someone else who has been hurt or scarred we have probably been the ones who have hurt others in the past. If this is so, there are various techniques we can use in the waking state to help us release others from the hurt we have inflicted. The healing that subsequently takes place may then be recorded in further dreams by the loss of the scar.

▦ An injury will suggest a recent hurt, whereas a scar in a dream suggests that there are old hurts, which have not been fully dealt with. These may be mental and emotional as much as physical, and can remain unnoticed until we are reminded of them. Just as in physical injury there can be many kinds of scars, so there can also be in the other areas. We may, for instance, be left with a pattern of behaviour which is irritating to other people, but without the clear connection given by the dream image, we are unable to understand it.

## INK

❀ Ink has significance, particularly in magical practices, when it is used to reflect powers that are outside the norm. In written magical spells it is often important to use particular inks in order to achieve the required results. Spiritually this creates the correct vibration and this concept often surfaces in dreams.

On a more intellectual level, ink signifies the ability to transcribe and understand knowledge in a more sophisticated way. When a particular flow of energy or information is needed, ink can symbolize that flow.

Since very few people now use fountain pens, the significance of ink on a physical level is no longer quite so valid. As a child, learning the art of handwriting could be difficult and pen and ink thus became 'instruments of torture' and can often appear as such in difficult dreams in later life. Formerly in dreams, ink also suggested the ability to communicate in a lucid fashion. *The entries for Paper/Parchment, Pen and Writing will help with further clarification.*

## INQUEST

An inquest in dreams from a spiritual perspective is an attempt to understand something that is, for the time being, incomprehensible.

Emotionally in dreams an inquest may signify the need to study events and feelings so that we understand our own reactions.

Sometimes in everyday life we fall short of what we expect of ourselves or others. Dreaming of an inquest – a proper inquiry – will help us to work out what we must do. It is as though we need someone in authority to sort us out. *You might like to consult the entries for Death, Law and Authority Figures in People.*

## INSANE – *see* MAD

## INSCRIPTION

The image of an inscription often appears in dreams as we reach a certain stage of spiritual development, almost like a message from beyond. Spiritually, this usually indicates the type of knowledge that needs to be recorded and can be passed onto other people.

In dreams, an inscription appearing on, for instance, a rock would suggest old knowledge or wisdom. An inscription appearing in sand would suggest that the knowledge is either impermanent, or must be learnt quickly.

Any inscription in a dream is information that needs to be understood and internalized. Reading an inscription can suggest that something is understood in some way already, whereas not being able to read it suggests that more information or knowledge is required in order to complete a task. *Also consult the entries for Ink, Paper/Parchment, Stone and Writing.*

## INSECTS

Psychically, insects can appear in dreams as some kind of threat. This is one reason why they are often used in psychological thrillers and science fiction. Some form of spiritual 'infection' may have taken place. Fleas are symbolic of the type of disruption that is likely to hurt, rather than destroy, such as gossip. A mantis represents deviousness, particularly of a spiritual kind. It is that Trickster part of us that can create problems when things are effectively working out for us; it is that aspect of our personality which perhaps preys on the other parts and will not take its place within our overall integration. More positively, insects such as ants can appear in dreams as reminders of instinctive behaviour.

♥ Insects tend to signify negative feelings and link us to primal instinctive behaviour, that of survival against all odds. In dreams, we often translate a quality or a situation we are struggling with into an object such as an insect; psychologically, insects can represent feelings we would rather do without. This could be something niggling at our consciences, or guilt. We may additionally be aware that we are not being treated properly and that people who should be our friends are not being fair. To be aware of a predatory insect such as a mantis may indicate that we are conscious of trickery around us. Whatever threatens us does so on a very basic level, and we may have no defences, except those of our own nature.

▣ Insects in dreams can reflect the feeling that something is irritating or bugging us. They may also indicate our feelings of insignificance and powerlessness and it will depend on the particular insect in the dream as to the interpretation. Thus, a wasp might indicate danger, whereas a beetle could mean either dirt or protection. Fleas are an irritation; there may be people or situations in our lives that are causing us difficulty, or that we feel are being parasites, and we need to go through a process of decontamination in order to be free. Flies are always associated with something nasty, which does not allow for the fact that they also devour rotten material, and thus are cleansing. So to dream of flies is to be aware that we have certain negative aspects of our lives that need dealing with. To dream of a swarm of flies indicates the deliberate intention of a large group of individuals. Where one insect may appear to be moving aimlessly, large numbers do not. Often we can only succeed in changing matters by group behaviour. As with most insects, the mantis often represents something devious within our lives.

## INSIDE (IN)

☀ Spiritually, inside may have connotations of protectiveness and of a degree of introversion. Being inside suggests the need for some spiritual awareness, of being permitted to enter an inner sanctum.

♥ Being shut in suggests that we are emotionally restricted and may feel we cannot express ourselves properly. Going into a building in dreams, for example, suggests we should explore the structure of our lives.

In dreams, exploring the inside of something as opposed to the outside suggests that we need to explore motivation in some way. Being stuck inside suggests we are aware of circumstances around us that are preventing us from moving forward. This may, of course, be due to our own attitudes.

## INSERT

To be inserting an object into a space or area is trying to ensure that it, or whatever it represents, is drawn to our attention and given relevance in a spiritual sense.

Dreaming of an insert in a paper or making an insertion in a document signifies that there is an idea or concept that we must include in our considerations.

With relevance to working life, making an insertion suggests that we are wishing to influence an outcome. For someone else to be doing so suggests that there is an influence we have not considered.

In both men's and women's dreams, insertion frequently has the same connotation as penetration, albeit from their different perspectives.

*Consult the entry for Penetration for further clarification.*

## INSTALMENT

Spiritually, when we recognize that something – payments perhaps, or information – is occurring in instalments we must understand that what is represented must happen, or occur to us, gradually. Perhaps we need to learn in bite-sized chunks.

In dreaming of instalments, from an emotional perspective we must accept that there is a degree of conditional acceptance, either in ourselves or others. We may not be ready to make a full commitment.

To install something is to put it into position. A new programme on a computer in dreams would, for instance, mean accepting a new way of working. A new instalment of a story suggests a different phase in a project.

## INSTRUMENTS – *see* MUSIC/RHYTHM, MUSICAL INSTRUMENTS AND SURGERY/SURGICAL INSTRUMENTS

## INSULATE – *see* WADDING

## INSURE/INSURANCE

Spiritual insurance is a sure and certain knowledge that we are protected from harm. We may also be trying to protect ourselves against trauma.

When we feel emotionally secure and safe against any loss we may dream of insurances or of trying to take out insurance. While to insure our possessions against loss and theft is natural in everyday life, to dream of doing so probably means that on some level we feel insecure.

▦ On a mundane level, insurance is trying to mitigate against possible loss in the future. It will often have this meaning in dreams, though the loss we are protecting ourselves against need not be financial.

*You might also like to consult the entry for Lose/Loss/Lost.*

## INTERMEDIARY

☼ An intermediary is someone who can plead our case or relay information. In spiritual terms this might be represented by a religious teacher or a medium (spiritual channeller). As we try to achieve a balance between the demands of the spiritual and physical realms, an intermediary such as an angelic figure may appear in dreams.

♡ When emotions run high we need someone who can 'filter' our energy to the point where it becomes manageable. Dreaming of an argument or conflict where an intermediary is present allows us to regain control and listen to reason.

▦ In working life an intermediary performs the function of a negotiator. In dreams dealing with mundane matters, when two points of view need to be balanced, such a figure may appear.

*You might like to consult the entries for Angel, Argue/Argument and Conflict for further clarification.*

## INTERNET – *see* COMMUNICATION AND WEB

## INTERSECTION

☼ When we meet an intersection in dreams, for instance two roads or paths crossing or meeting, we are having to make choices which may have a greater impact on others than they do on us.

♡ If we are conscious of an intersection – perhaps in a pattern that appears in a dream – we are being offered choices, and perhaps have to differentiate between right and wrong.

▦ An intersection that appears in a dream – such as a T-junction – indicates there is a choice of two ways forward. Two opposites may be coming together in our waking lives, and we are able to make changes and move forward in a more focused way.

*You might also like to consult the entries for Crossroads, Path and Road in Journey for further clarification.*

## INTERVIEW

☼ An interview in the spiritual sense suggests some test of worthiness for a task, particularly one that is for the Greater Good or has spiritual overtones.

♡ There is always a fear that we may be found wanting, so in dreams an interview may be seen as testing our belief in ourselves.

🔲 Dreaming of an interview suggests we may be questioning whether the work we do is satisfying us and giving us the feedback we need.

🔲 In a woman's dream, if she is being interviewed by a panel of men, she may be confronting aspects of her own drive and tenacity. In a man's dream, if his interviewers are feminine he is coming to terms with his sensitivities and softer skills. Women being interviewed by women, and men by men, suggests that they are being judged by their peers.

**INTESTINES –** *see* **ABDOMEN AND EXCREMENT IN BODY**

**INTOXICATION –** *see* **ALCOHOL/ALCOHOLIC, DRUGS AND DRUNK**

**INTRUDER**

🔲 Spiritually it is possible to put ourselves in danger of being open to desecration. The Self is a sacred space, but until we understand that it is inviolable, we can be open to challenge. The appearance of an intruder in dreams can indicate this.

🔲 To dream of an intruder has an obvious connection with sex and threats to one's sexuality. The intruder is also that part of ourselves that does not handle our fears and doubts properly, but makes us feel insecure. In dreams, this figure needs to be challenged.

🔲 As human beings, we are very conscious of our own personal space. Dreaming of an intruder or prowler indicates that we are feeling threatened in some way.

🔲 Particularly in women's dreams, the intruder is often masculine, indicating a need to defend ourselves. In a man's dream an intruder is more representative of his unruly side.

*Also consult the entries for Burglar and People.*

**INVADE/INVASION**

🔲 An invasion in spiritual terms is a desecration of our own spiritual space, that part of us that we hold sacred and normally free from harm. When rendered insecure by too many demands, we can feel invaded and under attack.

🔲 When we are ourselves invading somewhere in a dream, this presupposes that a degree of force is necessary, particularly on an emotional level. Normally an invasion suggests that there are many aspects involved, which could be feelings, needs or ideas.

🔲 To invade is to plan an organized movement or takeover and this can have relevance in dreams of a business environment. An invasion suggests a concerted movement against us or, if we are one of the invaders, against a weaker opponent.

🔲 Dreams of an invading force in a woman's dream suggest a violation of her personal space. In a man's dream he is perhaps more likely to dream of himself as the invader, particularly if he is aware of his partner's sensitivities, whatever their gender.

*Consult the entries for Armed Forces and Force for further clarification.*

## INVENT/INVENTOR

🔆 The inventor in us is the part that takes spiritual responsibility for our progress. He often signifies our ability to 'create' new ways of being, but needs assistance from us on a conscious level.

💚 When we dream of an inventor, psychologically we are linking with that side of ourselves that is wiser but at the same time perhaps more introverted than our waking selves. We can give ourselves permission to be creative.

🔲 Dreaming of an inventor or a professor type links us with the more creative sides of ourselves. Usually this is more the thinker rather than the doer; someone who is capable of taking an idea and making it tangible.

*You might also like to consult the entry for Laboratory.*

## INVEST – *see* MONEY AND WEALTH

## INVESTIGATE/INVESTIGATION

🔆 An investigation in the spiritual sense suggests that concepts, precepts and beliefs need to be very carefully looked at.

💚 Many people do not like to look too closely at their own emotions, but to be investigating a building, for instance, can suggest that we are trying to understand ourselves and our own reactions.

🔲 When we are unsure of our own position within a work hierarchy or family structure we may dream of an investigation in order to feel comfortable. If we are being investigated in dreams we may feel we have not fulfilled a task to our own satisfaction. Such a dream may also suggest that we are being too closely monitored for our own liking.

*You might also like to consult the entry for Question.*

## INVISIBLE

🔆 Spiritually, the Invisible is God Unmanifest, that is, prior to Creation. Also known as the Absolute, it is invisible because it is not experienced or comprehended by any of the five conscious senses.

💚 When we are conscious that something is invisible in a dream, it indicates that we simply need to be aware of the image's presence, without necessarily having to interpret it immediately.

🔲 Actually becoming invisible in a dream – disappearing – would indicate either that we are not ready to face the knowledge that understanding would bring us, or that there is something we would rather forget.

⚡ Sometimes a figure (either a man or woman), though seeming to be invisible, can represent the Shadow. In both men's and women's dreams it will have the same gender as the dreamer.

*Also consult the information on the Shadow in Archetypes in the Introduction.*

**IRIS – see EYE AND FLOWERS**

**IRON**

⚜ Iron usually symbolizes power. In a dream it can signify the part of ourselves that is capable of discipline – an iron will. However, before being tempered by fire (life's challenges) and made into hard steel, iron requires protecting against corrosion. It is this quality of the development of protection against spiritual 'corrosion' (eating away) that needs to be dealt with so we can progress.

♥ When we dream of using a clothes iron we are attempting to make ourselves more presentable to the outside world. We may also be trying to 'smooth things over'.

▦ When the metal iron appears in dreams, it usually represents our strengths and determination. It can also signify the rigidity of our emotions or beliefs. We should consider being more flexible.

*You might also like to consult the entry for Metal.*

**IRRITATION – see ANGER, INFECTION AND INSECTS**

**ISLAND**

⚜ In dreams an island can signify a spiritual retreat – somewhere which is cut off from the world – which will allow us to contemplate our own spiritual Self.

♥ Occasionally we all need to recharge our batteries, and to dream of an island can help, or warn us, to do this. Dreaming of a desert or treasure island indicates there is something to be gained by being alone and exploring our ability to cope with such a situation. We may actually function better in some way.

▦ Dreaming of an island signifies the loneliness one can feel through isolation, self-imposed or otherwise. We may feel out of touch with others or with situations around us. An island can also represent safety in that, by isolating ourselves, we are not subject to external pressures.

*Also consult the entry for Isolate/Isolation.*

**ISOLATE/ISOLATION**

⚜ Spiritual isolation signifies the hermit, or recluse – any person living in seclusion, whether through religious belief or not. This suggests the need to spend time alone in tranquility.

♥ When we isolate ourselves (for example, on an island) it suggests that we do not wish or need to become emotionally involved with someone.

When we find ourselves in isolation in a dream we should decide if it is by our own volition or because of others. If by our own wish, then there is a quality in us which has difficulty in relating to others; if because of others, we perhaps need to explore rejection and our feelings about it.

**IVY**

Spiritually, ivy symbolizes immortality and eternal life. It also represents fertility. It is a plant sacred to Bacchus and, therefore, in dreams can suggest Joy.

Because ivy has the symbolism of constant affection, we can recognize that, psychologically, we are in need of love and affection. In dreams it may signify a binding promise.

Dreaming of ivy harks back to the old idea of celebration and fun. It can also symbolize the clinging dependence that can develop within relationships.

In a woman's dream ivy may represent relationships, but in a man's dream may signify responsibility.

*Also consult the entries for Bonds, Plants and Weeds.*

## JAB

⚜ A jab, whether in the sense of a punch or an injection, may be seen as an act of aggression. From a spiritual perspective we may need to ascertain what is causing that aggression.

♥ By its nature a jab is a short sharp action, often containing an element of surprise. It will depend on other circumstances in the dream how this element of surprise is interpreted. We may need a short sharp shock to move us from our present emotional stasis.

▦ Jabs are straight, arm-length punches thrown from the leading hand. In dreams we must decide whether the action is defensive or offensive before we interpret them in terms of what is occurring in everyday circumstances. If the fight is structured as in a boxing match this action may refer to working difficulties.

*You might like to consult the entries for Fight, Inject/Injection and Vaccination.*

**JACKAL –** *see* **ANIMALS**

**JACKET –** *see* **COAT IN CLOTHES**

**JADE –** *see* **GEMS/JEWELS**

**JAGUAR –** *see* **ANIMALS**

**JAIL –** *see* **PRISON**

## JAILER

⚜ We may be feeling a degree of spiritual difficulty, a sense of being held back.

♥ To dream of a jailer suggests we feel we are being restricted in some way, maybe by our own emotions or by somebody else's personality or actions. There will be a sense of self-criticism and of alienation which makes it difficult to carry out our ordinary, everyday tasks.

▦ When we are in a situation from which we cannot escape, the personality that appears in our dream often gives information as to how we have got ourselves into that situation. For instance, being unfairly treated by our jailer would indicate that not only may we have been party to the entrapment, but also that we have become victims of our own circumstances.

*Also consult the entries for Authority Figures in People and Prison.*

## JAM/JAMMED

⚜ If a door or machine is jammed we recognize that there may be spiritual obstacles ahead of us.

⊘ To be in a traffic jam suggests that other people's concerns may be, or seem to be, more important than our own.

▥ If we have caused the jam – that is, stopped the movement or flow – we must work out what is causing the difficulty and take avoiding action. Jam as a fruit conserve (a mixture of fruit and sugar) suggests that only by blending the components of a project can we come up with something fresh and new.

**JAR**

◉ The Ancient Egyptians preserved the bodily organs of the dead in canopic jars to ensure that when the soul returned to the physical realms it had everything it needed. A jar thus symbolizes a receptacle for the Soul.

⊘ To be conscious of being jarred – of being shaken in some way – indicates that we are not controlling the way we are moving forward. We are putting ourselves in a position where we can be knocked about, hurt or put off balance. While this may be shocking or upsetting it can also present opportunities for us to gain understanding.

▥ A jar very often represents the feminine containing principle, perhaps some aspect of mothering or of conservation which we recognize within our lives. It often has the same symbolism as the vase – that is, an article which is beautiful in its own right and also the receptacle for something beautiful or necessary. If the jar is broken, it suggests that something essential has been lost.

⦂ In a woman's dream a jar will represent her own femininity whereas in a man's dream it is more likely to signify a nurturing nature or need.

*Also consult the entry for Vase.*

**JAVELIN** – *see* **SPEAR**

**JAW** – *see* **BODY**

**JAZZ** – *see* **MUSIC/RHYTHM**

**JEER**

◉ To be jeered at for our beliefs is often part of a spiritual testing, so experiencing it in dreams helps to clarify those beliefs.

⊘ To experience being taunted or mocked in dreams may be interpreted as an attack on our self-esteem.

▥ When we do not seem to be experiencing success in waking life that part of our personality which inhibits that success may appear in dreams to jeer at us.

⦂ In a man's dream the one who jeers may often appear as a parental figure, sometimes of the opposite sex. In a woman's dream it may be her Shadow which mocks.

**JESTER** – *see* **JOKE/JOKER**

**JET** – *see* **AEROPLANE**

**JEWELLERY**

🔆 Jewellery represents honour and self-respect without the attendant posturing. Spiritually, it usually indicates that we have, or can have, something valuable in our lives. Jewellery can also indicate love given or received.

♥ Very often, jewellery can represent our own feelings about ourselves, and how we present ourselves to the world. For it to appear in a dream – either as something which is very valuable or as something we know to be false (such as costume jewellery which masquerades as something valuable) gives an indication of our own self-esteem. It may also give an indication as to how others feel about us.

▦ Being given jewellery suggests that someone else values us; giving jewellery signifies that we feel we have something to offer to other people. Those qualities we have learnt to value in ourselves through hard experience are those that we display most easily to other people.

⌘ For a woman to be giving a man jewellery in dreams usually indicates that she is attracted to him and perhaps is able to offer him her own sexuality and self-respect. In a man's dream if he is giving a woman jewellery, he may be offering commitment.

*You might like to consult the entries for Gift or Gems/Jewels.*

**JEWELS** – *see* **GEMS/JEWELS**

**JIGSAW**

🔆 A jigsaw puzzle in dreams suggests a spiritual conundrum, a difficult problem to be solved.

♥ A jigsaw tool is capable of cutting around shapes. It is this interpretation which may be relevant in dreams, we are able to circumvent a difficulty.

▦ To see a jigsaw puzzle in dreams represents a mental challenge or a problem in waking life that needs to be solved. If there are pieces missing in the puzzle, then it suggests that we do not have all the facts in order to make a considered decision. If the pieces do not fit we may be at odds with a given way of working.

**JINX** – *see* **HEX**

**JOKE/JOKER**

🔆 A joker in dreams is a free spirit or a self-actualized personality, one who has come to terms with life on the physical plane of existence.

♥ Emotionally, a joke can bring about a release of tension and a bizarre occurrence in dreams which causes amusement can do the same. The aspect of our personality which shows itself as a joker has the same meaning as a jester – someone who can make us laugh at ourselves and arouse a sense of the ridiculous.

🀫 A joke in dreams can be an image presented in an odd way. It is as though the mind develops the oddity in order to have us remember what it is attempting to present.

*You might also like to consult the entries for Balloon and Clown.*

## JOURNAL/JOURNALIST

🌞 As a record of our daily lives a journal allows us to keep track of our spiritual progress. In dreams it signifies a tool that we might need in order to understand and monitor our own way of taking in knowledge. A journalist symbolizes the recorder and observing part of our Higher Self which witnesses how we maintain our spiritual integrity.

❤ An actual journal in which we record our dreams keeps track of our 'inner' life – what is going on in the unconscious while we live in the real world. When this image occurs in a dream it is time we paid more attention to this hidden side of ourselves. The journalist in this context makes judgements as to how much of this can be shared with others.

🀫 In ordinary mundane terms a journal or any type of manual keeps track of the progress of a particular task or project. To be writing in such a book suggests that we may need to monitor what we are doing more carefully. A journalist or newspaper reporter in such a dream suggests that care needs to be taken in putting across the right information and ensuring that detail is not lost.

📲 In both men's and women's dreams a journal suggests a private part of the psyche and perhaps the need for privacy. The gender of the journalist will suggest a more emotional approach if the figure is female and a more logical approach if male.

## JOURNEY

🌞 The idea of life being a journey or of journeying towards maturity is a large part of spiritual discipline. There is the Hero's journey as he (or she) discovers the meaning of life, overcomes challenges and reaches autonomy. In addition there is the journey as depicted by the Major Arcana in the Tarot which illustrates the main processes that the incarnate soul (living being) goes through in the search for spirituality. The image of a journey becomes more apparent as time goes on and death approaches. We become more aware of reaching our final destination.

❤ The image of a journey is a very potent one in dream work. Any time the idea of a journey becomes apparent, it is to do with the way that we carry on our everyday lives and how we move forward. Every step that we take towards understanding ourselves and the world we live in can be pictured in terms of a journey, and the dreams that a person has reflect that movement. Making a long journey, for example, suggests leaving friends and family, as would running away to sea. Making a short journey would be investigating an idea or principle in the short term. A difficult journey now behind us means we have come through the difficulties and set-backs of the past. In our ordinary everyday speech we use idioms to suggest our understanding. We speak of the ups and downs of life, of being at a standstill and so on. Each moment is totally unique, and that uniqueness is reflected in our dreams. Mostly dreams are about the here and now and give a snapshot picture as to what is happening at this particular moment, on our individual journey and are therefore a rich source of information as to our psychological or inner state.

▣ The images that appear in dreams will reflect how we are feeling, what obstacles there are, possible courses of action and what our ultimate goal should or may be in our everyday lives. The dream will bring in images from the past or recognizable scenes to help us interpret what is going on and move forward to meet our destiny. The mode of transport we use for our journey is also important. *Consult the entry for Transport.*

Some important images to do with journeys are as follows:

Avoiding an accident means we are able to control our impulses, whereas collisions or other such accidents represent arguments and conflicts which are often caused by our own aggression. *Also consult the entry for Accident.*

**Completing a journey** – arriving home, touching down and so on – indicates the successful completion of our aims.

**Corner** – this shows we have accepted the need for a change of direction. We may have made a major decision. *Also consult the entry for Corner.*

**Departures from airports, stations, etc.** – formerly all departures were interpreted as death. Nowadays the symbolism is much more of a new beginning. We are leaving our old life in order to undertake something new. When someone in our lives leaves us, we may dream of departures and the grief that parting causes. In certain circumstances, to dream of wanting to leave but not being able to suggests that there is still further work to be done. To be conscious of the time of departure might suggest that we are aware of a time limit within an area of our lives. *You may also like to consult the individual entries for Airport and Departing.*

**Destinations**, when they become apparent, will give some ideas about the aims and objectives we have. Our declared hopes and ideals may not correspond with those we subconsciously have – our inner motivation may be totally different to our outer behaviour – and dreams will highlight this discrepancy. The exact nature of our objective is often not known to us until after we have confronted the obstacles and challenges along the way. It is often enough just to have an aim for that particular section of the journey.

**Hills** – going uphill suggests extra effort is necessary, while going downhill will suggest lack of control. *Also consult the individual entry for Hill.*

**Obstacles ahead** – these indicate that we are aware of difficulties which may occur. We do need to be aware that we ourselves create the problems. Our own attitude to life is perhaps responsible.

**Passenger** – it will depend if we are a passenger in a vehicle or are carrying passengers as to the interpretation. If the former, we may feel that we are being carried along by circumstances, and have not really thought out our own way forward. If the latter, we may have knowingly or inadvertently made ourselves responsible for other people in some way. Travelling with one other passenger suggests we may be considering our relationship with that person or whatever they represent. *Also consult the individual entry for Passenger.*

**Road or path** – the road or path in a dream suggests our own individual way forward. Just as in dreams, an individual vehicle represents the dreamer's body and external way of being, so the road reflects the way of doing. Any obstacle in the road will reflect difficulties on the chosen path whereas turns in the road will suggest changes of direction. Crossroads will offer choices, while a cul-de-sac would signify a dead end or non-success. If a particular stretch of road is highlighted it may be a period of time, or may mean an effort. *Also consult the individual entries for Crossroads, Cul-de-sac and Path.*

**Road rage** – road rage appearing in dreams is an aspect of suppressed anger. It signifies a complete loss of control, both of our emotions and of common sense. It will depend on whether we are the victim of such rage or the perpetrator as to the interpretation.

**Standstill** – being at a standstill or blocked in some way indicates we are being prevented, or are preventing ourselves, from moving forward. This needs handling with care, since to stop may be appropriate. Frequently finding ourselves stopping and starting suggests there is conflict between laziness and drive or ambition.

**Walk** – if in our dreams we are aware of having to walk, it usually suggests that we are capable of making a part of our life journey by ourselves without any help. Hill walking or similar outdoor activities suggest that we enjoy challenging ourselves. Going for a walk shows we can enjoy the process of recharging our batteries and clearing our minds.

## JUBILEE

The time of a jubilee represents a fresh start. This has particular significance in some systems of belief in that it is the 49th part of the life cycle. After 7 x 7 years, the fiftieth year becomes sacred and gives a new beginning and additional insights.

Dreaming of a jubilee or jubilant occasion can represent the natural spontaneity with which we greet changes.

To be dreaming of a jubilee or jubilee celebrations would indicate a rite of passage – a passing from the old into the new, perhaps evidence of having reached the age of discretion. This image might be present after a promotion at work or a change of job.

## JUDGE/JUDGEMENT

Though from a spiritual perspective it is not right to judge others or to make judgements, in dreams we often find that we tend to do this. We need to be sufficiently spiritually advanced in order to accept matters as they present themselves, without passing an opinion.

Our own experience and, for that matter that of our families, can lead to problems with authority figures such as judges in dreams. These experiences can equally make us judgemental of others' difficulties and peccadilloes.

Within work situations our judgement is often an integral part of decision making. We must, for instance, evaluate whatever criteria are being applied and act accordingly, just as a judge in court must be as fair as possible.

*You might also like to consult the entry for Authority Figures in People.*

## JUG – see JAR AND VASE

## JUGGLE

Juggling presupposes a learned response and an expertise which we may need spiritually to balance our lives.

The image of a juggler or of someone juggling suggests that we need to keep control of our own emotions or of those around us.

In waking life we often find we have to carry out a number of tasks at the same time. This may translate in dreams as juggling, The colour of the balls may help us to interpret the relevance.

*You might like to consult the entry for Colour*

## JUMBLE

The jumble of images in dreams are spiritually a little like tasters at a meal, and sometimes not easily interpreted. As we become more proficient in understanding we begin to understand the themes of our dreams.

A jumble of objects in dreams suggest that there is some kind of mess or confusion in our waking lives which needs to be sorted out.

🎲 Jumble can have the same meaning as junk in that there is no particular order – it is a confused mess. If in everyday life there are aspects which have this quality we may be wise to try to create some kind of order, and decide what is worth keeping or continuing with and what is better discarded.

JUMPING

� In certain religions, spiritual ecstasy is induced by jumping. This is a way of employing physical action in order to reach spiritual realms, and has this significance in dreams.

♥ Repetitive movement of any sort in a dream usually indicates the need to reconsider our actions, to look at what we are doing and perhaps to express ourselves in a different way. On a psychological level, jumping up and down in a dream may indicate being caught up in a situation without having the power to move either forwards or backwards.

🎲 The act of jumping can be somewhat ambiguous in a dream. It can indicate either jumping up – attempting to attain something better for ourselves – or jumping down, which can mean going down into the unconscious and those parts of ourselves where we may feel we are in danger. Jumping on the spot can indicate joy and has the same significance as dance. *You might also like to consult the entry for Dance/Dancing.*

JUNCTION

� Because a road is such a potent image in a spiritual journey, a junction has equal resonance. It suggests that there are choices to be made which may well change the whole course of our lives.

♥ When in dreams we come to a junction, a joining together of more than one way, we perhaps need to look at what has brought us to this particular point. With this in mind, assessing what happened in the dream, such as hesitating before moving or having the feeling that we are waiting for someone can then be interpreted. Emotionally we may have to wait for others to catch up.

🎲 Dreaming of a junction presupposes that there is an element of duality in a project. We will have to weigh up the various options and make a decision as to which course of action we should take. If the way is clearly indicated the choice is obvious. If less clearly marked or the way is obscured, there will be other factors to be taken into consideration. *You might like to consult the entries for Crossroads and Journey for further clarification.*

JUNGLE

� The jungle can symbolize spiritual chaos due to its unpredictability. It suggests a rite of passage – a journey which must be taken to reach maturity.

⬦ Psychologically, without the ordering of information that we receive, our minds can simply become a jungle of information. We need to use logic to apply order so that we can make sense of ourselves and our environment. To be trapped in a jungle indicates that we are trapped by negative and frightening feelings from the unconscious, perhaps from those areas which could be considered to be uncivilized. To be conscious of having come through a jungle would indicate that we have passed through, and overcome, those aspects of our lives which we have never dared approach before.

▣ The jungle in dreams is an image belonging to mysticism and fairy tales, often representing chaos, which can be either positive or negative depending on the circumstances of the dream. In myths the jungle symbolizes an obstacle or barrier that has to be passed through in order to reach a new state of being. With this meaning it has the same significance in dreams as the enchanted forest.

⬒ In a man's dream of a jungle he is often helped by a feminine figure – his Anima – in his search for a clear passage. In a woman's dream she must frequently overcome the negative aspects of femininity before she can reveal her true identity or power.

*You might also like to consult the entries for Animals and Forest.*

## JUNK

⬥ Spiritually junk represents outmoded or unwanted concepts and ideas. A Chinese junk has the same significance as the lunar barque or boat.

⬦ From an emotional perspective we all tend to accumulate a great deal of rubbish which periodically needs sorting and disposing of. A cupboard or room full of junk would suggest we need to take action to clear ourselves of hang-ups and difficulties.

▣ When 'mental' junk accumulates we are not able to think clearly and dreams have the facility of enabling us to create order so that we can sort out our lives. Being able to categorize what seems to be rubbish in dreams means we can plan or decide on a course of action.

*You might like to consult the entries for Baggage, Boat/Ship and Rubbish.*

## JUROR/JURY

⬥ Often in the process of personal development we may have to make judgements which are not popular. We sometimes have to act as our own juror. Provided we adhere to our own inner spiritual truth, we cannot be judged.

⬦ Sometimes in life we may not feel we can go along with a group decision. If in dreams we are a member of the jury, a juror, it will depend on other aspects of the dream whether we can agree with the rest of the jurors or not.

We might have to decide to 'go it alone' and make a unilateral decision. Such a dream would probably reflect a situation in our everyday lives. Conversely, in dreaming of trying to reach a consensus of opinion, we must carefully consider our own beliefs as to how we should live our lives, perhaps taking into account all aspects of our personality.

⊞ When a jury appears in a dream on a mundane level we are usually struggling with an issue of peer pressure. We may fear that others will not understand our actions, that they could judge us and find us wanting.

*Also consult the entries for Justice and Verdict.*

## JUSTICE

⚙ In spiritual progression there needs to be a balance between our more spiritual selves – what might be called ideal behaviour – and the physical or material realm. This balance can be difficult to both attain and maintain. Such a difficulty can be symbolized by the figure of Justice.

♡ Often when we are attempting to balance two different states or ways of being, Justice – complete with scales – can appear within a dream. This shows that we need to use both sides of ourselves successfully. To be brought to justice can signify that we must pay attention to our actions or to our attitude to authority. It may be that we are offending against some aspect of society.

⊞ Very often in a dream we do not seem to be capable of expressing our right to be heard, to articulate those things we believe are correct. Therefore, to dream of either justice or injustice can indicate that the unconscious mind is trying to sort out right from wrong. This is usually on a personal level, although it can have a wider implication as to what is morally right and the norm within society.

*You might like to consult the entries for Authority Figures in People, Balance, Juror/Jury and Verdict.*

## KALEIDOSCOPE

In dreams we are able to appreciate the beauty of basic patterns. In a kaleidoscope, any arbitrary pattern of objects shows up as a beautiful symmetrical pattern because of the reflections in the mirrors from which the kaleidoscope is constructed. The patterns, both regular and irregular as seen in nature, can symbolize the patterns and matrices that we make to comfort ourselves in times of self-doubt.

The magnification and myriad reflections of the patterns created by small objects as they are tumbled together permits us to recapture the sense of wonder that is felt in being human. We become aware of our own 'smallness' within the larger scheme of things.

A kaleidoscope connects us with our childlike selves, and the patterns that such a toy creates reminds us of the Fibonacci perfect ratios that occur in nature, symbolizing the perfection of natural form. Just as a child is fascinated by the pattern that a kaleidoscope creates, so the dream image can introduce us to our own creativity, which can often become trapped.

*Consult the entries for Colour, Mirror, Mosaic, Reflection and Shapes/Patterns for further information.*

## KANGAROO – *see* ANIMALS

## KARMA

Karma is a man-made spiritual law, which dictates that any action, good or bad, brings upon oneself inevitable results, either in this life or in a reincarnation. Dreaming of karma suggests that we are aware of the consequences of our actions.

Emotions in waking life are difficult to control. Through a belief in Karma we can use our dreams to help us gain control of those emotions.

In pragmatic terms karma is the law of cause and effect – what goes around comes around. When we have not always acted with integrity we may find that dreams warn us of what the effect might be.

## KEEPSAKE

A keepsake in the spiritual sense is an object which, because of the high regard the owner has for it, is sacred. It will probably have been blessed in some way and when it appears in dreams highlights its sacred nature.

Romantic memories loom large in dream imagery. To dream of something that is very precious to us, has been given by someone else in recognition of their regard for us, or signifies a relationship which stands the test of time, allows us to appreciate and understand the beauty we hold within.

A keepsake in olden times was something which was often exchanged by lovers. To be conscious of having such an object in a dream signifies our ability to love and be loved. Any object that links with the past reminds us of what we have been capable of doing or being, and can take us back to perhaps happier times.

*You might like to consult the entries for Camelot and Jewellery.*

### KEG

As a hollow vessel, which helps in the preservation of food and nourishment, a keg is another symbol of spiritual nourishment. A beer keg in particular may also be a symbol of pure hedonism.

A keg will often symbolize our emotions and family loyalties. A broken keg may suggest lost dreams and ambitions.

A keg, particularly an old wooden one, suggests craftsmanship. If it is full, craftsmanship and expertise have fulfilled their purpose. If it is half full or empty, there is much work to be done. A beer barrel will have the same significance.

*Consult the entry for Cask for further information.*

### KERB – *see* EDGE

### KERNEL – *see* NUT

### KETTLE

A kettle, being a hollow vessel, can symbolize magic and magical forces working for the Greater Good, and can have the same significance as a cauldron. It is often taken to symbolize transformation and change.

A kettle just coming to the boil suggests that a plan or project is about to come to fruition. To dream of a kettle in this context suggests that we need to accelerate a process of learning and growth.

Because a kettle is such a mundane, everyday object, to dream of one indicates our more practical, pragmatic side. Perhaps we are taking certain things for granted. If the kettle is unusual – such as an old fashioned copper kettle – it denotes outworn, but still appreciated, beliefs.

As a cooking utensil, a kettle combines the power of fire and water to create usable nourishment. In a woman's dream a broken kettle, or one with a hole in it, can signify a perhaps temporary loss of energy or power. In a man's dream a kettle may denote aspects of interdependency within his relationships – a kettle is no use without fire or power.

*You might also like to consult the entry for Cauldron and Magic/Magician.*

# KEY

☼ A key can represent our need for liberation from a stressful situation and then the initiation of a positive spiritual move. Silver and gold keys represent – respectively – temporal and spiritual power. These keys crossed are part of the Papal regalia and signify belonging to both realms.

♥ We hold within us many of the answers to our own difficulties, but often in dreams need a down-to-earth, mundane symbol to trigger off our ability to work out solutions. When we experience ourselves as trapped, the key to freedom symbolizing what action we must take can often appear as if by magic. The image of a simple key can indicate that the solution is easy. An ornate key can suggest a more complex solution. When we cannot find a key in dreams we may have to wait until the time is right or circumstances are working in our favour.

▦ Keys often appear in dreams. They represent fresh attitudes, thoughts and feelings which are capable of unlocking memories, experiences and knowledge which we have previously hidden. If we can decide which way we turn the key, we can decide whether we are locking things up or freeing them. A bunch of keys signify responsibilities and success and the need to open up the whole of our personalities to new experiences.

▣ In a woman's dream a key can suggest that her own assertiveness needs to be sensitively used. A man may need to understand the 'mechanism' of his assertiveness and how to use it without force.

*Consult the entries for Keyhole, Lock and Prison for further information.*

## KEYBOARD – *see* COMMUNICATION

## KEYHOLE

☼ A keyhole can symbolize our tentative entry into the Sublime or transcendent state. Our vision is somewhat restricted and even in dreams we do not yet have confidence to remain in that state, but must accept the need to remain grounded.

♥ Since a key usually requires a keyhole, to dream of one without the other indicates some kind of confusion between the inner and outer self. A keyhole by itself can represent gossip or treachery by a close associate.

▦ When we dream that we are peering through a keyhole, we are conscious of the fact that our ability to see and understand is somehow impaired. Conventionally, the keyhole has been taken to represent the feminine, so that impairment could result from our attitude to the feminine and to feminine qualities such as intuition.

When a woman dreams of a keyhole without the key she will be conscious of her own vulnerability. In a man's dream he will need to look at the sensitivities of people around him. Not being able to find the keyhole suggests he has not yet quite understood those sensitivities either in personal or work relationships.

*You might also like to consult the entries for Key and Lock.*

## KICK

A kick can be taken symbolically as a need for spiritual motivation; it may be the kick that we need in order to continue (or maybe even begin) our spiritual journey.

Kicking a ball around in a dream signifies our need for self-control, but also our control of external circumstances. To dream of being kicked highlights a propensity to be a victim.

Aggressiveness can be represented in many ways, and to dream of kicking someone often allows the expression of aggression in an acceptable way. There will be some anxiety in everyday life that cannot be properly expressed. Being kicked in a dream may reveal a feeling of being bullied or made to react to situations that are not to our liking.

For many men, ball games such as football or rugby are simply a release of tension and will appear as such in dreams. For women, any action of kicking will be more to do with her own aggression.

*Consult the entries for Games and Sport for further clarification.*

## KIDNAP

Spiritually, dreaming of a kidnapping suggests that someone or something is draining our essential energy and possibly using it in an inappropriate way. This might, for instance, be a family argument or an anxiety that we are not able to deal with properly.

In dreams, we may find ourselves trying to kidnap someone, suggesting that we are trying to influence someone else, perhaps trying to absorb some quality that is not freely available, or making demands that they are not prepared to meet.

If we find ourselves being kidnapped within a dream, we are conscious of the fact that our own fears and doubts can make us victims. We feel out of control and perhaps need to 'negotiate' with the frightened part. We are being overcome by our own 'demons', which have ganged up on us and caused us to become insecure.

*You might like to consult the entry for Abduct.*

**KIDNEYS** – *see* BODY

**KILL**

❖ Killing almost inevitably symbolizes a violent ending of some sort. Often there is a struggle involved and spiritually it is important in dreams that we are the one who overcomes our opponent.

♥ Killing is an extreme answer to a problem. It is such a final act that in dreams it can often represent our perception of the need for an act of violence. In particular this may be against ourselves or a part of our personality that is no longer acceptable. The impulse may not be correct, though some adjustment needs to be made.

▣ To dream of being killed suggests we are under an influence – usually external – which is making us, or an aspect of our personality, ineffective in everyday life. Killing someone in a dream is attempting to be rid of the influence they have over us.

*Also consult the entry for Murder/Murderer.*

**KING** – *see* PEOPLE

**KINGFISHER** – *see* BIRDS

**KISS**

❖ A single kiss (particularly on the forehead) has often had spiritual and religious undertones, and here the image symbolizes a blessing of a spiritual kind. A kiss represents tranquility, peace and harmony.

♥ We are sealing a pact – perhaps coming to some sort of agreement or recognizing different ways of co-operating with others. We may also be moving towards unity and acceptance within ourselves. Being kissed indicates that we are appreciated and loved for our own qualities.

▣ When we dream about kissing someone, whether of the same gender as ourselves or not, it can suggest an acceptance of a new relationship with that person. Such an act can also signify that, on a subconscious level, we are seeking to develop a quality belonging to that other person in ourselves.

⦿ For both men and women a kiss in dreams is an acknowledgement, often of aspects of our personality that we have not been able to integrate successfully. Women may choose to understand their own drive and assertiveness and men their more sensitive side.

**KITCHEN**

❖ The rituals associated with the hearth and with fire were, and still are, a significant part of spiritual development. Even in today's climate of convenience foods there is the sense of work in the kitchen being a spiritual offering. There are folk tales in most cultures to do with the kitchen, and spiritually it represents transformation and transmutation. This is much more to do with desired transformation, rather than one that is enforced.

🜲 The kitchen is a place of creation, and usually of warmth and comfort. It has, therefore, come to represent the nurturing aspect of woman. In dreams, the kitchen can often represent the mother, or rather the mothering function.

🜲 For most people, the kitchen represents the 'heart' of the house. It is the space from which we go out into the world and to which we return. It is the place that is usually busiest and, therefore, where many relationships are cemented, and where many exchanges take place.

🜲 In a man's dream, a kitchen is more to do with the way that he is, or has been, nurtured and the effect this has on him, whereas in a woman's dreams a kitchen symbolizes how she nurtures others.

*Also consult the entries for Fire, Hearth, House and Oven for further clarification.*

### KITE

🜲 A kite represents our need for, or recognition of, forthcoming spiritual freedom. In Chinese lore, the kite symbolized the wind. We need to be free of constraints and to be 'pulling our own strings', while remaining grounded. The bird of prey also soars with the wind, and again represents freedom.

🜲 While flying a kite, we are at the mercy of the wind unless we have a fair degree of expertise. In dreams it is recognizable that we have some expertise in our everyday lives and that that expertise needs recognition.

🜲 To dream of flying a kite can remind us of the carefree days of childhood when we were without responsibility. Often the colour is important, as may be the material from which it is made. In more mundane terms, to be flying a kite may suggest ambition and career goals.

*Consult the entries for Colour and Wind for further clarification.*

### KITTEN – *see* BABY ANIMALS IN ANIMALS

### KNEAD

🜲 As bread is the 'staff of life', to dream of kneading bread suggests working hard on our own lives on order that we ourselves can effect change.

🜲 Kneading has the same symbolism as cooking: that is, combining ingredients to make something else. It also signifies working with tension to relieve pain as in massage.

🜲 In waking life, the act of kneading can be therapeutic. In dreams, this significance can be highlighted, allowing us to work at a problem or resolve a difficulty.

*You might like to consult the entries for Bread and Cooking.*

**KNEE/KNEELING** – *see* BODY

**KNIFE**

&#9775; A knife is a symbol of division. There may be something in life that needs to be cut out and got rid of. Alternatively, the knife may be representative of the need to view something from a dual perspective – the spiritual and the physical.

&#9829; It can be important in a dream about a knife to notice what type is being used. For instance, a table knife would be interpreted very differently to a Swiss Army knife. Both are functional, but the former would only be appropriate under certain circumstances, whereas the latter might have a more universal application. To dream that we are carrying a knife signifies anger, aggression and/or separation. We may be attempting to cut ties or feel that we need protection.

&#9632; If we are using a knife we may either be freeing ourselves from restrictions or trying to sever a relationship. If we are being attacked with a knife, it indicates either violent words or actions may be used against us. If we are aware that the knife is blunt, the words may be particularly hurtful. If sharp, matters can be dealt with quickly.

&#91;&#9832;&#93; In a woman's dream the symbol of a knife is probably more to do with her own fear of penetration and violation, whereas in a man's dream it is highlighting his own aggression.

*You might like to consult the entries for Dagger and Weapon for further information.*

**KNIGHT**

&#9775; A knight is a follower, or someone who has taken an oath of allegiance. Hence in dreams such a figure signifies initiation, in order to develop our finer spiritual qualities.

&#9829; Psychologically, the knight in a dream signifies the guiding principle. He is that part of ourselves that is sometimes known as the Higher Self, the spirit guiding the physical. The black knight is often seen as the embodiment of evil. It is interesting that often the white knight appears with his visor up, whereas the black knight appears with his visor down.

&#9632; In pragmatic terms, a project or task may require dedication and focus. Since a knight is expected to show loyalty he may appear signifying this in dreams. Being made a knight in the modern day is still considered to be something of an honour and may have this meaning in dreams.

&#91;&#9832;&#93; A knight appearing in a dream, particularly a woman's, can have the obvious connotation of a romantic liaison: the knight in shining armour. This actually is a manifestation of her own Animus – her own inner masculine –

and is to do with her search for perfection. In a man's dream it indicates he may be searching for the Hero in himself.

*You might also like to consult the entries for Camelot, Castle, Hero/Heroine and Quest as well as the information on Hero in Archetypes in the Introduction.*

## KNITTING

⚙ Knitting, as with weaving and knotting, can symbolize a form of creativity, the ability to form something new out of raw material.

♡ We are working on emotions, or at creating a relationship.

▦ The primary symbolism connected with knitting is that of creating something new out of available material, often having a pattern from which to work. If the pattern is intricate much care needs to be taken. A project or idea that is being worked on is beginning to come together. To be unravelling knitting suggests that a project that is being worked on needs reconsideration.

⊡ In a woman's dream knitting can represent the basic feminine skills. As many women become more business-oriented, knitting as a recreation – embodying a different form of creativity – may surface in dreams representing domesticity.

*Also consult the entries for Colour, Knot, Weaving and Wool.*

## KNOB

⚙ Since a knob of any sort is usually used to gain access to something, spiritually it can suggest changes occurring in the way we approach our unconscious self.

♡ To be dreaming of a knob such as a doorknob can indicate some kind of turning point in our life. A noticeable contrast between the door and the knob can present the dreamer with certain insights. For instance, a very plain knob on an ornate door may indicate that the process of moving forward from a situation is very easy. The knob coming off in our hands suggests a missed opportunity. We may need to turn or change issues or conditions.

▦ When we are turning a knob we need to decide whether we are turning it clockwise or anti-clockwise. Clockwise will signify a positive move, anti-clockwise perhaps an initially more difficult one, but one which will ultimately present further opportunities.

⊡ Since many people still have difficulty in calling 'private parts' by their correct name, a knob appearing in a dream can represent the penis or, if the dreamer is a man, his masculinity.

*You might also like to consult the individual entry for Door and also Door in Buildings.*

## KNOCK/KNOCKING

🌀 To hear knocking suggests we are being given permission from our spiritual self to progress on our current journey. Some believe that it is a way of alerting the psyche to the realms of spirit.

♡ If we ourselves are knocking on a door, we may be wanting to become part of someone's life, looking for a particular type of information asking for help or seeking different opportunities. We are waiting for permission before moving forward.

▦ To hear knocking in a dream generally alerts us to the fact that our attention needs to be re-focused. For instance, we may be too introverted when in fact we need to be paying more attention to external matters.

## KNOT

🌀 The knot symbolizes spiritual continuity or connection. It suggests a pause, perhaps for contemplation or assessment. As something to hold, a knot suggests capturing a fleeting idea or concept.

♡ A simple knot seen in a dream could represent the need to take a different direction in a project. A more complex knot could indicate that we are bound to a situation by a sense of duty or guilt. Ultimately the only way to escape from such restraint is by loosening the ties in our relationship with someone else, or with a work situation.

▦ A knot is one of the most interesting symbols to appear in dreams, since it can have so many meanings. Negatively, particularly if it is seen as a tangle, it can represent an unsolvable problem or difficulty. The answer can only be 'teased out' gradually. Positively, a knot can represent the ties or bonds that we have to family, partner, friends or work.

⬗ In a man's dream tying the knot is likely to have some aspect of being restrained or bound to a partner. In a woman's dream it is more likely to represent commitment.

*You might also like to consult the entry for Tangle.*

## KNOW/KNOWLEDGE

🌀 Spiritual knowledge and awareness can develop gradually. If we are prepared to allow it, this knowledge can come intuitively through dreams.

♡ In dreams we often know something without being sure of how we do. Many believe that in the dream state we have easier access to the collective Unconscious – the repository of all knowledge – than when we are awake.

▦ In mundane terms knowledge and experience go hand in hand. In dreams the mind may trigger an association, which allows us to reach viable conclusions.

## LABEL

❋ In the spiritual sense a label can give us a sense of spiritual identity.

♥ Having the wrong label suggests that we are aware that we are not perceiving something in the correct way. To be re-labelling something suggests that we have rectified a misperception.

▦ Often, dreaming of labels links with our need to name things. Our sense of identity comes from the name we are given, and our 'label' is much to do with the way that others see us and understand us.

## LABORATORY

❋ Dreaming of a laboratory indicates that we may need to make a more objective or perhaps scientific (knowledgeable) assessment of what is going on in our lives.

♥ A laboratory can suggest a very ordered existence, and it will depend on whether we are working in or are specimens in a laboratory how we interpret the dream. To be a specimen suggests that we feel we are being monitored in some way.

▦ Dreaming of working in a laboratory indicates that we need to be more ordered in our approach to life. We may have certain talents that need to be developed in an objective fashion, or we may need to develop our thinking faculty further.

*You might like to consult the entry for Invent/Inventor.*

## LABOUR

❋ The 12 labours of Hercules are reputed to represent the passage of the sun through the 12 signs of the Zodiac. They are also the hardships and effort man uses to attain self-realization.

♥ To be labouring at something, in the sense of working hard, suggests that we have a goal we wish to achieve. We are prepared to put effort in to achieve success.

▦ To dream of 'hard labour' will alert us to a tendency towards self-flagellation or self-punishment in our personality.

▤ If a woman dreams of being in labour she should look at her wish and desire to be pregnant. If a man dreams of his wife or partner being in labour, it may show his readiness to take on the responsibility of a family, or even new responsibilities at work.

*Also consult the entry for Work.*

## LABYRINTH

☀ Spiritually the labyrinth experience marks a watershed. It is a symbol for the transition stage between the physical, practical world and a deeper understanding of all mankind. The route in one type of labyrinth is 'unicursal' – that is, it goes by a straightforward route, which covers maximum ground straight to the centre and out again. The second type is designed with the intention to confuse, and has many blind alleys and unexpected twists. This can represent spiritual progress in dreams, through having to work out the key or code. Many trials and tribulations are met and overcome or negotiated on the path to attainment and the labyrinth may be a recurring image. Each individual will undertake his or her own route to the centre of his existence.

♥ Psychologically, in undertaking our own life journey, we must at some point go through a form of labyrinth experience. It is undertaken at a point when we must travel into the differing areas of our subconscious and come to terms with our fears and doubts, before confronting our own Shadow.

▦ On a purely practical level, the labyrinth appearing in dreams signifies the need to explore the hidden side of our own personality. With its many twists, turns and potential blind alleys when it is not unicursal, it is a very potent representation of the human being.

▸ In dreams the labyrinth can be suggested by any dream that has us exploring a series of underground passages. It is held by some to be an exploration of the hidden feminine, whether in the sense of Sophia (eternal wisdom) or the Anima in men.

*Also consult the entries for Maze and Minotaur.*

### LACE

☀ As a handworked adornment in vestments and altars within religious rites, lace has an extremely ancient history. In dreams, therefore, it comes to symbolize worship and perhaps the capturing of Spirit in craft of knotting. When joining two pieces of material such as linen, it signifies the transition between the physical and the spiritual realms

♥ Much symbolism can be worked into lace, so it is useful to note what, if anything, is depicted pictorially in this manner in dreams. Altar cloths, for instance, might contain Christian images such as the cross or fertility symbols might be included in Wiccan robes. As a creative art, which is less practised nowadays, lace may alert us to our own creativity.

▦ As a pastime, which kept women usefully employed and indeed was often the only source of income, from a practical perspective lace signifies gainful employment. More mundanely, to be tying our shoelaces suggests careful preparation. To be untying them suggests relaxation and informality. To lose shoelaces suggests insecurity.

*Also consult the entries for Linen and Shoes.*

## LADDER

🔆 In a dream, the rungs of the ladder are often either seven or 12 in number, these being traditionally the stages of growth towards spirituality. Jacob's dream of a ladder is one such potent image.

♥ The ladder denotes our ability to break through to a new level of awareness, moving from the physical to the spiritual, but also being able to move downwards again. It also suggests communication between the physical and spiritual realms as a stage of transition. Occasionally it may also represent death, though this is more the death of the old self, or way of being, rather than a physical death.

▦ The ladder in dreams denotes how secure we feel in moving from one situation to another. We may need to make a considerable effort to reach a goal or take an opportunity. Often this dream occurs during career changes and so has obvious connotations. If the rungs are broken we can expect difficulty. If someone else is carrying the ladder it could suggest that another person, perhaps a manager or colleague, has a part to play in our progression.

*You might like to consult the entry for Levels/Layers for additional clarification.*

## LAGOON/LAKE

🔆 A lagoon or lake represents our inner world of feeling and fantasy. It is the unconscious side, which is a rich source of power when it can be accessed and understood. The primordial substance is often pictured as a lagoon or lake. The Chinese concept of a kind of soup from which came all existence, links with the lagoon, a stretch of water that has become enclosed.

♥ Often thought to be the home of the magical feminine and of monsters, the lagoon stands for the darker side of femininity, and this is seen clearly in the legends of King Arthur and those of the Siren. This type of image will appear in dreams as we lose our fear of the depths of our own emotion.

▦ If the lake is contaminated, we have taken in ideas and concepts that are not necessarily good for us. A clear stretch of water would indicate that we have clarified our fears and feelings about ourselves.

▢ Perhaps one of the reasons that a lake or lagoon is so enticing is because of its association with relaxation and ease. In both men's and women's dreams this quality will often come across albeit from slightly different perspectives; a stormy lake, for instance, may well signify a woman's anger, whereas for a man it is likely to represent his partner's distress.

*Also consult the entry for Water.*

**LAMB –** *see* **ANIMALS AND SPIRITUAL IMAGERY IN THE INTRODUCTION**

**LAME**

☀ Lameness in the spiritual sense suggests the imperfection of creation, when an imperfect world is formed. Haephestos, one of the forge gods, was lamed when he was thrown out of heaven by his father Zeus.

♥ To be aware that someone else is lame has two meanings. If the person is known to us, we need to be aware of their vulnerability and uncertainty. If they are not known, it is more likely to be a hidden side of ourselves, which is insecure or perhaps damaged. If the left side is damaged the sensitive side is affected, if the right, then the more assertive side is in trouble.

▦ Dreaming of being lame suggests a loss of confidence and strength. If we ourselves are lame there can be a fear of moving forward or a fear of the future.

*You might like to consult the entry for Limp.*

**LAMP**

☀ Spiritually the lamp can suggest the idea of a personal guiding 'light in darkness'. The hermit in the Tarot demonstrates this in his protectiveness of the light and his need to be able to move forward despite the darkness around him. The lamp can also signify the light of the Divine and immortality.

♥ The lamp in dreams often signifies guidance and wisdom. If it is an old-fashioned lantern, it can also represent previously held beliefs, which may need to be updated.

▦ In dreams a lamp or a light can represent life. To be moving towards a lamp suggests a clarity of perception, which may be slightly old-fashioned. The lamp in its most practical aspect in dreams signifies the intellect and perception.

*You might like to consult the entries for Candle and Light.*

**LANCE**

☀ The lance is a phallic image initially of solar, and later of spiritual, power.

♥ A lance as a surgical instrument is penetrative and thus has a healing connotation. It is designed to release the negative, as in lancing a boil. We may need to take short, sharp action in order to improve a situation.

▦ A lance – as in a Knight's lance – in a dream suggests an aspect of masculine power, penetration and, therefore, sometimes the sexual act.

▸ In a woman's dream a knight with a lance will signify chivalry and dedication. In a man's dream a lance will suggest his own ability to fight his own corner.

*Also consult the entries for Arrow, Knight and Weapons.*

## LANDSCAPES

🏵 Spiritually, the landscape in a dream can suggest improvements that we can make in handling our own moods and attitudes.

💟 Dream landscapes can have a bizarre quality about them in order to highlight a particular message. For instance, there may be trees made of ice, or rocks made of sugar. The plot of the dream may be important in arriving at the correct interpretation of these symbols. The landscape in a dream can also indicate how we relate to other people. To be in a desert might represent loneliness, whereas to be in a jungle might represent a very fertile imagination. If the landscape changes between the beginning and end of the dream, we perhaps need to make corresponding changes in everyday life.

🔲 The landscape in a dream can be an integral part of the interpretation. It usually mirrors feelings and concepts that we have and, therefore, reflects our personality. A rocky landscape would suggest problems, whereas a gloomy landscape might suggest pessimism and self-doubt. A recurring scene may be one where in childhood we felt safe, or may reflect a feeling or difficulty with which we have not been able to come to terms. Landscapes do tend to reflect habitual feelings rather than momentary moods.

*Also consult the entry for Places for further clarification.*

## LAPSE

🏵 Any kind of spiritual lapse or falling away from our beliefs will reflect itself in dreams, sometimes by a sense of foreboding or other negative image.

💟 A slip of the memory or an inability to hold on to information can manifest in dreams as a lost object or a sense of searching for something we know we have once had.

🔲 When we have not been totally true to our own principles we may experience this in dreams as a lapse of attention or lack of attention to detail.

**LAPTOP** – *see* **COMMUNICATION**

**LARGE** – *see* **SIZE**

**LARK** – *see* **BIRDS**

## LASER

🏵 Because of its intensity, a laser beam has the image of light cutting through the non-essential to reveal complete truth.

💟 As it can be focused with pinpoint accuracy, from an emotional perspective this represents a kind of healing – that of cutting out emotional 'demons' and the pain associated with them.

🔲 Any laser beam suggests a clarity of perception is required. This can have an intrinsic danger, however, in that if the insights gained are not sensitively handled it can be hurtful.

*Also consult the entry for Light.*

## LASH – *see* WHIP

## LAST

🌞 There are two spiritual interpretations for last. The last supper, as in the sense of the final time, suggests the time just before we have completed one of our earthly tasks. A shoe last signifies a pro-forma from which we can achieve a better fit, albeit after some effort.

💗 When we realize that we are last, for instance in a queue, we should perhaps decide whether we are following all others or bringing up the rear. In the latter sense this requires some courage because our back is exposed. Following others may mean that others take the risk.

🔲 If we are last in a dream there may be a situation in reality where our feelings are not being taken into account. Being the last to be chosen highlights an insecurity about our viability which may be a legacy from childhood.

*You might also like to consult the entries for Running and Win/Winning.*

## LATCH – *see* KEY AND LOCK

## LATE – *see* TIME

## LAUGH

🌞 Laughter in the spiritual sense signifies pure joy. It is now known that laughter has a healing quality, so to be conscious of it in dreams suggests that a healing has taken place.

💗 If we ourselves are laughing we may be experiencing a release of tension. Often the object of our amusement will give a clue to the relevance of the dream in everyday life. It can also be seen as a sign of rejection. To hear a crowd laughing suggests a shared enjoyment, if we do not have a sense of being laughed at.

🔲 Being laughed at in dreams suggests we may have a fear of being ridiculed, or may have done something which we feel is not appropriate. We may find ourselves embarrassing.

## LAUNCH

🌞 In the sense of setting a boat afloat, a launch picks up the spiritual significance of a boat and also suggests some kind of initiation or the beginning of a process.

💗 Launching is associated with throwing – particularly a lance – and, therefore, emotionally represents perhaps an initial enthusiasm or enjoyment.

◼ Launching a project in a dream suggests the beginning of an exciting time. A launch was initially a smaller boat for use on a larger one, so therefore can suggest an offshoot of a task or idea.

*Consult the entries for Boat/Ship, Lance and Spear for further clarification.*

## LAUREL/BAY LEAVES

◈ The laurel or bay tree symbolizes chastity and eternity. It also suggests immortality.

◈ The laurel wreath is often used to indicate triumph and victory and, therefore, is an acknowledgement of success. Traditionally, the laurel or bay is difficult to grow, so it will symbolize triumph over difficulty.

◼ The laurel or bay tree is less likely to appear in dreams nowadays with a mundane explanation, unless the dreamer is either a gardener or has a particular knowledge of symbolism. In former times, it would have represented a specific type of success.

## LAVA – *see* VOLCANO

## LAVATORY – *see* TOILET

## LAW

◈ A law is an instruction or way of working deliberately laid down or fixed so a spiritual law is a universal code which works for all mankind, sometimes more accessible in dreams than in reality.

◈ When our emotions are called into question, we can find that an appropriate way of operating is offered in dreams. We work according to unwritten laws that are correct for us. The Law in the guise of a policeman is an aspect of a higher authority there to give guidance.

◼ Any aspect of the law appearing in dreams is as much to do with our own code of behaviour in waking life as with 'the law' in the sense of authority. In dreams, our own internal sense of justice tends to take precedence over the laws of society.

*You might also like to consult the entries for Judge/Judgement, Juror/Jury and Justice.*

## LAYERS – *see* LEVELS

## LEAD (METAL)

◈ Lead in spiritual symbolism stands for a consciousness of the physical realms as opposed to the spiritual. It is the metal of Saturn and has this planet's symbolism of blocking progress unless it is moving forward in the correct way for ultimate success. As we become more spiritually proficient, the old magical and alchemical definitions become more relevant.

◈ Lead as a substance is less used nowadays than it used to be, but still has the connotations of a base metal. In dreams it can indicate that the time is ripe for transformation and transmutation. We need to instigate changes to give a better quality to our lives.

🏛 The conventional explanation of lead appearing in a dream is that we have a situation around us, which is a burden to us. We are not coping with life as we should, leaving us heavy-hearted. Lead, as in a lead of a pencil, has obvious connections with the life force and masculinity.

*Also consult the entries for Alchemy and Metal.*

## LEAD/LEADING/LEADER

☼ We are able to take authority by virtue of our spiritual knowledge, though with humility and without ego. In dreams we will often find ourselves taking the lead before we are consciously able to do so.

♡ Leadership qualities are not necessarily ones that everybody has or will use. Often we can surprise ourselves in dreams by doing things that we would not normally do, and becoming a leader is one of them.

🏛 Dreaming of a dog lead symbolizes the connection between ourselves and our lesser nature. To have lost the dog lead would indicate a loss of control. Leading someone in a dream pre-supposes that we know what we are doing and where we are going. Being led suggests that we have allowed someone else to take control of a situation around us.

*You might also like to consult the entries for Harness and Halter.*

## LEAF/LEAVES

☼ Leaves signify fertility and growth. Since each leaf is completely unique, we may be becoming aware of the beauty of creation and the perfection of spiral patterns in Nature.

♡ When looking at our lives as a whole, leaves can signify a particular period of our lives – perhaps a period that has been meaningful and creative, a period of growth. Following a dream about leaves we may need to assess how to go forward in order to avail ourselves of the opportunities offered.

🏛 A leaf very often represents a period of growth and can also give a measurement of time. Green leaves can suggest hope and new opportunities, or the Springtime. Dead leaves signify a period of sadness, barrenness or Autumn.

*Also consult the entries for Autumn and Trees.*

## LEAK

☼ A leak of any sort suggests spiritual wastefulness and inattention to resources.

♡ A leak can indicate carelessness. We may not be paying attention to necessary repairs either on a physical, emotional or mental level.

▦ Dreaming of a leak suggests we are wasting or losing energy in some way. If it is a slow leak we are perhaps not aware of the drain on our energies. If it is gushing we need to look at 'repairing' the leak, perhaps by being more responsible in our actions.

⦂ There are times in a man's dream when a leak may suggest the sexual act. In a woman's dream it is more likely to have an emotional connotation.

*Also consult the entry for Water.*

## LEAP

✦ Making a leap of faith suggests a degree of trust in whatever we might consider to be a divine plan.

♥ Leaping in dreams suggests a longer or more difficult action than a simple jump. Emotionally it signifies the need for courage or conversely a degree of foolhardiness.

▦ A leap suggests a particular kind of action, both taking a calculated risk in facing danger, and movement that is somewhat exaggerated – a running jump rather than a standing start. These conditions in an everyday project can be symbolized in dreams. In that a leap year changes the measurement of time, causing fixed festival days to 'leap' ahead one day in the week, this image suggests that we may need to adjust a schedule.

*Also consult the entry for Jumping for further information.*

## LEARN

✦ To learn is to accrue knowledge, and to be learned spiritually is to have acquired knowledge through study. Dreams are a way for us to link with other levels of consciousness and acquire knowledge.

♥ As we gather experience we learn more, and dreams can be a way of internalizing what we have learned. As a child learns more of the world in which he or she exists, dreams become a way of dealing with everyday experience.

▦ When life is stressful we are able to learn methods of coping through dreams, not just through interpreting images but also by practising different behaviour through techniques like lucid dreaming. When we find ourselves in a learning situation in dreams, we should perhaps look at how these lessons can be applied in everyday life.

*You might also like to consult the entries for Education, Teacher and School.*

## LEASE

✦ A lease implies an agreement between two parties, in spiritual terms between the spiritual and physical selves.

♥ When the various aspects of our personality are able to act in harmony we may dream of signing a lease or other type of contract.

■ Legal papers of any sort suggest contractual arrangements. As a lease is usually to occupy premises or to apportion cost in a manageable way, we may have to decide on the long-term validity of a project or course of action.

## LEAVE/LEAVING

☀ To leave a situation may suggest conscious rejection of the past in order to create spiritual progression.

♥ To be departing from a known situation, such as leaving home, indicates a breaking away from old or habitual patterns of behaviour. We may need to give ourselves the freedom to be independent.

■ We may have a strong desire to get away from responsibility or difficulties, but must be careful how we handle it.

*Also consult the entries for Journey and Transport.*

## LECTURE

☀ A lecture suggests the imparting of spiritual knowledge by an authority – one who has expertise.

♥ A lecture is a way of passing on information, often specialized or newly accrued, so such an image suggests there is something we need to know.

■ In waking life, knowledge may be passed on in an environment geared for study or research. The need for such a situation translates into the dream image of a lecture or lecture theatre.

*You might also like to consult the entries for Education, Learn, Teacher and School.*

## LEDGER – *see* BOOK AND RECORD

## LEFT – *see* LAST AND POSITION

## LEG – *see* LIMBS IN BODY

## LEGITIMATE

☀ In spiritual terms a legitimate act is one that has been sanctioned by a higher authority.

♥ When we offend against our own moral code we may have dreams about being legitimate and working within the framework of the law.

■ Working within societies that are not particularly permissive in outlook, we may dream of needing to have our actions sanctioned if our autonomy is threatened in waking life. We may also in dreams find ourselves rebelling through illegal acts.

⊞ Dreaming of being illegitimate for both men and women suggests a lack of self worth and sometimes a questioning of our right to a place in society.

## LEND/LENDING/LOAN

☀ In spiritual terms, the concept of lending is connected with healing and support.

♥ If we are lending money, we are creating a bond of obligation within our lives. If we are being lent money we need to look at the way we are managing our resources, but more importantly what help we need to do this.

▣ If in a dream we are lending an object to someone, we are aware that the quality that object represents cannot be given away; it is ours to have but we can share it. If someone is lending us an article then we are perhaps not responsible enough to possess what it represents on a full-time basis. Conversely, we may only need it for a short time.

## LENS

☼ A lens symbolizes concentration and visionary clarity.

♥ When a lens appears in a dream we need to be clear as to whether it is enlarging the object being looked at, or is intensifying it. Enlarging it suggests taking a wider viewpoint, intensifying it requires that we pay attention to detail. A full interpretation can only be made in the light of other circumstances in the dream. It is the context of the dream that is important.

▣ Just as in everyday life a lens helps to focus the attention, so in dreams it can signify our need to perceive something very clearly.

*You might also like to consult the entries for Glasses/Spectacles, Goggles and Magnifying Glass.*

## LEOPARD – *see* ANIMALS

## LEPER

☼ Spiritually, a leper in a dream can suggest that we are having to deal with a moral dilemma that takes us away from compassion and caring. This image is less prevalent today as such diseases become more treatable.

♥ If we are caring for a leper we need to attend to those parts of ourselves we consider unclean, rather than trying to dispose of them. If the leper is offering us something, it may be that we have a lesson to learn about humility.

▣ To dream of a leper suggests that we are aware of some aspect of ourselves that we feel to be unclean. We feel that we have been rejected by society without quite knowing why. We may also feel that we have been contaminated in some way.

*You might like to consult the entries for Heal/Healing and Ill/Illness.*

## LETTER

☼ In dreams, hidden and perhaps private psychic information often comes in the form of a sealed letter, which we must make the effort to understand.

♥ Often we dream about a letter without knowing what the contents are. This suggests some information that is at present being withheld. If a particular letter of the alphabet is highlighted, we may understand more if we can name someone with that initial.

■ If we receive a letter in a dream we may be aware of some problem with the person it is from. It is possible that the sender is known to be dead, in which case there are unresolved issues with that person or the situation connected with them. If we are sending a letter we have information we feel may be relevant to that person.

*Also consult the entries for Communication, Email and Reading for further information.*

## LEVELS/LAYERS

✸ A level in sacred architecture represents knowledge out of the norm. All religions are based on worshipping a cosmic order, which means that a key aspect of religion is trying to recreate this order, something we often try to do in dreams. A *stupa*, for instance, a memorial instigated by Buddha himself, is essentially made up of the following five levels:

a) A square base
b) A hemispherical dome
c) A conical spire
d) A crescent moon
e) A circular disc

Each of these components is rich in spiritual significance and is identified with one of the five cosmic elements of creation. These are, from the base up, Earth, Water, Fire, Air and Space.

♥ There are many levels of awareness that are available to us in the dream state. It will depend on our stage of advancement at which level we choose to interpret our dreams. As a child grows in maturity he will go through different ways of understanding his world, commensurate with his particular stage of growth, which will be reflected in dreams. These levels of understanding resonate even in adulthood.

■ Usually a level surface suggests ease and comfort. Dreaming of a road being level would indicate our way ahead is fairly straightforward. A level crossing suggests that we are approaching a barrier or blockage that requires our attention. We may not yet have enough information to take avoiding action.

## LEVER

✸ A lever may appear as a symbol in dreams when we are attempting to reach a different level of spiritual awareness.

♥ A lever implies that we need to use some mechanical means to raise or lower an object. From an emotional perspective, this signifies that we need help in handling our emotions at this time.

▦ To be levering an object in dreams – for instance, using a crowbar – suggests that a project or idea needs to be freed up from some kind of restriction.

▸ A lever is a mechanical means of altering position, so in both men's and women's dreams such an image can suggest manipulation from an outside source.

## LIBRARY

☀ A library represents the Collective Unconscious – all that is, was and ever shall be. It is often taken as the Akashic records – the spiritual records of existence. At a certain stage in psychic and spiritual development, the library is an important symbol. It suggests both the wisdom and skills that we have accumulated, but also the collected wisdom available to all humanity.

♡ As we are able to look more objectively at our lives we have more access to universal knowledge. A chaotic, untidy library would suggest that we have difficulty in dealing with information and emotion.

▦ A library in a dream can often represent the storehouse of our life's experience. It can also represent our intellect and the way we handle knowledge. A well-managed library would suggest the ability to create order successfully.

## LICE – see INSECTS

## LID

☀ A lid closes a container and can, therefore, symbolize the division between the physical and spiritual realms.

♡ To be trying to open a lid suggests that we may need some kind of emotional release. To be closing a lid indicates that we are repressing some aspect of our personality.

▦ To be keeping a lid on a container indicates that we suspect that some task or situation may run out of control.

## LIE/LYING

☀ To lie, as in speak falsely, is to speak against a truth, though interestingly not necessarily against what we believe to be true. If we have sworn to tell the truth and do not, this would be spiritual perjury.

♡ We can become conscious of deliberate falsehood in dreams when our emotions are called into question and we are not true to our principles. To be lying prone suggests that we should adopt a different perspective.

▦ In waking life there is lying by commission and lying by omission; this is a deliberate manipulation of the truth. Dreams can often help us to clarify our awareness. We often can rely only on intuition to reveal the real truth.

## LIFEBOAT

❀ There is always risk in undertaking a difficult task. When we make mistakes or the risk is too great, spiritually we can only be 'rescued' by a greater knowledge and wisdom.

♥ Since a lifeboat requires a degree of dedication from the members of the crew, we may be alerted to the need for such selfless dedication in our lives. We may also be becoming aware of the degree of skill we require to navigate life's difficulties. Because the sea can represent deep emotion, in dreams a lifeboat may be of help in learning to handle our own emotions.

▦ Dreaming of a lifeboat could indicate that we have the feeling that we need to be rescued, possibly from our own stupidity or from circumstances beyond our control. If we are at the helm of a lifeboat we are still in control of our own lives, but are perhaps aware that we need to offer assistance to someone else.

*You might also like to consult the entries for Boat/Ship and Sea in Water.*

## LIFT

❀ A lift is an enclosed space and can, therefore, symbolize the physical body from a spiritual perspective. Being lifted up suggests Ascension.

♥ Going up in a lift suggests aspiration and a desire for something better. Going down may indicate difficult or depressing circumstances.

▦ A lift, particularly in a work situation, may indicate the possibility of promotion or demotion, but may also indicate the way to achieve this. An old-fashioned lift might signify the need for effort or, conversely, perhaps an out-of-date attitude.

## LIGHT

❀ Spiritually in dreams a bright light symbolizes the manifestation of divinity, truth or direct knowledge. Often this knowledge is beyond form and, therefore, appears as energy, which the dreaming mind translates as light.

♥ When light appears in dreams we are usually in process of trying to improve who we are. A very bright light often symbolizes the development of intuition or insight. There are various techniques using candle flames and other sources of light, which can be used in the waking state to enhance this faculty.

▦ Light in a dream usually means illumination. For instance, 'light at the end of the tunnel' suggests coming to the end of a difficult project. 'He saw the light' means recognition of the results of actions. It is much to do with confidence. To feel lighter signifies feeling better about ourselves.

*Also consult the entry for Lamp.*

**LIGHTHOUSE**

   ☼ A lighthouse highlights the correct course of action to help us achieve our spiritual goals. It can also take on the symbolism of the tower.

   ♡ A lighthouse can act as a beacon and can lead us into calmer waters. It is also a warning system, and in dreams it tends to warn us of emotional difficulties. It can often have this significance in dreams whether emotionally or spiritually.

   ▦ It will depend on whether we are aware in the dream of being on land or at sea. If we are on land we are being warned of difficulties to come, probably from our own emotions. If we are at sea we need to be careful not to create misunderstandings for ourselves by ignoring problems and be sure to steer the right course.

*You might also like to consult the entries for Beacon, Light and Tower.*

**LIGHTNING**

   ☼ Spiritually, lightning denotes some form of spiritual enlightenment, literally something which had not 'struck us' before. In dreams, a lightning flash can also represent the Holy Spirit or the travelling of energy through the various planes of existence into manifestation.

   ♡ When we dream of lightning we are marking a discharge of tension in some way. There may be a situation in our everyday lives that actually needs to be 'blasted' – apparently negatively – in order for something to happen which will change the circumstances. If we take all the known facts into account, our intuition will make us aware of the correct action.

   ▦ Lightning in a dream denotes unexpected changes, which are taking place or are about to take place. This may be the sudden realization of a personal truth, or of a more universal awareness. Often such a revelation has the effect of knocking down the structures we have built in as safeguards in our lives. Alternatively, we may have to make changes in the way we think while leaving our everyday structure and relationships in place. Lightning can also indicate strong passion – such as love – which may strike suddenly but be devastating in its effect.

*You might also like to consult the entries for Thunder/Thunderbolts and Weather.*

**LILY**

   ☼ Spiritually, lilies are a symbol of resurrection and of everlasting life. They are often used in religious ceremony to denote this and are a symbol of the Virgin Mary.

   ♡ One symbol of lilies is that of purity and, particularly in a teenager's dream, lilies can suggest virginity. Lilies in dreams, other than the white funerary arum lily, can also suggest aspects of femininity.

Because of their connection with funerals, for some people lilies can symbolize death. They can also, however, symbolize nobility and grace, and the interpretation needs to be carefully thought out. If we are planting lilies we are hoping for a peaceful transition in some area within our lives.

If we are gathering lilies, particularly in a woman's dream, we are developing a peaceful existence. In a man's dream the fleur-de-lys has a connection with heraldry representing faith, wisdom and chivalry.

## LIMB – *see* BODY

## LIMP

Limp, as in being lifeless, suggests that there has been a loss of essential spiritual energy.

To have a limp in dreams suggests that we are out of balance in some aspect of our lives. It may be worthwhile trying to remember which leg is favoured, since the right side represents the assertive masculine and the left the more equable feminine.

Recognizing that a character in a dream is limping suggests that there may be a problem in waking life with a project or relationship. It may need rethinking or reassessing as to its viability.

*You might like to consult the entry for Lame.*

## LINE

Spiritually in dreams a line can have great significance. The straight line can represent time and the ability to go both forward and back. When horizontal the line is the earthly world and the passive point of view; when vertical it is the spiritual world, the active aspect and the cosmic axis.

Psychologically, we tend to need boundaries or demarcation lines, and those lines can be demonstrated in dream symbolism in ways that might not be feasible in everyday life. For instance, jumping over a line would suggest being brave enough to take risks. A line of objects might signify the choices we are offered. Line dancing implies synchronized movement.

A line in a dream often marks a boundary or denotes a measurement. In dreams, it can also signify a link between two objects to show a connection that is not immediately obvious. A straight line suggests a direct approach, the shortest way between two objects or places. A line of people or queue would suggest an imposed order for a particular purpose. If we are waiting in line, the purpose of the line will be important in interpretation.

## LINEN

Spiritually, fine linen signifies purity and righteousness. By its fineness and the care it needs it suggests reverence and love.

❤ In today's world, where everything is done as quickly and as easily as possible, linen appearing in a dream would suggest a slowness of pace and caring, which enables us to appreciate our lives better.

▦ Linen in dreams on a purely practical level can suggest an appreciation of fine things. Linen tablecloths, for instance, may suggest some kind of a celebration in the sense of only using the best. Linen bed sheets might signify sensuality.

*Also consult the entry for Fabric.*

## LION

❀ Spiritually, the lion symbolizes all those attributes that belong to the fiery principle. However, it is also an ambivalent symbol, since it represents both good and evil. It plays a part in the recognition of the four Elements – Fire, Earth, Air and Water – and represents Fire.

❤ In psychological terms, the lion represents all those qualities it shows: majesty, strength, pride, courage and so on. It is easier to recognize the necessity for such qualities in ourselves when symbolized in something else.

▦ The lion in dreams signifies both cruelty and strength. It also symbolizes the astrological sign of Leo and epitomizes the qualities of leadership depicted in that sign.

*You might also like to consult the entry for Animals.*

## LIP – *see* EDGE

## LIQUID

❀ A strong symbol in spiritual development is golden liquid which can represent both power and energy. Its appearance in dreams suggests we have reached a certain level of understanding.

❤ Liquid in dreams can have more than one meaning. Because it is always connected with 'flow', it can represent the idea of allowing feelings to flow properly. The colour of the liquid in the dream can be important since it can give an indication of exactly which feelings and emotions are being dealt with. For example, red might represent anger, whereas violet might signify spiritual aspiration.

▦ When something is unexpectedly liquid in a dream, we need to be aware that in everyday life we are in a situation that may not remain stable. At that point we need to be ready to 'go with the flow' in order to maximize the potential within that situation. One of the symbols of liquid is to do with liquidity – that is, having assets or possessions that can be realized. This can be on either a physical or emotional level.

*You might also like to consult the entries for Colour and Water.*

**LIST**

☀ Dreaming of a list of any sort suggests an attempt to create some kind of spiritual order.

♥ In dreams, lists can represent logical or linear thought, in that there is a progression from one item to another.

▦ To be making a list suggests trying to impose some sort of order in our lives. To be given a list suggests that order has been reached but we must take steps to implement whatever is suggested.

**LITTER**

☀ Litter in dreams can alert us to a disorderly mess, a spiritual problem not properly thought through.

♥ Just as a newborn litter of puppies has not yet developed individual qualities, so such an image in dreams suggests perhaps unformed or undifferentiated thought. Interestingly, a litter was initially a portable bed; it may be that we need to look at how permanent we feel an aspect of our lives to be.

▦ Recognizing litter as thrown away objects suggests that some aspects of day-to-day life are no longer of use to us and a degree of clearing unnecessary problems is important.

**LITTLE –** *see* **SIZE**

**LIVE/LIVING**

☀ When something is live it is full of – perhaps unspent – spiritual energy. Considering such energy may alter our perception of the life we live.

♥ If we consider that to live is to use energy effectively, any image in dreams that highlights this, constitutes a reminder. Live ammunition, for instance, suggests that care and control of danger is necessary.

▦ The implication that an animal or person in dreams is living suggests that it still exists. To dream of a dead relative as being alive suggests either their existence in memory or within the spiritual dimension, depending on our beliefs.

**LIVER –** *see* **BODY**

**LIZARD –** *see* **REPTILES IN ANIMALS**

**LOAD/LOADED/LOADING –** *see* **BAGGAGE AND LUGGAGE**

**LOAN –** *see* **LEND/LENDING/LOAN**

**LOCK/LOCKED**

☀ A lock can suggest that either a new spiritual freedom is being offered to us or that the way forward is barred. Our actions are not appropriate.

♥ It is very easy to lock away the emotions, supposedly to keep them safe. A lock appearing in a dream may alert us to the fact that we need to free up whatever we have shut away. To force a lock would indicate that we need to work against our own inclinations to lock things away in order to be free of inhibitions. To be mending a lock suggests that our personal space has been trespassed upon and we need to repair the damage.

🔲 To recognize in a dream that a part of our body has become locked suggests that we are carrying extreme tension. We need to release that tension in a physical way in order to be healthy. To realize a door is locked suggests that somewhere we thought of as sanctuary is no longer available to us. It may also be that a course of action is not right.

*Also consult the entries for Key and Prison.*

## LOCUST

🔅 Spiritually, locusts signify divine retribution, a force that cannot be opposed, and also a misuse of resources.

🛡 As a flying insect, the locust can signify scattered thought and concepts that have not been properly thought out and marshalled. Put together, they may be a very powerful tool, albeit somewhat dangerous.

🔲 The image of a plague of locusts is so strong in Western thought that even in dreams it has come to represent retribution for some misdemeanour.

*You might also like to consult the entry for Insect.*

## LOG – *see* TREE

## LOOK – *see* SEARCH

## LOOM

🔅 The loom in spiritual terms symbolizes Fate, time and the weaving of destiny.

🛡 A loom picks up on the symbol of weaving and the idea of creating our own lives. We are given certain basic materials that can lay down an elementary pattern, but we must add our own touches through knowledge and experience, which give individuality to the overall 'woven' existence.

🔲 A loom in dreams will obviously have a different significance if it is a work tool, or if one is a creative artist. By and large a loom suggests creativity, whether more mechanical or craft-oriented. We all have the ability within ourselves to create beautiful objects and the loom is one of these symbols.

*Consult the entry for Weaving for further clarification.*

## LORD – *see* AUTHORITY FIGURES IN PEOPLE

## LORRY – *see* TRANSPORT

## LOSE/LOSS/LOST

🔅 The search for the lost object or the lost chord epitomizes the search for enlightenment. In spiritual terms we do not know what we are looking for until we have found it.

◈ To experience ourselves as being lost denotes confusion and perhaps a sense of rejection. This may be emotionally or mentally as much as physically. We have lost the ability or the motivation to make clear decisions.

▦ To lose something in a dream may mean that we have forgotten matters that could be important. This may be an opportunity, a friend or a way of thought that has previously sustained us. To suffer loss suggests that part of ourselves or our lives is now dead and we must learn to cope without it.

## LOTTERY

✿ Spiritually, a lottery represents our ability to take chances, to rely on fate rather than good judgement. The 'lottery of life' has the same basic meaning as the luck of the draw, in that certain conditions seem to be predestined through our genetics, our way of life or our intrinsic decisions. We appear not to be in control.

◈ A lottery can highlight all sorts of belief systems, some valid and some not. The idea of random selection – particularly mechanically – links with belief in a mechanistic universe. The lottery also denotes our attitude to greed and poverty and to the principle of winning through luck rather than effort.

▦ A lottery suggests the idea of gaining through taking a risk with money. Gambling is part of human nature almost since time began, but a lottery is less immediate and in today's society much less to do with trying to guess the will of the Divine. To dream of winning a lottery would suggest that one has either been lucky or clever in waking life. To dream of losing might suggest that someone else was in control of our destiny.

*You might like to consult the entries for Gambling, Ticket and Win/Winner.*

**LOUD –** *see* **NOISE**

**LOVE –** *see* **EMOTION**

**LOW –** *see* **POSITION**

**LUCK/LUCKY –** *see* **DICE/DIE AND GAMBLING**

## LUGGAGE

✿ Spiritually, if we are to travel 'light' we must often find a way of unburdening ourselves. Luggage in a dream, particularly as luggage on wheels becomes more available, can help us to envisage this.

◈ When luggage appears as a symbol in our dreams we should perhaps look at whether it is ours or someone else's. If ours, it signifies those views, attitudes and behaviours that we have brought through from the past. If it is someone else's, then we may be looking at family or global concepts that no longer are useful to us.

Luggage in a dream can be slightly different to baggage in that luggage will symbolize what we feel is necessary to have us go forward. It can be those habits and emotions that have helped us in the past, but which can now be reappraised before being 'repacked' for more efficient use.

As more people travel on business, luggage in both men's and women's dreams can signify work problems or information needed in that environment.

*Consult the entry for Baggage for further clarification.*

## LUMINOUS

If an article is luminous it contains its own light, which is a spiritual attribute.

Usually in dreams, when something appears as luminous, what is represented is transparent, easily understood and with a quality beyond the norm.

As a reflection of a piece of work or project that has been well executed, an image may appear in dreams as filled with its own light, i.e. luminous.

In both men's and women's dreams, love and passion can give a luminous quality to images. It is as though the energy has taken on a different quality.

## LUNGS – *see* BODY

## LUXURY

Spiritually, in a dream luxury signifies sinful self-indulgence, which might be counted as a spiritual misdemeanour.

To be in luxurious surroundings suggests that we have given ourselves permission in some way to have a degree of comfort in our lives. To be uncomfortable in such surroundings suggests a poor self-image.

Luxury tends to equate with wellbeing, so from a mundane perspective suggests that we are trying to create such feelings.

## LYNCH

A violent act such as lynching – sentencing to death by mob rule – suggests an abrupt end to a great negativity.

Lynching appearing in a dream indicates that there is a complete lack of control of our emotions and we are unable to put a stop to our own destructiveness.

When we are having to defend our own corner, our way of working, or our own beliefs, a violent reaction can lead to dreams of lynching. Such dreams are less likely in this day and age, but could be classed as nightmares when we are under extreme pressure.

## LYNX – *see* ANIMALS

**MACHETE –** *see* **AXE AND WEAPON**

**MACHINE**

☀ A machine may well represent the machinations of life, which would be interpreted as The 'Life Process'. In Chinese medicine *ch'i* or spiritual energy flows in certain ways around the body and the life process aids in that flow.

♥ In dreams, machines represent the brain and the logical thinking processes, so psychologically it is the actual process of thinking that is important in this context, rather than what we are thinking about. If a machine seems large and overpowering, we perhaps need to reassess the effect our actions are having, both on us and those around us.

▦ When a machine of any sort – particularly one that operates automatically like a robot – appears in a dream, it is often highlighting the body's automatic functions. These are the ordinary everyday actions that take place, such as breathing, heartbeat, elimination – those mechanical drives towards life that help us to survive. The 'mechanics' of the body are an important part of our well-being and often when we perceive a machine breaking down in dreams, it warns us that we need to take care, that perhaps we are over-stressing a particular part of our body, such as the lungs or the intestines.

*You might also like to consult the entries for Body and Engine.*

**MAD**

☀ Madness can be translated into feelings of Spiritual Ecstasy, an altered state of consciousness.

♥ Being mad in a dream represents the uncontrollable – and out of control – aspects of extreme emotion. If we are conscious of being at odds with other people, and therefore considered to be mad, we are not integrating fully within society or the group to which we belong.

▦ When we are confronted by madness in a dream, we are confronting those parts of ourselves that, within our present situation, have not been integrated internally or properly focused. We are facing an aspect that is out of control and that, under certain circumstances, can be frightening if allowed to 'escape' or take us over.

*You might like to consult the entry for Emotions for further clarification.*

**MAGGOTS**

💮 Maggots in dreams may reflect our own fears about death and illness. No-one likes the idea of the physical body being consumed by maggots, although, in fact, the spiritual does remain whole.

💚 Though the old use of maggots to cleanse wounds is receiving attention today, maggots can represent impurities in the body. They also link with the sense of being eaten up from the inside by something – such as an idea, feeling or emotion – that is alien to us and can, therefore, overtake and overcome us.

🔲 Maggots appearing in dreams in their correct context can represent the feelings we have about death. If a fisherman was using maggots we would be referring to power and energy, but if someone else was using maggots, their use of nastiness might be in question.

*Consult the entry for Death, Dead People and Ill/Illness for further clarification.*

**MAGIC/MAGICIAN**

💮 Magic and the use of powers beyond ourselves has always had an appeal. Classified as any extraordinary or mystical (beyond oneself) influence, charm, or power, in dreams this power can seem more easily accessible than at other times.

💚 Psychologically, when there is magic in a dream it indicates our ability to link with our own deepest powers. Initially, they can be the powers of sexuality, the powers of control, or of power over our surroundings. By learning, often through dreams, to control our emotions and channel them properly we are able to access energy beyond our own little world and use it to improve our own, or others', lives.

🔲 When we are using magic both in dreams and in everyday life, we are using our energy to accomplish something without effort or difficulty. We are capable of controlling the situation that we are in, to have things happen for us and to create from our own needs and wants. The figure of a magician appearing in a dream signifies the arrival of a wise guardian and counsellor, whether that is from an internal perspective or in everyday life.

*You might also like to consult the entries for Mystic, Witch and Wizard.*

**MAGISTRATE**

💮 Spiritual authority coupled with spiritual knowledge is often represented by a dream of a magistrate. It signifies that we can be susceptible to both.

💚 It may well be that a part of us knows best what we should be doing, and our conscious, everyday working self is deliberately flouting that inner authority. A magistrate in dreams has sufficient authority to correct our misdemeanours.

🔲 There are times when we need to be told what to do, or perhaps to have somebody who is more powerful than we are take control within our lives. A magistrate in everyday life imposes the laws of society for the good of the community in which we live. A judgement must be made as to what is for the good of all. In dreams, this figure will perform the same function, generally guiding us towards more acceptable behaviour.

*Also consult the entries for Authority Figures in People and Judge/Judgement.*

## MAGNIFYING GLASS

� Making Spirituality manifest would initially mean being more aware of our own actions. We need to examine ourselves minutely.

♥ Where it strikes us that the magnifying glass itself and not what we are looking at is important, we are recognizing our own abilities, our own power within a situation.

▦ When anything is magnified in a dream it is being brought to our attention. To be using a magnifying glass indicates that we should be making what we are looking at conscious. It needs to be made part of our everyday working life and we do have the power to create something out of the material that we have.

*You might also like to consult the entry for Lens.*

## MAGPIE – *see* BIRDS

## MAIL

� Mail in dreams is communication from the spiritual realms.

♥ Emotion is one of the most difficult things to communicate, so 'wrapping it up' in letters or emails is a strong dream image. Trying to send mail may be trying to communicate how we feel.

▦ Mail in the sense of armour suggests defences that we put up, but may also signify the masculine gender. Retrieving lost mail suggests that we need to increase our motivation.

▪ In a woman's dream mail may represent her more assertive side, whereas in a man's dream he may wish to reveal his true self.

*You might like to consult the entries for Armour, Communication, Email and Letter for further information.*

## MAIM – *see* ACCIDENT, INJURE/INJURY, TRAUMA AND WOUND

## MAKE-UP

� Spiritually, we must be aware of the way we are 'made-up' (constructed) and must be conscious of the facade we present to other people. In dreams we can become conscious of that facade and whether it differs greatly from the person we feel ourselves to be.

♥ To be dealing with make-up means that we have a choice as to the sort of person we want to be. We can choose our outward appearance and can create an impression that perhaps is different from the one we naturally make use of. To make-up, in the sense of bringing about a reconciliation, in our dreams suggests that we need to allow positive emotion to flow more fully.

▦ Make-up indicates our ability to change the impression we make on others. If we are making ourselves up it can very often indicate a happy occasion. We need to put on a facade for people – we may even need to put on a facade for ourselves – so that we feel better about our own self-image. If we are making someone else up, then often we are helping them to create a false – or perhaps better – impression.

*You might also like to consult the entry for Cosmetics.*

## MALLET

☼ A mallet, usually made of wood, suggests a form of spiritual power and energy. However, because of the symbolic qualities, particularly evident in Freemasonry, of the mallet – those of authority and ownership – we need to be assured that power and energy are being channelled correctly.

♥ The mallet is a symbol of the will correctly directed and to have such an item in a dream indicates that we may be attempting to make things happen in a particular way. Rather than brute force, finesse can be used, for correctly applied the mallet and chisel are shaping tools.

▦ For something like a hammer or a mallet to appear in a dream indicates that we may be using undue force or power to achieve a certain outcome. A mallet is a hammer for a particular purpose, and in dreams will suggest that we choose tools that are right for our task.

*Also consult the entry for Hammer.*

## MANDALA

☼ The mandala is a sacred shape, which is so powerful that it is found in one form or another in most systems of belief, but most frequently in Eastern religions. Typically, it is a circle enclosing a square with a symbol in the centre representing the whole of life. It is mostly used as an aid to meditation. It moves us into a space that enables us to create a whole new concept of the principles of existence.

♥ In dreams this pattern often appears without us knowing what it really represents. It is only when it is drawn afterwards that is it recognizable as a mandala. This would suggest that it is a true expression of our individuality and connection with Unity, whatever we consider this to be.

▦ The mandala is often consciously depicted as an eight-pointed star and represents both Man's aspirations and his burdens. It often appears in recurring dreams in this form and then becomes a personal symbol of the journey from Chaos to Order. It has also been found that in a healing process this symbol will occur in dreams over and over again. The particular shape, number of sides and colours in a mandala will be significant.

*Consult the entries for Chaos, Colour, Meditation, Mosaic, Numbers and Shapes/Patterns for additional information.*

## MANE – *see* HAIR AND HORSE IN ANIMALS

## MANIA/MANIAC/MANIC

❈ Mania suggests behaviour that is without reason, and previously was thought to be a visitation by the Gods or spirits. In dreams such behaviour is a warning of spiritual overload.

♡ Manic behaviour, such as hyperactivity, in dreams suggests that the emotions are having a bad effect on us and causing us to be out of control.

▦ In dreams, a maniac is a personalization of that destructive part of our personality that is not properly under control.

*Consult the entry for Emotions for further information.*

## MANSION – *see* HOUSE IN BUILDINGS

## MANTRA

❈ Spiritually, sound repeated over and over induces a change of consciousness and awareness. The Mantra is the creation of a sound, corresponding to a name or an aspect of God, and is a creative vibration, frequently used in meditation. Often it is three syllables long, and is an aid to becoming closer to the centre of both oneself and the universe. As such, in dreams it opens up possibilities for enhanced wisdom and knowledge.

♡ If dreams are considered to be alert restfulness, the use prior to sleep of Mantra – using intense concentration and constant repetition – can have a profound effect on the dream state in allowing us to be more focused in our dreaming. We fill the mind with one concept of God, whatever that might be – coupled with a sense of spiritual union.

▦ In dreams we frequently hear the sound of our own name and can develop this into a mantra. It is (or rather becomes) the personal 'key' to universal knowledge. When the images evoked by Mantra in waking life also appear in dreams, we are thus able to accept their validity.

*You might also like to consult the entry for Meditation as well as the information on Spiritual Imagery in the Introduction.*

## MANUSCRIPT – *see* INK, PAPER/PARCHMENT AND WRITING

## MAORI – *see* INDIGENOUS PEOPLES

## MAP

❈ A map can obviously help us in our quest to find the spiritual way forward. It is worth remembering that though others can read the map for us, ultimately we must make the journey ourselves and, therefore, we are our own guides.

❤ When we first set out on the journey of discovery that makes us grow into capable human beings, we often need clarification of the way that we must undertake the journey. In dreams this often appears as a map, whether this is an old-fashioned map denoting perhaps out-of-date information, or a computer-generated one symbolizing that others have made the same journey. The direction we are being shown to take is important: i.e. forwards, backwards, left or right and we are often helped by the idea of having a course to follow.

🀙 For a map to appear in a dream often indicates the clarification of the direction we should be taking in life. We may feel that we are lost and need something to indicate the way forward, particularly so far as ambition or motivation is concerned. A map that has already been used by other people would, therefore, indicate that we are capable of taking a direction and learning from those people.

*Consult the entry for Position for further clarification.*

## MARATHON – *see* RACE AND RUNNING

## MARE – *see* HORSE IN ANIMALS

## MARKET/MARKETPLACE

🔆 A marketplace can be viewed as a place of spiritual exchange in dreams. We can establish a balance between our everyday reality and our spiritual or inner world.

❤ A market is a bustling, happy place and to dream of one may indicate that we need to look after ourselves more and to spend time with more people. An open air or farmers market suggests that we should pay more attention to the good things in life. It could also suggest that we need to become more commercial in the work that we are doing, or perhaps to be more creatively influenced, rather than doing something purely and simply because it is commercial – thus it has quite an ambivalent meaning.

🀙 Dreaming that we are in a market indicates our ability to cope with everyday life, of being able to relate to people, but particularly to relate to crowds. It is also the place of buying and selling and, therefore, often gives us some sort of indication as to how we value our various attributes, whether we have something to sell or whether we are buying.

*You might also like to consult the entry for Food.*

## MARRIAGE

🔆 Spiritually there is a process of integration that needs to come about. This is usually known as a Mystic Union or mystic marriage. Here the physical and spiritual sides need to harmonize and when they do we are suffused by a sense of bliss. The sense of rightness is sometimes felt first in dreams.

♥ Firstly the masculine and feminine sides (drive and receptivity) of our personality need to unite, then emotions are allowed to settle. In dreams this can manifest as a sense of peace.

▦ On a more mundane level, as these processes of integration are taking place we will often dream of marriage. In previous times, the sexual act was seen as symbolizing the union of the sacred and the secular. The concept of the sacred marriage or sacred love ceremony originated with the ancients, who enacted annual ceremonies to bring fertility and prosperity, signifying commitment. Today dreams of marriage have that symbolism of dedication to someone else.

▣ As an actual wedding ceremony tends to become less important but commitment is, both men and women may dream of an act of commitment, a proposal or making a vow when they feel secure within a relationship. Dreaming of monogamy highlights this commitment.

*You might like to consult the entries for Propose/Proposal, Vow and Wedding/Wedding Dress/Wedding Ring.*

## MARSH

❀ A marsh being a mixture of earth and water suggests spiritual and emotional conflict. Water symbolizes emotion and earth symbolizes security, so an excess of emotion is not allowing us to feel at ease.

♥ Dreaming of marshy ground very often represents difficulty on an emotional level. Our emotions are clouded by practical concerns. Perhaps we are creating emotional difficulties for ourselves – or even having them created for us – which make it difficult for us to feel secure.

▦ When we dream of a marsh or a swamp, it can indicate that we are feeling 'bogged down'. We feel that we are being held back in something we want to do, and perhaps we lack either the self-confidence or emotional support that we need to move forward. A marsh or a swamp can also indicate that we are being swamped by circumstances, being trapped in some way by the events round us.

*Also consult the entries for Mud, Earth/Earthquake, Swamp and Water.*

## MARTYR

❀ In previous times being a martyr inevitably meant that suffering was involved. We may perceive the need, spiritually, to become a victim, sacrificing ourselves on others' behalf and thus give our life some meaning. Such actions can be perceived as honourable provided they arise from the correct motivation.

💗 Dreaming of a religious martyr often signifies that we need to question our own religious beliefs and upbringing, and our strength of purpose and commitment. We are perhaps allowing excessive enthusiasm to guide us.

🔲 Actually experiencing ourselves in dreams as playing the martyr highlights our tendency to do things without being sufficiently assertive to say no, and to act from a sense of duty. When we are aware of someone else being a martyr we may have too high expectations of that person.

*You might also like to consult the entries for Fanatic and Victim.*

## MASK

🔆 In primitive Shamanistic societies, to wear an animal mask gave the wearer the powers of that animal. If we dream of wearing such a mask, we may need to consider that animal's qualities and how they can be, or are, applied in our waking lives. The Death Mask, either our own or another's, can appear in dreams as a signal that it is time to put an end to a spiritual game we are playing.

💗 When we are trying to protect ourselves and prevent other people knowing what we are thinking or feeling, we 'mask' ourselves. A mask appearing in a dream can, therefore, represent concealment, perhaps of emotion, perhaps of finer feelings.

🔲 Most people have a facade they put on for others, particularly at a first meeting. To dream of a mask often alerts us to either our own or other people's facade. When we are not being true to ourselves we can often experience this in dreams as a 'negative' or frightening mask.

*You might also like to consult the entries for Animals and Shaman.*

## MASOCHISM

🔆 Spiritual masochism suggests an act of self-inflicted pain, such as self-flagellation. The pain perversely brings pleasure. It can be an aspect of martyrdom.

💗 Pleasure from pain, in the emotional sense in dreams, can alert us to our propensity to be a victim, albeit through a self-inflicted injury.

🔲 In a mundane sense masochism in dreams can highlight our tendency towards lugubrious acceptance that we can do nothing about the circumstances we are in.

🔛 Sado-masochism in dreams, while seemingly sexual in nature, may well show a propensity to tolerate an extreme attitude within a relationship, for both men and women.

*You might like to consult the entry for Martyr for further clarification.*

**MASS** – *see* **RITE/RITUAL AND SPIRITUAL IMAGERY IN THE INTRODUCTION**

## MASSACRE

☀ A massacre is an indiscriminate killing and is of little spiritual value except to alert us to the violence of others' belief.

♡ Indiscriminate killing in dreams suggests that emotions have been allowed to get out of control and taken over from reasonable behaviour.

▦ In mundane terms, when business methods become both heartless and ruthless this can be translated into dreams as a massacre. This may also suggest that there is little we can do personally to prevent this.

*You might like to consult the entries for Death and Kill.*

**MATTRESS – *see* BED/BEDROOM AND ALSO THE INFORMATION ON BED/MATTRESS IN FURNITURE/FURNISHINGS**

**MAUSOLEUM – *see* CATACOMB/CRYPT, MEMORIAL AND TOMB**

## MAYPOLE

☀ The maypole in a spiritual sense is a representation of the phallic, of masculine spirituality and of life-giving energy.

♡ Psychologically, festivals, celebrations and occasions for ceremony are necessary for the human being to be at ease with himself. Often the maypole may be one such symbol – of celebration, of new life. It may also represent time in a dream and the way in which a dream indicates the type of timing that is necessary within certain situations.

▦ A maypole in a dream can very often represent the masculine and may indicate the 'dance' that we go through when coming to terms with our own universe. It is the central pole of the world that we create for ourselves; thus to dream of a maypole may have sexual connotations, but also may indicate the way in which we handle our own lives.

⊞ As a symbol of fertility, the maypole can appear in a woman's dream as a promise of things to come. In a man's dream it may well mark the taking on of responsibility. In former times, relationships begun on Mayday, when the maypole dances took place, lasted for a year and a day, thus honouring the goddess of fertility.

## MAZE

☀ A maze is a path of initiation into divine knowledge. It also represents the feminine, and in its twists and turns signifies – at one and the same time – confusion and innate wisdom.

♡ Psychologically, the maze may represent the variety of opinions and authoritative beliefs that we come up against in our ordinary, everyday world. We may be trying to find our own way through this mass of detail and we picture this in a dream as actually trying to find our way through a maze.

■ A maze often represents a confusion of ideas and feelings. There are conflicting urges and opinions and we often discover that, in attempting to find our way through the maze, we have learnt something about our own courage, our own ability to meet problems. Often there is the apparently irrational fear and doubt that arises from not being able to find our way in and out of the maze. This can allow us to release feelings of self-doubt and fear. *Also consult the entries for Initiation and Labyrinth.*

## MEAL

◉ The sacred meal has always been an integral part of most systems of belief. Food is such a vehicle for the life force and for sharing in community that this type of meal becomes an important spiritual concept. It carries this significance in dreams.

♥ Banquets, festivals and feasts in dreams all represent man's capacity for enjoyment. A meal, whether in company or alone, signifies our appreciation of the gifts of nature.

■ From a purely practical viewpoint a meal eaten alone represents an aspect of self-nurturing; when eating in company, a convivial social process. In dreams, such images help to widen our perspective to encompass the needs of others. Offering a meal to a beggar would signify our need to share what we have.

*You might also like to consult the entries for Festival, Food and Party.*

## MEANDER

◉ It was Jung who recognized that dreams appear to meander (wander) all over the place, and it is only by perceiving the overall spiritual picture that we can make sense of them. The Spiritual Spiral is a concept whereby physical manifestation takes place, moving very quickly from the spiritual to the physical realms. In dreams this can often be perceived as a slow-motion meandering. We should look at whether it is a downward spiral, an aimless wandering or a purposeful – if indirect – exploration.

♥ Water moves in its own way, and often to be conscious of a river or a road meandering around us indicates that we should be more aware of our own emotions, that we are capable of dealing with these emotions in a much gentler way than by being very direct. This may also refer to our relationship with other people. It could be that we need to recognize that other people cannot be as straightforward as we are.

■ In a dream, to have a path or the road in front of you meandering – that is, not going in any particular direction – suggests that we very often have to 'go with the flow', to simply follow what happens without actually thinking of the direction in which we are going. Sometimes the meandering has a kind of purpose, in that by wandering about in an apparently aimless fashion we are learning to live in the moment and understand our own reactions and responses to the outside world.

*You might also like to consult the entries for Journey, Path, Wander/Wandering and Water.*

## MEASURE

✸ A measure in dreams – whether of capacity, length or weight – suggests a comparison, often against some kind of spiritual standard.

♡ Emotionally, when we attempt to find some kind of tranquility we will measure it against previous experience. In dreams this may come across as an overflowing cup, gauge or measuring stick.

▣ In waking life, we will try to measure our performance against correct practice or a set standard. This will surface in dreams with actual physical instruments of measurement such as rulers, scales and other measuring devices. To be measuring standards is to be applying a preset code of behaviour.

*You might also like to consult the entries for Cup, Scales and Weighing/Weight for further clarification.*

## MEDAL

✸ Just as a medal acknowledges our prowess, from a spiritual perspective it reminds us to adhere to a spiritual code of conduct.

♡ Human beings both like and need to feel good about themselves. A medal in a dream acknowledges our talents and/or successes – not just in the immediate moment – but gives a permanent reminder of what we have done.

▣ A medal is often a reward for good work or for bravery, so when one appears in a dream it is recognition of our own abilities. If we are giving someone else a medal then we are honouring that part of ourselves represented by the dream character.

*You might also like to consult the entries for Badge/Brooch and Win/Winning.*

## MEDIA

✸ In its truest meaning 'the media' signifies all means of mass communication. Spiritually, therefore, in dreams it comes to mean the dissemination of knowledge, particularly from a cosmic perspective.

♡ Radio, television and other media all feed our need to know and emotionally give a false sense of ownership, particularly of celebrities and their lives. In dreams, where once media would have meant the possession of facts, now it can symbolize a form of intrusion on our part. To be aware of any of the tools of the media suggests that we need to be conscious of our sense of responsibility towards other people.

▦ Dreaming of hearing information through any forms of media indicate that we need to pay due regard to events beyond our own everyday concerns giving careful consideration to community and worldly matters.

*You might also like to consult the entries for Actor, Celebrity, Communication, Newspaper, Radio and Television.*

## MEDICATION/MEDICINE

✷ The spiritual need for a healing influence in our lives is indicated by medicine appearing. It may be symbolic of spiritual healing or of the need to potentize (make more powerful) any medicine we have to take so that it can work to our best advantage.

♡ When in waking life we need medication and either cannot take it, or have difficulty in obtaining it, our dreams will often present a way – or the courage – to overcome the difficulty in waking life. Sometimes an experience that we have in waking life can be unpleasant in the immediate moment, but ultimately is good for us. In dreams, medicine can stand as such a symbol.

▦ To be taking medicine in a dream suggests that on some level we are aware of part of ourselves, possibly our self-image, that needs healing. Often we are aware of what the medicine is for and are thus alerted either to a potential health problem, or to a situation that can be changed from the negative to the positive.

*You might also like to consult the entries for Doctor, Drugs, Hospital, Nurse/Nursing and Tablet.*

## MEDITATION

✷ As a discipline, meditation helps us to become more aware of changes in consciousness. It also has the effect of opening our minds to dreaming as a spiritual learning tool. After learning meditation, our dreams take on a different depth and clarity. For instance, the mandala seen in dreams can become a gauge for spiritual progression.

♡ Often on an unconscious level we are aware of the need to change consciousness or attitude. To dream of meditating, particularly when we first learn this art, can highlight this for us. We can access our more creative, spiritual side and thus mandala and mantra become second nature, both asleep and awake.

▦ Interpreting the act of meditation will depend on whether we meditate in real life. In someone who does, it will suggest a discipline that is helpful, putting them in touch with intuition and spiritual matters. In someone who does not, it may indicate the need to be more introverted in order to understand the necessity to be responsible for oneself.

*Consult the entries for Mandala and Mantra for further clarification.*

## MEDIUM

☀ Mediumistic aspects in a dream can represent our wish to be in contact with the dead. This does not necessarily have to be dead in literal terms, it can merely be what is 'dead' in our life, that which we may wish to resurrect. During spiritual development, our perceptions widen from the ordinary everyday to other aspects and dimensions of knowledge that have become available to us. Whether these are aspects of our own personality or of the spirit realm is immaterial, since ultimately their function is to help us progress. The spiritual self has access to the Collective Unconscious in its entirety.

♥ To dream of being mediumistic would indicate that we are aware of greater powers than we believe we have in ordinary everyday life. When spirits appear in dreams, their function may be to help us through various states of transition. While we cope with everyday fears, there are many unconscious memories and feelings, which can surface unexpectedly. When we are conscious of a kindly or helpful spirit we are aware that we can move on. When we see the spirits of dead people we usually need reassurance.

▦ Dreaming of visiting a medium very often means that we are looking for some kind of contact with our own unconscious, or with the dead. We may also be attempting to alert our own intuition and use it differently to a way we have done previously. At a very basic level, we all have fears and feelings about death, and the actual appearance in dreams of spiritual entities can help us to come to terms with these.

*You might like to consult the entry for Dead People.*

## MEET/MEETING

☀ As part of our spiritual learning process, in dreams we at some point will meet (come face to face with) a figure who is representative of a spiritual teacher.

♥ A meeting is a gathering of people with a common aim or purpose. In dreams, this can often signify the integration of several aspects of our personality.

▦ A work meeting or consultation in dreams may signify an attempt to gain a consensus of opinion or an agreed course of action. This may be a way of dealing with our own inner confusion, or that which is actually in an everyday situation.

*Also consult the information on the Wise Old Man in the Introduction.*

## MELT

☀ On a spiritual level, melting suggests losing form and has sometimes had connections with the overcoming of negativity and evil. This is pictured most successfully in horror movies and dream images often follow the same format.

⊗ To see something melting in a dream is an indication that our emotions may be softening. We are perhaps losing the rigidity we have needed to face the world with previously. We are undergoing a change and are becoming softer.

▦ When we feel ourselves to be melting we may be becoming more romantically inclined and less likely to drive ourselves forward. We perhaps need to sit and simply let a situation develop around us to the point where it is safe for us to give up control.

*You might also like to consult the entry for Ice/Iceberg/Icicles.*

## MEMORIAL

❁ A memorial is a tangible representation of homage and esteem. Seeing the Cenotaph, or indeed any other war memorial, in dreams is a timely reminder of the sanctity of life.

⊗ A memorial may simply be recognition of a happier time that needs to be remembered. A mausoleum in a dream, since it holds many tombs, may be a memorial to family and inherited values.

▦ To see a memorial such as a war memorial in a dream takes us back to a previous time, to a memory that may be 'cast in stone'. We need to be able to come to terms with this memory in order to move on.

*You might also like to consult the entries for Catacomb/Crypt, Inheritance and Tomb.*

## MEND/MENDING – *see* REPAIR

## MERLIN – *see* CAMELOT AND WIZARD

## MERMAID/MERMAN

❁ The mermaid and merman symbolize the ability to integrate the spiritual aspects of the personality with the emotional. In being part fish and part human, they also symbolize the evolutionary journey from pure instinct to wisdom.

⊗ Mermaids and mermen are feminine and masculine representations of the link between the darker forces – which we do not necessarily understand – and the conscious self. In dreams the mermaid epitomizes how difficult it is to integrate the two sides of our nature. This lack of integration can result in capriciousness. The merman, however, is said to be less 'intrigued' by humans so, therefore, represents unification, but in a way that is more isolated.

▦ Traditionally, the mermaid or merman belongs to the sea as well as being able to exist on land. This symbolically represents an ability to be deeply emotional and also entirely practical. Until these two separate parts are properly integrated, the human being cannot fully exist in either the emotional or practical realms.

⊡ Many stories exist of the human's attempt to mate or link with these creatures of the sea, though the merman is less fascinated than his counterpart by humans. Most attempts end in hurt and distress for one party or the other and men's dreams of such a creature of fantasy in particular can reflect this. Women's dreams may contain an element of coming to terms with her own capriciousness.

*You might also like to consult the entry for Sea in Water.*

## MESSAGE

⚙ Receiving a message – by whatever means – in dreams signifies communication, probably from the Higher Self. Sending a message from a spiritual perspective suggests trying to make contact with Spirit.

♡ Dreams themselves were, and still are, considered to be messages from the gods or spiritual realms. As such, they require careful interpretation; images of letters, parcels, emails and other technology can all signify messages from the unconscious or instinctive realms.

▦ In dreams, receiving or sending a message highlights the importance of information *per se*. Particularly if we work in the creative fields and information technology, messages in dreams will represent our ability to handle such input. To remember the input suggests the information is useful, to forget, that we have the information but must rediscover it. A message in a bottle signifies that contact is being made from the less accessible parts of our personality.

*Consult the entries for Bottle, Communication, Email, Letter and Parcel/Package for further clarification.*

## METAL

⚙ The ancients recognized the importance of metal, particularly as offerings to the gods, and much of that symbolism is still relevant in dreams today as we find our magical roots and progress on our spiritual journey.

♡ Most metals have symbolic meanings. They can also be connected with various planets: Sun is represented by gold, the Moon by silver, Mercury by quicksilver, Venus by copper, Mars by iron, Jupiter by tin, Saturn by lead. In dreams these ancient symbolisms begin to surface as we learn more. For instance, Mars the warrior wielding an iron sword suggests that we need to fight our own corner and become more assertive.

▦ Any metal appearing in dreams represents the restrictions of the real world. It can represent basic abilities and attributes, but also can be hardness of feeling or emotional rigidity. An article made of lead suggests a heavy responsibility.

*Consult the entries for Alchemy, Gold, Iron, Lead and Planets for further information and clarification.*

## METAMORPHOSIS – *see* TRANSFORMATION AND TRANSMUTATION IN THE INTRODUCTION

## MICROCHIP

✺ In dreams a microchip will signify something that is small but powerful, such as the information we need to make spiritual progress.

♥ A microchip, being the essential driving force behind some much of today's technology, can represent the whole plethora of emotions available to us if we have the courage to access them.

▦ Having to become aware of a microchip in dreams suggest that we need to become aware of our motivations and drives. Computers are now such an integral part of our lives that any part of them will be easily decipherable in their symbolism – for instance, a computer screen may have the same relevance for some as a picture does for an artist.

## MICROSCOPE

✺ A degree of detailed introspection is called for, either spiritual or physical.

♥ We have the ability to look at things in dreams in much finer detail than we would necessarily do in the waking state. While the mind can be creative, it sometimes also needs to apply scientific – and perhaps logical – thought to a problem, and the symbol of a microscope can draw attention to this.

▦ A microscope in a dream very often indicates that we need to pay attention to detail. Also we may need to be somewhat introspective in order to achieve a personal goal.

*Also consult the entry for Laboratory.*

## MIGRANT – *see* IMMIGRANT

## MILITARY – *see* ARMED FORCES

## MILK

✺ One of the theories of Creation is that a celestial milk was stirred in order to create form. Milk in this context becomes a symbol for Creation and Chaos.

♥ As a nourishing food milk represents nurturing and, therefore by association, the qualities of mothering. It may also suggest the faculty of intuition.

▦ Milk in a practical sense in dreams can represent the flow of creativity. It can also suggest a requirement for simplicity and a return to basic ideas and knowledge. Milk that has gone sour indicates there is a problem in the completion of a project.

⊡ As a symbol associated with the Great Mother, in a woman's dream milk can symbolize her own femininity, ability to nurture and her intuition. In a man's dream, it is more likely to represent his need to be cosseted and cared for, though it can also signify the flow of ideas and concepts.

*Consult the entries for Chaos, Food and Great Mother in Archetypes in the Introduction for further clarification.*

## MILL/MILLSTONE

🔆 A mill symbolizes transformative energy, turning the crude into the usable. The two large stones that make up a millstone are said to signify will and intellect, the tools we use in transformation.

🜂 There is a transformation that occurs when any material is ground down and changed into a more useable material. A dream containing a mill will signify that transformation and echoes the process of Creation.

▦ A mill extracts what is useful from the crude material it is fed. It is this quality that is symbolized in dreams. We are able to extract from our experiences in life what is useful to us and what we can convert into nourishment.

## MINE/MINER

🔆 Mines spiritually suggest the ability to 'mine', or learn from the emerging unconscious.

🜂 The word 'mine' initially signified crude ore and has since come to mean the place from which crude ore is taken. In this sense dreaming of a mine suggests prospecting for crude material, which can be refined, whether that is raw emotion or unexpressed feelings. This is also one of those symbols that can actually be a wordplay. The objects in the dream are 'mine'. Dreaming of a miner is that part of us that is prepared to explore and use the crude material.

▦ Dreaming of mines signifies bringing the resources of the unconscious into the light of day. We are able to use the potential we have available. Interestingly in dreams mines can also represent the workplace.

*You might also like to consult the entries for Digging/Excavation and Metal.*

## MINOTAUR

🔆 The Minotaur is a mythical beast – half man and half bull – that was trapped within the first labyrinth created. Spiritually, it is symbolic of man's instinctive urges overcome by sheer bravery.

🜂 In dreams, depending on our personality, the Minotaur can be seen as a figure either to be pitied or feared. His conquest is part of the Hero's Journey to self-actualization or realization of our own power.

■ As a recognizable fabulous beast, viewed from a practical perspective, the overcoming of the Minotaur denotes the solving of problems in a well thought and logical manner (mind against instinct).

*Consult the entries for Fabulous Beasts, Labyrinth and Monster for further information.*

**MINUTE – see SMALL**

**MIRROR**

✷ The mirror in dreams suggests self-realization, which reflects spiritual wisdom. As a means of understanding ourselves on a deeper level, we can set up a dialogue in real life between our mirror image and ourselves. Many of the insights gained can be quite startling. As a symbol in dreams it allows us to search our self-image and make whatever changes are necessary.

♡ To be looking in a mirror can signify trying to look behind us without letting others know what we are doing. We may have a concern over past behaviour. We may also need to 'reflect' on something we have done or said. When the image in the mirror is distorted we are having a problem in understanding ourselves. When the mirror image speaks to us we should be listening more closely to our inner selves.

■ Dreaming of a mirror suggests concern over our self-image. We are worried as to what others think of us, and need self-examination in order to function correctly. There may be some anxiety over ageing or health.

*You might also like to consult the entry for Reflection.*

**MISCARRIAGE**

✷ Dreaming of a miscarriage, whether our own or someone else's, suggests that we are conscious of the fact something is not right. Spiritually, we must reject whatever is wrong.

♡ Dreaming of a miscarriage can also suggest the loss of work, a project or even a part of ourselves, and we need time to acclimatize. A miscarriage of justice suggests that all aspects of a story have not been taken into consideration.

■ A miscarriage can represent aspects of early death and the fear it can engender. Also it can signify the early finishing of a project or task before it has really had a chance to reach its peak.

⊡ In a woman's dream it will depend on whether she has suffered a miscarriage, since nowadays she may not have given herself time to grieve properly. When a man dreams of his partner's miscarriage, it highlights fears over changes in responsibility.

MISER – *see* MONEY

MISSIONARY – *see* SPIRITUAL IMAGERY IN THE INTRODUCTION

MIST

🔆 Mist can symbolize spiritual initiation, a passage through an area where we cannot perceive things properly. Mist in a dream can indicate a transition state, a way from one state of awareness to another, and will often manifest to signify this.

♡ Mist is a symbol of loss and confusion – particularly when it comes to emotions – so when this image appears we may need to sit down and reconsider our actions, and how they may affect us, or indeed others – in waking life.

▥ In waking life, many states of confusion can arise. Swirling mist in a dream may signify that the confusion arises from others. To be moving through stationary mist suggests that we are capable of reaching our goal provided we take into account our own confusion.

MISTLETOE

🔆 Mistletoe represents the Essence of Life. In myth it was used to kill Baldur the Norse god of peace. Thought by the Druids to be an 'in between', or a gateway to other worlds, it is a divine healing substance.

♡ As a parasite, mistletoe has the ability to draw strength from its host, but also to be useful in its own right. It can, therefore, symbolize relationships where there is a dependency on one partner. It is said that mistletoe takes on some of its hosts' characteristics, apple-grown mistletoe being different to oak-grown.

▥ In mundane terms mistletoe obviously is most often dreamt of around Christmas. Conventionally, mistletoe represents a time of celebration, love and partnership. To dream of kissing under the mistletoe symbolizes a relationship that may be transitory.

*You might also like to consult the entry for Flowers.*

MOB – *see* CROWD

MOLE – *see* ANIMALS

MONEY

🔆 Money in dreams can represent our spiritual currency and also spiritual 'change', small or otherwise. Symbols of money such as gold coins or money bags can signify our spiritual resources, which we can call on in times of difficulty. In the spiritual sense, savings suggests those talents and abilities that we have or have developed, but have not yet used, particularly those for the Greater Good.

⚜ Money can represent our own personal resources – whether material or spiritual – and our potential for success. In some circumstances a dream of money can be linked with our view of our own power. When we dream of savings we are aware of the need for conservation. This may be on a personal level or in a more global sense. A refund of money suggests that we have put effort into en emotional commitment, but have had to accept that that 'payment' is not valid. A mortgage in dreams suggests ownership of an asset – whether emotional or material – for which we must pay in the future.

▦ Money in dreams does not necessarily represent hard currency, but more the way in which we value ourselves. This symbol appearing in dreams would suggest that we need to assess that value more carefully, and equally to be aware of what we 'pay' for our actions and desires. If there is a feeling of self-denial in our making savings, particularly to the point of miserliness, we may not have managed our resources properly in the past and are having to suffer for it now. We may also fear the future. If someone else gives us their savings, we are able to use their knowledge and expertise.

*You might also like to consult the entries for Debt, Lend/Lending/Loan and Wealth.*

## MONK

⚜ In dreams, as someone who has dedicated himself to his God or Ultimate Power, a monk represents spirituality, obedience and discipline.

⚜ In his devotion to the mystical life, the monk in dreams symbolizes an emotional response to a vocation, perhaps to a life of asceticism. He symbolizes holiness – and no matter what religion – that part of us that searches for the divine. He can have the same significance as the hermit or wanderer.

▦ As a shadowy representation of the part of us that prefers to exist in isolation, the monk can appear in dreams when our self-belief is under threat. When he is cowled or hooded he signifies hidden information, but with his face uncovered he represents Truth.

⊡ In a man's dream a monk can signify the need or wish for celibacy. In a woman's dream he may be a representation of the Animus.

*Consult the entries for Ascetic, Hermit, Mystic and Wanderer/Wandering for further information.*

## MONKEY – *see* ANIMALS

## MONSTER

⚜ A monster is usually large and, therefore, can highlight a childlike fear – perhaps the fear of death and all that goes with it – or the fear of failure. Such an image tends to be encountered at some point in the Hero's Journey.

⚇ When, in everyday life, events get out of proportion we often have to suppress our reactions. In dreams we cannot do this and so our minds create some way of dealing with the problem. Often the colour of the monster will give us some indication of what the problem is; a red monster would indicate anger (possibly uncontrolled), whereas a yellow one might suggest resentment.

▦ Any monster appearing in a dream represents something that we have made larger than life. We have personalized it so that whatever is worrying us appears as a creature. It usually indicates our negative relationship with ourselves and fear of our own emotions and drives. If we vanquish the monster, it is said that we must take care not to kill it, since we may be killing off part of our personality. Equally it should not be allowed to overcome us; self-survival kicks in and we will normally wake up before it does.

*You might like to consult the entries for Colour, Dinosaurs, Fabulous Beasts, Minotaur and also the Introduction for the Hero's Journey.*

**MONOGAMY –** *see* **MARRIAGE**

**MOON**

✸ The Great Mother, the darker, unknown side of Self, is symbolized by the moon. It is also symbolic of the unapproachable feminine.

⚇ It has always been known that the moon has a psychological effect on the human being. In Pagan times, it was suggested that she ruled men's emotions and guarded women's intuition. Even today, that symbolism still stands. Moonlight in dreams signifies romanticism and in some cases entry into a different dimension of being.

▦ The moon has always represented the emotional and feminine self. It is the intuition, the psychic, love and romance. To dream of the moon, therefore, is to be in touch with the side of ourselves that is dark and mysterious. Often in dreams the moon can also represent our mother or the relationship with her.

⊞ When the moon appears in a man's dream he either has to come to terms with his own intuitive side or with his fear of women. In a woman's dream the moon usually indicates her inter-relationships with other women through their collective intuition.

*You might also like to consult the entry for Planets.*

**MORNING –** *see* **TIME**

**MORTGAGE –** *see* **DEBT, MONEY AND WEALTH**

**MORTUARY**

✸ A mortuary may symbolize a spiritual transition phase. We are dead to the old way of life and have new spiritual awareness. When a mortuary appears in a dream, we are usually having to consider our fears and feelings about death.

🕉 If we are viewing a dead body we may be having to consider a part of ourselves that has died or changed irrevocably, or perhaps a now defunct relationship. If we are the body in the mortuary, we may have induced a state of inertia that does not allow us to enjoy life properly.

🔲 In everyday life, a mortuary is a frightening place, connected as it tends to be with the trauma of death or endings. A mortuary's clinical atmosphere may mean that we should simply observe without judgment what is occurring around us.

*You might also like to consult the entries for Dead People and Death.*

## MOSAIC

🔆 The Kaleidoscope of Life, with its many facets, is a potent spiritual symbol represented in dreams by the mosaic.

🕉 Within a mosaic, made up of many small parts, there is a deliberate act of creation. When we are working with a mosaic in dreams we are being alerted to our abilities as a creator. The colours and shapes used will be important.

🔲 Any intricate pattern appearing in dreams usually signifies the pattern of our lives. We probably need to consider life as a whole, but also to understand and respect the many separate parts of it.

*Consult the entries for Colours, Kaleidoscope, Mandala and Shapes/Patterns for additional information.*

## MOSES – *see* SPIRITUAL IMAGERY IN THE INTRODUCTION

## MOTH

🔆 The moth symbolizes the Self, but perhaps in its darker, more worldly sense. As the butterfly symbolizes the soul, so the moth symbolizes Spirit trapped in the physical realms.

🕉 The moth symbolizes the darker side of us that uses fantasy. The moth emerging from darkness signifies our need to recognize this shadowy self so that we can survive difficulties unscathed.

🔲 The moth is largely associated with nighttime and therefore connects with the hidden side of our nature. Also, because the moth can be self-destructive when there is light around, it may highlight personal weakness. It also tends to symbolize our dream self and the more transient side of our personality – that part that finds difficulty in settling to proper tasks.

*Consult the entry for Butterfly for further information.*

## MOTHER – *see* ARCHETYPES IN THE INTRODUCTION, FAMILY AND MUMMY (EGYPTIAN)

## MOTORBIKE – *see* TRANSPORT

## MOULD/MOULDY

🌑 Mould or mouldiness in dreams suggests that the essential energy has dissipated. There is no longer a link to the spiritual dimension.

◈ When in dreams something has gone mouldy or has putrefied, it has been contaminated. Emotionally there is a negativity present, which indicates that we can no longer appreciate a sense of clarity; our vision is clouded and has upset our balance.

▦ There is a sense that the life has gone out of a project or task, perhaps that in waking life they have gone on too long or lost focus. If, in dreams, food has gone mouldy we no longer have some essential support. If mould is growing, for instance on a wall, there is a negative energy around, which suggests there may be difficult times ahead if it is not dealt with properly.

*Consult the entries for Decay and Food for further information.*

## MOUND – *see* HILL

## MOUNTAIN

🌑 Representing the centre of our existence in earthly terms, the mountain is an image that can be worked on over and over again. It represents the higher, more spiritual aspects of the personality.

◈ We all have difficulties to face in life. Often it is how we face those difficulties that is important. The symbol of the mountain offers many alternatives and choices, such as whether to choose the apparently easier route or the more difficult. This means we can work out, through dreams, our best course of action in everyday life.

▦ In dream sequences the mountain usually appears in order to symbolize an obstacle that needs to be overcome. By daring to climb the mountain we challenge our own inadequacies and free ourselves from fear. To reach the top is to achieve our goal. To fall down the mountain indicates carelessness and that we should perhaps consider our actions more carefully.

*Also consult the entry for Hill for more information.*

## MOURNING

🌑 Mourning expresses grief, a coming to terms with loss. In the spiritual sense we may believe in life after death but we still no longer have the physical presence of the individual.

◈ In many cultures less emotionally repressed than our own, the period of mourning is seen as a way of assisting the departing soul on its way. In dreams we may find that we are helping ourselves to create a new beginning through our mourning for the old. Psychologically, we need a period of adjustment when we have lost something (for instance when a relationship ends) and need to grieve for ourselves as much as for what we have lost.

🏛 The process of mourning is an important one in all sorts of ways. We not only mourn death but also the end of a relationship or a particular part of our lives. Since sometimes mourning or grieving is seen as inappropriate in waking life, it will often appear in dreams as a form of relief or release.

*You might also like to consult the entries for Death, Funeral, Weeping and Wake.*

**MOUSE – *see* ANIMALS**

**MOUTH – *see* BODY**

**MOVEMENT**

� A movement towards Spiritual Acceptance can be undertaken when the time is considered to be right. Movement in dreams is usually highlighted to make us aware of our progress. Spiritually, movement such as dance is an act of worship or adoration.

♡ The way we move in dreams can indicate a great deal about our motivations. For instance, to be moving briskly would suggest an easy acceptance of the necessity for change, whereas being moved – such as on some kind of moving walkway – would signify being moved by outside circumstances or at the wish of other people.

🏛 Moving forward suggests an acceptance of our abilities, while moving backwards signifies withdrawal from a situation. Moving sideways would suggest a deliberate act of avoidance.

*Consult the entries for Dance, Immobile/Immobility and Walking for further information.*

**MUD**

🌎 Spiritually mud represents the very basic materials of earth and water from which we are all formed, and thus its appearance in dreams indicates the need to go 'back to basics'.

♡ Mud represents the fundamental substance of life, which, handled properly, has a tremendous potential for growth but, handled badly, can be dangerous. Many cultures believe mankind was fashioned from clay mud to give him structure. In dreams, if the mud is too dry we have suppressed emotion, if too wet, like marshland, we cannot develop a proper way of working.

🏛 Mud in a dream suggests that we are feeling bogged down, perhaps by not having sorted out practicality and emotion (earth and water). Mud can also represent past experiences or our perception of them, which has the ability to hold us back.

*You might also like to consult the entries for Earth/Earthquake, Marsh and Water.*

## MUMMY (EGYPTIAN)

🔆 The Egyptian mummy symbolizes death, but also preservation after death and, therefore, the afterlife. It also symbolizes the Self, the unbending Mother and self-preservation.

💙 Egypt for many represents magic, and the mummy in this case its more sinister side and hidden secrets. We may be trying to understand such a concept in real life, or we may realize that life will continue despite setbacks.

▦ The Egyptian mummy in dreams can symbolize our feelings about someone who has died. There is also an obvious connection between 'mummy' and 'mother' as a play on words. As a mummy preserves the body for life in the hereafter, its appearance in dreams indicates that we should honour the best of what our mother is or was.

## MURDER/MURDERER

🔆 Murder suggests willful destruction of another life. Spiritually we need to understand what has taken us in dreams to the extreme position of trying to kill.

💙 To be angry enough to kill suggests that we are still holding some kind of childhood anger, since it is quite natural for a child to wish somebody dead. If we are trying to murder somebody else in a dream, we first need to understand what that person represents to us before recognizing the violence of our own feelings. To dream of a murderer suggests that we are conscious of violence around us.

▦ We may be denying, or trying to control, a part of our own nature that we do not trust. We may also have feelings about other people, which can only be safely expressed in dreams. If we ourselves are being murdered, a part of our lives is completely out of balance and we are being destroyed by external circumstances.

*Consult the entries for Anger, Emotions and Kill for further clarification.*

## MUSEUM

🔆 The past is a learning tool that can be observed at some length, and a museum, like a library, is a place where knowledge and expertise can be accessed and given due reverence. Gaining spiritual knowledge in particular allows us to progress.

💙 A museum can represent a place where we store our memories and, therefore, can represent the subconscious – it is that part of ourselves that we will usually only approach in an effort to understand who we are and where we came from.

🎴 A museum in a dream denotes old-fashioned thoughts, concepts and ideas. We may need to consider such things but perhaps more objectively than subjectively.

*You might also like to consult the entry for Old.*

## MUSIC/RHYTHM

🔅 Sacred sound has always been used in acts of worship, as has dancing. Spiritually, music expresses ideas and emotions through the elements of rhythm, melody and harmony. Rhythm expresses the essential pulse of life, melody an individual sound and harmony a combination of several sounds to make a pleasing combination. In dreams this symbolism expresses man, his concerns and his society.

♥ Sacred music – such as chanting, drumming and pipe playing – has often been used to soothe emotions and induce an altered state of consciousness. In dreams hearing such music offers the opportunity to make such a shift in awareness. Listening to music before sleep can also heighten dream imagery. Modern day ambient music is particularly effective.

🎴 Music and rhythm are both expressions of our inner selves and of our connection with life. In dreams, though in waking life we may not be musical, music gives us the opportunity to understand that connection. To be listening to music suggests that we are able to appreciate the rhythm of life and all its associations.

*You might also like to consult the entries for Dance/Dancing, Musical Instruments and Orchestra.*

## MUSICAL INSTRUMENTS

🔅 Musical instruments and the skill required to play them are both aspects of Man attempting to be close to the Divine. Ways of self-expression (for example, playing a musical instrument) are offerings of our own creativity and are spiritual acts. In dreams, we have access to vibrations and rhythms not always accessible in waking life.

♥ Sound produced by musical instruments is evocative of emotion. The symbolism of the instrument itself appearing may allow us to come to terms with that emotion in a slightly more objective way. Not being able to play a particular instrument suggests we do not have access to that emotion.

🎴 Musical instruments in a dream often stand for our skills and abilities in communication. Wind instruments tend to suggest the intellect, whereas percussion instruments suggest the basic rhythm of life. Stringed instruments calm the nervous system, so when these appear in dreams we are able to act accordingly in waking life.

*Consult the entries for Drum, Flute and Organ for further information.*

**MUTILATE** – *see* **INJURE/INJURY AND WOUND**

**MUTINY** – *see* **CONFLICT**

**MYSTIC**

☸ Mysticism signifies union with the divine and the search for hidden knowledge. The mystic is someone who has dedicated their life to that search, so in dreams represents our own search for spirituality. Such a vibration in dreams opens up countless possibilities for exploration.

♡ Emotionally, mysticism requires complete submission to the idea of ultimately returning to Source, whatever our belief, and to understanding our present place in the world. In dreams, an objectivity develops that allows us to view our own and others' foibles with tolerance and dispassion. This spills over into waking life.

▦ From a mundane viewpoint, the figure of a known mystic such as Mahatma Gandhi or the Persian poet Rumi alerts us to the possibilities that are available to us if we are prepared to widen our perspectives. Mystics appear in their guise of spiritual leaders to enable us to progress.

*Consult the entries for Ascetic, Hermit, Monk and Nun for further understanding.*

**MYSTIC KNOT**

☸ The mystic knot suggests Infinity. Traditionally it consists of 8x8 knots and is never ending. As a symbol it appears in places as far apart as China and countries of Celtic origin. The mystic knot usually appears in dreams as we are attempting to understand ourselves and our relationship with the spiritual.

♡ Mystic Knots are one of the eight Buddhist symbols that symbolize long life unaffected by setback. Their traditional meaning in Celtic lore is the interconnection of life and humankind's place within the universe. Both these meanings are highlighted in dreams and will suggest that we can live life accepting what it has to offer.

▦ Traditionally, the mystic, or in mundane terms the Gordian knot had no beginning and no end. Its basic meaning suggests an unsolvable problem. We probably need to leave such a problem until it is solved either by time or correct action.

## NAG

�} To nag almost always has a negative connotation, but when a spiritual idea or feeling keeps coming back and nagging at us we would be very wise to pay attention.

🌻 In dreams, if we are being nagged or scolded we will have recognized that we are not heeding our own inner truth.

🎑 From a mundane viewpoint, if we are nagging someone else in dreams we may actually be trying to justify our own actions. There may be a play on words here in that a nag is also an old horse, often one that does not deviate from a particular routine.

⊡ In old-fashioned parlance a nag was a scold or cantankerous old woman. If in waking life we are used to negative reinforcement, nagging may have this relevance in both men's and women's dreams.

## NAIL

🌻 Spiritually the nail represents necessity and fate. Nails also signify Ultimate Sacrifice and pain and may suggest instruments of torture, either spiritual or physical.

🌻 The penetrative power of the nail may be significant when we are having difficulty with issues of either masculinity or of sexuality.

🎑 Dreaming of nails, as in woodworking, suggests our ability to bond things together. The holding power of the nail may also be significant. Fingernails and toenails usually suggest claws or the capability of holding on.

⊡ In a man's dream nails may signify his own sense of self or his assertiveness, whereas in a woman's dream the same things are likely to be much more representative of the masculine around her.

**NAKEDNESS – *see* NUDE/NUDITY**

**NANNY – *see* NURSE**

**NARCOTIC – *see* DRUGS**

## NARROW

🌻 One-pointedness and bigotry are not qualities that are particularly spiritual, but self-discipline may require us to keep to the 'straight and narrow'.

🌻 A narrow bridge might suggest a difficulty in communication, perhaps in putting our ideas across. We should take care not to be narrow-minded and judgemental in our dealings with other people. We may be intolerant and parochial in our opinions.

⊞ When we dream of anything that is narrow, we are aware of restrictions and limitations. Sometimes we have created them ourselves, sometimes other people will have created them for us. A narrow road would perhaps suggest some kind of restriction, and a warning that we must not deviate from our path. A narrowboat highlights the meaning of a boat with the tendency to put additional restrictions in place.

*You might like to consult the entry for Boat/Ship.*

## NAUGHTY – *see* WILD

## NAVEL

✹ The navel or solar plexus is the point of connection between the spiritual and the physical. It is our emotional centre and also, as adults, initially the seat of our inherent power. Any distress in this area in dreams signifies an imbalance of energy.

♥ The navel in a dream can signify our dependency on others, particularly our mother. Often in nightmares we become conscious of something, perhaps a Devil or Demon sitting on our navel, and this can be a personification of our own fears.

⊞ To be conscious of the navel, or more subtly the solar plexus – whether our own or another's – is to be aware of the way in which we connect our inner-self with the rest of the outside world. It is through the umbilical cord that a baby in the womb first becomes aware of its physicality.

*Also consult the entries for Demon, Devil and Umbilical Cord for further information.*

## NAVY – *see* ARMED FORCES

## NAZI

✹ The figure of a Nazi still holds associations of extreme cruelty and bigotry. While the belief system was the wish for a pure race, such intense fanaticism is misplaced; it will have this significance in dreams.

♥ Emotionally such a figure will represent repression of our own emotions and often rigid self-control.

⊞ If there are circumstances in waking life under which we feel oppressed, the figure in Nazi uniform – whether male or female – will often appear.

## NECKLACE

✹ The necklace is an acknowledgement of honour and power. Prayer beads strung together are found in most religions to help with the recitations of devotions and prayers.

♥ Necklaces first arose from the wearing of a chain of office and, therefore, in dreams suggests a dignity or honour that has been conferred on the wearer.

The composition of the necklace may be an important part of the interpretation of the dream.

■ A necklace suggests a special object, and thus translates into special qualities or attributes. There is a richness to be acknowledged. This may be of feeling or of emotion. An old interpretation of a man giving a woman a necklace was that he would soon ask for her hand in marriage.

*You might also like to consult the entries for Beads and Gems/Jewels.*

## NEEDLE

☀ The needle can often suggest masculine sexuality, but also the type of penetrating insight that changes our view of life. A sewing needle will suggest spiritual repair, a knitting needle may suggest creativity and a hypodermic healing, or sometimes self-harm.

♡ The ability to have some penetrating insights about our own state of being can help us to cope with everyday life. It will depend if the needles are being used by us or on us in dreams. By us suggests that we have a need for others to share our viewpoint; on us suggests that we must internalize some kind of knowledge, unpleasant or otherwise, before matters improve.

■ In dreams hypodermic needles suggest irritations, but can also signify the power to heal through penetration. A concept or knowledge has to be introduced from the outside, which may hurt, but will ultimately improve our wellbeing.

⟨⟩ In a woman's dream using needles will probably require assessment of her more creative aspects, whereas for a man the assessment will be of his softer skills such as communication, listening and negotiation.

*Consult the entries for Inject/Injection and Syringe for further information.*

**NEGATIVE/NEGATIVITY** – *see* **THE INTRODUCTION AND REFUSE**

**NEIGHBOUR** – *see* **PEOPLE**

**NEPHEW** – *see* **EXTENDED FAMILY IN FAMILY**

## NEST

☀ The spiritual significance of a nest is that of security within our known environment.

♡ It is perhaps interesting to note that just before giving birth many women have what is known as a nesting instinct, the need to clean, tidy and make ready. This will sometimes emerge in dreams before it is recognized in waking life.

■ The nest symbolizes safety and perhaps home life. We may be emotionally dependent on the people around us and afraid of 'leaving the nest'. A nest egg was initially a device to improve a hen's ability to lay eggs and carries with it the idea in dreams of improving a situation.

## NET/NETWORK

🌞 A network, like a spider's web, symbolizes relationships unlimited in their scope.

💗 Women are often more able to create a network of 'sisters' through the use of intuition, and often will symbolize this in their dreams as a tangible bonding. In modern day technological parlance a network – particularly the internet – suggests a number of people working or playing together with a common aim

🔲 A net in dreams usually indicates that we are feeling trapped and entangled in a scheme or situation. A network, on the other hand, may be more supportive.

🔳 In a woman's dream she will be aware of her own seductive power, whereas in a man's dream he will be conscious of his fear of women. As old crafts die out, the physical act of netting as the old fisherwomen did has less relevance. In olden times it was said that a witch could catch the wind in a net.

*Also consult the entry for Web.*

## NEW

🌞 What seems to be new to us may be information that comes to us at the right time to enable us to progress spiritually. It has impact because we have not previously been aware of it.

💗 To be doing something new in a dream highlights the potential in a fresh learning situation. We are stimulated and excited initially. When we first move into a new situation in waking life our dreams can highlight our fears and difficulties. We may often dream of possible scenarios where we are not functioning as well as we should, or of actions we might take to enhance our performance.

🔲 Dreaming of something that is new suggests a new beginning, a new way of looking at or dealing with situations, or perhaps even a new relationship. Thus, new shoes might suggest either a different way forward or a way of connecting with the earth. A new hat might suggest a novel intellectual approach, whereas new spectacles indicate a fresh way of seeing things.

## NEW YEAR

🌞 Spiritually, in any culture, the New Year with its attendant celebrations can signify enlightenment or new knowledge becoming available. We are no longer in the depths of darkness.

💗 Psychologically, when there is a need for renewal or a new growth in understanding, we need to acknowledge the effort we must make. This is often symbolized as a New Year, a new beginning.

To dream of the New Year is to recognize the need for a fresh start. It may also signify the measurement of time in a way that is acceptable, or a time when something can happen.

## NEWSPAPER

Spiritually, we should be aware that what we do needs to be for the Greater Good. We probably need to be more publicly visible, though we are not particularly comfortable with this.

Newspapers in dreams signify new information available to us of which we are now aware rather than it being held subconsciously. A blank page in a newspaper can have two meanings: firstly, the information may not be available to us for various reasons; secondly, it may be for us to provide the information for other people to make use of.

Largely in dreams a newspaper will suggest knowledge that is in the public domain. It might be information that we require in order to make sense of the world around us, or something that is specific to us. A tabloid newspaper in theory may suggest sensational material, whereas a quality one would suggest better researched data. A Sunday newspaper indicates that we have the ability to assimilate the knowledge we need in periods of rest and relaxation. A local newspaper signifies that the facts we require are close to hand.

*You might like to consult the entries for Communication and Media.*

## NICHE

The niche in most religions is consecrated so that it itself is a fit place to contain the Divine. It then symbolizes the holiness and special powers relevant to the particular deity. If an icon is placed within the niche, then the god or goddess is there also.

In new situations we have a need to understand the world we are entering. Often our dream scenarios can open up possibilities by showing us what niche we need to find for ourselves. Not only must we find the space where we belong but we must also know which external factors are going to help us and which will hinder. Dream images connected with the niche will give us such information.

Everyone has a basic need to belong and often we are conscious in dreams of finding our particular place. It manifests itself in dreams as a place where we are protected on all sides except from the front. It has been suggested that this is a return to the childhood state prior to the age of four, when the child begins to realize that he is vulnerable from the rear. A niche is, therefore, our 'spot' – the place where we are safe.

*Consult the entries for Icon and God/Gods for further information.*

**NIECE** – *see* **EXTENDED FAMILY IN FAMILY**

**NIGHT**

🌑 Night symbolizes the intense darkness that occurs before rebirth or initiation. There is a disintegration, which has to occur before there can be any possibility of enlightenment. Night can also signify death or drastic change.

💗 Physiologically, night is a time when the body is supposed to be renewing itself. Dreams at different times of the night may highlight emotions formerly associated with various organs.

🔲 Night signifies a period of rest and relaxation, both in dreams and in ordinary life. It can, however, also suggest a time of chaos and difficulty. More positively, it is a period that allows us to create a new beginning with the dawning of the new day. Used constructively, night is, therefore, the fallow period before fresh growth.

*Also consult also the entries for Dawn/Day and Night and Time.*

**NIMBUS** – *see* **AURA AND HALO**

**NO** – *see* **REFUSE**

**NOAH/NOAH'S ARK** – *see* **SPIRITUAL IMAGERY IN THE INTRODUCTION**

**NOISE**

🌑 Any noise in dreams is a way of catching our attention, of focusing our minds. 'White noise' is a noise containing all of the audible frequencies of vibration; it is a good 'masking' agent when meditating or preparing for sleep used as a spiritual discipline.

💗 Any external noise can often be incorporated into dreams as part of the dream content. A bell ringing, for instance, might become a school bell.

🔲 When we hear a strange noise in our dreams, we can expect the unexpected and the unknown in waking life.

**NOMINATE/NOMINATION**

🌑 To nominate or be nominated suggests calling or being called for a special task often of a spiritual nature.

💗 When in dreams we are nominated by someone we perhaps should look at the level of commitment we have to our various tasks. When we are nominating someone else, it may be that we do not feel up to a particular emotional responsibility.

🔲 From a purely mundane perspective a nomination is quite literally a naming, so a dream where this occurs may have a great deal to do with who we think we are.

*You might also like to consult the entry for Vote for further clarification.*

**NOOSE**

At its simplest, the noose represents a traumatic death. In a more complex sense it can represent the binding – or capturing – of spiritual intent, and the harnessing of spiritual energy.

A noose, like the halter, harness and other symbols of restraint, suggests the taming of a perhaps wild untamed part of our personality. A noose can also imply the prevention of self-expression.

A noose in a dream suggests that we have a fear of being trapped, perhaps by others' actions. We are also aware that we can create a trap for ourselves, thereby 'putting a noose round our own necks'. Traditionally, a drawing of a hangman's noose was a threat of death and it can still have that association in dreams. As always, this 'death' may be of part of our personality being unduly restrained. For a young woman wishing to leave home, a noose might represent a fear of becoming trapped in the parental home.

*Also consult the entries for Halter, Hang/Hanging, Harness and Rope.*

**NORTH**

The North in spiritual terms suggests the winter, a time for old age and reflection. The Archangel is normally Uriel, administrator of Peace, but sometimes Ariel, Keeper of Wisdom.

We are looking towards night-time and rest and the right to use the wisdom we have accrued. The magical element is Earth and the color white. There is often the completion of a cycle associated with dreams of the North.

When we dream specifically of the North, we are searching for patience and understanding. We need firm foundations.

**NOURISHMENT/NURTURING**

The symbolism of nourishing the soul and conferring immortality all belong to the nurturing function of the Mother Goddess.

All symbols of containment (the vessel, cup, cauldron, bowl etc.) are symbols of nurturing and femininity. Food-producing animals are also associated with the nourishing aspects of the mother and, therefore, of Mother Earth.

In dreams, all symbols of nourishment are associated with basic needs. Firstly, we require warmth and comfort; secondly, shelter and sustenance. Initially we experience this as coming from mother. Any dream in which we become aware of our needs then has an impact on our relationship with mother. If our need for nourishment and nurturing is not met we experience rejection and hurt. In dreams these things become interchangeable.

Nourishing and nurturing are such intrinsically feminine functions that any dream containing such images are to do with survival. For a woman, nurturing is perhaps more physical in feeling, whereas for a man, his focus will be on growth to maturity.

*You might also like to consult the entries for Food and Fruit.*

## NUCLEAR EXPLOSION

🔅 Spiritually, a nuclear explosion would suggest a discharge of power, which, if not handled properly, could be destructive. Treated carelessly, that power can destroy ourselves as well as others.

💚 When we have suppressed certain parts of our personality rather than handling them, there may be some type of synergy (combined energy) that can become destructive. We would be alerted to this by dreaming of causing a nuclear explosion. The threat of such a huge explosion is enough to generate fear, sometimes unfounded.

🔳 A nuclear explosion is not always an act of war, but can sometimes be accidental. Such an accident can unintentionally have very far-reaching effects. To dream of a nuclear explosion can highlight our anxiety about great change in our lives. We do not yet know what effect that change may have. We do, however, know we must undertake radical change, but would prefer it to be a more gradual process.

*Also consult the entries for Apocalypse, Atom Bomb and Bomb.*

## NUDE/NUDITY

🔅 Nudity often suggests a new beginning, a rebirth, stripping away the non-essential. It is the paradise state and the state of natural innocence we all, at one time, had. It can also represent renunciation of the material world.

💚 Nudity signifies innocence. It may be that there is a situation in our lives that requires honesty and truth. If we are sufficiently secure within our own self-image, we will not be afraid of being 'stripped' in public. Dreaming of appearing nude, for instance in a strip show, could suggest we have anxiety about being misunderstood.

🔳 Freud assumed that dreaming of being nude was linked with sexuality. It is, however, more to do with self-image. We have a desire to be seen for what we are, to reveal our essential personality without having to create a facade. To interpret a dream of walking down a street naked will depend on whether we are seen by other people or not. If we are seen by others, there may be something about ourselves that we wish to reveal. If we are alone we may simply have a wish for freedom of expression

▸ For both men and women, returning to a sense of innocent pleasure and appreciation of the human body can be perceived in dreams as nudity. If in dreaming of someone of the opposite sex they are naked but we are not, they may be more vulnerable than we are.

**NUGGET –** *see* **METAL**

**NUMBERS**

When numbers are drawn to our attention in dreams they can have either a personal or a symbolic significance. Often a number will appear that has personal meaning, such as a particular date, or the number of a house we have lived in. Our minds will often retain the significance of the number even though we do not necessarily consciously remember it ourselves.

🔅 Spiritually, as we progress we put ourselves in a position to make the best use of the vibratory effect of numbers. It has long been accepted that by combining numbers in certain ways, influence can be brought to bear on our environment. The more esoteric interpretations are:

**One –** oneself, the Beginning, the first, Unity.

**Two –** duality, indecision, balance, male vs. female, two sides to an argument, opposites.

**Three –** the Trinity, freedom.

**Four –** the square, strength, stability practicality, the earth, reality, the four sides of human nature: sensation, feeling, thought, intuition. The Elements of Earth, Air, Fire and Water.

**Five –** the human body, human consciousness in the body, the five senses.

**Six –** harmony or balance.

**Seven –** cycles of life, magical, spiritual meaning; human wholeness.

**Eight –** death and resurrection, Infinity.

**Nine –** pregnancy, the end of any cycle and the start of something new, spiritual awareness.

**Ten –** new beginnings, the male and female together.

**Eleven –** eleventh hour, the Master Number.

**Twelve –** Time, a full cycle or wholeness.

**Zero –** the Feminine, the Great Mother, the Unconscious, the Absolute or hidden completeness.

🛡 Symbolically, numbers have some kind of significance in all systems of belief and religions. Below are the most often found meanings; the positive qualities are given first, followed by the more negative:

**One –** independence, self-respect, resolve, singleness of purpose. Intolerance, conceit, narrow-mindedness, degradation, stubbornness.

**Two –** placidity, integrity, unselfishness, gregariousness, harmony. Indecision, indifference, lack of responsibility, bloody-mindedness.

**Three –** freedom, bravery, fun, enthusiasm, brilliance. Listlessness, over-confidence, impatience, lackadaisical behaviour.

**Four** – loyalty, stolidity, practicality, honesty. Clumsiness, dullness, conservatism, inability to adapt.

**Five** – adventurousness, vivaciousness, courage, health, susceptibility, sympathy. Rashness, irresponsibility, inconstancy, unreliability, thoughtlessness.

**Six** – idealism, selflessness, honesty, charitableness, faithfulness, responsibility. Superiority, softness, impracticality, submission.

**Seven** – wisdom, discernment, philosophy, fortitude, depth, contemplation. Morbidity, hypercriticism, lack of action, unsociability.

**Eight** – practicality, power, business ability, decision, control, constancy. Unimaginativeness, bluntness, self-sufficiency, domination.

**Nine** – intelligence, discretion, artistry, understanding, brilliance, lofty moral sense, genius. Dreaminess, lethargy, lack of concentration, aimlessness.

🔲 Many people do not realize that numbers can be extremely significant in everyday life. A knowledge of numbers will enhance your ability to interpret your dreams successfully.

## NUN

🔆 In today's somewhat promiscuous society it is unlikely that we will dream of virgins. Nuns, however, as holy women epitomize devotion to the Divine and as a feminine archetype signify the Priestess, one who has a spiritually satisfying relationship with God.

💚 The nun, as a woman who has dedicated her life to service of her God, signifies our emotional need to commit to something beyond ourselves.

🔲 For many, whose experiences of nuns in real life have not been pleasant, they will be figures of fear and disciplinary action. For others, nuns will symbolize the devoted caring of which they are capable.

*Also consult the entries for Mystic and Caring Professions in People as well as the information on Priestess in Archetypes in the Introduction.*

## NURSE/NURSING

🔆 To nurse originally meant to suckle, to keep alive, and for this reason spiritually signifies the nourishing aspect of the Great Mother.

💚 The figure of a nurse in dreams will suggest either that part of our character which cares for others who are sick, or that part of us which is off-balance and needs particular nurturing at this time.

🔲 From an everyday perspective a nurse suggests that all is not well with a project or task and some kind of corrective care is needed. As the profession of nursing is given less status, the uniform unfortunately becomes less relevant than it once was.

*Also consult the entries for Doctor, Hospital, Ill/Illness, Medicine/Medication and*

*Caring Professions in People as well as the information on Great Mother in Archetypes in the Introduction.*

**NUT**

🔆 Nuts were reputed to be the food of the Gods, and so spiritually enhance the psychic powers. Edible nuts, because of their shape, have significance as inner nourishment.

♥ It was thought that nuts fed the brain, thus giving wisdom. They can still have this significance in dreams. Again, because of their shape, there is a connection with masculine sexuality and fertility. To dream of nuts may suggest that we are trying to de-personalize issues to do with sexuality.

▦ To dream of a metal nut, as in nuts and bolts, is highlighting our ability to construct our lives in such a way that it will hold together. In engineering terms a nut is considered to be feminine, and the screw masculine.

⊟ Because of their association with fertility and divinity these significances can surface in both men's and women's dreams as they move towards a more spiritual understanding of life.

**NYMPHS**

🔆 Nymphs are Earth spirits that deal with pure energy. Their charm is their youthfulness, beauty and vitality. Their significance spiritually is that they epitomize most of the feminine qualities in their purest states.

♥ Psychologically the nymph most clearly has associations with the princess. She is the carefree, fun-loving aspect of energy that glories in movement and light. As pure energy, when we work with dreams, the nymph allows us the opportunity to connect to the qualities of purity and grace.

▦ Nymphs are personifications of feminine universal productivity. They have an innocent and carefree energy, which is naive and clear. They tend to be guardians of sacred spaces such as woods, mountains and lakes, and often manifest in dreams as such.

⊟ In dreams nymphs are connected with a woman's sense of beauty and her own femininity. Each group of nymphs has their own particular role and guardianship of specific areas, such as forests and lakes, woods and valleys, mountains and grottoes, which has a certain resonance with different aspects of our personality. In a man's dream nymphs will often represent a perception of innocence.

*Also consult the entry for Fairy as well as the information on Princess in Archetypes in the Introduction and in the People entry.*

**OAK** – *see* **TREES**

**OAR**

🌞 An oar, being a tool that both propels us forward and allows us to move in a particular direction, signifies a spiritual guiding principle.

♡ To 'put our oar in' indicates our ability to interfere with other people's lives. To lose an oar indicates the loss of an ability we have formerly valued.

▦ The oar is a tool that enables a boat to move forward successfully, but its use requires some skill. Thus it stands for our own set of personal skills. We have certain skills that help us to 'navigate' our lives.

⊟ In dreams, a woman is more likely to be passive when an oar is used. If she is using the oars she is in control of any final decision. In a man's dream, since rowing faces away from the direction of travel, he must perhaps trust his own judgement.

*You might like to consult the entries for Boat/Ship, Journey and Transport for further clarification.*

**OASIS**

🌞 An oasis, in spiritual terms, represents refreshment and the idea of being able to put difficulties to one side for a time.

♡ Most people see an oasis as a place of refuge in a desert. Because of its association with water, in dreams it becomes a place where we can give and receive whatever emotional refreshment is required.

▦ When people are in difficulty, they need a place where they can express themselves – or perhaps renew their own strengths and ability to cope. In dreams, an oasis, particularly when we are lost, represents such a place. It highlights a particular type of sanctuary.

*You might also like to consult the entries for Desert, Lose/Loss/Lost and Water.*

**OATH** – *see* **PROMISE AND VOW**

**OBEDIENCE/OBEY**

🌞 To be obedient, in the spiritual sense, suggests an acceptance of the principle of the Greater Good, and the recognition that our individual struggles are a necessary part of our development.

♡ If we find ourselves in the position of being obedient to someone we know in an unexpected situation, we can often expect to have an easier relationship with them in the future; perhaps because we are able to acknowledge them in a different way.

When in dreams we expect obedience from someone, we are acknowledging our own power and authority over others. To dream of having to be obedient to others indicates we are aware of their greater authority and knowledge, and also that a degree of disempowerment has occurred.

## OBELISK

An obelisk is often representative of a Sacred Stone, a marker outlining a particular area such as a sacred space, helping us to be clear regarding our spiritual beliefs or marking a particularly sacred area within which it is safe to practise our spiritual beliefs.

An obelisk is a man-made needle-shaped stone, larger at the bottom than the top. It is usually taken today to indicate old instinctive knowledge – man reaching for the unknown. In dreams it suggests just that.

Any carved stone appearing in a dream suggests we are considering how we have shaped our own basic nature. The simpler it is, the more room we have for improvement; the more ornate it is, the more successful we are at using our creative energy.

Because of its shape, the obelisk obviously has phallic connotations. In both men's and women's dreams it may also represent a hard unforgiving 'core' within the personality.

*Also consult the entries for Needle and Stone.*

## OBESE – *see* FAT

## OBJECT/OBJECTION

An object in dreams can often give tangibility to spiritual concepts. A cross, for instance, will suggests sacrifice to some, conviction to others and refusal to even more. To object to something suggests that we cannot accept information given at this time.

To object to or disagree with a statement or idea in dreams suggests that we may have already formed an opinion in waking life or that the statement opposes our own code of conduct. From an emotional perspective we cannot make a commitment.

Often in waking life we are unable to speak out against an injustice or a wrong move. Our dreams will often give us the opportunity to object or protest against such things.

*Also consult the entry for Opponent/Oppose.*

## OBSCURE/OBSCURITY

Obscurity originally signified the absence of light, so spiritually has that connotation. The truth has not yet been revealed.

When we have not clarified how we feel about something, a representative image can often be obscured in dreams.

⊞ In the sense of being dark or dim, anything obscured in dreams requires us to uncover what is hidden and to discover the relevance in everyday life. We may not have the full facts of a situation. If we are able to admit in waking life that something is unknown, an image in recurring dreams, which has previously been obscured, becomes clear.

**OBSERVE – *see* WATCHING AND WITNESS**

**OBSESSION**

🜚 Obsessive behaviour, regarded from a spiritual perspective, would indicate an imperfect link between the spiritual and the physical realms. Spiritual possession was once seen to manifest as obsession. A real-life stalker will be acting out the belief that they have the 'right' to possess their victim.

♥ Obsessive or repetitive behaviour in dreams is often used to ensure that we have fully understood the message being conveyed by the unconscious.

⊞ Obsession is an unnatural focusing on a feeling, belief or object, and may simply indicate that we need to take time to work a difficulty through. There is often anxiety about a past occasion or deed, with which we have not been able, or allowed, to deal. When such an unnatural feeling appears in dreams we can appreciate how harmful this can be.

**OBSTACLE/OBSTRUCT/OBSTRUCTION**

🜚 Difficulty, indecision and doubt are the three main blocks we will come up against in any spiritual journey or quest. We will have to overcome each of these blocks at some time if we are finally to achieve our spiritual goal. Indecision and self-doubt can often translate themselves in dreams into actual physical objects, and the difficulty manifests in how we deal with these obstructions.

♥ At times, our own inhibitions and anxieties cannot be faced unless they are first given tangible forms in dreams. In allowing ourselves a visual representation, these anxieties can become more manageable. What has seemed to be a huge obstacle in dreams can be consciously made smaller until we feel capable of dealing with it. For example, a patch of weeds in dreams might be cut back until we can continue on our way.

⊞ Obstacles and obstructions in dreams can take many forms – a wall, a hill, a dark forest perhaps. The object will be symbolic of the problem in waking life. Largely we are aware that these obstacles need to be overcome. How we do this in a dream can often suggest how to tackle a problem in everyday life.

*You might like to consult the entries for Block and Quest for further clarification.*

**OCEAN** – *see* BAY AND WATER
**OCTAGON** – *see* SHAPES/PATTERNS
**ODOUR**

&#9673; If a sweet odour is particularly noticeable in dreams it will signify saintliness and spirituality. Traditionally, incense and other sweet smelling herbs are ways of connecting with the Divine and will have this meaning in dreams.

&#9672; Our sense of smell is extremely delicate, but just as the other senses such as touch and sound are suspended or transmuted into something slightly different in dreams, an odour in a dream may be a way of reminding ourselves of another time or place. Odour is highly evocative and for the dreaming self to register a known smell or perfume suggests that we are trying to make some sort of connection with conditions we have known in the past.

&#9635; If there is an odour in a dream at all and we become aware of it, it is usually highly significant. If it is a pleasant one it suggests good times; if a bad one then it is more likely to be a warning of bad things.

*Also consult the entries for Incense and Smell.*

**OFFENCE/OFFEND**

&#9673; A suggestion of spiritual wrongdoing may be relevant. A sin is a moral evil, but a wrongdoing is less culpable and in dreams may simply manifest as a warning, which allows us to assess the seriousness of the offence in waking life and then to act accordingly.

&#9672; To be committing an offence suggests that we are not, either consciously or unconsciously, following our own code of moral behaviour. We have put ourselves outside the norms of society.

&#9635; To take offence in a dream is to allow a display of emotion and feeling about our own sensitivity, which may not be appropriate in waking life. To give offence to someone in a dream is to recognize that we are not as aware of other people's feelings as we should be.

*Consult the entries for Burglar, Intruder and Vice for more information.*

**OFFICER/OFFICIAL** – *see* ARMED FORCES AND ALSO AUTHORITY FIGURES IN PEOPLE
**OGRE** – *see* GIANT AND MONSTER
**OIL**

&#9673; Oil, particularly that containing fine perfumes, represents consecration and dedication. Chrism or Holy Oil is of the highest spiritual vibration. Initiates were anointed (literally, smeared with oil) to signify that they were especially blessed and oil will often have this significance in dreams.

&#9672; Psychologically, we may recognize that a situation can only be dealt with by removing the stress – 'pour oil on troubled water'. Ointment was initially either oil- or grease-based, so today to dream of massage oil or ointment suggests caring and pampering.

▣ It will depend on which type of oil is being used in the dream. Cooking oil, for instance, will often signify the removal of friction, or a way of combining different components, whereas engine oil will highlight our ability to keep things moving. As the world becomes more polluted by petroleum oil products, dreams of oil may suggest contamination rather than purity.

*You might also like to consult the entries for Engine and Odour.*

## OINTMENT – *see* HEAL/HEALING AND MEDICINE

## OLD

✿ The Wise Old Man is a part of ourselves, which is not always consciously available to us. An old man appearing in our dreams puts us in touch with this part of ourselves. He can also represent our feelings about time and death.

♡ Old people in dreams tend to suggest traditional thought or wisdom arising from experience. We may also need to consider our attitude to death. Old buildings can signify a past way of life, which we thought we had left behind. Antiques will often represent elements of our past experience, which might be worth keeping. If something seems particularly ancient, the meaning may be ambiguous; either it has outlived its usefulness or has been imbued with special significance because of its antiquity.

▣ When we dream of old things, we are touching into the past and perhaps need to bring some kind of knowledge forward, so that we can make use of it in the present day. Dreaming of historical figures usually means we are aware of the qualities that those people possessed. Perhaps we need to develop those qualities within ourselves.

*Also consult the entries for Death, Museum and People as well as Wise Old Man in Archetypes in the Introduction.*

## OLYMPICS – *see* GAMES, RITUAL AND SPORT

## ONION

✿ In its many-layered aspect the onion symbolizes the Cosmos, and revelation. In dreams, we find that what we are doing with the onion reveals our intrinsic way of exploring creation. In removing each layer we come to an understanding of how we create from small to large.

♡ Chopping onions can signify an attempt to increase the energy available to us in some way. We quite literally want to ensure that we have allowed the essence of our being to permeate throughout our lives. As a reflection of the various levels of understanding we explore as we mature, the onion provides an apt symbol. If the onion is dried or dried up we have to make more emotional effort to understand.

▣ Oddly enough, the onion can appear in dreams and meditation as a symbol of wholeness, but a wholeness that is many-layered. Peeling an onion can suggest trying to find the best part of ourselves, or of somebody else. It may also indicate attempting to understand the various facets of our own personality.

*Consult the entry for Food for further information.*

**OPAL** – *see* **GEMS/JEWELS**

**OPERATION**

🕯 An operation is a carefully planned procedure, whether that is a military or surgical one. Spiritually, therefore, it represents incisive healing, or the restoration of equilibrium. An operation in dreams can, therefore, highlight the need for healing of the spirit, the eradication of 'dis-ease'.

♥ If we are performing an operation we are recognizing our own level of skill within a situation in waking life. If the operation is being performed on us we are attempting to access some inner knowledge but are possibly fearful of the outcome. Modern surgical methods are less invasive than early surgery and when these appear in dreams will suggest more subtle ways of managing distress.

▣ An operation in hospital is usually frightening and invasive. In dreams it can signify our awareness of our own fears of illness and pain, but also a recognition of our need to be healed on some level. A military operation signifies the need for careful planning and management and the establishing of order.

*Also consult the entries for Heal/Healing, Hospital, Surgery, Waiting and War.*

**OPPONENT/OPPOSE**

🕯 An opponent in dreams, from a spiritual perspective, is that part of us that is not co-operating in the grand scheme of things and is, therefore, introducing an element of negativity. It is also, as we become more aware, negative elements, which we may be required to confront and overcome, or at worst understand, before there can be progress.

♥ When we find ourselves opposed to someone in dreams, we often have some kind of emotional difficulty, which prevents us from understanding a conflict within ourselves. Once identified, we are able to resolve our problem in waking life.

▣ In mundane terms, any conflict in waking life could manifest as a personalized opponent or as opposition in dreams. How that opponent presents itself will often give us the information we need to deal with the problem. For instance, an imp as an opponent might mean that we will have to deal with minor irritations first.

**OPPOSITE –** *see* **POSITION**

**ORACLE**

   ❁ An oracle is a divine pronouncement and, therefore, suggests Hidden Knowledge. Prediction and foretelling both work on the assumption that the person concerned has received knowledge prior to the event.

   ❤ The need to know is very strong and the assumption is that an oracle – in this case an actual person – has more information than we do. Often that information has to be unscrambled, since particularly in dreams, it is presented in odd ways. Sometimes it cannot be made sense of until such time as we have considered it in waking life, taking into consideration our own personal circumstances.

   ▦ Most of us like to know what is going to happen to us and also like to be told what to do, so dreaming of an oracle links us with that part of ourselves that knows what our next moves are. Often an oracle can appear as a person, for instance as a goddess or wise old man, or we can dream that we are using one of the many systems of prediction that are available in everyday life.

**ORANGE –** *see* **COLOUR AND FRUIT**

**ORCHARD –** *see* **TREE/TREES**

**ORCHESTRA/ORCHESTRATE**

   ❁ Originally a place where dancers and musicians gathered, an orchestra now symbolizes the group of musicians itself. Such an image suggests that we are capable of operating in spiritual harmony.

   ❤ When we wish to orchestrate something, we want to make it happen. This means that we must take action that enables us to be heard and to have people understand us. When we find we are conducting an orchestra in a dream, we feel we can accept we are in control. When we are a member of an orchestra we are simply part of a greater task.

   ▦ We all have certain aspects of our personality that must work in harmony with one another for us to function properly. Dreaming of an orchestra represents ways in which we are capable of bringing all those aspects together and making a coherent whole. A discordant orchestra suggests that we have not succeeded in integrating all aspects successfully. A disciplined orchestra suggests that we have succeeded in that integration.

*You might also like to consult the entries for Music/Rhythm and Musical Instruments.*

**ORDER**

   ❁ Spiritually, to be trying to establish order suggests that we are attempting to make sense of something. We are trying to establish a logical progression when apparently there is no such thing. To be in holy orders suggests that we are imposing a degree of discipline on ourselves.

❤ Ordering others around in dreams suggests that we recognize the need for leadership. Emotions that are under pressure or difficulty can cause havoc in our lives. Dreams will often help us to establish a natural order by reflecting the order and method we need to deal with such chaos.

🔲 Lists and such techniques help us to maintain order in our everyday lives, Dreaming of such things often allows us to prioritize basic tasks. In dreams, finding that we are being ordered to do something suggests that we have instinctively recognized a greater authority.

*You might also like to consult the entries for Chaos, List, Nun and Monk for further information.*

**ORE – *see* METAL**

**ORGAN**

🌑 In theory, perfect health of mind and body would be possible provided we understood the workings of the physical body – how the organs inter-relate. Spiritually, if through dreams we can become aware of what perfect is, then self-healing ensures proper working of the organs. A musical organ has a richness of sound that is capable of changing a person's consciousness, so in dreams will tend to highlight or heighten our views and feelings about union with the Divine.

❤ In Chinese medicine, the different organs of the body represent different qualities. For instance, the gall bladder deals with the ability to make decisions, while the liver is the seat of irritability. In dreams, therefore, being conscious of a bodily organ would require us to be aware of what is bothering us and learning how to deal with it in an appropriate manner in waking life.

🔲 The various organs of the body can represent the different aspects of the self. In dreams they can signify diverse weaknesses and strengths. A musical organ, having many systems to produce sound, often symbolizes the bodily organs. Anything that is organic is characterized by a natural arrangement of parts, so in dreams comes to mean anything that is natural rather than manufactured. To dream we are growing food that is organic suggests we need to pay attention to the quality of our lives.

**ORGY**

🌑 An orgy was initially an esoteric religious ritual, characterized by wild dancing, singing and drinking. It has, therefore, from a spiritual perspective, come to mean any spiritual excess.

❤ Behaviour that would not necessarily be appropriate in ordinary, everyday life can be used in dreams to balance a difficulty. Since many people struggle with their self image, which can be closely connected with their sexuality, dreaming of an orgy or licentious behaviour can indicate the way in which we can release the blocked energy.

🔲 An orgy relates to a tremendous release of energy, which can take place when we give ourselves permission to access our own basic passion. This permission will often be given subconsciously first, and can be expressed in dreams more fully than we would allow ourselves to do in everyday life. To dream of an orgy can also highlight the way we relate to other people. The need for other people to love and understand us is quite strong and, when seen as an orgy, can perhaps indicate that we are afraid of loss of control.

⊞ While most people will think of an orgy as being sexual in nature, in dreams it is more about letting go of our inhibitions. In a woman's dream an orgy may show her a way of releasing her emotional hang-ups, whereas for a man it may be more about being able to express himself properly.

**ORIENT** – *see* **INDIGENOUS PEOPLES**

**ORPHAN**

❀ From a spiritual perspective the one thing that we all fear is rejection. To dream of being an orphan highlights this spiritual desertion, a moving away from Source into the uncharted waters of being human.

♥ We have to come to terms with our ability to grow up and to move away from our parents. When our lives force us into losing them at any age, either through death or other circumstances such as moving away, we may experience the feeling of being orphaned.

🔲 To dream of an orphan indicates that we may be feeling vulnerable and possibly abandoned and unloved. If we are looking after an orphan we are attempting to heal that part of us that feels unloved. If we experience ourselves as having been orphaned it may indicate that we need to be more independent and self-sufficient.

*Consult the entry for Family for further information.*

**OSTEOPATH** – *see* **THERAPY/THERAPIST**

**OSTRICH** – *see* **BIRDS**

**OTTER** – *see* **ANIMALS**

**OUIJA BOARD**

❀ Spiritually, the ouija board was – and indeed still is – a rather crude way of communicating with the spirit world. In dreams, it shows we may be aware of our need to communicate with spirit, rather than have the spirit world communicate with us. We are the instigators of communication.

♥ Psychologically, we all need some way of making contact with the unconscious side of ourselves. To dream of the ouija board alerts us to different ways of accessing the unconscious. It may be a symbol for all we have suppressed and refused to recognize.

⬛ The use of the ouija board holds within it certain inherent dangers. Dreaming of one may simply be a way that the psyche has of alerting us to further exploration of those things we do not understand. To be playing with the ouija board in dreams – as well as in waking life – denotes being prepared to take certain risks, particularly with our own peace of mind. When the ouija board seems frightening we are touching in on our deep fear of the unknown.

## OUROBOROS – *see* SPIRITUAL IMAGERY IN THE INTRODUCTION

## OUT/OUTSIDE

☀ Any sense of being outside in dreams – in the open air – will suggest a degree of spiritual freedom. We are free from the restrictions of the mundane world.

♥ Being shut out suggests rejection by others but if we ourselves are shutting something out then we are not prepared to include what is represented in our lives.

⬛ In the mundane world a sense of not belonging to a peer group can lead to a feeling of isolation, of being an outcast. In waking life we are aware of restrictions and boundaries that are not necessarily self-imposed. Any sense of being beyond some kind of boundary can mean one of two things: either we have deliberately put ourselves 'beyond the pale' or we have inadvertently offended against the rules of the society or group.

## OUTLAW – *see* THIEF

## OUTLINE

☀ Spiritually, to be conscious of a line marking the perimeter of an object suggests that we are recognizing a duality – the existence of two things. To be outlining an idea suggests that we have some basic concepts that are worth exploring.

♥ An outline is usually a brief statement of intent, and with practice in dreams we are often able to formulate such a statement. An outline document in dreams can symbolize this. The problem is that when we wake up, unless we are used to recording our dreams, such a statement of intended action can be lost.

⬛ An outline in dreams is intended to give emphasis or to mark the edge of something. Under these circumstances we should consider our actions in waking life a little more carefully.

## OVAL – *see* SHAPES/PATTERNS

## OVEN

☀ The oven's function of cooking represents spiritual change – the transformation of raw basic ingredients or qualities into something usable.

It thus suggests spiritual transmutation through the application of heat (fire).

⚕ As a hollow object, in dreams an oven can also represent the womb. With its ability to change ingredients into something else, the oven can also represent the process of gestation and birth. In dreams, this can suggest the ability to transform character traits and behaviour from something coarse to the more refined.

▨ An oven is representative of the human ability to deliberately start a process of the adaptation of raw material into something that is functional. This can apply within a work situation, for instance at the beginning of a project or in personal life. The oven thus symbolizes a creative process.

⊡ In a woman's dream a warm oven might signify her willingness to become pregnant or to begin a new relationship. In a man's dream it might signify positive change.

*You might also like to consult the entries for Bake/Baker/Bakery, Fire and Kitchen.*

**OVERDOSE** – *see* **ALCOHOL/ALCOHOLIC, DRUGS AND DRUNK**

**OVERFLOW** – *see* **WATER**

**OWE** – *see* **DEBT**

**OWL** – *see* **BIRDS**

**OX** – *see* **ANIMALS**

**OYSTER**

✸ The oyster represents spiritual transformation. In nature it is almost unique because of its ability to transform a grain of sand into a pearl. It is this quality that tends to be brought to notice in dreams to demonstrate how we can change an irritant into something beautiful. We can spiritualize it.

⚕ The oyster symbolizes our ability to make use of difficulty and negativity and create a new positive focus. In dealing with an irritant we are able to protect ourselves from further harm.

▨ Practically, the oyster is reputed to be an aphrodisiac food; in fact, this is because of its high zinc content, which affects the production of semen. For this reason a dream about oysters may be highlighting fertility issues. In dreams, as nowadays they can be expensive, they may well also represent the act of seduction.

⊡ In a woman's dream oysters may signify seduction, but can also suggest sacrifice. Hypatia, an Alexandrian mathematician and philosopher, was flayed to death by Christians using oyster shells in 415 CE for her beliefs. In a man's dream, oysters themselves may symbolize his own sexuality.

*You might also like to consult the entries for Food, Sacrifices and Sand.*

**PACKAGE** – *see* **PARCEL**

**PACKING**

🔆 With packing, as with any act of preparation, we need to make a choice about what spiritual information needs to be retained and what is relevant for the task in hand.

♥ We need to establish some kind of order in our lives. To dream of packing suggests an internal selection process must be undertaken in order to decide what is important to us. To dream of unpacking suggests qualities which may have been hidden from view.

🔲 When we dream of packing suitcases, as though going on a journey, we are highlighting the need to prepare carefully for the next stage of our lives. There is a need, or want, to get away from past ideas and difficulties. To be packing a precious object very carefully indicates we are aware of the intrinsic value to ourselves, or others, of what is represented by that object.

*You might like to consult the entries for Baggage, Luggage and Wadding.*

**PACT**

🔆 When we make a pact in dreams we are usually making a treaty or agreeing to a particular course of action.

♥ When two parts of our personality are at odds with one another, dreams of a pact can show us how to have them working in harmony, bringing about a state known as integration.

🔲 Reconciling two opposing ideas or principles is an integral part of day-to-day living. Reaching agreement is often a process of negotiation, which works itself out in dreams.

**PADDLE** – *see* **WADING AND WATER**

**PADLOCK**

🔆 We are preserving or, quite literally, locking up our spiritual integrity sometimes for future use.

♥ Often when our security is threatened, a symbol which reinforces our need for defence mechanisms appears, and the padlock comes into this category. It offers sanctuary and an element of control. If the padlock is of an ornate design, such control may be more complicated than we first thought.

🔲 Dreaming of locking a padlock suggests that we are attempting to shut a feeling or emotion away. We are not able to explore these at this time. This may either be through fear or possessiveness. Conversely, if we are opening a padlock we may be trying to open up to new experiences.

*You might also like to consult the entries for Key and Lock.*

## PAGAN

🔅 From a spiritual perspective a pagan is one who does not belong to a major religion, but believes in all gods. However, in dreams such a figure is likely to suggest someone who worships, and is in touch with, the forces of nature.

💟 In returning to basic beliefs about the world in which we live we can reveal our pagan side, in its true meaning. This part reacts and responds to natural forces. This tends to happen when we begin a journey of self-exploration.

🖼 When a work or personal situation contains elements that we have difficulty understanding, this may be symbolized by the appearance of a pagan type of figure. Intrinsic in this is the idea of going back to very simple beliefs.

🔳 For many people the concept of paganism is of a somewhat chaotic freedom oriented religion, which deals with the balance of masculine and feminine. For this reason, both men's and women's dreams will reflect whatever rebalancing is required. Dreaming of the various Gods and Goddesses, for instance, highlights those qualities that need to be developed.

*Consult the entry for God/Gods and Goddess/Goddesses for further clarification.*

## PAGE

🔅 The symbolism of a Book of Life in which our lives are recorded for assessment is a strong image in spiritual work. It might be said that we have our own special page.

💟 A blank page suggests a fresh start in our emotional make-up. We have no given course of action and the freedom to begin again. A page that we cannot read suggests that guidelines are available but have not yet become apparent.

🖼 Manuals and procedures are an integral part of today's world, so being unable to find the right page in such a booklet suggests there may be a problem with how to complete a task in a working environment. The page being missing suggests we have not been given the correct information in the first place. Such dreams can be categorized as anxiety dreams.

🔳 There is a supplementary meaning of page, which can surface in dreams. In medieval times the page was the youth preparing to be a knight, hence the immature male. This image occurs in both men's and women's dreams as an archetype.

*You might like to consult the section on Archetypes in the Introduction and also the entries for Book and Paper/Parchment.*

**PAGODA** – *see* **RELIGIOUS BUILDINGS IN BUILDINGS**

**PAINT/PAINTING**

🔆 Often we do not recognize our own creative ability and thus the potential we have to be in touch with the spiritual dimension. We each have the capability of 'reflecting' the Divine. This allows us to live mindfully – with awareness.

💚 Because painting has such a lot to do with self-expression, the way that we are painting in a dream may be important. If, for instance, we are painting miniatures we may need to concentrate on detail. If we are painting large pictures we may need to adopt a more global perspective. Colour in a painting is also important, as is the subject.

🔲 We may not actually have the ability to paint successfully in everyday life, but such a dream may alert us to other talents we have not realized we possess. To be looking at paintings in dreams indicates that we are questioning or paying attention to different ideas and concepts. Painting as in decorating suggests we are making recognizable changes in how we think and feel. A picture that we ourselves have painted might have more emotional impact than an Old Master – an Old Master can also suggest our attitude to the past.

*You might also like to consult the entries for Colour and Decorate/Decoration.*

**PAIR/PAIRS**

🔆 The use of pairs in dreams is drawing attention to the idea of duality. We are trying to achieve a balance between the spiritual and material realms.

💚 A dream clarifying the masculine side of ourselves may be followed by a dream clarifying the feminine. The juggling that goes on in this way can take place over a period of time. Often in dream interpretation looking at the opposite meaning to the obvious can give us greater insight into our mental processes.

🔲 The unconscious mind appears to sort information by comparing and contrasting. Particularly when we are aware of conflict within ourselves, we may dream in pairs (e.g. old/young, masculine/feminine, clever/stupid). It is almost as though there is some kind of internal pendulum, which eventually sorts out the opposites into a unified whole.

🔳 It is quite natural for us to seek partnership, and in dreams both men and women will dream of duality as a way of sorting out emotional and spiritual complementary aspects.

*You might like to consult the entries for Numbers and Partner/Partnerships for further clarification.*

**PALACE –** *see* **CASTLE**

**PAN/POT**

🌣 As always, any receptacle suggests the containing Feminine Principle, usually the nurturing side. A pot can have the same spiritual significance as a jar.

💟 Just as a cauldron can be taken to indicate the transformative process, so a pan or pot can symbolize the ability to combine several 'ingredients' to make something completely different. This can apply under any circumstances.

▦ In dreams a pan or a pot signifies nurturing and caring. It can also suggest a receptive frame of mind.

🔆 In a woman's dream it will depend upon what stage of life she has reached as to the symbolism of pans. The three stages of femininity of Maid, Mother and Crone or Wise Woman are recognizable. In a man's dream a pan is more likely to represent his attitude to the feminine.

*You might like to consult the entries for Cauldron and Jar for further clarification.*

**PANCAKE –** *see* **BREAD**

**PANE –** *see* **WINDOWS IN BUILDINGS**

**PANEL**

🌣 There are several symbolisms of panel that might occur in dreams. The first is that of a spiritual picture – an icon such as a triptych, which may reflect aspects of our spiritual state. Such a picture has been thought to protect against visitation by the Devil.

💟 The second image is that of a control panel. This suggests that we have the ability to make adjustments in our lives, some of which may be only small but are important.

▦ A panel of people such as an interview panel or a panel of judges signifies that we have a situation in our lives where we are being judged or are allowing our fate to be decided by others in authority.

**PANTHER –** *see* **ANIMALS**

**PANTOMIME –** *see* **CLOWN AND THEATRE**

**PAPER/PARCHMENT**

🌣 There is potential for Spiritual growth through both learning and creativity. A parchment scroll suggests acknowledgement of in-depth study or ancient knowledge.

💟 Blank writing paper points to a lack of communication, or need to communicate with someone, but can also suggest a new beginning. Brown paper can highlight the utilitarian side of our nature. Old-fashioned parchment scrolls (which were originally made from animal skins) would suggest longlasting information.

▦ Paper is one of those images that, in dreams, are dependent on the circumstances in the dreamer's life. For instance, in a student's life, paper would suggest the need to pay attention to the studies, whereas festive wrapping paper could indicate the need for, or the possibility of, celebration. The art of making paper or creating parchment indicates a highly skilled individual.

*You may also like to consult the entry for Page.*

**PARADE – *see* PROCESSION**

**PARADISE**

※ To dream of Paradise is to be aware of the perfect Soul. In this state there is no right and no wrong, only completion and totality. Paradise is used instead of Heaven to describe the ultimate pleasurable place after death. It is the part from which we can develop perfect union with the universe.

♡ Psychologically, Paradise is that part of ourselves that is enclosed within and does not need to be available to anyone else – it is an unblemished, sacred space.

▦ To dream of Paradise is to link with our innate ability to take pleasure in being perfect. We can experience total harmony within ourselves and be totally innocent. When this is reflected into everyday life our universe co-operates with us.

⊟ In both men's and women's dreams, Paradise reflects a perfect relationship both with ourselves and others.

*You might also find it helpful to consult the entry for Garden.*

**PARALYSIS**

※ Paralysis can signify a sense of spiritual inadequacy, the inability to create movement, and inertia. There is a condition, which sometimes occurs during psychic development, when sleep paralysis – a state which has a neurological explanation – forces us into facing our own fears.

♡ Imagination can often play tricks on us, and we experience as real some kind of reaction we would not normally allow ourselves. Strong emotional feelings may be experienced as paralysis in dreams in order to highlight the effect those feelings can have within the physical realm.

▦ When paralysis is felt in a dream we are probably experiencing great fear or suppression. Literally we are unable to make a move in any direction. Dealing with conscious fears will allow us access to those fears that have only been available in the dream state.

*You might also like to consult the entry for Immobility.*

**PARAPET –** *see* **BALCONY**
**PARASITES –** *see* **INSECTS**
**PARCEL/PACKAGE**

🔅 Parcels and packages can suggest latent potential gifts, skills and talents They can equally suggest opportunities offered from a spiritual perspective.

♦ Parcels and packages in dreams can also represent the gifts and assistance that we receive from others. Whether we are directly receiving the parcel from the person concerned or whether we are simply aware who the donor is is worth noting. It is something that we can receive with joy. The wrapping may also be important, brown paper being more utilitarian than a more festive kind.

🔲 When we receive a parcel in a dream, we are being made aware of something we have experienced but not explored. At this stage, we do not quite know what the potential of the 'gift' is, but by exploration can find this out. If the address is wrong or we discover that the parcel is not for us we have probably some doubts about our own abilities. When we are sending a parcel or package we are sending our energy out into the world.

*Consult the entries for Paper and People for further clarification.*

**PARCHMENT –** *see* **PAPER**

**PARENTS –** *see* **ARCHETYPES IN THE INTRODUCTION AND FAMILY IN PEOPLE**
**PAROLE**

🔅 Parole strictly means our word of honour and in that sense signifies a promise to conform to whatever laws are appropriate – with awareness, spiritual laws.

♦ To be on parole indicates that there is some way in which we feel we have offended against natural laws. When we give someone else parole we are aware that we can trust them to act with honour.

🔲 To have been judged by a higher authority and then to have been put on parole suggests that someone who in real life has some kind of authority over us is trusting us to do our best, but that trust is conditional on a job well done.

**PARROT –** *see* **BIRDS**
**PART/PARTING**

🔅 Recognizing that there is a part of something rather than a whole signifies that spiritually we have not seen the whole picture. Parting suggests division, as in the parting of the waters.

♦ When in dreams it strikes us that we can only see part of something it is the unseen part that needs careful consideration. A parting in the hair signifies a duality in our nature. Parting from a dear friend suggests there may be some difficulty to overcome in that relationship.

▦ When an object or drawing is divided into parts we can decide to break an everyday task into its various components to help us succeed. The number of parts may be significant.

*Consult the entry for Hair in Body, Friend and Numbers for further clarification.*

## PARTNER/PARTNERSHIP

❀ Partnership of any sort in dreams signifies a joint spiritual responsibility. Being aware of having a partner highlights the fact that burdens and difficulties can also be shared.

♥ Most of us look for qualities in others that enhance or complement our own, so whether we dream of our actual partner or of being in partnership we are searching for such attributes. We require some kind of integration within ourselves.

▦ From a mundane perspective, partnership often denotes a shared task, ideal or project. Such a dream suggests that looking at the work in hand from a different perspective might bring about a solution to problems.

⊞ In both men's and women's dreams, dreaming of a partner, particularly in a mixed gender relationship, will probably highlight the Animus or Anima. In many cases, a partner will represent the Shadow, a ready recipient for aspects of our own negativity.

*You might like to consult the entry for People as well as the information on Animus and Anima in Archetypes in the Introduction.*

## PARTY

❀ When a group celebrates a belief, which can be spiritual, it is an occasion for a party or festival. The joining up of several people enhances the atmosphere and creates additional power.

♥ The human being often has need of celebration in his or her life. To be attending a party such as a dinner party or other specific purpose in a dream can indicate our need for celebration, for joining with other people to create a potentially happy atmosphere.

▦ When we find we are attending a party in a dream, we are often alerted to our social skills – or lack of them. In waking life we may be shy and dislike such gatherings, but in dreams if we are coping with the groups involved, we have a greater awareness of our own ability to belong and to take enjoyment from that. To belong to a political party would indicate that we are prepared to stand up for our beliefs, that we have made a commitment to a particular way of life.

## PASS

❀ A pass signifies that permission has been given to move in selected areas and, therefore, that we have reached a certain level of spiritual recognition.

🏵 To lose a library pass suggests that we have not been careful to keep our knowledge up to date. To lose a bus or travel pass signifies that we have not planned our next moves carefully. To pass an examination or interview means that we have worked hard and well enough to have gained approval.

🔲 As nowadays many workplaces use electronic passes to gain entry, to forget a pass might denote a lack of interest in what we are doing or that if we are honest we do not feel our work is good enough or of value. To find a pass that is not our own signifies that we feel we have a right of entry but others do not necessarily feel the same way.

**PASSAGE** – *see* **HALL/PASSAGES IN BUILDINGS**

**PASSENGER**

🏵 When we take responsibility for someone else's spiritual development we may dream of carrying a passenger.

🏵 If we feel that someone known to us is drawing on our resources we may dream of having a passenger. If we are ourselves a passenger we should take warning that we are not taking full responsibility for ourselves or our actions.

🔲 Often in teamwork or family life one or more individual has to be 'carried' for a time to ensure success. This might give rise to images of carrying passengers on a journey in either party.

*You might like to consult the entries for Car, Journey and Transport to enhance your understanding.*

**PASSPORT**

🏵 A passport to a better life can be achieved by Spiritual Awareness. Such a document suggests that permission has been given by a higher authority – that some kind of initiation has taken place.

🏵 Often the passport can appear as a symbol of the permission we need to give ourselves or others to move on to new things or situations. To lose a passport suggests we are not committed to such an action.

🔲 The passport is normally regarded as proving our identity, to prove that we have reached the age of maturity or acceptance as a valid member of society. In waking life, we may experience difficulty in maintaining a good self-image and in dreams may reassure ourselves by producing a passport. Not being able to obtain a passport suggests that there is a lack of trust.

*The entries in Journey may give you a greater understanding of your dream.*

**PAST** – *see* **TIME**

**PATCH** – *see* **FABRIC**

**PATH**

🏵 A path in a dream can indicate the direction that we should take spiritually. The idea that there is a path in life resonates with Chinese thought, which calls the Tao 'The Way'. In some schools of thought the left hand path represents evil or black magic.

◈ Often a path can represent the way we feel a relationship or situation is developing. It can also suggest a way of following up a concept or line of enquiry. A pavement introduces the idea that the path is already prepared for us.

▦ A path in a dream signifies the direction we have decided to take in life. The type of path, e.g. whether it is smooth or rocky, meandering or straight, may be just as important as the path itself. In waking life, it is often the way a clairvoyant 'sees' the way in which the enquirer's life is changing.

*Also consult the entries for Journey, Line, Meander and Rock.*

**PATTERN** – *see* **SHAPES/PATTERNS**

**PAY/PAYMENT**

◉ In spiritual terms, to pay for something is to be accountable for it. To make payment signifies taking responsibility.

◈ If in dreams we are paying a bill we may be accepting that we have received something of value. It may be that we must make good use of our resources.

▦ Payment, as in a monetary transaction, can often show our attitude to finance. To be paying cash suggests a more immediate use of our money and resources, whereas paying by credit card signifies a need to satisfy our immediate needs without thought of the consequences. A cheque nowadays could well show a slightly outdated attitude.

**PEACE** – *see* **TRANQUILITY**

**PEACOCK** – *see* **BIRDS**

**PEAK**

◉ A peak experience is one that takes us beyond our normal capabilities. From a spiritual perspective we have not allowed the limitations of the mundane world to hold us back.

◈ Reaching the peak of a mountain or hill in dreams signifies that we have put in a good deal of effort to reach for the best that we can be.

▦ In the sense that a peak is a high point, after which the energy begins to fall away, such a dream image may show that we have reached a point of completion and the next stage of the journey will be easier.

⊡ Men's and women's perceptions of a peak experience will differ in dreams, although both will transcend the self-imposed boundaries and limitations that occur.

**PEARL** – *see* **GEMS/JEWELS**

**PEEP/PEERING** – *see* **INSPECT**

**PELICAN** – *see* **BIRDS**

## PEN/PENCIL

✺ The ability to transcribe and translate spiritual knowledge into recognizable images and to keep a record of that information is a necessary part of personal development. Such records and especially the ability to keep a journal are an invaluable part of dream recording. Dreaming of a pen or pencil may also suggest that we could attempt automatic or inspired writing.

♡ We all have an ability to learn but need to have some way of transmitting our learning to other people. A pen would suggest the learning would be more permanent than a pencil. Learning through dreams is an increasing part of modern day understanding of the psyche.

▦ If a pen or pencil appears in a dream we are expressing or recognizing the need to communicate with other people. If the pen will not work we do not understand information we have been given. If we cannot find a tool to write with we do not have enough information to proceed with an aspect of our lives.

*You may also wish to consult the entries for Ink, Inspire, Paper/Parchment and Writing.*

## PENALTY

✺ Incurring a penalty in the spiritual sense indicates that we have transgressed against a particular code of behaviour. We may not necessarily be aware of this code.

♡ A penalty is in normal parlance a fine levied for a misdemeanour. It is a punishment imposed by others, often our peers, and will have this meaning in dreams. We will have upset someone without necessarily being prepared to take the consequences.

▦ Dreaming of a penalty goal can mean, if we are shooting this goal, an opportunity to be in the limelight because of someone else's mistake. If the opportunity for such a goal is our fault, it is a warning to be more careful.

## PENANCE – *see* SPIRITUAL IMAGERY IN THE INTRODUCTION

## PENDANT – *see* NECKLACE

## PENDULUM

✺ A pendulum is both a measurer of time and of energy. Spiritually it represents the rhythm of life. It is for this reason that a weighted object can be used in divination.

♡ A pendulum in dreams may be a symbol of indecision, swinging from one course of action to another. It may also suggest the oscillation between two states of emotion.

🖾 In the dream image of an old-fashioned clock, a pendulum can signify outdated ideas. It can also suggest that a period of time must pass before a plan is allowed to come to fruition. On its own a pendulum signifies a swing between two polarities; if it comes to rest in our dream we have resolved a dilemma.

*Also consult the entry for Time.*

## PENETRATION

🔆 Any article that penetrates or pierces another, such as a knife or laser beam, signifies that the normal boundaries and limitations by which we live are illusions when viewed from a spiritual perspective.

♥ In today's world people tend to view penetration from a purely sexual viewpoint. In dreams it usually signifies getting to the heart of a matter. Any pointed object represents male sexuality but can also be interpreted in the above manner.

🖾 Inherent in the idea of penetration is a piercing of defences and this meaning is one which arises frequently in dreams. When we are feeling particularly vulnerable or at risk, dreams such as of castle walls being penetrated can occur.

🖄 Myths and fairy tales often give information that resonates in dreams. Women and men exploring their sexuality or their need for partnership can have dreams that highlight both penetration of a sexual nature and that of personal space.

*Consulting the entries for Castle, Dagger, Knife and Sex/Sexual Images might help with further clarification.*

## PENGUIN – *see* BIRDS

## PENTACLE/PENTANGLE/PENTAGRAM – *see* MAGIC/MAGICIAN

## PEOPLE

🔆 When we begin to work spiritually with ourselves, there is a gargantuan store of knowledge that can be worked on, and with, to enhance our lives. By and large it can be accepted that dream characters are aspects of ourselves and that the dream is first and foremost about us. It often helps, therefore, to view the dream through not just our own eyes but as though we are experiencing it as our dream character. The interaction that takes place between us and our dream character is an attempt either to understand that aspect of ourselves or to achieve some kind of integration with it in order to have a wider perspective on life. As such integration progresses we achieve a wholeness and awareness, which enable us to work in a more spiritual focused fashion.

♥ In order to disentangle the various types of 'information' that each character brings to the dreamer, it is often necessary to decide what or who each one makes us think of. That way we will reveal the deeper meanings and connections. Some of the following entries can also be found in the individual letters and we suggest that you consult these entries for extra information. Where archetypes such as the Anima, Animus, Great Mother, Shadow, Self and Wise Old Man are referred to, please consult the relevant section in the Introduction.

**Adolescent** – if we dream we are an adolescent we are focusing on our undeveloped side. Dreaming of an adolescent of the opposite sex usually means dealing with a suppressed part of our development. The emotions associated with adolescence are very raw and clear and such emotions are accessible often only through dreams. There may be conflict over issues of freedom.

**Ancestors** – our customs, ways of behaving, morality and our religious feelings are all handed down from generation to generation. When we become conscious of our ancestors in a dream we are focusing on our roots. We may understand ourselves through our relationship with the past.

**Authority figures such as judges, teachers etc.** – our concept of authority first develops through our relationship with our father or father figure. Depending on how we were treated as children, our view of authority will be anything from a benign helper to an exploitative disciplinarian. Most authority figures will ultimately lead us back to what is right for us, although not necessarily what we might consider good for us. Authority figures in dreams initially appear to have power over us, though – if we are able to work with them properly – will generate within us the power to succeed.

**Baby** – to dream about a baby that is our own indicates that we need to recognize those vulnerable feelings over which we have no control. We may be attempting something new. If the baby is someone else's in the dream, we need to be aware of that person's ability to be hurt, or that they may be innocent of something. Psychologically we are in touch with the innocent, curious side of ourselves, with the part that neither wants nor needs responsibility. Dreaming of a baby can indicate that, on a spiritual level, the dreamer has a need for a feeling of purity.

**Boy** – to have a dream about a boy shows the potential for growth and new experience. If the boy is known to us he reflects recognized qualities in the dreamer. Psychologically, we may need to be in touch with ourselves at that age and with the innocent youthfulness and enthusiasm that a boy has. We are contacting our natural drives and ability to face difficulties.

**Boyfriend** – to dream of a boyfriend, whether present or former, connects with the feelings, attachments and sexuality connected with him. To dream of having as a boyfriend someone whom you would not anticipate, indicates the need to have a greater understanding of the way you relate to men. Consideration may need to be given to the loving, nurturing side of masculinity. We are still searching for the ideal lover.

**Caring professions such as nurses, nuns etc.** – often these characters represent the side of us that has been 'called' or has a vocation; this suggests the more compassionate, nurturing side. When such characters appear in a man's dream the relationship that is represented is often non sexual in nature.

**Child (who could be one of the dreamer's own children)** – dreaming of a child gives us access to our own inner child. We all have parts of ourselves that are still child-like and curious. When we are able to get in touch with that side of ourselves we give ourselves permission to return to a state of innocence, which we may not previously have wished to do.

**Dictators (Hitler, Stalin etc.)** – if we have, or had, an overbearing father, a known dictator may appear in dreams as representing that relationship. It is as though our dreaming self cannot face confrontation with father as such. Such a figure may also appear where issues affecting the community in which we live are of concern to us.

**Emperor or Empress** – *see King and Queen in this section.*

**Esoteric figures (Astrologers, Magicians etc.)** – any character within our dreams who appears to have knowledge of magical practices or similar types of knowledge is usually our first introduction to the Higher Self. It is as though we can only become privy to this deeper knowledge by meeting our teacher first. *Also consult the individual entries for Magic/Magician, Witch and Wizard.*

**Girl** – if a girl of any age appears in our dreams it shows we are attempting to make contact with the more sensitive, innocent side of ourselves. Those qualities of intuition and perception may be somewhat undeveloped but can be made available. If the girl is known to us we probably are aware of those qualities, but need to explore them as though we were approaching them from the girl's point of view. If she is unknown, we can acknowledge that a fresh approach would be useful.

**Girlfriend** – when a girlfriend or ex-girlfriend appears in a man's dream there are usually issues to do with masculinity and femininity involved. There may be fears to do with sexuality. If a girlfriend appears in a woman's dream, there can either be a concern about her in our mind, or we need to search for – and find – qualities belonging to the friend in her.

**Hero or any heroic figure** – in today's world the hero has taken on many guises, particularly in psychological parlance. For many people their own heroic figure, from footballer to successful businessperson, will act as a role model in the journey of life. *Also consult the individual entries for Hero/Heroine and Quest.*

**Inadequate Person** – we would be unwise to ignore this aspect of ourselves and shouldn't dismiss such an image when it appears. We must acknowledge this dream figure as a reflection of ourselves in order to deal with a learnt sense of inferiority. If we do not, we will be continually faced in life by our own sense of inferiority. It is a lot easier to confront our own inadequacies in the dream state where we are safe. Often this is the first opportunity we have to meet the Shadow.

**Indigenous Peoples such as Aboriginal, Maori, Native American** – *see individual entry.*

**Intruder** – the intruder in a woman's dream is often a personification of her own Animus. In a man's dream it characterizes his Shadow. In either case it suggests the need for a change in attitude in order for the dreamer to be able to have a full and meaningful relationship with himself. *You may like to consult the entry for Burglar as well as the individual entry.*

**King** – almost invariably a king appearing in a dream represents the father or father figure. A personality such as an emperor may indicate that some of the father's attitudes are alien to the dreamer, but should perhaps be accepted. When the king is old or on the point of dying the dreamer will be able to reject outworn or old-fashioned family values.

**Magistrate** – *see individual entry.*

**Man** – any man appearing in a dream shows an aspect or facet of our character in a recognizable form. Each of us has a repertoire or portfolio of behaviours, some of which are acceptable and some of which are not. In dreams those behaviours and characteristics can be magnified so that they are easily identified, often as personalities. By working with the characteristic, more energy and power becomes available. Even when we are threatened by a negative character trait, we can still access room for improvement. A man in a dream can identify the Shadow for a man, and the Animus for a woman. An older man (if the man is white-haired or holy) can represent the innate wisdom we all have. Such a person can also signify the father in dreams. When a large man appears in our dreams we are usually appreciating the strengths, certainties and protection that our basic beliefs give us. A man in a woman's dream signifies the more logical side of her nature. She has, or can develop, all the aspects of the masculine that enable her to function with success in the external world. If the man is one she knows or loves she may be trying to understand her relationship with him. An unknown man is generally that part of the dreamer's personality that is not recognized. In a woman's dream it is the masculine side of herself, and in a man's dream it is the Self.

**Old People** – in dreams, old people can represent either our ancestors or grandparents, hence wisdom accrued from experience. If the old person is male – depending on the gender of the dreamer – he will stand for either the Self or the Animus. If female then she will signify the Great Mother or the Anima. All father figures, or representations of the father, will often appear old as if to highlight their remoteness. A group of old people often appears in dreams. Usually this signifies the traditions and wisdom of the past – things sacred to the 'tribe' or family. Older people usually stand for our parents even though the dream figures may bear no relationship to them. *Also consult the entries for Man and Woman in this section.*

**Pirate** – the pirate can represent the anarchic part of our personality, which in flouting convention causes us difficulty and tends to separate us from our own integrity.

**Police** – dreaming particularly of police can indicate a kind of social control and a protective element for us as members of society. Often a policeman will appear in dreams as one's conscience. We may feel that our wilder, more renegade side needs controlling.

**Priests, priestesses and ministers of all religions** – these figures all hold a special place in the dream hierarchy. Sometimes intermediaries between an ultimate power and Man, and sometimes authority figures, their power comes from beyond themselves. There is, therefore, a sense of 'otherness' about them, and in dreams it is usually the former function that they perform. *Also consult the entries for Archetypes in the Introduction and Authority Figures above.*

**Prince/Princess** – these figures represent those parts of ourselves, or others, who exist by right; that is, those aspects that have been brought into conscious awareness and authority. As the hero has taken responsibility for his own journey, so the prince and princess take responsibility for the lives they live. *Also consult the entry for Camelot.*

**Queen** – this usually represents our relationship with our mother or mother figure, and thus with women in authority generally. This applies to a dream image of any regal figure – not only the present queen, but also a historical one such as Victoria. An empress will also have the same connotation.

**Security personnel (including caretakers)** – in performing a dual function, that of authority figures and guardians of property, security personnel appearing in dreams tend to represent a curb on enjoyment.

**Stranger** – the stranger in a dream represents that part of ourselves that we do not yet know. There may be a feeling of awe or of conflict with which we need to deal before we can progress. *Also consult Shadow in the Introduction.*

**Twins** – twins in a dream can suggest two sides of our personality. If they are identical we may be recognizing our ambiguous feelings about ourselves. If not identical they suggest the inner self and the outer reality. Twins may also signify our projections into the world of our own personalities. These interpretations are also valid if there is a mirror image of a dream figure. *Also consult the individual entry for Twin.*

**Woman** – in a woman's dream a woman, such as a family member or friend is often representative of an aspect of her own personality, but often one she has not yet fully understood. In a man's dream such a figure denotes his relationship with his own feelings and with his intuitive side. It may also show how he relates to his female partner. A goddess or holy woman signifies the highest potential for working with the Greater Good that the dreamer has. Oriental women appearing in dreams usually suggest the mysterious side of the feminine. In a man's dream such a figure will often reveal his attitude to sexuality, while in a woman's dream it will reveal more about her own intuitive transcendent powers. An older woman mostly represents the dreamer's mother and her sense of inherited wisdom. An unknown woman in dreams will represent either the Anima in a man's dream, or the Shadow in a woman's. It is the qualities of surprise and intrigue that allow us to explore further the relevance of that figure. We can gain a great deal of information because the figure is unknown.

🔲 The people who appear in dreams are the characters with which we write our 'play'. Often they appear simply as themselves, particularly if they are people we know or have a relationship with in the here and now. We may introduce them in order to highlight a specific quality or characteristic. We may also permit them into our dream scenario as projections of our inner life or state of being, or as ways of handling problems in our everyday life. Sometimes, rather than trying to decipher the meaning of the dream, it is enough to look at what bearing the dream character's actions have on our everyday life. Below are interpretations of some of the most common interactions with people in dreams.

**Crowds in dreams** can indicate how we relate to other people, particularly in a social sense. They may indicate how we can hide ourselves, or indeed how we hide aspects of ourselves and do not single out any one attribute. We may also be attempting to avoid responsibility. A huge crowd suggests information that we may not be able to handle.

**An individual from the past** could link us with that period of our lives and with specific memories that may, or may not, be painful.

**A neighbour or close associate** usually appears in a dream to highlight a particular quality in that person.

**Somebody else's mother, father, brother etc.** may suggest our own family members or possibly jealousy. To interpret why we have adopted a particular role we would need to examine their lifestyle.

When there is some conflict within us between **love and aversion for a particular person** we are more likely to dream about them. Often in dreams there may be a noted difference between two of the participants to illustrate two sides of our thoughts and feelings. Similarly there may be a marked contrast in the way we handle a situation with two of our dream characters. It is as though two options are being practised.

As with composite animals, **the composite character** will emphasize one characteristic or quality in order to draw our attention to it. The fact that it is not just one person emphasizes the many-faceted human being. Every character who appears in our dreams is a reflection of a facet or part of our own personality and can often be better understood if we put ourselves in the position of that person.

## PERFECT/PERFECTION

🌞 Our search for perfection is an effort to return to our spiritual source. In dreams this is often signified by a sense of wonder.

♥ If we subscribe to the belief that everything is inherently perfect, dreams are one way in which we try to understand that perfection. They are also a way of coming to terms with anything in life that is less than perfect, of becoming aware of those things that need adjustment.

▦ Frequently in dreams we are aware of the ephemeral nature of perfection, a sense or feeling that is difficult without practice through meditation or other disciplines to retain in working life.

## PERFUME – see ODOUR

## PERFORM/PERFORMANCE – see ACTOR AND THEATRE

## PERJURY – see LIE

## PERMIT/PERMISSION

🌞 A permit suggests that recognition has been given by authority. In spiritual terms this indicates that permission has been given, or initiation has taken place to enable us to act in a certain way.

♥ When we permit certain actions this suggests that we approve of what is being done.

🔲 When we find ourselves seeking permission in dreams it may be that we are uncertain of a particular course of action and feel that we need to have our decisions validated.

🔅 In both men's and women's dreams, a permit can suggest the right to a relationship. Permission may be required from either party or from others for such a relationship. A backstage permit indicates the ability to get to know somebody better.

## PERSECUTE/PERSECUTION – *see* TORMENT

## PET

🌞 Pets will offer us unconditional love and acceptance without question. In many ways this is a lesson in spirituality. In being sensitive to our immediate emotional distress or pain, they can be of comfort. It has been recognized also that they frequently channel healing energies.

💠 On a subliminal level, when dreaming of pets we may be aware that someone else has control over our lives. Conversely, if we own a pet in a dream we perhaps need to question or recognize our ability to look after something or someone more vulnerable than ourselves.

🔲 Whereas in the waking state we may not be aware of our need for love and affection, when a pet appears in a dream we are reacting to a natural drive in ourselves to give or receive love.

*You might like to consult the individual entries for various animals as well as the entry for Animals to discover their qualities.*

## PETITION

🌞 A petition is a supplication, request or prayer and has this meaning in a spiritual sense. Nowadays it has the additional meaning of a request from like-minded people.

💠 It is worthwhile deciding which is more important in the dream, the petition itself, the cause or the people with whom we are working. We can then consciously decide where our loyalties lie in what is represented.

🔲 To be signing a petition indicates committing to a deeply held belief. To refuse to sign means we question our commitment. To have a petition refused signifies disappointment in a working environment.

## PETROL – *see* OIL

## PEW – *see* SPIRITUAL IMAGERY IN THE INTRODUCTION

## PHEASANT – *see* BIRDS

## PHOENIX

🌞 A mythical bird of great beauty, the phoenix is often an emblem of immortality or of resurrected idealism and hope.

💠 Since the phoenix rises from its own ashes ready to live its life all over again, it signifies our ability to pick ourselves up and begin again, after what appears to be disaster.

▣ The phoenix was believed to live for 500 or 600 years, then to burn itself on a funeral pyre, knowing it would rise again. In dreams, therefore, it can symbolize knowing when to move on, when to let the past go, being aware that there is more energy available if we do so.

*Also consult the entry for Birds.*

**PHOTOCOPY – *see* COPY**

**PHOTOGRAPHS**

☀ Photographs in dreams can represent a spiritual need to understand the past. In a sense they are a microcosm within a macrocosm – a small part within a greater whole.

♡ Obviously photographs represent memories, past occasions, perhaps past difficulties. To be looking at photographs of someone from the past is to be looking at that person's qualities – perhaps bringing them forward into our own lives – and making use of those same qualities within. In magical work a photograph is used as a representation of someone else and can have this meaning in dreams, rather than dreaming about the person concerned.

▣ When we dream of looking at photographs we are often looking at an aspect of ourselves, perhaps our younger self or a part of ourselves that we no longer feel is particularly valid. To be given a photograph of oneself would indicate that we need to be taking an objective view of situations round us or perhaps of ourselves within that situation. We need to stand back and look very clearly at what is going on.

*You might also like to consult the entry for Picture.*

**PHYSICIAN – *see* DOCTOR**

**PIANO – *see* MUSIC/RHYTHM AND MUSICAL INSTRUMENTS**

**PICK – *see* CHOICE/CHOOSE**

**PICKET – *see* DEMONSTRATE/DEMONSTRATION**

**PICNIC – *see* FOOD**

**PICTURE**

☀ A picture can be a visual depiction of a person or object, an icon – in itself a sacred object – or a representation of spiritual significance.

♡ The condition of the picture may be important, as may also the colours. A torn picture suggests that what is depicted has been damaged. The subject matter may give us suggestions as to what we should be 'looking at' in our lives more objectively.

▣ A picture in a dream is usually an illustration of something that is important to us at that time. If the picture is framed we may assume there is a degree of protection. The interpretation will depend on whether the picture is painted, a print of another picture, or perhaps a photograph.

*For further clarification consult the entries for Colours, Frame, Icon and Photograph.*

**PIERCE** – *see* STAB AND PENETRATION

**PIG** – *see* ANIMALS AND BOAR

**PIGEON** – *see* BIRDS

**PILL** – *see* MEDICATION/MEDICINE AND TABLET

**PILGRIM/PILGRIMAGE**

⚜ A seeker of Spirituality must always undertake a journey of some kind. This is often represented in dreams by a pilgrimage to a holy place of any denomination.

♥ A pilgrim can often represent the hermit or Wise Old Man within. That part of our personality that is secure and may not need much input from others has the ability to direct our lives, provided we create the correct circumstances.

▦ When we are undertaking a pilgrimage in a dream we are recognizing the purposeful, directed side of our personality. We have a goal in life, which may require faith to achieve.

*Consult the entry for Journey and the information on Archetypes in the Introduction.*

**PILLAR**

⚜ The contrast between spiritual and material power is seen as two pillars in dreams. Esoterically, for there to be two pillars in a dream highlights the difference between the masculine and the feminine. The left pillar represents the feminine, and is often seen as being black. The right is masculine, and is seen in dreams as white.

♥ Pillars mostly indicate a sort of support, so to become aware of supporting pillars indicates that the structure that we have given our lives may need some attention.

▦ One symbolism of a pillar is phallic, but another one is probably more accurate. We are able to create stability and to stand firm in the presence of difficulty. In dreams, to find that we are a pillar of the community suggests that we should be taking more responsibility for our actions.

*You may also wish to consult the entry for Column.*

**PIMP** – *see* PROSTITUTE

**PIMPLE** – *see* SPOT

**PIN**

⚜ We may not be able to solve a spiritual difficulty immediately. A temporary solution may be necessary and this can be symbolized by the use of a pin.

❤ Occasionally in a dream we are reminded of a feeling we have in everyday life. To experience a feeling of pins and needles in our dream suggests that we are not ensuring an adequate flow of energy in a situation around us. A PIN (Personal Identification Number) suggests the need for a sense of security and recognition.

▦ It depends whether the pin is holding something together or is being used to pierce us, or an object, in our dreams. If it is holding something together it indicates the emotional connections or bonds we use. If it is piercing an object a trauma is suggested, although it may be quite small.

## PIPE

❋ A pipe of any sort suggests some kind of spiritual conduit.

❤ When we are in difficulty in everyday life, a simple symbol such as a pipe will indicate how making connections between the various aspects of a situation will help resolve it.

▦ On a purely practical level a pipe can symbolize many things. A water pipe can give information as to how we might handle our emotions (the size and type in this case will be significant); a clay pipe might suggest former times or an old-fashioned attitude. A tobacco pipe or chillum might suggest a means of escape, whereas a musical pipe indicates our connection with the rhythm of life.

## PIRATE – *see* PEOPLE

## PISTOL – *see* GUN, SHOT/SHOOTING AND WEAPONS

## PISTON

❋ The spiritual drive – that is, the need to be complete – requires effort which can be enhanced by using our resources properly. A piston symbolizes this drive.

❤ A piston may also represent a person's drive for success. We need to assess the amount of effort that is necessary for us to be able to achieve our goals. We may need to recognize that concentrated effort – which is fairly mechanical – may, at this stage, achieve more than creative flair. The piston, being only part of an engine, does require the rest of the components to operate successfully. Often a great deal of help can be gained by considering the way in which the piston works. In other words, though at a particular stage of development our actions may have to be mechanical, we do have to consider the 'engine', not just its component parts.

▦ A piston in a dream can be taken to mean sexual drive or activity. In this context it is more of a mechanical action than a loving act, and may show a particular attitude to sex.

⊞ In a woman's dream a piston may reveal her fear of being hurt sexually. She may also be aware that she is simply being used, and that there is no tenderness. In a man's dream such an image may indicate his sense of identity and masculinity. If the piston is not rigid a man may fear impotence, whereas a woman will feel perhaps that she cannot trust her partner.

*Consult the entry for Engine for further clarification.*

## PIT

🔅 The pit, like the abyss, represents the Void and possibly death – not necessarily a physical death, but more a death of the old self. We have no choice but to go forward, knowing that we may fail, but also that if we do succeed our lives will change for the better. To face the pit requires extreme courage.

♥ Rescuing others from a pit, particularly if they are members of our own family, suggests that we have information which may be of use to them to enable them to overcome their problems. We may also be showing our concern over certain actions, which seem irrevocable. Pushing someone into a pit indicates that we are trying to suppress a part of our personality. To be conscious that the pit is bottomless signifies that we do not have the resources to recover a previous situation.

▦ Many people talk about the pit of despair and of feeling trapped within a situation. A pit in a dream makes us more conscious of this particular feeling. We may be in circumstances that we cannot get out of, or may find that if we are not careful we will put ourselves in such a situation. If we are digging the pit in the dream, we may be creating the situation ourselves. If others are digging the pit, we may feel we have no control over our circumstances and that doom and disaster are inevitable.

*You may also wish to consult the entry for Abyss.*

## PLACES

🔅 In the sense that a place suggests a 'spot', places appearing in dreams allow us to orientate ourselves in order to make the best use of information we are given. Interpreting the symbolism of certain places gives us an insight into our own 'inner landscape'. A place that becomes fertile or lighter in the course of the dream indicates that an aspect that we have not previously appreciated – or have found unpleasant – is now developing possibilities and potentials, possibly for spiritual development. Dreary, unfriendly places, or tranquil favourable landscapes may well refer to our subjective view of the world. To find such landscapes changing in the course of a dream suggests that our attitudes are changing.

❤ The country where the dream takes place may have certain resonances for the dreamer. For example, America for most people will signify a rather brash, commercially oriented culture, England tends to be seen as inhibited and dutiful, while France will represent the temperamental masculine, and so on. Other places that offer information for consideration are as follows:

**Our birthplace** represents a secure space where we feel at ease.

**A bright and sunny place** suggests fun and liveliness, whereas a dark, shadowy, murky scene signifies despondency and gloom.

**Darkened places** can also represent the unconscious.

**Countryside** can suggest a particular mood or feeling, especially of freedom.

**Composite scenes** consisting of many images recognizable to us are usually drawing attention to particular qualities, ideals and moods. These all enhance the information content of the dream, may have particular associations for us or have been included because of frequently encountered associations.

**A familiar place** will often take us back to childhood or a time of learning and a particularly beautiful place may allow us to fantasize so that we can make more use of creative visualization.

**Jungles** connect with the labyrinth and ways of understanding our sexuality, whereas a place that feels oppressive has formerly been a sanctuary, but is no longer. A sheltered place offers peace and security. *Also see the individual entry.*

**Unknown places** indicate aspects of ourselves of which we are not yet aware. Such places can lead to an environment that seems familiar and yet we do not know it. This signifies a situation we are continually re-running in our lives.

**Wide-open spaces** offer us freedom of movement.

▦ When the environment or setting of a dream is particularly noticeable there is usually some kind of message or information being given. Sometimes the place reflects our inner state of mind or mood. It can be a reminder of a particular place, which had meaning at a specific time in our life, and sometimes a reminder of particular people.

PLAGUE – *see* EPIDEMIC/PLAGUE

PLAIT

❁ Very subtle influences come into play when we begin to develop spiritually. Hair plaited into the shape of a crown – or wound round the head – indicates spiritual attainment. Hair is often used as a representation of the individual in magical spells.

❤ Plaited hair was formerly a means of creating order and cleanliness. Often in dreams to see a plait reminds us of the talisman – or favour belonging to his lady – that a knight of old would carry into battle. Nowadays it is more of a lucky charm. To be plaiting string, rope, hair etc. highlights our ability to weave the different influences of our, or someone else's, life into a coherent whole.

▦ In olden times, a plait using three strands indicated the interweaving of body, mind and spirit. It also represented the influences that were assimilated by a growing girl and taken into her understanding of herself as a woman.

⊞ In dreams, a plait represents womanhood. In the present day, the more creative men will often wear their hair longer, and for this to happen in a dream suggests that they are in process of recognizing their emerging sensitivity.

*To clarify this interpretation further, consult the entries for Crown, as well as Hair and Head in the Body section.*

## PLAN/PLANS

🔅 Plans are diagrams designed to help in certain tasks, whether that is construction or in the sense of a map. They are of assistance in spiritual development in that they let us see the way forward.

♡ Normally, if we have a plan we have considered what our future actions must be. In dreams this may appear as an actual document. To be at a planning meeting signifies the need for order in our lives.

▦ As planning is such an integral part of business life today, the image or idea will surface in dreams quite frequently. When a plan or plans are dropped in a dream the significance is obvious.

⊞ When a woman dreams of visiting a family planning centre, she may be becoming aware of her wish to be pregnant. In a man's dream this may suggest his wish or need to take responsibility.

## PLANETS

🔅 Spiritually, once we become aware of how the subtle energies can help us live our lives successfully, we can learn to make use of planetary energy. This is a belief that goes back to ancient times and is the basis of astrology.

♡ The interpretations of the planetary significances are:

**Jupiter** suggests growth and expansion, and also freedom from limitation.

**Mars** indicates activity and war but also drive.

**Mercury** signifies communication, intuition and mental powers.

**The Moon** represents our emotions and our links with our mother.

**Neptune** works with illusion – but also with inspiration.

**Pluto** has charge of the unconscious and transformation.

**Saturn** is a restraining influence and rules the past.

**The Sun** usually symbolizes the Self and the energy that we have.

**Uranus** governs sudden changes.

**Venus** highlights love and beauty.

🏮 Dreaming of planets is to be linking with very subtle energies, which surround us and have an effect on our lives, even though we may not be consciously aware of them. Often as we begin to study the esoteric arts we become more aware of these influences.

## PLANTS

☀️ Plants in a spiritual sense signify both the life force and the cycle of life. Because they die only to grow again, they also suggest death and rebirth.

♥️ If the plants are growing wild, there is a part of us that needs freedom. If they are grown in regimented rows we are aware of too much concern for the views of other people. Many plants have both healing and magical qualities. Equally, without proper knowledge, plants can be harmful.

🏮 Because of the process of growth and decay that plants go through naturally, they become a symbol for progressive change. If the plants are cultivated, then we should be aware of our ability to cultivate potential. If the plants are dying we may have reached a stage where there is no more advantage within a situation.

*You might also like to consult the entries for Garden and Weeds.*

## PLATEAU

☀️ Many dreams will hold images of climbing and of reaching a plateau. Spiritually this offers us choices. We can rest on our laurels and take time out to assess our progress, or we can use the plateau for calm and peace.

♥️ If the plateau is barren, we may need some further stimulus to help us move on. If it seems to be a place of safety, we may not wish to move on and perhaps need to take time out to recuperate.

🏮 After a great deal of effort we reach a place that is even and not difficult to cross. Sometimes it can represent a period of peace and quiet, sometimes stasis where there is no energy left for change. When this happens in a work situation we eventually need to decide on and initiate whatever further action is needed.

## PLAY

☀️ From a spiritual perspective, the life that we have creates a play, which gives us the best opportunity to learn lessons through experience. If people we know are in the play we should be aware of the 'drama' we are playing out with them.

♥️ In dreams, the play that takes place is a distillation of our experiences, knowledge and abilities. The creator in us directs the performance to enable us to get the best benefit of the information it contains. Images in dreams are put together to have the greatest impact and to make the interpretation as easy as possible. Sometimes, however, to catch our attention the unexpected occurs, which means that we have to seek explanation from a source outside ourselves.

▦ When in a dream we are watching a play, we need to decide whether it is a drama, a comedy or a tragedy. This is because we often are trying to view our own lives objectively. The content of the play may give us clues as to what our course of action should be in everyday life.

*You might also like to consult the entries for Actor, Audience and Theatre.*

## PLEA/PLEADING

❀ Spiritually a plea has the same meaning as prayer. It also suggests applying to arbitrators of spiritual law such as priests and holy men.

♥ When we find ourselves pleading for something – begging or appealing – we have some extreme need for whatever is represented. This might, for instance, be some kind of assistance or sanctuary.

▦ A strongly held feeling or principle will deepen to a plea in dreams, particularly if we feel we are not understood.

*Also consult the entry for Prayer.*

## PLOUGHING

❀ We are in process of creating new opportunities to develop spiritually.

♥ We may have a situation within our lives which needs 'turning over'. By looking at it from a different perspective we are able to make the situation more productive.

▦ As more people move away from working with the land, this symbol has become less relevant in dreams. It does mean, however, working at clearing ourselves for new growth and being able to prepare for change, particularly in regard to conservation issues.

## PLUMAGE – *see* FEATHERS

## PLUMBING

❀ We are beginning to become aware of the flow of spiritual energy within our lives, though this may be in the background.

♥ Emotional security is important to almost everybody, and mostly such feelings are hidden from view. When we are looking at plumbing we are actually looking into our subconscious to where we have stored information and emotion. We need to be able to access the subconscious in order to create clarity within our lives.

▦ Dreaming about plumbing looks at the way we direct our emotions. It indicates how we make use of our emotions to bypass obstacles in order to create security for ourselves and to control the flow of emotions within. Another interpretation is that of the internal plumbing. Often, to dream of plumbing in this sense alerts us to something that is perhaps out of kilter with ourselves, with our bodies. A leaking steam pipe might suggest, for instance, a problem with hypertension. A pump might symbolize the heart. Obviously, such images should not be used as diagnostic tools in any way.

*You might also like to consult the entry for Pipe.*

**PLUNGE**

🔆 Spiritual risk pushes us into a situation where we must take the plunge. The Fool in the Tarot gives a visual image of this conundrum. He steps out into space secure that he will be safe.

◈ When facing uncertainty in waking life we very often need reassurance that we have both the courage and the daring to go ahead with a particular activity. Very often, to dream of plunging is to recognize that we do have the ability to go forward. To dream of a plunger – as in something that clears a blockage – usually indicates that we need to use some force to enable us to deal with difficulty. Frequently, this can be because we have internalized a problem – we have either worked too hard and don't have the energy to move the difficulty away from us or we have created a problem for ourselves in that we have not acted appropriately.

▦ To dream of plunging into something is to recognize that we are facing uncertainty. We are going into something unknown – something that we have perhaps not done before – and are taking a risk. That risk will very often take us into our emotional depths and we will learn new things about ourselves, of which we will then be able to make use. The sports of bungee and parachute jumping epitomize this.

*You may like to consult the entries for Diving and Plumbing.*

**POACH** – *see* **STEALING**

**POCKET**

🔆 A pocket suggests hidden matters or the Occult. In a spiritual sense it is anything that occurs in the realms of the intuitive feminine.

◈ A pocket in a dream can also indicate a sense of ownership and possession. To have something in our pocket means that we have appropriated it, that we have taken ownership. This can represent a situation in the everyday world, or it can represent emotions that we may have previously hidden and now need to own, in the sense of being able to make use of them.

▦ To dream of a pocket is to be dealing with our personal secrets or thoughts – those things that we have deliberately chosen to hide rather than done so on impulse. They are perhaps secret thoughts that we do not want to share with anyone else. There may also be thoughts about our own abilities and the value that we have within our own personal community.

## POINT

❁ A point is the Beginning of all things, the Soul or Completion, the place from which everything else emanated.

♥ Psychologically and intellectually, to have integrated ourselves means that we have reached our own centre. This is often symbolized in dreams by a point or dot.

▥ To be aware of the point of decision is to come to a resolve that something has to be done. We must bring about change in one way or another and at that particular 'point' there is nothing else to be done. From this arises all other creative solutions.

⊞ Anything pointed normally refers to male sexuality and has this symbolism in both men's and women's dreams.

## POINTING

❁ A particular way forward is being indicated; there is a goal we must reach.

♥ Pointing in a dream, particularly by one of our dream characters, indicates either that we are being given a sense of direction, or that we are being pointed away from a present action and should leave it behind. If we are being pointed at we may also be being singled out for a particular task.

▥ When we dream of someone pointing, normally we are having our attention drawn to a particular object, feeling or even place. We need to take note of both who is pointing it out to us, to gain some idea of the relevance and equally what they are pointing at. We may feel that we are at the receiving end of an aggressive act or accusation – that we are being accused of wrongdoing and need to look at the validity of our conduct.

*Also consult the entry for Direction in Position.*

## POKE/POKER

❁ The poker in this instance suggests rigid and unbending discipline, which is sometimes necessary. There is often the necessity for aggressive action, but also rigid attitudes and behaviour in spiritual development. To poke someone is to goad them.

♥ Playing a game of poker in a dream, whether on-line or otherwise, suggests that we are taking a risk in everyday life. It may be important to note who we are playing with. A poker face is one that shows no emotion whatever the circumstances. As the game of poker becomes more popular in the field of gambling, many of the terms used have relevance in today's world.

▥ A poker obviously has links with masculinity, but also with rigidity. Inherent in the idea of such an object is that it causes a shift in perception.

When we are being poked in a dream we need to ascertain what the irritant is in our waking lives.

⚏ The use of a poker can be seen as the sexual act in both men and women's dreams but may also be seen as an inflexible attitude to the physical body.

*You might also like to consult the entries for Cards and Gambling.*

**POLICE – *see* PEOPLE**

**POLLUTION**

⚏ Pollution suggests that ideas, concepts and principles can be contaminated in some way and thus made less than perfect.

⚏ In its original meaning of desecration, such a strong image makes us aware of how easy it is for us to lose sight of our aims and objectives in life. On an emotional level we can become conscious of a kind of pollution when we are not in line with our own truth.

⚏ As we become more aware of the consequences of pollution in waking life, dream images will take on a relevance that has not been evident before. On a personal level we ourselves, our bodies, can become polluted by the food we eat, the medications we need, the air we breathe and so on, giving rise to distorted dream images.

**PONY – *see* HORSE IN ANIMALS**

**POOL/POND**

⚏ A pool can have the same connotations as a doorway – an entry into the unconscious and our deepest emotions. A pond will tend to represent a man-made construction. Esoterically, a puddle – a small body of water – can be used for scrying, that is, looking towards the future as though into a magic mirror. To be looking into a puddle may be trying to decide what future action needs to be taken.

⚏ In order to understand ourselves we may need to explore the pool by totally immersing ourselves in it, that is, to become involved in our own emotions. How we deal with what arises (in more senses than one) will teach us a lot about ourselves. The pool may suggest a form of cleansing, particularly of old traumas and emotions or of past misdeeds. The most potent image of that is baptism by immersion.

⚏ Dreaming of a pool deals with our need for the understanding of our own emotions and inner feelings. A pool in a wood, for instance, would suggest the ability to understand our own need for peace and tranquility. An urban swimming pool might signify our need for structure in our relationships with other people, whereas a pool in the road would suggest an emotional problem to be got through before carrying out our plans. A pond might suggest the emotions associated with the workplace in that this is an environment where relationships are artificially constructed.

*Consult the entries for Lagoon/Lake and Water for further clarification.*

**POOR – *see* POVERTY**

**POPE**

🏵 Our spiritual mentor or Higher Self will sometimes be seen as the Pope. He may also be someone to whom we have given authority.

♡ The Pope often appears in dreams as a substitute for the father, or as a personification of God.

🎴 Often to meet the Pope in a dream is to meet the side of ourselves that has developed a code of behaviour based on our religious beliefs. He may be benign or judgmental, depending on how we perceive the head of the Catholic church. It will also depend on how the figure of the Pope was presented in childhood.

**POSITION**

🏵 When a particular position is highlighted in a dream it usually signifies our moral or spiritual standpoint, or our position in life. It can also give an indication of how we are handling situations in our lives. For instance, something in the wrong position means we are going about things in the wrong way.

♡ Status is an important aspect of self-esteem. In dreams we often picture our sense of self by becoming conscious of our position relative to other dream objects. Often in dream interpretation position is not considered. However, much additional information can be gleaned by carefully considering these such placings:

**Higher or above** – our spirit, intellect, ideals and consciences are being brought to our attention. This applies also when dreaming of the upper part of anything (of a building or body, for example). Our altruism may be being brought into question.

**Underneath, below or downstairs** – this signifies the anarchic or immoral side of our personalities. The sexual impulses can also be characterized in this way.

**Upside down** – the potential for chaos and difficulty is being emphasized.

**Ups and downs** – the personality has a need to balance the heights and depths of its experience, and if this does not happen a warning will usually appear in dream form. Situations in life can be experienced in dreams as the actual movement of our position.

**Back and front** – the back of anything signifies rejection, and the front acceptance. Conflict between rejection and acceptance can be shown in a dream as seeing both the back and front of something.

**Backward/forward** – when a backward and/or forward movement is prominent this usually indicates a regressive, backward-looking tendency. We may want to retire into the past, rather than tackling fears and moving ahead.

**Centre** – to be particularly conscious of the centre of any aspect of a dream indicates we are aware of a goal or objective, or perhaps even of our real Self. We may need to be the centre of attention whatever the circumstances. *Also consult the section on Archetypes in the Introduction.*

**Far/Near** – in dreams, space and time can become confused. Dreaming of something that is far away may indicate that it is far away in time. This may be future or past, depending on the dream. A long way in front would be future, a long way behind would be past. Near or close would mean recently, or in the immediate future.

**Horizontal and Vertical** – the horizontal usually symbolizes the material world whereas the vertical in dreams tends to represent the spiritual realm.

**Left** – the left side suggests the less dominant, more passive side. Often it is taken to represent all that is dark and sinister and those parts of our personality that we try to suppress. It is, however, more to do with instinctive behaviour, what feels good inside, and with personal behaviour without attention to moral codes.

The left side is supportive in expression, and receptive by nature, so anything appearing in dreams on the left side can be accepted as a symbol of support. Any pain experienced on the left side is interpreted in terms of sensitivity. The left expresses the more feminine attributes and often the past. Any conflict between right and left indicates the differences between logic and intuition. Indecision over left or right suggests an inability to decide whether to rely on drive or instinct. Feelings of being left behind suggest a sense of inadequacy, of disintegration and of having to leave the past behind.

**Low** – in dreams, feeling 'low' can suggest a sense of inferiority or humility. Often we will give way to submissive behaviour, and put ourselves in a lower position than others. Occasionally, to be below something or someone can indicate a need to explore the underside or negativity of a relationship or situation.

**Opposite** – anything in a dream that is opposite us may suggest difficulty in reconciling two paradoxes (good/bad, male/female etc.). This can sometimes suggest conflict. One thing deliberately put opposite another suggests a deliberate attempt to introduce discord. When something is deliberately moved from being opposite in a dream, any differences that we have may be reconciled.

**Right** – the right side represents the more dominant, logical side. It is the consciously expressed, confident side that perceives the exterior world in perhaps a more objective sense. It is to do with 'rightness' – that is, correctness and moral and social behaviour. Anything observed on the right side in dreams usually becomes more significant as we progress. Any pain experienced on the right side can also be interpreted in terms of drive. It also expresses the more masculine attributes. Movement to the right indicates that something is coming into conscious awareness.

**Top** – to be at the top of anything shows we have succeeded in our endeavours. Trying to reach the top suggests more effort is needed, whereas to be on top is to have assumed control.

**Under/underneath** – being underneath something suggests either taking shelter or submitting to someone else's handling of us. It may also represent the part of us that we hide, or the part that is less capable.

**Up/upper** – this shows that we have the capability of achieving a degree of supremacy. We are capable of getting the 'upper hand' in particular situations. We can move away from the mundane, ordinary, everyday world into a more spiritual way of life.

When any direction is indicated or particularly noticeable in a dream, we need to consider the esoteric implications and how these are applicable in our everyday lives. Based on the Chinese method of interpretation and used by those systems of belief that adhere to the natural forces, the points of the compass can be read symbolically. **The North** signifies the Unknown, and hence sometimes darkness. It is spirituality within the world. **The East** traditionally suggests birth and mystic religions. It also represents becoming 'conscious'. **The South** is representative of earthly passion and sensuality. **The West** can symbolize death, but more properly the state after death when there is increased spiritual awareness. Traditionally, it can also represent the more logical side of our natures.

## POST

A post in spiritual terms may signify a support or a marker. As a marker it has the same meaning as flag or banner. As a support it will be useful to look at what help we need to advance our spiritual understanding.

To be posting a notice suggests making a declaration. When in dreams we are posting a letter it is to communicate information or intention.

To be 'in a post' suggests that someone else has made the decision to employ us – we become a support. A large quantity of post being delivered in a dream may indicate that we are under pressure.

**POVERTY**

&#9775; Spiritual poverty occurs when we become conscious that there is something lacking in our lives. It can also be recognized as self-denial.

&#9829; Poverty can be conveyed by poor surroundings in a dream. It may be that we need to deal with our surroundings; there is something lacking in our environment rather than ourselves. When we feel poor we do not have the wherewithal to look after ourselves properly.

&#9635; To experience poverty in a dream highlights a sense of being deprived of the ability to satisfy our basic needs. We may feel inadequate, either emotionally or materially. Often we need to go right back to basics to discover what our real needs are.

*You might also like to consult the entries for Money and Wealth.*

**POWDER** – *see* MIX

**PRAYER**

&#9775; There are two aspects of prayer. One is supplication – asking for something – and the other is worship – acknowledging the supremacy of the Ultimate.

&#9829; Psychologically, the human being has always needed to feel that there is a greater power than himself available to him. To be praying in a dream reinforces this, since we need to use our own inner sense of self to access the Greater Power.

&#9635; Prayer suggests the idea that we need to seek outside help for ourselves. We may need someone else's authority to succeed in what we are doing. It also can indicate our ability to draw on our own inner resources.

*You might also like to consult the entry for Spiritual Imagery in the Introduction.*

**PREACH** – *see* **PRIEST/PRIESTESS AND MINISTERS OF ALL RELIGIONS IN PEOPLE**

**PRECIPICE**

&#9775; A precipice will indicate a perceived spiritual danger. In fact, there is no way forward except to acknowledge that danger and continue on our way.

&#9829; The image of the Fool in the Tarot shows him at the beginning and the end of his journey. He is unmindful of the precipice and initially is not aware of the danger he is in. Conversely, he does not care because he is aware he is capable of stepping off the edge and taking flight. This type of dream often appears when we are in a position of great risk.

&#9635; The fear of failure is a very strong emotion. Often it can be represented in dreams by a precipice. To step off a precipice is taking risks, since we do not know the outcome of our action. To try to climb a precipice is to be making a tremendous effort to overcome obstacles that have arisen.

*Consult the entry for Cliff to help with clarification.*

## PREGNANCY

⚙ There is always a gestation period in spiritual work. We may have to be patient and wait for a natural process to take place so that we can fulfil a task.

♡ To dream of someone else being pregnant suggests that we are in a position to observe part of ourselves developing new skills or characteristics. We may be unaware of what the outcome of this process will be. To dream of a man being pregnant, particularly if it is a woman's dream, is probably a projection of her own wish for the man to take responsibility within her life.

▦ Dreaming of pregnancy usually denotes a fairly protracted waiting period being necessary for something, possibly the completion of a project. A new area of our potential or personality is developing.

⦂ Interestingly enough, for a woman to dream of pregnancy seldom actually means her own pregnancy, although it can indicate pregnancy in someone around her. For a man, dreaming of the pregnancy of his wife or partner can indicate his willingness to take on extra responsibility.

## PREHISTORIC

⚙ Spiritual progression requires us to understand our physical, emotional, mental and spiritual urges. The prehistoric images indicate either the lack of ability to integrate the various parts of ourselves successfully, or to integrate with society. There are still aspects perhaps of family history that need to be understood.

♡ Often in dreams the landscape or scenario appears to be prehistoric. This is 'before thought' and before we had the ability to properly record our impressions. If we believe that babies are conscious of the world they will enter before birth, then these impressions can appear in later life as prehistoric images. For instance, a barren landscape might indicate a lack of love.

▦ Being aware in a dream that something is prehistoric is to recognize that feelings and emotions we have arise literally from before the time we were able to understand ourselves. When we have not fully integrated and comprehended the basic urge for survival, it is possible for us to be self-destructive without necessarily appreciating why.

*You might also like to consult the entry for Dinosaur.*

## PRESCRIPTION – *see* HEALING

## PRESENT/PRESENTS

⚙ One of the requirements of spiritual advancement is that we learn to live in the present (literally the pre-sent). We need to be able to take advantage of anything that life offers us – to use it for ourselves, but also to recognize that it has relevance for other people and can affect the way that they live.

♥ To present something in a dream (as in making a presentation) is offering work that we have done for approval and recognition. We appreciate that the work we have done is more important than we ourselves are.

▦ When a present appears in a dream, it can first of all be a play on words. We are being given a 'here and now'. We are being reminded to live in the moment and not the past or future. A present can also indicate a talent or gift. If we are receiving a present we are being loved and recognized and are also gaining from the relationship. If we are giving a present, we appreciate that we have characteristics we are able to offer other people. A pile of presents in a dream can signify as yet unrecognized talents and skills. If the presents give some indication of time – e.g. birthday presents – we may expect some success around that time.

*Consult the entry for Gift/Give/Giving for further information.*

**PRESERVE – *see* PROTECT/PROTECTION**

**PRIEST/PRIESTESS – *see* ARCHETYPES IN THE INTRODUCTION, MONK, NUN AND PEOPLE**

**PRINCE/PRINCESS – *see* ARCHETYPES IN THE INTRODUCTION, HERO/ HEROINE AND PEOPLE**

**PRISON**

✹ Duty and guilt are opposite sides of the same coin in a spiritual sense. Duty can be a liability and therefore a trap, and guilt can prevent us from seeing a way forward. When we feel trapped either by duty or guilt we will dream of a prison.

♥ Often we create a 'prison' for ourselves through a sense of duty or guilt and this can often be shown in dreams. The types of locks and bolts we perceive in our prison may show us how we are imprisoning ourselves. For example, a lock with a key would suggest that we know how to escape, whereas a bolt shows that we have to make a greater effort. A barred window would suggest that we are being prevented from using that which is external to us.

▦ We may feel that outside circumstances are making life difficult, but in actual fact we are creating those circumstances ourselves. This can be on an emotional, material or spiritual level and is translated into the dream image of a prison.

*Also consult the entries for Bolt, Key and Lock.*

**PRIZE**

✹ In spiritual terms, gaining a prize or accolade in a dream means having used our instincts and intuition in harmony and so can use inspiration.

♥ To prize an object (as in a prize possession) is to give it its proper value. This does not necessarily mean being materialistic, but being able to gain from an appreciation of its intrinsic value. This may indicate the need to concentrate on the material world for a time.

▨ In dreams, to win a prize is to have succeeded in overcoming our own obstacles. We are also being acknowledged by other people for having made the effort to succeed and achieving what we set out to do. To be giving away prizes suggests that we are giving public acknowledgement to efforts others have made.

⊞ In a woman's dream a prize often suggests emotional satisfaction. In a man's dream it will signify success.

## PROCESSION

❀ Spiritually, a procession is indicative of a group of like-minded people but also of people who have great knowledge. In dreams we are recognizing the importance of whatever system of belief or religion we belong to. We recognize respect must be paid.

♥ A procession is often a way of marking a special occasion with pageantry and dignity. In dreams such an image can often represent our need to have our own successes and abilities recognized. To be taking part in a procession is acknowledging our need to belong to a like-minded group. To be watching a procession is to appreciate other people's single-mindedness.

▨ A procession means an orderly approach and often makes a statement of intent. In a dream, to see a line of people who all appear to have a similar goal or set of beliefs in mind, indicates that it is the intention behind the group which is important. Often a procession is hierarchical, with the most important people either first or last. This could be important in a dream in enabling us to adopt priorities for ourselves.

## PROFIT

❀ In spiritual terms, profit is energy or power gained commensurate with the amount of effort we are prepared to put in, in anything we do.

♥ Simply, if we profit from something we gain benefit. In dreams we are made aware of possible emotional or material benefits through the symbolism of profit.

▨ The idea of profit and loss comes from the material world and the need to control resources. In dreams the meaning is widened to all sorts of resources not just financial, though if there are financial worries we may well dream of some kind of accounting procedure.

*You might also like to consult the entries for Money and Wealth.*

## PROPOSE/PROPOSAL

🌑 A proposal is a statement of intent and spiritually represents the sacred marriage, the union of spiritual and physical. To propose in the spiritual sense is to make an offer or offering of our abilities.

♡ To propose an action in a dream is to promote it as a good idea, as something that should be considered. In the sense of a marriage proposal we are marking the potential integration of two sides of our personality.

▦ A business proposal in dream parlance is a properly thought out course of action to bring about some kind of merger or autonomy. It is often the first step in a new understanding of the world we live in.

⊟ Both men and women will dream of proposals with personal and business connotations. The type of proposal made or given will highlight the seriousness or emotional impact of the integration that is taking place. Contrary to popular belief, it does not necessarily mean that a proposal will take place in real life.

*Consult the entries for Contract, Marriage and Wedding/Wedding Dress/ Wedding Ring for further information.*

## PROSECUTE – *see* TRIAL

## PROSTITUTE

🌑 Spiritually we need to accept other people's values. A prostitute originally meant 'one who stood before', and in ancient times was a woman who initiated men into the mysteries of the sacred marriage, a rite of sacrifice.

♡ In dreaming of prostitution, we may actually be connecting with a poor self-image. We are minimizing our abilities and talents – this may be in a work situation as much as in our personal life. Very often, when we are expected to 'perform', inadequacy or ego makes us feel that we are 'prostituting' our talents.

▦ Dreaming of a prostitute often suggests a hidden sexual need. Often, dreaming of a prostitute forces us to look at our own sense of guilt or uncertainty about ourselves. A pimp is one who procures business for a prostitute and this has obvious resonance in the business world. To be paying a prostitute may suggest that we do not trust our own abilities, sexual or otherwise. To be paid for the sexual act may suggest that we feel relationships will cost us. In both cases there may be a fear of loving relationships.

⊟ The appearance of a prostitute in a woman's dream can highlight her own unexpressed need for sexual freedom. In a man's dream it may signify his need for relationship at any cost.

## PROTECT/PROTECTION

🌑 Spiritual protection appears in many guises in dreams from images such as a cloak to a mist. It will depend on the type of protection needed – a cloak would suggest a closer, more intimate level than a mist, which is more ephemeral or disparate.

◈ It is a natural reaction to need to protect ourselves from harm and for many people an emotional attack will cause us to dream of trying to find some sort of protection. When we feel that a principle or idea needs preserving we will often dream of protection of something.

▦ When we have been made vulnerable in daily life our dreams will offer an image in order to help us deal with the problem. The mind has a habit of imaging the necessary type of protection needed.

*Also consult the entry for Garlic.*

**PROTEST –** *see* **ARGUE/ARGUMENT AND DEMONSTRATE/DEMONSTRATION**
**PROVOKE –** *see* **GOAD**
**PROWL/PROWLER –** *see* **THE INDIVIDUAL ENTRY FOR INTRUDER AND ALSO THE ENTRY IN PEOPLE**
**PSYCHOLOGIST/PSYCHIATRIST –** *see* **ANALYST**
**PUDDLE –** *see* **LAGOON/LAKE, POOL/POND AND WATER**
**PULL/PULLING**

❀ At a certain stage of spiritual development, we can find ourselves being pulled in a certain direction. We may be compelled to do certain things without necessarily knowing where the impulse comes from. The call could be, for instance, because of someone's distress or to give us information we need. Dreams are a very effective way of implanting such ideas into our psyche.

◈ We may in everyday life find ourselves being pulled by our emotions and feel that we are powerless to resist. This can translate into the dream image of being pulled. We may feel that we have to go along with something and do not have the ability to refuse.

▦ Pulling suggests a positive action. We are being alerted to the fact that we can do something about a situation. In dreams, if we are pulling we are making the decisions within a project. If we are being pulled we may feel that we have to give in to outside pressures. Extra effort to have something happen may be necessary. The object we are pulling, and the means by which we are pulling it, may be important. *For examples, see Bridle, Rope etc.*

⊞ In slang terms, pulling means picking up a potential partner. In dreams this can actually translate itself into a physical feeling.

**PUMP –** *see* **PLUMBING**
**PUNCH –** *see* **FIGHT**
**PUNISH/PUNISHMENT**

❀ The concept of Divine Retribution – that is, being punished by a force greater than ourselves – suggests a judgemental God. Spiritual punishment is much more, however, the idea of self-flagellation for not having achieved what is required of us. When in dreams we are punishing another, the inference is that we are standing in judgement over them.

◈ When there is conflict in our lives, if we cannot resolve it we will often dream of being punished. This may be the only way out of our particular dilemma. We would rather suffer pain than resolve the difficulty. Inflicting punishment suggests that we feel some aspect of our personality is out of alignment.

▣ When a child recognizes that he or she is not conforming to what is expected, the threat of punishment is often present. In later life, when there is fear of retribution from an external source, we will often dream of being punished when there is no evidence of such. Self-punishment occurs when we have not achieved the standards we expect of ourselves and in many ways might be considered self-abuse.

## PUPPET

◈ At certain stages of development, we can become aware that we are powerless without a spiritually motivating force behind us. We are like puppets in the greater scheme of things.

◈ When a puppet appears in a dream there is perhaps a sense of being able to manipulate circumstances or people around us. A puppet can also represent the more mechanical processes of our being, those activities that go on automatically in the background.

▣ If someone else is working the puppet, we may feel that we are being manipulated. It would be wise to look at how we are co-operating in everyday life in becoming a victim. If the puppet is manipulating us we have become aware that bureaucracy is causing us difficulty. What should be working for us has, in fact, turned into some kind of manipulation.

*The entry for Toys may give further clarification.*

## PUPPY – see ANIMALS

## PURPLE – see COLOURS

## PURSE

◈ One symbolism of a purse is the same as that of a bag: the feminine and the containing principle. We are attempting to conserve our Spiritual energy or power.

◈ The material that a purse is made from can have an important significance. A fine material could suggest affluence and a purse that is not appropriate for the occasion symbolizes literally being out of our comfort zone. The old saying 'You cannot make a silk purse out of a sow's ear' has relevance in dreams.

▦ A purse is normally used to hold money, or something of value to us. In dreams it therefore becomes something of value it its own right. To find a purse would suggest that we have found something of value, whereas to lose a purse suggests that we may be being careless.

⬚ For a woman to lose her purse in dreams would suggest that her essential nature as a woman is being compromised, whereas in a man's dream he may be losing the security he finds in his primary relationship.

## PUSHED/PUSHING

⬢ When one is developing psychically, it is possible to become aware of the subtle forces and energy around. This can be experienced as being pushed.

◈ When in a dream we are being pushed, there is an energy around us that enables us to achieve what we want. If we are pushing, then we are usually exerting our will positively. Pushing something uphill, such as a car or snowball, suggests that we are trying to resist natural forces.

▦ When in everyday life we are aware of pressure, this can surface in dreams as being pushed and can sometimes indicate a fear of illness. In certain forms of mental illness, the patient experiences a feeling of being pushed around and made to do something he does not want to do. Occasionally, when experienced in dreams, this can actually be a form of healing.

## PYJAMAS – see CLOTHES

## PYRAMID

⬢ Spiritually, the pyramid is a symbol of integration of the Self and the Soul. In dreams it can represent death, but also indicates rebirth. It is a guardian of power.

◈ The pyramid always signifies a wider awareness of power and energy. There is a point inside the pyramid where all the planes intersect. This will regenerate any matter that is placed there, for instance razor blades will become sharp again. In a larger pyramid, that particular spot can be used for enhancing mystical experiences. In dreams, to enter a pyramid is to be searching for the meaning of life.

▦ A pyramid is a very powerful image. On a physical level, it is a building of wonder. On a mental level, it is a structure of regeneration. It will depend on our level of awareness as to which interpretation is valid.

## PYTHON – see SNAKE

## QUADRUPLE

✹ When a thing is quadrupled it is made four times as large or four times as important as previously. In spiritual terms this suggests that there is four times the amount of power available – it is power 'squared'.

♥ The symbolic meaning of number four deals with stability and invokes the ability of all things to be grounded, so anything that is quadrupled is linked to the proper manifestation in the physical realm. Things must manifest through the four elements of Fire, Air, Water and Earth to become real.

▦ As we become more aware, the ancient symbolisms become more relevant. Anything which is represented as being quadrupled in size or power picks up on the symbolism of numbers. Fours represent solidity, calmness and home in the sense of sanctuary. On a mundane level, this means we may need to consider our need for security.

*Consult the entries for Elements and Numbers.*

## QUAINT

✹ When something is considered to be quaint it is old-fashioned but with a charm of its own. The spiritual significance of this is that ideas may be outmoded but still worth pursuing for their intrinsic value. Many folk tales are seen as quaint yet have within them a grain of truth or self-awareness.

♥ Any object seen as quaint in dreams bears further scrutiny in order to understand its relevance. We may be dealing with behaviour patterns from the past which are charming but out of date.

▦ On a mundane level an image that is quaint is perhaps a curiosity – of interest but not much use. In today's technological age, dreaming of an old typewriter, for instance, might highlight an antipathy to new technology.

## QUAIL – *see* BIRDS

## QUAKER

✹ The name 'quaker' was initially given to religious sects given to fits of shaking during religious fervor. Only later did it become a popular name for those of the Society of Friends who 'trembled at the Word of the Lord'. Religious beliefs and the acceptance of an ability to cope because of those beliefs is a great part of spiritual development.

♥ The human being has a need for a belief system that can support them in times of difficulty. To dream of being a Quaker allows us to link with our own inner self-sufficiency.

To dream of somebody else being a Quaker indicates the recognition of the ability to maintain a strongly held belief, come what may. It indicates a tranquility and peacefulness that is not necessarily available to us in the waking state.

## QUALIFY/QUALIFICATION

In spiritual terms, a qualification suggests that we have been invested with a particular quality or ability. This suggests effort on our part to understand and make use of the hidden meaning in those things we have learnt.

To dream that we have qualified – that is, passed an examination – suggests that we have been tested by an external authority and given permission to use our abilities.

In purely mundane terms, to qualify an action or project is to justify its existence. In dream parlance, we may find that tasks or projects that have given us difficulty sort themselves out in dreams and enable us to move forward.

## QUALITY

Quality suggests the best that we can be. Poor quality means we are falling below our own spiritual aspirations. Good quality being highlighted in a dream can suggest some hidden approval.

When quality is an issue in dreams we are perhaps not certain that we have put our best efforts into what we are doing. Emotion may be getting in the way.

When we find ourselves in dreams dividing things into separate groupings – for instance into good and bad, or best and worst – we are questioning our own ability to differentiate.

## QUANTITY – *see* AMOUNT

## QUARANTINE

Quarantine, in a spiritual sense, means isolation; that is, retreating from the world for a time, perhaps to gain a different perspective, perhaps to preserve our own truth or belief.

When in waking life we feel isolated, this may translate itself in dream language into being in quarantine. We are aware that we have been cut off from normal contact with others. It would seem that some internal 'authority' has taken over to give us a breathing space or time to consider our actions. While frightening, this can be a time of rest and replenishment.

Dreaming of having to put an animal into quarantine signifies our inability to look after a vulnerable part of ourselves or others. It may also indicate our awareness of having to cut off the lower, more animal side of ourselves. To put someone else in quarantine suggests that we cannot handle what that dream character represents.

**QUARREL**

🔅 Spiritual conflict or a conflict between the spiritual self and the physical can appear in dreams as a quarrel. It is a passionate dispute, so suggests that there is extreme feeling.

💧 Depending on the other aspects of the dream, quarrelling can suggest that there is conflict between what we have been taught and what we believe, or rather what we have come to believe. Often such a conflict can only be resolved through an outburst of emotion.

🔳 To dream that we are quarrelling with someone indicates an inner conflict. To be quarrelling with authority, e.g. police, indicates a conflict between right and wrong.

🔹 For a man to be quarrelling with a woman, or vice versa, signifies a conflict between drive and intuition.

*Consult the entries for Argue/Argument, Conflict and Police in People for additional clarification.*

**QUARRY**

🔅 Both in the sense of something which is hunted and that which is dug out, a quarry signifies a spiritual search which may require us to unearth information in order to progress.

💧 Seeking a quarry (that is, pursuing someone or something) in a dream can indicate that we know what we are looking for and have a goal in mind. It is the act of finding it that is important, however.

🔳 Dreaming of a quarry means quarrying the depths of our personality, 'digging out' the positive knowledge and perceptions we may have. Often dream symbols are created which link with childhood or past experiences which we may have buried and which now need to be brought into conscious understanding.

*You might like to consult the entries for Chase/Chased, Digging/Excavation, Hunt/Hunting/Huntsman and Mine/Miner.*

**QUARTER – see FRACTION/FRAGMENT**

**QUARTET**

🔅 Spiritually the quartet – a set of four similar things considered as one object – links with the Quaternity, which signifies manifestation on the physical plane. The Quaternity, from a theological perspective, is the Holy Trinity – Father, Son and Holy Ghost – plus the feminine principle of Wisdom.

💧 Anything repeated more than once emphasizes the significance of that object to the dreamer. The dream object will be reproduced four times at the same moment, rather than being seen sequentially, in order to make the emphasis apparent.

⊞ Dreaming of a quartet of any kind signifies a link with the material or practical aspects of other objects in the dream. It could be necessary to concentrate on pragmatic solutions to a problem. A musical quartet symbolizes harmony.

*Also consult the entry for Four in Numbers.*

## QUARTZ

✺ The quartz is recognized as both receiving and transmitting spiritual energy.

♥ The crystallization process was seen by the Ancients as the trapping of light and, therefore, power, and, on a subliminal level, this is still recognized by many dreamers. To dream of quartz, therefore, signifies a recognition of developing power.

⊞ Quartz seen in dreams tends to represent the crystallization of ideas and feelings. It touches into our deep internal processes, often enabling us to express that which we have found impossible before.

*You might like to consult the entry for Gems/Jewels.*

## QUAY

✺ Spiritual progress can be suggested by a quay, since it is a point of departure. This image has obviously had more relevance in the past when travel by sea was more prevalent than air travel.

♥ Because anything associated with water is connected with emotion and how we feel about things, being on a quay can indicate how we need to handle other people's emotions as we move into a new phase of life. It also signifies being prepared to participate in the flow of life.

⊞ Standing on a quayside in a dream can indicate either moving forward into a new phase of life or leaving an old one behind. If looking forward with a sense of anticipation, it is the new phase that needs understanding. If looking back, there may be something in the past which needs attention before we can move on.

▣ Oddly, a quay, presumably because of its shape, can represent the masculine principle. In a man's dream it is the quay itself which will be relevant; in a woman's dream it will be the water and her emotions.

*You might like to consult the entries for Boat/Ship, Journey and Water.*

## QUEEN – *see* PEOPLE

## QUEST

✺ Undertaking a spiritual quest in order to understand our place in the world and the pursuit of spiritual knowledge is a way of developing our own personal attributes.

❤ Often, the trials and tribulations we have to go through in achieving something we feel to be important are translated in dreams into a quest or search. The way these events are faced is as important as the actual achievement itself.

▦ Many fairy stories and mythological tales have as their main theme the search for something rare or magical (e.g. Jason and the Argonauts). Such themes can be translated into dreams in a personally applicable way. We eventually find the rare and magical within ourselves.

◗ The Hero's Quest for both men and women is a fundamental pattern of human experience which can appear in many guises in dreams. It is a rite of passage and usually signifies some kind of initiation. To be searching for something usually indicates that we are aware that we must undertake a frightening task in order to progress.

*Also consult the entries for Hero/Heroine, Initiation, Knight, Rescue, Search and Task.*

## QUESTION

✹ Spiritual questioning and enquiry lead to greater knowledge. The question of the meaning of life is, of course, a perennial one. Questions of any type will often appear in dreams when we are reaching a new stage of spiritual awareness.

❤ If we have a question in waking life which needs answering, by keeping it in mind before going to sleep we may often find the answer through dreams.

▦ When we ask questions in a dream we are indicating a degree of self-doubt. To have someone asking us questions in dreams shows that we are aware that we have some kind of knowledge available to us. If the question cannot be answered, we may need to seek the answer ourselves through other means.

## QUESTIONNAIRE/QUIZ

✹ Questioning the inevitable is a way forward spiritually. A questionnaire suggests a formalized form of questioning, whereas a quiz tests knowledge.

❤ A questionnaire depicts the use of our mental faculties in a focused, decision-making way. By being rational, we are able to evaluate a problem. Taking part in a pub quiz suggests a group activity which tests awareness and knowledge.

▦ To be answering a questionnaire or quiz in a dream suggests we may be making an attempt to change our circumstances without being certain of what we should actually do to bring about the change. We may also be trying to come to terms with other aspects of our personality.

**QUEUE** – *see* **LINE**

**QUICK**

🌑 Formerly, quick was used to designate full of life and it is this meaning that can be used from a spiritual perspective.

♡ The word 'quick' is often used as a command to speed up an action or process. It will tend to have this connotation in dreams and it is worth considering what actions are taking too long in waking life.

▥ In pregnancy, a baby 'quickens' when it makes its presence felt in its mother's womb. A project or idea in workaday life takes on a life of its own and this is symbolized in dreams by a sense of speed.

**QUICKSAND**

🌑 Spiritual quicksand suggests a situation where we may be on insecure ground insofar as our beliefs are concerned.

♡ To find ourselves trapped in quicksand suggests that we have been put in a difficult situation which is not necessarily of our own making.

▥ In old-fashioned dream interpretation, quicksand represented business difficulties – often due to circumstances beyond our control. Today it tends to signify a lack of security. This is represented by the ground beneath our feet not being stable and indeed being somewhat dangerous.

**QUIET**

🌑 Peace and tranquility give us the opportunity for contemplation.

♡ Becoming aware of how quiet it is in a dream shows that we need to cease being active for a while, perhaps in order to restore our emotional or spiritual balance.

▥ Experiencing a need for quiet in a dream suggests that we need to listen more carefully to either ourselves or others in waking life. Our lives may be lived at such a pace that we have no time to 'stand and stare'.

**QUILT**

🌑 Spiritual comfort and caring can be suggested by a quilt.

♡ Old fashioned patchwork quilts often told a story, both in their materials and the way they were constructed. They therefore became heirlooms and treasured objects. Modern day quilts tend to be more functional and, therefore, the colour and patterns will have less significance. The colour, material and pattern of a quilt in a dream, however, may have more significance than the quilt itself.

▥ The quilt or duvet can often represent our need for security, warmth and love. To be aware of one in a dream, therefore, is our identification of that need. A particular quilt may have a special significance. For instance, a childhood quilt in an adult dream would suggest the need for some kind of reassurance.

*The entries for Colour, Fabric and Shape will enhance your understanding.*

## QUIT

🕉 Somehow quitting has a different impact to leaving. To quit suggests a premeditated action, one in which we have considered the spiritual consequences of our action.

💚 Quitting a responsibility or feeling is to gain a sense of freedom from concern and it is this sense of freedom that allows us to experience new ideas and concepts.

🔲 If in dreams we find ourselves quitting a job, it suggests that a task we have set ourselves in waking life is not fulfilling its purpose. Such a dream may also be among what is classed as anxiety dreams.

## QUIVER

🕉 A state of spiritual ecstasy can be induced which is accompanied by quivering, a kind of shivering. This was initially how the Quakers got their name, as did the Shakers. A quiver in the sense of an arrow holder may be a symbol of words being used as weapons.

💚 A physiological reaction can be translated into dreams as an action. To be quivering in a dream may simply be the effect of feeling cold.

🔲 Quivering indicates a state of extreme emotion. Such a reaction in a dream would signify that we need to consider the emotion and deal with it in everyday life. For instance, an extreme fear reaction may be the residue of something that has happened to us previously and can only be dealt with in waking life.

## QUIZ – *see* QUESTIONNAIRE/QUIZ

## QUOTE/QUOTATION

🕉 A quote in a spiritual sense signifies Truth.

💚 To utter or hear a quote – e.g. Shakespeare – indicates that we should consider the sentiment and power expressed within the quote.

🔲 To be giving a quote – as in a building estimate – can signify the value that we put on our services or talents. We may have difficulty with the accuracy – or the acceptance – of the quote and, therefore, in waking life, will need to reconsider not only our own self-image, but also how we think others see us.

**RABBIT** – *see* ANIMALS

**RABBLE** – *see* CROWD

**RACE** – *see* RUNNING

**RADAR**

🔆 Radar in a dream represents our own personal intuitive faculty. It is our way of picking up subtle messages and signals that other people are giving out, often on a subliminal level.

💟 For many, radar will register in dreams as a sort of 'Big Brother is watching you' feeling. We are monitoring ourselves, perhaps as to whether our behaviour or thoughts are appropriate.

🎴 In today's surveillance society we are conscious of being watched and observed. In dreams this can translate into the image of radar. Its appearance shows that our personal 'antennae' are on the alert for trouble.

*Consult the entries for Watching and Witness for additional information.*

**RADIANCE**

🔆 True radiance, being a quality of light, is a sign of pure spirituality. It is pictured in representations of Holy figures and has the ability to dazzle us – to stop us in our tracks – and at the same time draw us in and enlighten us. Radiance represents something out of the ordinary or supernatural. It also suggests purity of thought, wisdom and the transcendence of the mundane.

💟 When something appears as radiant in a dream it is being marked as having some kind of special quality, which we may need to explore further. Heightened emotion in dreams can be seen as radiance and charisma also has its own quality of light.

🎴 Filmic images of extraterrestrials give a stereotypical image that is often characterized by a type of radiance and this can be carried over into dreams. Whether it is menacing or not will depend on other dream content, but the eeriness will certainly need to be considered.

*Consult the entries for Halo, Light and Extra-terrestrials for further clarification.*

**RADIO**

🔆 A radio is symbolic of spiritual communication. We should be alert and aware of all the subtler vibrations at this time and be open to any eventuality.

💟 Often in dreams a radio can stand for the voice of authority, or of commonly held ideas and ideals. As a method of communication, a radio suggests information that is available to everyone and therefore is widely understood.

🔲 To dream of hearing a radio playing suggests a form of connection with the outside world. What we are hearing is also important: speech would suggest the transmission of information whereas music would indicate a more subtle vibration.

*You might also like to consult the entries for Communication and Media.*

## RAF – *see* ARMED FORCES

## RAFFLE – *see* GAMBLING

## RAFT

🔆 The raft is an image connected with the spiritual transitions we must make in life. It is less secure than the idea of a boat, but more secure than doing it alone. If we are feeling 'lost' and can see no respite, then we may dream of a raft, a solid – yet impermanent – structure beneath us.

💟 It can sometimes be meaningful to find out what the raft is made of. It can often appear in dreams as a symbol of transition, so the material can give us some idea of how to act. If it were made of wood, for instance, it would suggest a readily available rigidity; if of car tyres or other waste material we need to recycle, or reuse the information we already know.

🔲 A raft is a place of safety, often amid turbulence. While it may not be overly secure, it has the ability to support us. This is the kind of dream that occurs when we are dealing with emotional upset or difficulties.

*You might like to consult the entries for Boat/Ship, Journey, Transport, Water and Wood.*

## RAGE – *see* ANGER

## RAILWAY

🔆 Spiritually, the railway suggests a chosen direction that is usually fairly straightforward. It may also indicate a predictable routine.

💟 Psychologically, a railway points to the idea of keeping to one goal (which may be a group one) and being single-minded about it. One early symbolism of the railway was the facility of being able to ignore obstacles, to go round, through or over anything that stood in the way. Seeing the points on a railway line change would signify a change of direction.

🔲 A railway in a dream signifies the way we wish to go in life. We can take a way forward and can make informed choices. A single track suggests that there is only one way to go, whereas a multiple track suggests many more opportunities. A railway station would suggest a planned break.

*Also consult the entries for Journey and Trains in Transport for further information.*

## RAIN

✦ Rain, by virtue of its 'heavenly' origins, symbolizes divine blessing and revelation. It brings about creativity and growth.

♥ Rain can also have a more universal meaning, in that it is the realization of potential on a group level. We should all be able to make use of the fertility that it can bring. The various types of rain have different meanings: heavy rain suggests depression and perhaps isolation whereas gentle rain indicates a time of relative prosperity. Realizing that rain has passed can indicate fresh opportunities are available.

▦ In its simplest meaning, rain stands for tears and emotional release. We may have been depressed with no way to release our feelings in everyday life. Rain in dreams often becomes the first realization that we can let go

⊞ Rain in a woman's dream can suggest the sexual act and the release that that brings. For a man it may bring understanding of his own and his partner's emotions.

*You might also like to consult the entries for Emotions, Water and Weather for further information.*

## RAINBOW

✦ A rainbow symbolizes the spiritual glory that is available to us through understanding and learning. More esoterically, a rainbow is said to represent the seven steps of awareness necessary for true spirituality. It is the connecting 'bridge' between the physical and the spiritual realms.

♥ The raising of consciousness and appreciation of something as ethereal as a rainbow suggests the need for a heightened sense of awareness. When it was realized that white light could be split into its component parts the various colours came to have meaning. For instance, red indicates passion, green fertility, and purple dignity.

▦ A rainbow appearing in a dream is the promise of something better to come. The old story of the pot of gold at the end of the rainbow is so firmly entrenched in folklore that this meaning often comes across in dreams.

*Consult the entries for Cauldron, Colour, Gold and Light for further information.*

## RAM – *see* ANIMALS

## RAPE – *see* SEX

## RARE

✦ If an object is rare it is rendered so by its scarcity, so spiritually suggests ancient knowledge and practices, which we have not yet uncovered.

♥ If something is rare it is precious and thus not seen often. This can be translated in dreams into emotions that we do not often allow to surface.

▦ In dreams, as in waking life, if meat is rare it is only partially cooked and thus represents ideas that are not yet fully formed or concepts that have been put forward without having been finalized. This does not mean that they are any less valid and this would be the same if we dreamt of any other rare article or object.

**RAT – *see* ANIMALS**

**RAVEN – *see* BIRDS**

**RAW**

Raw as in tender or sore is recognized spiritually in, for instance, martyrdom where all pretence is stripped away and there is an element of suffering for our beliefs.

Raw emotion is present in dreams when we are able to access hose things we choose to cover up in everyday life. Where we have difficulty in expressing this, such feelings can be given vent to in dreams.

Images in dreams that highlight a state of rawness may be bringing to our attention that elements of our lives have not been worked on or worked with to their best advantage. Raw meat might represent a wound and raw vegetables a dietary deficiency, particularly if they are those we do not like.

*You might also like to consult the entries for Food and Martyr.*

**REACHING OUT – *see* YEARN**

**READING**

Reading, or being in a library, appears in dreams as a symbol of the realization of spiritual truths. Reading a Holy Book in dreams suggests that we are attempting to understand a particular belief system, or that there is information in it pertinent to us at this time.

Until comparatively recently, the only way to record events was to write them down. Reading is an activity that assists us in recalling things from memory – our own or joint memories. To be aware that we are reading a novel is to begin to understand our own need for fantasy. A psychic reading often works with the symbolism of many basic dream images. To dream of having such a reading suggests a need to understand ourselves on a deeper level.

Reading a book in a dream suggests that we are seeking information. Reading a letter signifies receiving news. Reading a list – e.g. a shopping list – indicates a need to give some order to our lives.

*Consult the entries for Book, Letter, Library, List and Medium as well as the information on Spiritual Imagery in the Introduction.*

**REALITY TELEVISION – *see* MEDIA AND TELEVISION**

**REAPING**

The scythe was an ancient symbol for Harvesting – gathering in. The Grim Reaper – Death – is always pictured as carrying a scythe.

🛡 The saying 'as ye sow, so shall ye reap' can be interpreted as – if we do good deeds, then that good will be returned. When we dream of reaping a reward for something we have done, we approve of our own activities. More negatively, a harmful act will return to haunt us.

🖼 In former times, the whole community took part in the reaping (gathering) of the harvest. This ensured that everybody gained in some way from this activity. Nowadays, to dream of reaping suggests a way of gaining from our activities.

*Also consult the entries for Harvest and Scythe and also the information on Spiritual Imagery in the Introduction.*

## REBEL/REVOLUTION

🌞 A rebel is someone who sets his face against the norms of society and held belief, so spiritually is one who cannot accept given teachings. A revolution takes place when a number of rebels can bring about a change in belief.

🛡 We will only rebel if we feel sufficiently strongly about something. For there to be a rebel or anarchist in our dreams suggests that we have allowed that part of ourselves a 'voice'. We can then understand it and decide on the validity of the feelings.

🖼 In working situations we are not often able to express our rebelliousness, perhaps at being asked to perform a particular task we don't consider necessary. As a dream character we can find out from the rebel what it is that is really disturbing us. A rebellion or revolution would occur in dreams if a position became completely untenable.

*Consult the entry for Conflict for further clarification.*

## RECLUSE – *see* HERMIT

## RECORD/RECORDS/RECORDING

🌞 The idea of keeping spiritual records is quite a powerful one. These may range from the Akashic records, an accounting of our personal thoughts words and actions in a Cosmic sense, through to keeping notes of our own progress as we travel the spiritual path. The first is an idea that exists in most religions in one form or another and the latter allows us to take full responsibility for who we are and also to chart our progress.

🛡 The content of dreams is, in a sense, a record of those things that have affected us on an emotional level, which become accessible to us through dream images. The ability to access those records becomes almost like that of a computer. Keeping records in dreams highlights our need to have some kind of order in our lives.

▣ When we dream of consulting records we are trying to access information. To be consulting company records would suggest we need to know how the company, or the community in which we live, functions. To be consulting public records may mean we need to know how to fit in. To be recording music or other material indicates that there is something we need to remember.

*You might also like to consult the entries for Communication, Order and Music/Rhythm.*

**RECYCLING –** *see* **RUBBISH**

**RED –** *see* **COLOURS**

**REDUCE –** *see* **SIZE**

**REDUNDANT**

☼ Spiritually to be redundant is not to be needed, to be surplus to requirements – which is the challenging of the basic human need to be wanted and a fear of rejection.

◊ In dreams, to be redundant can be equated with being rejected and will often reflect such a situation in our personal lives.

▣ To dream of being made redundant can be interpreted as an anxiety dream, not so much about our job situation but more to do with our own self-worth. In today's climate, when employment is less secure, redundancy is a risk, so such a dream may also reflect our ability to take risks.

*You might also like to consult the entry for Work.*

**REFEREE –** *see* **GAMES AND SPORT**

**REFERENCE**

☼ Reference books in a spiritual sense can symbolize knowledge or the Akashic records. A personal reference suggests a record of how we live our lives.

◊ To be asking for or receiving a reference is to be seeking some kind of validating process. We need to know we are 'fit for purpose'.

▣ When we are giving someone else a reference in dreams, we are giving approval to some of our own ideas and beliefs. If giving references is a normal part of our everyday behaviour, to do so in dreams may suggest we need to question some of our own beliefs. To be reluctant to give a reference suggests a lack of trust.

*You might also like to consult the entry for Work.*

**REFLECTION**

☼ Symbolically Spiritual truth that is available to us at any particular stage of understanding is often shown to us as though in a reflection. It is as if we need an image that gives us tangibility.

❤ Often, to see a reflection in a dream is to try to be understanding the inner self and the way that we cope with the outside world. If in a dream the two images do not correspond, we will need to make some kind of adjustment in order to live comfortably within the everyday world. Our inner self must give the impetus to the outer reality.

▦ A reflection seen in a dream has a great deal to do with the way we see ourselves at that particular moment. Our self-image is important to us, as is the way other people see us. If the reflection is in a mirror, then our image will be perhaps more 'solid', whereas one seen in water will be more transient. The story of Narcissus and the way he fell in love with himself (or rather his own image) is a warning to all of us against self-worship.

*You might also like to consult the entry for Mirror.*

## REFRIGERATOR

✺ As a preserver of basic sustenance, a refrigerator will symbolize the asceticism or dispassion which is developed by some seekers of spirituality.

❤ To dream of refrigerating leftover food indicates we are storing up resentment. This, in turn, will 'cool down' our own responses to love and affection.

▦ The refrigerator is a symbol of preservation. In dreams this becomes self-preservation and suggests we may be turning cold emotionally or sexually. To dream of rotten food in a refrigerator suggests we feel we may not be being sustained properly by those around us.

*You might also like to consult the entries for Ascetic, Decay, Food and Mould/Mouldy.*

## REFUGE/REFUGEE

✺ Dreaming of needing refuge suggests the need for some kind of sanctuary for the spirit. Spiritually, dreaming of being a refugee indicates that we are trying to escape from some anxiety or terror or from some authority greater than ourselves.

❤ If in dreams we are conscious of a place being a refuge, we can assume that we are temporarily emotionally secure. Dreaming of giving refuge indicates that we are capable of offering others that security.

▦ In more mundane terms only those who have been refugees themselves can know what it truly feels like, so any dream of being a refugee is going to be a dramatization of our circumstances. We need to identify the feeling and deal with it. Being in a refugee camp in dreams will highlight our feelings of displacement.

**REFUND – see MONEY**

**REFUSE/REFUSAL**

  ❀ To refuse in the spiritual sense is not to recognize the long-term benefit to ourselves or others of what is being offered or suggested. We may need to identify what fears are holding us back. Intuitively we may feel something is wrong.

  ♡ Emotionally many people find difficulty in saying 'no' so any refusal in dreams will come from a strongly held inner feeling. Refuse in the sense of abandoned material may be a pictorial representation of such a feeling and may highlight our own fears of abandonment.

  ▤ To be aware in dreams of a refusal suggests that on some level we have not given ourselves the necessary permission. If an authority figure refuses us something, we may assume that we are not acting in the way we should in waking life.

**REHEARSAL/REHEARSE – see THEATRE**

**REINDEER – see DEER IN ANIMALS**

**RELATIONS – see FAMILY**

**RELEASE**

  ❀ When we release a previously strongly held belief we are moving into a different stage of spiritual awareness. The release of birds, for instance at funerals, has the symbolism of letting the soul go free.

  ♡ Emotional release in dreams can give rise to a number of images, such as rushing water, a raging fire or a mighty wind.

  ▤ To be released in dreams from an institution such as school, prison or hospital is to gain a type of freedom. Whatever was bothering us is now behind us and we can move on.

*Also consult the entry for Emotions for further information.*

**RELIGION/RELIGIOUS BUILDINGS/RELIGIOUS IMAGERY – see SPIRITUAL IMAGERY IN THE INTRODUCTION**

**REMOVE**

  ❀ When a dream object is deliberately removed it can be thought of as being spiritually unnecessary. However, we need to decide if we are being possessive over it, or what it represents.

  ♡ In dreams, to be removing an object suggests that we do not appreciate the principle of sharing. If someone else is removing it we should reassess our need for whatever it represents. A removal as in changing location suggests that we need change in our lives.

  ▤ It will depend on whether a dream object seems to have disappeared or has been deliberately removed. The interpretation if it is deliberate will suggest that we are rejecting some aspect of our waking life.

**RENT**

✿ Often, in spiritual terms, we must relearn how to handle money and value. We are 'on loan' to the physical realm. The image of paying rent gives this concept a focus.

♦ There comes a time when, if we wish to maximize our potential, we must find a space of our own. Paying rent allows us to be independent within someone else's space.

▦ Paying rent in dreams is to undertake a personal responsibility. We are prepared to look after ourselves and to take responsibility for who we are. Receiving rent suggests that we have entered into a transaction that will benefit us.

*You might like also like to consult the entries for Home, Money and Tenant.*

**REPAIR**

✿ An older meaning of repair was 'to go back' and it is this meaning that is most spiritually relevant. The idea of going back to where we came from – to Source – is an accepted spiritual belief.

♦ Dreaming of repairing something suggests that we still have needed of whatever the dream object represents.

▦ Making repairs from a mundane perspective suggests that we are not satisfied with what we have done in a project or task. The implication is that we need to make it work better, that until we do there is an essential flaw.

**REPEAT INCLUDE REPEATED BEHAVIOUR – *see* RITE/RITUAL AND TELEVISION**

**REPLY – *see* RESPONSE**

**REPTILES**

✿ With understanding of the basic urges and the way to manage them we can create a firm foundation. From there we can progress spiritually.

♦ When there is a need to understand why we do things, we first need to control our basic drives. Many reptilian dreams are about control or management. Control of a crocodile would suggest some fear of an aggressive nature. Feeding a lizard or stroking a snake symbolizes taking care of our natural basic urges.

▦ Reptiles in dreams link with our basic and instinctive reactions and responses. When there is a basic urge – such as a need for food, sex, etc. – we sometimes cannot face it full on, but will symbolize it as a reptile.

*You might find it helpful to consult the information for Reptiles in the Animals entry as well as the entry for Crocodile.*

**RESEARCH**

🔆 To be carrying out Spiritual research, for instance with Holy Books in dreams, suggests a need to understand accepted thought.

💗 To be doing research in dreams, particularly if it is beyond our field of knowledge in waking life, indicates that we need to widen our focus, take in extra knowledge and not be narrow minded.

🔳 Research and development in waking life is a large part of many companies way of working, so in dreams we will often find that this concept points us to new ways of operating, not just in our working but also in our personal lives.

*You might also like to consult the entries for Invent/Inventor and Laboratory.*

**RESCUE**

🔆 Rescuing someone in the spiritual sense is saving someone who is less fortunate than we are, whether that is through compassion or otherwise. Spiritual rescue is a technique where the souls of the departed are turned towards the Light – direct knowledge – and helped to move on.

💗 When we have put others in danger, we are required to rescue them in dreams. We are then able to show a degree of nobility and courage that engenders a feel-good factor and allows us to have the capability to reach for the best within ourselves.

🔳 Being rescued in dreams is a powerful image, since it leaves us indebted to our rescuer. Rescuing someone else, particularly someone known to us, often suggests that we wish to have a, or form a different type of, relationship with that person. If we do not know them, then the character may represent part of our own personality that we need to pay attention to. The knight rescuing the maiden signifies the idea of the untouched feminine being rescued from her own passion.

*Also consult the entries for Danger, Knight, Light, Quest and Threat/Threaten for further information.*

**RESIGN**

🔆 Spiritual resignation is the giving in to inevitability if possible with patience. We no longer have any need or wish to fight back any more.

💗 Resignation is a state of mind brought about through having to face difficulties in life. It is as though we come to a point where we are not capable of making any further effort or decision. Indeed, it may be better not to, but simply to resign ourselves to whatever may happen. In dreams this resignation is recognizable as not wanting to go on.

🔳 In dreams to resign is to give up. To dream of resigning from work means we are aware of major changes in our lives. We perhaps need to look at our lives and accustom ourselves to the idea that there are areas that would bear improvement. To be resigned to something suggests that we have accepted the status quo in our lives.

*You might also like to consult the entry for Work.*

## RESPONSE

✹ A spiritual response is one that affects every part of our being and is a reaching out to whatever we deem the Ultimate to be. An instinctive response is often one drawn from us by a situation that has personal resonance.

♥ If a response is needed or if a reply is given there must have been a question. This will often have been a subconscious one. In dreams it is unfortunate that we sometimes have one without knowing the other.

▦ To reply is to respond, usually in words to a question or an action. In dreams any response we make should be carefully considered as to whether it reflects our feelings accurately in a waking situation.

*Also consult the entry for Question.*

## RESTORATION

✹ When something is restored it is made whole again and in spiritual terms such an image can suggest healing or a return to a former state.

♥ Carrying out a restoration in dreams suggests that we are still connected with the past and are trying to recreate it in some way.

▦ There is an interesting anomaly from a mundane perspective since in carrying out a restoration we are referring to the past but working for a future, towards the tangibility of something permanent.

*You might also like to consult the entries for Old and Repair.*

## RETREAT

✹ A spiritual retreat is a place that allows us an environment and ambience in which to meditate and contemplate. To dream of such a place suggests we have need of peace and quiet.

♥ When we dream of retreating from something we may need to decide whether it is a forced withdrawal or a strategic move. If the former then we may be under pressure, if the latter then we must formulate new plans.

▦ When in dreams we are conscious of retreating from a previously held position this may be because we need to reassess our resources.

## REVEAL

✹ A revealed (law-giving) religion is one that is considered to have been disclosed by God to Man. This presupposes an intimate relationship between the two. Revelation is that which has been revealed, and is often received in dreams.

♥ To reveal something is to make it plain. Dreams will often uncover our hidden truths, which we cannot necessarily deal with in waking life.

■ The meaning of a symbol can often be revealed in dreams and needs to be consciously retained. Such a symbol will often have relevance to what is happening in our daily lives though we may need to follow up with research.

**REVERSE** – *see* BACK AND FRONT AND BACKWARD/FORWARD IN POSITION

**RHYTHM** – *see* MUSIC/RHYTHM

**RIBBON** – *see* BRIDLE, HALTER AND HARNESS

**RICE** – *see* SPIRITUAL IMAGERY IN THE INTRODUCTION

**RIDE** – *see* TRANSPORT

**RIGHT** – *see* POSITION

**RING**

❂ Like the circle, the ring signifies eternity and divinity. It represents totality and infinity.

♡ We all need some kind of continuity in our lives, something that gives a sense of long-term comfort. A ring holds this symbolism because it is never-ending and is self-perpetuating. To be ringing someone in a dream suggests we are trying to make contact with something important.

■ A ring appearing in a dream usually signifies a relationship of some sort. A wedding ring suggests a union and a promise. A ring belonging to the family would represent old traditions and values. An engagement ring suggests a more tentative promise of devotion. An eternity ring would be a long-term promise. A signet ring would indicate setting the seal on something. A bullring suggests an element of cruelty.

*You might like to consult the entries for Hole, Telephone, Wedding/Wedding Dress/Wedding Ring as well as the information on Circle in Shapes/Patterns.*

**RISK**

❂ Spiritually we run into danger if we do not pay attention to perceived knowledge or accepted behaviour. Daring to question the status quo is a calculated risk.

♡ In dreams, an emotional risk can make itself felt if we have not acknowledged such a possibility. Then we may dream of some kind of potential disaster or breakdown.

■ In today's business climate there are many risks to be taken. This will often reflect in dreams as personal risk, such as standing on a cliff edge or drowning.

*Consult the entries for Cliff, Danger, Disaster and Drowning for further clarification.*

**RITE/RITUAL**

❂ Spiritually we are able to focus our energies in such a way that we can work for the Greater Good. Repetition helps to concentrate the power we are calling on, whatever our system of belief, and is used in prayer and in Mantra.

A rite is a customary form for a religious ceremony and in dreams is only distinguishable from a ritual in that it is given credence by its long usage. Such a rite would be that of baptism.

♥ Such rituals as getting up in the morning, because they are habits, simply have the purpose of getting us focused. Religious rituals have taken on a life of their own and help concentrate the power of the many. Magical rituals have become 'power centres' in their own right.

▦ Rituals can range from the 'sublime to the ridiculous'. They are actions that are repeated over and over again in order to achieve a certain result. In dreams, such an action can be a comfort mechanism or a way of learning a required behaviour.

⊞ Magical ritual often concentrates on the union of two polarities – male and female, drive and receptivity. Ancient religions symbolized this in the sacred marriage and many dreams – particularly as we begin exploring spirituality – echo this. Men will most often play the role of priest and women as priestess in such dreams – that is, fulfilling their gender roles.

*You might like to consult the entries for Baptism, Ceremony, Magic/Magician, Mantra and Ziggurat, as well as the information on Spiritual Imagery in the Introduction.*

**RIVER** – *see* WATER

**ROAD** – *see* JOURNEY

**ROB/ROBBER** – *see* BURGLAR, STEAL AND THIEF

**ROBE**

🕱 In spiritual terms the white robe is innocence and the seamless robe represents holiness, and in dreams would tend to represent different spiritual awarenesses. Magical robes with different symbols and of different colours would signify esoteric knowledge and the ability to use power correctly.

♥ A robe can suggest our attitude to sex and relationships. If it is clean we have a good self-image, if dirty, the opposite. A dirty robe could also suggest depression. A new robe might signify a new approach to the way we present ourselves, whereas an old one might suggest the comfort of a previous way of working.

▦ Dreaming of a robe such as a bathrobe can have two meanings: one is that of covering up vulnerability and the other is of being relaxed and at ease. The dream will indicate the correct significance. To be dressing someone else in a robe is to protect them.

*You might also like to consult the entries for Clothes, Colour and Magic/Magician.*

**ROBOT** – *see* MACHINE

**ROCK**

🔆 Spiritually we will need, at some point, to go through a transition that requires careful management This often presents itself as a rock barrier. Dual rocks through which we must pass suggest the same image as the passage between two pillars, such as the Pillars of Hercules; that is, passing from one state of awareness to the next. It is similar to an initiation.

♦ On an intellectual level, all the images that we think of in relationship to rocks prevail. There is reliability, coldness, rigidity and a foundation on which we can build. We need to recognize these qualities within ourselves so that we give ourselves the best options possible. We can find ourselves 'between a rock and a hard place', in a difficult situation in dreams.

▦ To dream of rock suggests stability in the real world. If we are on firm ground we can survive. We may also be aware that we must be firm and stand 'rock-like', and not be dissuaded from our purpose. Seaside rock can remind us of happier, more carefree times.

*You might also like to consult the entries for Barrier, Initiation and Stone.*

**ROCKET**

🔆 Because of the spiritual symbolism of reaching heights to which none have been before, and 'shooting for the stars', the rocket represents spiritual searching and adventure.

♦ Nowadays any symbol of power connects with our ability to do, or be, better than before. The rocket in this sense will have much of the same symbolism as the aeroplane except the destinations will be less easily accessible. The explosive power and energy available is something to be carefully looked at, since we need this type of power in order to make radical changes in our lives.

▦ The energy that is available to us in dreams can be indicative of what we have available in waking life. In popular parlance, to be given a rocket suggests recognizing that we are not functioning the way we should. To take off like a rocket means moving very fast in terms of some project we have. Giving someone else a rocket in dreams may mean we are trying to motivate a part of ourselves or that we know more can be done by others.

▣ The rocket in basic terms has a connection with male sexuality and can have this significance in both men's and women's dreams.

*Consult the entries for Aeroplane, Journey and Transport for further information.*

**ROD** – *see* **STAFF**

**ROOF**

🔆 The roof is protection from the elements and suggests the sheltering aspect of the feminine as the 'guardian of the hearth'.

❤ A roof is a basic requirement in man's need for comfort. Psychologically, it is important to be protected against the elements. The various types of roofs have different significances in dreams. A pitched roof signifies our ability to reach for the sky and attain our goals. A pagoda, with its many roofs, signifies a holy place.

▦ To concentrate on, or be aware of, the roof of a building in a dream is to acknowledge the shelter and protection it affords. If the roof leaks then we are open to emotional attacks. If we are on the roof we are not being protected and, therefore, could be vulnerable.

*Consult the entries for Hearth and Goddess/Goddesses for further information.*

**ROOMS – see BUILDINGS**

**ROOT – see TREE**

**ROPE**

☀ A rope, as in a mountaineer's rope, can offer security and also a sense of spiritual freedom. As a noose, such as a hangman's noose, it may suggest despair and possibly our attitude to death.

❤ If we are tied to the rope, something is holding us back from expressing ourselves. Being tied by a rope to something or someone else means we are bound to them and need to look at the ties that bind us – what holds us together. We should look at the limitations of that particular relationship and how much mutual freedom there is.

▦ A rope can suggest strength and power, though the power can turn against us. A rope and pulley suggests using the forces of weight to help us; a frayed rope signifies a lack of care. If the rope is made of an unusual substance such as hair or material, or is fashioned in a strange way, this will be a representation of the uniqueness of the bonds we have.

*You might also like to consult the entries for Hang/Hanging, Noose and Weighing/Weight.*

**ROSARY – see NECKLACE, BEADS AND SPIRITUAL IMAGERY IN THE INTRODUCTION**

**ROSE/ROSETTE – see SPIRITUAL IMAGERY IN THE INTRODUCTION**

**ROT – see DECAY AND MOULD/MOULDY**

**ROUGH – see TEXTURE**

**ROUND TABLE**

☀ Spiritually the table suggests a centre, but one from which all things can begin. Partly because of the tales of King Arthur, there are various myths associated with a round table, but essentially it indicates that everyone is equal in status and has an equal right to express an opinion.

❤ The round table is a representation of the heavens, since the 12 knights are the signs of the Zodiac. It also suggests resolution since it gives no one person status over another. In dreams we are continually trying to create perfection and this is one such dream that calls on archetypal images.

▦ A round table in a dream is a symbol of wholeness. In mundane terms it can suggest negotiation, since it is used to allow everyone the opportunity to express an opinion.

*You might also like to consult the entries for Camelot, Knight, Table and Zodiac as well as the information on Archetypes in the Introduction.*

ROW – *see* ARGUE/ARGUMENTS AND LINE

RUBBISH

✹ We may need to dispose of spiritual rubbish – outdated perceptions and truths that are no longer relevant. A dream about rubbish or garbage can indicate that now is the time to perform that task.

❤ Very often, rubbish or garbage is the remains of food preparation. Often we are being alerted to what we need to do in order to remain healthy – how we need to treat our bodies and make space for new experiences which will allow us to act for the Greater Good. Recycling of both rubbish and garbage suggests making best use of our resources.

▦ Rubbish in our dream creates a scenario where we are able to deal with those parts of our experience or our feelings that need to be sorted through in order for us to decide what is being kept and what can be rejected so we can progress. To be collecting rubbish or garbage can indicate that we are making wrong assumptions. To be recycling old rubbish suggests that we have learned the lessons we needed to.

RUINS

✹ We sometimes have to understand a destructive streak in ourselves if we are to move forward, perhaps building on mistakes from the past.

❤ If we have deliberately ruined something we need to clarify a self-destructive element in us. Sometimes by looking at the symbolism of what has ruined an object or an occasion will give us insight into our own processes. If someone else has ruined one of our possessions in dreams we should look at an emotional difficulty in waking life.

▦ When something is in ruins we have to discover if it is through neglect or vandalism. If the former, we need to pull things together. If the latter, we need to look at how we are making ourselves vulnerable.

*Also consult the entries for Buildings, Demolition and Wreck.*

## RUNNING

🌣 Running in dreams suggests the potential for anxiety or distress. Spiritually we may be trying to do something too quickly. The original marathon signalled victory and was a trial to the death. Running races or marathons in dreams are, therefore, tests of endurance.

♥ Obviously in dreams of running, time and place are significant. Running a marathon is today a group activity and will in dreams suggest competition. Where we are going will perhaps indicate why speed is needed. If we are being pursued this will also give some kind of reason. To be running something – managing – is to be taking responsibility.

▦ To be running in a dream suggests speed and flow. To be running forwards suggests confidence and ability. To be running away from someone or something signifies fear and an inability to do something. Running back to something indicates that a readjustment or reassessment is necessary. If we do not know our destination we may not have thought through a plan properly.

*You might like to consult the entries for Chase/Chased, Time and Win/Winning.*

## RUSH

🌣 Interestingly, rushes or reeds are an ancient symbol of Time. In both spiritual work and dreams, time and space are interchangeable. Thus, if we use our space successfully then we also use time properly. If we are rushing we do not see the best of our world.

♥ We need to learn how to manage time successfully in order to succeed, and to be rushing suggests that we have not done so.

▦ To be in a rush suggests that we are having to contend with outside pressures. To be rushing suggests that we ourselves are putting the pressure on. The pressure would be on our time.

*You might also like to consult the entries for Hourglass, Time and Quick.*

## RUST

🌣 Rust signifies old outdated attitudes. Spiritually, we may have to reconsider ideas that are harmful (corrosive) before we can progress.

♥ To dream of cleaning up rust suggests that we recognize our own negligence. Dreaming of rust appearing as we look at an object signifies that a project has reached the end of its useful life.

▦ Rust represents neglect and negligence. We have not looked after the quality of our lives properly and should look to address this oversight.

*Consult the entries for Iron and Metal for further information.*

## SACK

�};️ Formerly the appearance of a sack in a dream was taken as an indication of death. Today, it is more likely to indicate the liberation (freeing up) of part of our personality or difficulties that need to be overcome so we can progress spiritually.

♡ A sack shares much of the significance and symbolism of the bag, or any such receptacle, in dreams; the womb is often symbolised in dreams as a bag or sack. As an everyday object it acts as a container and its appearance in a dream can indicate that we should look making the best use of our resources.

🔳 At its simplest, to dream of a sack can link with word play such as 'getting the sack'. It brings a period of our lives to an end, possibly in a rather negative way. Perhaps in an effort to move on, we have created circumstances within our lives that make us feel bad about ourselves for a time.

🔳 In a woman's dream a bag can represent her feelings about pregnancy, while, interestingly enough, in a man's dream it is more likely to mean some kind of womb experience.

*Consult the entry for Bag as well as the information on Womb in the Body entry for further information.*

## SACKCLOTH – *see* SPIRITUAL IMAGERY IN THE INTRODUCTION

## SACRIFICES

🌐 Sacrifice is an important aspect of spiritual growth and signifies the renunciation of the lesser for the rewards of the greater. As a rule, sacrifice has two meanings. Firstly, it is to give something up and secondly to make something sacred or holy. When those two things are possible within a dream scenario we are prepared to give up our ego or individuality for the sake of something greater or more important than ourselves.

♡ There is usually some expectation of a forthcoming just reward (often spiritual) for having made sacrifices. There may be an element of deferred gratification in that we do not expect an immediate reward, except that of feeling good or knowing we have done the right thing. There is always an element also of giving up egotistic behaviour, which is no longer appropriate, and going with the flow of life.

🔳 Sacrificing an animal in dreams suggests that we are aware that our lower, more basic instincts can be given up in favour of spiritual power. We have to be prepared to recognize our own human fallibility, but to give up extravagance. A sacrificial altar may appear, or it may just be a question of killing and cooking an animal ritualistically. If the animal is willing to be sacrificed, then we are ready to transmute instinct into spiritual energy. If the animal is a hare or a rabbit, the symbolism is that of rebirth.

*You might also like to consult the entries for Animals, Hunt/Hunting/Huntsman and Rite/Ritual.*

## SADISM

⚘ Sadism appearing in a dream would suggest that it is probably a counterbalance to our conscious way of being in, and dealing with, the world.

⚘ It will obviously depend on whether we are being sadistic or if someone is being sadistic towards us as to the interpretation. We know that in dreams other people can represent parts of ourselves, so we need to consider whether we are causing ourselves harm deliberately or inadvertently. We may feel that we wish to punish ourselves for some supposed misdemeanour and, as a displacement activity, we dream of sadistic behaviour. The very fact that it is sadistic may also mean that it is masochistic – that is, self-involved.

▦ Sadism often arises because of anger still held – but suppressed – from childhood hurts. It is the wish to hurt or provoke a reaction – often in someone we love. In waking life most of us are not capable of being sadistic, but in dreams we can do what we like, so sadism becomes acceptable.

⚐ Sadistic behaviour that is not sexual in nature signifies a degree of childish cruelty in both men's and women's dreams. That cruelty may well be gender specific.

## SAILING/SAILS

⚘ Sails represent the Spirit – as in a force that moves us. Sailing suggests a sense of spiritual freedom and the ability to use our intellect.

⚘ To be tacking – sailing against the wind – suggests that we have created difficulties, possibly by setting ourselves against public opinion. To be sailing with the wind means we are using opportunities to the best of our abilities. Because a boat or ship is usually thought of as feminine, the sails in dreams can represent pregnancy and fertility. By association, they can also signify how a woman will use her intellect.

▦ Sails suggest the idea of making use of available power. Often the type of sail will be relevant. Old-fashioned sails would suggest out-of-date methods, whereas racing sails might suggest the use of modern technology. The colour of the sails may also be important. When we dream of sailing, we are highlighting how we feel we are handling our lives. We can either work with the currents or against them. If we are sailing in a yacht there is more of a sense of immediacy than if we were sailing in a liner. The former is more to do with one-to-one relationships, while the latter suggests a group effort.

*Also consult the entries for Boat/Ship, Colour, Journey, Transport, Wind and Water.*

## SAILOR

⚜ Spiritually, the sailor can signify communication. The aspect of freedom links with a quality of the god Mercury who, having been given a task, then forgets what it is.

♥ Most people have a rather antiquated idea of the sailor. It is this image that usually appears in dreams. He represents freedom, both of movement and of spirit, and is a representation of the Tramp archetype.

▥ The sailor suggests someone who is totally in control of his own destiny, who 'sails with the tide'. A modern-day sailor in waking life would have the added benefit of being in control of his own environment and it is this image that is likely to surface in the dreams of the modern entrepreneur.

⊟ If a sailor does appear in a dream, particularly in a woman's, he is usually a somewhat romanticized figure and can represent the Hero. In a man's dream he represents the part of himself which seeks freedom, but that needs to be given permission or authority to take that freedom.

*Also consult the information on Hero and Tramp in the information on Archetypes in the Introduction.*

## SALMON

⚜ A potent image in mythology is the Salmon of Knowledge, which signifies knowledge of other worlds (the lands beneath the sea) and of other-worldly things. This conforms to Shamanistic belief that creatures have the ability to visit other dimensions.

♥ In common with most fish when they appear in dreams, the salmon signifies our basic urges – most often the need for survival. By being able to put in effort we reap the rewards of our actions.

▥ In modern medicine the omega 3 oil that is in salmon is a powerful brain food. When the salmon appears in dreams we may need such a substance or be being warned that we need to pay attention to our intellectual pursuits.

⊟ The salmon signifies abundance and masculinity and is also phallic. In its fight to mate by swimming upstream it can also symbolize the sperm and may do so in men's dreams. Often a salmon can appear in a woman's dream as a symbol of her wish for pregnancy, whether this is a conscious wish or not.

*You might also like to consult the entry for Fish as well as the information on Shaman in Spiritual Imagery in the Introduction.*

## SALT

☼ As a distillation of everything we know, salt represents wisdom. As a symbol of permanence and incorruptibility, spilt salt is thrown over the shoulder, supposedly in the face of the Devil.

♡ As in the old days salt was paid as salary, so nowadays to be given salt in a dream shows we are aware of our value. There are many customs associated with salt. In Scotland, along with coal and bread, it is the first thing to pass over the threshold to greet the New Year, symbolizing health, wealth and happiness and will also appear in dreams as a symbol of the savour of life.

▦ In dreams, salt highlights the subtle qualities we bring to our lives, those things we do to enhance our lifestyle. We run most of our lives through our emotions but the more subtle aspects are just as important. It has been suggested that if the water was removed from the human body there would be enough minerals and salt left to cover a fifty pence piece.

## SAND

☼ Spiritually, sand represents the impermanence of the physical life and can suggest having to approach death or change in some way. The sands of time is an image much used in poetry and lyricism.

♡ Sand in a dream suggests a degree of instability and lack of security. When sand and sea are seen together we are not feeling particularly emotionally secure. When the sands are shifting we are probably unable to decide what we require from life. If we are conscious of the sand in an hourglass we are aware of time running out; we perhaps need to be certain we are making best use of our resources.

▦ Sand can represent impermanence. Because they will inevitably be washed away by the tide, building sand castles in dreams suggests that there is some doubt about the validity of a project in which we are involved. They also indicate that the structure we are trying to give to our lives does not necessarily have permanence and may be an illusion.

*You might also like to consult the entries for Beach, Digging/Excavation, Hourglass and Time.*

## SARCOPHAGUS – *see* TOMB

## SATAN – *see* DEVIL

## SATELLITE

☼ A satellite can represent spiritual communication from a discarnate source.

♡ A satellite can appear in a dream to indicate the dependency that one person can have upon another. Often in relationships one partner is considered to be more important than the other and either could, therefore, recognize the symbol of the satellite.

🔲 Before satellites were invented, the stars were used as fixed points in communication. Nowadays a satellite would suggest efficient, effective contact. We are more globally aware of the effect we can have both on our environment and on other people around us.

*You may also find it helpful to consult the entries for Astronaut, Communication and Space.*

## SATYR

🔆 The satyr is a spirit of nature and of natural power. When man was less civilized than he is now, his animal nature was closer to the surface. It was possible for him to see and identify patterns of energy or spirits, both in himself and in nature, which then took on human or semi-human form. As we progress and learn more spiritually this ability can resurface in dreams.

♦ From a psychological standpoint the satyr is that part of nature that is not controlled, and is beyond restraint. It owes allegiance to no one and is completely anarchic. If perceived as destructive then it will be so. If accepted as helpful then it will be equally obliging.

🔲 While most of the time in the waking state we suppress such figures, in dreams – where there is no conscious control – they will sometimes appear. The satyr is usually pictured with the horns, legs and tail of a goat and is recognizable as Pan, the Horned God. He represents the wilder lustful side of our personality.

*Consult the entries for Centaur, Fabulous Beasts and Horns for further information.*

## SAVINGS – *see* MONEY

## SAW – *see* TOOLS

## SCAFFOLD/SCAFFOLDING

🔆 A scaffold suggests an enforced code of spiritual behaviour and the need for self-control. Scaffolding indicates spiritual support.

♦ Sometimes in dreams a scaffold indicates an enforced ending. This can be death, but is more likely to suggest the 'death' of part of our personality. This suggests that because at this time we cannot integrate that part, we must stop the behaviour or activity that is causing a problem. Otherwise we will have to take the consequences of behaving in such a way.

🔲 A scaffold or scaffolding in a dream usually indicates that there is some kind of temporary structure in our lives. If builders' scaffolding appears we should decide whether it is there to help us build something new or whether we are repairing something old. In either case, it indicates we need a temporary structure of some sort to help us reach the heights we wish, or achieve our goals. If we are building something new, the scaffolding will support us while we build, whereas if we are repairing the old it will support the previous structure while we make the necessary changes. A hangman's scaffold will suggest that a part of our lives must come to an end. We may, for instance, be aware that we have offended against some of society's laws and beliefs, and must be held to account. We also may need to look at our propensity to be a victim.

*You might also like to consult the entries for Hang/Hanging, Martyr, Noose and Rope.*

### SCALES

🌞 The Scales of Justice represent spiritual balance and harmony, and also good judgement. By association, they also represent the astrological sign of Libra.

♡ Scales in a dream suggest the necessity for balance and self-control. Without that balance we cannot make a sensible decision as to potential courses of action. We must 'weigh up' all the possibilities. Scales will also suggest standards – for instance, standards of behaviour – to which we are expected to adhere. We may be weighed and found wanting. If the scales are unbalanced in a dream we need to search our conscience and discover where we are not functioning properly in our lives.

▣ The various types of scale we see in our dream will have slightly differing meanings. For example, bathroom scales would suggest a more personal assessment than a public machine, whereas a weighbridge might suggest that we need to take our whole lives into consideration. If they were doctor's scales we may be alerting ourselves to a potential health problem.

*You might also like to consult the entries for Justice, Weighing/Weight and Zodiac.*

**SCALP –** *see* **HEAD IN BODY**

**SCAPEGOAT –** *see* **VICTIM**

**SCAR –** *see* **INJURE/INJURY**

### SCEPTRE

🌞 The sceptre is representative of royal power and sovereignty. Spiritually it signifies the transmission of divine power from above rather than below.

♡ The sceptre can represent the magic wand and in dreams can indicate our right and ability to use such magic. If we are holding the sceptre we have the ability to transmit the life force. If someone else is using the sceptre and is bestowing honour or power on us, then we can accept that we have succeeded in a particular project.

▓ When it appears in dreams a sceptre indicates that we have given someone authority over us. We have abdicated responsibility to the point where the inner self has to take over.

⚏ The sceptre has the same symbolism as most rods and staves: that of a phallic object. In a woman's dream it suggests the power for action. In a man's dream it signifies the power to take authority.

*Also consult the entries for Magic/Magician, Staff and Wand.*

## SCHOOL

✸ Spiritually it is often considered that life itself is a school. It is an arena for learning and experiencing so that we can maximize our best potential; life is a testing-ground for the reality that comes afterwards.

♦ The school or classroom will often appear in dreams when we are re-learning how to deal with our own personalities idiosyncrasies. Such images will often appear at times when we are attempting to get rid of old outmoded ideas and concepts. Also, when we are learning different ways of dealing with authority and with feelings of inadequacy, our feelings about school will surface.

▓ School is an important part of everyone's life. In situations where we are learning new abilities or skills, the image of a school will often surface in dreams. It is also the place where we experience associations that do not belong to the family, and can in dreams, therefore, suggest new ways of learning about relationships. School may also be indicative of how we learn about competitiveness and belonging to groups.

*Consult the entries for Education, Teacher and University for further information.*

## SCISSORS

✸ Spiritually, scissors can have two meanings. They can cut the Thread of Life, but can also represent unity and the coming together of the spiritual and physical.

♦ Scissors in dreams suggest the idea of cutting the non-essential out of our lives. This may be feelings we do not think are appropriate, emotions that we cannot handle, or mental trauma that needs to be excised. To dream of a hairdresser using scissors signifies our fear of losing strength and status.

▓ Scissors can also suggest a sharp, hurtful tongue or cutting remarks. Dreaming of sharpening scissors suggests that we need to be more precise in our communication, whereas using blunt scissors suggests that we are likely to create a problem through speaking too bluntly. The type of scissors may also be important. Kitchen scissors would, for instance, be more utilitarian than surgical scissors, which would suggest the necessity to be more precise.

*Consult the entries for Kitchen, Surgery and Thread for further clarification.*

## SCROLL

☀ A scroll can signify the letter of the law and the respect that it deserves. If we are given a scroll in dreams, we are deemed responsible enough to use the information we have gained.

♡ A scroll can represent hidden knowledge, and also the passing of time. Thus, in most dreams, dreaming of a scroll signifies having to wait until the knowledge we have gained can be used at an appropriate time. The type of script used in the scroll may also need interpreting.

▦ Nowadays, a scroll will represent an acknowledgement of a learning process – i.e. the scroll presented to graduating students. We are endorsing either our own knowledge or information that has been given to us, so that we can enhance our lives.

*Consulting the entries for Ink, Paper/Parchment, Seal, Time and Writing will give further information.*

## SCYTHE

☀ The scythe, like the hourglass, is often held by the figure of Death and represents the ending of physical existence. We are becoming aware of the fact that the cutting off of life – or energy – may be imminent around us, although it need not be our own death.

♡ The scythe is a very old-fashioned symbol for the passage of time. Its appearance in dreams shows we are linking with very deeply held concepts and ideas. It is time to harvest our own experience and ensure that we can acquire all that we need.

▦ The scythe is a cutting instrument, and therefore has the same significance as a knife. In dreams it usually suggests that we need to cut out non-essential actions or beliefs. We need to be fairly ruthless in order to achieve a desired end.

*You might also like to consult the entries for Death, Harvest, Hourglass, Knife, Reaping and Time.*

## SEA – *see* WATER

## SEAL

☀ Spiritually a seal suggests hidden knowledge. Not all esoteric and occult information is available to everyone; such information is only entrusted to someone who has the courage to break the seal.

♡ When we dream of legal documents, and are particularly aware of the seal, it can indicate that a conclusion has been reached in waking life which is both binding and secret. To be breaking a seal indicates that we are possibly breaking a confidence or someone's trust in us. In dreams, the possession of a seal gives us the authority to take responsibility for our own actions.

▣ Historically, a wax seal confirmed authority and power. It was also a symbol of identity. Nowadays in dreams it is much more likely to signify legality or correct moral action.

▣ It has been suggested that in a woman's dream a man breaking a seal suggests that she will lose her virginity or purity at some level. In his own dreams, it will suggest that he is aware of the seriousness of his actions.

*You might also like to consult the entry for Wax as well as the information for Seal in Animals.*

**SEANCE** – *see* **MEDIUM AS WELL AS SPIRITUAL IMAGERY IN THE INTRODUCTION**

**SEARCHING**

✾ The movement towards spirituality often begins from a feeling of searching for something.

♥ Searching in a dream for something we have lost can suggest either that we need information from the past, or that we feel we have lost our identity. Searching also suggests more of a commitment to actually finding than just simply looking.

▣ To be searching in a dream is an attempt to find an answer to a problem. If we are searching for someone we may be conscious of our loneliness. If we are searching for something we may be aware of an unfulfilled need.

*Consult the entries for Find and Lose/Loss/Lost for further clarification.*

**SEARCHLIGHT** – *see* **LIGHT AND TORCH**

**SEASONS**

✾ The division of the year into Spring, Summer, Autumn and Winter gives occasion for celebrations and festivals which are vehicles for knowledge and inspiration.

♥ The need for us to be able to divide time into periods or phases arises initially from the necessity to co-operate with the seasons from a survival point of view. Given deadlines and limitations, the human being is able to survive through striving. In dreams we instinctively link with this inherent ability and need to live by the natural calendar.

▣ When we become conscious of the seasons of the year in dreams, we are also linking with the various periods of our lives; spring signifies childhood; summer, young adulthood; autumn, middle age; winter, old age.

▣ When we understand the natural cycle of the year, dreams by both men and women will link with the union of the God and Goddess.

*You might like to consult the entries for Autumn, Festival, Rite/Ritual, Spring, Summer and Winter for further information.*

**SEED –** *see* **GRAIN**
**SERPENT –** *see* **SERPENT AND SNAKE IN ANIMALS**
**SEX/SEXUAL IMAGES**

⚙ Dreams will often allow us to explore physicality in a safe way. Real spiritual growth takes place when we are not afraid of the curiosity that allows innocent exploration of our own body. When a child is first born, its first awareness is of itself as an individual. It has to learn that it is now separate from its mother and cope with the separation. It begins to become 'conscious' of itself, and of its need for warmth, comfort and love.

♥ Dreams highlight the whole range of the individual's sexuality. One vital stage of growth is the baby's fascination with its own body and the ability to be physical. Only if later we ignore our own sexual nature and fail to appreciate his own life force do the negative aspects make themselves obvious in dreams. This is a natural attempt to balance the waking state, which may have been over-intellectualized, or over-dramatized. Contact with others then becomes necessary, and often this need will manifest in dreams. There are many aspects of sex and sexuality that can surface in dreams unexpectedly or in an apparently bizarre fashion and they can generally be interpreted as follows:

**Bisexuality** – within us we all hold both masculine and feminine potentials. One is more overt than the other and when there is conflict between the inner and the outer selves this can sometimes show itself in dreams as bisexuality.

**Castration** – in a dream this suggests fear of loss of masculinity and sexual power.

**Clothes** – being fully clothed would suggest feelings of guilt or prudery.

**Contraception** – dreaming of contraception can indicate a fear of pregnancy and birth.

**Ejaculation/Emission** – the conflicts that arise in us because of our sexual desire for someone can be dealt with in the dream state through dreaming of emission or orgasm.

**Fetishes** – a fixation on an external object, in sexual terms it appears that there can be no sexual act without it – akin to a child being without its comforter. In dreams, therefore, a fetish can highlight fear, immaturity and lack of capability.

**Hermaphrodite** – dreaming of a hermaphrodite (someone who is both masculine and feminine) signifies our attitude to bisexuality, or androgyny – the perfect balance within one person of the masculine and feminine qualities.

**Homosexuality** – in dreams this is a desire for someone who is the same as oneself, i.e. has the same energies, thought processes etc. If we can identify similarities with the dream character that are not purely sexual, the dream can be fully interpreted.

**Incest** – usually characterizes the need for love expressed in a more tactile way. In dreams incest can highlight the guilty feelings we have about our parents or members of the family.

**Intercourse (or petting)** – the wish or need to be able to communicate with someone on a very intimate level can translate itself into intercourse in a dream. If intercourse is interrupted we may have inhibitions of which we are not consciously aware. Often intercourse in a dream can mark the integration of a particular part of our personality. If a child is then born in the dream that integration has been successful.

**Kiss** – this can indicate a mark of respect or a desire to stimulate the dream partner. It suggests we should be aware of what arousal we ourselves need.

**Masochism** – the desire to hurt or be hurt in dreams through sex arises from two causes. The first is to be a martyr (to suffer for one's 'sins') and the second to feel extreme emotion of one sort or another. We may not allow ourselves to feel deeply in everyday life.

**Masturbation** – the child learns to comfort himself through masturbation, so such a dream shows a need for comfort.

**Perversion** – when sexual perversion appears in dreams we are avoiding, or attempting to avoid, issues to do with closeness and bonding.

**Phallus** – any image either of or to do with the phallus signifies everything that is creative, penetrative and masculine. It is vitality and creativity in both its simplest and most complex form. It is resurrection and the renewal of life.

**Rape** – any image of rape appearing in dreams can be as much to do with violation of personal space as with the sexual act. Rape may only appear as an image when we as adults are ready to deal with trauma of any kind.

**Sadism** – in everyday life we may be very timid, in which case sadism in a dream is an escape mechanism. If we have to be dominant and controlling in everyday life, the unconscious shows its need to be controlled by such dreams.

**Semen** – the sign of masculinity and of physical maturity, semen is often seen in dreams as some other milky fluid. Dreams have an odd way of manifesting images of primitive rites and practices of which we may have no conscious knowledge, such as depositing semen in the earth.

**Transvestism** – signifies a confusion so far as gender is concerned in dreams.

**Venereal Disease** – in a dream this can suggest awareness of some kind of contamination. This need not necessarily be of a sexual nature, but could also be emotional.

▣ In dreams, sexuality, in the sense of feeling desire for someone else, is a basic, primeval urge for closeness and union. It is as though we are searching for a part of ourselves that we have lost and the other character in the dream represents the closest we can get to that part. If we were a fully integrated human being, we would have no need for sex with someone else, but most of us have an inherent desire to be united with everything that is not part of our own ego. Sexual activity is either the highest expression of love and spirituality between two people or, if purely physically based, is entirely selfish. It would be up to us and our understanding of ourselves to determine which it is.

*Consulting the entries for Androgen/Androgyny, Castration, Clothes, Hermaphrodite, Homosexuality, Incest, Kiss, Masochism and Sadism will help you clarify your dream.*

**SHADOW** – *see* **ARCHETYPES IN THE INTRODUCTION**

**SHAMPOO** – *see* **SOAP/SHAMPOO**

**SHAPES/PATTERNS**

✺ At a certain stage of spiritual development, geometric shapes that will give us a greater understanding of the abstract world begin to appear in dreams. It is as though our old perceptions of form are beginning to take on new meaning and interpretation.

♥ The number of sides a shape has will be significant, as will the colours. Considerable symbology has grown up around shape. Various shapes and patterns can be interpreted as follows:

**The centre** symbolizes the point from which everything starts. In relation to shape, it is the point from which the pattern grows.

**Circles** represent the inner being or the Self. They are also unity and perfection.

**Crescents (including the sickle and crescent moon)** signify the feminine, mysterious power that is intuitive and non-rational. The crescent is also recognized as the symbol of the Islamic faith.

**Crosses** signify the realization (in the sense of making real) of spirit into matter.

**Cubes** – *see Square.*

**Diamond shapes** in a dream indicate that we have both greater and lesser options available to us.

**The hexagon** is the geometric figure that makes the most efficient use of space. The cells of a honeycomb are hexagonal for this reason and this shape epitomizes nature's best use of resources.

**The hexagram** is a geometric figure that symbolizes the harmonious development of the physical, social and spiritual elements of human life and its integration into a perfect whole.

**Ovals** are symbolic of the womb, and also of feminine life. Called the *Vesica Piscis*, it is the halo that completely encircles a sacred figure.

**Patterns** of any sort that appear in dreams as part of the scenario can categorize how we handle the repeated patterns and behaviours in our lives.

**Spheres** have a similar meaning to globes and indicate perfection and completion of all possibilities.

**The spiral** is the perfect path to evolution. The principle is that everything is continually in motion, but also continually rising or raising its vibration.

**Square or Cube** – the square and cube both signify the manifestation of spirit into matter. They represent the earthly realm as opposed to the heavens. The cube is a more tangible representation of this.

**Stars**, particularly bright ones, indicate our hopes, aspirations and ideals. The star represents those things we must reach for.

**The swastika**, with its arms moving clockwise, portrays Ideal Man and the power he has for good. In Eastern symbolism it signifies the movement of the sun. The swastika moving anti-clockwise signifies all that is sinister and wrong.

**The triangle** represents Standing Man with his three parts: body, mind and spirit (or being). Consciousness and love manifest through his physicality. There is potential still to be realized.

We can accept the nature of things as they are and can look at the fundamental structure of our nature. We can appreciate the basic shape our lives are taking without placing inhibitions in the way. There is a game based on shapes in which you draw a square, a circle and a triangle, and then get someone else to elaborate each of the basic shapes into a drawing. Whatever they make of the square is supposed to relate to their outlook on the world, the circle to their inner being and the triangle to their sex life. Such images give potent material for dream work.

*You might also like to consult the entries for Archetypes, Colours, Globe, Labyrinth and Numbers, as well as the information on Spiritual Imagery and Symbols in the Introduction.*

SHAWL – *see* COAT IN CLOTHES
SHEAF – *see* INTRODUCTION
SHEARS – *see* SCISSORS
SHEEP – *see* ANIMALS

## SHELLS

⚜ Spiritually a shell is a miniature representation of the process of life and death.

♥ A shell carries within it a great deal of symbolism. It can be seen as a magical symbol which holds within it the power of transformation. The spiral of the shell suggests both going inwards and coming outwards. The ability to shelter is also symbolized, and as a receptacle it also links with the feminine, emotional side of nature.

▦ In dreams a shell represents the defences we use in order to prevent ourselves from being hurt. We can create a hard shell in response to previous hurt, or a soft shell, which would indicate that we are still open to being hurt. Shells were also once a unit of currency and in dreams can still be seen as this.

*You might also like to consult the entry for Snail as well as the information for Spiral in Shapes and on Transformation in the Introduction.*

## SHELTER

⚜ Shelter in the spiritual sense suggests sanctuary – a space wherein we will not be harmed but can be ourselves.

♥ The other image of shelter is protectiveness – that is, actively participating in giving shelter or sanctuary. If we are giving shelter to someone in dreams, we may be protecting a part of ourselves from hurt or difficulty. If we are being given shelter we are aware that there is protective power in our lives.

▦ Any shelter signifies protection. We are all aware of the need for a safe space, and this symbolism comes across in dreams quite strongly. The images used could be anything from a snail shell to an umbrella. Usually dreams about shelter highlight our needs or insecurities.

*You might also like to consult the entries for Shells and Umbrella.*

## SHIELD

⚜ In spiritual development the shield appears as a symbol of a particular stage of growth. It is at this point that we need to appreciate that we have control over our own destiny. This symbol often first appears in dreams representing this stage of development.

♥ In myths and legends the Amazonian woman is shown carrying a shield. This symbolizes woman's ability to be both protective and assertive.

A shield is a symbol of preservation. It can appear in dreams as a warrior's shield, or as a barrier between the dreamer and the rest of the world. If we are shielding someone else, then we need to be sure our actions are appropriate and supportive. If we are being shielded, we need to be clear as to whether we are erecting the shield or whether it is being erected for us.

*Consult the entries for Barrier and Warrior as well as the information on Amazon in Archetypes in the Introduction for further clarification.*

**SHIRT –** *see* **CLOTHES**

**SHOE –** *see* **CLOTHES**

**SHOP –** *see* **MARKET/MARKET PLACE**

**SHOT/SHOOTING**

Directed explosive energy, such as that from a gun, is a very effective spiritual tool, although it must be used with care. If we are noticeably aggressive we would have to be aware of our own motives and perhaps be a little more objective in taking action.

To be conscious of hearing a shot in dreams or of shooting someone highlights the need for a targeted release of energy, perhaps to clear the air or to achieve a particular end result. Being shot in a dream suggests that we may need to be aware of someone else's ill feeling towards us.

Unconsciously you may be feeling threatened in some way and need to be consciously pro-active in coming to terms with the fear that this brings. The type of weapon being used may have significance. When in a dream we are shooting someone we need to come to terms with aggressive or destructive tendencies which cannot be dealt with satisfactorily in waking life. Being in an environment where shooting is permitted, such as a shooting range or a war zone, indicates that certain safeguards should be put in place before planning on making any sort of assertive move.

In a woman's dream being shot or shot at can symbolize the sexual act and all that goes along with the idea of penetration. She might wish to explore her own feelings, particularly whether she feels targeted or victimized. In a man's dream the same idea of victimization or aggression can be apparent, but will be much less to do with the sexual act and more to do with everyday matters and his place in the world.

*Consult the entries for Explode/Explosion, Gun, Victim, War and Weapon for further clarification.*

**SHOVEL/SPADE**

A shovel is an implement or tool which can be used to help us uncover what is spiritually correct.

❤ Since a shovel or spade can suggest a degree of introspection, of covering up, what is being moved is important. We need to be mindful of the content of our lives. Digging compost, for instance, would mean considering the sum total and most fertile aspects of our lives, whereas shovelling sand, with its attendant dangers, might suggest trying to manipulate time.

▦ A shovel in a dream will signify a need to dig into past experiences for information. We may need to uncover a past joy or trauma, or possibly even a learning experience. The type of spade or shovel will be of relevance. A garden spade would suggest being totally pragmatic, whereas a fire shovel would indicate a need to take care.

*You might also like to consult the entries for Digging/Excavation, Sand, Time and Tools.*

## SHRINK

❀ Following the psychological recognition of our smallness, we equally can become aware of the sense of belonging to a much greater cosmic whole. This is represented in dreams by a feeling of shrinking.

❤ Psychologically we can learn to handle who we are by recognizing both how necessary and also how small we are in the general scheme of things. The latter can be accompanied in dreaming by a feeling of shrinking. We therefore become less threatening to ourselves and others.

▦ In dreams, to shrink is to have a desire to return to childhood, or to a smaller space in order to be looked after. In everyday life we may be aware of losing face or of feeling small and this can be translated in dreams as shrinking. To see something – or somebody – shrink can indicate that it is losing its power over us.

*Consult the entries for Analyst and Size for further information.*

## SHROUD

❀ In spiritual terms a shroud is a mark of respect for the dead. As a garment, it is meant to convey decency.

❤ In a dream a shroud can be a frightening image, since it is associated with death. It can also signify the covering up of something we do not fully understand. We know that it is there, but we do not wish to confront it.

▦ If we recognize that by shrouding something it becomes hidden, then the image is more manageable. In times gone by, the shroud was a set of ropes used by sailors. This image surfaces in dreams when we deliberately tie something up in order to make it safe – shrouded from view.

*You might also like to consult the entry for Sailing/Sails.*

**SICK –** *see* **ILL/ILLNESS AND VOMIT**

**SICKLE –** *see* **SCYTHE**

**SIGNATURE –** *see* **WRITING**

**SILENCE**

🏵 Spiritually, silence is a 'space' where there is no need for sound. Many religious orders are silent on the basis that there is then closer communication with God. In dreams it may suggest that contemplation and withdrawal from the everyday world is necessary.

💖 When we are silent in dreams we are unable to voice our feelings or opinions. We are either inhibited by our own selves or by outside influences. Conversely in silence we have no need to express ourselves.

▣ Silence in a dream can suggest uneasiness and expectancy. There is a waiting for something to happen or not. If a dream character is silent when we expect them to speak, we are unsure as to how we ourselves will react in waking life to external circumstances.

*You might also like to consult the entries for Hear/Hearing and Sound.*

**SILVER**

🏵 Spiritually, silver is said to represent the feminine aspect, gold being the masculine. This came initially from the gold of the sun and the silver of the moon. Metals were thought to be 'reflections'.

💖 Silver on a more psychological level has been taken to represent the emotional qualities of the moon. This may be in the sense that we are available, yet remote. The moon and silver both represent a quality of attraction and self-sufficiency at the same time.

▣ On a practical level, silver coins appearing in a dream suggest finance or money. Silver bars are metal in its raw state. In any case, silver is something of value that can be held in reserve against possible difficulty.

⸙ In a woman's dream, silver will often represent her essential core. In a man's dream it is more likely to represent his rather more diffuse qualities.

*The entries for Colours, Gold, Metal, Money and Moon will further enhance your understanding.*

**SING**

🏵 Spiritually when we sing we are capable of raising the vibration, either for ourselves or other people. We are in touch with the Higher Self.

💖 Singing as an act of worship is a vital part of many systems of belief. Singing as chanting has a valid place in religion – as in the Gregorian chant – where certain tones achieve a shift in consciousness. To hear this in dreams is to be in touch with a high vibration. Chanting of a mantra also achieves the same end. If we are singing alone, we have learnt to be skilled in our own right.

🎴 To hear singing in a dream is to link with the self-expression we all have. We are in touch with the flowing, feeling side of ourselves and of others. To be singing is to be expressing our joy and love of life and our need to perform and star in our own show. To be in a choir suggests our ability to worship or express ourselves in a peer group. To be singing a football anthem creates a fellow feeling. To find ourselves singing in a talent contest suggests that we wish for other people to become aware of our perceived abilities.

*You might also like to consult the entries for Mantra, Music/Rhythm, Musical Instruments and Worship.*

## SINKING

🪷 Both spiritually and physically, to be sinking is to be getting into a situation where we are unable to see clearly or to perceive the best course of action. For sensitives, this may be when the negativity of others threatens to overwhelm us.

💗 A sinking feeling in dreams usually suggests worry or fear. Emotionally we are unable to maintain our usual happiness. We may feel that we are not in control, and that we cannot maintain forward movement. To see an object sinking may suggest that we are about to lose something we value. A sink as a water receptacle symbolizes the way we hold onto our emotions.

🎴 To be sinking in a dream suggests a loss of confidence. We may be unhappy at something we have done, and feel hampered by the circumstances around us. We may feel we are losing ground within a relationship or situation. To see someone else sinking would suggest we are aware of a difficulty that perhaps needs our help. What we are sinking into could be important. To be sinking in water would suggest a particular emotion is threatening to engulf us. To be sinking in quicksand or a bog indicates that we feel there is no safe ground for us. Becoming conscious of a sink or basin suggests that some kind of cleansing is necessary.

*The entries for Drowning, Emotions, Quicksand and Water will provide additional information.*

## SIREN

🪷 As an archetype, it is only when it is understood spiritually that the Siren can ultimately restore man to himself that she becomes acceptable and can be worked with. After having rejected her enchantment, we are free to become whole.

💗 The Siren suggests deception and distraction of man from his purpose. In dreams this is usually sexually oriented and difficult to handle. In psychological terms she is Temptation and often appears in Greek or Roman attire, as if to enhance the erotic image. She can often be pictured in dreams sat by water, since she works mainly with the emotions.

■ To hear a siren – as in an ambulance or fire engine – is to be warned of danger. For some, the sound of a siren will evoke images and memories of war and destruction, triggering feelings of anxiety.

◧ In a woman's dream, if she has not come to an understanding of the Siren within her, such a character can appear ultimately to be destructive. In a man's dream, the Siren is generally an aspect of his Anima, initially alluring, then recognizably destructive, before he finally discovers how to handle her. For both men and women it is vital that they learn to integrate, or come to terms with, this part of the personality.

*You might also like to consult the entries for Emotions, War and Water as well as the information on Siren in Archetypes in the Introduction.*

### SISTER – *see* FAMILY

### SIZE

◉ Spiritually size is irrelevant. It is more the appreciation of feeling that becomes important. A 'big' feeling is something that consumes us, whereas a 'little' perception may be only part of what really exists.

♥ A child learns very early on to make comparisons, and this is one of the things that we never lose, particularly in dreams. Something is often bigger (taller) or smaller rather than simply big or small. In dreams size is relative. We might recognize somewhere we know, but find it is larger or smaller than we thought it to be. It is the size within the dream that is relevant.

■ To be conscious of size in a dream highlights how we feel in relation to a person, project or object. Big or tall might suggest important or threatening, whereas small might indicate vulnerability or something 'less than' ourselves. Thus a big house would be an awareness of the expansion of oneself, whereas a small house would indicate an intensity of feeling. The contrast between fat and thin, or thick and thin, is a subjective evaluation that will often depend on cultural differences. The issue of size in dreams is dependent on our own personal evaluation. To be actively reducing an article may mean that we are trying to make a project or task manageable.

### SKELETON/SKULL

◉ A skeleton in dreams alerts us to our attitude to the macabre. We are aware that the physical must 'die' or change, but that there is still a framework left. The skull in dreams can sometimes represent major changes such as death and all the adjustments necessary.

◈ Psychologically, we sometimes need to be aware of our feelings about death. The obvious image of the skeleton appearing in our dreams forces us to be aware of this. It can also suggest feelings or talents that we have forgotten and that, therefore, seem to have died. To be conscious of our own skull in dreams is to appreciate the intellectual structure that we have given our lives. To perceive a skull where there should be a head suggests that we are not using our intellectual abilities as well we might. When a skull is talking to us, a part of us that we have rejected or denied is beginning to 'come back to life'. To be talking to a skull is recognizing the need to communicate with those who are lost to us in any way; if we believe in life after death, we may feel that spirit is talking through the skull.

▦ A skeleton in a dream suggests the 'bare bones' of something, perhaps an idea or concept. A skeleton in a cupboard represents a past action or shame, both in dreams and waking life, we wish to hide. A dancing skeleton is an awareness of the life we have lived or are living. To dig up a skeleton is to resurrect something – perhaps a talent – we have buried or hidden away. The skull and crossbones in dreams could represent either a somewhat romantic appreciation of a pirate or freedom-lover, or perhaps is a symbol of danger. Since the skull is a representation of the head it can also symbolize intellectual ability, or rather lack of it.

*Also consult the entry for Death and the information on the Head in the Body entry as well as the information on Tramp in Archetypes and Spirits in Spiritual Imagery in the Introduction.*

**SKIN** – *see* **BODY**

**SKULL** – *see* **SKELETON**

**SKY**

☀ The sky spiritually suggests infinity and that which is above and beyond us – a representation of the Ultimate. It also signifies order, particularly that applied to the intuitive function.

◈ The sky signifies the unattainable. Whatever effort we make we can never make the sky tangible. This is one reason why the sky gods were so important in more primitive cultures.

▦ In dreams the sky can represent the mind and signify our potential. Floating or flying in the sky can be ambivalent, since it can either mean trying to avoid the mundane, or exploring a different potential. If the sky is dark or cloudy it may reflect our mood of gloominess; if it is bright, our mood of joy.

*You might also like to consult the entries. for Clouds, Float/Floating, Flying/ Flight and Order*

**SLOW** – *see* **SPEED**

**SMALL** – *see* **SIZE**

**SMELL**

🌕 As our spiritual senses develop, the ability to sense and recognize smells from the past on a clairvoyant level can be rather alarming. In dreams, provided this ability is recognized merely as a means of identifying a time, place or person, we need not be afraid.

♥ Childhood is a time when smell is very significant. Many smells that are associated with that time, e.g. baking bread, burning oil, flowers, school dinners, can still be very evocative for us as adults. A pleasant smell could represent happy times or memories, whereas a bad smell can hold memories of particularly traumatic times.

▦ To be conscious of a smell in a dream usually means that we are trying to identify an object or its source. Most other senses are sharpened in dreams, but the sense of smell is made available only if a specific interpretation is needed.

*Also consult the entry for Odour.*

**SMOKE/SMOKING**

🌕 Spiritually, smoke signifies prayer rising to heaven and is used with that significance in those belief systems that use incense. It also represents the raising of the soul to escape from space and time and the restrictions of the physical dimension.

♥ Smoke in dreams can represent passion, although it may not have 'flared' properly into being. Smoke can also represent either cleansing – as with incense – or contamination of some sort. If we are smoking tobacco or any other substance, we are trying to control our anxiety. If we smoke in real life, but recognize in dreams that we no longer do so, we have overcome a difficulty. Smokers who are attempting to give up in everyday life will often have many dreams focused around the issue of smoking.

▦ Smoke in dreams suggests that there is a feeling of danger around, especially if we cannot locate the fire. As smoking in public become less acceptable, in dreams it may be seen as an act of rebellion or deliberately choosing to go against the norms of society.

*Consult the entries for Fire, Incense, Rebel/Revolution and Tobacco for additional information.*

**SNAIL**

🌕 The snail shell symbolizes the perfection of nature's creativity, which is also echoed in mathematical fractals (repeated patterns). The spiral shape of the snail shell is symbolic of the labyrinth.

⬦ From a psychological point of view, the snail suggests steadiness and self-containment. To be moving at snail's pace suggests direct planned, careful movement.

▦ The snail appearing in dreams may engender, because of its sliminess, a feeling of repulsion in some people. It does, however, also represent vulnerability and slowness, along with the type of apparent rootlessness seen in the Wanderer.

*You might also like to consult the entries for Labyrinth, Shell, Spiral and Wanderer.*

## SNAKE – *see* SERPENT AND SNAKE IN ANIMALS AND ALSO SPIRITUAL IMAGERY IN THE INTRODUCTION

## SNOW

✺ Snow represents spiritual purity, beauty and the melting away of difficulties.

⬦ Psychologically snow in dreams can suggest emotional coldness or frigidity. When snow is lying on the ground it can symbolize a protective covering. When blowing around its interpretation is similar to that of rain.

▦ Snow is a crystallisation of water, and as such represents the crystallization of an idea or project. When melting, it can represent the softening of the heart.

*You might also like to consult the entries for Cold, Ice/Iceberg/Icicles, Rain, Weather and Winter.*

## SOAP/SHAMPOO

✺ From a spiritual perspective, soap and shampoo represent cleansing. It is an attempt to get back to basics and to clear our wants, needs and requirements. We are trying to make a new connection with the Spiritual Self.

⬦ Psychologically soap can indicate a need to clean up our act. We may feel a sense of having been contaminated by an experience and situation and our dream mind is alerting us to the fact that we need to deal with it. Because shampooing is connected with the head – which of itself represents intellect – there is a connection psychologically with needing to have clarity of thought. We may feel that our thought processes have been slowed down, or dirtied, by outside influences.

▦ Soap in dreams suggests the idea of being cleansed. We perhaps need to create an environment of cleanliness – both of physical cleanliness and appropriate behaviour. Shampoo in dreams has an obvious connection with cleansing and washing. On a practical level, we are trying to 'clear our heads' in order to think or see clearly.

▯ Often in emerging male sexual dreams soap and shampoo represent ejaculated semen. A woman will often dream of shampooing her hair when a relationship breaks down; presumably she is instinctively aware that she must intellectually free herself.

*You might also like to consult the entries for Clean/Clear, Dirty and Washing as well as the information on Hair and Head in the Body entry.*

**SON** – *see* **FAMILY**

**SOUND**

🔆 Sound in the spiritual sense is vibration from which everything is created. In dreams, purity of sound is a prerequisite of awareness.

♥ To the waking mind, sound is necessary – and is sometimes somewhat irritating. Sound can be a marker for the natural changes that occur in focus in the dream state and, therefore, becomes part of the dream scenario. A particularly sharp sound – such as a desk bell pinging – would suggest sudden change, whereas an apparently long, drawn-out sound – such as a foghorn – would signify a slower process.

▦ Literally, if what we do in waking life resonates with us – that is, satisfies our inner and outer being – we may become particularly aware in dreams of sound. A discordant note would signify difficulty, and a purer one success.

*Consult the entry for Noise for further information.*

**SOUP** – *see* **EATING, FOOD AND NOURISHMENT**

**SOUTH**

🔆 The South in spiritual terms suggests the summer, a time for fun and laughter. The Archangel is Michael, the Soldier of God.

♥ We are looking towards midday and the right to use the energy we have available. The magical element is Fire and the colour red. Dreams of the South often signify the high point of any endeavour.

▦ When we dream specifically of the South, we are looking to be able to direct our energies successfully. It is the will to do and to be, so a time for action.

*You might also like to consult the entries for Colour, Elements, Fire and Summer.*

**SOWING**

🔆 Sowing in a spiritual sense suggests creating the correct environment in which growth can take place. It is, above all, the creative act.

♥ The image of laying down a framework for success is implicit in sowing. The actions that have to be gone through – such as preparing the ground, tilling the soil and so on – are all evocative images even in today's technological society. When this image appears in dreams, we need to look at circumstances around us and decide what we can gain most.

▦ Sowing is a symbol that has certain basic ideas attached to it. It can represent the planting of an idea, the beginning of a new project or the careful planning of a multi-faceted task.

▣ Originally, sowing seed was taken to be a feminine occupation. With mechanization that emphasis has shifted. However, in women's dreams, the primary image of nurturing may be that of sowing seed. In a man's dream it is more likely to signify the sexual act, and well as suggesting good husbandry. *The entry for Harvest will help to clarify your dream.*

### SPACE

✸ Space is a representation of a cosmic centre – a place that 'is, was and ever shall be'. When it appears in a dream it shows we need to widen our present view of the world.

♡ Psychologically we often need space to make the best use of opportunities. We should be capable of going beyond our own concepts of limitation and restriction. As the exploration of space takes us beyond our own little world, we become more conscious of the need for best use of resources.

▦ In dreams, when we are aware of the space we occupy we are in touch with our own potential. We may be aware that our personal space is being, or has been, penetrated. To be 'spaced out' is to have widened our personal boundaries artificially through the use of stimuli.

*You might also like to consult the entries for Astronaut and Rocket.*

### SPADE – *see* SHOVEL

### SPARK

✸ The spark suggests fire and therefore love. The 'essential spark' is the vital principle in life; we need to appreciate our own lust for life.

♡ The spark of an idea suggests the germ of a creative potential that, given the opportunity, will become much bigger. Since the spark also represents the basic life force, emotionally we can accept the myriad possibilities offered to us.

▦ A spark in a dream represents a beginning. Being aware of a spark is to be conscious of the germ of an idea that may be brought to fruition in waking life. From a physical perspective it is a small thing that gives rise to a greater one.

*You might also like to consult the entries for Electricity, Fire and Lightning.*

### SPEAR

✸ Spiritually, the spear signifies directness and honour. It has the power of life and death.

♡ The spear is psychologically that part of ourselves that is fertile and assertive. To see a warrior with a spear is to recognize the aggressive male. To put a spear in the ground is to mark one's territory. If we are throwing a spear we perhaps need to be aware of our more assertive tendencies.

🔲 The spear has many meanings from a mundane perspective. It can represent the cut and thrust of business life or the wit of social interchange. In its more negative sense it can suggest sarcasm and bloody-mindedness.

🔲 A spear represents the masculine in dreams and is a phallic symbol. Whether it appears in a man's or a woman's dream, it allows us to be conscious of the need to cut out nonsense and get straight to the point.

*The entries for Arrow and Weapons will provide further information.*

SPECTACLES – *see* GLASSES/SPECTACLES

SPEED

⚙️ There is a point when, as we are developing spiritually, we lose our sense of time. Speeding things up may appear as slowing things down, and vice versa. This is all part of the spiritual growth process. The polarities of fast and slow – that is, speed and inertia – are a duality that, when handled properly, create a balance.

♥ Travelling at speed suggests trying to achieve a fast result. Speeding – as in a traffic offence – suggests being too focused on an end result, and not the method of getting there. However, as the opposite to fast, being slow in dreams gives a sense of greater tranquillity than such frenetic behaviour. To be taking, or to be given, speed (amphetamines) in a dream may have two meanings. If the substance is used in everyday life, we could be being alerted to a gift or talent that should be developed. If we do not normally use the drug, then we are putting ourselves in danger in some way. We may be trying to force an issue or pre-empt results.

🔲 Speed in dreams identifies an intensity of feelings that is not usually available in waking life. Because everything is happening too quickly, it engenders anxiety in us, which creates problems. In dreams, when everything slows down or seems to be going in slow motion, we need to consider very carefully each aspect of our lives at that particular moment. To be moving slowly suggests taking greater care.

*Also consult the entries for Drugs, Quick and Time as well as the information on Anxiety Dreams in the Introduction.*

SPHINX

⚙️ Spiritually the sphinx stands for vigilance, power and wisdom as well as dignity.

♥ Psychologically, and because even today little is known about it, the sphinx in dreams represents our enigmatic side. It will highlight the mysterious power that becomes available to us, particularly in times of trouble.

▦ The sphinx, for most people in dreams, will represent Egypt and all the mystery it contains. It may also represent a hardened attitude.

*You might also like to consult the entry for Mummy (Egyptian).*

## SPIDER

⊛ Spiritually the spider represents the Great Mother in her role as the Weaver of Life. She weaves Destiny from the body of her self and is, therefore, the Creator. In coming to terms with this aspect, we become weavers of our own destiny.

♥ In psychological terms the spider connects with the principles of the Mandala. The spider has the ability to create a perfect pattern, which both nurtures and protects at the same time.

▦ On a very mundane level spiders are generally disliked, perhaps because of their scuttling movement but also because of its association with dirt. In dreams it can also suggest deviousness, harking back to the innate fear of the Destructive Mother archetype.

▣ In a woman's dream a spider will often reconnect her with her essential femininity, whereas in a man's dream such an image is more likely to generate fear.

*Consult the entries for Insects, Mandala and Web as well as the information on Great Mother and Destructive Mother in Archetypes in the Introduction.*

**SPINE** – *see* **BACKBONE IN BODY**

**SPIRAL** – *see* **SHAPES**

## SPIRE

⊛ As a representation of our spiritual progression, the spire suggests the movement from the secular to the sacred. It has represented this from time immemorial.

♥ The spire represents ambition and striving. A fallen spire would suggest the collapse of hopes. To be building a tower or spire has connotations with the Tower of Babel and shows a need for more – or better – communication.

▦ To see a spire in a dream is to recognize a landmark, whether personal or more universal. In previous times, people oriented themselves by churches. Now a pub tends to be a marker, but in dreams the spire still persists.

▣ The spire can often be taken in dreams as a phallic symbol, particularly – and somewhat obviously – the erect one. In a woman's dream, the spire will usually represent her sense of the Ultimate, whereas in a man's dream it is more likely to represent his ambition.

*Consulting the entry for Tower as well as Religious Buildings in Buildings and also the information for Spiritual Imagery in the Introduction should help provide further clarification.*

**SPIRITS** – *see* **SPIRITUAL IMAGERY IN THE INTRODUCTION**

**SPIRITUAL IMAGERY** – *see* **INTRODUCTION**

**SPORT**

⚙ From a spiritual perspective, sport in dreams suggests the ability to keep the 'temple' of the physical body in peak condition. To be the best requires discipline and means calling on reserves of power and energy we may not know we have. Sporting activities were, and indeed still are, used to channel excess energy.

♥ Psychologically, any sport requires us to overcome our own inadequacies and to have courage beyond the norm. Taking part in competitive sport in dreams will signify our ability to be competitive in other areas in life. Tackling an opponent is confronting a problem, whereas fishing tackle is a means to an end.

▦ Sport, as a dream symbol of business and working life, is a potent image. Team games will represent the ability to work in harmony with others, whereas athletic activities in dreams may suggest personal excellence. Acting as a referee highlights our ability to control circumstances around us. To challenge the referee is to be challenging authority.

*Consult the entries for Compete/Competition, Games, Running and Win/ Winning for further information.*

**SPRING**

⚙ Spiritually within the cycle of nature, spring is a time of rebirth and rejuvenation. We can now afford to make a new beginning, particularly insofar as emotion is concerned.

♥ The saying 'spring forward, fall back' is also applicable in psychological terms, since effort and new energy is required to progress. To walk with a spring in one's step is to be looking forward to something.

▦ Springtime in a dream can suggest new growth or opportunities. Perhaps there is a fresh start in a relationship. A spring of water suggests fresh energy, whereas a bedspring or other type of coil would indicate latent power for movement.

*You might also like to consult the entries for Autumn, Seasons, Summer, Water and Winter.*

**SPRINKLE/SPRINKLING**

⚙ Spiritually we are aware of basic concepts and abilities. In some cultures, semen is sprinkled on the ground to propitiate the Mother Goddess and ensure a good harvest. In protective magical rituals herbs and salt are sprinkled.

♥ Sprinkling suggests the symbolism of impregnation, of conception and gestation. Psychologically we need to make a link with our creative side in order to function properly as human beings.

🔲 Sprinkling as a symbol in dreams suggests an attempt to make a little go a long way. Perhaps we need to get the best out of situations around us, by putting a little effort into many things.

*Consult the entries for Goddess/Goddesses, Harvest, Magic/Magician and Rite/Ritual for further information.*

## SQUARE – *see* SHAPES/PATTERNS

## SQUIRREL – *see* ANIMALS

## STAB

🌞 When we realize that we can use particular skills, they can assume an almost ritualistic feeling. Fighting and stabbing movements (as in martial arts) are a means of spiritual discipline. We need to understand appropriate behaviour.

💟 When we make ourselves vulnerable we are open to being hurt. Often a stab is a quick way of achieving a result. For instance, to be stabbing at something rather than somebody would suggest the need to break through some kind of shell or barrier in order to proceed.

🔲 To be stabbed in a dream indicates our ability to be hurt. To stab someone is, conversely, to be prepared to hurt but also with the faculty of being able to get straight to the point.

📑 Since a stab wound is penetrative it has obvious connections with aggressive masculine sexuality and will have this meaning in feminine dreams. In a man's dream it is more likely to be to do with his ability to get straight to the point.

*Consult the entries for Dagger, Knife, Rite/Ritual and Wound/Wounding for further information.*

## STAFF

🌞 Spiritually the staff is a symbol of the support we have, or will need, on our spiritual journey. As we progress, we move from using it as a support to using it as a tool and finally as a sign of authority.

💟 The staff in dreams symbolizes the journeying and pilgrimage that we must undertake. It also represents magical power in the form of a wand.

🔲 A staff, in the sense of a stick, is a support mechanism; staff, as in office staff, a support system. Dreaming of either should clarify our attitude to the support we require in life. It is worthwhile noting that one is passive in its use (the stick) and one is active.

*You might also like to consult the entries for Sceptre, Tool and Wand.*

## STAG – *see* DEER IN ANIMALS

## STAGE – *see* THEATRE

**STAIRS** – *see* **STEPS AND ALSO STAIRS IN BUILDINGS**
**STAR** – *see* **CELEBRITY, FAME, FAMOUS PEOPLE AND SHAPES/PATTERNS**
**STATION** – *see* **DEPARTURES IN JOURNEY AND TRAIN IN TRANSPORT**
**STATUE**

🔅 There is a basic side of nature that needs to look up to something and this can be symbolized in dreams by a statue, which is representative of an idea or concept rather than a person.

💗 When emotion is not allowed proper expression it is 'dead' and, therefore, has solidified. Often in dreams this will take the form of a statue. If the statue comes to life, the emotion can be rescued.

🏛 Dreaming of a statue is to be linking with the unresponsive, cold side of human nature. We may be worshipping or loving someone and not getting any response. We come up against the knowledge that we have given value to something that no longer has significance.

*You might also like to consult the entry for Stone.*

**STEALING**

🔅 Spiritually, stealing is using energy inappropriately. At each level of awareness we have certain power available to us that must be used wisely and well. For instance, 'black' magic could be interpreted as stealing. Psychic 'vampirism' is another form of stealing.

💗 Stealing is a very emotive word for most people, and it will depend on the dreamer's background as to how they feel about inappropriate behaviour. This image also comes up when dealing with the emotions. For instance, a 'needy' person may feel they are stealing affection.

🏛 To dream of stealing suggests that we are intent on taking something without permission. This may be love, money or opportunities. If someone steals from us we may feel cheated. If in dreams this act is by someone we know, then we need to work out how much we trust that person. If it is by someone we don't know, it is more likely to be a part of ourselves that we don't trust. However, if we belong to a gang of thieves, then we should carefully look at, and consider, the morals of the peer group that we belong to.

*You might also like to consult the entries for Burglar, Group and Thief.*

**STEAM**

🔅 We are looking at, and are aware of, the all-encompassing power of the Spirit.

💗 Because it is two substances uniting into one (fire and water), steam suggests transformation. It also suggests a transitory experience, since steam also melts away.

▣ Steam in dreams can suggest emotional pressure. We are passionate about something without necessarily knowing what it is.

*Also consult the entries for Fire, Machine/Machinery, Piston and Water, as well as the information on Transformation in the Introduction.*

**STEEPLE – *see* SPIRE**

**STEPS**

✿ There is still perceived to be a hierarchical structure in spiritual progression. We can achieve certain things at each level before moving on to the next.

♡ Steps in dreams almost invariably suggest an effort made to succeed. Going up steps suggests trying to make things better and improve them, whereas going down means going either into the past or the subconscious.

▣ Steps represent changes in awareness within a project, quite literally the steps necessary. Steps also represent communication of a progressive kind.

*Also consult the information for Stairs in Buildings.*

**STERILIZE/STERILITY**

✿ Sterilization in a spiritual sense is somewhat ambivalent. It can either suggest purity of spirit or a belief in austerity, which does not allow the Self to grow.

♡ To dream of sterilizing something suggests a need for cleansing at a deep level. We wish to get rid of hurts or traumas and are prepared to put in the effort to do so. 'Sterilizing' a situation may be taking the emotion out of it.

▣ Sterility suggests an absence of ideas and motivation. The need not to be sidetracked in everyday life can present in dreams as a sterile environment. Dreams of alienation, or of being captured by aliens, often have such an image.

⊡ For a woman to dream of being sterilized, either by an operation or otherwise, may be connecting with her feeling of powerlessness. In a man's dream sterilization may suggest sexual dissatisfactions or doubts about his self-image.

*You might also like to consult the entries for Abduct, Alien/Alienated and Operation.*

**STONE**

✿ Stone, as basic material, signifies the imperishability of Supreme Reality. Ultimately it is indestructible and returns to Source.

♡ Stone has many connotations on an emotional level. For stone to be broken up signifies being badly hurt. Being turned to stone would suggest that we have had to harden up our attitudes. Being stoned in dreams is being punished for misdemeanours.

▦ Dreaming of stone can suggest stability and durability, but also a loss of feeling. To be carving stone is to be attempting to create a lasting monument. *You might also like to consult the entries for Break, Emotions, Gems/Jewels and Statue.*

## STORM

❀ Spiritually a storm symbolizes the Creative Power. Thunder and lightning are the tools of the storm gods.

♡ When we are in difficulty, for instance, in a relationship, a storm can bring release. When an argument is not appropriate in everyday life, in dreams a storm can clear our 'emotional air'.

▦ In dreams a storm indicates a personal emotional outburst. We may feel we are being battered by events or emotions. It can also signify anger. *Consulting the entries for Anger, Emotions, God/Gods, Lightning, Rain, Thunder/Thunderbolts and Weather will provide further information.*

## STRANGER – *see* PEOPLE

## STRANGLE

❀ Spiritually, wisdom arises out of learning how to hold back inappropriate speech. In dreams the feeling of being strangled suggests a deliberate act of suppression.

♡ Strangulation suggests a violent act of suppression. Emotionally, our more violent, aggressive side may not allow us to act appropriately in certain situations. In dreams this can appear as strangling.

▦ To dream of strangling someone is an attempt to stifle our own emotions. To dream of being strangled is to be aware of our difficulty in speaking out about our emotions. *You might also like to consult the entries for Kill, Murder/Murderer and Violence.*

## STREAM

❀ The image of a stream is often quoted as being blessed by Divine Power. Spiritual energy is often experienced as a stream of light.

♡ Emotionally if we are to function properly we must feel loved and appreciated. To be in the flow of things suggests being part of a social group that will enable us to interact with people. This image often surfaces as a stream.

▦ Dreaming of a stream suggests the awareness of the flow of our emotions. To be in a stream suggests being in touch with our sensuality. *Also consult the entry for Water.*

## STRING

❀ String theory is a scientific attempt to explain a spiritual anomaly. Anything that binds suggests a direct relationship with our inner self. This is traditionally seen as the Silver Cord that holds the spiritual and physical together.

♥ In a psychological sense, string – like rope – can be seen as a link between two objects or aspects of our lives. We may not have made the connection before in waking life.

▦ String appearing in dreams signifies some sort of binding, perhaps to make something secure. It may also represent trying to hold a situation together.

*You might also like to consult the entries for Hold and Rope.*

## SUBMARINE

❂ Dreaming of a submarine indicates we have a spiritual need to understand the depths of our emotions.

♥ If we are to be comfortable with ourselves, we need to understand our unconscious urges. Since there can be some fear with this – and perhaps a need for protection – the submarine becomes quite a potent image.

▦ A submarine in dreams indicates the depth of feeling that is accessible to us. Usually we are looking at the subconscious depths rather than the spiritual heights.

*The entries for Boat/Ship, Deep, Torpedo and Water will provide further information.*

## SUCCUBUS – *see* DEMON AND DEVIL

## SUCKING/SUCKLE

❂ The snake that sucks its own tail – the Ouroboros – is a potent image of spiritual completeness and will appear as we become more spiritually advanced.

♥ Emotionally we all have needs which are left over from childhood. These may be unfulfilled desires or the need to be whole and complete. This need can surface in dreams as sucking something.

▦ To be conscious of sucking in a dream suggests a return to infantile behaviour and emotional dependency. Sucking a lollipop alerts us to a need to bring ourselves some sort of comfort. Sucking a finger symbolizes the primitive urge to suckle.

## SUFFOCATING

❂ Suffocation may appear in dreams when negativity is too strong for us to deal with and threatens to overwhelm us.

♥ If in waking life we are struggling within a relationship we may find that dreams of suffocation occur. Fears connected with the sexual act can also surface in dreams as suffocation.

▦ When we feel we are suffocating in a dream, it may be that our own fears are threatening to overwhelm us. It can also indicate that we are not in control of our own environment. To be suffocating a dream character may mean we wish to shut someone up in waking life.

**SUICIDE**

🔆 Often on the path of spirituality we must let go of the old Self. This can occur in dreams as suicide. It is also a sign of anger against the Self.

♡ Emotionally, when dreams of suicide occur, we may have come to the end of our ability to cope with a particular situation in our lives. It does not actually mean that we are suicidal. It simply marks the end of a phase.

▣ Dreaming of suicide alerts us to the sudden ending of something, perhaps a project or relationship. It may also signify the end of a business or business relationship, but one that we ourselves terminate.

*Also consult the entries for Anger and Death as well as the information on Self in Archetypes in the Introduction.*

**SUITCASE – see BAGGAGE AND LUGGAGE**

**SUMMER**

🔆 Esoterically, summer represents the mid-life. This is a time of spiritual success and of the ability also to plan for the rest of our lives. We have learnt by experience and can now put that experience into practice.

♡ The significance of summer on a psychological level is twofold. Because of its association with holidays and with fun and laughter, we are able to be more relaxed. We also have opportunities to meet with other people and to form new associations.

▣ To be aware in a dream that it is summer suggests that it is a good time in our lives. We can look forward to success in projects we have around us. We have the ability to make the most of what we have done to date.

*You might also like to consult the entries for Autumn, Seasons, Spring, Sun and Winter.*

**SUN**

🔆 The sun can symbolize spiritual enlightenment and radiance. The dreamer can 'soak up' and use the sun's power for further spiritual development. Because the sun is such a powerful image on its own as a life source, it can also appear in dreams as a symbol for other life energy.

♡ The sun in dreams suggests warmth and conscious awareness. If dreaming of a Native American Sun Dance, or any such worship, we may be wishing to acknowledge the sun for its all-encompassing power and energy. We are using the energy of the sun for guidance and vitality.

▣ A sunny day suggests happiness. To be drawn to the sun indicates we are looking for enlightenment. In turning towards the sun, the sunflower could be said to be a symbol of obsession, but also of worship. With its many seeds it also represents fertility.

⚡ There was an ancient belief that the sun was masculine and the moon feminine. The image of the sun and the moon appearing together in a dream follows that belief and suggests integration of masculine and feminine energies.

*You might also like to consult the entry for Planets.*

**SUNGLASSES –** *see* **GOGGLES**

**SURGERY**

☀ Spiritually we may feel that we have too much to deal with or that something needs altering.

♥ Surgery is a necessary, though unpleasant intrusion into our lives. Dreaming of having surgery performed on us shows we need to accustom ourselves to changes that may initially be difficult, but ultimately are healing and to our benefit.

▦ To find ourselves in a doctors' surgery in dreams would indicate that we should be considering our health and health matters. Performing surgery indicates that we need to 'cut out' contamination or a 'sick' part of our personality.

*Also consult the entry for Operation.*

**SWAMP**

☀ A swamp can symbolize the vast amount of spiritual knowledge that there is to be taken in. A swamp is so-called primordial material, out of which everything emerges; at this stage we have no idea what our potential is.

♥ Emotionally, when a swamp appears we are putting ourselves in touch with very basic feelings and emotions. The sheer vastness may leave us feeling utterly hopeless and out of our depth, but with perseverance we can pull ourselves through and have a much clearer outlook.

▦ To be swamped is to be overwhelmed by a feeling or emotion. A swamp in a dream symbolizes feelings that can undermine our confidence and wellbeing. To be swamping someone else in a dream may suggest that we are being too needy.

*You might also like to consult the entries for Marsh and Mud.*

**SWAN –** *see* **BIRDS**

**SWASTIKA –** *see* **SHAPES/PATTERNS**

**SWEEPING**

☀ We have attained much spiritual knowledge on which we are now reflecting and need to consider all options and how to make best use of them.

 Sweeping is a traditional image that symbolizes good management and clearing of our environment. In psychological terms it suggests an attention to detail and correctness, as much as to cleanliness. In modern-day technological symbolism it could suggest searching for viruses.

 To dream of sweeping suggests being able to clear away outmoded attitudes and emotions. To be sweeping up suggests putting things in order. There may be certain elements of confusion, which we can take time to clear away.

*You might also like to consult the entries for Broom/Brush and Clean/Clear.*

**SWEETS – see FOOD**

**SWIMMING**

 Swimming is an archetypal dream image. It suggests that spiritual energy is being used as we are moving towards a particular goal. It is said in dreams to symbolize the womb experience.

 To dream of being a good swimmer shows the ability to be able to handle emotional situations well, whereas being a poor swimmer in a dream could indicate the need to learn how to handle our emotions in a more positive way. Swimming in water will always be symbolic of the emotions, whereas swimming through the air connects with intellectual ability.

 Dreaming of swimming has much the same symbolism as immersion. To be swimming upstream in a dream would indicate we are going against our own nature. Swimming fish can have the same symbolism as sperm and, therefore, can indicate the desire for a child. Swimming in clear water indicates being cleansed, whereas dark water could symbolize the possibility of depression.

*Consult the entries for Drowning and Water for clarification.*

**SWINE – see PIG IN ANIMALS**

**SWORD**

 Spiritually the sword signifies the power of authority and protection. In dreams, to be given a sword signifies that we have the protection of the sacred. We are able to make our own decisions.

 The sword symbolizes justice and courage as well as strength. For the image of a sword to appear in a dream indicates there is an element of the warrior in us, and that we are prepared to fight for our beliefs.

 The sword in dreams invariably suggests a weapon of power. We may have the ability to create power and use energy properly through our beliefs. A ceremonial sword will confer status.

*Also consult the entries for Knight, Warrior and Weapon.*

**SYMBOLS** – *see* INTRODUCTION

**SYNAGOGUE** – *see* RELIGIOUS BUILDINGS IN BUILDINGS AS WELL AS SPIRITUAL IMAGERY IN THE INTRODUCTION

**SYRINGE**

⚜ Penetrative awareness, as symbolized by the syringe, can suggest a particular way of approaching our own spiritual selves.

♥ Dreaming of a syringe can indicate that we need to be conscious of the way we influence other people. We can be very specific and hit the right spot, or we can have a more 'scatter gun' approach. Those who use syringes regularly may well dream of contamination or associated problems.

▦ In dreams the syringe suggests an awareness of the influence that other people can have over us. It will depend on whether the syringe is being used to take something out or put something in as to the particular significance. A garden syringe (as in a fly spray) in dreams can suggest either masculine energy or decontamination.

*Consult the entries for Contamination, Injection and Needle for further information.*

**TABERNACLE** – *see* **SPIRITUAL IMAGERY IN THE INTRODUCTION**

**TABLE**

⚙ A table can represent spiritual judgement and legislation. As a dividing line between those with authority and those without, it signifies a barrier to be crossed.

♥ To dream of dealing with a table or list of objects, or perhaps actions, instils a sense of order in our lives. It represents our ability to create order out of chaos. In sitting around a table if rectangular the top end will suggest higher status than the bottom end.

▦ A table being a focus for meeting, whether socially or professionally, is usually recognized in dreams as a symbol of decision making. There can be an element of ritual associated with the image of a table. As a place for a family rendezvous, we may consider meals eaten around a table to be an important aspect of family life. In business and professional terms, the boardroom table can also introduce an element of ritual around it such as hierarchy of position.

*You might also like to consult the entries for Altar, Furniture/Furnishings, Rite/ Ritual and Round Table.*

**TABLET**

⚙ We all have access to esoteric and hidden knowledge. This can be represented in dreams by the Tablets of Moses. Taking tablets in dreams may suggest that spiritual or alternative methods of healing may be appropriate in a given situation.

♥ In magical terms, a tablet presupposes knowledge greater than our own and, therefore, represents an element of trust. We trust our destiny to someone else. Taking a pill in a dream may alert us to our ability to heal ourselves. We may also be conscious that we need to be careful over what we choose to include in our lives.

▦ Taking medicine in the form of tablets signifies we recognize our need to be healthy and suggests doing something to make ourselves feel better. We need to 'heal' something that is wrong. In dreams, taking such a course of action will signify putting ourselves through an experience we need in order to improve our performance or potential. If we are giving tablets to someone else we may be aware that their needs are not being satisfied.

*You might also like to consult the entry for Medication/Medicine.*

**TACKLE –** *see* **SPORT**

**TADPOLE**

&#9775; Spiritually, the tadpole represents the Germ of Life. Dreaming of tadpoles links to an awareness of the simplicity of life.

&#9829; A tadpole is the beginning of an idea, an opportunity, something that has not yet had time to grow. We are aware that there is growth, but either we, or someone else, has not yet reached full maturity of thought.

&#9632; To dream of many tadpoles can suggest a number of business opportunities, some of which will come to fruition and some which will not. If the tadpoles are already growing legs we should look at which options in waking life have the best chance of survival.

&#9635; In a woman's dream tadpoles may represent either her wish, or her ability, to become pregnant. In a man's dream tadpoles are more likely to symbolize his virility.

**TAIL**

&#9775; The tail symbolizes the completion of a spiritual action, the finishing touches. It brings our involvement to an end.

&#9829; The tail is necessary to the animal for balance, and thus in dreams can be recognized as a means of adjustment in difficult circumstances.

&#9632; To dream of a tail can signify some residue from the past, something we still carry with us. Just as our tailbone (coccyx) can be vulnerable to injury, so we also can be affected by the past.

&#9635; In a man's dream the tail can indicate sexual excitement, or possibly, by association, the penis. For a woman it will initially suggest her own basic energy, and perhaps later on her way of linking with her own latent powers. *For an additional interpretation consult the entry for Follow/Follower.*

**TALISMAN –** *see* **SPIRITUAL IMAGERY IN THE INTRODUCTION**

**TALKING**

&#9775; Talking in dreams signifies spiritual communication, whether that is the passing on of spiritual knowledge or communication from spiritual entities.

&#9829; We are perhaps afraid of not being listened to properly in waking life and this anxiety can express itself through hearing someone else talking in dreams. It is not necessarily the words that are important, more the sense of what is being said. If we cannot hear them properly we are perhaps not ready consciously to accept the information.

&#9632; To be conscious of people talking in a dream gives a sense of being in contact with our own ability to communicate. We are able to express clearly what we feel and think, whereas in waking life we may not feel confident. Stopping people from talking means we wish some information to be kept hidden. Translating what is being said suggests we view ourselves as an intermediary, or in some cases the medium for understanding.

*You might also like to consult the entry for Hear/Hearing.*

**TALL** – *see* SIZE

**TAMBOURINE** – *see* MUSIC/RHYTHM AND MUSICAL INSTRUMENTS

**TAME**

🔆 Spiritual energy is quite powerful and as part of our discipline we must learn self-control, to tame it.

🜨 To find that something is extremely tame – in the sense of being dull and boring – in dreams suggests that we should reconsider the way we live our lives. We should perhaps do more to ensure that we are interested and stimulated.

▦ To dream of taming an animal indicates our ability to control or develop a relationship with the animal aspect of ourselves. The animal may be of note, the lion representing courage for instance. To dream of being tamed, as though we ourselves were the animal, signifies the need for restraint in our lives.

*Consult the entries for Animals and Wild for extra information.*

**TANGLED**

🔆 Cutting through a tangle of trees or undergrowth in a dream is part of the Hero's Journey towards spiritual autonomy. He must work hard to overcome chaos in order to succeed.

🜨 When something like hair is tangled, we need to be aware that our self-image or projection is coming across to other people as distorted, and not how we wish them to see us.

▦ Sometimes when we are confused in everyday life, we may dream of an object being entangled with something else. Often the way that we untangle the object indicates action we should take in waking moments. We can cut straight through quickly or patiently work at it.

*You might like to consult the entries for Chaos, Hero/Heroine, Knot, String and Rope.*

**TANK**

🔆 There are times when we need to be something of a 'Spiritual Warrior' and yet have our defences in place. A tank, as both a defensive and defended vehicle, would be likely to appear at this time in our dreams.

🜨 Often in dreams we become aware of our need to overcome objections and difficulties. Sometimes the only form of expression we have is to ride roughshod over those objections. The image of a war tank helps to highlight our ability to do this without ourselves being hurt.

🔲 Dreaming of a water tank is putting ourselves in touch with our inner feelings and emotions. Dreaming of a military tank connects us with our own need to defend ourselves, but to be aggressive at the same time. Such a dream would indicate that we are feeling threatened in some way.

*You might also like to consult the entries for Armed Forces, Conflict, War and Water.*

**TAO** – *see* **SPIRITUAL IMAGERY IN THE INTRODUCTION**

**TAP**

🔆 A tap is a means of controlling the flow of Spiritual energy. As visualization before sleep it can be a way of controlling imagery in dreams.

🔮 Water is considered to be a symbol of emotion, so a tap is representative of our ability to use or misuse emotion in some way. To be able to turn emotion on and off at will is indicative of great self-control. A dripping tap would indicate a difficulty in controlling emotions.

🔲 The tap is an image of being able to make available universal resources. To dream of not being able to turn a tap either on or off highlights our ability – or inability – to control those things we consider to be rightfully ours. To be tapping something suggests that we are trying to free up our energies. Tap dancing highlights a rhythmic approach to life.

*Consult the entries for Dance/Dancing, Emotions and Water for additional information.*

**TAPE**

🔆 The image of a tape – particularly the slightly old-fashioned recording tape – is spiritually a way of recording and measuring life's processes. This ties in with the idea of the Akashic records – when everything that is, was or ever shall be is noted.

🔮 Masking or parcel tape could be considered to be restraining – to create boundaries – within which movement becomes difficult. In dreams we become aware of the limitation we impose on ourselves in everyday life.

🔲 Dreaming of a measuring tape indicates our need to 'measure' our lives in some way. Perhaps we may need to consider how we communicate with, or 'measure up' to, other people's expectations. Equally, if we are doing the measuring we may be trying to create order in our lives.

*You might also like to consult the entries for Communication, Measure and Record/Records/Recording.*

**TAPESTRY** – *see* **THREAD AND WEAVING**

**TAR**

🔆 The symbolism of tar in a spiritual sense, because it is black and viscous, would suggest some kind of evil or negativity. Dreaming of tar on the road would suggest the potential to be trapped by such difficulties as we progress.

🔯 Dreaming of tar on a beach might suggest that we had allowed our emotions to become contaminated in some way. As tar was a basis for road-making and comes from oil it is now of concern to conservationists and may surface in dreams as a pollutant.

🔲 To be mending a road might signify that we can be repairing wear and tear in our everyday lives. To be tarring a fence could mean we must protect ourselves and also to reinforce our personal boundaries.

*Consulting the entries for Beach and Fence as well as the information on Road in Journey will enhance your understanding.*

## TARGET

🔯 Spiritually a target with its concentric circles can symbolize the total Self. The soul is in the middle, surrounded by spirit, mind, body and finally environment. To be shooting at a bull's-eye could be interpreted as a search for perfection.

🔯 Most of us need some kind of motivation in life, and a target as a symbol of our intellectual aspirations may not make much sense until we study the context of the dream. Aiming at a target in dreams would suggest we have a particular goal in mind. To be aiming at a person could suggest 'targeting' them on an emotional level for our own gratification.

🔲 In a work sense in dreams a sales or performance target might suggest our goals are imposed on us by others. On a more personal note, we will set our own targets – for instance health or education goals. If we were setting someone else a target in dreams, we would need to understand that the other person in the dream is a reflection of part of ourselves.

*You might also like to consult the entries for Arrow, Goal and Shot/Shooting.*

## TASTE

🔯 As we become more sensitive and aware, our tastes become more refined. As we progress spiritually we may find the crass and the gross harder to deal with.

🔯 In waking life we usually know what we like and what our personal standards are. In dreams those standards may be distorted in order to highlight a change. For instance, to discover that we like a colour in a dream that would not normally be appreciated in real life could suggest that we need to study the new colour more fully in order to discover what it has to offer.

🔲 When something is not to our taste in a dream, it does not conform to our ideals and standards. To be aware of a bad taste in dreams suggests that whatever is signified by what we are eating or experiencing does not nourish us. If we find something a bit tasty we are aware of fine living. To recognize that our surroundings are in good taste suggests an appreciation of beautiful things.

*Consult the entries for Colour and Food for further information.*

## TATTOO

🌀 Polynesian peoples believe that a person's *mana*, their spiritual power or life force, is displayed through their tattoo. In spiritual terms a tattoo can suggest a group identity, belonging to a tribe or cult. It will be on a more intimate level than wearing a badge.

♥ A tattoo in dreams can also signify something that has left an indelible impression. This could be great hurt, but could also be a good memory. Sometimes, the image that is tattooed is worth interpreting if it can be seen clearly. The colour and design can be important and, while fashions vary, the symbolism is evident.

▦ On a physical level, a tattoo will stand for an aspect of our individuality. We wish to be seen as different. To be having a tattoo done in dreams suggests that we are prepared to suffer for this. To be having a tattoo removed indicates that we have rejected some former belief or credo.

⊡ As both men and women will now have tattoos done, the symbolism of any particular dream tattoo will be easily interpreted. The position of the tattoo and its spiritual symbolism – its connection with a system of belief – may give us insights.

*You might also like to consult the entries for Badge/Brooch, Colours and Picture as well as the information on Symbols in the Introduction.*

## TAU CROSS – *see* SPIRITUAL IMAGERY IN THE INTRODUCTION

## TAX

🌀 Spiritually, any tax levied in a dream would indicate our attitude towards working for the greater, or communal, good. We need to take some responsibility for the universe we live in.

♥ In real terms, a tax represents the extra amount of effort necessary to enable us to belong to society. Thus, dreaming of car tax would indicate that greater effort is needed to move forward. To be paying income tax suggests that we may feel we owe a debt to society. To be paying council tax may suggest that we feel we have to pay for the 'space' in which we exist. Refusing to pay any taxes suggests an unwillingness to conform.

▦ In everyday life, a tax represents a sum of money exacted from us in return for the right to live a certain lifestyle. In dreams, therefore, having to pay a tax suggests some kind of a penalty for living the way we choose.

*Consult the entry for Money or further clarification.*

**TAXI**

🔅 A taxi can represent spiritual knowledge, coupled with practical know-how. This is an important attribute in spiritual and personal development.

🛡 A taxi is a public vehicle in the sense that it is usually driven by someone unknown to us. We therefore have to trust the driver's awareness and knowledge. In dreams, therefore, a taxi can suggest having the need to reach a destination without knowing how we will do so.

🔲 In a dream, calling a taxi signifies recognizing the need to progress – to get somewhere. We cannot be successful without help, for which though there may be a price, it is worth paying.

*Also consult the entry for Car as well as the information on Destination in Journey and Car in Transport for further clarification.*

**TEA**

🔅 Tea as a symbol suggests spiritual refreshment – based on a reverence for nature and the creation of a perfect moment in time.

🛡 The Japanese tea ceremony suggests a unique way of caring for and nurturing someone – as does afternoon tea, each having their own rituals associated with them. Dreaming of teacups in particular links with our need to know the future (reading tea leaves). A tea break in a work environment suggests a need for rest and relaxation from concentration.

🔲 It will depend on whether the dream is about tea as a commercial commodity, or a social occasion. On a practical level, tea as a commodity represents a unit of exchange, whereas the social occasion – and the ceremonies associated with this – suggests inter-communication and the gift of our time.

*You might also like to consult the entries for Ceremony and Rite/Ritual.*

**TEACHER**

🔅 A spiritual teacher usually appears either in dreams or in person when the individual is ready to progress. There is a saying in the Hindu religion, 'When the *chela* (pupil) is ready, the teacher will come.' Often that teacher will not appear as a Wise Old Man or Woman, but as a person appropriate to the level of our understanding.

🛡 When we are looking for guidance, the Animus/Anima can present itself in dreams as a teacher. Often the figure will be that of a headmaster or headmistress (someone who 'knows better'). If we dream of ourselves as a teacher we will need to look at what information we have that should be passed on.

🔲 For many people, a teacher is the first figure of authority they meet outside the family. That person has a profound effect on the child and the teacher is often dreamt about in later years. Teachers can also generate conflict if their expressed views are very different to those learnt by the child at home. This may be something that has to be resolved through dreams in later years.

*Consult the entries for Education, School and Authority Figures in People, as well as the information on Animus, Anima and Wise Old Man in Archetypes in the Introduction.*

**TEAM – *see* GAMES AND GROUP**

**TEAR/TEARS/TORN**

    ✳ Tears can represent hurt or compassion, and it is often this latter meaning that applies spiritually. Experiencing compassion in a dream can make us more aware of the necessity for it in waking life.

    ♦ To dream of being in tears and then to wake up and discover that we are actually crying, suggests that some hurt or trauma has come sufficiently close to the surface to enable us to deal with it on a conscious level. To interpret tearing something up in dreams will depend on whether the action is destructive or one of division in order to share. If the article is already torn, then there is an aspect of our lives that is less than perfect and has been damaged in some way.

    ▦ Tears in dreams can indicate an emotional release and a cleansing. If we are crying we may not feel we are able to give way to emotion in everyday life, but can do so in the safe scenario of a dream. If we dream of someone we know in tears we perhaps need to look at our own conduct to see if it is appropriate. If we do not know them then we have offended against our own code of behaviour.

*Consult the entries for Emotions and Weeping for further information.*

**TEASE – *see* TORTURE/TORMENT/TEASE**

**TEETH – *see* BODY**

**TELEGRAM – *see* COMMUNICATION, EMAIL AND LETTER**

**TELEPHONE**

    ✳ Because communication via the telephone usually means that we are not able to see the recipient, using the telephone in a dream can signify communication with Spirit or with Guardian Angels.

    ♦ When we are aware of the telephone number we are ringing, it may be the numbers that are important. We also may be aware of the need to contact a specific person who we can help, or who can help us. If we are searching for a telephone number we are having difficulty in co-ordinating our thoughts about our future actions. Using the telephone suggests a direct one-to-one relationship. The type of phone will also have relevance; an old-fashioned one suggests ancient ideas or concepts. A modern up-to-date digital or mobile phone indicates we are easily able to make ourselves understood in various situations.

Using a telephone in a dream suggests the ability to make contact with other people and to impart information we feel they may need. This could actually be communicating with someone in our ordinary everyday lives, or establishing contact with a part of ourselves. Being contacted by telephone in dreams suggests there is information available to us at some level of awareness that we do not yet consciously know.

*You might also like to consult the entries for Angel, Communication and Numbers for further information.*

## TELESCOPE

Interestingly enough, a telescope in spiritual terms can signify the art of clairvoyance – the ability to perceive the future from an immediate perspective.

Using a telescope in a dream may mean that we should look at things with both a long- and short-term view. Without taking account of a long-term view, we may not be able to succeed in the short term. Conversely, by looking at the long-term view, we may be given information which will help us to 'navigate' our lives in the here and now.

Using a telescope in a dream suggests taking a closer look at something. A telescope enhances our view and makes it bigger and wider. We do need to make sure, however, that we are not taking a one-sided view of things.

*You might like to consult the entry for Lens.*

## TELEVISION

There are some aspects of spiritual learning that require an element of practicality about them. Often this will appear in dreams as a medium such as television. It is as though the dreaming mind requires a recognizable intermediary in order to accept the information.

Television, with its many repeats and 'reality' programmes, gives a rich source of dream images, from celebrities to fantasy scenarios. Many such images can, with a little thought, be identified as archetypal; football stars, for instance, representing both the Hero and the Tramp as freedom lover.

Dream images connected with television drama series and 'soaps' where we are able to follow a story are much to do with our ability to recognize archetypes that we can relate to, or situations that have resonance with us in our work or personal life.

*Consult the entries for Celebrity, Fame, Famous People and Media as well as the information on Archetypes in the Introduction for further information.*

## TEMPLE

☀ Both as a sanctuary for human beings and as a place where the Divine resides, a temple reflects the beauty of Heaven. It is a microcosm (small picture) of what is, after all, infinite.

♡ Psychologically, wherever there is a temple there is a sense of awe associated with creativity. Perhaps the biggest significance in dreams is the fact that it takes many to build one temple. This links with our awareness of the many facets of our personality that go to make a coherent whole.

▦ Often in dreams a temple can signify our own body. It is something to be treated with reverence and care. It has the same significance as a church since it is an object built to honour and pay respect to a god or gods.

*Also consult the information for Religious Buildings in Buildings and in Spiritual Imagery in the Introduction.*

## TEMPT/TEMPTATION

☀ Temptation is one of the biggest spiritual barriers we must overcome. Often it is a conflict between the Self and the Ego.

♡ Intellectually, when presented with options of action we may tend to go for a result that gives short-term rather than long-term satisfaction. The idea of giving in to temptation suggests that it is stronger or more powerful than we are. Often dreams can show us the course of action we should be taking. If we are being the tempter we need to be very sure of our own motives in waking life.

▦ Temptation is a conflict between two different drives. For instance, in dreams we may experience a conflict between the need to go out into the world and the need to stay safe at home. Temptation is yielding to that which is the easiest, and not necessarily best, course of action.

*Consult the entry for Siren and also the information on Ego, Self and Siren in Archetypes in the Introduction for further information.*

## TENANT

☀ Dreaming of having a tenant would link with the idea that within us we all have many aspects of personality that must be synthesized into a spiritually complete being. Evicting a tenant might signify the need to get rid of a belief or aspect that we cannot work with.

♡ If we follow up the idea of a tenant being someone with whom we have a commercial relationship, then we will have some insights into how we handle such transactions. As more people invest in buy-to-let property to give themselves security, a tenant in dreams will simply represent a means to an end.

🔲 To dream of being a tenant suggests that at some level we do not want to take responsibility for the way we choose to live. We do not want to be burdened by having full responsibility for our living space. To have a tenant signifies that we find it expedient to have someone be involved in what we consider to be our 'space'. This may also be the type of dream that occurs as we are preparing to become involved in a full-time relationship.

🔲 If the dreamer is a man and the tenant a woman then the tenant is likely to represent his Anima. If the situation is reversed then the tenant will epitomize her Animus.

*You might also like to consult the entries for Home and Rent as well as the information on Anima and Animus in Archetypes in the Introduction.*

## TENT

⚜️ The biblical and nomadic image of being able to pack up one's tent and steal away is the spiritual meaning here. We are not tied to any one place, but can move to where we need to be at short notice, thus satisfying the requirements of the Wanderer and the ascetic.

♦️ We perhaps need to get away from everyday responsibilities for a time, and rediscover our relationship with the forces of Nature. There is benefit to be gained by being self-sufficient and not dependent on anyone.

🔲 A tent in a dream would suggest that we feel we are on the move, and not able to settle down at this time and put down roots. Anywhere we settle is only going to be temporary. This might be so in a work situation as much as a personal.

*You might also like to consult the entries for Ascetic and Wanderer/Wandering as well as the information for Temporary Buildings in Buildings and Tramp in Archetypes in the Introduction.*

## TENSE/TENSION – *see* ANXIETY DREAMS IN THE INTRODUCTION

## TERROR/TERRORIST

⚜️ Spiritual terror could be identified as extreme fear of perceived evil. The fanaticism of a terrorist could be seen to be an effort to handle this extreme fear. This exaggerated reaction leads to drastic action and the endurance of the inevitable results.

♦️ Terror in a dream is often the result of unresolved fears and doubts. It is only by experiencing such a profoundly disturbing emotion that are we likely to make an attempt to confront those fears. If someone else is terrified in our dream we are in a position to do something about it, and need to work out what course of action should be taken. The appearance of a terrorist is a negative manifestation of our predisposition to be intensely emotional.

■ Fear or terror dreams can be one of the triggers towards a deeper understanding of oneself. If we know we are fearful we can do something about it. Terror in dreams is more difficult to handle since in that state we will not know what the cause is and may well be paralysed by the feeling itself. When we are able to identify what prompts it in waking life, we can again take action to disperse it.

*Also consult the entries for Fanatic, Immobility, Paralysis and War as well as the information on Terror Dreams in the Introduction.*

## TESTS

❀ A spiritual test is one that is created from the circumstances around us, perhaps to test our resolve. Having to justify a course of action in dreams might be one such test.

♥ Testing something in a dream suggests that there has been some form of standard set, to which we feel we must adhere. This need not mean that we are setting ourselves against others, simply that we have resolved to maintain a certain standard.

■ Dreaming of tests of any sort can indicate some form of self-assessment. Medical tests may be alerting us to the need to watch our health. A driving test would suggest a test of confidence or ability, whereas a written test would signify a test of knowledge.

*You might also like to consult the entry for Exam/Being Examined.*

## TEXT

❀ A spiritual text is an encouraging message to enable us to progress. For a text such as this to appear in a dream would signify the need for encouragement and perhaps wisdom. An elaborately illustrated text or manuscript gives us access to ancient knowledge and belief.

♥ Text from a book or play indicates the need for us to carry out instructions in a particular way in order to achieve success. A manual of instruction in dreams suggests we need to take particular care over our actions.

■ A text is taken to mean a collection of words that have a certain specific meaning. As mobile phone texting catches on, such an image suggests short pithy communication.

*Consult the entries for Book, Communication, Telephone and Writing for extra information.*

## THAW

❀ A spiritual thaw would suggest the ability to come to terms with old barriers and constraints and to become warm, loving and less rigid in our judgements.

❤ Psychologically we have the ability to 'warm up' a situation, and to melt coldness away. If we are aware of coldness within ourselves, on an emotional level we need to discover what the problem is or was, and why we have reacted as we did.

▦ In dreams, to be conscious of a thaw is to note a change in our own emotional responses. We no longer have a need to be as emotionally distanced as previously.

*You might also like to consult the entries for Emotions, Ice/Iceberg/Icicles and Water.*

## THEATRE

☀ Spiritually the idea of a theatre in a dream highlights the idea of the microcosm within the macrocosm – the small within a larger framework. A stage is a representation of our own life play. We are able to observe and be objective about what is going on. By externalizing the 'play' into a particular framework such as a rehearsal we can manipulate our lives.

❤ The theatre is a scenario that has meaning for many. Because it is a social venue, it has relevance in people's relationships with one another. To be in the spotlight, for instance, might signify our need to be noticed. To be up in 'the gods' might suggest that we need to take a long-term view of a situation. To be on stage in a dream is to be making ourselves visible.

▦ In dreams about the theatre it will depend which part of the theatre is highlighted: if the stage, then a current aspect of our lives being drawn to our attention. If it is the auditorium, then our ability to listen and understand the relevance is what is significant. An open-air stage suggests communication with the masses rather than a selected audience. A moving stage signifies the need to keep moving, even while performing a role. The play we create in our dreams as an aspect of our lives is particularly relevant. If we are not involved in the action, it indicates we are able to stand back and take an objective viewpoint. If we are very involved it will be from an emotional perspective.

*You might also like to consult the entries for Actor and Audience.*

## THEFT – *see* THIEF AND STEALING

## THERAPIST – *see* ANALYST

## THIEF

☀ A spiritual thief is that part of us that has no respect for our or others' beliefs.

❤ When a thief appears in dreams, we are aware of part of our personality that can waste our own time and energy on meaningless activity. It literally steals from us.

⊞ Dreaming of a thief links with our fear of losing things, or of having them taken away from us. We may be afraid of losing love or possessions.

*Also consult the entry for Stealing.*

**THIGH – *see* LIMBS IN BODY**

**THIN – *see* SIZE**

**THIRD EYE – *see* SPIRITUAL IMAGERY IN THE INTRODUCTION**

**THIRST**

⊛ Thirst in a dream is symbolic of our quest for spiritual knowledge and enlightenment. It may well be an unquenchable one.

♥ To satisfy a thirst indicates we are capable of satisfying our own desires. By being prepared to take in what we need, we are able to experience life in the best way possible. If we are thirsty in a dream we need to look very carefully at either what we are being denied, or what we are denying ourselves, in waking life.

⊞ Dreaming of being thirsty suggests we have an unsatisfied inner need; we may be emotionally at a low ebb and need something to give us a boost. Anything that gives us emotional satisfaction – whether short- or long-term – would suffice.

*Consulting the entries for Drink, Emotions, Quest and Water will provide further information.*

**THISTLE**

⊛ The thistle can represent our spiritual defiance in the face of physical adversity and difficult conditions. This is one of the reasons why it became the emblem of Scotland. Magically it is a fire herb and, therefore, represents courage.

♥ The thistle has a meaning of rebelliousness and spite, but also of affording protection. When dreaming of a thistle we may be being made aware of those qualities, either in people around us or in ourselves. The colour of the thistles may also be important.

⊞ To be conscious of thistles in a dream is to be aware of some discomfort in waking life. A field of thistles would suggest a difficult road ahead. A single thistle would indicate minor difficulties.

*You might also like to consult the entries for Colour, Plants and Weeds.*

**THORN**

⊛ The thorn may signify that we are dedicating ourselves to a difficult element of our spiritual quest – we are suffering for our beliefs.

♥ The thorn stands for physical suffering in dreams. In matters of health, it may indicate a vulnerability to infection.

▣ To dream of being pierced by a thorn or splinter signifies that a minor difficulty has got through our defences. If the thorn draws blood, we need to look at what is happening in our lives that could make us vulnerable.

⊟ In a woman's dream a thorn, being penetrative, could represent the sexual act, or rather fear of intercourse. For a man thorns may represent sacrifice of some sort.

*Consult the entries for Crown, Sacrifices and Weeds for further information.*

## THREAD

⚜ Thread is a vivid image in dreams and in spiritual work. We have the thread of life spun for us by the Fates who determine the life and death of all mortal beings; Klotho spins the thread; her sister Lachesis determines the length of it and Atropos cuts the thread when the proper time has come for death. The various threads of our spirituality are being interwoven into the Tapestry of Life.

♡ To be aware of thread is to be aware of the way our lives are going. A tangled thread suggests a difficulty that needs unravelling. A spool of thread suggests an ordered existence; the colour of the thread is also important. The image of tapestry or weaving suggests a degree of competence and creativity. The relevance of the 'picture' we produce may well represent emotional concerns.

▣ Thread in dreams represents a line of thought or enquiry and, in today's way of communicating, a blog. In terms of our ordinary everyday lives we perhaps need to remain focused on our goals. Threading a needle has an obvious sexual reference. It can also, because of the perceived difficulty in threading a needle, suggest incompetence in ways other than sexual, such as hitting work targets.

⊟ In a woman's dream a basket full of spools suggests the various aspects of her personality. This is because of its association with the Archetypal feminine. For a man, such an image may represent his attitude to the complexity of the feminine.

*You might also like to consult the entries for Colour, Needle, Sew, Tangled and Weaving.*

## THREAT/THREATEN

⚜ A spiritual threat is one that forces us to reassess our beliefs. Most often it will contain options of action that lead to a degree of inevitability either way. Once on that particular path we have no choice but to continue. In dreams the image of a divided path or road will often occur at this time, or of going up or down.

❤ To feel threatened in dreams approaches anxiety and nightmare. Taking us out of our comfort zone whether emotionally or otherwise results in fear and distress, which we can suppress in waking life but often not in dreams. If we ourselves are threatening someone in dreams we perhaps need to seek out the source of our own negative emotions and what it is we feel so strongly about.

▦ A threat to our security or way of life can translate itself in dreams to an image of a threatening situation or environment. The Shadow – that part of us which contains a great deal of negativity – can manifest in dreams literally as a dark shadow and at that point needs to be confronted either through working with the dream or by careful analysis.

⊟ In both men's and women's dreams the opposite gender can pose a threat. Thus a man might feel threatened by the image of a vengeful goddess (an aspect of the Anima) and a woman by an overbearing Ogre (an aspect of the Animus).

*You might also like to consult the entry for Path as well as the information on Archetypes, Anxiety Dreams and Nightmares in the Introduction.*

## THRESHOLD

❂ We may be standing on the threshold of a new spiritual awareness. We need to be particularly alert as to what changes are occurring. At this time we are often aware of a personal guiding force known as the Guardian of the Threshold. The Guardian of the Threshold to the Underworld (a different entity) is often seen in dreams as a dog.

❤ When we are about to take on new responsibilities, we can dream of standing on a threshold. We may be moving into a new life, or perhaps a new way of living. The threshold experience is a particularly strong one in Masonic imagery and Initiation rites and surfaces in dreams when we are emotionally ready for such a ceremony. Even in Parliament, permission must be asked to cross the threshold.

▦ Crossing the threshold in dreams indicates new experiences. To be lifted across a threshold may suggest marriage, or in this day and age, a new relationship.

*Consult the entries for Ceremony, Edge, Freemason, Initiation and Rite/Ritual for further information.*

## THROAT – *see* BODY

## THRONE

❂ Spiritually we could be at a point where knowledge and understanding are finally within our grasp at last. A throne, as a symbol of power, epitomizes this.

♦ A throne is a seat of authority or power. In dreams it can represent our ability to belong to groups, or even to society; we may need to take the lead in a project or scheme. The throne usually suggests that we have attained an element of control on all levels of existence, both spiritually and physically.

▦ When we dream of sitting on a throne, we are acknowledging our right to take authority. When the throne is empty, we are not prepared to accept the responsibility for who we are. It may be that we are conscious of a lack of parenting. When someone else is on the throne, we may have passed over authority to others.

*You might like to consult the entry for Crown as well as the information on King and Queen in People.*

## THUMB – *see* BODY

## THUNDER/THUNDERBOLTS

❀ Spiritually, the rumblings of thunder can demonstrate deep anger, or in extreme cases Divine anger. This originates from the ancient belief in the Thunder Gods.

♦ Thunder has always been a symbol of great power and energy. In conjunction with lightning, it was seen as a tool of the gods. It could bring doom and disaster, but also was cleansing and has this significance in dreams.

▦ Hearing thunder in a dream can give a warning for the potential of an emotional outburst. We may be building up energy that eventually must reverberate. Hearing thunder in the distance signifies that there is still time to gain control of a potentially difficult situation.

*Also consult the entries for God/Gods, Lightning, Storm and Weather for further information.*

## TIARA – *see* CROWN AND DIADEM

## TICKET

❀ Spiritually, a dream of a ticket will symbolize our recognition that all knowledge must be somehow 'paid for' and that we have a right to that knowledge.

♦ One interpretation of a ticket – in the form of a certificate or voucher – is that of us requiring recognition of the effort we have put in. To dream of receiving such a ticket indicates it is we who are being recompensed. A winning lottery ticket would have the same significance.

▦ Generally, a ticket suggests that there is a price to pay for something. A bus ticket would indicate that there is a price for moving forward, as might a train ticket. A ticket to a theatre or cinema may suggest we need to take a back seat and be objective over a part of our lives. Tickets to a football or rugby match might mean that we will have to pay for some area of conflict in our lives.

*You might also like to consult the entries for Gambling, Lottery and Win/Winning.*

**TIDE**

🌣 Spiritually, it may well be a simple image, such as the tide turning, which indicates that we are finding our way and can progress on our spiritual journey with confidence.

💙 In waking life there are two times in the year when there are very high tides – the spring and the autumn. Thus, in dreams, an exceptionally high tide might signify those times or that our emotions are running at a particularly high level. A moon over a moving tide would, at a certain stage of development, suggest the powers of the feminine.

▦ Dreaming of a tide is attempting to go with the ebb and flow of life or, rather more specifically, with the emotions. As a tide also removes debris, the symbolism of cleansing is relevant. A high tide may symbolize high energy, whereas a low tide would suggest a drain on our abilities or energy.

*Consult the entries for Autumn, Emotions, Moon, Spring and Seasons as well as the information for Seas in the Water entry.*

**TIDY –** *see* **ORDER**

**TIE –** *see* **BONDS, CHAINS AND HALTER**

**TIGER –** *see* **ANIMALS**

**TILL**

🌣 A till is symbolic of the resources we have accumulated spiritually, not necessarily financially. They are being stored up until such times as we need them.

💙 When we put money in a till, it is being put there for safe-keeping and will allow us to quantify how much we have accumulated. Nowadays this accumulation will be deposited with a bank for safe-keeping. This is where the more practical and psychological meanings coincide. We need to save or conserve what we have – both energy and resources – to get best benefit. To be withdrawing money from a cashpoint in a dream signifies our need to make use of those resources.

▦ There are two meanings of 'till'. One is to till or tend the ground, and while that is a less potent image nowadays, the image still appears in dreams in the sense of cultivating opportunities. The other meaning is as a safe, temporary repository for money. It is this symbolism of a commercial transaction which is the one most understood. In dreams, a broken cash register would symbolize the breakdown of our ability to accumulate resources and also possibly signify debt.

*You might like to consult the entries for Debt, Garden and Money for further information.*

**TIMBER –** *see* WOOD

**TIME**

In a spiritual sense time has no relevance, being a man made construct. The Realization of Age and Time, being a valid concept, is signified by a clock. The image of Father Time as an old man signifies changes brought about by the passage of time.

For time to be significant in a dream there is usually the necessity to measure it in some way, or to use a period of time as a measurement. Usually we are only aware of the passage of time – often symbolized by a clock or watch – or that a particular time is meaningful in the dream, it is part of the dream scenario. The time in the dream may symbolize a particular period in our life as follows:

**The daylight hours** will thus suggest our conscious waking life. Where **several days (or other long periods)** appear to have passed we are conscious that some other activity, which is not particularly relevant to us, has been going on in the dream.

**If we think of our lives as being a day long,** the hours of the day will refer to a specific time in our lives. Thus, **afternoon** is a time of life when we can put our experience to good use; **evening** shows a more relaxed time; **mid-day** indicates we are fully conscious and aware of our activities. **In the morning** the first part of our life or our early experience is being highlighted, whereas **night** may be a period of depression or secrecy. We may be introspective or simply at rest. **Twilight** can indicate a period of uncertainty and possible ambivalence insofar as our direction in life is concerned.

Watching the clock indicates the necessity to make time work for us. The clock hands or digital numbers in a dream may be indicating those numbers that are important to us. To be early for an appointment in a dream suggests having to wait for something to happen before we can carry on our lives. Being late shows our lack of attention to detail or the feeling that time is running out. *Consult the entries for Calendar, Dawn/Day And Night, Evening, Night and Numbers for further information.*

**TITANS –** *see* GIANT AND GOD/GODS

**TOAD –** *see* REPTILES IN ANIMALS

**TOBACCO**

We may be interested in the idea of spirituality, but as yet have not found the right stimulation. The symbolism of tobacco as a giver of visions may be relevant to our situation.

❦ Native Americans are reputed to use tobacco to drive away bad spirits, and it is true that initially tobacco will give the person a mood lift. In dreams it is this symbolism of impending change that is meaningful. Trying to give up smoking in dreams suggests that we are attempting to live without false stimulation. Tobacco appearing in dreams will have different meanings depending on whether we smoke in waking life or not. If we do, then tobacco, in the dream, is probably a comfort tool, though nowadays something of a guilty pleasure. If not, then the symbolism is probably more to do with the idea of using tobacco to achieve a particular state of mind. If the dreamer is smoking a pipe, there may be issues of masculinity to deal with.

*Also consult the entries for Indigenous Peoples and Smoke/Smoking.*

## TOILET

❁ Spiritually, a toilet suggests that we have the means at our disposal to cleanse away negativity we have taken in.

❦ Something wrong with the toilet could suggest that we are emotionally blocked. If it is overflowing, the blockage is causing a difficulty in controlling our emotions at the present time. Going to an unfamiliar toilet suggests we are in a position where we do not know what the outcome to a situation will be. Cleaning a dirty toilet suggests we are losing our 'prudish' attitude, and may have gone through some kind of internal epiphany.

▦ For many people the toilet has in dreams been until recently a symbol for dirt and lack of appreciation. There has also been the inevitable association with sexuality. Nowadays the symbolism is much more to do with notions of privacy, and the ability to reach a state where we can release our feelings in private.

⊡ In both men's and women's dreams, toilet dreams can often be about self-worth and clearing childish confusion.

*You might also like to consult the entries for Clean/Clear and Dirty as well as the information for Bathroom in House.*

## TOMB

❁ Spiritually we may feel that we have entered into a world that is all at once mysterious and dark – dark in the sense of the light being obscured. Although we perhaps fear this darkness, we are also excited. It is worth remembering that we are not trapped, but in a brief state of panic which can be overcome by belief.

❦ If we are trapped in a tomb in a dream we may be trapped by fear, pain or old outdated attitudes in our waking life. If there are bodies in the tomb, these are usually parts of ourselves we have either not developed or have killed off. If one of those bodies comes alive, the attention we have given to that aspect of our personality has been sufficient to resurrect it, and a little thought will allow us to identify it.

🁢 Going into a tomb suggests going down into the darker parts of our own personality. We may be fearful to begin with, but later more at ease. Finding ourselves in a tomb suggests we are ready to face our intrinsic fears of death and dying. A sarcophagus is similar to a tomb, but is much more of a memorial, marking how important the occupant is or was. To dream of such an edifice is to recognize the importance of death and the rites of passage associated with it.

*Consulting the entries for Catacomb/Crypt, Death and Skeleton/Skull will provide further information.*

**TONGUE – *see* BODY**

**TOOLS**

🌣 Spiritual tools which can be symbolized in a practical way are love, hope, compassion and charity. As tools of understanding, Tarot cards, Runes and other divinatory devices will appear in dreams as our knowledge increases.

♥ Each tool will have its own significance in dreams A drill suggests working through emotions and fears as well as attitudes that have become hardened. Both a hammer and a mallet provide the energy to break down old patterns of behaviour and resistances. A saw suggests being able to cut through all the rubbish we have accumulated in order to make something new. The garden spade is another such tool.

🁢 Tools in dreams suggest the practical tools we have at our disposal for enhancing our lifestyle. Our profession or work will give ready images of tools we use and to be using tools that are not ones we normally use will highlight skills or abilities we may need to develop.

*Consulting the entries for Chisel, Hammer and Mallet will provide further information.*

**TOP – *see* POSITION**

**TORCH**

🌣 We may feel that we need some spiritual guidance, and this can sometimes be symbolized as a torch. A searchlight, in pinpointing and lighting the way ahead, enables us to reject the unnecessary.

♥ A torch can be used not only for ourselves, but also for other people. Dreaming of a torch shows we can have the confidence to know that, because of our own knowledge, we have the ability to see the way forward. A searchlight, being more focused, can symbolize the insights we need.

In dreams, a torch can represent self-confidence. It can also suggest the need to be able to move forward, but at the same time carry our own light. Firebrands, having an open flame, will have the same symbolism as fire, whereas a battery torch signifies a more contained energy. If a searchlight or torch is trained on us we need to consider our actions and behaviour and whether they are appropriate.

*You might also like to consult the entries for Fire and Light.*

**TORMENT** – *see* **TORTURE/TORMENT/TEASE**

**TORN** – *see* **TEAR/TEARS/TORN**

**TORNADO**

Our early ventures into spirituality may make us feel powerless, and at the mercy of all the elements. This can be symbolized by the tornado. However, within the centre there is peace and tranquillity.

While a tornado can be very destructive, interestingly it can also be very cleansing and it is in this context that it is often met on a psychological level. It sweeps all in front of it, but after its passage there is the potential for new life and new beginnings.

A tornado appearing in a dream is a symbol of violent energy of one sort or another. Often it is emotions and feelings against which we feel powerless. It is a recognizable symbol of energy, which has turned in on itself, and has therefore become destructive.

*Consult the entries for Weather and Wind for additional clarification.*

**TORPEDO**

A torpedo is symbolic of spiritual directness. In terms of being able to home in on its target, the torpedo suggests directed energy.

Since a torpedo passes through water to reach its target, the symbolism is of using emotion as a means to an end. This may be the type of honest getting to the point which we can do with friends, or it may be a warning that such directness could be harmful or upsetting.

In dreams the torpedo may signify destructive power, often unrecognized until too late. In waking life we may 'expect the unexpected' though, as a torpedo is a missile, there will have been an element of pre-planning in that unexpectedness.

The torpedo, because of its shape, has obvious connections with masculine aggressiveness and will have this significance in both men's and women's dreams. It will depend on whether we are on the receiving end or are firing it. Rather obviously, men are more likely to be firing a torpedo, whilst women will be receiving it.

*You might also like to consult the entries for Submarine, Target and War.*

**TORTOISE**

🌞 In Chinese lore the tortoise is a revered figure of wisdom and knowledge. He is said to carry the pattern of all existence on his back. He also represents Creation.

💟 The tortoise may, of course, simply be an image of a pet as an object that is loved. It may also, however, be a symbol for long life. For those undertaking esoteric studies, the tortoise in dreams may signify the need to consider Chinese systems of belief.

▣ The tortoise for most people suggests slowness but also perhaps thoroughness. It also in dreams signifies a shell that perhaps we – or others round us – have put up in order to protect or defend ourselves.

*Consult the entries for Chinese in Indigenous Peoples and Pet as well as the information on Reptiles in Animals.*

**TORTURE/TORMENT/TEASING**

🌞 Spiritual torture can be a conflict between right and wrong and spiritual torment is the mental agony, which ensues when we must make choices between two or more courses of action. Often the idea of such torture for the benefit of the majority – that is, the Greater Good is part of the process of growth. Spiritual teasing is the sort of irritation engendered by the imp.

💟 Being teased in dreams may reveal a fear of becoming a laughing stock. If we are being physically tortured in dreams, we need to look at the other images and personalities in the dream to discover what significance such action has in our everyday life. It may be that we tend to put ourselves in the position of victim without realizing it. Torment has a hugely emotional charge behind it and reveals an element of sadism in our dream tormentor. This can amount to persecution and is the sort of dream that will surface in Post-Traumatic Stress Disorder.

▣ When an image connected with torture appears in a dream, often we are trying to come to terms with a great hurt. This does not need to be on a physical level – indeed, it hardly ever is. It is more likely to be emotional or mental pain. If we are unable to deal with the hurt, the dream may escalate into one of torment.

*You might also like to consult the entries for Imp, Sadism and Victim as well as the information on Nightmares in the Introduction.*

**TOTEM/TOTEM POLE**

🌞 Both in its symbolic meaning of a protector and as a representative of spiritual matters, the totem pole suggests strength and power. In a dream a totem pole can link us back to a very basic human need for protection. It is not the protection afforded by a father, but by those natural forces whose energy is powerful enough to be used by us.

◉ When an object revered as a sacred article is given enough power by a joint belief, the thing itself is perceived as taking on a power of its own. One such object is the totem. When it appears in dreams we need to be looking at our belief systems to discover whether we are really living according to those beliefs.

▦ In ordinary everyday terms, a totem pole in dreams will signify a standard or representation of ethics. It suggests a hierarchy of importance that may or may not have seemed significant to us thus far.

*You might also like to consult the entry for Native American in Indigenous Peoples as well as the information on Spiritual Imagery in the Introduction.*

## TOURIST

◉ The tourist in a dream in spiritual terms represents the Hermit or Wanderer.

◉ To play the tourist in a dream is to be aware of the fact that we have the necessary information to do what we want, when and how we want but that ultimately we are choosing not to do so.

▦ A tourist in a dream is someone who does not know his way around. If we are the tourist then we need to look at that aspect within ourselves. If someone else is the tourist then we need to be aware of what help we can give other people.

*Consult the entries for Hermit and Wanderer/Wandering for further information.*

## TOW – *see* TRANSPORT

## TOWER

◉ The tower has duality in the spiritual sense, since it can be feminine in the shelter it affords and masculine because of its shape. It suggests ascent to the spiritual realms, but also descent to the practical. The inner aspects of the tower represent our inner life, whereas the outer signify the structure we present to the world.

◉ A tower in a dream usually represents the construction of our lives – our inner attitude, outer life or both. The tower or tall building is such a rich source of imagery that it is feasible to give only the most easily identifiable. Familiarity with our own tower in the waking state will act as a trigger for many other potent images. Thus:

**To dream of a tower** with no door suggests we are out of touch with our inner selves.

**A tower with no windows** signifies that we are unable to see and appreciate either our external good points or our inner ones.

**An ivory tower** suggests an innocent approach.

**A square tower** signifies a practical approach to life, whereas a round tower is more spiritually geared.

**A round tower** at the end of a square building is the combination of the practical and spiritual.

From a mundane perspective if we are to live life as fully as we can, we need to understand our own tower. In dreams it may appear initially as far away and later coming closer. How we get into the tower is also important. Shallow steps indicate that we have easy access to our inner self. More difficult steps suggest that we are fairly private individuals. If the door is barred or particularly difficult to open we are not yet ready to explore our unconscious self. If the door is closed we must make an effort to get in. If inside the tower is dark, we are still afraid of our subconscious. The hidden room in the tower would have the same significance as in a house.

*Also consult the entries for Escape, Rescue, Shapes and Trap/Trapped as well as the information on Tower in Buildings for further clarification.*

**TOWN –** *see* **PLACES**

**TOYS**

Toys, as small copies of larger objects, symbolize the microcosm within the macrocosm. Appearing in dreams, they may be alerting us to our ability to create our own lives. Just as a child will imagine himself creating his own little world through his toys, so also can we create as dreamers.

When there are toys in a dream we may be aware of children around us, or of our more childlike selves. Toys will highlight the creative side of ourselves, and the more playful innocent part.

Perhaps we need to look at the types of toys that appear. They often give some indication of what we are playing with. We may be mulling over new ideas or new ways of relating to others. Equally we need to 'play' more, to relax and have fun.

It will depend on whether the toys are gender specific in dreams. Boys' toys in men's dreams indicate the need to learn different masculine skills and girls' toys suggest learning about sensitivity. Girly toys in women's dreams might suggest that she needs to rediscover her hidden femininity, whereas boys' toys would show that she needs to appreciate her more assertive side.

*You might also like to consult the entries for Doll and Puppet.*

**TRACK –** *see* **PATH AND ALSO TRAIN IN TRANSPORT**

**TRAFFIC –** *see* **TRANSPORT**

**TRAIN** – *see* **TRANSPORT**

**TRAITOR**

   ☼ Spiritually, to be a traitor is to deny our basic beliefs. We do not have the courage of our convictions.

   ♡ When in a dream we are betrayed by others with whom we thought we shared beliefs – and discover that they have let us down – it would mean they are traitors to the relationship.

   ▦ To dream of a traitor suggests that we are subconsciously aware of deviousness. This may be in someone else, or it could be a part of our personality that is letting us down. We may feel that our standards are not appreciated by others.

**TRAMP**

   ☼ Spiritually, although this image initially appears to be negative, if we are prepared to work with it, it can have great positivity – since ultimately he is always in the right place at the right time for the right reasons.

   ♡ The tramp personifies in us the wanderer, the freedom lover. In dreams he will often appear at a time when we need freedom, but can also show that that need can bring difficulty and sadness. He can also appear in dreams as the jester or fool. There is a part in all of us that is anarchical, and the tramp represents this aspect.

   ▦ To dream of a tramp in the sense of a decrepit old wanderer links us back to the part of ourselves that is seldom expressed fully in real life. It is the 'drop-out' or gypsy within us. We may be conscious of our need for irresponsibility.

*Also consult the entry for Wanderer/Wandering as well as the information on Tramp in Archetypes in the Introduction.*

**TRANQUILLITY**

   ☼ Tranquillity is sought by all those – such as the ascetic or monk – who search for the spiritual within themselves. Known by many names, it is one concept which spans all religions, and is the 'peace which passeth all understanding'.

   ♡ As a sanctuary from the hurly burly of waking life, tranquillity in dreams can be encouraged by choosing to empty the mind of daily concerns before sleep. This gives the dreaming mind the ability to work more efficiently to process the material of the unconscious and reach for true peace.

   ▦ Tranquil environments and landscapes in dreams have the facility to allow us to rebalance ourselves and our mental processes. Stress in daily life requires us to take in more and more information and at a certain point chaotic dreams can often be contrasted or followed with peaceful ones as though the mind is demonstrating the possibilities.

*You might also like to consult the entries for Ascetic, Chaos, Landscape and Monk.*

**TRANSCRIBE** – *see* WRITING

**TRANSFIGURATION** – *see* INTRODUCTION

**TRANSFORMATION** – *see* INTRODUCTION

**TRANSLATE** – *see* TALKING

**TRANSPARENT**

✦ Transparency in the spiritual sense represents honesty, integrity and responsibility.

♥ When we are aware in dreams that things around us are transparent, we become our ability to 'see through' situations and people's behaviour. We are able to be discerning in our judgement.

▦ When something is transparent in a dream we may be feeling vulnerable, but may also be aware of insights we would not normally have. To be inside a transparent bubble, for instance, would suggest visibility and vulnerability in our lives, perhaps taking on new responsibilities. For a dream character to be behind a transparent shield suggests they or what they represent are somewhat remote and unavailable to us.

**TRANSPORT**

✦ In a spiritual sense transport is being carried from one state of consciousness to another. This change in consciousness is not necessarily by our own volition. Riding either a horse or a vehicle suggests that we are happy to have the changes take place. The lift in mood can just as easily be due to external circumstances such as a beautiful day or extreme emotion and this can be reflected in dreams.

♥ The type of transport used in dreams may suggest how we are moving through this particular stage of our lives. Previously the horse was used as an image to depict how we dealt with life, although nowadays the car, the aeroplane and other more modern forms of transport have been substituted. A vehicle that appears in our dreams often conforms with the view we hold of ourselves. For instance, we may be driving a very basic type of car or a Rolls-Royce. In today's modern world there are so many diverse means of transport that each has developed its own symbolism. Some of these are given below.

**Aeroplane** – an aeroplane suggests a swift easy journey with some attention to detail. We may be embarking on a new journey of discovery about ourselves or someone else. An airman or pilot is a romanticized picture of either the Animus or of the Self. *You might also like to consult the individual* *entry for Aeroplane and the section on Archetypes in the Introduction for further information.*

**Bicycle** – this suggests youth, freedom and movement without a supporting structure. With two wheels and, therefore, a symbol of duality, it can suggest the first forays into relationship and adult behaviour.

**Boats** – it will depend on what kind of boat is in the dream as to its interpretation. A ferry or piloted boat holds all the symbolism of the journey across the River Styx after death. Today it signifies the giving up of selfish desires. Having been able to do this, we may be 'reborn' into a better life, or way of living. A small rowing boat would suggest an expedition of emotional discovery but one often undertaken alone. A yacht might suggest a similar journey done with style, whereas a large ship would suggest creating new horizons but in the company of others. Early seafarers referred to their ships as 'she' largely, it is thought, because of the close dependence they had on them for life and because they were difficult to manage. Today ships have lost that personal association. What a boat does in the dream will have relevance as a reflection of our waking life, e.g. running aground, pulling into harbour etc. To dream of disembarking indicates the end of a project, successful or otherwise. If we dream of missing a boat it shows we have not paid enough attention to detail to a project in our waking lives. *Also consult the individual entry for Boat/Ship.*

**Bus** – a bus signifies that part of our life journey that we are able to undertake in the company of others. More public than private, we perhaps have a common aim with the people with whom we travel. Trouble with timetables, missing the bus, arriving too early, missing a connection all indicate we are not in control of our lives and perhaps should sit down and replan how we wish to continue. Dreaming of getting on the wrong bus, or it going the wrong way, shows that there are conflicting aims or desires that need to be considered and we should listen to our own intuition. This is usually a warning of a wrong action, and we do not need to get carried away. To dream of not being able to pay the fare signifies we do not have enough resources to set out on a particular course of action. It may be that we have not paid enough attention to detail. *You may also like to consult the individual entry for Bus.*

**Car/carriage/cart/chariot** – any wheeled vehicle is by tradition a reflection of us and how we handle life. Carts, chariots and carriages tend to have a more old-fashioned resonance, whereas a car is more up to date and in keeping with modern thinking. All such vehicles reflect the physical body, so anything wrong with the vehicle may alert us to a problem. A car in particular is a reflection of a person's self-image and possibly sexuality and indeed any part of a car has significance. The back tyres might suggest our support system, the steering wheel the way we control our lives and so on. If the brakes are not working we are not exercising proper control over our lives. Too many people in the car would suggest that we feel overloaded by responsibility. *Also consult the entries for Car, Carriage/Cart/Chariot, Passenger and Wheel for additional information.*

**Caravan or motor home** – a caravan that is static will represent temporary security on a small scale, being similar in meaning to hotel. A moveable caravan or motor home will have the same symbolism as that of a snail, in that we are able to carry our security with us, giving us a sense of freedom.

**Driving any sort of vehicle** – this symbolizes our self-control and awareness of how external circumstances can affect us.

**Engine** – this represents our basic motivation our instinctive drives and possibly the sexual impulse. If the engine is not working properly we are not able to summon up enough energy to go on. If the starter motor is not working this would suggest that we need help to start a project. It is for us to be able to translate the symbolism into our own lives. *Also consult the individual entry for Engine.*

**Lorry/Van** – a lorry or van in a dream will have the same significance as a car, except that the drives and ambitions will be connected more with our work and how we relate on a business basis to the world in general. Being towed by a lorry or vehicle more efficient than our own suggests we need some kind of assistance with our motivation.

**Motorbike** – the motorbike is a symbol of masculine youth and daring. In dreams it is an image of independent behaviour and a symbol of freedom. A group of Hell's Angels would suggest some kind of anarchical behaviour, which may or may not be appropriate.

**Trains** – a train will often highlight our attitude to social behaviour and relationships with other people. It will also clarify our attitude to ourselves. A steam train would suggest that we feel ourselves to be somewhat outdated and old-fashioned but still viable, whereas an up-to-date electric turbo might suggest speed and efficiency. Catching the train shows we have been successful in having outside circumstances co-operate with us in achieving a particular goal, whereas missing the train indicates we do not have the resources to enable us to succeed in an appropriate way, either because we have forgotten something or because we have not been sufficiently careful. We fear that we will miss an opportunity. Equally, we may feel that external circumstances are imposing an element of control over us. Often dreams of missing a train and then catching either it or a later one, suggest that we are managing our inner resources better. Dreams of missing a train, alternating with those of catching one, show we are trying to sort out our motivations. Getting off the train before its destination or it has reached a station implies we are afraid of succeeding at a particular project. We do not appear to be in control. Getting off the train before it starts suggests that we have changed our mind about a situation in waking life. Railway lines and tracks will have significance as ways of getting us to our destination. Being conscious of the way the track runs ahead may give us an inkling as to what direction we are going. Recognizing the signals up ahead would have the same significance. Coming off the rails might suggest doing something inappropriate or of not being in control. Not wanting to be on the train might indicate we feel we are being unduly influenced by outside circumstances. Arriving at a station indicates we have completed a stage of our life journey. We may be ready for a new relationship with the world in general. The carriages on a train suggest the various compartments or sections of our lives and the way we feel about them. For example, if a carriage is untidy or dirty, we are aware that we need to 'clean up' an aspect of our lives.

▦ Images of vehicles and methods of transport often represent either our physical body or our personality. If we are driving, we perhaps feel more in control of our own destiny. If a passenger, we feel others are trying to control our life. If we are with friends we may be aware of a group goal whereas if we do not know the other people we may need to explore our ability to make social relationships. Heavy traffic symbolizes external pressure and stress. Traffic accidents and offences can arise in dreams when we have perhaps not been paying sufficient attention to detail. We have offended a code of conduct that is important for our own safety. *Consult the entries for Accident and Passenger for additional clarification.*

**TRANSVESTISM** – *see* **SEX/SEXUAL IMAGES**

**TRAP/TRAPPED**

♘ Spiritually we are holding ourselves back. We may also be aware of being trapped by the restrictions of the physical body. As we gain in spiritual knowledge, the wider perspective makes us more aware, particularly in dreams, of our lack of freedom.

♦ When we feel trapped in dreams, we are not usually able to break free of old patterns of thought and behaviour. We need outside help. The type of trap will give an indication of our psychological state. A gin trap would, therefore, suggest something is biting us and, rather obviously, a box trap that we are restricted in thought. We can gain insight into what is restricting us by taking careful note of our surroundings if we are trapped or locked in a room.

⊞ To be in a trap in a dream signifies that we feel we are trapped by outside circumstances. To be aware of trapping something or someone is attempting to hold on to them. To be trapping a butterfly is to be trying to capture the inner self.

⊡ The mythology surrounding the princess in the ivory tower has resonance in both men's and women's dreams. A woman is often trapped by her own imperturbability and needs help to escape and a man needs to find and release his trapped feminine.

*Consult the entries for Box, Escape, Lock/Locked, Key, Keyhole and Tower as well as the information on Rooms in Buildings for further information.*

**TRAVELLING** – *see* **JOURNEY AND TRANSPORT**

**TREASURE**

❁ To search for treasure symbolizes man's search for enlightenment, his search for the Holy Grail. Expecting treasure and finding a negative as in the story of Pandora's box is part of our learning how to deal with disappointment.

♥ To find a box that has treasure such as gems and jewels in it is to understand that we must break through our own limitations before we find what we are looking for. The search for treasure epitomizes the search for tangible value in the everyday world.

⊞ Treasure in dreams always represents something that is of value to us. It is the result of personal achievement and effort. To find buried treasure is to find something we have lost, perhaps a part of our personality. To be burying treasure is to be trying to guard against the future and potential problems.

*You might also like to consult the entries for Box, Chest/Box, Digging/Excavation, Gems/Jewels and Money.*

**TREES**

❁ Spiritually the tree symbolizes the Tree of Life and represents the union of heaven, earth and water. When we learn and understand our own Tree we are able to live life successfully on all levels.

♥ The tree is symbolic in dreams of the basic structure of our inner lives. When one appears in our dreams it is best to work with the image fairly extensively. A tree with wide branches would suggest a warm loving personality, whereas a small close-leafed tree would suggest an uptight personality. A well-shaped tree would suggest a well-ordered personality, while a large, messy tree would suggest a chaotic personality. Branches signify the stages of growth we go through, and leaves suggest the way we communicate to the rest of the world. To be climbing the tree suggests we are looking at our hopes and abilities, in order to succeed. To be chopping a tree down indicates the need for a complete overhaul of our beliefs and ideals and symbolizes radical change.

▦ The roots of a tree are said to show our connection with ourselves and the earth. It could be more accurate to suggest that they signify our ability to belong to the practical side of life, to enjoy being here. Spreading roots would indicate an ability to relate well to the physical, and, conversely, deep-rootedness would suggest a more self-contained attitude. The trunk of the tree gives an indication of how we use the energies available to us, and also what exterior we present to the world. A rough trunk suggests obviously a rough and ready personality, whereas a smoother trunk would indicate more sophistication.

*Consult the entries for Trees and Wood for further information.*

## TRESPASSING

✸ We are approaching areas of knowledge where we cannot go without the permission of a higher spiritual authority. Trespassing indicates that we have not yet been initiated into the correct level of awareness.

♥ If it is our personal space or area that is being trespassed upon, then we need to look at our own boundaries and whether we are comfortable with them in waking life. Sometimes it is interesting when interpreting the dream to find out whether we feel that the trespasser is there voluntarily or has just wandered in. We can then work out whether we are a victim or not.

▦ When we find ourselves trespassing in a dream, we are perhaps intruding on someone else's personal space or area of expertise in waking life. This may also suggest that there is a part of ourselves that is private and feels vulnerable. We should respect those boundaries.

*You might also like to consult the entries for Initiation, Intruder, Invade/Invasion and Victim.*

## TRIAL

✸ A trial in the spiritual sense is anything that tests our spiritual beliefs and understanding to the limits. Often such a dream will highlight our weakest points – sometimes ways in which we can be most judgemental – in which case we have the opportunity to reach more understanding in waking life.

♥ To dream of a scenario where we are being prosecuted suggests that we feel that authority has us on trial and we must justify ourselves, usually from an emotional perspective, but sometime in our actions or demeanour. Trial by ordeal, such as the supposed witched went through in previous times, appearing as a dream image signifies that we may be feeling persecuted.

▦ When in waking life we are on trial, such as on probation at the beginning of a job, images of legality such as justice, judges and so on can appear in dreams. Understanding the relevance of these images can help us to overcome our own doubts.

*You might also like to consult the entries for Judge/Judgement, Juror/Jury and Justice for further clarification.*

**TRIANGLE** – *see* **SHAPES/PATTERNS AND TRIO**

**TRICKSTER**

✺ This is the spiritually irresponsible part of our nature. We have not yet put ourselves on the correct spiritual path and need to do so.

♡ Psychologically, if we have been too rigid in our attitude to life – for instance, struggling to be good the whole time or always taking a moral stance – the trickster can appear in dreams as a counter-balance. When we are under stress this personage can present himself in dreams as the character who points us in the wrong direction, answers questions with the wrong answers etc.

▦ In dreams, the trickster is literally that part of ourselves that can create havoc and chaos in our lives. A kind of practical joker, possibly presenting as the jester or fool, he symbolizes the anarchic aspect of the personality. It is our choice as whether we choose to confront or integrate him.

*Consult the entries for Chaos and Joke/Joker as well as the information on Villain in Archetypes.*

**TRIGGER** – *see* **WEAPONS**

**TRIO**

✺ Spiritually any group of three – e.g. triplets or a musical trio – appearing in dreams symbolizes The Divine Trinity. Events or situations should be looked at carefully in terms of physical wants, emotional needs and spiritual requirements, then there can be the development of spiritual stability. Negative energy challenged three times is banished.

♡ The triangle in dreams can represent the family – mother, father and child – with all its attendant relationships. It then represents emotional stability. It can also suggest the process of realization – making something tangible. Anything in triplicate or repeated three times in dreams signifies an enhanced sense of awareness. In magic, any ill wish is returned to the originator threefold.

▦ In mundane terms, when there are three similar articles in dreams, they represent body, mind and spirit. If one of the three is different to the others, what is different will give information that we require to help us.

*You might also like to consult the entries for Family, Magic/Magician and Numbers.*

**TRIP** – *see* **FALL/FALLING AND JOURNEY**

**TRIPLETS** – *see* **TRIO**

## TROPHY

✸ A trophy would signify a Peak Experience (having moved into an expanded state of awareness) in order to achieve a spiritual goal.

♥ Formerly, trophies such as animal heads were much sought after. This is no longer so, but the symbolism of overcoming our basic fears, inadequacies and idiosyncrasies in order to achieve and be rewarded still remains.

▦ Dreaming of a trophy is to recognize that we have done something for which we can be rewarded. It depends on what the trophy is for as to its significance. The trophy will take on the significance of the object being presented. A cup would suggest receptivity and a shield, protection.

⊡ A common dream that men have is the presentation of a football cup. They are the 'first among men'. Women will give trophies a totally different connotation and will give symbolism to a much more individual memento.

*You might also like to consult the entries for Cup, Shield and Win/Winning.*

## TRUE/TRUTH/TRUST

✸ A spiritual truth is seldom provable but is one that has been given credence through belief over time or through subjective observation. It is something that, for most people, they 'just know'. In dreams such intuition is valid. Trust is belief in such truth.

♥ Perceived truth in dreams is a reality which works within the context of the dream. We believe it to be true at the time.

▦ In the mundane world we have to learn to trust our own truth. In dreams we will often receive information that helps us to verify – or not – our own appraisal of a situation.

## TRUMPET

✸ The trumpet sounds a spiritual vibration, which requires awareness. The trumpet is closely associated with power. Representations of angels are often shown blowing trumpets, a stylized depiction of the trumpet's dominion over lesser spirits.

♥ As a wind instrument, the trumpet in dreams represents the call to maximize our potential, particularly our intellectual expertise. We reach for the best within ourselves to have the maximum effect and benefit in our lives.

▦ A trumpet in a dream will most often suggest either a warning or a 'call to arms'. From a practical point of view it will often be alerting us to some potential danger. When there is conflict around us we may need some kind of warning to be ready for action and a trumpet can be one such symbol. The sound of the trumpet is an invitation to sheer joy.

*You might also like to consult the entries for Angels, Music/Rhythm, Musical Instruments and Sound.*

**TRUNK**

�€¢ Dreaming of a trunk has the same connotation as a treasure chest and indicates that spiritually we need to explore our hidden depths and the knowledge we have stored in order to get the best out of ourselves.

◈ We have the ability to store all sorts of rubbish, useful or not – both physically and mentally. When a trunk appears in a dream it is time to 'open the box' and have the courage to sort out what is there, what we can keep and what we can now reject. Often, when we should do this but do not do so, the image of the trunk will appear over and over again in different dreams. To find a jewel in a trunk indicates the good that can be found in doing a personal spring-clean.

▦ In previous times to dream of a trunk was supposed to foretell a long journey. Nowadays, as people tend to travel light, it is much more likely to represent the baggage that we have accumulated in our day-to-day life. An elephant's trunk, by association with the idea that elephants never forget, could signify memories.

*Consult the entries for Animals, Baggage, Box, Chest/Box, Gems/Jewels, Luggage and Treasure for additional information.*

**TUG OF WAR**

�€¢ A spiritual tug of war suggests the need to resolve the conflict between two polarities and make intelligent informed spiritual choices.

◈ A tug of war may indicate the need to maintain balance through tension between opposites. To be on the winning side suggests that what we wish to achieve can be managed with help. To be on the losing side requires us to identify the parallel situation in everyday life and decide whether to continue.

▦ To dream of a tug of war suggests a conflict between good and bad, male and female, positive and negative – any two opposites. In everyday life our personal ethics may be at odds with the ethics of the group we belong to.

⟐ In both men's and women's dreams a tug of war may represent a degree of tension between the more assertive side of the personality and the more passive. Much information can be gained by noting whether the two teams are male, female or mixed.

*You might also like to consult the entries for Balance, Conflict, Lose/Loss/Lost and Win/Winning.*

**TUMBLE** – *see* **FALL**

**TUNNEL**

�€¢ A tunnel in dreams at times represents the birth canal and, therefore, the process of birth, the transition between the spiritual and physical realms. The image of a tunnel both helps us to escape from the unconscious into the light and also to go down into the depths.

♦ A tunnel in a dream usually represents the need to explore our own unconscious and those things we have left untouched. If there is a light at the end of the tunnel in dreams, it indicates we are reaching the final stages of the exploration we have undertaken. If something is blocking the tunnel, some past fear or experience is stopping us from progressing.

▨ Finding ourselves in any kind of a tunnel in dreams suggests some kind of constriction in our everyday lives. We may need to focus on an end result to the exclusion of everything else. Going backwards into a tunnel suggest we may have to review the past for answers while working 'blind'.

*You might also like to consult the entries for Block and Light.*

**TURF** – *see* **GRASS**

**TURKEY** – *see* **BIRDS**

**TURN**

✹ To turn in dreams is to change direction spiritually. A right turn may be towards good and a left turn towards wrongdoing. A right turn may also be towards the logical while the left is to the intuitive.

♦ Turning round or back in dreams is to look to the past for information. Turning on the spot suggests reaching for a different state of awareness. To turn our bodies over signifies attempting to gain a different viewpoint, whilst turning an object over is to try to uncover hidden information or ideas.

▨ In mundane terms to turn a project round is to make it viable. The image of turning a lever or wheel may symbolize this in dreams. We make it work. To be turning our cupboards or draws is an attempt to clarify our ideas.

*Consult the entries for Lever, Positions and Wheel for further clarification.*

**TWILIGHT** – *see* **GLOOM AND TIME**

**TWINS**

✹ Twins illustrate the idea that two spiritual concepts or ideas, while separate at the moment, can achieve unity. A spiritual conceptualization is that while Unity is the Original State and splits into Duality, Duality must eventually reunite into Unity.

♦ Often in everyday life we come up against conflicts between two opposites. Twins in dreams can actually represent two sides of our personality acting in harmony.

▨ In dreams twins may, if known to us, simply be dream characters. If they are not known to us then they may represent two sides of one idea.

*Also consult the information for Twins in the People entry.*

**TYPHOON** – *see* **STORM AND WIND**

**UFO** – *see* ALIEN/ALIENATED AND EXTRA-TERRESTRIAL

**ULTIMATUM**

☀ We become aware of a spiritual ultimatum – a final demand – when we realize that we have no option but to conform to our inner beliefs; we must follow the path of spiritual integrity.

♥ To be given an ultimatum in dreams signifies that we must bring a situation to a conclusion. Often there will be considerable emotion, either negative or positive, attached to such action.

▦ We may dream of an ultimatum – a final proposal or statement of conditions – when all other methods of working have not borne fruit. This will often contain the germ of an idea that eventually solves our problem.
*You might like to consult the entry for Choice/Choose.*

**UMBILICAL CORD**

☀ The Silver Cord is an image seen psychically as the connection between body and soul, and is also perceived in dreams. As we begin to grow spiritually this is often seen as being connected at, or near, the solar plexus or belly button.

♥ The umbilical cord particularly represents the life-giving force and the connection between mother and child. Severing the umbilical cord often appears in teenage dreams as the child grows into adulthood.

▦ Often in life we can develop an emotional dependency on others, and the umbilical cord in dreams can signify that dependency. We have perhaps not yet learnt to take care of our own needs in a mature way.

⊡ In a woman's dream, an umbilical cord is more likely to be about her subtle connection to someone else, particularly if she has been pregnant, whereas for a man it is more likely to be about their connection to him. Some men will dream of the umbilical cord when trying to escape from an over-possessive mother.
*Also consult the entry for Navel.*

**UMBRELLA**

☀ As a sunshade conferred status and power, along with the need to protect, so does the umbrella.

♥ As we mature we need to develop certain emotional coping skills. In dreams these can be seen as a protective covering, hence the image of the umbrella.

▨ An umbrella is a shelter and a sanctuary, and it is this symbolism that comes across in dreams. Often in a work situation we need to work under someone's teaching, and this feeling of safety can be recognized in dreams. Occasionally, as in the term 'umbrella organization', the umbrella is seen as all-encompassing.

## UMPIRE

☼ As an umpire in sport has the right to a final decision, he takes on the function of the Higher Self in dreams.

♥ In sport, an umpire or referee must take a number of factors into consideration before making a decision. It is this need for objectivity that surfaces in dreams of an umpire.

▨ The umpire or referee must arbitrate between several differing opinions, and it is this function that gives rise to dreams of such a figure. This may mirror work or family disputes. As spectators in waking life we are at liberty to disagree, yet we must abide by his decision.

*You might like to consult the entries for Games and Sport.*

## UNCLE – *see* EXTENDED FAMILY IN FAMILY

## UNDER/UNDERNEATH – *see* POSITION

## UNDERGROUND

☼ The subconscious or the unconscious is often perceived in dreams as a cave or place underground. We usually need to explore the unconscious before embarking on our own spiritual journey.

♥ To be on the underground or subway usually signifies the journeys we are prepared (or forced) to take towards understanding who we are.

▨ Just as Alice dreamt of falling down the rabbit hole in *Alice in Wonderland*, so we all have opportunities to explore our own hidden depths through dreams. We cannot usually access the unconscious in waking life, unless we practise some form of meditation or other technique, and to dream of being underground will often allow us to come to terms with the unconscious in a very easy way.

## UNDERWORLD

☼ Almost every culture has a concept of the underworld, a place we go to after death. Dreams of the underworld, Hades or Hell are thought to help us come to terms with the illusions we have developed on the physical plane of existence and to prepare us ultimately to cope with death. The Underworld or Afterlife was once thought to be a place that was full of terrifying monsters and dangerous animals, which had to be traversed before one was free of karma.

♥ Any dream of a descent into an underworld signifies a journey into the unconscious and a way of coming to terms with inappropriate emotions or actions. Possibly the best known such journey is that of Persephone when she was captured by Hades or Pluto and thus became Queen of the Underworld. There are two meanings that might be given from a practical perspective to dreams of the underworld. One deals with the criminal underworld, an area of organized flouting of the law; the other is the more frightening transitional stage. Dreaming of the first suggests that we instinctively feel we are doing something wrong, whereas the other suggests that we are hampered by fears and doubts.

*You might also like to consult the entries for Death and Hell.*

## UNDO

Spiritually, to be undoing something suggests we are trying to reverse a process. This action is not always negative in that we recognize that a situation was better previously.

We often recognize through the medium of dreams that an action will have unforeseen circumstances. To be undoing a knot or tangle suggests the necessity to sort a problem out.

Pragmatically, when matters in everyday life have taken a turn for the worse, we may dream of undoing or loosening a stuck object to allow matters to move more smoothly.

*You might also like to consult the entries for Knot and Tangle.*

## UNDRESS

To be undressing suggests a need for Spiritual openness and honesty.

To be watching someone else undressing often indicates that we should be aware of that person's sensitivity. To be undressing someone else suggests that we are attempting to understand either ourselves or others on a very deep level.

When we find ourselves undressing in a dream, we may be putting ourselves in touch with our own sexual feelings. We may also be needing to reveal our true feelings about a situation around us, and to have the freedom to be totally open about those feelings.

*You might also like to consult the entries for Clothes and Nude/Nudity.*

## UNEARTH

Spiritually, when we are prepared to move on we are able to confront the hidden Self. Dreams of unearthing objects are not unusual around this time.

Occasionally, we may be aware of knowledge and potential within ourselves or others that requires hard work to realize. It has to be properly unearthed lest it remains hidden.

When we are trying to unearth an unknown object in a dream, we are attempting to reveal a side of ourselves that we do not yet understand. When we dream that we know what we are searching for, we are trying to uncover aspects of our personality that we may have consciously buried.

*Also consult the entries for Digging/Excavation and Hide/Hidden.*

## UNEMPLOYMENT

☼ A sense of spiritual inadequacy and inability can translate itself into the image of unemployment. This is more to do with not being motivated enough to accept a spiritual task.

♥ Unemployment is a fear that almost everyone has. When an event connected with unemployment occurs, e.g. redundancy, dole payments etc. in a dream, our feelings of inadequacy are being highlighted. We need to experience that fear in order to deal with, and overcome it.

▦ Dreaming of being unemployed suggests that we are not making the best use of our talents, or that we feel our talents are not being recognized. Equally such a dream may highlight a level of stress that requires we take a break from responsibility.

*You might like to consult the entries for Employment and Work.*

## UNHAPPY – *see* EMOTIONS AND WEEPING

## UNICORN

☼ The unicorn signifies unconditional love and symbolizes high ideals, hope and insight in a current situation. It also suggests power, gentleness and purity.

♥ There is a story that unicorns missed being taken into Noah's Ark because they were too busy playing. They represent intuitive knowledge; in this context we need to be mindful of what is going on in the real world if we are to survive.

▦ Traditionally, the only people who were allowed to tend unicorns were virgins. When a unicorn appears in a dream, we are linking with the innocent, pure part of ourselves. This is the instinctive, receptive feminine principle.

*Also consult the entries for Animals and Fabulous Beasts.*

## UNIFORM

☼ Identification of a common spiritual goal and an agreement as to 'uniform' behaviour is an important aspect in spiritual development.

♥ Often, in collective groups, the right to wear a uniform has to be earned. Dreaming of being in a group of uniformed people indicates that we have achieved the right to be recognized.

▦ Dreaming of uniforms is all to do with our identification with a particular role or type of authority. However rebellious we may be, a part of us needs to conform to the ideas and beliefs of the social group to which we belong. Seeing ourselves in uniform confirms that belonging.

*Consult the entry for Clothes for further information.*

## UNION/UNITY

❋ Unity in a spiritual sense is usually perceived as a return to Source, to the One. Union presupposes that there are two (duality) that need to be brought together.

♡ We all attempt to achieve unity from duality – to create a relationship between two parts or opposites. Dreaming of achieving union depicts this relationship. Psychologically, the human being is consistently looking for a partner.

▦ Union indicates a joining together, and this can be of pairs or of multiples. Union in pairs suggests the reconciliation of opposites and the added energy this brings. A union, in the sense of a trade union, suggests collective action that is for the good of all.

## UNIVERSITY

❋ Spiritual Knowledge and the ability to use it can only be achieved in 'The University of Life'. Often we need to graduate or be initiated with some ceremony, such as a rite of passage, into such learning.

♡ Since a university is a place of 'higher' learning, we are being made aware of the breadth of experience and increase in knowledge available to us. Dreaming of being at university signifies that we need to move away from the mundane and ordinary into specific areas of knowledge and awareness.

▦ Dreaming of being in a university highlights our own individual potential and learning ability. We may not be particularly academic in waking life, but may be subconsciously aware of our ability to connect with people of like minds. As universities nowadays become somewhat less selective, they can also in dreams represent a potentially carefree transition between childhood and adulthood.

*Also consult the entries for Education and School.*

## UNKNOWN

❋ The hidden or the Occult in spiritual terms remains both unknown and unknowable unless we have the courage to face it. This we can often do through dreams.

♡ When we are conscious of the unknown in dreams, we should try to decide whether it is threatening or whether it is something we need to know and understand. It is the way we handle the information – rather than the information itself – which is important.

⬛ The unknown in dreams is that which has been hidden from us, or that which we have deliberately made secret. This may be the 'occult' – that is, knowledge that is only available to initiates. It may also be information that we do not normally need, except in times of stress.

**UP/UPPER** – *see* **POSITION**

**URINE** – *see* **BODY**

**URN**

✦ The urn represents the feminine receptive principle.

♥ Just as all receptacles signify the feminine principle, so does the urn, although in a more ornate form. In earlier times, a draped urn signified death. That symbolism is still carried on today in the urn used in crematoriums. Thus, to dream of an urn may alert us to our feelings about death.

⬛ For many people the tea urn is a symbol of community life. To dream of one suggests our ability to belong to a community and act for the Greater Good.

*Consult the entries for Death, Jar and Vase for further information.*

## VACCINATION

🔅 Vaccination in dreams suggests spiritual indoctrination, knowledge we must have if we are to be protected.

♡ Vaccination indicates that we can easily be affected and influenced by other people's ideas and feelings.

🎴 In normal everyday life, vaccination is an action that initially hurts but is ultimately for our benefit. To dream that we are being vaccinated therefore suggests we are likely to be hurt by someone (perhaps emotionally), though ultimately it will be for our own good.

*Consult the entries for Injection and Needle for further clarification.*

## VALLEY

🔅 Fears of death and dying are often translated in dreams as entering into a valley – the so-called Valley of Death. The less fear we have over dying the easier our transition, which is symbolized by the valley, will be. In Spiritual terms it is simply recognizing that death is inevitable for all of us.

♡ Being in a valley can represent the sheltering, feminine side of our nature and also being down to earth. Leaving a valley suggests coming out of a period of introversion in order to function properly in the everyday world.

🎴 Dreaming of going down into a valley can have the same significance as going downstairs – that is, going down into the subconscious or unknown parts of ourselves. The result of this can be two-fold, sometimes depression and gloominess and sometimes finding new areas of productiveness.

## VAMPIRE

🔅 Negativity, which has the effect of draining our essential energy, is represented by the vampire in dreams, particularly if there is an assault on our spirituality and beliefs.

♡ Often the fear of emotional and sexual relationships can be represented in dreams as a vampire. Because the human being still has a fear of the unknown, ancient symbols that have represented this fear can still appear in dreams.

🎴 When heavy demands are made on us that we do not feel capable of meeting, a vampire can appear in a dream. We are figuratively being 'sucked dry'. The vampire or blood sucker is such a fearful figure that it is accepted as an embodiment of total negativity.

⊡ The succubus, a female demon believed to have sexual intercourse with sleeping men, and the incubus (the opposite) preying on a dreamer's vital energy has traditionally been pictured as a vampire in both men's and women's dreams. Such dreams may originally arise from childhood trauma.
*You might also like to consult the entry for Blood.*

## VAN – *see* LORRY IN TRANSPORT

## VANDAL/VANDALIZE

⚙ Spiritual vandalism takes place when our basic beliefs are destroyed or trashed. Under these circumstances the dream content will have a sense of violence and violation.

♡ Vandalism suggests a degree of mindless damage and a vandal is the perpetrator of such mindlessness. From an emotional perspective such a dream may manifest when there has not been a natural respect for our feelings.

▩ When in waking life there are so many examples of wanton destruction, it is not surprising that such images become part of our dream content. When perhaps our professional integrity is called into question we may translate that as vandalism. That part of our being that has no respect for the norms and customs of society may be pictured in dreams as a vandal.
*You might like to consult the entries for Damage and Violence.*

## VANISH

⚙ One of the most annoying things about dreams is that images will vanish unexpectedly. The mind has a great capacity for 'magic'; to dream of things vanishing, and then possibly reappearing, means that we have to work a little harder from a spiritual perspective to understand.

♡ Just as a child believes in the world of magic, so the dream state is one that at the time is totally believable. When images vanish in a dream, they will very often become more tangible in the waking state and available for interpretation.

▩ There is also the tendency for us to forget various parts of the dream on waking. The reason is that the subject of the dream has not yet fully fixed itself in consciousness. Working with dreams on first waking can help to 'fix' the information our subconscious is attempting to give us.

## VAPOUR – *see* WEATHER

## VASE

⚙ The Great Mother in all her glory is represented. Symbolically any hollow vessel has been taken to represent feminine spiritual qualities.

♡ The accepting, receptive, intuitive aspect of the feminine is often suggested by a hollow object such as a vase. Because of its association with the womb a vase can symbolize the potential for growth. When we dream of a vase containing plants or flowers they may also help to clarify the information we are being given in the dream.

🔲 As a holder of beautiful things, any receptacle such as a vase, water pot, pitcher or urn tends to represent the feminine within a dream. Such an object can also signify creativity, and may suggest practical or emotional help in a project. If the vase is cracked or chipped our basic premise may be faulty.

*You might like to consult the information for Great Mother in Archetypes in the Introduction and the entries for Flowers, Jar and Urn.*

## VAULT

🔆 A vault represents the meeting place of the spiritual and physical. Consequently a vault can also symbolize death, though this may not necessarily be a physical death but rather a leaving behind of non-essential material.

🔷 Collective wisdom (or the Collective Unconscious – information available to all of us) often remains hidden until a real effort is made to uncover the knowledge available. While a vault can represent a tomb, it also represents the 'archives' or records to which we all have access. As a transition image it suggests darkness and perhaps fear of the unknown.

🔲 In dreams any dark, hidden place suggests sexual potency or the unconscious. It can also represent our store of personal resources, those things we learn as we grow and mature. To be going down into a vault represents our need to explore those areas of ourselves that have become hidden. We may also need to explore our attitude to death.

*You might also like to consult the entries for Catacomb/Crypt, Death and Tomb.*

## VD – *see* INFECTION

## VEGETABLES – *see* FOOD AND HARVEST

## VEGETATION

🔆 Vegetation in a dream symbolizes abundance and the capacity for growth on a spiritual level.

🔷 While the obstacles we create for ourselves in life may cause difficulty, vegetation suggests that there is also an underlying abundance and fertility that is available to us. In dreams, a pictorial image can help us to understand this. To be clearing vegetation, for instance in a vegetable garden, can suggest clearing away that which is no longer of use to us. If vegetation is sparse enough in dreams for this to be noticeable there is a lack of emotion or passion in us.

🔲 Vegetation in a dream can often represent the obstacles that we put in front of ourselves in order to grow. For instance, a patch of brambles can

suggest irritating snags to our movement forwards, whereas nettles might represent people actually trying to prevent progress. The image of vegetation also links with the forest and with the archetypal image of the jungle.
*Consult the entries for Forest and Jungle for further clarification.*

## VEIL

🌣 A veil can represent all that is hidden and mysterious – and this often translates into aspects of the Occult. To take the veil suggests becoming a nun and, therefore, adopting a spiritual path. The veil is also a way of shrouding the feminine in order to avoid temptation and is for many women a badge of faith.

♡ The mind has different ways of indicating hidden thoughts in dreams. The veil is one of these symbols. When an object is veiled in a dream, there is some kind of secret, which cannot be revealed except to the initiated or those 'in the know'.

▦ We may, as dreamers, be concealing something from ourselves, but we could also be being kept in ignorance by others. Depending on our own attitude the veil may symbolize submission to an external authority.
*Also consult the entry for Clothes.*

## VERDICT

🌣 A verdict in a dream suggests that a judgement from a more spiritual source has become relevant. The spiritual law of cause and effect results in a 'ruling' being made.

♡ To dream we are on trial and a verdict has been given means that we have become aware that we have been judged, perhaps by our own moral code, perhaps by others.

▦ When we feel subject to scrutiny or judgement by others in waking life, perhaps having done something that could get us into difficulties, in dreams judges, courts and juries may hand down a verdict on our behaviour.
*You might also like to consult the entries for Judge/Judgement, Juror/Jury and Justice.*

## VERMIN – *see* ANIMALS

## VERTICAL – *see* POSITION

## VETO

🌣 In dream terms a spiritual veto – the right to forbid an action – can be experienced in many ways: a straightforward refusal, a withdrawal of approval or a definite denial of rights.

♡ In emotional terms a veto happens in dreams when we have a strongly felt reason for not agreeing to a particular course of action. Sometimes it is not until the dream action occurs that we realize the strength of our feeling.

When or if an action offends in real life against a code of behaviour, we may find our dreams directing us to operate the right of veto.

## VICAR

A vicar is a man of God and spiritually has authority over us. He is often the authority figure to whom we have given control.

When a vicar appears in a dream, we are usually aware of the more spiritual, knowledgeable side of ourselves – that part that sits in judgement on our own actions.

Just as the priest was given spiritual authority over many, and was often a figure to be feared, so the vicar is also given this authority. He is perhaps less daunting than the priest in dreams.

*Also consult the entries for Priest in the Archetypes section in the Introduction and in the People section.*

## VICE

A moral fault or wickedness is a sin regularly practised and a basic moral code offended against. Unacceptable behaviour may manifest in the form of vice in dreams. The Cardinal (principal) Vices are considered to be: Lust, Sloth, Pride, Greed, Envy, Wrath and Gluttony.

Often dreams allow us to behave in ways that are not those we would normally try in waking life. Being conscious of a particular vice, e.g. sloth, envy, apathy etc., in one of our dream characters may enable us to handle that tendency within ourselves.

There are obviously two meanings to the word vice. One is a tool which clamps and the other a wrong action. Dreaming of a vice in its first sense may suggest that we are being constrained in some way. The second indicates that we are aware of the side of ourselves which is rebellious and out of step with society. We may in both cases need to make adjustments in our behaviour.

*You might also like to consult the entry for Offence/Offend.*

## VICTIM

If we are repressing our ability to develop spiritual potential, we will experience ourselves in a dream as a victim, often of our own doing.

When we are continually creating 'no-win' situations this tendency is highlighted in dreams, but may be done so somewhat dramatically. We may find we are victims of burglary, rape or murder, for instance. These will not necessarily be precognitive dreams apart from alerting us to the potential to become a victim. The nature of our particular difficulty may reveal itself through the dream content.

In dreams we are often aware of something happening to us over which we have no control. We are the victim – in the sense that we are passive or powerless within the situation. Sometimes we are aware that we are treating others incorrectly. We are making them victims of our own internal aggression, and not handling ourselves properly in waking life.

*You might also like to consult the entries for Burglar, Intruder and Martyr.*

**VICTORY –** *see* **WIN/WINNING**

**VIDEO –** *see* **CAMCORDER/CAMERA, FILM, RECORD/RECORDS/RECORDING**

**VILLAGE**

🔅 Often village life was centred around the church and the pub, providing many contrasts. Spiritually, we often have to look at balancing two parts of our lives. A village appearing in a dream suggests a fairly tightly knit community. It may illustrate our ability to form supportive relationships and a community spirit.

♦ A village can present certain problems. For instance, everybody knows everybody else's business – which can become trying. In this case we may be highlighting the oppression felt in close relationships.

▨ A village can symbolize restriction and an unsophisticated attitude. Because the pace of life is slower, we may find that the village in a dream in today's busy world is a symbol of relaxation.

**VINE/VINEYARD**

🔅 A vine or vineyard can symbolize growth of a spiritual nature. We are linking with the more spiritual side of ourselves that has grown through shared, rather than individual, experience. It can also represent fertility.

♦ When we dream of the vine we are often referring to the various members of our family, including our ancestors. Quite literally we are making a link with our family tree and all that has gone before.

▨ The vine in dreams can suggest growth and fruitfulness. This can be of one's whole self, or the various parts. A vineyard can symbolize our place of work as well as the effort we put in. A fruitful vine or vineyard suggests success and prosperity, whereas a neglected vineyard signifies that we have not previously taken enough care. Matters may have gone beyond our control.

**VIOLENCE**

🔅 A sense of spiritual injustice may be represented by scenes or acts of violence in a dream. A violent reaction to something in dreams suggests some kind of spiritual distress.

♦ When we are unable because of social pressures or circumstances to express ourselves properly, we can find ourselves behaving violently in dreams. If others are behaving violently towards us we may need to take care in waking life not to upset others, or it may be that subconsciously we are aware of others' distress.

▣ Any violence in dreams is a reflection of our own inner feeling, sometimes about ourselves, sometimes about the situations around us. Often the type of violence – fighting or extreme behaviour, for example – is worthy of notice if we are fully to understand ourselves.

*Also consult the entries for Anger and Fight.*

**VIPER – *see* SERPENT AND SNAKE IN ANIMALS**

**VIRGIN**

✸ Spiritually there is a kind of innocence and purity which can often be dedicated to the service of mankind. This quality can often manifest more clearly in dreams than in waking life. In ancient Rome Vestal Virgins served the goddess Vesta as priestesses for thirty years, after which they were free to leave and marry. Most Vestal Virgins preferred to remain single after retirement. Before that, they had to maintain chastity or face a frightening death.

♥ In dream parlance, the virginal mind – that is, a mind that is free from deception and guile – is perhaps more important than physically being a virgin. It is this freedom that often becomes evident in dreams. Dreams of the loss of virginity can suggest the ending of all innocence.

▣ To dream of being a virgin suggests a state of dedication and purity, and may symbolize the life of a single, unromantically attached woman, one perhaps known to us. To dream that someone else is a virgin highlights the ideals of integrity and honesty.

⊟ In a woman's dream such a figure suggests she is in touch with her own psyche, her own essential being. In a man's dream a virgin may symbolize an innocent understanding of romance or a chivalrous approach.

**VIRGIN MOTHER – *see* SPIRITUAL IMAGERY IN THE INTRODUCTION**

**VIRUS**

✸ A virus is an infectious agent so from a spiritual viewpoint is a pollution or corruption of information or knowledge.

♥ Dreaming of an infectious virus has the connotation of us having caught a contaminant or had it passed on to us. Our emotions and feelings may be out of sorts.

▣ Dreaming of a computer virus suggests that a system of communication has broken down or been contaminated and we should perhaps try a different approach. A health virus suggests something a little more personal and is more concerned with our own reaction to actual physical infection.

*You might also like to consult the entries for Ill/Illness and Infection.*

**VISA**

✵ As a visa gives permission to be in a certain place, the spiritual interpretation is that we are in the right place at the right time for the correct spiritual reason.

♥ A visa signifies a permission given by an authority, which is not the normal one under which we operate. Interestingly this image can manifest when we are embarking on a new course of action.

▦ From a purely mundane perspective, a visa signifies that we have given ourselves permission to undertake a new project or task, have sought permission from a higher authority and are ready to begin.

**VISIONS –** *see* **HYPNOPOMPIC AND HYPNOGOGIC IN THE INTRODUCTION**

**VISIT**

✵ Our spiritual guide often first makes itself available by a visit in the dream state. Any visitation by an apparently discarnate being or a dead relative suggests information from the Higher Self.

♥ To be paying someone else a visit in a dream signifies that we may need to widen our horizons. It requires us to move beyond our own boundaries towards other people. This may be physically, emotionally or spiritually.

▦ To be visited by someone in a dream can suggest that there is information, warmth or love available to us. If it is someone we know then this may apply in a real-life situation. If it is not, then there may be a facet of our personality that is trying to make itself apparent.

**VOICE**

✵ The Voice of God is a term that is used to describe the energy and seriousness of a summons – a call to spiritual duty.

♥ A voice that speaks through, or to, us as in trance work (an altered state of consciousness) has two areas of significance. Through us suggests information for others, whereas to us is more personal. If we believe in the spirit realm, this is communication from a discarnate spirit. More psychologically, when we suppress certain parts of our personalities they may surface in dreams as disembodied voices. This does not constitute a form of madness.

▦ The voice is a tool that we use to express ourselves. We all have inner awareness of our own state that is sometimes difficult to disclose. In dreams we are frequently able to use our voices in more appropriate ways, for instance in singing and chanting, which we would not normally do in waking life. Many times we are spoken to in dreams so that we remember the information given.

**VOID** – *see* **ABYSS**

**VOLCANO**

☀ A volcano is representative of spiritual deeply held passion. This can sometimes erupt with frightening results, if we do not learn to express ourselves properly. Frustration often gives rise to the image of an active volcano.

♡ An erupting volcano usually signifies that we are not in control of a situation or of our emotions – of which there may be a hurtful release. If the lava is more noticeable, feelings will run very deep. If the lava has cooled there has been a deep passion that has now cooled off. If the explosiveness is more noticeable, and seems more recent, anger may be more prominent.

▦ The image of a volcano in dreams is a very telling one, partly because of its unpredictability. To dream of a volcano being extinct can indicate either that we have 'killed off' our passions, or that a difficult situation has come to an end. This may be one that has been around for some time.

*You might like to consult the entries for Eruption and Explode/Explosion.*

**VOLUNTEER**

☀ In spiritual terms by volunteering for something we are promising to make a commitment – apparently an anomaly, since we are promising to make a promise. To volunteer, however, requires dedication (setting aside) of what resources we have.

♡ Volunteering in dreams shows that we have made an emotional commitment to whatever is represented.

▦ In everyday life there are certain projects and tasks that require more effort than others. Dreaming of volunteering suggests that we are aware of the extra effort required. We have decided to take part before we have consciously registered that fact.

**VOMIT**

☀ Vomiting is a symbol of a discharge of negativity. We may have held on to bad feeling for so long that it has caused our spiritual system some difficulty.

♡ Intuitively, we can often be aware of problems around us and be affected by them. When we become overloaded, we may need to 'throw up' (or away) the distress it is causing us. To wake up feeling sick intimates that we have been affected on an emotional level by any release that occurred in the dreams that we have had.

▦ To dream of vomiting suggests a discharge of disagreeable feelings and emotions. It is the cleansing of inner distress that makes us extremely uncomfortable. To dream of watching someone else vomit indicates that we may have upset them or what they represent in our lives and need to have compassion and understanding.

**VORTEX –** *see* **WHIRLWIND**

**VOTE**

🔅 Spiritually when we have given unconditional acceptance to something, we have placed our trust in it. A votive offering is a spiritual request.

🔷 While the process of voting is supposed to be fair and just, when we dream of this we may question the process or the decision. To dream of being elected to a position is to seek power.

🔲 Dreaming of voting in an election, whether general or within the workplace, highlights our wish and ability to belong to groups. Being voted for signifies acceptance by our peers. If we are conscious that we are voting with the group we are happy to accept group practice. Voting against the group indicates a need to rebel.

*Also consult the entry for Election.*

**VOUCHER**

🔅 Spiritually, a voucher signifies acceptance of our wants, needs and requirements and denotes our right to have these satisfied.

🔷 A voucher opens up our opportunities and suggests that these are a gift. Because it is usually an exchange between two people, it can indicate the help that others can give us. In today's more commercial society, a voucher in dreams can also signify a way of pacifying distress.

🔲 A voucher – in the sense of a promissory note – can be taken in dreams to suggest our ability to give ourselves permission to accrue resources. If, for instance, it is a money-off voucher we may not be valuing ourselves properly, or alternatively we could be looking for an easy option.

**VOW**

🔅 A vow is a spiritual promise made between us and our universe, a pact between two people or between ourselves and God.

🔷 Because a vow is normally made in front of witnesses, we need to be aware of the effect that it will have on other people. In dreams we are expecting others to help us honour our promise. To be listening to or making marriage vows indicates our commitment to totality.

🔲 A vow is dedicating ourselves to a course of action and to dream of making a vow is to be recognizing responsibility for our own lives. It is more solemn than a simple promise and the results are consequently more far-reaching.

**VOYAGE –** *see* **BOAT/SHIP AND JOURNEY**

**VULTURE –** *see* **BIRDS**

## WADDING

❂ Wadding, in spiritual and psychic terms, suggests security. It is an image that often arises when we are looking for protection.

♥ Sometimes bodily changes can be reflected in the images that we produce in dreams. Wadding can represent a fear of getting fat or becoming ungainly.

▦ In dreams our need for security can become more noticeable than we allow it to be in ordinary, everyday life. Because wadding is normally a protective material, we may decide that we should take action to protect ourselves rather than defend ourselves.

*Also consult the entry for Fat and Packing.*

## WADING

❂ Spiritually, wading suggests a cleansing process, which ties in with baptism. Many meditations also use the symbolism of walking through water.

♥ Often the feeling associated with wading can be more relevant than the action of wading itself. To recognize that we are not actually in water – for example, we are wading through treacle or another substance which impedes our progress – can give us a clue to how we feel about ourselves or our circumstances.

▦ Dreaming of wading puts us in the position of recognizing what effect our emotions can have on us. If we are impeded by the water then we need to appreciate how our emotions can prevent us from moving forward. If we are enjoying our wading experience, then we may expect our connection with life to bring contentment. Sometimes the depths to which our bodies are immersed can give us information as to how we cope with external circumstances. For instance, if the water is chest high we should consider how much our knowledge of ourselves is being threatened.

*Consult the entries for Baptism, Emotions and Water for further clarification.*

## WAGES

❂ Spiritually, wages can represent recompense for our actions and the reward we so richly deserve coming our way after all our hard work. Initially, wages were paid for work already done, whereas salary was initially an allowance to buy salt in advance – a basic commodity.

♥ Most actions we take have a result. Often when we are doing something that we do not want to do – or that we do not enjoy – the only pay-off is in the wages we receive. To dream of wages may signify that this is all we can expect from a situation in everyday life. In dreams, we tend to think of wages as a short-term payment and salary as long-term reward.

▦ Wages are normally paid in exchange for work done. In dreams, to be receiving wages signifies that we have done a good job. To be paying somebody wages implies that we feel we have to pay for services rendered. To receive a wage packet suggests that our value is tied up with other things such as loyalty and duty. To receive a salary in dreams suggests an element of trust between ourselves and our employers in waking life.

*Also consult the entry for Money.*

## WAIL

✹ The making of sounds in mourning is used spiritually to banish bad spirits and summon the good. In dreams, therefore, wailing can suggest that we are trying to get in touch with a power that is greater than ourselves. We should look at what we feel needs 'banishing' from our lives.

♦ Wailing is reputed to be a method of summoning the spirits used in ancient times by the Oracles. It is also a long, protracted way of releasing emotions. When we hear someone wailing in a dream, we become conscious of another person's sadness.

▦ When we ourselves are wailing in dreams, we may be allowing ourselves an emotional release which would not be seen to be appropriate in everyday life. We may be attempting to make contact with a part of ourselves that has stopped functioning. It may also be a way of expressing frustration that we have not yet consciously recognized.

*You might also like to consult the entries for Emotions, Mourning and Weeping.*

## WAITER/WAITRESS

✹ Spiritually we must learn two lessons – service and patience. These must be learnt before we can really progress.

♦ When such a person appears in a dream, there may be a play on words and we must become a 'waiter'. Part of us needs to be conscious that for complete fulfilment in any task we need to wait and be less anxious.

▦ The interpretation of this dream depends on whether we ourselves are waiting at table, or whether we are being waited upon. If we are in the role of waiter, we are aware of our ability to care for other people. If we are being waited on, we perhaps need to be nurtured and made to feel special.

## WAITING

✹ In developing spiritually we must often learn to wait until the time is right for a particular event. We have to wait for the passage of time and develop patience in the interim.

♦ When we become aware that something is expected from us, and other people are waiting for appropriate action, we may need to consider our own leadership qualities in waking life. When we dream of waiting lists such as that for operations we become aware that we must wait our turn, though not necessarily over a health issue. We perhaps feel that we are not sufficiently important.

▣ To be waiting for somebody, or something, in a dream implies a need to understand the relevance of anticipation. We may be looking to other people, or outside circumstances, to help us move forward or make decisions. If we are impatient, it may be that our expectations are too high. If we are waiting patiently, there is the understanding that events will happen in their own good time.

*Consult the entry for Time for further clarification.*

## WAKE/WAKING UP

❀ Spiritually, to wake up signifies becoming aware. The dream state alerts us to various ideas and concepts we should be looking at, although it may take us a little time to 'wake up' to them. A wake signifies appropriate grief and watching over the body of a loved one so they come to no spiritual harm.

♦ In most religions, there is a period around a death when it is appropriate to express our feelings. Sometimes it is easier to do this in company and with the support of other people. A wake such as this in a dream indicates we may need support to overcome a disappointment. To seem to wake up in a dream can indicate that we have become more aware of our selves and have come out of a period of emotional withdrawal.

▣ A wake, in the sense of a funeral rite gives us an opportunity to grieve properly. When in dreams we find ourselves attending such an occasion, we need to be aware that there may be some reason in our lives for us to go through a period of grieving. We need to let go that which we hold dear.

*You might also like to consult the entries for Death, Funeral, Hearse and Mourning.*

## WALKING

❀ A walk becomes spiritual when it is a journey of exploration into unknown realms. Walking the labyrinth is a spiritual exercise in contemplation.

♦ Walking may be used as a relaxation from stress, and it is this significance that often comes up in dreams. If we are alone in our dream then our walk can be silent and contemplative. If it is in company, then we are able to communicate and converse with anyone without fear of interruption.

▣ In a dream, walking indicates the way in which we should be moving forward. To be walking purposefully suggests we know where we are going.

To be wandering aimlessly suggests we need to create goals for ourselves. To take pleasure in the act of walking is to return to the innocence of the child. To be using a walking stick is to recognize our need for support and assistance from others.

*You might like to consult the entries for Labyrinth and Journey for further clarification.*

## WALL

✿ A wall symbolizes the boundaries of a sacred space. We need to be aware of what our limitations are, not just spiritually but also emotionally.

♡ A wall has the symbolism of a dividing line – a marker between the inner and the outer, privacy and open trust. A hole in a wall suggests a breach of trust or privacy. If the wall is imprisoning us we are being held prisoner by our own fears, doubts and difficulties. If the wall appears and disappears, we have only partly dealt with our problem.

▦ In dreams, walls usually indicate the limits we have set ourselves. These may be created as defence mechanisms or support structures, and it is sometimes helpful in the interpretation to decide whether the walls have been created in order to keep ourselves in, or other people out.

*Also consult the entry for Walls in Buildings.*

## WALLET

✿ A wallet has the same significance as a bag, so spiritually represents our life and all it contains. As something that carries money, symbolically it signifies the value we place upon ourselves.

♡ The wallet, through its development from a money bag, can also suggest the feminine aspects of care, prudence and containment. It can highlight our attitude to intuition and awareness.

▦ In dreams, the wallet is a representation of where we keep our resources safe. These need not simply be financial resources, but can be of any kind. Many dreams can suggest our attitude to money, and to dream of a wallet is one of those dreams.

*You might also like to consult the entries for Bag and Money.*

## WALNUT – *see* NUT

## WALTZ – *see* DANCE

## WAND

✿ Obviously a wand works in tandem with magic, so to dream of a wand can symbolize 'magical' powers that may influence us or that we are capable of using. It is only when we fully understand these powers that we can use them effectively.

⬥ Conventionally the wand is an instrument of supernatural forces, and it is often this image that is the most important. We are aware of some force external to ourselves, which needs harnessing. From an emotional perspective, learning to use and direct the innate power we have gives us the ability to change our circumstances.

▦ When we dream of using a wand we are aware of our influence over others. Conversely, if someone else uses a wand we are aware of the power of suggestion, either for negative or for positive within the situation.

▣ As an instrument of power, the wand can rather obviously suggest the penis. However, as more people become intrigued by magic it will revert to its older meaning of a magically charged tool. In a woman's dream it is possibly used from a more emotional perspective, whereas in a man's dream its use will be dispassionate.

*Consult the entries for Magic/Magician, Witch and Wizard for further information.*

## WANDERER/WANDERING

✲ Wandering as a spiritual concept means going wherever life's path takes us. It is particularly recognized in the Taoist religion and signifies going with the flow.

⬥ As we learn to live in the moment we are prepared to listen to our intuition and not to plan. Wandering in dreams may be alerting us to this faculty within.

▦ Meeting the wanderer in dreams is actually learning to understand that part of us that is the freedom lover, who on a practical level can take life as it comes and not be thrown by external circumstances.

*You might also like to consult the entries for Hermit and Tramp as well as the information on Tramp in Archetypes in the Introduction.*

## WAR

✲ As a symbol, the disintegration of order inherent in war signifies some kind of conflict in us. The natural order is breaking down and identifying the source of the conflict – often a difficulty in achieving some kind of balance between the inner and outer selves – will help to bring a sense of peace or closure.

⬥ War is ultimately a way of dealing with distress and discomfort. In theory, the outcome should be the re-establishing of order, but this can often only happen over an extended period of time. In dreams, when war breaks out we are dealing with destructive feelings that cannot easily be expressed in any other way.

▦ War is often deliberately engineered rather than spontaneous and tends to have a more global effect than mere skirmishes. It therefore suggests that we need to be fully aware of the consequences that our actions may have on others.

⚡ Dreams of war will depend on the experiences in waking life of the dreamer. In a woman's dream traditionally she would have been on the periphery though this may no longer be true. In a man's dream he is much more likely to be combative.

*Additional information might be gleaned by consulting the entries for Argue/Argument, Armed Forces, Conflict and Fight.*

**WARDEN – see JAILER**

**WARDROBE – see CUPBOARD/WARDROBE IN FURNITURE/FURNISHINGS**

**WARMTH – see HOT**

**WASHING**

🔆 A spiritual cleansing may be necessary in order to preserve our integrity, such as before a magical ritual. Such an image will often arise spontaneously as our knowledge increases.

♦ Since water is a symbol for emotion and the unconscious, washing stands for achieving a relationship with our emotional selves and dealing successfully with the results.

▦ Dreaming of washing either ourselves or, for instance, clothes suggests getting rid of negative feelings. We may need to change our attitude, either internally or externally. Washing other people touches on our need to care for others.

*Consult the entry for Water for further information.*

**WASP – see INSECTS**

**WASTE**

🔆 To be conscious of waste may mean that we are becoming aware of problems beyond our own small concerns and becoming aware of global issues. Equally, our spiritual energy may have calls upon it of which we are not consciously aware.

♦ If we are being wasteful in dreams we need to reassess how we are running our lives. We may be giving too much in relationships, or putting too much effort into trying to make things happen.

▦ Waste in dreams signifies matter or information we no longer need. It can now be discarded. Often the colour will have significance. Waste can also suggest a misuse of resources – we may initially be using too much energy on a particular project.

*You might also consult the entries for Colour, Climate and Rubbish for further information.*

**WATCH – see TIME**

**WATCHING**

🌑 There is a need for us to monitor our own actions, to be objective in our self-assessment, particularly if new forms of spiritual discipline have recently been taken on.

◈ In dreams, we are often conscious of the Self or the observer in us, which is both watching and participating in the dream. If we are to achieve the best interpretation, we probably need to be aware of both perspectives.

▣ To be aware of being watched in a dream suggests that we feel threatened by someone's close interest in us. This may be in a work situation, but could also be in personal relationships.

*You might also like to consult the entry for Witness.*

**WATER**

🌑 Water is such a life giving force that it symbolizes the flow of life energy itself. It is a rather mysterious substance, given that it has the ability to flow through, over and round objects. It has the quality of being able to wear away anything that gets in its way. It can symbolize spiritual rebirth. In baptism, water is a cleanser of previously held 'sins', often also those inherited from the family.

◈ Water symbolizes our emotions under all sorts of different circumstances so images associated with it are very evocative. Below are some such representations:

**Bathing** suggests purification.

**Canals** symbolize the birth process.

**Dams, islands and other obstacles** are conscious attempts to control the force of the water, and, therefore, our emotions.

**Diving** represents going down into the unconscious, or perhaps trying to find the parts of ourselves that we have suppressed.

**Drowning** highlights our ability to push things into the unconscious, only to have them emerge as a force that can overcome us.

**Floods** represent the chaotic side of us, which is usually uncontrollable. This side requires attention when it wells up and threatens to overwhelm us.

**Fountains** suggest womanhood, and particularly the Great Mother.

**A lake**, like **a pool**, can signify a stage of transition between the conscious and the spiritual Self. When come upon unexpectedly it can give us the opportunity to appreciate and understand ourselves. To be reflected in a pool indicates we need to come to terms with the Shadow. We must learn to accept that there will be a part of ourselves that we do not like very much but, when harnessed, it can give much energy for change.

**Overflows and overflowing** can signify an excess of energy, often emotion that is too much to be contained.

**Rivers or streams** always represent our lives and the way that we live them. It will depend on our attitude as to whether we see our life as a large river or a small stream. If the river is rushing by we may feel that life is moving too quickly for us. If we can see the sea as well as the river, we may be aware that a great change needs to occur or that attention must be paid to the unconscious within. Crossing a river indicates great changes. If the river is very deep we should perhaps be paying attention to the way we relate to the rest of the world. If the river is frightening we are perhaps creating an unnecessary difficulty for ourselves. If the water in the river appears to be contaminated we are not doing the best we can for ourselves.

**Seas or oceans** very often represent Cosmic Consciousness – that is, the original chaotic state from which all life emerges. Inherent in that state is all knowledge – i.e. completeness – although that may be obscured by our fear of deep emotion; we do not fear that which we understand. A shallow sea suggests superficial emotion. The waves in the sea represent strong emotion and passion. A calm sea suggests a peaceful existence, while a stormy one signifies passion, either negative or positive. To be conscious of the rise and fall of the tides is to be conscious both of the passage of time and of the rise and fall of our own emotions.

**Waterfalls** symbolize any emotion that reaches the stage where it must 'spill over' in order to become manageable.

▣ Water is usually taken in dreams to symbolize all that is emotional and feminine. Water can also stand for our potential and our ability to create a new life for ourselves in response to our own inner urgings. Water also represents cleansing, being able to wash away the contamination that we may experience in everyday life.

Water appears so often in dreams as an image, with so many different meanings, that it is possible only to suggest some probable ones. **Entering water** suggests new beginnings and **being immersed in water** is a return to the womb and can suggest pregnancy and birth. **Flowing water** signifies peace and comfort, while **rushing water** can indicate passion. **Deep water** suggests the unconscious and can also indicate that we feel out of our depth, while **shallow water** represents a lack of essential energy. To be **on the water** (as in a boat) can represent indecision or a lack of emotional commitment, while to be **in the water** but not moving can suggest inertia. **Going down into water** indicates a need to renew one's strength, to go back to the beginning, while **coming up out of the water** suggests a fresh start.

*You might also like to consult the entries for Boat/Ship, Drowning, Emotions, Lagoon/Lake and Swimming as well as the information on Great Mother and Shadow in Archetypes in the Introduction.*

## WEALTH

�</> There is a wealth of spiritual knowledge to be gained, and to dream of pecuniary wealth indicates that this knowledge is within our grasp. Symbols of finance such as accounts or bills suggest that we should record very carefully what we do know and also what we pass on to others.

💗 Wealth and status usually go naturally together, so often when we are having problems in dealing with our own status in life we will have dreams about wealth. It can also often indicate the resources that we have or that we can use from other people. We have the ability to draw on our experiences or feelings and to achieve a great deal within the framework of our lives. Our savings may represent resources, either material or emotional, that we have hidden away until such times as they are needed. They can also represent our sense of security and independence. To dream of savings we did not know we had would suggest that we are able to summon up extra energy or time, perhaps by using material or information from the past.

🔲 Dreaming of being wealthy is to dream of having in abundance those things that we need. We have possibly come though a period where we have put in a lot of effort and to dream of having a great deal of wealth indicates that we have achieved what we have set out to do. A mortgage in dreams can suggest a false sense of security in that we apparently have access to a resource that is only comparative in value and not readily realized. If we are aware of our goal in making savings in a dream we should perhaps be making long-term plans in waking life. If we are giving our savings away, we no longer have need of a particular practical resource.

*The entries for Debt, Lend/Lending/Loan and Money should help with clarification.*

## WEAPONS

🌎 Various weapons can suggest differing degrees of spiritual power. This power should always be used with relevant caution.

💗 To have a weapon used against us means that we have to look at how we are party to people being aggressive around us. It may be that we have done something to upset the other person, which results in aggression, or it may be that we have put ourselves in a position of becoming the victim of circumstance. Different weapons have various meanings:

**An arrow** indicates being pierced by some kind of powerful emotion, of being hurt by someone else through words or actions. In order to make ourselves feel better we must turn our attention inwards.

**The gun or pistol** traditionally represents male sexuality and for a woman to dream of being shot often indicates her thoughts about sexual aggression. If we are shooting the gun ourselves we may be using our masculine abilities in quite an aggressive way, in order to defend ourselves.

**A knife** represents the ability to cut through debris, to 'cut into' whatever is bothering us and to cut out the hypocrisy that perhaps is prevailing in a situation.

**The sword** has more than one meaning. Because of its hilt – which is a cross shape – it often represents a system of belief that is used in a powerful way. Equally it can be used to suggest spiritual strength, creating an ability to cut away the unnecessary more powerfully than the knife. The sword when sheathed is the soul or the Self in the body.

To dream of weapons usually suggests our desire to hurt someone or something. We have internalized our aggression and it is marginally more acceptable to dream of weapons and of using them against people, than actually having to deal with such circumstances in everyday life. Depending on the weapon that we use we may get a fairly good idea of what the real problem is in the waking self. To dream of squeezing the trigger of a gun, for instance, suggests that we may be at fault.

*Consult the entries for Armour, Arrow, Dagger, Gun, Knife and Sword for further information.*

**WEASEL –** *see* **ANIMALS**

**WEATHER**

Different types of weather may be symbolic of a spiritual response. Sunshine suggests good feeling and happiness, whereas rain might suggest tears. Wind symbolizes the intellect, a windy day might suggest a time for intellectual pursuits.

Weather can indicate our internal responses to situations. If, for instance, there was a storm in our dream our emotions would be stormy, perhaps angry and aggressive. If we are watching a very blue, unclouded sky, we may be recognizing that we have the ability to keep the situations that we are in under control. We do possess the ability to control internal moods and emotions that may not have been possible in the past. Being aware of the weather would indicate that we need to recognize that we are part of a greater whole rather than just individuals in our own right.

🔲 Weather, as being part of the 'environment' of the dream, usually indicates our moods and emotions. We are very much aware of changing external situations and have to be careful to adjust our conduct in response to these. *You might also like to consult the entries for Emotions, Lightning, Rain, Storm, Thunder/Thunderbolts and Wind.*

## WEAVING

🌞 Weaving is one of the strongest spiritual images there is. In most cultures there is an image of our fate being woven in a particular pattern. We are not supposed to be in control of that pattern, but must accept that the gods or God know what is best.

💗 Weaving is taken to signify life itself and often symbolizes our attitude to the way we run our lives. The fabric of our emotions is what we have to work with; the patterns that we weave consist of our experiences as we go through life.

🔲 Weaving is a very basic symbol and suggests the need to take responsibility for our own lives. Handicrafts of any sort symbolize our hold on life and on the situations around us. To make a mistake in weaving suggests that we need to take a situation back to its roots and rework it. *You might also like to consult the entries for God/Gods, Knitting and Web.*

## WEB

🌞 The spider's web is the Cosmic Plan. It is within the 'web of life' that the divine powers have interwoven fate and time in order to create a reality in which we can exist. There is a belief that we are the spiritual entrapped within the physical and not able to 'escape' back to our own spiritual realm.

💗 When we dream of a web we are linking into one of the most basic of spiritual symbols. Interestingly in today's technological age it will also symbolize a network of communication as in the world wide web on the internet. In dreams this 'web' can stand for our own personal group of friends and acquaintances.

🔲 In everyday life we may well be caught up in a situation that could trap us. We could be in a 'sticky' situation and not quite know which direction to move. This can result in the symbol of a web appearing in the dream. We are 'caught in the middle' or we are trapped. Because the situation is extremely complex we have no idea which way is going to be most advantageous for us. *Consult the entry for Communication for further clarification.*

## WEDDING/WEDDING DRESS/WEDDING RING

🌞 A wedding can symbolize the sacred union between the spiritual and physical. In former times it was seen as a ritual that brought fertility to the earth. Within the human being there is the need to make vows, to give promises and above all to symbolize the making of those promises Traditionally, the wedding ring was a symbol of total encircling love because it is in the shape of a circle. It is complete, with no beginning and no end.

🛡 To dream of a wedding can give some indication of the type of person we are looking for as a partner. We may, for instance, dream that we are marrying a childhood friend – in which case we are looking for somebody who has the same qualities as that person. We may dream we are marrying a famous figure and again the qualities of that particular person will be important. The wedding ring, worn on the finger that represents the heart – that is, the fourth finger of the left hand – suggests that we have made a commitment or promise. To dream of a wedding ring being on any other finger than that particular finger may indicate that the promise is not valid or we feel the wedding ring to be a constriction or an entrapment in some way.

▦ A marriage or a wedding in a dream often indicates the uniting of two particular parts of us which need to come together in order to create a better whole. For instance, the intellect and feelings – or perhaps the practical and intuitive sides – may need to be united. To be dreaming of wearing a wedding dress is to be trying to sort out our feelings and hopes about relationships and weddings. To be dressing someone else in a wedding dress can indicate one's feelings of inferiority – 'always the bridesmaid, never the bride'.

To dream of losing our wedding ring would very often symbolize a problem within a marriage, or perhaps highlight a problem in our commitment. To dream of finding a wedding ring might well indicate that a relationship is being formed that could result in marriage. To be attending a wedding in dreams when we are not expecting to attend one in waking life suggests that we are aware of a relationship between two people, but it has not yet registered on the conscious level.

*You might also like to consult the entries for Marriage, Partner/Partnership and Propose/Proposal.*

## WEEDS

🌸 Weeds, by courtesy of their irritating qualities and refusal to be quickly eradicated, symbolize spiritual difficulties.

🛡 Mental attitudes and old patterns of behaviour that clog us up and do not allow us to move forward can very often be shown in dreams as weeds. We may need to decide which of these weeds are helpful to us – that is, which could be composted, transferred into something else and made use of to help positive growth – or which need to be thrown away. Often plants growing wild have healing properties and by using these properties we can enhance our lives. Such information can be given intuitively in dreams.

🔲 Weeds are generally plants that grow on waste ground and their symbolism in dreams reflects this. They may indicate misplaced trust, misplaced energy or even misplaced attempts at success. They do not contribute a tremendous amount to our lives and if allowed to run riot or to overgrow can stop our own positive growth. To be digging up weeds would show that we are aware that by freeing our life of the non-essential, we are creating space for new growth and new abilities.

*You might like to consult the entries for Garden and Plants.*

## WEEPING

🔅 Weeping suggests mourning for some spiritual quality we have lost. Something exuding moisture so that it seems to be weeping is often deemed to be miraculous, and this dream can appear quite often in stages of transition as we are moving from one state of awareness to another. The excess energy can be shown as a weeping plant, tree or some such image.

💠 Weeping suggests uncontrollable emotion or grief, so to experience either ourselves or someone else weeping in dreams is to show that there needs to be a discharge of such emotion. We may be sad over past events or fearful of moving into the future.

🔲 It is worthwhile exploring the quality of weeping. Are we sobbing and, therefore, not able to express ourselves fully? Are the tears that we shed for ourselves or others? We may simply be creating difficulty within ourselves, which enables us to express the feelings we have bottled up.

*Consulting the entries for Emotions, Mourning, Tear/Tears and Wail should help your understanding.*

## WEIGHING/WEIGHT

🔅 Weight in a dream indicates gravitas and seriousness. We may wish to make clear in our conscious minds our own spiritual worth. Anubis, the Egyptian god, assumed the role of the guide who holds steady the scales on which the hearts of the dead are weighed against the feather of Ma'at, goddess of Truth.

💠 Weighing something up is to be trying to make an accurate decision to assess what the risks are. If we are trying to balance the scales we are looking for justice and natural balance within our knowledge. Weight in a dream may well indicate the need to be practical and down-to-earth in waking life. We need to keep our feet on the ground.

🔲 To be weighing something in dreams is to be assessing its worth. This image connects with the calculation of our needs and what is of value to us, whether materially or spiritually. Experiencing a weight or heaviness in a dream is to be conscious of our responsibilities. It may also suggest that we should assess the importance and seriousness of what we are doing.

*Consult the entries for Measure and Scales for additional information.*

**WELL**

✸ A well can symbolize a form of contact with the depths – possibly the depths of emotion. It is also a symbol for the Abyss, though perhaps less frightening. We can access its vastness through our emotions.

♥ The image of a well in a dream suggests our ability to be 'well'. We have the ability to be healed and to fulfil our dearest wish, if we so desire. By putting ourselves in touch with our intuitive, aware selves we open up the potential and possibilities for healing and success.

▦ A well in dreams is a way of accessing the deepest resources of feeling and emotion that we have. Without such access we are not going eventually to be whole and completely understanding ourselves. If there is something wrong with the well – we cannot reach the water for example – it indicates that we are not able to get in touch with our best talents.

*Consult the entries for Abyss, Emotions and Water for further clarification.*

**WEREWOLF – *see* SINISTER ANIMALS IN ANIMALS**

**WEST**

✸ The West in spiritual terms, from ancient times has suggested Autumn, a time for harvesting. The archangel is Gabriel, keeper of Wisdom.

♥ We may be looking towards a time of rest and reward. The magical element associated with the West is Water and the colour is blue. These significances will often reveal themselves initially in dreams.

▦ Specifically dreaming of the West indicates that we are looking at the sensitive creative side of ourselves. We link with the flow of life and the wisdom of experience.

*Consulting the entries for Colour, Elements, Harvest and Water will provide additional information.*

**WET – *see* WATER**

**WHALE – *see* ANIMALS**

**WHEAT – *see* GRAIN**

**WHEEL**

✸ In Buddhist teaching the Wheel of Life symbolizes the ideal way to live life, and how we see ourselves fitting in. As Eastern religion becomes more widespread this image becomes both more present and more pertinent.

♥ To lose a wheel from a vehicle is to lose motivation or direction – to be thrown off balance. A large wheel, such as the Ferris Wheel in a fairground, suggests an awareness of life's ups and downs.

A wheel in a dream indicates the ability and need to make changes – to move forward into the future without being thrown off course. It is also used in business and therapy as a symbol for work/life balance.

*You might also like to consult the information for Circle in Shapes/Patterns as well as the entries for Mandala and Transport.*

## WHIP

A whip suggests corrective punishment and self-flagellation. We need to consider whether such behaviour is appropriate as we progress spiritually.

Because the whip or lash is an instrument of punishment we need to be aware that in trying to force things to happen in waking life, we may also be creating problems for ourselves.

The whip is an instrument of torture. For it to appear indicates we have either the need to control others, or to be controlled by them. We may be trying to control by using pain – either physical or emotional.

## WHIRLPOOL/WHIRLWIND

These images are symbols of the vortex, a representation of life and natural energy. Harnessed, this energy gives rise to a whirl of creativity. Unharnessed, it can be destructive.

Intellectually we may know that we have control over our lives, but are caught up in an endless round of activity that appears to be unproductive, but in fact contains a tremendous amount of energy.

There are usually conflicting currents in both the whirlpool and the whirlwind. When they appear in dreams we are aware of the quality of power we have within. The whirlpool, being made up of water, will more properly represent emotional energy, whereas the whirlwind (air) will suggest intellectual power. We perhaps need to consider which one is most appropriate to use.

*Consult the entries for Water and Wind for further information.*

## WHISTLE

A whistle can signify a spiritual summons and shares the significance of a wind instrument.

A whistle may be heard and recognized in dreams about games. As a means of imposing control and training, it may be relevant as to how it is blown. For instance, if it is blown harshly, we may be being made aware that we have transgressed a known code of conduct.

A whistle being blown in a dream can mark the end of a particular phase of time. It can also sound as a warning to alert us to a particular event.

*To clarify your interpretation consult the entries for Games and Musical Instruments.*

**WHITE – see COLOURS**

**WIDOW/WIDOWER**

🔮 A widow can signify the Crone or Wise Woman and the widower the archetypal Wise Old Man. They have the wisdom of experience.

💗 Psychologically we all seek within ourselves complete harmony in partnership. This is a security that allows us to express parts of our personality which are not normally accessible otherwise. Dreaming of being a widow or widower when we are not suggests that we have lost part of ourselves. A husband represents the masculine principle, the drives and ambition, and a wife the intuitive sensitive principle, so to have lost either is to have lost an essential part of the Mystical Union that everyone requires in order to become spiritually complete.

🔲 Dreaming of being a widow or widower can suggest loss and sadness, but can also suggest the independence of old age. Sometimes such a dream can mark the change in a woman's awareness as she moves towards the 'Crone' or Wise Woman. A woman to dream of a widow highlights her ability to be free and use her own innate wisdom.

🔳 In a man's dream a widow may signify a deeper understanding of a woman's needs. He may recognize that all women do not necessarily need to become dependent on him. In a woman's dream a widower may signify her awareness that she has a right to companionship without losing her ties to her husband.

*Consult the entries for Marriage and Wedding/Wedding Dress/Wedding Ring as well as the information on Family in the People entry.*

**WIFE – see FAMILY**

**WIG**

🔮 A wig, as in a judge's wig, is a symbol of Spiritual authority and judgment. In Jewish belief a woman was expected to hide her hair lest anyone other than her husband saw it. Nowadays it would be under a wig.

💗 Sometimes a wig highlights the fact that we have something to hide. We are perhaps not as competent, as youthful, or as able as we would like others to believe.

🔲 In previous times, covering the head was considered to be a way of hiding the intellect, of giving a false impression, yet also of indicating wisdom and authority. A judge's wig can suggest all of these on a temporal level. A hairpiece or toupée highlights false ideas or an unnatural attitude.

*You might also like to consult the entries for Bald and Hairdresser as well as the information for Hair in the Body entry.*

**WILD**

🌕 In a dream to be, or feel, wild often suggests a lack of spiritual control. Within each of us there is a part that dislikes being controlled in any way. It is the part of ourselves that needs to be free, and is creative and independent.

♡ Anything that grows wild is not subject to the same constraints which normal society puts upon us, so in this context wildness may signify anarchy and lack of stability. In its more positive sense, there is profusion and promise in whatever we are trying to do.

▦ In dreams anything wild always represents the untamed. A wild animal will stand for that aspect of our personality that has not yet committed itself to using rational thought.

⬒ Depending on whether the dreamer is masculine or feminine, a wild woman will represent the Anima or the Shadow.

*Also consult the entries for Animals, Flowers, Tame and Weeds, as well as the information on Anima and Shadow in Archetypes in the Introduction.*

**WILL**

🌕 Determination in spiritual matters is represented here. This can also suggest the resolution of a problem with which we have been dealing.

♡ We may dream of a will at a time when we need everything to be done properly and with certain levels of correctness. There is the obvious play on words where a will would indicate the will to do or to be – the determination to take action, for instance. Because for many making a will is a very final action, in dreams it can indicate a recognition that we are entering a new phase of life.

▦ To dream of a will or any legal document is connected with the way in which our unconscious side can push us into taking notice of our inner needs. To be making a will is to be making a promise to ourselves over future action. It may also have overtones of attempting to look after those we love and care about. To inherit from a will means that we need to look at the habits, characteristics and morals we have inherited from our ancestors.

*You might also like to consult the entry for Inheritance.*

**WILLOW** – *see* **WOOD**

**WIN/WINNER**

🌕 In spiritual terms a winner is someone who has overcome their own fears and doubts to 'win through' to their own personal excellence.

♡ To win in dreams is to be able to acknowledge our own supremacy. To be a champion is to be best overall, to have competed and won.

▦ In the everyday world there is much competition and to dream of winning a contract, for instance, may suggest that, though this may not be our normal function, we have done a good job. To win a race signifies we have the application and dedication needed to come out on top.

◆ In both men's and women's dreams winning can be a potent image. For a woman to win in a dream when the other competitors are women indicates that she has the right to a high opinion of herself. To win over men can signify that she has overcome her own fears of inadequacy. For a man, winning over other men may suggest he is aware of his abilities. To come in before women highlights his own ability to use the softer skills. Such dreams would need to be carefully interpreted.

## WIND

◆ Wind signifies the Power of the Spirit and the movement of Life. Just as the Holy Spirit in Christianity was said to be 'a mighty rushing wind', so such a dream can represent a Divine revelation of some sort. A gale can be symbolic of the spirit we have within us. The intensity and power of our spiritual belief is depicted by a hurricane – an unpredictable force. To be winding something up, such as a clock, suggests that we are priming ourselves for action.

◆ On a slightly more psychological level, wind in a dream can suggest the beginning of a new, much deeper awareness of ourselves. Since wind in a dream often denotes spiritual matters, if we are conscious of a gale or strong wind we may be taking ourselves too seriously. We are allowing those forces within us, that will lead us forward of their own accord to something else, to have too much meaning. A hurricane can represent the power of our own passion, or passionate belief, which picks us up and carries us along.

■ In dreams, wind symbolizes the intellect. It will depend on the force of the wind how we interpret the dream. For instance, a breeze would suggest gentleness and pleasure. An idea or concept we have is beginning to move us. A gale might indicate a principle we feel passionately about, whereas a north wind might suggest a threat to our security. Actually being in a gale indicates that we are being buffeted by circumstances that we feel are beyond our control. We are allowing those outside circumstances to create problems for us when actually we may need to look at what we are doing and either take shelter – to withdraw from the situation – or battle through to some form of sanctuary. When we experience a hurricane in a dream, we are sensing the force of an element in our lives that is beyond our control. We may feel we are being swept along by circumstances – or possibly someone's passion – and are powerless to resist.

*You might also like to consult the entry for Breeze.*

**WINDOWS –** *see* **BUILDINGS AND GLASS**

**WINE**

⚜ Wine can represent potential spiritual abundance (as in the parable of turning water into wine). It can also signify the taking in of spiritual power.

♥ As a symbol of 'the liquid of life', wine highlights our ability to draw the best out of our experiences and to make use of what is gleaned to provide fun and happiness. The wine glass can have two meanings. Firstly, it stands for the container of our happiness and secondly it can stand for pregnancy. Because of wine's association with blood, a broken wine glass and spilt wine can depict sorrow, or in a woman's dream, miscarriage.

▦ In dreams, wine can suggest a happy occasion. As a substance it has an influence on our awareness and appreciation of our environment. A wine cellar, therefore, can represent the sum of our past experiences, both good and bad. A wine bottle, as a source of enjoyment, is taken by some to indicate masculinity.

*You might also like to consult the entries for Alcohol/Alcoholic, Blood and Drunk.*

**WINGS**

⚜ Wings generally symbolize the protecting, all-pervading power of God. An angel's wings would depict the power to transcend our difficulties, as also would the wings of a bird of prey.

♥ Wings can be protective, and this symbolism often appears in dreams. Folded wings can suggest sorrow, whereas open wings would seem to signify unconditional love.

▦ Because wings make us think of flight, to dream of, for instance, birds' wings would suggest attention is being drawn to our need for freedom. A broken wing indicates that a previous trauma is preventing us from 'taking off' and progressing in our lives.

*You might also like to consult the entries for Angel, Birds and Flying/Flight.*

**WINTER**

⚜ Within the cycle of nature, winter can represent a time of lying fallow before rebirth; hence winter can mean death as part of the inevitable spiritual cycle of death and rebirth.

♥ At a period in our lives when we are emotionally cold, images associated with winter – such as ice and snow – can highlight the appropriateness, or otherwise, of the way we feel. In clairvoyance, the seasons can also indicate a time of year when something may happen.

▦ In dreams, winter can represent a time in our lives that is unfruitful. It can also represent old age, a time when our energy is running down.

*You might also like to consult the entries for Autumn, Ice/Icebergs/Icicles, Seasons, Spring, Snow and Summer.*

**WIRELESS —** *see* **RADIO**

**WISH**

    A wish is a statement of intent and when looked at from a spiritual perspective is often in dreams a directive from the Higher Self.

    Emotionally, we are able to 'power up' our wishes in dreams. By bearing our intent in mind prior to sleep, we can add the additional energy of the unconscious to making things happen. This is called manifestation.

    By regarding a wish as an appeal to the powers that be, from a mundane viewpoint we need to be very clear that what we wish for is what we want. Dreams can have the function of sorting out what we really want and getting rid of the non-essential.

**WITCH**

    Spiritually a witch is someone who has come to understand the intrinsic power they have and learnt to use it properly. Because this power, which is based in strongly held beliefs and codes of behaviour, is perceived as dangerous there are many ideas as to the protection necessary, such as hanging garlic.

    The conventional picture of the warty-nosed old crone is actually a personification of malevolence. Any blemish that comes to our attention in dreams can be accepted as evidence of there being a distortion in our view of the world. In dreams we have the opportunity to confront our fears, overcome them and use the power thus generated successfully.

    In mundane terms we may dream of witches when we do not fully understand the use of personal power. Dreaming of warts, which are often associated with witches, links with that part of ourselves which remains superstitious and afraid of an energy we have not fully comprehended.

    In dreams a woman will recognize the appearance of the witch as the opportunity to come to terms with the sacred duty she has to pass on her knowledge. A man may use the appearance of the witch to overcome his fears of the powerful woman.

*Consult the entries for Magic/Magician, Wand and Wizard as well as the information on Witch in Archetypes in the Introduction.*

**WITNESS**

    We are acknowledging a degree of Spiritual Testament or statement of truth in our life, which we need in order to continue along our spiritual path. Witnessing is a term used when spiritually we observe without judgement.

◈ Testifying as a witness suggests that we feel we are being called to account for our actions or beliefs. We may feel somewhat insecure until we have been accepted by our peers.

▦ When we find ourselves in the position of being a witness to, for instance, an accident, it may be that our powers of observation are being highlighted. We need to take very careful note of what is going on around about us. Our interaction with authority may also be being called into question.

*Also consult the entries for Court and Crime/Criminal.*

## WIZARD

◈ The figure of a wizard in dreams is he who has learned to use his powers of manifestation in a dispassionate manner. He is Merlin, the sorcerer and the magician. As a stage on the journey to Wise Old Man, he is a recognizable Archetype.

◈ Conventionally pictured in long flowing robes with a long beard, he tends to be seen as somewhat otherworldly. In dreams he appears when we are struggling with the idea of being able to use natural power in a magical way. He usually epitomizes the alchemical idea of transmutation – turning the crass into the beautiful.

▦ In a workaday environment a wizard is a set of computer instructions which enables you to complete a task. Both practically and magically this image is one that can enable us to use the expertise we inherently possess.

⬚ In a man's dream the wizard may well represent his own sense of power and control of the energies. In a woman's dream he will suggest the non-emotional use of authority.

*Consult the entries for Alchemy, Magic/Magician, Wand and Witch as well as the information on Sorcerer in Archetypes in the Introduction.*

**WOLF** – *see* **ANIMALS**

**WOMAN** – *see* **PEOPLE**

**WOMB** – *see* **BODY**

## WOOD

◈ The wood is often a manifestation of the Spirit. If it is a wild wood, it suggests the untamed spirit – as in nature – and we perhaps need to exercise some self-control.

◈ When our behaviour becomes rigid or wooden, dreams will often attempt to make us aware of this and of the necessity to balance our feelings. We might then dream of willow, a tree that bends in the wind.

▦ Dreaming of wood, in the sense of prepared timber, suggests our ability to appreciate the past and to build on what has gone before. We are capable of building a structure, which may or may not be permanent. Dreaming of a wooden toy highlights our connection with the more natural side of ourselves.

*You might also like to consult the entries for Forest and Trees.*

**WOODPECKER –** *see* **BIRDS**

**WOOL**

 Wool is symbolic of Spiritual Protection. Lamb was sacrificed by the Jews at Passover, Christ was the Lamb of God so the spiritual significance of wool is obvious.

 Wool has, from earliest times, represented warmth and protectiveness. Nowadays it particularly represents gentleness and mothering.

 How we interpret wool depends on whether the image we have is of lamb's wool or of knitting wool. Lamb's wool may stand for blurred thoughts and feelings. We have not really sorted our thoughts out. 'Pulling the wool' over someone's eyes, though generally accepted as being devious, can also be a protective act.

*Also consult the entry for Knitting.*

**WORD**

 Spiritually the Word is the Logos, the Sacred Sound, the beginning of creation. In dreams we can appreciate words of power, such as Mantra and the Names of God.

 Certain words have esoteric meanings, such as the Hebrew word *JHVH* (Jehovah). Such words are more likely to appear initially in the dream state than in ordinary everyday life at a particular stage of development. We are more open to such information while we are asleep.

 The repetition of words creates a particular vibration. When in dreams we are conscious of a word being repeated, we must decide whether it is the sound or the meaning that is significant.

*Also consult the entries for Sound and Talking as well as the information on Spiritual Imagery in the Introduction.*

**WORK**

 There may be some degree of activity of the spirit ahead. We could be being moved towards new spiritual tasks.

 Often what we do as a job or daily occupation bears no relation to what we consider to be our real work. Dreams can very often help us to change our situation by giving information as to our real talents and gifts. When we dream of working at something which does not have a place in our ordinary everyday lives, it may be worth exploring how we could use those skills to enhance our lives.

▣ Dreaming of being at work highlights issues, concerns or difficulties we may have within the work situation. We could be actively trying to make changes in our lives and these changes, in dreams, become reflected into the work situation.

▣ There used to be a strong division between men's and women's work. In dreams if we find ourselves doing work that traditionally belonged to the opposite gender we perhaps need to develop some of the qualities of that occupation. For instance, to dream of being an engineer might suggest we need to use precision and vision.

## WORKSHOP

❁ A workshop often holds within it creative outlets – this creativity can be used for our spiritual progression.

♡ A workshop may often be where we meet others of like mind, people who are creative in the same way as we are. It therefore represents group interaction and talent.

▣ A workshop is a place that is productive. In dreams it symbolizes the part of ourselves that creates projects which then become profitable for us, though not necessarily financially.

*You might also like to consult the entry for Garage.*

## WORLD

❁ As we progress spiritually we become conscious that, just as on an individual level we belong to the family, so the world belongs to the Cosmos. Being aware of the world in this sense means we must take responsibility for the way the world functions.

♡ To dream of other worlds and dimensions suggests different ways of experiencing our own lives. We perhaps need to become less rigid in our opinions.

▣ The world represents the area of experience in which one lives, and our everyday activities. Often to dream of a world beyond our sphere of influence suggests the necessity to take a wider viewpoint in a situation around us.

*Consult the entry for Globe for additional information.*

## WORM

❁ 'Being given to the worms' is a metaphor for death, so we need to be aware that on a spiritual level changes – not necessarily death – may shortly be taking place.

♡ The worm in dreams can also highlight our feelings of ineffectiveness and insignificance (whether this is about ourselves or others). If the worm is bigger than we are then this would suggest that our own sense of inferiority is a problem. If we are particularly conscious of a wormcast – that is, the earth the worm has passed through its body – then this is a transformation image and indicates we are capable of changing our lives into something more fertile.

▦ Most dreams about worms are fairly ambivalent. The worm is not necessarily seen to be particularly clean, so phrases like 'the worm turning' suggests that we have decided to state our case. A can of worms could be transformative or a difficult mess.

▯ At its very basic interpretation, the worm can suggest the penis. Depending on the dreamer's attitude to sexuality and gender, there may be a sense of threat.

**WORSHIP** – *see* ALTAR, ICON, RITE/RITUAL AS WELL AS SPIRITUAL IMAGERY IN THE INTRODUCTION

**WOUND**

✾ A wound symbolizes an experience, which may have been unpleasant, that we should take note of and learn from.

♡ Any wound or trauma in dreams will signify hurt feelings or emotions. If we are inflicting the wounds, our own aggression and mistrust are being highlighted, if the wounds are being inflicted on us we may be making ourselves into, or being, the victim.

▦ The type of wound will be important in interpreting the dream. A large, ugly wound will suggest more violence, whereas a small one may indicate a more focused attack. This wound may be to our reputation, self-esteem or pride.

*You might also like to consult the entries for Attack and Weapon.*

**WREATH**

✾ A wreath has triple spiritual significance – dedication, sacrifice or death (change). The shape, often circular, will be important as thus signifying continuity and completeness, as well as everlasting life.

♡ A wreath in dreams can have the same significance as any of the binding symbols, such as a bridle. It forms a bond that cannot be broken, or an acknowledgement that must be accepted.

▦ A wreath in a dream can suggest honour and celebration. Dreaming of being given a wreath suggests being singled out, perhaps for some honour. It formerly warned of the potential for one's own death, which is why wreaths are still part of funeral rites. Dreaming of giving someone else a wreath – not a funerary one – validates our relationship with that person.

*Consult the entries for Bridle, Flowers and Laurel/Bay Leaves for further information.*

**WRECK**

&#9673; A wreck of any kind symbolizes a spiritual defeat. Although frustrated on this occasion, we should continue to 'battle' through to reach our intended goal.

&#9673; Since a wreck can happen due to circumstances beyond our control, such a dream can indicate a greater need for control, or management of resources.

&#9632; Dreaming of a wreck – such as a car or shipwreck – indicates that our plans may be thwarted in some way. It is necessary to decide in waking life whether we are at fault for the failure of our plans or someone else is.

*You might also like to consult the entries for Accident and Disaster.*

**WRITING**

&#9673; We may not be consciously aware of our spiritual progression. A manuscript would suggest some aspect of ancient knowledge. Dreaming of writing suggests a subconscious record is being kept. Spiritually our signature is a reflection of ourselves; it is a representation of who we perceive ourselves to be.

&#9673; Writing as a creative art is meaningful, and as a form of self-expression it perhaps allows us to communicate when spoken words are inadequate. In dreams we may learn how to communicate with ourselves in differing ways. Computers are a way of writing just as much as pens. Transcribing information in a dream signifies committing it to memory. At those times when we are arranging legal matters or agreements, but are actually not sure if we are doing the right thing, our signature can appear in dreams as obliterated or illegible.

&#9632; To dream of writing is an attempt to communicate information that we have. Sometimes the instrument we are writing with is important. For instance, a pencil would suggest that the information is less permanent than with a pen. Our signature in a dream suggests that we have an appreciation of ourselves. We are prepared to recognize who we are and to make our mark in the world.

*Also consult the entries for Ink, Paper/Parchment and Pen/Pencil for further information.*

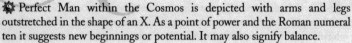

**X**

☀ Perfect Man within the Cosmos is depicted with arms and legs outstretched in the shape of an X. As a point of power and the Roman numeral ten it suggests new beginnings or potential. It may also signify balance.

♥ If a cross appears in the shape of an X, this usually represents the idea of sacrifice or perhaps of torture.

▦ If an X appears in a dream, we are usually 'marking the spot'. It can also represent an error, a misjudgement or possibly something we particularly need to note. Written as a kiss it signifies unification of two entities.

*Also consult the entry for Cross in Shapes/Patterns.*

**X-RAYS**

☀ Spiritually, an X-ray can symbolize a new clarity that you are about to experience. This 'clear-sightedness' should enable you to move ahead more confidently and face the future with equanimity.

♥ Within waking life, it may be that there is something we need to 'see through'. This can be a play on words, in that we need to finish off a task, or we may need to have a very clear view of the situation around us.

▦ Dreaming of X-rays can be significant in a number of ways. There may be something influencing your life on an unconscious level which needs to be revealed. If you are carrying out the X-ray it may be necessary to look more deeply into a situation. There may also be a fear of illness, either in yourself or others. This image is obviously more likely to occur when you have health concerns or work in a hospital situation.

**Y**

⚜ The Y is said to represent the human form with outstretched arms, reaching to the Cosmos, sometimes in supplication, otherwise in glorification. It is also thought to represent the choices that Man must make between good and evil.

♥ Moving from the bottom upwards, the point at which the Y forks suggests the point at which you may demand autonomy for yourself, the right to make your own choices. From the other perspective, in two halves coming together it suggests androgeny or a perfect blend of two polarities.

▣ On a purely mundane level this letter may denote the dividing of the ways or a change in direction.

*You may also like to consult the entry for Androgen/Androgeny.*

**YACHT** – *see* **BOAT IN TRANSPORT.**

**YARN**

⚜ In former times storytellers were known as weavers of stories, which is where the symbolism arose. The myths and stories of the old heroes who undertook their own spiritual journey are archetypal and can help us identify a strategy for life.

♥ A yarn – as in a tale or story – is most often to do with our sense of history or of continuity. To be being told a yarn or story links with our need for heroes and heroines, and perhaps our need for a mentor.

▣ Yarn in the sense of knitting yarn or twine often signifies our ability to create order out of chaos. In olden times it suggested spinning, an archetypal symbol for life, and often in dreams it is this image that is portrayed. Tangled yarn may suggest a complex situation. We fashion our lives out of what we are given.

▣ It was once said that yarn in a woman's dream signified that she would marry well, but in a man's dream suggested that he would find himself a dutiful wife. It has less such significance nowadays, but yarn always has the overtones of industriousness and hard work.

*You might like to consult the section on Archetypes in the Introduction.*

**YAWN**

⚜ In the physical world a yawn is a way of taking in more oxygen. In the spiritual sense it is our inner selves attempting to assimilate more knowledge or power.

❤ In the animal kingdom a yawn often is a warning against aggression, and to actually be yawning in dreams may be a way of controlling our own or other's abusive or overly assertive behaviour.

▦ If we become conscious of yawning in a dream it can indicate boredom and tiredness in the everyday. We may also be attempting to communicate with someone, but have not yet thought through what we wish to say.

**YEAR** – *see* TIME

**YEARN**

☼ To yearn is to long for. One stage of spiritual development is a yearning to free yourself from mundane matters. You may have become impatient in a seemingly never-ending search for your spiritual self. This feeling is often heightened in a dream.

❤ If we have suppressed our needs through long habit or self-denial, an urgency may emerge in dreams for the very thing that we have consciously denied.

▦ Feelings in dreams are often heightened in intensity. A need which may be perfectly manageable in ordinary everyday life becomes a yearning and seeking in dreams. Such a dream would highlight an emotion which we may need to look at in order to understand.

⊟ In some senses yearning is a more feminine feeling than masculine. However, it is also a somewhat chaotic feeling, and therefore somewhat adolescent. In both men's and women's dreams it can be given this interpretation.

**YELL** – *see* SHOUT

**YES**

☼ We are being given – or have given ourselves – permission to spiritually grow and flourish. With this permission, you can look towards a more directed lifestyle.

❤ Often, before we are able to make changes in our ordinary, everyday lives, we need to give ourselves permission on an unconscious level. Recognizing this in the dream state can be an important part of our growth process.

▦ Occasionally in dreams and in the hypnogogic state, we become aware that we have 'said' yes. This is an instinctive acceptance or acknowledgement of the validity of whatever has been happening.

*Consult the Introduction for clarification.*

**YEW**

☼ A yew tree outlives most other trees, and regenerates when its branches take root, so even if the main trunk dies it still continues. Thus it symbolizes transformation, great age and spiritual immortality. Ancient peoples were in the habit of planting yew trees as acts of sanctification near to where they expected to be buried.

🕉 Considered to be the most powerful tree for protection against evil, the yew is a means of connecting to your ancestors and a bringer of dreams and journeys into other dimensions. There can also be an aspect of word-play here as sometimes happens in dreams, in that the 'yew' is focusing your attention away from yourself as the dreamer to some other aspect of the dream.

🏛 In former times the yew tree symbolized mourning and sadness and was a symbol of the old magic. While few people would necessarily recognize a yew tree, there is, on an unconscious level, awareness of such knowledge in everyone. Such a symbol can surface as instinctive awareness in dreams.

*You may also like to consult the entry for Tree.*

## YIELD

🌞 You may have been contemplating the idea of a more spiritual existence for some time, and have now finally yielded, or submitted, to the notion. In *T'ai Chi* (an art of personal discipline) knowing when to yield in order to succeed in the end is an important lesson.

🕉 Yielding is one of the more feminine attributes and signifies our need to let go and simply 'go with the flow'.

🏛 To yield in a dream is to become aware of the futility of confrontation. To understand this we may need to look at situations within our everyday lives.

🔯 In a man's dream yielding suggests submission to the inevitable, whereas in a woman's dream it suggests submission to a stronger force.

## YIN AND YANG

🌞 Perfect Spiritual Balance is created by the energy created between two complementary opposites, the passive feminine principle and the active masculine. Each contains within itself the 'seed' of the other, creating a state of inner stability. This image occurs in dreams when we begin to approach such a state.

🕉 We are continuously searching for balance, though not necessarily a state of inertia. The yin-yang symbol signifies a state of dynamic potential, the sense that anything is possible.

🏛 A representation of the Cosmic egg, the beginning of all things, this symbol has become much better known in the last thirty years in the West as the balance of two complementary opposites. In dreams it indicates the balance between the instinctive, intuitive nature of the feminine and the active, rational nature of the masculine.

🔯 As a symbol, this will only appear in both men's and women's dreams when a certain state of internal equilibrium is becoming apparent.

## YOB

✺ In spiritual terms the yob, as in the uncontrolled and uncontrollable youth, signifies a quality of waywardness seen in gods such as Loki and Mercury. It is an untamed part of the psyche.

♥ In not having respect for the rules laid down by society, the yob draws our attention to those aspects of ourselves and others which refuse to conform.

▦ More mundanely, such a figure in dreams can highlight a threat or difficulty in our work or personal field of endeavour.

### YOGA/YOGI

✺ The word 'yoga' comes from Sanskrit language and means union or merger. The practice is in itself a spiritual discipline and in dreams symbolizes that which is needed to achieve union with the Divine.

♥ The practice of many of the different forms of yoga actually opens many pathways to perception and can enhance our dreams, allowing us access to universal truths. To be dreaming of doing yoga suggests a need for a deeper understanding of our own impulses.

▦ Yoga can play an important role in maintaining a balance between work and healthy mind. Because yoga is a physical discipline, a philosophy of mind/body connection and a spiritual way of life, any or all of these significances can become apparent in dreams. A yogi (spiritual practitioner) in dreams is a representation of a wise person or teacher and alerts us to the need in us to find such a person.

*You might also like to consult the entry for Yin and Yang.*

### YOUTH – *see* ARCHETYPES AND PEOPLE

### YULE/YULE LOG

✺ In Pagan times a log was decorated and burnt at the time of the Winter solstice (Yule) in order to clear away the Old Year, and to celebrate the return of the sun. In dreams it is seen as a symbol of light and new life.

♥ In modern times, the Yule log is often symbolized by a celebration cake. Decorated in a traditional fashion with greenery and candles, it honours the Holly King, who dies at this time, giving way to the Oak King who brings light. Therefore it tends to suggest the New Year and new beginnings in dream language.

▦ A Yule log represents an offering or sacrifice, particularly at the time of a spiritual or religious celebration when we pay homage to the gods. Originally the bringing in of the Yule log was a whole ritual in itself, requiring special prayers and offerings to ensure the next year's prosperity. In dreams such an image may suggest a time of celebration or of prosperity.

*Also consult the entry for Fire as well as Spiritual Imagery in the Introduction.*

## ZEAL/ZEALOT

🔯 It is more likely that we would dream of a terrorist rather than a zealot, yet they both have the same fanatical belief in and love for one principle. There comes a time in spiritual development where we can, if we are not careful, develop extremist behaviour. The presence of a zealot in dreams can help us focus.

♡ Zeal is love in action and in the psychological sense suggests service to others and denial of the self. In dreams it suggests that some of our behaviour may be 'over the top'.

▦ Historically, the Zealots were a group who objected to Roman rulership and sought to violently eradicate it. This kind of 'love in action' has relevance in today's world when we come up against fanaticism in all its forms. Dreaming of a zealot suggests that we may need to act more circumspectly to achieve our aims.

## ZEBRA – *see* ANIMALS

## ZEN – *see* SPIRITUAL IMAGERY IN THE INTRODUCTION

## ZERO – *see* NUMBERS

## ZIGGURAT

🔯 The ancient ziggurats of Mesopotamia were temples built by kings to celebrate their sacred marriage with the Divine, which at that time was matriarchal. Spiritually, when this image appears, therefore, it celebrates our awareness of our own potential for such union.

♡ The seven steps or stages up to the entrance into the secret chamber at the top of the ziggurat, leading where union took place, correspond to the different stages of awareness in Eastern religions known as chakras. So to find ourselves in dreams at, say, the fourth step or stage would signify the need to come to terms with our ability to love and be loved.

▦ On a purely mundane level the ziggurat symbolizes a sacred secure space and the ability to access that space within ourselves.

⊞ Because the ziggurat signified union, in a woman's dream it suggests her receptivity, while in a man's dream it suggests his willingness to be of service to mankind.

*You might like to consult the entries for Pyramid and Temple.*

## ZIGZAG

🌞 A zigzag is symbolic of a lightning flash which represents new potential and growth. It is the transmission of energy between the spiritual and physical realms – in essence, a revelation.

♥ In a psychological sense, we are able to achieve a new level of awareness which will radically change our perceptions.

🔲 When we see a zigzag in dreams there is the potential to be struck by some mishap, such as in a bolt of lightning. Usually an event will occur which brings about a discharge of energy; circumstances will then be brought back into balance.

## ZIP

🌞 A zip fastener symbolizes spiritual connections and the interlocking of the physical and spiritual realms. In technology, a zip drive is an efficient means of storing information and can therefore represent the Akashic Records – all of life's vicissitudes.

♥ Psychologically, we are capable of being either open or closed to our friends and family. Often a zip can highlight this in a dream.

🔲 A zip appearing in a dream may indicate our ability – or difficulty – in maintaining relationships with other people. A stuck zip suggests a difficulty in keeping our dignity in an awkward situation. As computers themselves become more efficient, a zip drive in dreams can symbolize our working environment.

## ZODIAC

🌞 The zodiac wheel is symbolic of our relationship with the universe. Sometimes the signs of the zodiac are used in dreams to demonstrate time or time passing, and also suggest courses of action we might take. Each sign also rules (has responsibility for) a particular part of the physical body, and any imbalance is reflected into dreams through the symbolism of the zodiac.

♥ Hidden information often comes to us through dreams. As we become more knowledgeable these symbols tap into arcane wisdom which allows us to live our lives in tune with the universe. The spheres of influence of the planets were first described by Plato and modern astrology stills tend to follow his teachings.

By then using the correspondences we can harness the energy of the zodiac in everyday life – its colours and gemstones. Below are some of the most important correspondences:

**Aries** – the symbol is the Ram and it governs the head. The colour associated with the sign is red; its specific gemstones are amethyst and diamond.

**Taurus** – the symbol is the Bull and it governs the throat. The colours associated with the sign are blue and pink; its specific gemstones are moss agate and emerald.

**Gemini** – the symbol is the Twins (often shown as masculine and feminine) and it governs the shoulders, arms and hands. The colour associated with the sign is yellow; its specific gemstones are agate and beryl.

**Cancer** – the symbol is the Crab and it governs the stomach and higher organs of digestion. The colours associated with the sign are either violet or emerald green; its specific gemstones are moonstones and pearls.

**Leo** – the symbol is the Lion and it governs the heart, lungs and liver. The colours associated with the sign are gold and orange; its specific gemstones are topaz and tourmaline.

**Virgo** – the symbol is the Virgin and it governs the abdomen and intestines. The colours associated with the sign are grey and navy blue; its specific gemstones are pink jasper and jade.

**Libra** – the symbol is the Scales and it governs the lumbar region, kidneys and skin. The colours associated with the sign are blue and violet; its specific gemstones are opal and lapis lazuli.

**Scorpio** – the symbol is the Scorpion and it governs the genitals. The colours associated with the sign are deep red and purple; its specific gemstones are turquoise and ruby.

**Sagittarius** – The symbol is the Archer and it governs the hips, thighs and nervous system. The colours associated with the sign are light blue and orange; its specific gemstones are carbuncle and amethyst.

**Capricorn** – the symbol is the Goat and it governs the knees. The colours associated with the sign are violet and green; its specific gemstones are jet and black onyx.

**Aquarius** – the symbol is the Water-Bearer and it governs the circulation and ankles. The colour associated with the sign is electric blue; its specific gemstones are garnet and zircon.

**Pisces** – the symbol is The Fishes and it governs the feet and toes. The colour associated with the sign are sea-green and mauve; its specific gemstones are coral and chrysolite.

■ Everyone has a fascination for horoscopes, without necessarily understanding the significance of the zodiac wheel. It is often only when we begin the journey of self-discovery that images and symbols from the zodiac will appear in dreams. Frequently, the animal or creature associated with our own star sign will appear, almost as a reminder of basic principles. The way we deal with that image will give us insight into how we really feel about ourselves.

**ZOO**

🔅 Dreaming of being in a zoo suggests the need to understand some of our natural urges and instincts. We perhaps need to be more objective in our appraisal than subjective.

♡ There may be an urge to return to simpler, more basic modes of behaviour. Some people are natural observers, and we may be being alerted to the fact that we also need to be capable of participating in conduct appropriate to the group to which we belong. We also, of course, may be conscious that we ourselves are being observed, perhaps in the work situation.

▦ Dreaming of a zoo can alert us to the necessary and appropriate customs and behaviour or the hierarchical structure in an impending situation.

*You might also consult the entry for Animals for further clarification.*